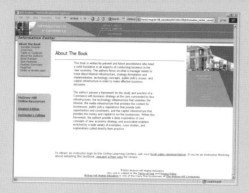

Introduction to e-Commerce Website—For students, online materials include chapter overviews and quizzes to help them master essential concepts and competencies. For instructors, there is a link to the MarketspaceU website where they can download sample syllabi, lecture notes, PowerPoint slides, and other multimedia materials.

marketspaceU (www.marketspaceU.com)—Instructors in the e-commerce field continually confront the challenge of staying current with industry events. Securing fresh classroom material and staying on the cutting edge of theory and practice are among the most important and time-consuming of instructor duties. MarketspaceU solves these problems by offering outstanding instructor support, including regular case updates, news feeds, PowerPoint case timelines, and video segments. Instructors will also find lectures (including teaching notes and PowerPoint slides), sample syllabi, and multimedia materials for each chapter.

E-Commerce PowerWeb – Online access to current full-text articles, quizzing and assessment, validated links to relevant material, interactive glossaries, weekly updates, and interactive web exercises.
http://www.dushkin.com/powerweb

McGraw-Hill/marketspaceU
Mission Statement

McGraw-Hill/marketspaceU was created to develop exceptional higher-education teaching materials on the latest business practices and theories by leading thinkers in the field of e-commerce. McGraw-Hill/marketspaceU is committed to providing business instructors with a comprehensive set of pedagogical tools in an easy-to-use learning system with the most current materials, which include textbooks, casebooks, video interviews, and a website. We aim to help present and future executives, managers, and strategists become successful creators of value in the networked economy.

To accomplish this task, we offer a suite of cutting-edge tools to help you navigate the networked economy:

- *e-Commerce*
- *Cases in e-Commerce*
- *Introduction to e-Commerce*
- *Internet Marketing: Building Advantage in a Networked Economy*
- marketspaceU.com
- *Introduction to e-Commerce* website

For more information about these tools, see Supporting Materials, page xv.

Acknowledgments

We are grateful the outstanding colleagues who made the preparation of this second edition possible. While we acknowledge the original contributors to each chapter throughout the book, here we would like to thank those who did such a great job revising the original chapters. Michael Yip rewrote Chapter 3, "Market Opportunity Analysis," while Katherine Jocz contributed to Chapter 6, "Market Communications and Branding," and Chapter 7, "Implementation." We truly appreciate the work of Jennifer Sturak and Jenny Johnston, both in revising some of the chapters and copyediting the entire book. Jennifer worked on the "Market Communications" chapter, as well as Chapter 5, "Strategy Formulation: Customer Interface." Jenny revised Chapter 2, "Basic Technology of the Internet..." and Chapter 11, "Human and Financial Capital." We would also like to thank David Ruben for writing the wonderful caselets that open each chapter and for updating or writing many of the Drill-Downs; and Jon Davis for updating all of the Market-Watch.com examples. We would also like to thank Ian Findlay and Pete Giorgio for going beyond the call of duty to write Chapter 9, "Website Development Process," and Chapter 10, "Site Architecture," respectively.

Much appreciation goes to Steve Szaraz, who not only is responsible for the marketspaceU website, but also revised two of the chapters (Chapter 12, "Media Transformation," and Chaprer 13, "Public Policy") and provided much needed last-minute support throughout this process. Also, a big debt of gratitude goes to Marie Claire Guglielmo for coordinating the the entire revision process. We would also like to thank our marketspaceU team: Craig Thompson and Katarina Gizzi, who provided content; and Blair Hotchkies, Bryan Barkley, and Greg Robinson, for their technical development and support of the website. We would also like to thank Dickson Louie, for laying the groundwork of the Media Chapter.

We would like to thank Kimberly Basile and Kristia DeRoche for both their fact-checking help and their administration and design efforts. We are grateful to Allison Reese for her coordination efforts on the project. We also appreciate Max Kalehoff of comScore Media Metrix for his assistance.

We gratefully acknowledge the editorial support at Irwin/McGraw-Hill of John Biernat, Barrett Koger, and Scott Becker. We would also like to thank Rich Wright for his project management efforts during the production of the book.

We would especially like to recognize the contribution made by JoAnn Kienzle to this book and to the marketspaceU series in general. JoAnn single-handedly organized this book's extensive revisions, working patiently but firmly with its authors, as well as working as a reviser, writer, and editor thoughout the book. She ultimately oversaw the completion of all our second-edition textbook revisions. For this service "above and beyond" and for tireless good cheer and good advice, we thank you.

Finally, this book would not have been possible without the generous support and enthusiasm of Mark Fuller, Joe Fuller, and Mark Thomas, cofounders and leaders of Monitor Group, a strategy consulting company and merchant bank based in Cambridge, Massachusetts.

About the Authors

Jeffrey F. Rayport

Jeffrey F. Rayport, founder of Marketspace, is widely regarded as one of the most influential thinkers in the field of e-commerce. Nearly eight years ago, he launched the first e-commerce strategy course at Harvard Business School, and he has written nearly 100 case studies on e-commerce. His second-year elective course on this subject consistently enrolled nearly half of the Harvard Business School class of 800 students. For three years in a row, he was voted "best professor" at Harvard Business School by the student body, the first Harvard Business School professor to receive the honor that many times consecutively.

Dr. Rayport's research and client work has focused on breakthrough service and marketing strategies for information-intensive businesses, and has involved a wide array of high-tech and service firms, industry associations, and professional practices. In addition to his Harvard Business School case studies, he has written numerous articles that have appeared in industry publications and popular business magazines.

Dr. Rayport earned a bachelor's degree from Harvard College, a master's in international relations from the University of Cambridge (United Kingdom), and a master's in the history of American civilization and a doctorate in business history from Harvard University. His doctoral research examined diversification strategies among the regional Bell operating companies after the breakup of AT&T, with a focus on the transformation of high-tech companies from technology-driven to marketing-oriented firms.

Bernard J. Jaworski

Bernard J. Jaworski is a cofounder and senior adviser at Marketspace. In 2001, Bernie was the corecipient of the Sheth Foundation/*Journal of Marketing* Award. This award honors the *Journal of Marketing* article that has made the greatest long-term contributions to the field of marketing in a given year.

Dr. Jaworski has been the Jeanne and David Tappan Marketing Fellow and a tenured full professor of marketing at the University of Southern California. He previously served on the faculty of the University of Arizona and was a visiting professor at Harvard Business School. In 1997, he received a Golden Apple Award as the MBA teacher of the year at USC. Dr. Jaworski is one of a few two-time winners of the prestigious Alpha Kappa Psi award for the best marketing-practice article published in the *Journal of Marketing*. He currently serves on the review boards of the *Journal of Marketing*, the *Journal of Marketing Research*, the *Journal of Business-to-Business Marketing*, the *Asian Journal of Marketing*, and other journals. His client work has focused on a variety of projects involving single-channel to multi-channel optimization. Moreover, he has been involved in a variety of executive education initiatives including recent work on building organization-wide marketing capabilities.

About MarketspaceU

MarketspaceU is a community of award-winning academics and talented business practitioners dedicated to preparing managers for the networked economy. MarketspaceU is a part of Marketspace, a Monitor Group company. Marketspace was founded in 1998 and specializes in strategic advisory services and research focused on the needs of leading information industry companies.

Drawing upon the resources at Marketspace and other Monitor Group companies, as well as a network of academic institutional partners and CEO visionaries, marketspaceU brings together the diverse talents of practitioners, management consultants, academics, and writers.

Preface

We are in the midst of a period of economic uncertainty. At the center of this uncertainty is the role of technology in reshaping how individuals live, learn, work, and play. A significant part of this technology change is the Internet and, more specifically, e-commerce. Our purpose in writing this comprehensive textbook was to take a point of view about the scope of activities that fall within the responsibilities of the business practitioners who must cope with this change.

Narrowly conceived, it is possible to write a book about the technology that powers the Internet. More broadly, one can address how firms compete and win in this arena, which is the heart of business strategy. Alternatively, one can address the culture of capital formation and investment that has paved the way for the revolution. We believe that each of these views provides only one piece of the more general understanding that is necessary. The successful practitioner must know all of the above—and more. He or she must also comprehend the fundamental changes in laws, public policy, and regulation that affect e-commerce. Moreover, the Internet is a media vehicle at its core. Therefore, the manager must also understand the economics and strategic choices of media businesses.

How can all of this be accomplished? We believe that this textbook captures all of these issues in a simple "four infrastructures plus strategy" framework. Strategy will always be center stage in the board room. However, a deep understanding of the four infrastructures—technology, media, public policy, and capital—is also a requirement for the senior executive.

Approach

This book is written for present and future practitioners who desire to know more about all aspects—strategy, technology, public policy, capital, and media—of the networked economy. As such, it provides a deep exploration of core concepts of online strategy and associated enablers, and it is enriched by a wide variety of examples, case studies, and explanations culled directly from practice.

We take this approach for a variety of reasons.

Management and strategy are being invented in real time as we go to press. Every online business we have studied—and our work is based on nearly 100 case studies completed at Harvard Business School over the last six years, as well as significant client work—has been engaged in the creation of a new (albeit challenging) way of doing business. The true insights will be generated at this stage by deep observation of both new and established businesses wrestling with networkded-economy challenges. Thus, we take a militantly field-based and practitioner-focused perspective in this book. This is not to say that management theory is irrelevant. Existing concepts and theories such as network effects and increasing returns to scale do apply. However, in general, practice is far ahead of theory at this time in history.

This book is a collection of rigorous concepts, frameworks, and approaches that represent an entire suite of tools for doing business in the networked economy. Observation of business practices, while often fascinating and instructive, is not enough. We have taken our knowledge of practice, as developed through case studies, and followed through with conceptualization. Our tools represent a critical source of competitive advantage for companies and their managers; we have tested them with students in our MBA and executive-education programs and with our consulting clients in their own businesses. In other words, these are "road-tested" tools, not theoretical approaches to doing business

This book reflects the rich-media or new-media environments in which today's businesses operate. We provide deeper exploration of topics that appear in the text through sidebars called Drill-Downs. Point-Counterpoints highlight the two sides of some unresolved business debates. Points of View include commentary from leading practitioners. We transcribe excerpts from our videotaped conversations with thought leaders and present them as Marketspace Interviews. At the end of each chapter in the strategy module, MarketWatch.com serves as a living case study to which we apply the ideas and concepts presented in that chapter. We show exactly how these ideas have created real and substantial value for a company doing business in the real world.

Content and Organization

This book serves as a comprehensive introduction to the field of e-commerce. At the core of e-commerce activities is the strategy of the enterprise. Wrapped around this strategy process are four critical infrastructures: technology, capital, public policy, and media. These four infrastructures provide the context—both the opportunities and the constraints—within which the strategy operates.

The Strategy Process

We begin with a discussion of the strategy process, which comprises interrelated, sequential decisions in six areas: market opportunity analysis, business model, customer interface, market communications and branding, implementation, and evaluation. To fully understand how these six decisions interrelate, we apply them to the well-known website MarketWatch.com. This discussion includes our secondary analysis of the MarketWatch.com strategy, as well as our interviews with its senior management team.

Technology Infrastructure

In this two-chapter section, we take the reader through the basics of how the Internet and the World Wide Web work, including the core software, applications, and hardware that underlie them. In the second and third technology chapters (Chapters 9 and 10), we discuss the process of building a website and then explain the architecture behind websites.

Capital Infrastructure

Where does the money to launch new businesses come from? How does one find the right managers, build a business plan, and find funding? This chapter provides a primer on what we call the capital infrastructure of the networked economy.

Media Infrastructure

Just as we observe the convergence of multiple technologies, we have also observed the convergence of digitized content—from radio, TV, magazines, books, and other print media. We discuss the evolution of each of these media and the convergence of these media, both technologically and organizationally. We further discuss the challenges facing media corporations.

Public Policy Infrastructure

All of the previous decisions—related to strategy, technology, capital, and media—are based on public policy decisions. In this section, we introduce and discuss some of the most important regulatory issues that confront firms today.

The sequence and topics of chapters reflect the intellectual architecture of our approach to managing in this field. Our chapters are organized to reflect the framework sequence of the strategy process and associated infrastructures.

Overview of the Book

Chapter 1: Framework for e-Commerce

Many of our students and clients have asked us what is different about managing in the networked economy. In this chapter, we set forth those differences in detail, attempting to frame the unique attributes of the networked economy and the implications for managers and strategists. In doing this, we present a working definition and framework for the study and practice of electronic commerce, discussing both the strategy involved in running an e-commerce company and the four infrastructures—technical, capital, media, and public policy—that can influence that strategy.

The Basic Technology of the Internet and the Web

Chapter 2: Basic Technology of the Internet and e-Commerce Businesses

In the first part of this chapter we look at the history of the Internet and the underlying technology that powers it. This chapter explains basic technology concepts, including webpages, hyperlinks, and protocols. The second part of this chapter discusses the new challenges and opportunities that the Internet has brougth to companies. We look at several aspects of selling, including traffic, customer service, and fulfillment, and compare how bricks-and-mortar companies and e-commerce companies deal with these issues.

Strategy Formulation for Online Firms

Chapter 3: Market Opportunity Analysis

In this chapter, we revisit the basics of any business to construct an original approach to formulating business strategy. We focus on the company, competition, technology, and customers. The goal is to understand what market analysis becomes in this new world and to introduce a process not only to understand the market, but also to identify those portions of the market that are unserved or underserved. This chapter presents a seven-step process that can help a company determine if there is a market opportunity.

Chapter 4: Business Models

While some once believed that Internet businesses did not need to worry about having a business model, even for online businesses, a comprehensive strategy is critical to success. Having a business model is essential to competing in the online world. Here, we introduce the four components of the online business model: (1) the value proposition, or "cluster," (2) the online offering, (3) the resource system that the firm selects to deliver the offering, and (4) a revenue model that enables the business to generate cash flows and, ultimately, profit margins. These four choices are the foundation of the strategy decisions that we explore throughout the book.

Chapter 5: Strategy Formulation: Customer Interface

The visible storefront of most e-commerce businesses is a digital or rich-media interface. While online businesses may make substantial use of traditional offline interfaces—such as retail points of sale, printed catalogs, stand-alone kiosks, and call centers—they rely primarily on a virtual storefront connected to the Internet. In this chapter, we fully develop the set of design tools and elements that we refer to as the 7Cs of the customer interface: content, context, community, commerce, customization, communications, and connection. In particular, we focus on the levers that managers can use to create competitive advantage and generate customer value through these essential elements of interface design.

Chapter 6: Market Communications and Branding

In the demand-oriented business world, there is nothing more valuable than mind share, or the ability to attract and hold the attention of markets and customers. The traditional tools of attention management are marketing communications. In this chapter, we explore the variety of traditional and new-media communications approaches that provide competitive advantage to businesses, and delve into the extraordinary power of brands in this new information-enabled world. Many believed that the Web would create a world of downward price pressures and rapid commoditization of goods and services of all kinds. As we explain, the opposite has occurred. Brands are more important than ever—and some would argue that, at least in business-to-consumer ventures, they are essential to success.

Chapter 7: Implementation

If strategy is about what to do, implementation is about how to do it. In this chapter, we discuss how implementation of an online strategy is different from implementation of an offline strategy and what occurs when implementation is poor. We discuss the seven factors of successful implementations: human assets, processes, organizational structure, systems, culture, leadership, and partnerships.

Chapter 8: Metrics

The dynamic relationship between strategy and market feedback demands new approaches to the measurement and evaluation of business results. We know that e-commerce businesses offer unprecedented opportunities for capturing information on how markets operate and how customers engage in search and shopping behavior. Because this kind of data is available in rich granular forms and, as importantly, in real time, we introduce a management tool called the Performance Dashboard. It is a set of metrics that reflect both the early-warning indicators of the progress of an e-commerce strategy and outcome measures such as customer satisfaction and financial performance.

Technology Infrastructure

Chapter 9: Website Development Process

Once an e-commerce company creates a strategy, it is time to develop the interfaces it will use to reach its customers. In this chapter, we discuss the process of creating a website. We explain the stages that the development team must go through, from starting the website to going "live." We then discuss the user-experience definition (how the team chooses its target customers and understands what those customers will do on the website), architecture design process, implementation, test/build process, and rollout.

Chapter 10: Site Architecture

As websites have increased in complexity and size, the number of choices that the company must make has also increased. While cost, time, and performance are the biggest tradeoffs, other variables include maintenance, security, flexibility, and scalability. It is important for e-commerce managers to understand these types of choices and make intelligent decisions so that the website clearly reflects the company's strengths.

Capital Infrastructure

Chapter 11: Human and Financial Capital

While a business may have the best idea or new technology, getting capital—both human and financial—is critical. In this chapter, we explore the relationship between human and financial capital, namely, the elements of a business plan, the roles and responsibilities of an entrepreneur, how to articulate an idea, and how to form a management team. We also discuss the different types of capital that online companies pursue, concentrating on venture capital and angel financing. We describe the various stages of funding, with emphasis on the beginning and liquidity stages (including explanations of the IPO process and mergers and acquisitions), and end with methods of valuation and how the negotiation process works.

Media Infrastructure

Chapter 12: Media Transformation

In this chapter, we discuss two types of convergence: technological convergence, in which all types of media converge to a digital platform, and organizational convergence, which companies have tried to achieve through megamergers. Among the key reasons for technological convergence are the proliferation of media, the resulting increased fragmentation of media usage among consumers, and the shift of media to a digitized platform. Organizational convergence, illustrated by the mergers such as the one that joined AOL and Time Warner, was supposed to optimize many types of digitized content and show immediate rewards to consumers and shareholders. These megamergers, however, have not lived up to their promise. We conclude this chapter with a discussion of the pros and cons of media megamergers.

Public Policy Infrastructure

Chapter 13: Public Policy

In this chapter, we explore how government is currently regulating the Internet and what it may regulate in the future. We discuss self-regulation versus government regulation and how the Internet's lack of boundaries has created regulatory challenges. We explore issues such as access, privacy, free speech, and intellectual property—and determine how the laws and regulations currently governing these issues will affect e-commerce and Internet businesses.

User's Guide

Textbook Navigation

Because online businesses operate in networked environments, we have endeavored to make this book a rich information environment. You will see that every chapter has a variety of features to augment the text. You can count on these to enrich your understanding of the material covered, to introduce new and often controversial perspectives, and to provide greater detail on topics of current and future salience. Look for these features as you read:

- *Drill-Downs.* These sidebars deeply explore topics that appear in the text. Not every reader will want to uncover the intricacies of collaborative filtering or viral marketing, but many will find these additional materials useful. Think of Drill-Downs as hypertext—there when you need them, out of your way when you do not.

- *Point-Counterpoints.* These segments acknowledge the reality that many issues—such as whether profits matter or whether Internet-company valuations are rational—remain unresolved. Rather than take an artificial approach to these issues and present the "right" answers, we make the cases for and against. Of course, we do have our opinions, and you will find these clearly indicated.

- *POVs (Points of View).* Throughout the chapters, we have included sidebar commentary from leading practitioners in the networked economy—people who have invented new business approaches, developed new network architectures, created major Web brands, and influenced policy in the field.

- *Marketspace Interviews.* These are transcribed excerpts from our ongoing videotaped conversations with contemporary business thought leaders, such as Netscape cofounder Marc Andreessen, Ethernet inventor Bob Metcalfe, and ICQ instant-messaging creators Yair Goldfinger and Sefi Vigiser. These interviews represent exclusive perspectives on the state of play in our field. Longer streaming-video excerpts are available on our website at *www.marketspaceU.com,* and full interviews are available on videotape for purchase.

- *MarketWatch.com case study.* At the end of every strategy chapter, we visit one company, the financial-news website MarketWatch.com (*www.marketwatch.com*). MarketWatch.com serves as a living case study to which we apply the ideas and concepts presented in each chapter. We show exactly how these ideas apply, and we help you see the ideas in action in ways that have created substantial value for a company doing business in the real world.

Supporting Materials

We realize that instructors need teaching support materials, so we have developed a comprehensive support package that includes materials available in print and on the Web, at *www.marketspaceU.com* and at *www.mhhe.com/marketspace*.

- *Marketspace multimedia materials (www.marketspaceU.com)*. We draw upon the extensive professional media capabilities of the Marketspace media group and of our partners to let the networked economy speak for itself.
  - The Marketspace media archives contain more than 100 broadcast-quality interviews with leading CEOs, investors, inventors, and implementers conducted at leading business conferences around the world. Streaming-video excerpts are available on our website at *www.marketspaceU.com,* and full interviews are available on videotape for purchase.
  - We have captured Professors Rayport and Jaworski in a series called "Dot-Com Debates," where they discuss lively issues in the networked economy. Do profits matter? Do the valuations make sense? Who has it better, dot-com startups or dot-coms backed by bricks-and-mortar giants? Does segmentation matter on the Web? Tune in by visiting us at *www.marketspaceU.com* as Dr. Rayport and Dr. Jaworski provide educational and entertaining discussions.
- *Our cases (www.marketspaceU.com)*. Our library includes cases written for top business schools and our own cases written by our team of scholars and practitioners. Case studies—long used in clinical psychology, medical, and business school programs—are designed to facilitate a dialogue or, more appropriately, a healthy debate on the alternative solutions to a particular problem.

  Today, there are precious few case studies that illustrate "what works" in the networked economy. Our casebook provides a unique and comprehensive selection of cases that are both timely and relevant. The interesting challenge in crafting cases on evolving firms is that the solution seems to be changing as rapidly as the practitioner is able to diagnose the problem. We use the word "seems" because there are some basic strategy principles that last. Our intent in providing these case studies is to challenge your thinking about the business principles that have emerged and will emerge in the networked economy.
- *Case Dashboards (www.marketspaceU.com)*. For each case, we offer an enhanced multimedia teaching note to keep instructors informed on the case and in control in the classroom. Each dashboard provides a quick summary of the case since the date it was written, as well as a list of key articles, teaching aids (for example, a time line of company developments), discussion questions, Point-Counterpoint debates, and real-time company news updates.
- *Lecture Dashboards (www.marketspaceU.com)*. For each textbook chapter, we offer enhanced PowerPoint slide decks designed to capture key chapter themes and insights. These slide decks offer visual aids to assist instructors who are using our textbook to teach an e-commerce course

or module presentations on various networked-economy topics. Similar to the case dashboards, we provide 24/7 news feeds on themes related to the lectures as well as streaming videos with various business leaders.

- *Syllabus (www.marketspaceU.com).* For instructors using our textbook to teach an e-commerce course or module, we offer a 13-week course syllabus with suggested course timing, class session summaries, and class preparation questions.

- *Irwin/McGraw-Hill website (www.mhhe.com/marketspace).* Our online instructor's manual is designed to help faculty using our textbook to teach an e-commerce course or module. Our online manual offers a concise summary of each chapter's key themes, classroom questions (and answers) that highlight those themes and spur lively classroom debates, and relevant student project assignments designed to reinforce key learning points in each chapter. The *Introduction to e-Commerce* Instructor's Manual provides teaching tips for each chapter, PowerPoint slides (10 to 15 slides per chapter), test and discussion questions, exercises, and associated websites that illustrate the chapter content.

For Faculty

The changes taking place in the networked economy have energized the classroom and brought a new set of teaching challenges. Students have unprecedented access to sources of information and data, and they have had a greater range of experiences—from investments in dot-coms to their own startup battle scars—so support for teachers in the classroom has advanced from a blackboard or two to a multimedia toolkit to make lessons more immediate.

These developments make the job of staying on top of the new businesses and effectively conveying their lessons more difficult. Given the speed of change, how can we prevent being blindsided by late-breaking developments? Since the "old warhorse" cases often no longer work, what can we repurpose, and where do we turn for new frameworks?

- Our *Introduction to e-Commerce* textbook, along with our *e-Commerce* and *Internet Marketing* textbooks, provide a strong knowledge foundation to help chart your course through these challenges.

- Our casebook and stand-alone cases raise key issues to show how new knowledge is applied in the business world and to drive productive discussions.

- Our teaching-support materials give you unequaled confidence in the classroom: Our teaching notes outline the issues and chart the questions; our case updates give you real-time intelligence on the case, time lines of case developments, key articles, and focused Point-Counterpoint questions.

- Our articles and forums provide in-depth insight into what academic and business leaders are thinking and doing.

- Our extensive media library of interviews provides the first—and the last—word on networked-economy issues from the men and women who are driving them.

For Students

You are riding the wave of a technological revolution that is changing the way the economy operates. Businesses, entrepreneurs, governments, academic institutions, and nonprofit organizations are all scrambling to hire students who understand, can operate in, and can lead in this economy.

- Our *Introduction to e-Commerce* textbook, along with our *e-Commerce* and Internet *Marketing* textbooks, provide a strong business knowledge foundation.
- Our case studies show how this knowledge is applied in the business world.
- Our articles and forums provide in-depth insight into what academic and business leaders are thinking and doing.

Jeffrey F. Rayport
Cambridge, Massachusetts

Bernard J. Jaworski
Los Angeles, California

September 12, 2002

Brief Contents

Contents

CHAPTER 1

Framework for e-Commerce   1

CHAPTER 2

Basic Technology of the Internet and e-Commerce Businesses   27

CHAPTER 6

Market Communications and Branding 193

CHAPTER 7

Implementation 235

CHAPTER 8

Metrics   273

Framework for e-Commerce

OVERVIEW

Many of our students and clients have asked us to explain how managing an e-commerce business is different than managing a traditional business. In this chapter we set forth those differences in detail while attempting to frame the unique attributes of the networked economy and their implications for managers and strategists. In doing so, we present a working definition and framework for the study and practice of electronic commerce, discussing both the strategy involved in running an e-commerce company and the four infrastructures—technical, capital, media, and public policy—that can influence that strategy. We conclude the chapter with an overview of each of the remaining chapters in the book.

PLEASE CONSIDER THE FOLLOWING QUESTIONS AS YOU READ THIS CHAPTER:

1. What are the categories of e-commerce?
2. What are the new views of strategy in the networked economy?
3. What is the framework for the field of e-commerce?
4. Why does a senior manager need to know all four infrastructures?
5. What are the roles and responsibilities of senior e-commerce managers?
6. What key challenges do senior leaders face today?

INTRODUCTION

After several years of turbulence for Internet stocks and the resulting failure of many companies, it is easy to underplay the impact of e-commerce in daily life. Yet, every day in the newspaper we read articles about companies that are helping the growth of the Internet. These articles cover companies that engage in e-commerce (such as Amazon.com or eBay), provide access to the Internet (America Online), create software for the Internet (Ariba and Commerce One), or supply the hardware that supports the Internet (IBM, Cisco, and Nortel Networks). Television programs carry 30-second ads for both pure dot-coms and the online outlets of well-known bricks-and-mortar stores. As we drive to work, we see billboards that point us to websites for entertainment, commerce, information, or community. We pass office buildings that display the corporate signage of dot-coms. Many of us carry handheld devices such as personal digital assistants (PDAs) or wireless phones that are connected to the Internet. Despite recent layoffs, many of us still work for (or have friends and family that work for) online companies. And so the day goes—with constant stimuli related to the Internet, e-commerce, and the networked economy—as we work, shop, dine, or drive through our communities.

One of the outcomes of this proliferation of Internet companies is the emergence of new terminology, including the phrase **networked economy**. There are many definitions of this term, but most people agree that networked-economy businesses have several key traits in common:

- They create value largely or exclusively through the gathering, synthesizing, and distribution of information. Their success is predicated on creating value by tapping the power of electronic information networks and new-media interfaces.
- They formulate strategy in ways that make management of the enterprise and management of technology convergent.
- They compete in real time rather than in "cycle time" and operate in constantly responsive dialogue with their customers and markets.
- They operate in a world characterized by low barriers to entry, near-zero variable costs of operation, and—as a result—intense, constantly shifting competition.
- They organize resources around the demand side (e.g., customers, markets, trends, and needs) rather than the supply side, as businesses have traditionally done.
- They often manage relationships with customers and markets through "screen-to-face" channels and interfaces, which means that technology, rather than people, manages these relationships.
- They use technology-mediated channels and have ongoing operations that are subject to measurement and tracking in unprecedented and granular ways.

Putting these characteristics together does more than give a rigorous understanding of what business managers and pundits alike mean when they talk about doing business in the networked economy. Each of these statements indicates changes in how practitioners determine strategy, deploy resources, operate firms, manage relationships with their markets, and measure results. This does not mean that everything we previously knew about business becomes irrelevant and obsolete, but it does mean that significant changes in the business environment justify new approaches to thinking about strategy and management.

The purpose of this book is to provide an overview of the entire field of e-commerce. Hence, the book is written for present and future practitioners who desire to know more about all aspects—strategy, technology, capital, media, and public policy—of the networked economy. Our intent is to deeply explore the core concepts of online strategy and associated enablers, enriched by a wide variety of examples, case studies, and explanations culled directly from practice.

In the next section, we discuss the various forms of e-commerce activities, including traditional, retail-like companies such as Amazon, Yahoo, and Gap.com, as well as business-to-business players such as Dell, Cisco, and General Electric.

Definition and Scope of e-Commerce

Definition

Digital technology has changed the economy. The primary source of value creation for consumers has shifted from physical goods to service and information. In essence, e-commerce is characterized by several attributes:

- *It is about the exchange of digitized information between parties.* This information exchange can represent communications between two parties, coordination of the flow of goods and services, or transmission of electronic orders. These exchanges can be between organizations or individuals.

- *It is technology-enabled.* E-commerce is about technology-enabled transactions. Web browsers are perhaps the best known of these technology-enabled customer interfaces. However, other interfaces—including automated teller machines (ATMs) and electronic banking by phone—also fall in the general category of e-commerce. Businesses once managed transactions with customers and markets strictly through human interaction; in e-commerce, such transactions can be managed using technology.

- *It is technology-mediated.* Furthermore, e-commerce is moving beyond technology-enabled transactions to technology-mediated relationships. Purchases in the marketplace at Wal-Mart are technology-enabled in that shoppers have human contact with a cashier whose cash register does PC-based order processing. What is different in e-commerce is that the transaction is mediated much less through human contact and more by technology—and, in that sense, so is the relationship with the customer. The place where buyers and sellers meet to transact business is moving from the physical-world "marketplace" to the virtual-world "marketspace." Hence, the success of the business rests on the screens and machines that manage customers and their expectations. Compared to a time when all transactions involved human-to-human contact, that is a big difference.

- *It includes intra- and interorganizational activities that support the exchange.* The scope of electronic commerce includes all electronically based intra- and interorganizational activities that directly or indirectly support marketplace exchanges.[1] In this sense, we are talking about a phenomenon that affects both how business organizations relate to external parties—customers, suppliers, partners, competitors, and markets—and how they operate internally in managing activities, processes, and systems.

A Contemporary Definition

In summary, **e-commerce** can be formally defined as follows: technology-mediated exchanges between parties (individuals or organizations) as well as the electronically based intra- or interorganizational activities that facilitate such exchanges.

Distinct Categories

There are four categories of e-commerce (see Exhibit 1.1): business-to-business, business-to-consumer, peer-to-peer, and consumer-to-business.

Business-to-Business

Business-to-business (B2B) activity refers to the full spectrum of e-commerce that can occur between two organizations. Among other activities, this includes purchasing and procurement, supplier management, inventory management, channel management, sales activities, payment management, and service and support. Major players such as FreeMarkets, Dell, and General Electric may be familiar names, but there are also some exciting emerging consortia that combine the purchasing power of traditional competitors such as GM, Ford, and DaimlerChrysler, which jointly created Covisint. Similar initiatives are under way with industry groups, including pharmaceuticals, commercial real estate development, and electronic subcomponents.

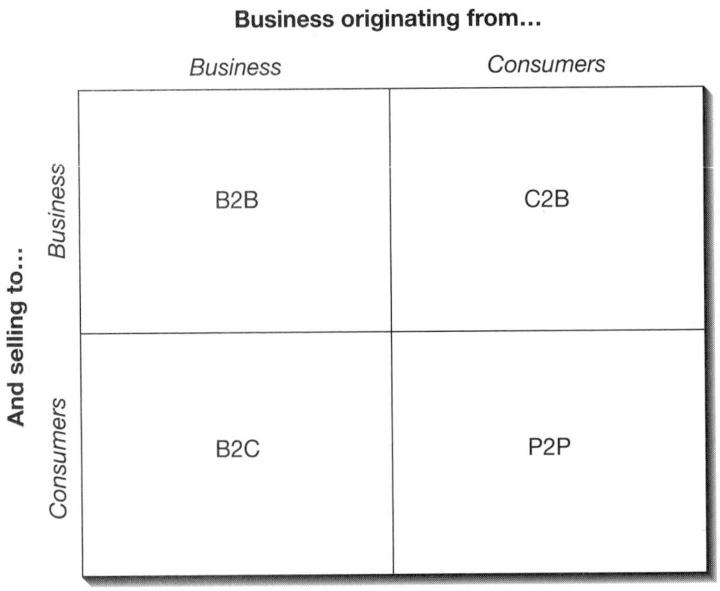

Business originating from...

	Business	Consumers
Business	B2B	C2B
Consumers	B2C	P2P

And selling to...

EXHIBIT 1.1   Four Categories of e-Commerce

Business-to-Consumer

Business-to-consumer (B2C) e-commerce refers to exchanges between businesses and consumers, such as those managed by Amazon, Yahoo, and Charles Schwab & Co. B2C transactions can include the exchange of physical or digital products or services and are usually much smaller than B2B transactions.

Peer-to-Peer

Peer-to-peer (P2P) exchanges involve transactions between and among consumers. These exchanges can include third-party involvement, as in the case of the auction website eBay. Other operations that support peer-to-peer activity include Owners.com and Craigslist (classified ads), Gnutella (music), Monster (jobs), and Lavalife (personal services).

Consumer-to-Business

Consumers can band together to present themselves as a buyer group in a **consumer-to-business** (C2B) relationship. These groups may be economically motivated, as with demand aggregators, or socially oriented, as with cause-related advocacy groups at SpeakOut.com.

Converging Categories of e-Commerce

Some authors argue that a single chain of e-commerce will ultimately emerge. This chain will be a superset of the categories noted above. Therefore, it is increasingly important to think of a single demand-and-supply chain that can be most accurately characterized as initiating with end-customers and rippling backward through a supply chain to the eventual raw-materials producers. Moreover, the chain can ripple through the P2P to C2B exchanges as well.

Consider, for example, the purchase of a Harry Potter book at Amazon.com. Exhibit 1.2 illustrates how the sale of Harry Potter books can ripple throughout the four e-commerce quadrants. In the first time period, thousands of consumers buy the most recent Harry Potter book through Amazon. This purchase triggers an electronic exchange between Amazon and the publisher to request more books. This order forces the publisher to print new copies. The new copies trigger orders of paper products, shipping materials (from cardboard suppliers), and ink. Meanwhile, consumers may be able to "demand aggregate" through public websites or through corporate bulk-purchase rates. Finally, after the books are read, they can be sold on eBay. Thus, it could be argued that the categories of e-commerce are not distinct, but rather intimately linked in a broader network of supply and demand.

Strategy Making in a Rapidly Changing Environment

The online environment changes faster than the offline environment, so it is difficult for a company to select a strategy and stay the course. Indeed, a hallmark of online companies is their ability to shift resources, revenue models, and content. How can a company faced with these changes set a strategy? In this section, we begin with a discussion of a classical approach to strategic analysis and planning. Next, we discuss how recent authors have challenged this perspective and how the Internet may force a reconsideration of central tenets of this approach. We conclude with a discussion of emergent strategy.

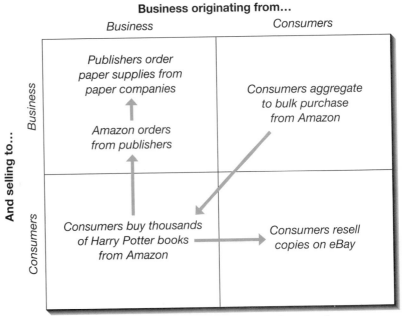

EXHIBIT 1.2   Convergence of e-Commerce Categories

Classical Strategic Planning

Exhibit 1.3 shows a classical framework for the strategic management process. This process begins with the identification of the mission, or vision, of the firm. A mission specifies why the organization exists, with a particular focus on the benefits it provides to chosen customers. Once the mission is spelled out, the firm can begin to address its specific goals; these goals may be financial, customer oriented, internally focused, or shareholder based. Given the broad company goals, the firm is in a position to carefully analyze its core strengths and competencies, as well as the forces that operate outside its official boundaries. This includes competitive forces as well as broader developments related to economic, political, and social conditions.

The careful balance of internal and external analysis leads to a choice of strategy for the company as a whole, called "corporate strategy." Strategies that relate to specific divisions within a company are termed "business-unit strategies." Once the strategies have been agreed upon by the senior managers, the firm can implement the strategies in the marketplace through a series of specific policies, programs, procedures, and budgets. Then, the senior management team can monitor marketplace success and take corrective action as needed.

The New Views of e-Commerce Strategy

The speed of change and adaptation must be figured into the classical strategic-management equation. While the basic tools of strategy remain the same—external and internal analysis, strategy choice, and implementation—the speed of change in the online environment has forced companies to act and react more quickly. In this section, we discuss two new perspectives

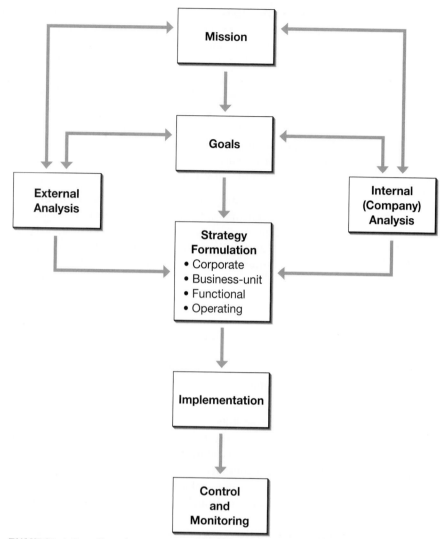

EXHIBIT 1.3   Classical Framework for Strategic Management

on strategy. The first perspective, termed "sense and respond," focuses on the agility of the firm in the face of rapid change. The second, termed "strategy as simple rules," points to the need for simple decision rules—as opposed to massive strategy analysis—that can guide managers in spotting and acting on market opportunities. Finally, we conclude by looking at two key consumer-based aspects of Internet commerce: customization (i.e., individualization) and interactivity.

Sense and Respond

In 1998, Professors Stephen Bradley and Richard Nolan of Harvard Business School noticed a shift had taken place from what they called the "make and sell" approach that characterized traditional business to more of a "**sense and respond**" approach.[2] Amid so much experimentation and unexpected change, the sense-and-respond paradigm was important for two reasons:

- *It provided an approach to strategic thinking that was intuitive, actionable, and easy to implement.* Executives were no longer paralyzed by attempts to overanalyze the unknown challenges and problems that they were facing; they could start experimenting with solutions instead.

- *It made companies focus on listening in a new manner to customers to reduce the high levels of uncertainty.* The make-and-sell paradigm made most companies "very good at responding, but not very good at sensing [the customer]."[3] It had also become increasingly difficult to predict what was going to be successful in the first Internet age. By proactively soliciting feedback from customers, companies could get a better sense of what was—or was not—going to be hot in the market.

The sense-and-respond approach has two shortcomings, though. First, it is a reactive approach that appears most appropriate for incremental competitive moves. The starting point is always the customer. By sensing what the customer likes and dislikes, the company can figure out how to best respond. At no point is there an attempt to proactively change or influence the likes and dislikes of the customer. This is not very apt for strategies that require significant customer education (such as those for breakthrough innovations) or in industrial markets.

Second, this approach is more appropriate for traditional offline companies defending themselves against new Internet entrants in their markets. And even then, no sensing in the world would have predicted the rise of Napster, or provided companies in the field with a means to react to it.

Strategy as Simple Rules

A second perspective on strategy has recently emerged that stresses the need to focus the organization on **simple rules** rather than complex strategic planning exercises.[4] Environments are viewed as both rapidly changing and unpredictable. Thus, it is impossible to anticipate all of the possible market conditions that may unfold. In light of these situations, organizations should follow very simple decision rules (e.g., Cisco's early rule that companies that it acquired should have fewer than 75 employees, 75 percent of whom should be engineers). Much like the U.S. Marine Corps' rules of engagements, these simple decision rules are doctrines that guide choices in the heat of battle. Just as all future military battlefields cannot be anticipated, all future business environments cannot be predicted. Hence, simple rules help senior e-commerce managers recognize positive (or negative) situations and react accordingly. Psychologists—or, more specifically, decision scientists—term these cognitive approaches "pattern recognition." For example, expert chess players intuitively recognize various board patterns as they emerge and can anticipate the reactions of competitors and perhaps even the winning moves as the battle unfolds.

Exhibit 1.4 illustrates the recent ideas of Kathleen Eisenhardt and Donald Sull on the strategy of simple rules. They highlight the differences among three strategy approaches: the "position" approach typically taught in marketing or strategy courses, the resource-based view of the firm (which emerged in the past decade), and the simple-rules approach. Perhaps the most interesting aspect of this chart is the key strategic question. The positioning approach asks, "Where should we be (versus the competition)?" The resources approach asks, "What should we be?" And the simple-rules approach asks, "What process should we follow?"

	Position	Resources	Simple Rules
Strategic Logic	• Establish position	• Leverage resources	• Pursue opportunities
Strategic Steps	• Identify an attractive market • Locate a defensible position Fortify and defend	• Establish a vision • Build resources • Leverage across markets	• Jump into the confusion • Keep moving • Seize opportunities • Finish strong
Strategic Question	• Where should we be?	• What should we be?	• How should we proceed?
Source of Advantage	• Unique, valuable position with tightly integrated activity system	• Unique, valuable, inimitable resources	• Key processes and unique simple rules
Works Best In	• Slowly changing, well-structured markets	• Moderately changing, well-structured markets	• Rapidly changing, ambiguous markets
Duration of Advantage	• Sustained	• Sustained	• Unpredictable
Risk	• It will be too difficult to alter position as conditions change	• Company will be too slow to build new resources as conditions change	• Managers will be too tentative in executing on promising opportunities
Performance Goal	• Profitability	• Long-term dominance	• Growth

Source: Kathleen M. Eisenhardt and Donald Sull, "Strategy as Simple Rules," *Harvard Business Review* (January 2001), 109.

EXHIBIT 1.4 Three Approaches to Strategy

Within the context of the classical strategic-management framework (Exhibit 1.3), the positioning approach emphasizes the external environment, the resource approach emphasizes the internal environment, and the simple-rules approach focuses on the organization process within the internal environment. Hence, all focus on one part of the framework. While we agree that firms need to move very quickly—much like a battlefield commander—it also makes sense that the commander is able to bring resources to bear on the field and his position versus the competition. Hence, it may be that all three approaches have important contributions to the strategy formulation and execution process for networked-economy firms.

Factors of Consumer Behavior in the Online Environment

The notions of sense and respond and strategy as simple rules have evolved in response to increasingly unpredictable and rapidly changing business environments. We now turn to two factors that, having increased in importance with the rise of the Internet, are now the consumer-behavior constants of online businesses: customization and interactivity.

Customization

Customization, or individualization, refers to the personalization of communications between users and a website. This customization can be initiated by the firm (i.e., the firm customizes its site for the user) or by the user (i.e., user builds a custom version of the site, such as MyYahoo). This ability to create a custom experience through the use of technology is one of the profound changes affecting the evolution of consumer behavior.

Interactivity

The second force that affects consumer behavior is the two-way communication between users and the site. **Interactivity** is defined as the users' ability to conduct two-way communication. This includes user-to-user and firm-to-user communication. Typically, strategy execution—or, more narrowly, market communication—has focused on mass-market programs that involve large sums of money allocated for one-way communication (such as television, radio, or magazine advertising). With the advent of direct mail and telemarketing, we have witnessed the emergence of so-called one-to-one marketing. However, it should be stressed that the communication in these situations is typically one-way and, often, a one-time occurrence. In sharp contrast, the Internet affords the opportunity for a dialogue, which may be in real time or asynchronous (over hours or days). This ability to converse is at the heart of the revolution. It puts the customer in control of the interaction and, hence, increases the probability of a positive outcome for both parties.

The Process of Emergent Strategy

Consider a final note on strategic change. Much has been written about how the emergence of the Internet has forced companies to react more quickly—perhaps even with limited forethought. There is evidence in prior strategic-management literature of a phenomenon that closely parallels this view. Henry Mintzberg, one of the foremost contributors to the field of strategic management, observed what he terms "emergent strategy."[5] A firm first sets out its intended strategy; this strategy is what the firm hopes to achieve in a certain timeframe—say, a fiscal year. However, a series of developments unfolds in the marketplace—or within the firm itself—that give rise to unplanned, or emergent, strategies. According to Mintzberg, these emergent strategies are the unplanned responses to unseen changes. They are not the classical top-down analyses of the formal planning process; rather, they are the real-time changes in strategy that are often felt and initiated by the troops.

Thus, emergent strategy is not unlike the sense-and-respond approach discussed earlier. The major difference is that the sense-and-respond approach is typically directed by senior managers, while emergent strategy often comes from the executives who are at the front lines executing the strategy. Regardless of approach, it is clear that firms often modify their intended strategy as the forces of the four infrastructures change.

The Framework for the Field of e-Commerce

Now that we have explored e-commerce and the new challenges it brings to strategy development, we will set up a framework that best illustrates how to learn and think about the networked economy. Exhibit 1.5 shows how we view the dynamics of the field and, consequently, how this book is structured.

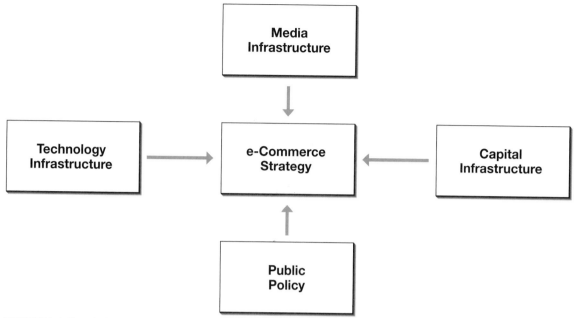

EXHIBIT 1.5   A Comprehensive Framework

At the core of e-commerce activities is the strategy of the enterprise. Wrapped around this strategy process are four critical infrastructures: technology, capital, media, and public policy. These four infrastructures provide the context—both the opportunities and the constraints—in which the strategy operates.

The Strategy Formulation Process

There are six interrelated, sequential parts to this strategy: market opportunity analysis, business models, customer interface, market communications and branding, implementation, and metrics (see Exhibit 1.6). To fully understand how these six decision areas interrelate, we apply them to MarketWatch.com at the end of each strategy chapter, using both our secondary analysis of the MarketWatch.com strategy and interviews with the company's senior leadership team.

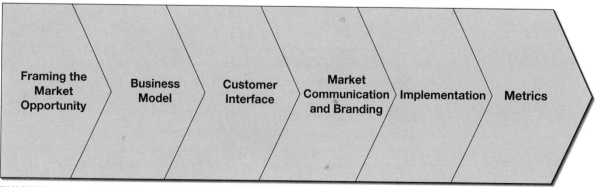

EXHIBIT 1.6   e-Commerce Strategy

The Context of Strategy Formulation: The Four Infrastructures

Successful strategies emerge from a deep understanding of where the market—and, hence, the cash flow—will be in both the short-term and long-term future. The important word in this sentence is *market*. While the market certainly involves the customer—indeed, the customer is at the center—a market also includes the buyers and sellers as well as the broader contextual forces that shape the nature of the marketplace exchange. We argue that there are four critical forces that the e-commerce manager must know and manage if the online firm is to be successful. These four forces are technology, capital, media, and public policy. We review each of these forces and provide a simple illustration.

Technology Infrastructure

The **technology infrastructures** of the Internet and websites are both enablers and drivers of change. An infrastructure is defined as "the foundation of a system." In this case, the technological foundation of the Internet and websites enables the running of e-commerce enterprises. Understanding technology infrastructure is essential to managing a successful online business. Knowing what technology is available (as well as understanding the tradeoffs involved) and then being able to make the appropriate choices so that the website can be a reflection of the company's strategy is critical.

Capital Infrastructure

Where does the money to launch these new businesses come from? How does the process work, from finding the right managers to building the business plan and seeking funding sources? Finally, how should this venture be valued? Any successful senior e-commerce manager must understand the **capital infrastructure** and know how to secure funding for a venture (whether independently or in a global 2000 company) and, subsequently, value that business.

Media Infrastructure

Why is the **media infrastructure** an important issue for all e-commerce managers, whether they run GE Medical Systems, USAToday.com, or Gamesville.com? The answer is that the Internet is a mass communication platform. Just as technology evolution sets the context for technology choices and the capital markets set the context for funding, media convergence provides both opportunities and constraints for the practicing manager. Managers who run e-commerce enterprises must learn to manage a staff responsible for design interface, stylistic choices, editorial policies, and, most important, content choices associated with this new communication venue. Thus, in addition to all other tasks, the e-commerce manager is now a publisher of digital content on the Web.

Public Policy Infrastructure

All decisions related to strategy, technology, capital, and media are influenced by laws and regulations—in short, public policy. The **public policy infrastructure** affects not only the specific business but also direct and indirect competitors. Senior managers must understand the current laws and how the laws may change to hurt or help their businesses and those around them.

Why a Senior Manager Needs to Know All Four Infrastructures

Consider the media company Bertelsmann and, in particular, Bertelsmann Music Group (BMG). Bertelsmann is a major player in the music industry; in fact, recent statistics place it as one of the largest music companies in the world. Music companies are organized around several functions, including (1) artist and repertoire, (2) recording, (3) manufacturing, (4) distribution, (5) marketing, and (6) music sales. At the core of the revenue stream is the CD recorded by the artist. The lion's share of the revenue in this industry is garnered by the record companies (e.g., BMG or Sony) and the retail outlets. The artist typically receives approximately 10 percent of the revenue from each CD sale.

Historically, the most significant challenge for BMG was the discovery of new talent. Once artists were discovered, BMG invested significant sums of money in marketing those individuals or groups through radio play on local FM stations, concert tours, publicity tours, and so on. The cash cow for BMG was CD sales. Because BMG was vertically integrated—it owned, or controlled, the production and manufacturing of each artist's CDs—it was able to achieve healthy sales margins.

Enter the Internet. Since 1999, file-swapping software such as Napster, Gnutella, and Aimster has allowed users to swap digitized music files without the intervention of a third party such as a music company. Hence, a student in a dorm at the University of Southern California could swap music with a student at the University of New Hampshire. The effect has been significant: Recent data suggest that Napster successors Morpheus and Kazaa have 90 million and 75 million registered users, respectively, and Kazaa alone had 1.1 billion files downloaded in April 2002.[6] Also, in the past few years, MP3 players—devices that play the digitized music files—and CD burners have become more prevalent. So, the ability to use digitized music files has risen along with the ability to swap them.

In this new file-swapping era, music companies such as BMG could disappear altogether. So what could BMG do? One move would be to try to shut down file-swapping websites—as the Recording Industry Association of America and other record labels have tried to do. Another move would be to ignore the new technology and simply focus on product sales. Another move—which is what BMG decided to do—would be to try to use the new technology by forming a partnership with Napster. After making significant investments in Napster, Bertelsmann agreed to buy it on the condition that Napster file for bankruptcy. In August 2002, that deal was still pending.

We now provide the types of questions that BMG executives should have been asking at the time this book was written, in the summer of 2002. Consider the following set of sample questions in each domain.

e-Commerce Strategy
- Has the digitization of music revealed unmet or underserved needs that BMG can exploit?
- Who, other than the other record labels, are BMG's competitors? Has the Internet brought new, indirect competitors?
- Can BMG find a sustainable revenue model on the Internet?

- With an agreement to buy Napster's post-bankrupt assets, how can BMG utilize its technology and users?
- Will the Internet change how talent will be discovered? Will BMG be able to retain its big-name artists?
- How can BMG use the Internet to market both itself and its artists?
- What is the impact of NTT DoCoMo Inc.'s wireless service and Sony's delivery of music over wireless networks in Japan?

Technology Infrastructure

- How effective are streaming files versus downloadable files? Which do customers want?
- How can BMG leverage Napster's software for its own benefit? What other technologies will emerge?
- Should BMG wait for other major music firms to solve the problem, or should it acquire or partner with other emerging technology players?
- Should BMG invest in a large website to distribute its music?

Capital Infrastructure

- What is the business plan for BMG in the file-swapping era?
- How does BMG continue to secure funding inside of Bertelsmann?
- What is the new pitch to the office of the chairman?
- How does Bertelsmann invest in online, digital music? What portfolio does it support?
- How should BMG be valued?

Media Infrastructure

- Bertelsmann is a media empire. What media integration—print, audio, or video—is necessary to support its music websites? Does it integrate only its media, or does it access competitor media?
- What are the implications of media convergence for BMG?
- Do customers want rich media or simple music files?

Public Policy Infrastructure

- How does the recent emergence of digital rights management (DRM) technology affect music distribution?
- What is the effect of recent legislation on patents, copyright infringement, and taxation on BMG?
- How will legislation regarding broadband affect whether BMG should invest heavily in delivering digitized files to customers?
- How will recent moves by the Recording Industry Association of America to take action against users of file-swapping websites affect record sales? Will there be a backlash by consumers?

These questions highlight the central point of our framework (Exhibit 1.5), namely, that strategic online choices cannot be made without considering these four infrastructures, which provide the context for BMG's online strategy. Most notably, the legal outcome of the copyright infringement suits of the major record companies against file-swapping sites may (or may not) influence the evolution of the recording industry. Moreover, software such as Aimster, which allows users to control access to their own PCs, could change the fact that it is now exceptionally difficult to track who is swapping with whom. Finally, the biggest play for BMG is likely to be related to media convergence—how it brings its vast magazine, music, TV, and Web properties together in a single, bundled offering.

The Roles and Responsibilities of a Senior e-Commerce Manager

Given the evolving online environment, what is the role of the senior e-commerce manager? The previous section focused on the strategic questions and choices that confront the senior management team at BMG. Now, we shift our focus to the roles and responsibilities of all senior e-commerce managers. Do these managers need the same skill set as senior executives at leading bricks-and-mortar companies, or do the skill sets of e-commerce managers need to vary? The answers, naturally, are "yes" and "yes." Senior managers need to have the basic business skill set as traditional managers but must also incorporate new knowledge, skills, and capabilities.

Cross-Discipline, Integrative Position

Exhibit 1.7 provides one perspective on the evolving skills, knowledge, and capabilities that are expected of senior leaders in the e-commerce arena. The exhibit highlights a few observations about the role. First, entrepreneurship is at the heart of any online business. Keep in mind that the Internet has been a significant commercial entity only since the 1990s. By definition, therefore, almost all online businesses are new. The e-commerce manager must be able to make strategic decisions quickly and with authority—much like the classic entrepreneur of offline business. Second, the executive must be trained in a variety of traditional disciplines, including marketing, logistics, accounting, and finance. To assume the role of general manager, the individual must be

Marketspace Interview

Lise Buyer, Venture Capitalist

There's a really smart fellow by the name of Paul Saffo—he's with the Institute for the Future—who has a great line that is just so applicable to the Internet. He says that we always overestimate what a new technology can accomplish over two years and grossly underestimate its impact over 10 years. And that's just what we've seen with the Internet. We've way overestimated how quickly it would "change everything," so now we're dumping all these stocks and wondering whether the whole thing was just a bubble. But the truth is that over the next 10 years, the Internet will inspire huge, profound changes to all kinds of businesses, from core industries to new enterprises.

In many ways, the Internet is like the telephone. Those who embrace it and struggle in the short term with how it changes their businesses should ultimately turn out to be big winners. And those who ignore it will likely find themselves in some degree of difficulty.

well schooled in the basic business disciplines. Third, the senior manager must add two new disciplines to the mix: technology sophistication and media knowledge. The senior executive must be comfortable with the hardware and software that make the business run. Finally, because we noted earlier that an Internet business is a media business at its core, the manager must understand the role of mass communication and what works in terms of media choices and media integration.

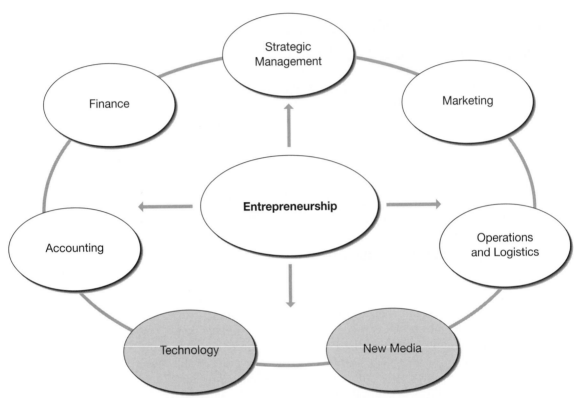

EXHIBIT 1.7   Relevant Disciplines for a Senior e-Commerce Executive

Responsibilities of the Position

While Exhibit 1.7 provides an overview of the senior e-commerce manager's areas of responsibilities, in the next section we take a deeper look at the day-to-day responsibilities (see Exhibit 1.8).

Provide a Vision

One of the most important tasks of the senior manager is to establish the vision for the online business. As Patricia Seybold notes in her book *Customers.com*, this is a tricky exercise, because focusing too narrowly means one is probably describing the world as it exists today, while looking too far into the future does not provide concrete direction for employees—or revenue for the business.[7]

So, how does one balance the need to be concrete while providing a vision that gives direction to the troops? In *Built to Last: Successful Habits of Visionary Companies,* James Collins and Jerry Porras note that superior visions often

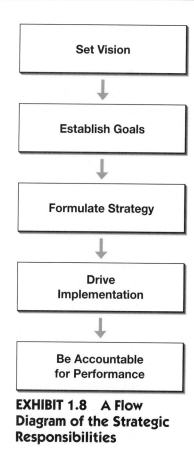

EXHIBIT 1.8   A Flow Diagram of the Strategic Responsibilities

reflect something more than simple revenue or business goals. They point to visions that stress higher-order effects on society.[8] Hence, a vision that says, "We want to be the largest online supplier of ethical, over-the-counter drugs" is not as motivating as one that says, "We want to help people recover from illness to improve their social, medical, and family welfare."

Strong visions provide direction for employees to rally around, encourage investors to "bet" on the company, and send a signal to the market that the firm is able to provide leadership in the evolution of industries. This last point is particularly critical for networked-economy firms.

Set Process and Outcome Goals

The second major task for the senior leader is to set the strategic direction of the company by specifying clear performance targets. As will be discussed in Chapter 8, the metrics for success vary depending on the stage of the business life cycle. As online companies have matured, the metrics to track their success have changed. At first, metrics such as unique visitors and customer base were important for new Internet companies; then, metrics such as conversion rates became the new buzzwords. Now, financial returns are the metrics most discussed. What is important in this environment is for the senior manager to decide what goals are in line with the company's strategy and life cycle and not just what metrics are most popular at the moment.

As we discuss in Chapter 8, we believe that the successful e-commerce executive must track both "process" measures of success and "outcome" measures of success. In this context, outcome measures reflect the concrete financial measures that appeal to investors, while process measures illustrate the firm's performance in variables such as customer satisfaction, employee recruitment, new-product development, and access to new markets. These process measures provide the triggers for financial success.

Formulate Strategic Direction and Choices

After communicating the vision and target goals of the firm, the senior manager must specify its strategy. This involves making concrete choices—and associated tradeoffs—related to each phase of the e-commerce strategy process, including market opportunity choice, business-model specification, the design of the customer interface, and other aspects.

This process is typically managed by the most senior executive. Much of the groundwork comes from careful analysis of the market and the firm's capabilities, and while it is not one person's job, the most senior manager leads and directs the process. It is that manager's responsibility to build consensus, make the tough calls, and be accountable for the strategic direction.

Drive Implementation

Strategy implementation is about making the right choices related to the people, structure, systems, and processes to execute the strategy. The most senior manager must make these choices, which (as noted earlier) require a deep understanding of technology implementation as well as new-media integration.

Accountable for Performance

The senior manager is responsible for the performance of the organization. While the organization as a whole produces (or does not produce) the desired results, it is the senior leader who is accountable to the board or other relevant stakeholders.

Location in the Organization

Senior e-commerce managers can be found in many parts of a conventional bricks-and-mortar company. In Exhibit 1.9 we provide a framework for understanding the organization of e-commerce businesses and, hence, senior e-commerce managers within traditional companies. The framework is composed of a cross between the responsibilities (e.g., line executive versus staff executive) and location within the organizational hierarchy (e.g., corporate, business unit, stand-alone company).

Line Executive

The senior manager may be a line executive who is responsible for the profit and loss of an online initiative. Think of a general manager who is responsible for all aspects of the business: setting strategy, hiring, supervising technology choices, and taking responsibility for success or failure. This is particularly true when the firm shifts its focus to become demand-centric and attempts to aggregate products or services across the business units of

	Corporate	Business Unit	Stand-Alone
Line Executive	• Corporate site management • Cross-business-unit integration site	• Report to general manager of business unit	• Separate business from corporate parent
Staff Executive	• Supports corporate-wide initiatives	• Supports and advises strategic business unit e-commerce initiatives	—

Note: Line executives are accountable for profit and loss of the business; staff personnel provide support services to line personnel

EXHIBIT 1.9   Where to Find Senior E-Commerce Managers Within Existing Bricks-and-Mortar Companies

the corporation. Or the senior manager may be responsible for a business within a particular corporation. Here it is likely that the firm has a digital equivalent of its traditional business. Finally, the company could have a stand-alone e-commerce business, perhaps with its own brand name.

Staff Executive

A staff executive does not have formal profit-and-loss responsibility for a business. His role is to support the efforts of the line executives in the execution of their strategy. The senior e-commerce executive may be a staff function at the corporate or business-unit level (see Exhibit 1.9).

Key Challenges for Senior Leadership in Today's Environment

As the growth of Internet companies slows, several challenges must be confronted by the firm's most senior e-commerce executives. These challenges are caused by forces related to factors inside the firm, such as the integration of online and offline operations, as well as forces outside the firm, such as changing customer dynamics and the evolution of technology. The following sections briefly review five major challenges.

Understanding Customer Evolution

Customer behavior evolves. Winning firms anticipate the features and functions that matter most to target customers. Currently, Amazon and Barnes & Noble.com compete on a set of benefits—convenience, price, variety of offerings, trustworthiness, and security—that matter most to the various segments of their customers. However, as these benefits that once differentiated each firm are taken for granted—or perceived as simply the cost of doing business—each firm must continually innovate to stay abreast of changes in consumer tastes, desires, and needs. They must invest ahead of customer tastes to produce a product or service that matches the evolution of the market.

Amazon's well-regarded 1-Click shopping service is one such innovation. When people started shopping on the Web, checkout speed was not an important variable. Customers were most concerned about reliability, correct invoices, and receiving the order. Once these benefits became expected, speed became important. To address this concern, Amazon invested ahead of consumer tastes to develop its 1-Click service, which automatically stores customers' shipping and billing information. Amazon's introduction of the service was timed exactly with the evolution of consumer desires and, hence, was a great success.

The challenge for senior executives is to invest heavily in understanding the evolution of customer needs—and to invest ahead of these needs, so that the launch of the innovation coincides with customer desires.

Charting Changing Technology

It is almost impossible to stay on top of changing technology. By the time this book is printed, technologies discussed in later chapters may be replaced by next-generation products and services. Much like the evolution of consumer tastes, the evolution of technology—and a firm's investment in it—must coincide with the development of the market. Consumer tastes and technology choices need to match to ensure competitive advantage.

It is perhaps obvious to state that what matters most is not the technology itself, but the evolution of consumer needs and how new technology can support and reinforce those needs. The senior executive must be well schooled in basic and emergent technologies. Hence, the role of chief technology officer is critical to online firms. New technologies are constantly emerging and disappearing. Picking the right ones, and investing ahead of the curve, is a constant, high-stakes gamble for the senior management team.

Balancing Irrational Exuberance and Irrational Doom

In summer 2002, when this book was written, large layoffs had been common in the dot-com sector for more than two years. So is the e-commerce sector dead? Hardly. Many pundits who follow the evolution of technology-intensive innovations argue that this is part of a normal pattern. The impact of new technologies in the first two to three years is typically overestimated, but the impact over 10 years is severely underestimated. Thus, the market had expectations that were too high for the year 2000, but perhaps too low for the year 2010.

What is the senior executive's role in this investment environment? To some degree, it is a matter of riding out the storm. That is, the executive must continually reassure the workforce that the company will weather the current environment, reassure investors that the business model makes sense, spell out the path to profitability (if necessary), and paint a vision that can rally all relevant stakeholders, including partners, customers, and employees.

Integrating Offline and Online Activities

Certainly one of the most important unfolding business trends is the increasing pressure on offline firms to integrate their online activities. This is particularly true for "customer-facing" activities such as advertising, branding, retail and online store design, service, warranties, and returns. Depending on the executive's position within the firm (see Exhibit 1.9), the importance and degree of influence on this integration will vary. However, regardless of their location in the hierarchy, we anticipate the senior executives will be under increasing pressure to be closely aligned—in terms of systems, structure, processes, compensation, and employee welfare—with the traditional offline business.

Identifying the Key Levers of Competitive Advantage

Consistent with the idea that the senior leader needs to anticipate changing consumer and technology trends, the executive must also realign the resource system of the firm in advance of these trends. Stated differently, the key levers of competitive advantage are likely to evolve as the market evolves. The best senior leaders are able to reallocate their resources and capabilities in anticipation of an evolving competitive landscape.

Overview of the Book

As noted before, this book reflects our framework for understanding e-commerce. We now discuss each chapter as part of the overall "five box" framework of the book—strategy decisions at the core, with the four infrastructures influencing those decisions. We begin with a discussion of basic Internet technology. With this foundation in mind, we turn to an overview of the strategy formulation and execution process. This process is applied to MarketWatch.com throughout the chapters in the strategy section, for which we interviewed key executives of MarketWatch.com. We then turn to the four key infrastructures: technology, capital, media, and public policy. Below are brief previews of each chapter.

Introduction to the Web and Internet

Chapter 2: Basic Technology of the Internet and e-Commerce Businesses

To provide both the novice and expert reader with an understanding of technology infrastructure, we divide this chapter into two parts. The first part focuses on the basics of Internet hardware and software—specifically, how the Internet and the Web work. We give a basic history of the Internet and its underlying technology to provide a knowledge base for the later chapters on technology. The second part of the chapter discusses the new challenges and opportunities that the Internet has brought to companies.

We look at several aspects of selling, including payment, security, and fulfillment, and compare how a bricks-and-mortar company and an e-commerce company would deal with these issues.

Strategy Formulation for Online Firms

Chapter 3: Framing the Market Opportunity

In this chapter, we revisit the business basics to construct an original online approach to formulating business strategy. In doing so, we focus on the company, competition, technology, and customers. The goal is to understand what market analysis becomes in this new world and to introduce a process not only to understand the market but also to identify those unserved or underserved portions of the market. This chapter presents a seven-step process that can help a company determine if there is a market opportunity.

Chapter 4: Business Models

While some believe that many Internet businesses do not need business models, we strongly disagree. There may be poorly articulated models out there, but business-model definition is essential to competition in this new space. We introduce the four components of the Marketspace Business Model: (1) the value proposition or cluster; (2) the online offering; (3) the resource system that the firm selects to deliver the offering; and (4) a revenue model that enables the business to generate revenues, cash flows, and, ultimately, profit margins. These four choices constitute the foundation of the strategy decisions that we explore throughout the book.

Chapter 5: The Customer Interface

The visible presence of most e-commerce businesses is a digital- or rich-media interface. While networked-economy businesses may make substantial use of traditional offline interfaces—retail points of sale, printed catalogs, stand-alone kiosks, or call centers—they rely primarily on a virtual storefront connected to the Internet. In this chapter, we develop the set of design tools and elements that we refer to as the 7Cs of the customer interface: content, context, community, commerce, customization, communications, and connection. In particular, we focus on the levers that management can use to create a competitive advantage and generate customer value through these essential elements of interface design.

Chapter 6: Market Communications and Branding

In the demand-oriented world of the new economy, there is nothing more valuable than "mindshare," or the ability to attract and hold the attention of markets and customers. The traditional tools of attention management are marketing communications. In this chapter, we explore the variety of traditional and new-media communications approaches that provide competitive advantage to networked-economy businesses, and we delve into the extraordinary power of brands in this new information-enabled world. Many believed that the Web would create a world of downward price pressures and rapid commoditization of goods and services of all kinds. As we will explain, the opposite has occurred. Brands are more important than ever—and some would argue that, at least in business-to-consumer ventures, they are essential to success.

Chapter 7: Implementation

While it is important to create a strategy, implementation of that strategy is vital to a company's success. In this chapter, we discuss how implementation of an online strategy is different than implementation of an offline strategy, and what occurs when there is poor implementation. We then discuss the different aspects of implementation, including human assets, organizational structure, and systems.

Chapter 8: Metrics

The dynamic relationship between strategy and market feedback demands new approaches to measurement and evaluation of business results. We know that e-commerce businesses offer unprecedented opportunities for capturing information on how markets operate and how customers engage in search and shopping behavior. Because these kinds of data are available in rich granular forms and in real time, we introduce a new management tool called the Performance Dashboard. It is a set of metrics that reflects both the early warning indicators of the progress of an e-commerce strategy as well as outcome measures such as customer satisfaction and financial performance.

Technology Infrastructure

Once a company creates an online strategy, it needs to build the website. Our technology chapters help managers understand what is involved—both in the process and in the technology—in building a website.

Chapter 9: Website Development

In this chapter, we discuss the process of creating a website. We explain the stages that the development team must go through, from starting the website to going live. We discuss the user-experience definition (how the team chooses its target customers and understands what those customers will do on the website), the architecture design process, implementation, the test/build process, and rollout.

Chapter 10: Website Architecture

As websites have grown in complexity and size, the choices that the company must make have also increased. While cost, time, and performance are the biggest tradeoffs, other variables include maintenance, security, flexibility, and scalability. It is important for e-commerce managers to understand these types of choices and make intelligent decisions so that the website created clearly reflects the company's strategy.

Capital Infrastructure

Chapter 11: Capital Infrastructure

This chapter is designed to give the student an understanding of how a startup can obtain capital. We focus on the types of capital most online companies pursue: venture capital and angel financing. While a business may have the best idea or new technology, getting capital—both human and financial—is critical. In this chapter, we explore the relationship between human and financial capital, namely, the business plan and management team. We also discuss sources of financing and how to choose the right mix for a startup, as well as the various stages of funding.

Media Infrastructure

Chapter 12: Media Transformation

In this chapter, we discuss the convergence of media to a digital platform, as well as the organizational convergence of media through "megamergers." Among the key issues of media convergence are the increased fragmentation of media usage among consumers and the resulting megamergers of the past decade, in which the ultimate goal was to maximize the use of similar content across multiple media platforms. This chapter also provides a starting point for a lively discussion about the future of the media. With continued media fragmentation expected—especially with the increased usage of new applications such as broadband access, video-game players, and handheld computers—several possible scenarios of future media use emerge.

Public Policy Infrastructure

Chapter 13: Regulation

In this chapter, we explore how the government is currently regulating the Internet and what it may regulate in the future. We discuss self-regulation versus government regulation and how the Internet's new technology and lack of boundaries have created regulatory challenges. We explore issues such as access, privacy, free speech, and intellectual property, and determine how the laws and regulations currently governing these issues will affect e-commerce and Internet businesses.

Summary

1. What are the categories of e-commerce?

Four distinct categories of electronic commerce can be identified: business-to-business, business-to-consumer, peer-to-peer, and consumer-to-business.

Business-to-business refers to the full spectrum of e-commerce that can occur between two organizations. Many of the same activities that occur in the business-to-business sector also occur in the business-to-consumer context. Peer-to-peer activities include auction exchanges, classified ads, games, bulletin boards, instant-messaging services, and personal services. In a consumer-to-business relationship, consumers can band together to form buyer groups.

2. What are the new views of strategy in the networked economy?

Several new views have emerged, changing the classical strategic planning process. The sense-and-respond view offers an approach that is intuitive, actionable, and easy to implement. It also makes companies listen in a new manner to customers. The sense-and-respond approach makes companies reactive to consumer opinion, though, instead of proactive in trying to change the market.

The simple-rules approach stresses that an organization should focus on simple rules instead of complex strategy planning. It creates a battlefield mentality that causes the company to recognize pattern behavior and respond quickly, instead of developing grand strategies that are pushed into the marketplace.

3. What is the framework for the field of e-commerce?

E-commerce does not consist only of the businesses themselves. While business strategy (market opportunity, business models, customer interface, market communications and branding, implementation, and metrics) is at the core of e-commerce, it is important to note that the four infrastructures—technology, capital, media, and public policy—all affect it. Technology consists of the hardware and software upon which the Internet is built. Finding the right source and amount of capital—both human and financial—affects whether or not the business can become, or stay, a business. Media affects opportunities and constraints placed on a company. Government regulations affect what a company can and cannot do. Exhibit 1.5 illustrates how, in the field of e-commerce, strategy is influenced by the infrastructures.

4. Why does a senior manager need to know all four infrastructures?

A senior manager needs to know all four infrastructures because they will affect the strategy he or she chooses for the firm. Bertelsmann is a good example of a company whose managers need a strong understanding of all four infrastructures. Knowledge of the technology infrastructure is important in understanding issues such as streaming files versus downloadable files and how BMG can potentially leverage Napster's software to its own benefit. A manager must understand the capital infrastructure in order to make decisions about BMG's business plan in the file-swapping era and how the music group should be valued. He must also understand the media infrastructure in order to figure out how best to leverage Bertelsmann's media empire on the Internet. Finally, he must understand public policy issues in order to understand issues such as the regulation of copyright, patents, and trademarks on the Internet.

5. What are the roles and responsibilities of senior e-commerce managers?

Senior e-commerce managers have many roles and responsibilities. They must make strategic decisions quickly and with authority; they must understand the traditional disciplines associated with offline managing such as marketing, finance, logistics, and accounting. Senior managers must also have an understanding of technology and media. Finally, they must understand the role of mass communications to be able to make the best choices in terms of media integration.

6. What key challenges do senior leaders face today?

The key challenges include understanding customer evolution, charting changing technology, balancing irrational exuberance and irrational doom, integrating offline and online activities, and identifying the key levers of competitive advantage.

1. Find examples of each of the categories of e-commerce: B2B, B2C, P2P, and C2B.
2. For each of the examples found in Exercise 1, describe the levels of interactivity and/or customization on the website.
3. How is Bertelsmann BMG affected by the four infrastructures today? What issues from each of the infrastructures would affect a manager from Yahoo? From Salon.com?

networked economy	consumer-to-business	technology infrastructure
e-commerce	sense and respond	capital infrastructure
business-to-business	simple rules	media infrastructure
business-to-consumer	customization	public policy infrastructure
peer-to-peer	interactivity	

Endnotes

[1]David Kosiur, *Understanding Electronic Commerce* (Washington: Microsoft Press, 1997).

[2]Stephen Bradley and Richard Nolan, *Sense and Respond* (Cambridge, MA: Harvard Business School Press, 1998).

[3]Ibid.

[4]Kathleen Eisenhardt and Donald N. Sull, "Strategy as Simple Rules," *Harvard Business Review,* January 2001, 107–16.

[5]Henry Mintzberg, "Patterns in Strategy Formulation," *Management Science* 24 (1978): 934–48.

[6]Jefferson Graham, "File Sharing Is a Hit, Despite Legal Setbacks," *USA Today*, May 13, 2002
(URL: *http://www.usatoday.com/life/cyber/tech/2002/05/14/music-sharing.htm*).

[7]Patricia B. Seybold, *Customers.com* (New York: Random House, Inc., 1998).

[8]James C. Collins and Jerry I. Porras, *Built to Last: Successful Habits of Visionary Companies* (New York: HarperCollins Publishers, 1996).

Basic Technology of the Internet and e-Commerce Businesses

CASELET: E-COMMERCE, THE BEGINNING

In 1992, riots scorched Los Angeles, Wayne's World *partied on at the box office, Billy Ray Cyrus had an "Achy Breaky Heart" . . . and a Cleveland bookseller named Charles Stack plugged in a couple of modems and waited for the ring that would signal Book Stacks Unlimited's first online customer.*

"We waited days," Stack would later tell the Cleveland Plain Dealer. *"Finally the modem rang and we all ran over and watched. The person was going very slowly through the site, so we broke in with a chat function and asked if he needed help. It turns out he was a blind person who had a machine that was reading the text."*

Not exactly "Watson, come here, I need you," but a significant moment in the early history of e-commerce. For this phone call predated the first Web browser (Mosaic) by a year and that other pioneering online bookstore—Amazon—by more than two years. In fact, though the precise history is murky, Stack may be able to claim the title "First Internet Retailer."

Whether or not he was first, his early success certainly presaged the commercial explosion that would soon rock the heretofore largely academic and techie Internet. Soon after that first call, Stack was fielding orders from around the world and had expanded to 12 dial-in lines. In 1993, he changed the name of his business to Books.com and added a telnet site with eight more lines. In 1994, he launched a bona fide website that would soon feature literary news, electronic texts, even audio clips of author readings and interviews. By 1996, ready to move on, Stack sold his venture to CUC International (now Cendant) for nearly $5 million. Today, Books.com's auspicious URL belongs to Barnes & Noble, and the store itself is gone. But the e-commerce revolution it helped to usher in is very much alive.

This chapter was coauthored by Jeffrey Rayport, Bernie Jaworski, Eugene Wang, and Joseph Hartzell.

PLEASE CONSIDER THE FOLLOWING QUESTIONS AS YOU READ THIS CHAPTER:

1. What is the Internet?

2. What are four components of Joseph Carl Robnett Licklider's original vision that make the Internet easy to use?

3. What are the content types on the Web?

4. How are websites created?

5. What are the key similarities and differences between e-commerce and bricks-and-mortar selling in regard to location?

6. How does e-commerce payment differ from bricks-and-mortar payment?

7. What role does security play in e-commerce?

8. What challenges exist in e-commerce fulfillment?

INTRODUCTION

This chapter provides a history of the Internet and the underlying technology that enables it. We begin with the development of the basic technology that powers the Internet, including TCP/IP, routing, and packet switching. Next, we talk about the World Wide Web—how Web documents are created, what web-pages can contain, and how Web browsers work.

This chapter also introduces the fundamental concepts behind e-commerce. We create a framework for understanding the basic tenets of traditional commerce and then apply those tenets to e-commerce. In the process, we uncover key similarities and differences in conducting business across offline and online channels. In addition to identifying and exploring these fundamental concepts, we provide brief overviews, where appropriate, of the technologies that support these basic business concepts on the Web.

What Is the Internet?

Early Networks

The Internet's beginnings can be traced back to a series of memos written in 1962 by the Massachusetts Institute of Technology's Joseph Carl Robnett Licklider outlining what he called the "Galactic Network" concept. Licklider envisioned a global network through which everyone could share and access data and programs. Shortly after writing the memos, he became the head of computer research at the Advanced Research Projects Agency, later referred to as ARPA. ARPA would play a large role in spearheading and funding the Internet's early development.

Over the next decade, great advances were made in network technology, specifically in packet switching and the beginnings of what would eventually become TCP/IP, the basic protocol that defines how information is exchanged over the Internet. By the late 1970s, network computing began to flourish. Several computer manufacturers introduced minicomputers with enough computational power to support multiple users. As these minicomputers became less expensive, they began to populate businesses and other organizations. To connect these computers and permit the transfer of information between them, many organizations began installing **local area networks (LANs)**—essentially, a web of personal computers and work stations able to communicate with one another. Also by the late 1970s, ARPA had several operational computer networks and had begun to introduce the technology to the military. However, LAN technology was limited by geographical distance: It could only connect computers and networks that spanned a few square kilometers or less. To allow computers and networks separated by larger geographical distances to communicate, ARPA developed a **wide area network (WAN)** called the ARPANET. WAN technology allowed engineers to build networks to connect computers and LANs separated by large geographical distances.

However, organizations that employed multiple networks faced a problem: Because no standard for networking existed, each manufacturer took its own approach, building hardware that would read a certain type of software or that could only communicate with hardware from the same manufacturer. As a result, individual networks had no way of communicating with one another because computers built by different manufacturers could not connect with one another. Computer networks of that time formed isolated islands, with no paths existing between them.

Compatibility

Before the development of internetworking technology, an organization with networks had two options. The first was to choose one set of network technologies that would satisfy the entire organization. While this option enabled communication between all networks and computers within the organization, it came with tradeoffs, such as inflexibility and increased functional and switching costs. The second option was to allow groups within the organization to choose the network technology that best suited them, without regard to compatibility issues. While this option did give organizations more flexibility in negotiating and purchasing network hardware and applications, there was a downside: More often than not, computer networks within the same organization would be unable to communicate with one another.

To solve the compatibility issue, ARPA researched how to connect all computers in a large organization, regardless of the manufacturer or the type of software that the LAN connecting the computers was running. The result was a new approach to connecting computer networks known as internetworking. The Internet that we know today is named after this technology. Many pieces of software enable internetworking, but the two most well known are **Internet Protocol (IP)** and **Transmission Control Protocol (TCP)**. IP software sets the rules for data transfer over a network, while TCP software ensures the safe and reliable transfer of the data. Together, these components are referred to as TCP/IP. Because these two components are the best-known internetworking software, the abbreviation TCP/IP is commonly used to represent the whole suite of internetworking software.

Open System

To encourage the adoption of a standard network communications protocol, ARPA decided to publish its research results and make public the internetworking technology it developed. The idea was to encourage network builders to adopt the same standards, making it possible for networks to speak to one another. **Standards** are rules that companies agree to adhere to so that their products can interact. For example, there is a standard in the United States that everyone drive on the right side of the road; if everyone failed to adhere to this standard, traveling on U.S. roads would be slower and more dangerous.

At the time, the decision to develop networking standards was shocking. Most network-building companies advocated the "closed system" approach, in which individual companies' internetworking technology remained proprietary rather than shared; they believed that keeping their technology private was crucial to retaining customers and maintaining their competitive edge. But because large organizations typically needed to purchase different brands of computers to serve a variety of purposes, the inability to link these computers together had quickly grown impractical.

The "open system" development of TCP/IP not only helped to establish TCP/IP as the Internet standard but also played a key role in the rapid development and success of the Internet. The TCP/IP standard ensured universal access to the Internet by preventing any one company from controlling that access and helped ensure compatible communication among diverse hardware. This universal compatibility allows the Internet to function like a single network, even though the Internet is actually a collage of many networks. Without the TCP/IP standard, the Internet could not function as it does today.

How the Internet Works

Although the Internet seems like a single, giant network to which many computers attach, it is not. The Internet is a consortium of networks; it connects millions of computers and thousands of networks. Wide area networks allow the Internet to overcome physical boundaries by providing efficient long-distance technology that can connect many networks. The term **backbone network** is often used to describe a major WAN to which other networks attach. The backbone reaches some, but not all, sites; these locations are called backbone sites. In fact, the building blocks of the Internet are often described as a collection of WAN backbones connected to LANs that, in turn, connect to individual computers.

Several components of Licklider's original vision of a Galactic Network were important in creating this network of shared access and data. These include human-friendly addressing and the domain name system, packet switching, routing, and TCP. We now discuss each of these in more detail.

Addressing and the Domain Name System

With so many computers connected to the Internet, it is important that each computer be uniquely identified—which is why each Internet-connected computer is assigned a unique Internet Protocol address. An **IP address** consists of four groups of numbers separated by decimal points; for example, the IP address for *The Chronicle of Philanthropy*'s main computer is 198.108.95.145. However, early network engineers recognized that numeric IP addresses are difficult to remember. Even if they could be memorized, the fact that IP addresses sometimes change makes accurate recollection a constant challenge. To remedy this situation, Sun Microsystems developed the **Domain Name System (DNS)** in the early 1980s. The DNS gives each computer on the Internet an address comprised of easily recognizable letters and words that could be used instead of a numeric IP address. For example, the DNS address *http://www.philanthropy.com* is much easier to remember than the IP address *http://198.108.95.145*, yet both addresses take the user to the same website.

The last portion of most DNS addresses is known as the top-level domain. The top-level domain characters refer to the nature of the organization that uses that particular address. Common top-level domains include .com for commercial, .org for organization, .edu for education, .mil for military, .gov for government, and .net for network. Other top-level domain standards in the United States include .biz, .aero, .coop, .info, .museum, .pro, and .name.

For computers located outside of the United States, an additional country domain appears after the top-level domain. Countries are identified with two letters; for example, .uk represents the United Kingdom, .au represents Australia, and .cn represents China. The address *http://www.amazon.co.uk* points to Amazon's U.K. site.

Packet Switching

Licklider's Galactic Network would also require an efficient way to transfer large amounts of data across a complicated network. Engineers realized early on that smaller pieces of data would be far easier to transfer. As a result, they developed the Internet Protocol. Every computer connected to the Internet must run IP software and follow the rules of the IP, which specify exactly how a computer is to communicate with other computers— including how large data files are to be broken up into smaller, more manageable data files, or **packets**. The IP defines exactly how a packet must be formed. In addition to breaking down large files into smaller packets, the Galactic Network notion would require a system for sharing the limited resources of a network. If only one data transfer can occur on a given wire at a given time, then multiple devices that share the same wire must take turns using the wire.

Early telephone networks worked on the same kind of system. Like early computer networks, they were also **circuit-switched networks**—networks in which only one data transfer can occur at a given time. All the subscribers in a neighborhood shared the same telephone line. If two neighbors were having a telephone conversation with each other, a third neighbor would be unable to use the telephone. The third neighbor would have to wait until the conversation was over before placing a call, as the shared telephone line would accommodate only one conversation at a time. The same applies for computers connected to a circuit-switched network.

This problem is compounded when the data being transferred are of varying sizes. Exhibit 2.1 presents a network of 10 computers that all share the same transmission line. Computer 1 wants to transfer a large amount of data to 7, while 4 wants to transfer a very small amount of data to 6. Although the data transfer from 4 to 6 is much smaller than the transfer from 1 to 7, 6 must wait until 1 has transferred all of its data to 7 before it can begin receiving data from 4.

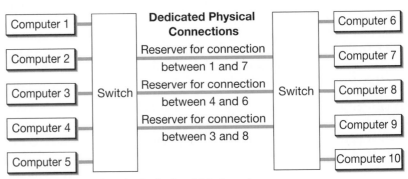

EXHIBIT 2.1   Circuit-Switched Network

To alleviate the delays associated with unequally sized data transfers, computer engineers developed **packet switching**, which has become the fundamental technique that computer networks use to ensure fair access to shared network resources. Instead of being transferred over a network in their entirety, files are broken up into data packets. In this way, the transfer of a large file does not delay the simultaneous transfer of a smaller file.

Exhibit 2.2 presents the same network of 10 computers shown in Exhibit 2.1, only this time the computers are part of a packet-switched network. Computer 1 still wants to transfer a large amount of data to 7, and 4 still wants to transfer a small amount of data to 6. In Exhibit 2.1, 6 was forced to wait until the transfer from 1 to 7 was complete before it could receive any data. In Exhibit 2.2, the IP mandates that computer 1 divide its data into many smaller packets. Because 4 wants to transfer a smaller amount of data, 4 can send its data in a single packet or divide it into smaller packets. Computers 1 and 4 then take turns sending the respective data packets. Packet switching is a more equitable method of transferring data, since it allows 4 to complete its smaller data transfer without having to wait for 1 to complete its large data transfer. Like most computer networks, the Internet is a packet-switched system. All data transferred across the Internet is broken into packets.

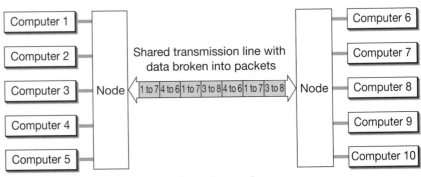

EXHIBIT 2.2   Packet-Switching Network

Routing

Another key piece to bringing the Galactic Network notion to fruition was figuring out how to efficiently route packets to the appropriate destinations within an environment comprised of many different networks. The solution was special-purpose computers called routers that connect the thousands of computer networks that make up the Internet. **Routers** serve as intermediaries between networks; that is, they direct traffic and translate messages so that different network technologies can communicate with one another. It is for this reason that routers are often referred to as the building blocks of the Internet.

Transmission Control Protocol

Another important Internet-enabling technology is Transmission Control Protocol (TCP). In addition to IP software, most computers also run TCP software, which ensures safe delivery of packets. Often, routers will route too many packets to a network so that the network is unable to accommodate and process all of the data. When this occurs, the network is forced to discard some of the packets. Without TCP, these discarded packets would never reach their intended destination.

TCP requires the destination for each packet to send a confirmation message once the packet is received. If this message is not received, then the TCP retransmits the packet. In addition, the TCP puts incoming packets in the correct order. Different packets from the same original message may take many different paths to their final destination—some paths may be short, others may be long. As a result, packets do not always arrive at their final destination in the order in which they were sent. TCP automatically checks the packets upon arrival and puts them in the correct order. Finally, because network hardware failure sometimes results in duplicate packets, TCP automatically checks for duplicate packets and accepts only the first copy that arrives.

Introduction to the Web

Every day, millions of people all over the world use the World Wide Web—61 million, to be precise, as of March 2002.[1] One reason behind the explosive growth in the popularity of the Web is the fact that no one company "owns" the right to create content for the Web; almost anyone with access to a computer can publish something. Another reason is the underlying simplicity of the Web's design. At its core, the Web consists of just three moving parts: *webpages*, which are the documents that a user sees when he opens a Web browser; the *links* that connect these webpages to one another; and the *servers* that store and transmit information to the browsers for display.

Webpages

Like the Web itself, a webpage is made of relatively simple components. In fact, all webpages are constructed of text, just like the sentences on this page. No special software is required to create a webpage. All that a potential Web

Drill-Down

TCP Retransmission Is Dynamic

One could imagine that if the TCP timer that resends a packet if there is no confirmation were static, the Internet would slow down or be prone to constant data transmission error. For example, packets do not always travel the same route or distance to their final destination. As a result, the delivery times for packets vary greatly. If the TCP timer were static, the packets that take a longer time to deliver might cause the timer to expire, triggering the retransmission of duplicate packets. In addition, with a static timer, lost packets whose destinations are close by would experience a delay in retransmission.

TCP does not encounter these problems because it adapts to maximize its efficiency everywhere on the Internet. For example, if the destination computer resides near the sender, TCP will allow only a short delay for receiving a confirmation message before resending the data packet. However, if the destination computer resides far away from the sender, TCP will allow a longer delay for receiving confirmation that the data packet has been delivered.

In addition, if Internet traffic is heavy and data transmission slows down as a result, TCP automatically lengthens the time before retransmission; if conditions change and packets begin traveling across the Internet more quickly, TCP automatically shortens the allotted time. TCP's ability to automatically adjust time-out values has contributed greatly to the success of the Internet. Without TCP's ability to adapt to changing Internet conditions, the Internet could not support the diverse network hardware and applications that it does today.

One alternative to TCP sacrifices quality for speed. User Datagram Protocol, or UDP, provides nonguaranteed packet delivery—that is, unlike TCP, UDP does not check for lost packets. As a result, UDP transmissions, although less reliable, are generally faster than TCP transmissions. Many types of streaming-media software, such as RealPlayer, use UDP because it is fast (important for video) and does not need to guarantee quality (small gaps are less noticeable in full-motion video).

Drill-Down

What Is the Difference Between the Web and the Internet?

A common misconception is that the Internet and the World Wide Web are the same thing. The terms "Internet," "World Wide Web," "Net," and "Web" are often used interchangeably. However, from a technical perspective, the Internet and World Wide Web are two separate entities.

The Internet is a collection of wires, protocols, and hardware that allows the electronic transmission of data over TCP/IP. Any data can be transferred over this collection of hardware and software components. Examples include e-mail, faxes, video, voice, and webpages. The Internet is the hardware and software infrastructure that allows for this data transfer and global networking.

The World Wide Web exists on the Internet. The Web is composed of hypertext pages viewed by a browser, which are served from a Web server over TCP/IP. Webpages always begin with http:// or https://, signifying that the content being viewed is hypertext and transferred using the Hypertext Transfer Protocol. Common webpages include *http://www.yahoo.com*, *http://www.amazon.com*, and *http://www.ebay.com*.

So while the Internet is the infrastructure, the Web can be thought of as an application for the Internet. It is important to note that there are other types of applications that use the Internet but are not part of the Web. For example, e-mail, file transfer protocol (FTP), and peer-to-peer applications such as Napster use the Internet, but not the Web.

author needs to get started is a simple text-editing program (Notepad in Microsoft Windows, for example) and an understanding of HyperText Markup Language (HTML), the language Web browsers interpret to display. Because the vast majority of computers are capable of creating text documents and the syntax of HTML is simple and straightforward, almost anyone with access to a computer has the ability to write webpages.

HTML

HTML is the most common text-based tagging language for creating documents and setting up hypertext links between documents on the Web. **HTML** stands for HyperText Markup Language—"hypertext" refers to the ability to link to other pages, and "markup" describes the way content is displayed. HTML can be thought of as a set of rules and conventions for designing text formats, and those rules and conventions are relatively simple to learn and use. HTML uses tags to structure text into paragraphs, lists, and so forth, and to indicate font size and style. HTML specifies what each tag means and what the text between the tags will look like on the computer screen. For example, if a person creating a webpage wants to have his name appear in bold on that page, he would type this: <b>name</b>, where the HTML tag <b> indicates the beginning of the bold and the tag </b> indicates the end. A sample of HTML source code is included in Exhibit 2.3.

An increasingly popular alternative to HTML is XML, or Extensible Markup Language—"extensible" because its format is changeable, not fixed like HTML. XML allows webpage builders to create their own customized tags and does not scrunch text and tags together as HTML does. XML was designed as an easy means of exchanging data on the Web (e.g., transmitting data to Web servers) and is more often used behind the scenes in applications and databases.

Although it is possible to create great-looking websites by writing each individual page with a text editor, most website authors rely on other tools once their sites exceed more than a few pages. There are a wide variety of tools available for this task. They fall into two main categories: content conversion tools and Web authoring tools.

Content Conversion Tools

Document conversion tools allow someone who has created a document in another application, such as a word-processing or desktop-publishing program, to convert that file into a standard markup language, such as HTML or XML. For example, someone who has created a document in Microsoft Word can convert it into a webpage by simply using the "Save As" command and choosing "webpage" under "Save as Type." Most word-processing and desktop-publishing programs support the creation of hyperlinks and other Web-enabled functions straight out of the box. Document conversion tools enable both existing documents and new documents to be created and posted on the Web with a minimal investment in learning a markup language. It should be noted, however, that using these simple tools significantly limits one's ability to control the look-and-feel of the pages created. Some document programs may not convert easily to HTML, resulting in a document that looks very different on the Web than it does coming out of a printer.

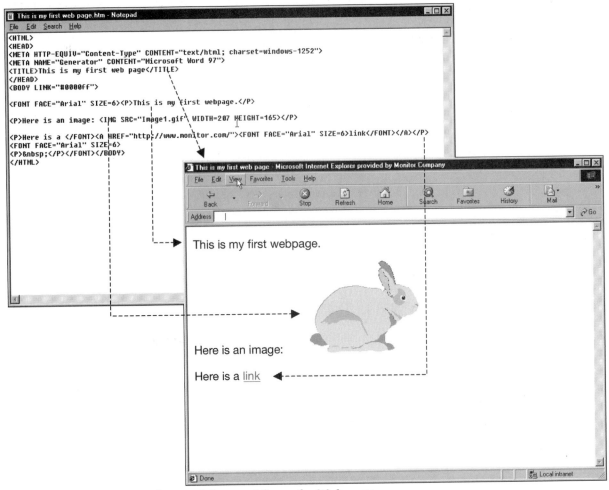

EXHIBIT 2.3   Browser View and Source View of a Webpage

In addition to converting text documents to HTML, it is possible to convert multimedia content from one format to another. Apple's iMovie will convert MPEG video into QuickTime video. Also, ripping programs from companies such as RealNetworks allows users to convert CDs to compressed audio formats (such as MP3) in one step.

WYSIWYG Editors

Not all webpage creation tools require users to work in a markup language such as HTML. **WYSIWYG editors** (WYSIWYG stands for "what you see is what you get") conceal the markup language from the user, allowing him or her to create the page in the exact look that they want without dealing with tags and codes. A WYSIWYG editor such as Microsoft FrontPage allows users not only to easily integrate text and images but also to add multimedia objects, such as sound and animation, to their webpages. In addition to content creation features, these programs usually offer website generation and management features. For example, if a page is moved or renamed, the program will automatically update all links to that page on the website, saving hours of work. High-end editing programs such as Adobe's GoLive and

Macromedia's ColdFusion Studio and Dreamweaver offer more powerful website creation and management features and allow expanded features such as database integration to be built into a website. But these capabilities come at a price: In addition to being expensive, they have steeper learning curves than their less powerful competitors.

Web Content Types

Unlike paper documents, hypertext documents are dynamic. When you read a paper document, what you see on the page is all there is. When you read a hypertext document, the information you see on the screen often serves as a gateway to more information. Hypertext documents might include links to other webpages or images that can be clicked on and downloaded. Although the Web does not limit the number of content types available, most content found on webpages falls into a few broad categories.

Links As mentioned earlier, hypertext links (aka hyperlinks) are used to connect webpages. Links are typically text or graphics that, when clicked, jump a user to another place in a document or to another webpage entirely. There are three basic categories of links: internal anchor links, page links, and mail-to links. *Internal anchors* provide shortcuts to various places within a single webpage, allowing users to jump to the exact section of the webpage that they want to see. Internal anchors save users from excessive scrolling and are most often used in long hypertext documents. A *page link* is simply a hyperlink that connects one webpage to another. *Mail-to links* let users send feedback directly to a website. When a user clicks a designated e-mail link, a message window opens with an e-mail address already entered in the "to" field.

Forms Another way that webpages can solicit information is through forms—basically, fields on a webpage that can be filled out by either typing in text or selecting from a list of preset responses. Users enter their information into the form, then click a "submit" button that transmits that information to a computer program that processes that form. For Internet companies, forms are useful for getting highly structured feedback as well as user information such as shipping addresses and phone numbers.

Images Images are one of the most popular content types on the Web. Before the advent of Tim Berners-Lee's WorldWideWeb browser in late 1990 (see Exhibit 2.4), the Internet was largely accessed with text prompts and text commands through browsers such as Lynx (a Web browser for text-based terminals). The Web consisted primarily of file directories and text, and rich-media webpages did not exist. However, with the introduction of graphical browsers such as Mosaic and Netscape in the mid-1990s, the way users viewed and interacted with the Web transformed completely.

The most widely supported image formats on the Web are Graphics Image Format (GIF) and Joint Picture Encoding Group (JPEG). Both are native MIME types to most browsers. MIME stands for Multipurpose Internet Mail Extensions and means that the browser recognizes certain file formats by their extensions (such as ".gif"). Users will be able to see these images easily, without having to change any settings within their browser, because all popular browsers support these file types.

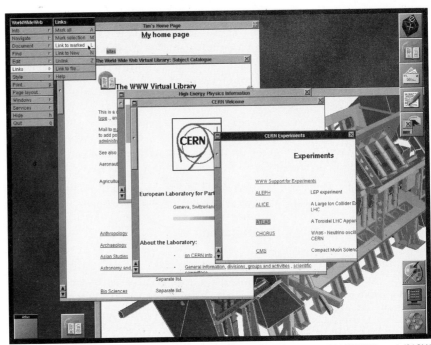

Source: (www.w3.org/History/1994/WWW/Journals/CACM/
screensnap2_24c.gif) © 1994-2001 W3C

EXHIBIT 2.4 WorldWideWeb—The First Graphical Web Browser

- *GIF.* The GIF format, originally developed for CompuServe in the late 1980s, was specifically designed for online delivery. It is an 8-bit file format, which means that it can support up to 256 colors. However, GIF files can do many things that other file types cannot, such as animation, transparency, and interlacing. In this regard, there are two different types of GIF files: GIF87a and GIF89a. GIF87a supports transparency (which allows images to have transparent sections) and interlacing (which allows images to be viewed as they are downloaded). GIF89a supports transparency, interlacing, and animation.

- *JPEG.* The JPEG file format is a 24-bit alternative to the 8-bit GIF format; it can support millions of colors rather than just 256. As such, the JPEG format was developed specifically for photographic-style images. JPEG files use "lossy" compression, which removes information from images and causes a loss in quality. However, the loss is often not visible. Unlike the GIF file format, the JPEG file format requires both compression and decompression. This means that JPEG files have to be decompressed before being viewed. Although a GIF and JPEG might be identical in size, the JPEG will take longer to render in a Web browser because of the added decompression time.

Multimedia The Web also supports multimedia file types such as audio and video. The ability to support multimedia formats plays a large role in the Web's current popularity. Video files such as AVI and MPEG and audio files such as WAV can be easily embedded into webpages.

Drill-Down

Compression

All computers and networks have a finite amount of critical resources. Limitations on processor speed, RAM, hard-drive space, and network bandwidth all affect how much Web content can be stored on servers and how quickly that content can be downloaded and displayed on users' computers. These resource limitations have been an issue for computer users and programmers since the inception of the computer. In fact, this resource scarcity was the key driver behind the "Y2K bugs" that caused such panic in the late 1990s. In the 1960s and 1970s, computer programmers discovered that they could save precious memory space by using a two-digit number to represent a calendar year instead of a four-digit number (68 instead of 1968, for example). Thirty years later, this shortcut had to be undone to prevent millions of computers worldwide from thinking that "00" meant the year 1900 instead of the year 2000.

Smaller Is Better

These hardware limitations, particularly limitations on network bandwidth, have made compression an important technology on the Web. Compression was critical in the evolution of graphical Web browsing, because the ability to compress graphics files made image-rich pages load fast enough to be usable over relatively slow Internet connections. Standard compression types vary for different multimedia content types. For example, JPEG and GIF are often used for images; MP3 and RealAudio (RA) are commonly used for music; and MPEG, QuickTime, and RV are often used for video. These file formats are used to compress otherwise enormous media files into smaller, more manageable units that require less Web-server space and consume less network bandwidth.

Lossy Vs. Lossless Compression

Web-based image file formats have to implement impressive schemes to compress large images to small file sizes. Unfortunately, there is a tradeoff. At times, compression results in a loss of quality. There are two main terms used to describe compression: lossless and lossy. Lossless compression means that even though the file is compressed, it will not lose any quality; a lossless image will contain identical data regardless of whether it is compressed or uncompressed. The GIF file format uses lossless compression.

Lossy compression is the opposite of lossless compression: Data are removed from the image file in order to achieve compression. Often this loss of data is not terribly significant, as the compression procedure was designed to reduce data that are not essential. The JPEG file format uses lossy compression.

Capturing Content

It is becoming much easier to capture, compress, and save content. Printed images can be captured with low-cost scanners, photos can be directly downloaded to a PC with digital cameras, and digital video cameras now make it easy for anyone to capture video content and save it to a hard disk for use on the Web. PC software is then used to compress the content to make it more Web-friendly.

Capturing Images

The two most popular tools for converting images into electronic files are digital cameras and digital scanners. Unlike regular cameras that use film, digital cameras store the pictures electronically in the camera's memory; the images can then be sent to a computer and stored on that computer's hard drive. Digital scanners, on the other hand, are more like copy machines. They scan pictures and then convert the scanned images into files. In the same manner as a digital camera, the image file is transferred to a computer and stored on the computer's hard drive, where it can then be compressed, stored, and used on a webpage.

Capturing Audio

Like images, sounds can also be captured, compressed, and stored for use on the Web. A simple way to record sounds from the real world is to use the microphone port on the sound card of a computer. To record a voice, for example, a person can simply plug a microphone into the microphone port (assuming it has sound capability) and record his or her voice using the recorder program included with the operating system. To capture sounds from recordings, a device such as a DVD player, CD player, cassette deck, or MiniDisc player can be connected to the microphone jack of the computer, and the recordings can be captured using the same method as a microphone. For a cleaner recording of CDs, however, the computer's own CD-ROM or DVD-ROM drive can be used to capture the audio digitally. Most media-player software has the ability to redirect CD output from the speakers to a file on the computer's hard drive. This is a fast and easy way to create high-quality recordings of CD audio.

Uncompressed audio files (e.g., those in WAV format) tend to be very large. An uncompressed three-minute song, recorded in CD-quality stereo on a hard drive, consumes about 25 megabytes of hard-drive space. The enormous size of these files has made compression technologies such as MP3 and RealAudio popular formats for downloading and streaming audio off the Web. Many vendors now offer "ripping" software that allows users to convert their CDs into highly compressed MP3 and RealAudio files. These files can then be played back on a user's computer or, in the case of MP3, on portable players/recorders. Currently, issues relating to the legality of distributing copyrighted music over the Internet remain unresolved. Although it may be possible for Internet users to access copyrighted music and video on the Internet, it may not always be legal.

Capturing Video

As more manufacturers recognize the opportunity the Web is creating for video, capturing video is becoming easier and less expensive. Video capture cards allow users to record the output of camcorders, VCRs, and DVD players onto a PC's hard drive. Some digital video cameras interface directly with PCs over a digital connection so that no quality is sacrificed in the capture process. This uncompressed video can then be converted to a compressed format, such as MPEG, to save storage space and reduce download times.

Web Browsers

All webpages are viewed through programs called **Web browsers**. Compared with other programs, browsers are designed to do a small set of tasks. Because browsers do not have thousands of features and functions embedded in them, they tend to be small in size and simple. This simplicity has contributed to their widespread adoption.

The flexibility of browsers allows new types of functions to be added constantly. For example, multimedia animation was not available on early browsers until a company called Macromedia created a content type called Shockwave to support animation on the Web. Now, support for Shockwave animation can be added in minutes to any computer with Internet Explorer or Netscape Navigator. The openness of browsers allows anyone with the initiative, ability, and a little bit of computer hardware to develop new content capabilities for the Web. These entrepreneurs can add functionality to the Web that can be accessed by millions of users worldwide without the prior approval of any person or company.

Web browsers are specifically designed to display content in a standard file type (such as HTML or XML) in the form of a webpage. Depending on the hardware that is running the browser, some or all of the content described by such a standard file will be displayed. For example, a webpage that contains text, photos, and sounds will display differently on a PC, PalmPilot, and mobile phone. A PC's Web-browsing software will most likely display all three of these content types; a mobile phone's browsing software will most likely display only text. Regardless of what type of content is included on a webpage, it is the browser's job to know what it is capable of effectively communicating to the user. The browser's capabilities are defined by both the hardware it relies upon and the capabilities programmed into it at the time it was designed.

How Browsers Work

The Internet provides access to an enormous quantity of content spread out over many computers using many services. Today's Web browsers attempt to allow users to access this content without having to think about which computer is actually storing the data, where that computer is, and what service is being used to access the data.

As mentioned before, webpages use links to connect users to other content that may or may not be located on the same server as the page from which it links. The address used to identify the location of this content is called a **URL**, short for Uniform Resource Locator. The URL tells the browser several things about how to access the desired content (see Exhibit 2.5):

- *The transmission protocol.* Several protocols are supported by browsers, including HyperText Transfer Protocol (HTTP) for webpages, File Transfer Protocol (FTP) for transmission of files, and the extended S-HTTP for a higher degree of security. One reason that browsers are so powerful is that they need to have the ability to integrate access to several Internet services with one easy-to-use interface. Because the type of transmission protocol required to access these services is defined in the URL, the browser can automatically access that service without requiring the user to run another program.

- *The name of the computer where the content can be found.* For identification purposes, all servers on the Internet are assigned an IP address. IP addresses work much like telephone numbers, making it easy for computers to uniquely identify other computers on the Internet; in fact,

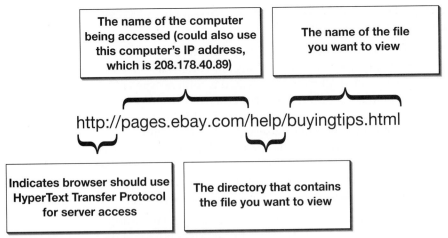

EXHIBIT 2.5   Components of a URL

you can use IP addresses to get access to a server through your browser. As discussed before, to prevent people from having to memorize long strings of numbers, domain names were introduced. Domain name servers basically function like electronic phone books that look up numerical IP addresses when they are given a server's name.

- *The directory on the computer where the content is stored and the name of the file containing the content.* Each file on a server is stored in a directory. The browser needs to know both the name of the file and the directory in which it is stored.

Functions That Browsers Support

Most popular PC-based browsers actually consist of a bundle of client programs that enable them to support multiple Internet services in addition to HTTP for Web access. For example, both Netscape Navigator and Microsoft Internet Explorer allow users to transfer files using the FTP protocol and also include powerful e-mail programs. As mentioned before, the protocol information at the beginning of a URL (http://) makes it possible for browsers to seamlessly integrate all of these services for the user. Many users surfing the Web end up accessing these services without realizing they have switched to a completely different transmission protocol.

Differences in Appearance

Although most webpages can be read by most browsers on the market today, the same page might look a little (or a lot) different depending on the system on which it is viewed.

Different Devices

Obvious variations exist among browsers run on different types of devices. For example, PC browsers tend to support myriad functions, such as high-quality graphics, multiple fonts, and multimedia, while a mobile phone browser will support a much simpler subset of these features—typically three to 10 lines of text. As a result, the same website might look significantly different when viewed on these two devices.

Drill-Down

IP Address Sharing

Although routers see each IP address on the Internet as identifying a unique computer, it is quite common for one IP address to be used for multiple computers or for one computer to use several IP addresses. For example, the vast majority of dial-up modem connections to the Internet are made using dynamic IP addressing. Dynamic IP addressing allows a dial-up service to own fewer IP addresses than it has customers. Because most dial-up subscribers are not on the Internet 24 hours a day, Internet service providers share a limited set of IP addresses among all customers. When a user dials in to his service, his computer sends a discovery packet that requests an IP address along with other connection information from a Dynamic Host Configuration Protocol (DHCP) server. The DHCP server responds to the computer with an assigned IP address that the computer can use while connected to the Internet for that session.

Also, dynamic IP addressing lets several computers on a LAN share the same Internet connection. For example, if you have three computers networked together at your home office and want to connect them all to the same cable modem or DSL modem, all three of these computers could simultaneously access the Internet on one account. Software such as Microsoft's Internet Connection Sharing program can be installed on the computer that is physically connected to the modem (this computer is called a *host computer*). The host would connect to the Internet service provider through this modem and be assigned a dynamic IP address by the provider's DHCP server. The Internet Connection Sharing software would then take packets from the other computers on the LAN (called *client computers*) and send them out to the Internet as if they were from the host. When the information (such as a webpage) came back from the Internet to the host, the host would forward the information to the client that had requested the information. In this scenario, all of the routers on the Internet act as if only one computer (the host) is associated with the IP address making the request. The client computers are visible only to other clients on the LAN and to the host computer.

Different Operating Systems

Although less significant, there are still substantial differences in the way that various computers and operating systems treat the display of visual content. For example, the display of the font named Helvetica renders slightly differently on a Macintosh computer than on a Windows-based PC. A Macintosh also tends to display Web fonts as if they were approximately two points smaller than on a Windows-based PC, even when both computers are running the same browser.

Different Browsers

In addition to device and operating-system differences, there are also differences in the way browser manufacturers choose to display the content described on a page. For example, tables look somewhat different in Internet Explorer than they do in Netscape Navigator.

Platform Independence

Historically, browsers' small size has made them easy to install on devices that are less powerful than PCs (although PC-based browsers are becoming large very quickly). Browsers are either currently or expected soon to be built into devices such as phones, TVs, cars, PDAs, and retail kiosks.

Dynamic Web Functionality

When the Web was first emerging, virtually all websites consisted solely of static pages of text and images. As the Web has evolved, the manner in which content is generated, as well as the way users interact with this content, has changed. Most of the websites run by large corporations, particularly corporations engaged in e-commerce, include pages that generate content in a dynamic manner instead of static webpages connected by HTML links. This is because users now expect more interesting and interactive websites, and because as websites get larger, it becomes much easier to manage the thousands of pages by modifying a few page templates instead of thousands of individual pages. Templates allow Web authors to format a single template page and then have copies of the template populated with information from a dynamic source, such as a database.

The type of information a company posts on the Web, as well as the anticipated level of usage of the site, will determine the way in which the back end of the system will be set up. There are essentially two options when creating a dynamic back end:

1. *Set up a database that generates new static HTML pages at regular intervals.* This type of system might make sense for a website that is reporting weather forecasts and wants to update them every 30 minutes by plugging new data from a weather service into HTML page templates. Because the pages that the browser is viewing are actually static, they can be served easily and quickly by Web servers. This allows the website to manage a lot of traffic without investing enormous amounts of computing horsepower in its servers. However, one drawback of this type of system is that the information is not in real time. The pages are generated on a periodic basis; the data on them do not automatically update, nor can calculations be done on the fly.

2. *Create a Web-based user interface to a computer program running on the server.* Allowing users to directly interact with a computer program over the Web allows far more flexibility and power when designing a site. For example, a person might use this type of system to get real-time stock quotes from her stockbroker's site. When the user submits a request for the current value of her portfolio, the program could contact the stock exchange and provide an immediate update of the prices of each of her stocks. The program could then calculate the sum values of each holding and the percentage value change from the previous day's closing prices. This type of real-time calculation is a major benefit to this server-side program approach to creating a website. One drawback, however, is the fact that such systems require much more processing power to serve many users in a timely manner.

Doing Business on the Internet

Although 2001 saw the failure of many online initiatives, e-commerce is playing an increasingly prevalent role in the lives of consumers. The U.S. Department of Commerce reported that in 2001, 31 percent of Internet users purchased products and services on the Internet, up from 13 percent in 2000.[2] The Commerce Department also estimated that in 2001, $33.7 billion was spent in retail e-commerce sales, up from $27.3 billion in 2000. Both bricks-and-mortar and pure-play e-commerce companies are making millions, and sometimes billions, in online sales. Retail Forward estimated that Amazon.com made $3.2 billion in online revenue in 2001, while Office Depot and Staples made $1.6 billion and $950 million, respectively.

Selling on the Web requires many of the same activities and components needed to conduct business in the offline world. In this section, we examine the similarities and differences between bricks-and-mortar and e-commerce selling as they relate to six key components of running an e-commerce store: placement, merchandise and audience size, presentation, payment, security, and fulfillment.

Placement

Bricks-and-Mortar

When deciding on a store location, a company must consider many factors, including geographic desirability, the other nearby stores, the number of customers the store must accommodate, and the attributes of the space itself. A store's location has a large effect on the number of customers and the type of customers who will flow into the store. For example, a store in a busy mall will likely have more traffic than a stand-alone store. Also, a store near a freeway is more convenient for customers who live far away. It is also important to consider the types of customers who will shop at the store. A high-end boutique would do better in a wealthy town with other exclusive stores than in a low-income neighborhood. A few customers who can afford—and appreciate—the merchandise are better than many customers who cannot afford anything in the store.

Competition

When choosing a location, merchants prefer to set up stores where there is little competition for customers. For example, a coffeeshop owner would be hesitant to open next door to a Starbucks.

Convenience

In addition to considering convenience for the customer, merchants also consider how convenient a location is for themselves. For instance, a merchant such as Wal-Mart, which usually chooses to put a store in a stand-alone location, must consider issues such as security, parking, and cleaning. On the other hand, mall merchants often do not have to worry about these additional responsibilities because they join together to outsource security, parking, cleaning, and even some advertising for all the stores.

e-Commerce

Placement is also an important issue when starting an online store, but in a very different way. While a bricks-and-mortar running store in New York would not worry about competition from a running store in Oregon, one of the fundamental properties of the Internet is that there is no perceived distance between websites. So while the physical location of an online business's headquarters (see the hosting discussion in Chapter 10) is of little concern to the consumer, it is important that the website is highly visible and easily found. Placement of links to the website is an important determinant of traffic for an e-commerce store. For example, just as a bricks-and-mortar store might choose a mall location to gain access to all of the traffic that flows through the mall, an e-commerce store could choose to locate itself in a virtual mall, such as Yahoo Shopping, for the same reason. Yahoo attracts traffic from many types of users. An e-commerce store on Yahoo Shopping could expect that it would receive some of Yahoo's traffic. As with physical stores, it is more important to attract traffic from people who are potential customers.

Unlike a physical location, a website (or links to the website) can be found in many different "places" on the Internet. As discussed earlier in this chapter, websites can be found through their domain names. Some companies have several domain names; Barnes & Noble owns the names *www.barnesandnoble.com*, *www.bn.com*, and *www.books.com*. Companies that do not own the domain name for their industry can still benefit from the domain name, as in the case with Monster.com, which has a link to its website on *www.jobs.com*. Also, as we will discuss in Chapter 4, many online companies partner with other companies. Links for 1-800-Flowers.com can be found on AOL, Yahoo, and the American Airlines website (*www.aa.com*). Search engines such as Google also help users find stores, which is why many online companies pay to ensure that when someone searches for their category, their name comes up early in the search results.

Competition

Like the bricks-and-mortar example of a coffeeshop opening near a Starbucks, competition is also an issue when considering e-commerce location. An online merchant selling books and CDs would probably not choose Amazon zShops as a store location. Because Amazon is one of the largest sellers of books and CDs on the Internet, a smaller merchant would certainly have trouble competing.

Convenience

Some e-commerce locations offer more convenience to the merchant than others. We already discussed the convenience that outsourced services in a mall provide to merchants. The e-commerce equivalent is that large online malls, such as Amazon zShops and Yahoo, can take care of many of the mundane aspects of running an online business, such as payment processing, hosting, and maintenance, allowing the merchant to focus on the core business.

Merchandise and Audience Size

There are two issues related to size. The first is what type of items the store sells—the size of the merchandise will influence the size of the store. The other issue is the number of customers who will be shopping in the store at once. A store where only a few customers trickle in each hour can get by with a smaller space than a store that needs to accommodate a large influx of customers at the same time every day.

Bricks-and-Mortar

After a manager has evaluated the amount of traffic the store should expect, he or she must consider how large the store needs to be to accommodate its products and customers. For example, some types of products require a larger store than others; a store selling furniture would need a larger showroom floor than a card shop. Also, stores that expect heavy traffic need to choose a location with adequate parking and entrances and walkways large enough to accommodate such traffic.

e-Commerce

Just as a bricks-and-mortar manager must evaluate how large a store must be to accommodate its customers and products, so must an e-commerce store manager. Stores that expect a lot of traffic need to be designed to handle that traffic. Just as bricks-and-mortar stores must have an adequate number of parking spaces and wide enough aisles and entrances, e-commerce stores need enough bandwidth, processing power, and data storage capacity to provide the proper service to their customers.

Bandwidth

Bandwidth is the amount of data that can be sent through a connection at once. Imagine a supermarket checkout area. Even though the store experiences peaks and lows in the number of customers throughout the day, the supermarket manager must make sure that the checkout area is large enough to accommodate all of its customers during peak hours. This is the reason most supermarkets always seem to have a few empty checkout stands; the additional checkout stands exist so that the supermarket can accommodate all of its customers during peak hours.

The same concept applies online—the merchant must plan to have enough bandwidth to accommodate customers during peak times. A general rule of thumb is that the average bandwidth utilization should not exceed 30 percent of the total bandwidth available, and during peak times, bandwidth should not exceed 70 percent of the total available.[3] Beyond these levels, performance of an e-commerce store will begin to deteriorate. Therefore, websites such as Amazon and Yahoo must have very large bandwidth capacities to adequately serve their customers.

Another factor that merchants consider when thinking about bandwidth is the type of products or content offered by the store. For example, are the products best displayed with graphics or streaming multimedia? If so, these types of stores need more bandwidth than stores whose products are best sold with simple descriptions.

Websites where customers download files also require a lot of bandwidth. For example, CNet's Download.com is dedicated to providing its customers with the latest software and applications for their computers. Because those types of downloads require the transfer of significant amounts of data, Download.com needs a lot of bandwidth to serve its customers.

Processing Power

Processing power, as we refer to it, is the amount of data that can be processed by a website at a given time. E-commerce merchants have varying needs for processing power. In general, the larger the e-commerce website is in terms of product breadth, number of transactions, and level of interactivity, the greater its need for processing power.

- *Product breadth.* Imagine an e-commerce store that is dedicated to selling only one book. Because the merchant has only one stockkeeping unit, or SKU, this business is fairly simple. Inventory and orders are easy to track and maintain, and the store requires little processing power.

  Now imagine the online bookselling behemoth, Amazon. Amazon claims to have more than 1 million SKUs available to its customers. As a result, managing and organizing these SKUs is a significant and complicated task. Amazon must be able to collect, organize, and display an enormous amount of data. For example, Amazon must provide its customers with a search engine capable of finding more than 1 million titles, authors, publishers, keywords, and topics. In addition, Amazon must be able to accurately track inventory levels and process (potentially) more than 1 million different types of orders. The complexity that Amazon's product breadth adds to its e-commerce store requires a significant amount of processing power.

- *Number of transactions.* Let's revisit the one-book store we mentioned earlier. Because this store sells only one item, it probably does not conduct very many transactions per day, perhaps even per month. Given this low number of transactions, the e-commerce store does not require much processing power.

  In contrast, Amazon.com may process thousands of orders per day. Many of these transactions occur simultaneously. Amazon must be able to simultaneously process orders from a customer in Memphis, Tennessee, who orders *The Works of Alfred Lord Tennyson*, a customer in Manila, Philippines, who orders John Grisham's *The Chamber*, and a customer in Palo Alto, California, who orders Richard Wright's *Black Boy*. Amazon's ability to process large numbers of transactions involving different SKUs requires copious amounts of processing power.

  Consider another example: the Nasdaq stock market. Nasdaq operates three websites—*www.nasdaq.com, www.amex.com,* and *www.american-stocks.com*—which receive more than 20 million hits and conduct roughly 2 million transactions per day.[4] Because Nasdaq must be responsive, providing instant and accurate market data to traders and investors, powerful servers are needed to quickly and reliably process enormous amounts of data. Surprisingly, though, a website such as eBay would need even more power, because its pages are more customized and it has many more products to display. As we'll discuss more in Chapters 9 and 10, each website has individual needs that have to be addressed when considering the processing power needed.

- *Level of interactivity.* In addition to product breadth and number of transactions, the level of interactivity on an e-commerce website also helps to determine the amount of processing power required. Continuing with the Nasdaq example, Nasdaq interacts with a variety of parties and data sources to serve its customers. For instance, Nasdaq interacts with the markets, traders, investors, and others to collect and display accurate market data. In addition, Nasdaq provides its customers with news, research, and financial analysis; it even allows users to customize their own content and track the performance of individual portfolios. These levels of interactivity and customization require that Nasdaq employ some of the most powerful servers available.

Data Storage Capacity

Our previous examples have focused on the power needed to process different types of data. We have also hinted at the enormous amounts of data involved in e-commerce and e-commerce transactions. Online businesses collect huge amounts of customer data such as demographics, purchase patterns, billing histories, and click streams (the sequence of pages visited). A relatively large B2C (business-to-consumer) website that receives about 100 million hits per day will log about 200 bytes of data per hit.[5] This amounts to about 20 gigabytes (1,024 bytes equals one kilobyte; 1,024 kilobytes equals one megabyte; 1,024 megabytes equals one gigabyte) of stored data per day. While 20 gigabytes of data does not seem overwhelming, given that large online merchants tend to keep this data for about three years, those 20 gigabytes can quickly add up to dozens of terabytes (1,024 gigabytes), more information than is contained in the entire printed collection of the U.S. Library of Congress![6]

Presentation

Presentation includes the variety of store components that add or detract from a product's appeal to customers. These components include store layout and customer service.

Bricks-and-Mortar

Store Layout

Store layout often speaks volumes about the image a store wishes to project and the type of customers it wishes to retain. As a result, marketers and merchants often pay great attention to how their merchandise is presented. Good examples of the importance of store layout include upscale restaurants and department stores, which are often able to charge a premium, not because of the quality of their products but because of the elaborate presentation.

Customer Service

Customer service is another important aspect of presentation. Customer service is a necessity for a successful merchant, and it has become a staple in U.S. retailing. Virtually every large U.S. retailer employs personnel dedicated to customer service. Customer service often defines a customer's experience and is a leading driver of customer retention. Similar to store layout, great customer service also often enables merchants to charge premiums for their products. Examples include the luxury hotel chain Ritz-Carlton and upscale department stores such as Nordstrom or Barneys New York.

e-Commerce

Store Layout

As in the bricks-and-mortar medium, store layout can help e-commerce stores draw and retain customers. Online presentation encompasses all customer-facing aspects of the store. Two especially important pieces of online presentation are user interface and customer service.

User Interface   A well-planned user interface is crucial to successful Web selling. An appropriate user interface should be representative of the store's theme, easy to navigate, and pleasing to the store's customers.

- *Ensure your customers see what you want them to.* With bricks-and-mortar stores, a merchant can be certain that the store layout he or she designs and implements will be accurately viewed by customers. However, this is not always the case online. Despite an online merchant's efforts, not all of a store's customers will see what the merchant intends for them to see. On the Web, what customers can see is often limited by the hardware, software, and bandwidth available to them. For example, websites that employ heavy Java applications within their webpages will be difficult for customers to view if they have older, less powerful hardware. Websites that employ Flash animation can be viewed only by customers who install the Macromedia Flash plug-in on their browser. Websites that are multimedia intensive can be appropriately viewed only by customers with high-bandwidth connections.
- *Know your customer.* The user interface should be designed both aesthetically and functionally for the optimum customer experience for the company's target customers. Also, the merchants must be aware of how technically savvy their customers are in terms of hardware, software, and bandwidth.

Online Customer Service

The biggest difference between the customer service experiences in a bricks-and-mortar store versus an e-commerce store is the lack of direct interaction between the customer and the purchasing environment. For example, in a bricks-and-mortar environment, customer service can often be conducted in person. On the Web, however, customer service needs are most often addressed over the Web or with Internet applications such as e-mail, chat, or discussion groups.

- *The Web.* If organized effectively and comprehensively, a website can be an excellent method for distributing static information to customers. Web-based customer service can take the form of informational webpages that anticipate customer questions, often referred to as FAQs (frequently asked questions). The Web can provide a lower-cost customer service alternative for Web-based merchants and faster access to information for consumers than the phone-based solutions of many bricks-and-mortar retailers. Once the website is set up, the cost of providing information is minimal, because no personnel need to be directly involved in the information distribution. Although webpages can be an effective means of customer service, it is important to note that the information contained on them is rarely comprehensive and often not suitable for customers requiring specific information. Bricks-and-mortar stores that have an online presence often use their websites for common questions such as nearest store location, hours, directions, and return policy.

- *E-mail.* One way to help customers get information that is not provided on the website is to allow e-mail inquiries to be sent directly to customer service representatives (CSRs). It is easy to provide e-mail links to the CSRs from a website, and in most cases (especially when the questions asked by customers can be answered in a concise manner), e-mail is more cost-effective than a phone-based customer service call center. Although the company does have to pay CSRs to respond to the e-mail inquiries, there are no phone bills to pay, and usually more customers can be served per CSR via e-mail than over the phone. The primary disadvantage of e-mail support for customers, as compared with telephone or other live support, is that it is not provided in real time. Customers must wait for a response and trust that the company will respond quickly.

- *Chat.* A potential solution to the lack of real-time interactivity of webpages and e-mail is chat-based support. Online chat rooms allow a customer to directly interact with a CSR over a text-based interface. Chat support lets companies provide real-time support with immediate answers to customer questions without incurring the cost of a phone call. In addition, chat support allows CSRs to handle multiple customers at once, which significantly reduces the cost-per-customer interaction. This low cost-per-customer makes chat support attractive to websites where revenue per customer is very low (e.g., advertising-supported websites).

- *Discussion groups.* Although e-mail support tends to be much less expensive than phone support, it still requires that a company pay the salaries of CSRs. Discussion groups are a low-cost form of customer service. A discussion group helps customers interact in a way that allows them to help each other. A discussion group is essentially an electronic bulletin board where customers can post questions and other customers can post responses. The company sets up the discussion group and assigns very few people to manage it. The result is essentially a user-generated list of frequently asked questions to which customers can refer. For example, Hewlett-Packard uses discussion groups to enable users of its printers to help each other with technical questions.

Another advantage to discussion groups is that the company can reference the questions posed on the discussion boards and see where customers are frequently having problems. This information can help in the redesign of product information, the website, and other company operations.

However, a major drawback of discussion groups is that the quality of the information posted on them is sometimes difficult for the company to control. TiVo Community (*www.tivocommunity.com*) was started by customers who wanted to talk about their TiVo digital recording systems, an alternative to VCRs. Because digital recording systems are a relatively new technology, it was helpful for customers to be able to answer each other's questions about how to best save and play back television programs. TiVo, understanding the importance of the website, helped lend support to the website, both financially and by encouraging employees from the company to post solutions to customers' problems. By doing so, users are encouraged to help each other (which saves money for TiVo), and TiVo is able to provide a certain amount of quality control on the website. Another drawback to discussion groups is that, like e-mail support, discussion-group support is not provided in real time. If a customer has a new question that has not already been answered by the group, he or she will have to wait to see if another customer posts a reply. Depending on the interest, activity level, and knowledge base of the customers in the discussion group, questions might get answered quickly or not at all.

Payment

A key component to conducting business is accepting payment. At a high level, payment seems very simple: A buyer receives some type of value from a product or service, and in return, the seller receives some form of payment. Here we examine some aspects of payment, uncovering different issues in the bricks-and-mortar and e-commerce mediums.

Bricks-and-Mortar

In the bricks-and-mortar world, customers pay in a variety of methods, including cash, personal check, traveler's check, debit card, credit card, coupon, and gift certificate. Each one of these payment types has distinct characteristics, and managers must carefully determine which types of payment to accept. Here we will briefly examine some of the issues a manager thinks about when accepting the two most popular payment forms: cash and credit cards.

Cash

Cash is the most popular form of payment in the bricks-and-mortar world. Virtually all offline stores accept cash, from the largest department stores to the corner hot dog stand. Cash is the simplest type of payment to accept, and the only type accepted by many small businesses, such as restaurants. These businesses are typically referred to as cash businesses.

Theft   The most pressing issue for managers whose businesses accept cash as payment is theft. Not only are cash businesses more susceptible to robbery, but employee theft is also a major concern. For example, consider cash register theft. Beyond the simple scenario where the clerk reaches into the cash register, the register provides employees many less obvious opportunities to steal. For example, a customer could pay for an item with exact change and not ask for a receipt. With no record of sale, the clerk could very easily pocket the customer's money. In another scenario, a clerk could enter discounted prices into the cash register for friends shopping at the store. These indirect methods of theft can be discouraged through standardized cash-handling procedures such as giving a receipt to every customer or having separate cash drawers for each employee.

Cash Fees   Another issue that managers must consider is cash fees. Although one would imagine that a cash-intensive business allows the manager to keep all revenue and eliminate bank fees associated with credit card or personal check transactions, this is not always the case. Banks often charge businesses a cash deposit fee. For example, banks regularly charge supermarkets a cash fee of up to 1 percent of cash deposits.

Credit Cards

Credit cards are another popular form of payment at bricks-and-mortar stores. Besides being convenient, credit cards allow consumers to extend their purchasing power. As a result, these cards are often used for larger purchases, when the consumer may not have enough cash on hand to complete the transaction.

Fraud   Theft is also an issue with credit card payments. For example, fraud occurs when someone purchases something with a card that does not belong to him. This can occur when the merchant does not request picture identification or check the back of the card for a signature match.

However, in the bricks-and-mortar world, the main difference between credit card and cash theft lies in which party assumes liability for the theft. With cash theft, the merchant typically assumes liability; however, with credit card purchases, as long as the merchant has a complete and legitimate record of sale (usually a receipt signed by the cardholder), the fraud is committed against the card company, not the merchant. In this case, the merchant still receives payment, and the card company assumes liability.

It is important to note that in some instances, the merchant may be held liable for the loss. For example, if a consumer contacts her credit card company to dispute a sale, a merchant's primary protection is a complete and valid record of sale, such as a signed receipt. Without such information, a consumer's claim may be deemed legitimate, in which case the merchant would have to pay back the money to the card company and the consumer. This is called a *chargeback*.

Fees   In return for their services, credit card companies charge transaction fees to participating merchants. Fees are a per-transaction charge plus a small percentage of the purchase price.

In addition to transaction fees, merchants often have to spend money to lease or buy the equipment necessary to accept credit card payments. This equipment might include a terminal that reads the magnetic strip on the back of a card, dials into an acquiring bank for validation, and prints credit card receipts.

e-Commerce

The main difference between e-commerce and bricks-and-mortar payment methods can be seen when evaluating the natures of the two media. Bricks-and-mortar implies the physical, while e-commerce implies the virtual. As such, an electronic medium prohibits the use of cash and encourages transactions that do not require physical funds but instead involve only data transfer.

Cashless Society

Given the security risks of mailing cash payments, few, if any, e-commerce stores accept cash as a method of payment. Many do, however, accept personal checks, cashier's checks, and money orders. Because these forms of payment are traceable, they are generally considered safer from theft than cash. To pay by check or money order, customers usually mail in the payment, and the merchant ships the purchased items once payment is received. Because of the delays involved with mailing payments, this form of payment is not especially popular on the Web.

Credit Cards

Despite the willingness of online merchants to accept checks and money orders, credit cards are the dominant form of payment on the Web. Their electronic nature allows customers and e-commerce stores to pay and receive payment immediately. While check and money order payments might take days to complete, credit card payment takes only seconds. As a result, credit cards account for the majority of online transactions.

Card-Not-Present Transactions   A major difference between offline and online credit card transactions is that in an offline transaction, the credit card is physically present, while in an online transaction (or a telephone transaction) the card is not physically present. Credit card companies often refer to online credit card transactions as card-not-present transactions. When fraud occurs online, e-commerce merchants are often helpless to protect themselves. Because the card was not physically present during the transaction, an e-commerce merchant is typically unable to produce a valid record of sale, such as a signed receipt. This is an important distinction between offline and online merchants because it shifts the onus of fraud away from the credit card companies and onto the merchants. In the online medium, merchants are forced to absorb all of the costs of their chargebacks.

Higher Fraud Rates   Given the virtual nature of e-commerce transactions, credit card fraud is much more prevalent online than offline. All a potential thief needs to commit a crime online is a valid credit card number, name, and expiration date. No signature or identification is required. The thief does not even need to physically have the card. As a result, credit card fraud occurs in more than 1 percent of all online transactions. This rate is at least 10 times greater than the credit card fraud rate in the offline world.[7]

Higher Fees   In addition to absorbing chargebacks and dealing with higher fraud rates, online merchants must also cope with higher credit card fees. Because credit card fees vary according to a merchant's risk category, on average, e-commerce merchants pay fees that are 66 percent higher than those paid by less risky bricks-and-mortar merchants. Offline retailers typically pay around 1.5 percent of the purchase price, plus an additional per-transaction fee of 10 to 30 cents. However, Web-based retailers pay an average of 2.5 percent of the purchase price plus an additional 20 to 30 cents per transaction.

However, the costs of accepting credit card payments online do not stop there. E-commerce merchants also have to connect their stores to credit card processing networks and fraud protection services, which can add up to 50 cents to the cost of each transaction.

Despite these higher fees, online merchants have no choice but to accept credit cards, because they are the customer-preferred and dominant form of payment on the Web.

Security   Given the increased opportunity for credit card fraud on the Web, security is an important component of enabling credit card transactions. Most credit card transactions are completed by submitting electronic information over the Internet. Data routed through the Internet can be easily monitored or intercepted if not secured. Merchants must take steps to ensure the security of their transactions.

Merchants must address three primary aspects of credit card security: the transfer of data from the customer's computer to the merchant's e-commerce store, the transfer of data from the merchant to the payment processors, and the protection of customer data stored in the merchant's database.

The first two issues concern data transfer on the Internet and are addressed with the use of secure protocols. The most popular security protocol in the United States is **Secure Sockets Layer**, more commonly referred to as SSL. SSL is used to encrypt both data sent between the customer's computer and the merchant's Web server and data sent between the merchant and payment processor. The two most popular Web browsers, Netscape Navigator and Microsoft Internet Explorer, are both SSL-capable. A customer using these applications can see if his or her connection is secure by checking for an icon shaped like a closed lock or a key at the bottom of the browser window or making sure the URL begins with "https" instead of "http."

The third issue concerns data, such as credit card numbers, stored by the merchant. To protect such data, merchants usually store the information in a secure database that cannot be accessed over the Internet. In addition, such data are often left in the database in encrypted form to protect the merchant from internal theft.

How to Implement Credit Card Transactions

To enable credit card transactions, an e-commerce company must establish connections with two parties. First, it must create a merchant account with a financial institution called an **acquiring bank**, and second, it must establish a **payment gateway** connection from the store to the credit card processing networks. The acquiring bank processes the credit card transaction through the card networks and then deposits the funds into the merchant's bank account. The payment gateway connection to the credit card networks allows the merchant to gain real-time authorizations of customers' credit cards.

There are two key components to implementing credit card payment on the Web. The first is integrating the orders coming to an e-commerce website with an existing credit card payment infrastructure that was originally designed for the bricks-and-mortar world. The second component is security. Not only must e-commerce websites be able to provide confidential transmission of payment information for customers when they place an order, but they also must be able to provide secure storage of customer payment information once it is received. Integrating these systems and providing customers with a secure transaction environment require significant technical expertise and technological investment.

Security

Keeping assets (including products, cash, and employees) secure has been an issue for merchants for as long as commerce has existed. As the technology of commerce has progressed, so have the threats. The worldwide economies of scale enjoyed by merchants on the Internet are also enjoyed by hackers (or cybercriminals) who have an unprecedented ability to steal from literally millions of e-commerce customers in an instant. Keeping a store safe has been and always will be a constant battle. As electronic commerce becomes a part of our daily lives, this battle will increasingly be fought on a front defined by technology.

Bricks-and-Mortar

Physical security of inventory, cash, and customer records will always be important in the bricks-and-mortar world. Security technologies include overt and covert cameras, alarms and security tags, and security guards.

Overt and Covert Cameras

To monitor both shoplifting and shrinkage (employee theft of inventory), store management may install cameras in areas where theft is likely. In locations where aesthetics are not an issue (such as in a warehouse or discount store) or in locations (such as at a bank) where preventing a robbery attempt is critical, easily recognized overt cameras are used. In situations where management is concerned about aesthetics, covert cameras allow managers to minimize the visual effect on the store while monitoring employee and customer activity.

Alarms and Security Tags

Stores can use alarms to monitor entry and exit activity during off-hours to reduce the threat of burglary and robbery. In addition, some stores with high-value items, such as designer clothing, place security tags on expensive items so that an alarm will sound if the items are taken from the store.

Security Guards

Security personnel monitor both in-store activity and off-hours activity. Guards can be uniformed or undercover.

e-Commerce

Physical security issues still exist for most e-commerce companies. For example, Web merchants who sell physical products (as opposed to downloadable products) still need to be concerned with shrinkage and burglary. But e-commerce security is complicated by several factors that are less prevalent or nonexistent in offline commerce.

Technologically Complex

Because selling products on the Web is so dependent on technology, significant technological expertise is required to secure an e-commerce site.

Many More Potential Attackers

Other issues exist due to the worldwide scale of e-commerce enterprises. Because the Internet allows a website to be accessed by a worldwide base of customers, it also allows it to be accessed by a worldwide base of hackers and criminals. Potential attackers can be anywhere and therefore are more difficult to avoid or prosecute.

Much More Potential Damage

Because an e-commerce website is functionally the equivalent of a large single store, the scale of crimes that can be committed against an online store is far larger than for any single outlet of a chain of physical stores. For example, if a cybercriminal gets access to the customer database of an e-commerce website, he or she probably has access to every customer's credit card. Someone rifling through records at a physical store, however, would most likely see data only for credit cards used at that location. Also, if a cybercriminal makes a website nonfunctional, it is the equivalent of closing the physical store for the same amount of time. Not only do e-commerce stores lose money, but they can lose business.

e-Commerce Security Technology

The unique nature of the threats to e-commerce companies requires new technologies and systems to provide a secure transaction environment. Due to the openness of many of the networks that make up the Internet, it is relatively easy for privacy to be compromised. (For example, without security measures, cable modem users could view the e-mail of neighboring cable modem users on the same system by downloading free software to their computers.) Although no website is ever 100 percent secure, several technologies can be employed to help reduce the risk to companies and their customers when conducting e-commerce transactions.

Passwords

Password protection may be the most common online security measure. Logins and passwords identify who is trying to access a website or part of a website. When attempting to access a secure area, customers are presented with a screen that requests a user ID or login and a password (the password protects secure accounts). After supplying the appropriate password for that user ID, customers can access confidential account information (e.g., order status, shipping address, and payment information). By setting up and using an account, customers do not have to retype their name, address, and payment information for every order. There are two primary drawbacks that tend to make passwords less secure than other security methods mentioned later in this chapter. First, people are not always diligent about keeping passwords secret. Users share their passwords with friends, write them down, or choose ones that are easy to guess. Second, many websites do not encrypt login information. Because of this, a cybercriminal with sniffing software (software that allows a cybercriminal to read packets moving between a website and its users) could inspect packets going to the server and steal user passwords.

Encryption

Because so much personal information (e.g., names, addresses, and credit card information) is sent across the Internet during e-commerce transactions, there is a need to ensure that this information is kept private while it is being communicated between the customer and the website. **Encryption** technology encodes and decodes information transmitted over the Internet so that only the sender and intended recipient can read the information. This is accomplished through the use of complex mathematical formulas. Well-designed encryption software uses formulas so complex that it would take the most powerful computers years to decode the messages. (Of course, as processor power increases exponentially, encryption standards must be regularly improved and upgraded.) This is why encryption is not used for every online transaction—the processing load to encrypt all data sent to a server would make that server too slow for practical use. Instead, encryption is reserved for the transmission of sensitive data such as credit card numbers.

How to Use Encryption Use of encryption requires that software be installed on both the sending and receiving computers. For example, to send a secure e-mail to a friend, the sender would write her message, use encryption software to encrypt the message, and then send the message. The friend would receive the message in encrypted form, use software to decrypt the message, and read it. If other people somehow got a copy of the message in transit or by other means, they would not be able to read the encrypted version.

Most people who have placed orders online have used encryption technology. The Secure Sockets Layer (SSL) discussed earlier in the payment section is a type of encryption software that automatically sets up an encrypted "pipe" through which the browser and server can communicate. This happens whenever the browser hits a secure section of a website. On most browsers, the lock or key icon will be shown as closed if a user is on a secure connection and will appear as open (or not appear at all) if the user is not on a secure connection.

Public Key Infrastructure

You might wonder if a third party who steals encrypted information could use any piece of encryption software to decrypt the stolen information. This cannot happen. Encryption software uses pieces of additional software called **keys** to ensure that only the creators and intended recipients of encrypted information can access it.

For encrypted data to be transmitted from one computer to another, a set of two keys is required. One of the keys is called a public key; the other is called a private key. The public key encrypts the data, which is sent to a computer that has the corresponding private key for decryption. Any user who wants to receive encrypted data from other users can use a set of these keys to accomplish the task.

For example, if you wanted all of your friends to send you e-mail in encrypted format, you would simply get a set of keys (one private key and one public key) and distribute copies of the public key to each friend. They would use their encryption software with your public key to encrypt their e-mail to you. You would use the private key (which only you possess) to decrypt and read the messages. However, if you wanted to be able to send encrypted replies to one of these friends, that person would have to get his or her own set of keys and send you a copy of the public key. Only then could you encrypt messages to send to her. Therefore, for two parties to send encrypted communication back and forth, each one has to have a set of two keys (one public and one private) for a total of four keys.

Public Key Infrastructure in e-Commerce

Public key encryption is commonly used on e-commerce websites to ensure that sensitive data from customers (such as credit card numbers) are kept private when transmitted across the Internet. Most e-commerce Web servers contain a private key for decryption. This private key, along with its corresponding public key, are often created and distributed by trusted third-party companies, such as VeriSign. When an e-commerce Web server is set up, it will have a private key and public key installed. Once running, the Web server will automatically send a copy of the public key to the browser of any customer who logs on to a secure page on the website for the first time. This public key (also known as a digital certificate, see Exhibit 2.6) is stored in the customer's browser and used for that session and all future sessions with that Web server until the private key changes. (Some users update their digital certificate as more secure encryption methods become available.)

The transmission of keys from server to browser is automatic. The only involvement the user has in the process is in agreeing that he or she trusts the Web server. Once the user agrees to trust the website, an encrypted "tunnel" that allows secure transmission of data is established between the browser and the server. This secure tunnel is known as Secure Sockets Layer (SSL) and is created automatically when a user connects to a page that requires secure data transmission (i.e., any page whose URL begins with "https://").

Once an SSL session has begun, the user can confidently send encrypted information that only that server can decrypt. This occurs through a process called *authentication*. Although e-commerce customers routinely use public keys to encrypt the data they transmit and servers use private keys to decrypt this information, the process can work in reverse as well. To prove their

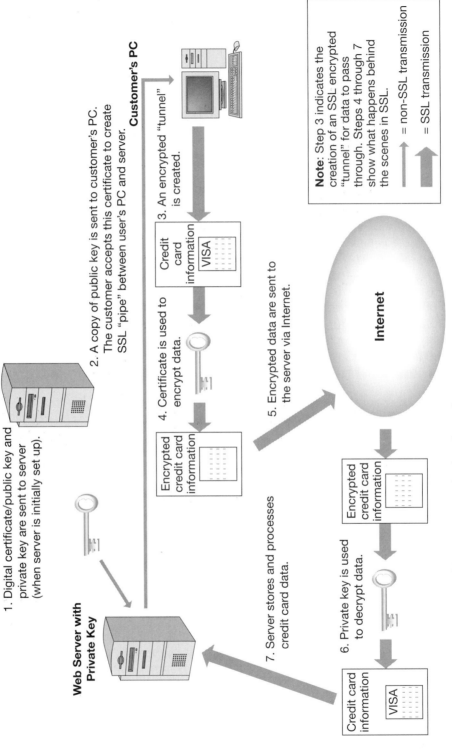

EXHIBIT 2.6   Digital Certificate Transmission in e-Commerce

authenticity, Web servers can encrypt a document called a digital signature (see Exhibit 2.7) and send it to a customer's browser. The customer's browser, with the public key, can decrypt the digital signature to see if it is legitimate. Because private keys are held only by the company that owns them, if the corresponding public key for that company (acquired from a third party such as VeriSign) successfully decrypts the digital signature, the customer knows it has come from the company he or she expects. Authentication is important because, otherwise, it would be possible for someone to make a copycat website and use it to illegally collect credit card numbers from unsuspecting customers.

Managing Secure Transactions   Although SSL eases the process of sending order information securely, many things still happen behind the scenes when an order is placed on the Web. To process the payment, the credit card number must be authorized by the cardholder's bank. **Secure Electronic Transaction** (SET) is a protocol that facilitates the secure authentication of online credit card transactions, as well as other payment-processing issues such as debit card transactions and credits back to credit cards.

Securing Companies from External Attack

Consumers are not the only ones who need to be protected from unscrupulous interests on the Internet. Companies need to protect themselves against a worldwide base of cybercriminals who can damage their reputations and profitability with attacks ranging from viruses to credit card theft.

Screening Routers   Most routers today can do more than just identify the best path for a packet and pass it on. Routers known as screening routers can screen packets as well. The primary difference in their function is that they look at not only whether they *can* forward a packet but also whether they *should* forward it. This determination is made based on rules that the network administrator sets according to the company's security policy. For example, if users inside a company need Web access but not File Transfer Protocol (FTP) access, a screening router can be configured to prevent all FTP traffic from traveling between the Internet and the company's internal network. This setup would prevent employees from accidentally downloading a virus via FTP. It would also prevent employees from setting up an Internet-accessible FTP server on their PCs that could allow cybercriminals or hackers to see sensitive files.

Proxy Servers   The primary purpose of a **proxy server** (also called a gateway) is to forward packets on behalf of PCs on a company's internal network to the Internet. When using a proxy, if a computer on the company's network wants to request something from the Internet (e.g., a webpage), instead of directly contacting the server it wants to access, it requests the information from the proxy server. The proxy server then contacts the website and requests the information as if it were for itself. After receiving the information, the proxy server forwards it to the appropriate computer on the internal network. The true identity of the computer requesting the information is never transmitted across the Internet. All requests for information from proxy server users appear to be coming from the proxy server itself. This has an important security benefit—it prevents the identities (in the form of IP addresses) of individual computers inside a company's network

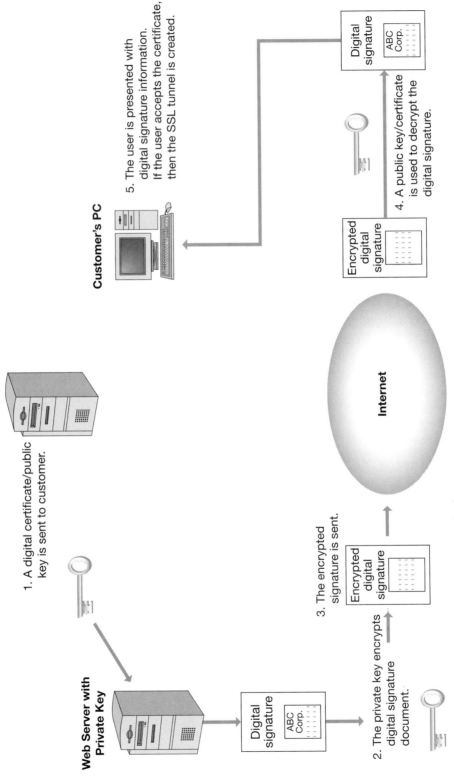

EXHIBIT 2.7   Digital Signature Transmission

from being "published" on the Internet whenever they access the Internet. This anonymity makes it more difficult for hackers to access computers on the internal network, keeping the network more secure.

Proxy servers provide other benefits, too. Many proxy servers support caching (temporary local storage) of recently requested information. This means that if several people in a company use the same website often, the proxy server will automatically store a copy of the viewed pages for that website on its local hard disk. When a user requests a page that is cached, the proxy server will send a copy of the page from its local hard disk over the company's fast local network instead of going onto the Internet and pulling the page down again. This saves users time, because obtaining the document is faster over the local network; it also preserves Internet bandwidth. Another benefit of proxies is that they increase scalability. Because individual computers on the company's local network are not directly accessing the Internet, they do not need to have globally unique IP addresses. Only the proxy server needs to have such an address because (according to other computers on the Internet) only it is making requests. This makes it simpler to add new users to the internal network because addresses for computers on the local network need to be unique only to the local network, not worldwide.

Firewalls A key piece of infrastructure used to keep hackers and cybercriminals out of a company's internal network is the firewall. A firewall is essentially a computer (or specialized appliance) that sits between the Internet and anything a company wants to protect (such as a Web server or the company's internal network). A firewall functions similarly to antivirus software for PCs, except that instead of looking on a hard disk for malicious content, it looks at packets coming over a network connection while they are in transit. Firewalls perform what is known as *stateful inspection.* This means that rather than just looking at source and destination information, or the type of service the packet is used for (such as FTP or HTTP), the firewall actually looks closely inside the packet to determine whether it could be harmful. If a packet looks dangerous, the firewall will prevent it from passing into the company's network. Firewalls can be actual computers with specialized software running on them, or they can be specialized pieces of hardware (such as routers) that are designed to perform firewall functions very quickly.

Fulfillment

Fulfillment is often considered the least glamorous component of e-commerce. Many early e-commerce startups spent millions on customer acquisition and brand building but paid little attention to fulfillment. As a result, many early customers complained of late or erroneous order delivery, which led those customers to look elsewhere for future purchases.

Fulfillment is, in fact, a crucial component of online selling. Fulfillment encompasses all activities that enable merchants to adequately complete customer orders. These activities include taking orders on the front end; processing, packing, and delivering those orders; and processing customer returns.

Bricks-and-Mortar

Fulfillment has long been a component of bricks-and-mortar selling. Fulfillment in the offline world can take many forms, depending on the type of business. For example, a chain of national discount stores, such as Wal-Mart, would have very different fulfillment needs than a catalog company such as Fingerhut.

Fulfillment for Wal-Mart includes all the steps necessary to distribute products to individual Wal-Mart stores, where customers can conveniently purchase them. These steps might include ensuring that there are enough Wal-Mart stores to adequately serve customers, building relationships with suppliers, creating a distribution network of warehouses and trucks to maintain inventory levels at individual stores, and providing customer service counters at individual stores to process customer returns.

Fingerhut has different fulfillment needs. Fingerhut must still build relationships with suppliers, but as a company that specializes in catalog sales, Fingerhut does not need to create a distribution network of regional warehouses, trucks, and retail stores. Instead of building retail stores where customers pick up their desired items, Fingerhut must take the extra step of delivering those items. In addition, customer returns must also be handled through delivery instead of through face-to-face interactions at a physical store.

e-Commerce

If you are beginning to think that catalog fulfillment issues look a lot like the fulfillment issues that e-commerce merchants must confront, you are right. In both types of businesses, the burden of delivery is placed on the shoulders of the merchant. Instead of bulk-shipping items to distribution channels, individual items must be packed and delivered to customers. This scenario creates a significant fulfillment challenge for both catalogers and e-commerce merchants, particularly when considering the challenge of managing thousands of individual orders and unique deliveries while controlling shipping costs.

A study by Jupiter reported that 44 percent of online retailers lose money on shipping and handling, while 37 percent cite the cost of shipping as their primary fulfillment challenge.[8] That many e-commerce merchants (particularly online retailers that must fulfill individual orders) are not profitable is well publicized. The online retailing graveyard is a large and illustrious one, filled with billions of lost dollars and former household names such as Pets.com and eToys.com (though, the eToys.com name has been resurrected).

Hope is not lost, though. The same study found that of catalog-based e-commerce plays, nearly 80 percent were profitable. Catalogers are experienced in fulfilling remote orders, and this experience filters down to the bottom line. Fulfillment capability is a significant factor in determining the profitability of an e-commerce venture. Major issues facing merchants as they consider e-commerce fulfillment are discussed in the following sections.

Customer Demand for Transparency

The Web provides customers with an easy interface to collect and track information. Web customers often demand increased information about their purchases, such as order status and delivery tracking. In contrast, most bricks-and-mortar mail-order businesses do not offer this level of transparency. With bricks-and-mortar merchants, after the order is placed either through mail-in forms or telephone, the customer typically has very little information about order status except a range of dates within which the order is likely to arrive. On the Web, however, customers demand much more, and most established e-commerce merchants try to please their customers by providing as much information as possible. This might include the ability to check product availability, order status, and shipping status at any time. Most major delivery services used by e-commerce retailers, including Federal Express, UPS, and the United States Postal Service, even offer package tracking to precise geographic detail; the customer always knows where her package is and when it should arrive. Yet providing this transparency creates significant challenges for e-commerce merchants. It requires the coordination of many systems and information sources into a seamless, Web-based information experience for the customer.

Many Activities and Parties

A key challenge for e-commerce fulfillment is handling the logistics of accommodating many activities and parties simultaneously. For shipping alone, an e-commerce merchant could use a variety of providers (UPS, FedEx, U.S. Postal Service, Airborne Express, etc.) simultaneously, depending on customer-preferred variables such as cost or delivery time. An e-commerce merchant might also use different providers to address customer service needs, electronic order processing, product sourcing, and warehouse logistics.

Multiple Systems

In addition to keeping track of these multiple parties, an e-commerce merchant must also coordinate between different platforms and multiple computer systems. For example, many catalog companies rely on older mainframe and minicomputer systems to handle their inventory and completely different computer platforms to handle payment. We already discussed some of the challenges of setting up a website capable of displaying the company's products and taking orders securely. In addition to these challenges, companies wishing to add e-commerce capabilities to existing fulfillment systems need to find ways to integrate all of their systems so that they can automatically process Web orders. Often, these legacy systems are not compatible with each other (e.g., they run on different operating systems) and were set up before the advent of the Web. Exhibit 2.8 shows ways in which systems must be integrated. Making all of these disparate technologies work together seamlessly requires significant planning, equipment, and technical expertise.

Capacity Utilization

Another issue that e-commerce merchants often cite as a major challenge is capacity utilization. According to a recent survey, online merchants struggle with order volatility.[9] About 60 percent of online merchants report that the number of orders during peak days is at least four times the number of orders for an average day. About 25 percent report peak days of more than eight times the number of orders on an average day.

Reluctant to turn away orders, early e-commerce merchants were forced to build the distribution and fulfillment resources necessary to fulfill orders during peak times. One example is Webvan, a $1.2 billion bet on revolutionizing the grocery business. Webvan designed its state-of-the-art San Francisco

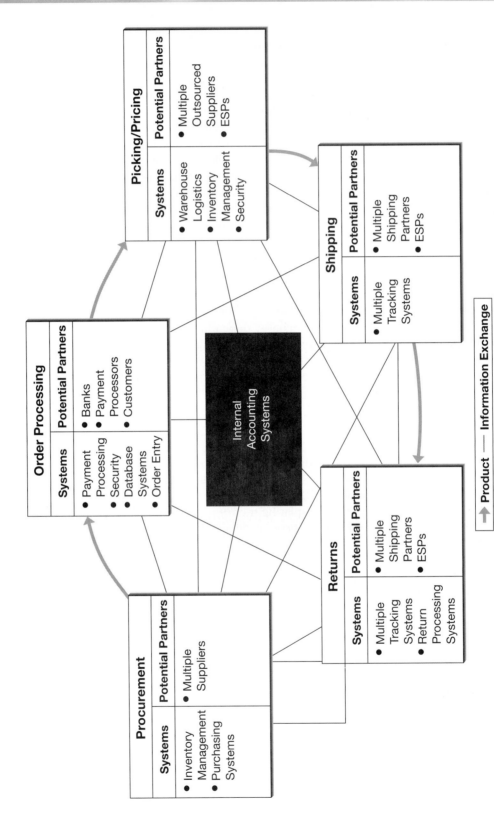

EXHIBIT 2.8   Fulfillment—Integrating Multiple Partners, Technologies, and Systems Is a Major Challenge

fulfillment warehouse to handle about 8,000 orders per day. However, Webvan fulfilled an average of only 2,100 orders per day, leaving three-quarters of the facility mostly unused.[10] In July 2001, Webvan filed for bankruptcy. Many other e-commerce companies made the same mistake, building large fulfillment centers that turned out to be liabilities. The costs of running these large, underutilized buildings kept the companies from making a profit.[11]

As a result, most e-commerce merchants are migrating toward flexible fulfillment solutions that can accommodate fulfillment peaks and valleys. These often include the use of third-party fulfillment providers (often referred to as e-commerce service providers, or ESPs) that serve a multitude of customers and can therefore reach the economies of scale associated with effective capacity utilization.

Summary

1. What is the Internet?

The Internet is a collection of wires, protocols, and hardware that allows the electronic transmission of data over TCP/IP. The Internet forms a global network of computers that can share data and programs. The computers are connected through a series of local area networks (LAN) and wide area networks (WAN) and transfer data through the communication rules set forth by the Transmission Control Protocol (TCP) and Internet Protocol (IP).

2. What are four components of Joseph Carl Robnett Licklider's original vision that make the Internet easy to use?

Four such components are human-friendly addressing and the domain name system, packet switching, routing, and TCP. The Domain Name System (DNS) gives each computer on the Internet a human-friendly address made up of easily recognizable letters and words. Packet switching is used by computer networks to ensure fair access to shared network resources and to remedy the delays associated with unequally sized data transfers. Routing directs traffic and translates messages so that different network technologies can communicate easily and efficiently with one another. Transmission Control Protocol (TCP) software enables reliable communication over the Internet.

3. What are the content types on the Web?

The four Web content types are links, forms, images, and multimedia. Links can be categorized into three general types: internal anchors, page links, and mail-to links. Forms allow the user to enter information in fields on a webpage by typing in text or selecting from a list of options. Image formats, such as Graphics Image Format (GIF) and Joint Picture Encoding Group (JPEG), allow users to see images easily, without having to change any settings within their browser, because all popular browsers support these file types. Multimedia files contain images, audio, and video that are embedded into webpages.

4. How are websites created?

A webpage is simply a text file that contains a text-based code called HTML. Web content, such as text, images, multimedia, and links, can easily be added to webpages through the use of HTML "tags," which describe Web content. Web-authoring tools help to expedite both page generation and website maintenance. Users can also use WYSIWYG editors to create a document in another application and convert that file into a standard markup language, such as HTML or XML.

5. What are the key similarities and differences between e-commerce and bricks-and-mortar selling in regard to placement and size?

The placement of an online or bricks-and-mortar store is important in driving traffic to it. An easy-to-remember and logical domain name for a virtual store increases brand awareness and makes locating the store easier for customers. Physical stores can locate on popular streets or in malls to maximize foot traffic, while online stores can place their stores in virtual malls to generate traffic. In addition, making sure there is enough capacity to handle the number of customers it will attract is critical. In a bricks-and-mortar store, having enough capacity involves making sure there is enough physical space to handle the foot traffic generated by the store. Online, having enough capacity involves maintaining enough server bandwidth and processing power to allow fast and reliable access to the store during peak hours of use.

6. How does e-commerce payment differ from bricks-and-mortar payment?

There are many popular forms of payment in the offline world. In the online world, however, the credit card is king. When a credit card is used in a physical store, the clerk can check the buyer's identification, and the store keeps a signed receipt in its records. Online purchases, however, do not have this paper trail and are therefore referred to as card-not-present transactions. Because of this difference, the financial responsibility for credit card fraud is placed on the credit card company for bricks-and-mortar purchases and on the merchant for online card-not-present transactions.

7. What role does security play in e-commerce?

The key components of online security are privacy and authentication. SSL is the most popular encryption technology used to ensure privacy during online purchases. Encryption utilizes public key infrastructure to encrypt and decrypt sensitive information. Digital signatures are used to authenticate the identity of websites so that consumers can be sure they are giving their payment information to a legitimate company. Firewalls are used to decrease the risk of Internet hackers gaining access to a company's private networks and sensitive information.

8. What challenges exist in e-commerce fulfillment?

Along with the complexities associated with warehousing, packing, shipping, and handling returns, e-commerce companies must also contend with issues specific to Web businesses. For instance, e-commerce customers expect more information on the status of their orders. Also, e-commerce businesses have to coordinate the activities of many different parties to ensure proper delivery, as well as contend with the difficulties of integrating Web order-taking capabilities with multiple systems for procurement, payment, inventory management, and delivery. Finally, online retailers must ensure that they maintain high-capacity utilization while having adequate capacity to handle customers' fulfillment needs during peak order cycles.

Exercises

1. Go to Salon.com (*www.salon.com*). Now go to the IP address 206.14.209.40. What site is it? What site is 216.239.51.101?

2. Go to an e-commerce site. Browse through some selections and then begin to make a purchase. Note where the site uses encryption and where it does not. Does the site use secure pages when you are entering credit card information, or when you are entering your e-mail address or looking at your shopping cart?

3. Go to RitzCamera.com (*www.ritzcamera.com*). What presentation factors do they consider? How does the presentation of this site differ from the Barneys New York site (*www.barneys.com*)?

Key Terms

local area network (LAN)	circuit-switched networks	Secure Sockets Layer (SSL)
wide area network (WAN)	packet switching	acquiring bank
Internet Protocol (IP)	routers	payment gateway
Transmission Control Protocol (TCP)	HTML	encryption
standards	WYSIWYG editors	keys
backbone network	Web browser	Secure Electronic Transaction (SET)
IP address	URL	proxy servers
Domain Name System (DNS)	bandwidth	
packets	processing power	

[1]"Global Internet Statistics (By Language)," *GlobalReach.com*, March 2002 (URL: *http://glreach.com/globstats/*).

[2]U.S. Department of Commerce, Economics and Statistics Administration, National Telecommunications and Information Administration, *A Nation Online: How Americans Are Expanding Their Use of the Internet*, February 2002 (URL: *http://www.esa.doc.gov/508/esa/nationonline.htm*).

[3]"E-commerce 101: Choosing an e-Commerce Host," *Tophosts.com*, 4 April 2002 (URL: *http://www.tophosts.com/pages/articles/ecom10101.htm*).

[4]"Success Stories: The Nasdaq Stock Market," *Intel.com*, 2002 (URL:*www.intel.com/eBusiness/casestudies/snapshots/nasdaq.htm*).

[5]Cassimir Medford, "Analytics," *PC Magazine*, 4 January, 2001 (URL: *http://www.zdnet.com/pcmag/stories/reviews/0,6755,2668446,00.html*).

[6]Roy Williams Clickery, "Data Powers of Ten," California Institute of Technology, 1995 (URL: *http://www.cacr.caltech.edu/~roy/dataquan/*).

[7]Avivah Litan, "E-tailers Squeezed by Higher Credit Card Fraud and Rates," *Gartner Group Market Analysis*, 28 July 2000.

[8]David Schatsky, "Internet Commerce and the Last Mile," *Jupiter Research Vision Report 7* (22 January 2001).

[9]David Schatsky, "Fulfillment Nets: Building a Hybrid Retail Supply Chain to Balance Cost and Customer Value," *Jupiter Research Vision Report 4* (29 August 2000).

[10]Saul Hansell, "Some Hard Lessons for Online Grocer," *The New York Times*, 19 February 2001.

[11]Miguel Helft, "Wanna Buy a Warehouse?" *The Industry Standard*, 12 March 2001 (URL: *http://www.thestandard.com/article/display/0,1151,22759,00.html*).

Market Opportunity Analysis

CASELET: AKAMAI'S MARKET OPPORTUNITY

Massachusetts Institute of Technology (MIT) business-school student Jonathan Seelig and his two mathematics colleagues, professor Tom Leighton and PhD candidate Daniel Lewin, knew they had an algorithm. What they didn't know was whether they had a business.

The algorithm was an innovative way to bypass what in 1995 was a growing problem on the increasingly trafficked World Wide Web, aka the "World Wide Wait"—congestion. The business would become Akamai Technologies, one of the Web's best-known early-stage success stories.

The algorithm-generating project had started as a theoretical puzzle, spurred by a conversation between Leighton and Web pioneer Tim Berners-Lee, who worried that traffic jams would eventually cripple the Web. It wasn't long, however, before Leighton and his team realized that they were coming up with the solution not just to a mathematical problem, but a business one.

"We saw that there might be a real market opportunity out there," Seelig says of the resulting breakthrough, a means of intelligently routing and replicating content over a large network of distributed servers. "But to seize it, we'd have to move fast. So we said, 'We're going to take six months, we're going to put our shoulders to the wheel, and we're going to see if we can build a service that matters to content providers.' "

Which is what they did, doggedly seeking out potential suppliers, partners, investors—and, most importantly, customers. They gathered data on the billions of dollars in e-commerce sales squandered each year as consumers lost patience with slow-loading websites. They even sent MIT undergrads into the field to canvas potential clients such as CNN and Yahoo. And they came up with a simple yet powerful value proposition: You pay us some money to make your site perform better, and you'll make a lot more as a result.

It turned out to be a compelling pitch. In 1998, the Akamai team entered its newly hatched business plan in the MIT $50K Entrepreneurship Competition. They didn't win, but they garnered a more valuable prize: $8 million in seed money from several prominent venture capitalists. Soon they launched with

This chapter was coauthored by Toby Thomas and Mark Pocharski. Substantive input was also provided by Robert Luvie, Leo Griffin, Yannis Dosios, Bernie Jaworski, Scott Daniels, and Michael Yip.

Yahoo as a charter customer, then made a splash with one of the hottest IPOs in an already sizzling capital market.

Seelig says that the kind of market opportunity assessment undertaken by him and his colleagues ought to be a no-brainer. But it's not. "I judged a business plan competition once in which only three of the five finalists could answer the question, Who pays you money for your service? Who is the constituent to whom you are beholden?" he recounts. "That's a disturbing phenomenon. You should know who is going to pay your bills. You should know who is going to make you a success."

PLEASE CONSIDER THE FOLLOWING QUESTIONS AS YOU READ THIS CHAPTER:

1. Is market opportunity analysis unique for online firms?

2. What are the two generic value types?

3. What is the framework for market opportunity analysis?

4. How do you identify unmet and/or underserved needs?

5. How does a company identify the specific customers it will pursue?

6. How do you assess advantage relative to competitors?

7. What resources does the company need in order to deliver the benefits of the offering?

8. How do you assess readiness of the technology needed to deliver an offering?

9. How do you specify opportunity in concrete terms?

10. How do you assess the attractiveness of an opportunity?

INTRODUCTION

In Chapter 1, we examined the effect of e-commerce and some of its distinguishing features. We also briefly reviewed the decision-making process that companies must go through in order to develop an e-commerce strategy. In this chapter, we answer the first question a company must address when formulating its strategy: "Where will the business compete?" Ideally, a company would like to compete in an arena in which the financial opportunity is considerable and the competitors are scarce, and in which it can position itself well to fulfill unmet customer needs either on its own or through partnerships.

Regardless of the reasons a firm seeks online business opportunities, a successful company defines its marketspace early in the business development process. The term **marketspace** refers to the digital equivalent of a physical marketplace. By defining the intended marketspace, a company identifies the customers it will serve and the competitors it will face. Over time, a company's defined marketspace may change as both the company and the market evolve, but a clear, initial definition is necessary to develop the business model.

In the last several years, we have seen an unprecedented launch (and failure) rate of startups. At the time of this writing, in August 2002, the Dow Jones industrial average had retained nearly 90 percent of its value from its high of 11,723 on

January 14, 2000. Meanwhile, the Nasdaq had retained only 35 percent of its value from its high of 5,048.6 on March 10, 2000. For some, enduring the risks associated with starting a new business will prove rewarding. But most will watch their businesses crash and burn—the historical failure rate of startup companies is about 80 percent within the first five years after launch.[1] With the current negative investor sentiment toward technology-related firms in general and Internet firms in particular, a quick but rigorous opportunity analysis is a requisite first step toward gaining support for any proposed new business initiative. The best-performing pure Internet stocks average at less than 5 percent of their historically highest values.[2]

Analysis of market opportunity is an essential tool for both entrepreneurs and senior managers who seek either to extend existing businesses or launch new businesses. The goal in performing this analysis is to identify high-potential opportunities and begin to form ideas about the essential elements of a business. We will need to gain greater understanding of the size and nature of the opportunity—as well as the resources of the firm—before considering the details of business models (Chapter 4).

While the resources available to a startup may vary dramatically from those available to an established corporate business unit, the manager seeking and evaluating market opportunities must have a sense of the following: the general attributes of an attractive opportunity, the company's domain expertise and ability to pursue an opportunity, and the firm's appetite for risk. Without an understanding of these elements, the manager has no way of deciding which opportunities to cultivate.

Also, in understanding the firm's risk tolerance, the manager must find a balance between overanalysis at one extreme, which can lead to paralysis and indecisiveness, and blind acceptance of uncertainty and risk at the other. Good strategy analysis will not guarantee success of a new endeavor, but a quick and rational process can provide a balanced approach to defining attractiveness and increase the likelihood of pursuing an attractive opportunity in a timely manner.

In this chapter, we review some of the tools that can be used to "frame" the market opportunity. Much of this spadework will be deepened and refined as the company moves toward developing and launching a market offering. Only when this work is complete can we begin to determine the value proposition, the exact offering, and a potential revenue model.

Unique Market Opportunity Analysis for Online Firms

Before exploring market opportunity analysis in greater depth, we should consider whether this type of analysis should be any different from an analysis of opportunities in more traditional sectors of the economy. Some authors and analysts believe that opportunity analysis in the marketspace is unique and requires a different approach. We summarize this reasoning in the section that follows.

Competition Across Industry Boundaries Rather Than Within Industry Boundaries

Web-enabled business models can operate across traditional industry boundaries because they often lack physical product manufacturing or service delivery. Consequently, these businesses can more accurately match value creation from the customer's perspective. For example, Cars.com (*www.cars.com*) allows customers to research and purchase new and used vehicles, finance them, insure them, and even purchase extended warranties through the website and its partners. Limiting opportunity assessment to traditional definitions of industry or value system could result in missed market opportunities.

Competition Between Alliances of Companies Rather Than Between Individual Companies

Many technology-based products have a high degree of reliance on other related, complementary products; for example, Web businesses are reliant on browser technology, and browsers are dependent on operating systems, PCs, and modem technologies. Furthermore, the networked nature of the Web means that several companies can easily team up to create a seamless offering. Companies can often find themselves in "**co-opetition**"[3] with each other, where they are both competitors and collaborators. For example, Amazon.com and Target.com directly compete online as suppliers of electronics, kitchen appliances, and housewares, yet they are also partners. Toys "R" Us and Target have each entered into third-party service agreements with Amazon. Amazon.com provides each with the technology to manage the entire virtual supply chain, complete with fulfillment services. In assessing the resources necessary to succeed, managers must examine both internal and external possibilities, rather than assume the company must perform all alone.

Competitive Developments and Response at Unprecedented Speed

Advances in technology and the adoption of creative business models are occurring at a rapid pace. During the "browser wars" between Microsoft and Netscape, each firm introduced a new version of its product approximately every six months. Any market opportunity assessment must be continually refreshed by keeping abreast of important trends or events that could redefine opportunity attractiveness.

Unique Ways to Bring Value to Consumers and Change Behavior

Most modern marketing textbooks emphasize the importance of being customer-focused. This means that businesses must analyze customer needs, define products that meet those needs, and implement defendable strategies. In the past, competitive battles were frequently fought over a well-defined set of consumer behavior patterns (e.g., consumers shopping in grocery stores). Now, new software and hardware have tilted the landscape of consumer behavior. Companies introduce products, leading to new behavior and new customer requirements. The challenge is to listen closely enough to today's customers to develop insights about opportunities without being lulled into simply meeting customers' established needs. To state the obvious: Customers do not know what they do not know. The company's task is to define new experiences that customers will recognize and seek, based on insights into how customers are acting today and why.

Take, for example, the emergence of file-sharing services such as Napster, Gnutella, Kazaa, and Morpheus, which enable users to search, share, and copy files of any format—including MP3 music, games, movies, software, and spreadsheets—across a global distributed network. Introduced in the fall of 1999, Napster revolutionized consumer behavior in the recorded music industry by providing users an easy way to "swap" electronic music files. Then, in the spring of 2000, a new version of Napster emerged that allowed the swapping of any file format. Soon, other free services won millions of users by imitating the Napster model. While part of the allure was that these files were free, consumers also enjoyed the benefit of being able to search for singles, find rare songs and/or rare performances by their favorite artists, and easily burn electronic files onto compilation CDs.

While Napster and other file-swapping companies have had well-publicized financial and legal problems, they still illustrate how companies can fundamentally change the way that consumers think about information, services, and products. At this writing, four legal online music services were available: Full-Audio's MusicNow (*www.fullaudio.com*), Listen.com's Rhapsody (*www.listen.com*), MusicNet (*www.musicnet.com*), and pressplay (*www.pressplay.com*). Bertelsmann Music Group (BMG), EMI Group, Sony Music, Vivendi Universal, and Warner Music—along with their trade organization, the Recording Industry Association of America (RAIA)—fear rampant online piracy. They argue that piracy is responsible for the 5 percent drop in worldwide music sales in the years 2000 and 2001. And while Napster will probably survive in some new form still to be defined, there is no doubt that consumers' attitudes and behaviors toward digital recordings of music have been permanently changed.

Industry Value Chains and Value Systems Rapidly Reconfigured

The Internet allows firms and industries to reconfigure their **value chains** (discrete collections of individual and organizational activities that work together to create and deliver customer benefits via products or services) or **value systems** (an interconnection of processes and activities within and among firms that creates benefits for intermediaries and end-consumers[4]) by increasing the level of information throughout the value chain, enabling constant contact between customers and businesses, and eradicating or significantly reducing the cost of stages in the value chain. For example, Dell Computer Corp. provides the ability for customers to purchase personal computers online (*www.dell.com*) or by telephone. Dell is unique in that it sells only direct-to-customer, and each computer is built-to-order. Dell uses the Internet and supply-chain management software to achieve extreme process efficiency. With improved material management by better inventory planning, forecasting, and execution, Dell was able to reduce computer parts inventory levels in its factories from days to hours. Inventory is procured from suppliers in real time, and materials are delivered to the factories every two hours based on customers' orders. The custom-configured computer system can be shipped to the customer for next-day delivery.[5]

Drill-Down

First Mover: Advantage or Liability?

Amazon.com launched in July 1995—the Cretaceous period of Internet time—and was the first national bookseller on the Web. Barnes & Noble, the nation's largest bricks-and-mortar book retailer, did not open its virtual doors until 1997. By then, Amazon was Tyrannosaurus Rex, king of the online booksellers, and it dominated the terrain. Barnes & Noble has yet to catch up.

Does being second—or late—to the Web mean a company will have to lag behind its competitors in sales and performance? Not necessarily. For some companies, being late to the online market can be an advantage. Virgin Megastores Online launched its e-commerce platform in May 1999, well after CDNow and Amazon had gained broad recognition for selling music and videos via the Web. "We didn't want to replicate existing entertainment online sites, and we had the advantage of watching our competitors, particularly in terms of marketing," said Dave Alder, Virgin Megastores Online's general manager and senior vice president. "We didn't want to spend $200 per head on customer acquisition."

Virgin leveraged the brand it had developed over 30 years in dozens of stores worldwide and tapped a loyal customer base through cross-marketing. Alder cites webcasts of exclusive in-store artist appearances as a particularly successful element of the company's clicks-and-bricks strategy. "We're very determined to utilize the marketing tools we've already got in the business. We can use online events to liven up the stores and vice versa." Alder said the website has already paid off, since it was used to create a system that tracks whether store revenues are affected by the online research of customers.

But what strategies can startups use to gain an edge? Underselling your competitors to attract a large customer base is one possibility. Latecomers can also employ new, attention-grabbing strategies to draw customers. When Hotmail introduced its free e-mail service in July 1996, several similar services were already on the market. But Hotmail managed to sign up 10 million subscribers in its first 18 months, surpassing competitors by turning its users into salespeople through viral marketing (see Chapter 6). "Latecomers," said Michele Pelino, program manager of the Yankee Group's Internet marketing strategies team, "can really learn from what early entrants have done in the past."

Two Generic Value Types

To explore the notion of value creation, we must first look for a set of activities ripe for positive transformation, either within a firm or across activities conducted by multiple firms. A firm is made up of a series of connected activities—from purchasing inputs to manufacturing to marketing and sales to product delivery to after-sales support—that result in the creation of an end product or the delivery of a service. In addition, there are supporting activities necessary to ensure a company's viability, from financial planning and control to employee recruiting and training to research and development.

In the same way that many of these activities are interconnected within one company, there are also connections with other companies or consumers. Both the activities within a firm (the value chain) and those connecting firms with other firms and customers (the value system) are potential candidates for value creation. Furthermore, if we look across several related industries in the same manner as customers, we may find cross-value chain opportunities.

Exhibit 3.1 shows a simplified value system for the automobile industry. The value system encompasses the value chains of multiple companies, each of which plays a part in the automobile industry. For example, this value system includes steel manufacturers, component manufacturers, auto manufacturers, dealerships, maintenance shops, and used-car dealers. Each of these industry members has its own value chain. The value chain of auto manufacturers includes primary activities (such as designing autos, building and testing prototypes, sourcing components and parts, and assembling the autos) as well as key support activities (such as marketing and finance).

A number of Internet businesses have chosen to compete in the automotive marketspace, in part because the value system is extremely complicated and presents many opportunities for value creation. Autobytel.com is one such company. Exhibit 3.1 includes a simplified value chain for Autobytel.com that shows how the company has aggregated several activities across the value system—including allowing car buyers to research vehicles, e-mail a purchase inquiry to a local dealer, arrange financing, schedule the delivery of the vehicle, compare insurance rates, set up a schedule to manage their car's maintenance, and post a classified ad to sell their old vehicle—without leaving the keyboard. Autobytel.com created value both within the value chain (e.g., by providing panoramic interior photos) and across the value system (by allowing users to check car inventories at dealers across the country).

Firms should look at the value system with a lens that yields ideas about new business possibilities. Specifically, a firm looks for either **trapped value** to be liberated, or **new-to-the-world value** to be introduced.

Trapped Value

Online companies have unlocked trapped value by delivering existing benefits better or reducing costs. Forms of trapped value include creating more efficient markets, creating more efficient value systems, enabling ease of access, and disrupting current pricing power.

Creating More Efficient Markets

By lowering search and transaction costs, the market is made more efficient—customers can buy what they want at a lower net cost. EBay, for example, allows almost anyone to trade almost anything on a local, national, or international basis. Users can trade online by auction-style or fixed-price formats for a wide variety of items such as automobiles, jewelry, musical instruments, cameras, computers, furniture, sporting goods, tickets, and boats.

Creating More Efficient Value Systems

Compressing or eliminating steps in the current value system can result in greater efficiencies in time or cost. For example, Federal Express has been moving its customer interactions into the marketspace since 1982, when the firm first started equipping its major customers with dedicated terminals; enabling customers to request pickups, find drop-off points, and track shipments over the Internet was a natural development. Today, the company estimates that it would need an additional 20,000 employees to handle the tasks

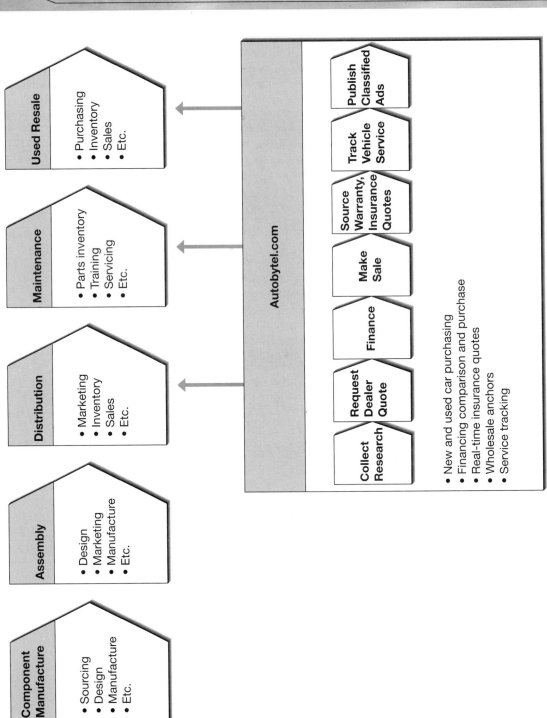

EXHIBIT 3.1   Car Manufacture and Sales Value System

that customers handle themselves. By connecting directly with its customers, FedEx removed the duplication of tasks such as the reentry of shipping data.

Enabling Ease of Access

Enabling ease of access entails enhancing the access points and the degree of communication between relevant exchange partners. The Internet allows bricks-and-mortar companies such as Target and Gap to be constantly available to their customers. Other companies make searching for products or services easier. Guru.com, for example, expedites access to hard-to-find professional experts across a wide range of fields.

Disrupting Current Pricing Power

Beyond making markets more efficient, this value-unlocking activity changes current pricing-power relationships. Customers can gain more influence over pricing and capture a portion of the vendor's margin when they have more information about relative vendor performance, a deeper understanding of vendor economics, or insight into the vendor's current supply-demand situation. For example, BizRate.com allows online shoppers to comparison-shop for price and quality of service. BizRate.com presents current vendor asking prices and customer satisfaction ratings (aggregated from customer responses) for each store.

New-to-the-World Value

In addition to reconfiguring existing value chains to release trapped value, online companies can create new-to-the-world benefits that can enhance an existing offering or be the basis for creating a new offering. In this section, we present five ways companies can create new value: customize the offerings, radically extend reach and access, build community, enable collaboration among multiple people across locations and time, and introduce new-to-the-world functionality or experience.

Customize Offerings

The Internet allows companies to tailor their offerings more flexibly than they ever could in the offline environment. By adding personalization to news and stock quotes through its "MyYahoo" function, Yahoo creates value for customers who previously had to navigate through "one size fits all" news and information services over the Web. A MyYahoo page contains just a small subset of all available information, but it is information that is relevant to the user.

Radically Extend Reach and Access

Companies may extend the boundaries of an existing market or create a new market by delivering a cost-effective reach. Keen.com created an entirely new market by building a virtual marketplace for advice. Anyone can advertise their services as an advisor on such subjects as "managing your love life" or "choosing a career." Customers log on to the site, choose an advisor, and are connected to the advisor for a per-minute fee.

Build Community

The Internet enables efficient community-building, as demonstrated by the explosion of chat rooms addressing myriad topics. Beyond chat rooms, companies also foster the building of public and private communities. MyFamily.com seeks to bring together the far-flung modern family by enabling conversation, picture sharing, and recipe exchange, among other things.

Enable Collaboration

In the networked world, people are working together more efficiently and more effectively than ever before. Autodesk Inc.'s ProjectPoint offers users in the building industry a secure, shared project workspace online. Project documents and communications are centralized in a single secure online location that is easily accessible by team members across the building design, construction, and management process.

Introduce New-to-the-World Functionality or Experience

The convergence of communications, computing, and entertainment, as well as the ever-changing form and functionality of access devices, is making new experiences possible. The Internet fosters broad access and participation in these new experiences. NNT DoCoMo, Coca-Cola, and Itochu Corp. have partnered to install what they refer to as "C-Mode" networked vending machines that will allow i-mode phone users throughout Japan to not only purchase Coke products but also access local information and buy tickets to local attractions via the vending machines.[6]

Value Creation

To define where in a value system or value chain a company should focus its development activities, two simple dimensions must first be considered—horizontal versus vertical plays. In the business world, horizontal plays improve functional operations that are common to multiple industries and types of value systems. In the software world, horizontal plays typically tackle improving functional areas such as accounting and control, customer service, inventory management, and standard computer-aided design/manufacturing (CAD/CAM) applications. In the consumer world, horizontal plays reflect common activities in which most consumers broadly engage (e.g., paying taxes).

Vertical plays, on the other hand, focus on creating value within or among activities that are central to a particular business. Movie Magic Virtual Production Office (*www.creativeplanet.com*) provides an advanced suite of tools for online real-time management and reporting for film and television production in the entertainment industry. Vertical plays can often be thought of as industry-specific plays (steel industry, chemical industry, automotive industry, etc.).

At its most extreme, a "white sheet" exercise—a thorough analysis beginning from a blank slate—could systematically look for and evaluate the trapped and new-to-the-world value potential across all functions and activities pursued by businesses and individual consumers. More typically, a group of managers will have some familiarity with or interest in a particular horizontal function or vertical activity. The challenge for this group is to map out the

major sets of activities related to that horizontal function or vertical business at a high level. After mapping out the activities, the group should consider a series of questions designed to guide a knowledgeable manager to uncover trapped value or recognize the opportunity for new value creation. These questions include, but are not limited to, the following:

- Is there a high degree of asymmetric information between buyers and sellers or colleagues at any step in the value system that traps value?

- Are significant amounts of time and resources consumed in bringing people together to make a transaction or complete a task?

- Do customers view activities as more collapsed than do industry participants?

- Are key participants in an activity able to collaborate effectively and efficiently at critical stages in a process?

- Do people have access to necessary advice and information to maximize their effectiveness or the ability to extract maximum benefits from a given activity?

- Are people forgoing opportunities to participate in an activity due to privacy or other concerns?

At this point, the manager has a sense of where the opportunity may lie in terms of business and customer activities. The next step is to identify customers and their unmet or underserved need. As the manager begins to specify the opportunity, the potential associated with the opportunity should become more apparent.

Drill-Down

Innovation

The following is a basic and useful definition of **innovation** that 3M, a leading innovator and global company, provides to its employees: "new ideas plus action or implementation that results in an improvement, gain, or profit."[7] Innovation is not an isolated act of creativity or the introduction of great ideas but a process that combines ideas with action and gainful result—ideas must be successfully brought to market as products and/or services and provide value directly to the customer or indirectly to the customer through benefit to the firm.

Types of Innovation

Dorothy Leonard describes five distinct types of innovation: (1) user-driven enhancement, (2) developer-driven development, (3) user-context development, (4) new application or combination of technologies, and (5) technology/market co-evolution. 3M categorizes innovation into three developmental types: line extensions, changes to the basis of competition, and creation of new industries.

User-Driven Enhancement   User-driven enhancements are no-risk improvements or incremental advances to a product. This is equivalent to 3M's notion of line extensions. Common types of user-driven enhancements include lowering product price; adding low-cost, high-value feature enhancements; and introducing cost-efficient quality improvements. For example, Windows XP is an improved version Windows 2000.

Developer-Driven Development   Developer-driven developments occur when a firm comes up with a new way to meet an existing consumer need. This corre-

continued

sponds with 3M's notion of innovations that change the basis of competition. The PalmPilot is a well-known example of a developer-driven development. Palm revolutionized the handheld organizer market by focusing only on the most important features that users needed to organize themselves. As a result, Palm products fueled the worldwide market for electronic PDAs.[8]

User-Context Development   User-context development innovations occur when firms invent products that meet a previously unexpressed need. In many cases, careful market research reveal these needs. A good example of user-context development is the positioning and further development of sport utility vehicles (SUVs) as spacious family vehicles. In today's SUV market, very few purchasers actually use SUVs for off-road travel or utilize their four-wheel-drive features. Although consumers apparently do not use many of the original design functions of SUVs, producers discovered that SUVs met the personal expressive needs of many consumers buying large, family-size vehicles.

New Application or Combination of Technologies   These innovations occur when an established technology is applied to a new industry. Radio-monitoring service Broadcast Data Systems (BDS) implemented this type of innovation. Music companies were interested in learning when music from their artists was being played on the radio. But when survey companies compiled the information, there was general concern over data integrity and frustration over the amount of play-list detail. BDS retooled existing technology by using a sophisticated monitoring system (created during the Vietnam War) that involved sampling snippets of records for unique electronic "fingerprints" or "patterns" into a computer. The computer scans thousands of radio stations in the United States every few seconds to make song matches. Every 24 hours, BDS provides clients detailed lists of the titles and exact playing times of songs played on specific radio stations.

Technology/Market Co-Evolution   Technology/market co-evolution innovations stand at the very frontier of innovation. This parallels 3M's notion of innovations that create new industries. Clayton Christensen similarly refers to disruptive technologies as innovations that create an entirely new market through the introduction of a new kind of service or product.[9] Yahoo and Schwab.com are organizations whose businesses depended entirely on this type of innovation. Portals such as Yahoo were extended search engines that served as an entry onto the Web, while Schwab.com provided online tools that allowed customers to manage their own financial lives. Often the firm has developed a great solution and then attempts to find its problem and market.

Framework for Market Opportunity Analysis

The goal in performing market opportunity analysis is to identify and assess the attractiveness of business opportunity. Is there an unmet customer need? Is the technology ready to deliver the offering? Does the company have the resources or have access to resources to deliver the offering? Is the competition strong? Is this an attractive opportunity? The outcome of an opportunity analysis should provide answers to these questions.

A "funnel process" is commonly used as a metaphor to describe idea creation—beginning with the generation of a broad input of ideas that are successively filtered through a series of developmental steps and decision gates until only the most promising ideas remain. The decision gates are sets of criteria defined by the firm to ensure that only the most attractive

and appropriate opportunities with the highest probability of success are pursued. The **market opportunity analysis framework**, which can be thought of as the initial investigative stages of idea creation, includes the following steps:

1. Identify the unmet and/or underserved *customer* need.

2. Identify the specific *customers* a company will pursue.

3. Assess advantage relative to *competition*.

4. Assess the *company's* resources to deliver the offering.

5. Assess the market readiness of the *technology*.

6. Specify the opportunity in concrete terms.

7. Assess opportunity attractiveness.

Exhibit 3.2 illustrates the steps of opportunity analysis that firms should satisfy in order to frame market opportunity. Taken together, these seven steps comprise the scope of a sound process for market opportunity analysis.

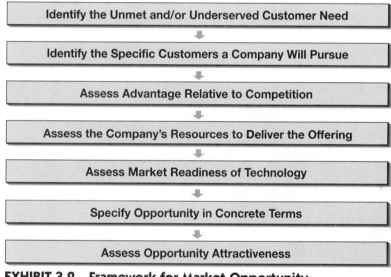

EXHIBIT 3.2   Framework for Market Opportunity

Notice that the seven steps revolve around **four key environments**: customers, company, technology, and competition. Analysis of the *customer* environment uncovers unmet or underserved customer needs, as well as the market they occupy. Identifying and choosing priority customers lead to a preliminary understanding of the potential audience the company could seek to serve. Analysis of the *technology* environment reveals the readiness of the particular technology, as well as any alternative technologies, on which the manager anticipates deploying the firm's offering. The manager must be able to estimate customer readiness to adopt these platforms. Key issues center on the evolution of technology and its adoption. Analysis of the *company* environment provides the current state of the company's resources. The manager must know the resources of the firm, as well as its strengths and weaknesses.

The manager must be able to identify the distinct benefits the company would bring to the offering to achieve advantage and win in the market, as well as to expose any missing or weak areas of its resource system. Analysis of the *competition* should reveal the structure of the industry and market, key competitors in the marketspace, and the firm's relative advantage to each of the key players. Key players should include industry-level competition as well as competitors that are not in the immediate space but can pose a threat to the firm in its anticipated offering.

Market opportunity analysis is complicated. Oftentimes a customer need exists but there is either a lot of competition or not the right technology to meet the need. Likewise, a company may have the perfect resources to provide a benefit but then realize too late that there is not enough of a customer need for that benefit. Exhibit 3.3 shows a Venn diagram for these four elements that make up the opportunity analysis. Once the seven steps of market opportunity analysis have been performed, a company should ideally pursue the opportunity that falls in the "sweet spot." This means that there is an unmet customer need, the company has the available resources, competition is weak, and technology is able to deliver the benefit. However, in practice, firms can often only find opportunities *near* the sweet spot—the technology is not perfect, there is more competition than would be ideal, there is an unmet need but perhaps not a critical unmet need. In these cases, managers must decide whether pursuing the close-to-perfect opportunity is worth the risk.

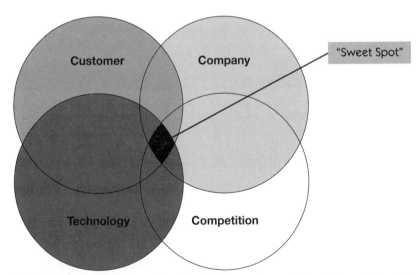

EXHIBIT 3.3   The Four Key Environments and the "Sweet Spot" for Market Opportunity

Step One: Identify Unmet and/or Underserved Customer Needs

New value creation is based on doing a better job of meeting customer needs. What customer needs will the new business serve? Are these needs currently being met by other companies in the market, and, if so, why will customers choose your business over the competition? The opportunity analysis framework describes the uncovering of an **opportunity nucleus**—a set of unmet or underserved needs.

Customer Decision Process

The **customer decision process** is an organizing framework that looks systematically for unmet or underserved needs. This process maps the activities and choices customers make in accessing a specific experience within a value system. Then the process lays out the series of steps: awareness of the experience, the purchase experience, and the use experience. The customer decision process may help generate new ideas about unmet or underserved needs. For example, an examination of the process people go through to buy books might identify that people rely on recommendations from others. Jeff Bezos successfully identified this need and created a function on Amazon whereby customers can read reviews and comments about books while they browse—a service not available to customers in a bricks-and-mortar bookstore.

To discover unmet or underserved needs, senior management should map out the customer decision process. When properly answered, the following questions will help structure that process:

- What are the steps that the typical customer goes through?
- Who gets involved, and what role does he or she play?
- Where does the process take place?
- How much time does the overall process take? How much time is associated with individual steps? Does the customer move through the entire process at once, or does he or she take breaks?
- What choices do customers *not* consider? What choices are they unaware of?
- Which customers are not participating in this customer decision process for a specific value system?

Exhibit 3.4 illustrates the customer decision process for buying a book. Each process is organized into three broad categories: prepurchase, purchase, and postpurchase. While some of the steps are highly linear and require either/or decisions (e.g., buying the book at a physical store versus buying the book online), other steps require weighing several factors at once (e.g., weighing availability against price and quality). Analyzing which factors are weighed during which process will help a company see how it can help the customer decide on a purchase. This process also shows each step a customer needs to take to become a satisfied and loyal customer of the company.

Of course, not all businesses involve purchases just by users. Access to CNN's website is free to all users but is paid for by advertisers, so the business has two sets of customers. In this case, it is worthwhile developing one customer decision process cycle for visitors and another one for advertisers.

Reveal Unmet or Underserved Needs

Having identified the steps in the customer decision process, the management team can look to uncover unmet or underserved needs. The following questions can help identify these needs:

- What is the ideal experience the customer wishes for, both functionally and emotionally? How does it vary step-by-step in the activity?

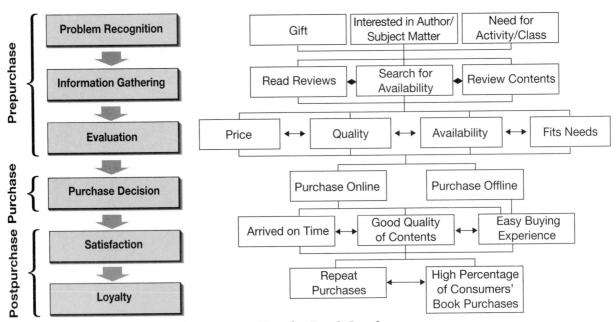

EXHIBIT 3.4   Consumer Buying Process Tree for Book Purchase

- How closely does the actual experience compare with the customer's view of the ideal? What are the key frustration points? What compensating behaviors do we observe (i.e., what actions does the customer engage in to overcome these frustrations)?
- Does the experience customers seek vary according to their environment?
- What are customer beliefs and associations about carrying out this activity? How do they view their relative competence and role? How positively or negatively do they view the current set of company offerings?
- What barriers block some or all participation by potential customers?
- What are the online opportunities to enhance or transform the customers' experience?

Uncovering these needs may be as straightforward as having a conversation with a number of customers, or may be as complex as creating observation opportunities to watch customers in action and identify behaviors of which they may be unaware. Immersion in the customer decision process can be an effective way to reveal opportunities for a better way of doing things.

Step Two: Identify the Specific Customers a Company Will Pursue

So far, we have talked about where a company is likely to play in the value system and how customers go through their decision-making process. Now we will discuss the specific customer segment that the company plans to pursue. What distinguishes *must-have* customers from *nice-to-have* customers who are seeking a solution to this unmet need? Companies need to develop a sense for the type(s) of customers they ultimately seek to serve. This understanding allows a company to assess opportunity attractiveness at a high level and to focus on crafting an offering that will best appeal to the target customer.

In analyzing the outcome of the customer decision process, companies are likely to identify subsets of customers with very different patterns of behavior, underlying needs, and behavioral drivers. **Segmentation** is the process of grouping customers based on their similarities. Once the different segments have been identified, the company must determine the segments (or customers) it will target in order to further refine the type of opportunity the company will seek to capture. Of course, the digital play that a company has in mind may radically change how customers act in this value system. Hence, a company would look for both segments that disproportionately benefit from some change in the status quo and those more predisposed to adopt an entirely new product or service.

Approaches to Market Segmentation

There are many approaches to segmentation, and the best way to segment a market is an often debated topic. The best segmentation for the opportunity depends on the value system that the opportunity is centered upon, how the

---

Drill-Down

Empathic Design[10]

All companies, particularly technology companies, rely on innovation to survive. A natural choice is to rely on customers to tell you how to serve them better. The problem is that customers are particularly bad at doing that. They rarely are able to imagine or describe innovations.

One solution is to use "empathic design," a set of techniques described by Dorothy Leonard and Jeffrey Rayport in the *Harvard Business Review* article, "Spark Innovation Through Empathic Design." Two things distinguish empathic design research techniques from those used in traditional market research. First, they are based on observation (watching consumers) rather than inquiry (asking consumers). Second, unlike traditional lab-based usability testing, which typically involves observing consumers using a product in a laboratory, empathic design research is conducted in the environment in which the consumers would commonly use the product.

Empathic design is not a substitute for traditional research, but it can yield the following five types of information that are not ordinarily revealed by traditional techniques:

- *Triggers of use*: What circumstances cause people to use a product?
- *Interactions with the user's environment*: How does the product fit with users' idiosyncratic environments and habits?
- *User customization*: Do users redesign the product to fit their needs? If so, how?
- *Intangible product attributes*: Intangible attributes may be important in creating an emotional franchise with the consumer.
- *Unarticulated user needs*: Observation can discover unarticulated user needs that can be easily fulfilled.

Different people notice different things, and the use of a small team with a diverse set of skills (e.g., interface design, product management) may observe otherwise unnoticed subtleties. The team should observe and record a subject's normal behavior. The team should also take detailed notes and minimize interruptions or interference with the subject. Photographs, videos, and sketches can all help the team record what it finds.

A common criticism of the innovative ideas that can emerge from empathic design is, "But users didn't ask for that." This is precisely the point of the exercise. By the time customers ask you for an innovation, they will be asking your competitors, too.

customer can and will make decisions within that value system, and what action a company is likely to take. Exhibit 3.5 provides a comprehensive listing of segmentation approaches that academic literature and textbooks often cite.[11]

Segmentation Type	Description	Examples — Variables
Geographic	▪ Divides the market into different geographical units	▪ Country, region, city
Demographic	▪ Divides the market on the basis of demographic variables	▪ Age, gender, income
Firmographic	▪ Divides the market on the basis of company-specific variables	▪ Number of employees, company size
Behavioral	▪ Divides the market based on how customers actually buy and use the product	▪ Website loyalty, prior purchases
Occasion (Situational)	▪ Divides the market based on the situation that leads to a product need, purchase, or use	▪ Routine occasion, special occasion
Psychographic	▪ Divides the market based on lifestyle and/or personality	▪ Personality (laid back, type A), lifestyle
Benefits	▪ Divides the market based on benefits or qualities sought from the product	▪ Convenience, economy, quality

EXHIBIT 3.5   Segmentation Approaches

Over time, segmentation has evolved from the use of observable and customer-external variables (age, income, geography) in the 1960s and 1970s to more meaningful customer-internal variables (needs, attitudes) in the 1980s and 1990s. The fact remains that neither is sufficient on its own to fully define a segment. The difficulty comes with selecting the segmentation approach and the variables that most effectively describe and reflect the nature of the opportunity being analyzed.

Actionable and Meaningful Segmentation

Unfortunately, most segmentation efforts fail to deliver on the intended objective—to be both useful and insightful. The segments either are often easy to recognize but do not provide much insight into customer motivations (actionable, but not meaningful) or generate real insight about customers but are difficult to address (meaningful, but not actionable). The goal of market segmentation is to identify the intersection or combination of marketplace variables that will generate actionable and meaningful segmentation of customers.

Point-Counterpoint

Which Is Better? Online Consumer Tracking Vs. Holistic View

In the online world, there is no lack of data. Click-stream information reveals purchase patterns, online habits, basic demographics, and potentially a host of other consumer information. Is this information sufficient to define new business opportunities?

Many argue that studying past and real-time behavior will yield enough information about customers to make choices about the services they need at that time. The Web enables companies to watch customers interacting in real time with their product with a high degree of precision and allows them to intervene while the customer is still in the buying process. Procedures such as collaborative filtering allow real-time suggestive selling. An example of this is Amazon.com's success at cross-selling customers.

An alternative view is that click-through-based data provide an insufficient picture of the reasons customers behave the way they do. In other words, click-stream analysis explains what customers do but not *why they do it*. A total customer view brings together consumer behavior and insights about motivations for that behavior; this view considers the behavior plus the customer context and environment, the functional and emotional desires of the customer, and the customer's beliefs and associations about the product, service, and current purveyors of the offering. Without a total customer view, managers are unlikely to generate real insight into key customer groups. Some companies are responding to this concern by trying to merge their online data with behavioral data gathered offline.

Actionable Segmentation   To be actionable, segmentation must be consistent with how a company can go to market, and it must be able to be sized and described. **Actionable segmentation** fulfills the following criteria:

- The segments are easy to identify.
- The segments can be readily reached.
- The segments can be described in terms of their growth, size, profile, and attractiveness.

Meaningful Segmentation   To be meaningful, segmentation must help describe and begin to explain why customers currently behave—or are likely to behave—in a specific way. **Meaningful segmentation** fulfills the following criteria:

- Customers within a segment behave similarly, while customers across segments behave in different ways.
- It provides some insight into customers' motivations.
- It corresponds to the set of barriers customers face when they buy or use a product or service.
- It corresponds with how customers currently (or could) buy or use the product or service.
- It correlates to differences in profitability or cost to serve.
- The segments and/or their differences are large enough to warrant a different set of actions by a company.

Step Three: Assess Relative Advantage to Competitors

To assess the competitive advantage the firm may be able to achieve relative to the competition, the manager must understand the context of competition at the industry level and specific competitors at the individual company

---

Point-Counterpoint

Is Segmentation Obsolete?

Some people have begun to question whether the segmentation concept applies in the online world. Because the online world enables consumers to customize products, services, and information specifically to their needs, the segmentation concept has been reduced to "segments of one."

Proponents of this notion have given it various labels, including "1:1," "segment-of-one," or "one-to-one" marketing. Furthermore, they argue that Web businesses such as eBay often attract an exceptionally wide variety of customers who weigh buying criteria (such as low price, most convenient buying method, best online information and reviews, broadest selection) quite differently. Hence, it is foolish to attempt to cluster these widely divergent groups. Rather, customization enables firms to uniquely meet the needs of each customer. Additionally, they argue that the back-office supply systems and infrastructure can easily accommodate every type of customer. Finally, multiple storefronts—even 1:1 storefronts—can be constructed in a real-time basis. (See Exhibit 5.16 in Chapter 5 for an example of this.)

Conversely, proponents of segmentation argue that all Web storefronts are, by definition, already segmenting the market. That is, if a given Web storefront simultaneously attracts selected customers and repels certain customers, it is segmenting the market. By disregarding these segments and focusing exclusively on 1:1 marketing, the company would miss the fundamental economics of which particular class of customer is most profitable or least profitable. For example, Dell requires its online customers to segment themselves into "consumer," "business," or "public" categories, then offers business users (and large-business users in particular) such perks as customized portals and "don't call us, we'll call you" sales rep service.

---

level. Competitive advantage is based on the customer value a firm creates that exceeds the firm's cost to produce that value. In his book *Competitive Strategy*, Michael Porter defines two basic types of competitive advantage: cost leadership and differentiation.[12] Value is not determined by the firm but rather by buyers, in the amounts they are willing to pay. Firms can create value by offering lower prices than competitors for the same benefits or by providing unique benefits that more than offset the higher price.

To measure relative advantage, a company obviously needs to identify the competitors it will face. The manager must understand individual competitor offerings, the reasons they do or do not offer the solution to the unmet customer need, and the reasons they can or cannot replicate the offering the firm intends to present. In the discussion of value systems, a company's key competitors would have been identified, and white-space opportunities (those in which there is no apparent competition) would have been isolated. At this stage, the task is to develop a better understanding of the threats and opportunities associated with various participants.

Identifying online competitors is both easier and more difficult than identifying offline competitors. On the one hand, the firm can simply use search engines to begin identifying competitors (although generic searches may deliver thousands of relevant pages), then visit the websites of these potential competitors to gain an understanding of their offerings. On the other hand, competition in the marketspace typically cuts across traditional industry boundaries. No matter what online business you are in, there is a good chance that either Microsoft or AOL Time Warner (or both) are your competitors.

In the online world, companies that one would not consider **direct competitors** (a company offering a similar or competing product) can become **indirect competitors** because they are reaching and attracting the same customers, or because they are developing a technology, platform, or offering that might compete with your offering. In other words, direct competitors are rivals in the same industry. Porter defines these firms as offering products or services that are "close substitutes" for each other.[13] Indirect competitors include two categories of companies:

- *Substitute producers.* Porter defines substitute producers as companies that, though they reside in different industries, produce products and services that "perform the same function."[14] Keen.com and Britannica.com are substitute producers. Keen.com is a switchboard that connects people with questions to individuals who can answer them knowledgeably. Britannica.com offers answers to a wide range of questions through its online encyclopedia.

- *Adjacent competitors.* Adjacent competitors do not currently offer products and services that are direct substitutes, but they have the potential to quickly do so. For example, adjacent competitors may have a relationship with a company's current customers.

A useful tool for identifying direct and indirect competitors is the profiling approach in Exhibit 3.6, which maps the different competitors in the picture-taking industry. Kodak is one of the only companies that competes along the entire spectrum of the picture-taking process. Most of its competitors provide either physical products for the initial steps of the process (providing cameras and film) or the service steps of picture taking (providing services to manipulate images, processing and developing services, and the ability to share photos). Although Kodak is one of the only companies to provide both physical goods and services for the picture-taking process, it does not integrate

---

Marketspace Interview

Jeff Hawkins, Inventor of the PalmPilot; founder Palm Inc. and Handspring

The Newton [Apple's early, unsuccessful handheld computer, introduced in 1993] was a real watershed event in this industry. It got tremendous publicity and tremendous ridicule. But at Palm, we went out and asked the people who bought the Newton, "Why did you buy this? You may not like it, but you must have expected it to do *something*." The technology pundits would say, well, it's supposed to be an intelligent agent, a communicator, talk to wireless. . . . But the users said, "I just wanted to organize my life." They would show me their paper organizer and they'd say, "I just can't keep my addresses; they're always getting out of order. And I can't keep coordinated with my secretary. I was hoping somehow this thing would just help me organize my life!"

So we began to realize that our competition wasn't technology or computers; our competition, the system we were trying to improve on, was *paper*. We looked at how people used paper organizers and we said, *that's* what we have to be better than. And paper's pretty good: It's fast, it's cheap, it's reliable. So we actually studied people doing things with paper—things like how long does it take to look up a name? How do people enter things? And where do they want to carry it? And in the end, those studies produced many of the design concepts that went into the original PalmPilot.

these resources to compete. Kodak produces the film, cameras, paper, and printers, while its Ofoto website provides the online processing services. Therefore, Kodak uses the same playing field to compete against other companies.

● Direct Competitor   ◐ Indirect Competitor   ○ Not a Competitor

	Kodak	Canon	Fuji	Shutterfly	Snapfish/ MotoPhoto	Yahoo
Purchase Camera	●	●	●	○	○	○
Purchase Accessories	●	●	●	○	○	○
Purchase Film	●	○	●	○	○	○
Look for Picture-Taking Advice	●	○	●	○	○	◐
Digitally Manipulate Pictures	●	○	○	●	●	○
Download and Choose Pictures to Print	●	◐	○	●	●	◐
Print and Receive Pictures	●	◐	○	●	●	◐
Share Pictures	●	○	○	●	●	◐
Store Pictures on CD	●	○	○	●	●	○

(Ofoto brackets the Kodak rows from "Look for Picture-Taking Advice" through "Store Pictures on CD.")

EXHIBIT 3.6   Competitor Profiling for Kodak

Competitor Mapping to Selected Segments

Current and prospective competitors can significantly shape the nature of a company's online opportunity. In previous steps, we identified the customer segments that the company wants to target and the competitors (direct and indirect) that a company may face. To assess competitive intensity, we need to map the competitors to the target segments. In other words, we need to map out where current competitor companies are participating and determine their effectiveness in delivering benefits to our target customers. This analysis will help the company do the following:

- Demarcate underserved areas in the market, as well as the most competitive areas.
- Identify the companies it will compete against, and gain preliminary understanding of their strengths.
- Spot companies that could be potential collaborators—in other words, companies that might offer a critical capability or unique access to customers at a specific stage of the customer decision process.

The competitor mapping of segments can also be used to record the relative strengths and weaknesses of current competitors and their offerings at each relevant cell in the map. Ultimately, the customer seeks specific benefits. Assessing the current players' performance in meeting the customer standard will provide an indication of the potential for a company to move in and win. Understanding current competitor capabilities will also give a sense of the height of the competitive hurdles a company may face in its selected space.

Exhibit 3.7 illustrates a mapping of Kodak's competitors to three segments. Kodak is a clear leader among cost-conscious consumers and middle-income families with children. Kodak provides inexpensive disposable cameras, along with low-end film and digital cameras that would appeal to those who want to take pictures but do not want to spend too much money doing so. Kodak appeals to middle-income families by supplying midline cameras and services that are easy to use and that allow families to take pictures of children and vacations, get them processed, and share them with grandparents. High-income, tech-savvy consumers, however, would probably only use Kodak for film or processing; they would likely buy more expensive cameras and printers that would allow them more options and better quality. If Kodak were to decide to pursue the higher-income bracket, it would have to either change its offerings or partner with another company in order to provide that segment with the benefits it wants.

Target Segments	Kodak	Canon	Snapfish
Cost-Conscious	◕ • Disposable cameras • Low-end film and digital cameras • No deals on developing	◔ • Limited low-end cameras • No services	◑ • Deals on services • No products
Middle-Income Families with Children	● • Midline cameras • Film • Photo services; developing, sharing	◑ • Mid-range cameras • No services	◑ • Services—developing, sharing, gift cards
High-Income/Tech Savvy	◔ • High-quality accessories (film, paper, CDs) • Products are less sophisticated	◕ • High-tech products • Software • Printers—consumers don't need to process	◔ • Services, though limited

● High performance level   ◑ Medium performance level   ○ Low performance level

EXHIBIT 3.7   Competitor Mapping to Selected Segments for Kodak

Step Four: Assess the Resources of the Company to Deliver the Offering

At this stage, the company should stake out what experience and benefits **the offering** will provide and what resources and technology will be needed to deliver the benefits of the offering. While the offering and the means to deliver its benefits will be revisited and refined many times, these details will play a vital part in influencing and determining the company's rationale for success in this endeavor.

Company Resources

Before spending a great deal of time crafting a specific business model to support a concept, the management team should assess whether or not it can identify at least three or four resources or assets that it can leverage successfully into the selected online space. These resources should be central to delivering new benefits or unlocking trapped value—the core of the company's value story. These resources should also hold the promise for advantage, considering the current and prospective players in the targeted space. With three or four such resources, the management team will have the beginnings of a robust business.

In this step, the team will already have a strong understanding of the following:

- The selected value system in which the company will be participating
- The key stages of the target's customer decision process and the benefits sought/value trapped at each stage
- The target customer segments

Looking across these insights, the management team should identify which winning resources it can create or provide through business partnerships. In Chapter 4, we introduce an analytical tool that we call the **resource system**; this is a useful framework for assessing the new business's resources. A resource system is a discrete collection of individual and organizational activities and assets that, taken together, create organizational capabilities that allow the company to serve customer needs. Resources that a company can bring to bear can be classified into the following three groupings:

- *Customer-facing.* Customer-facing resources include brand name, a well-trained salesforce, and multiple distribution channels.
- *Internal.* These resources are associated with the company's internal operations. Examples include technology, product development, economies of scale, and experienced staff.
- *Upstream.* These resources are associated with a company's relationship to its suppliers. Examples include partnerships with suppliers and the degree of operational seamlessness between the company and its suppliers.

Partners

On its own, a company may not be able to bring to bear all of the resources necessary to deliver value to its target segments. In opportunity assessment, a company must be realistic about any capability gaps. If a gap is insurmountable, the company should not proceed; if the gaps can somehow be closed, then a company must find a way to do so. Partnering may be an effective alternative to building or acquiring the capability. Online businesses find partnerships particularly relevant because their offerings span traditional value-system boundaries. In fact, effective partnering can be an important source of advantage. For example, AOL uses only Associated Press content for its online news alerts. Yahoo.com uses AP, Reuters, OneWorld.net, AP Features, and NPR for its world news coverage and Reuters, CNET, AP, Internet Report, ZDNet,

TechWeb, *USA Today*, NewsFactor, and MacCentral for its technology news. The potential partners for a company can be grouped into two categories: complementary partners and traditional, or capability, partners.

Complementary Partners   These partners provide offerings that are complementary to those of another company. For example, Intel is complementary to Microsoft. Also, an increase in the sales of a complementary offering is likely to lead to an increase in the partner company's sales. For example, a boost in the sale of Intel's Pentium processor is likely to lead to an increase in Microsoft Windows-based software sales and vice versa.

Capability Partners   Capability partners give and receive value from partnering with another company. Combining the benefits to be delivered with the way in which the company will deliver them fills in the business concept. With this high-level business concept in mind, we can assess the attractiveness of the opportunity from financial, technical, and competitive points of view. In Chapter 4, we consider in greater detail how the company can determine what capabilities it needs to develop and how to develop them.

Step Five: Assess Market Readiness of Technology

Technology Vulnerability

Beyond the competitive and customer arenas, the company must make a high-level judgment about the opportunity's vulnerability to technology trends, both in the penetration of enabling technologies and in the effect of new technologies on the value proposition.

Technology Adoption   The management team must also make a high-level judgment on technology transfer and the rate of adoption of relevant technologies. Is there sufficient penetration of the technologies (e.g., cable or DSL modems, scanners) that enables the customer to take advantage of or participate in the offering? What penetration is necessary to make the offering financially viable? When is the minimum penetration likely to be met? Is there an introductory version that could be upgraded as technology penetration increases?

Impact of New Technologies   What new technologies could radically alter the economics of delivering an offering or require adjustment of the actual features and functionality of an offering? How likely is it that your target population or competitors will use these technologies?

The pace and discontinuity of technological change make forecasting the future particularly challenging, and it is not our intent to provide an exhaustive treatment of the subject here.[15] Fortunately, several rules of thumb about technological development can guide entrepreneurs. Moore's Law forecasts that the processing power of successive generations of microchips will double every 1.5 years. Our definition of what a computer is will probably also change. Soon, every device will be a computer. Many believe these devices will all be connected by a vastly larger Internet. George Gilder, a technology forecaster who has given his name to Gilder's Law, predicts that total bandwidth of communications systems will triple every 12 months for the foreseeable future. The challenge for entrepreneurs is to understand what these macro-trends will mean for their proposed businesses.

Step Six: Specify the Opportunity in Concrete Terms

At this point, the management team should have a clear picture of the market opportunity. Its members should be able to describe the value system for the industry and have a strong sense of how intervention into this value system and the customer decision process could create new benefits, enhance existing ones, or unlock value trapped in the current system. The team should be able to clearly identify the customer segments that it will be targeting and support its determination with data or strong hypotheses about the underserved or unmet needs of one or more of these customer segments. This understanding provides the basis for creating a high-level value proposition and determining capabilities that the team can bring to bear to participate successfully in the business. The examination of potential competitors enhances the team's thinking about where to participate in the identified market and what to bring to the opportunity.

To specify the opportunity in concrete terms, the management team should craft an **opportunity story**—in essence, the first rough outline of the business plan. The opportunity story should:

- Briefly describe the target segment(s) within the selected value system.
- Articulate the high-level value proposition.
- Spell out the expected elements of customer benefits (we largely focused on functional benefits in this chapter; however, needs can be emotional or self-expressive).
- Identify the critical capabilities and resources needed to deliver the customer benefits.
- Lay out the critical "reasons to believe" that the identified capabilities and resources will be a source of relative advantage over the competition.
- Categorize the critical capabilities (and supporting resources) as in-house, build, buy, or collaborate.
- Describe how the company will monetize the opportunity (i.e., how it will capture some portion of the value that it creates for its customers).
- Provide an initial sense of the magnitude of the financial opportunity for the company.

If there is uncertainty about one or more of the gating questions, the management team must judge whether additional analysis would remove the uncertainty. The team should not proceed too far down the path toward business-model development if members cannot reach a consensus on passing these initial gates.

Step Seven: Assess Opportunity Attractiveness

At this point, the management team should have a clear picture of the market opportunity. Its members should be able to describe the value system for the industry. They should also have a strong sense for how intervention into this value system and the customer decision process could provide exceptional value to the customer by creating new benefits, enhancing existing ones, or unlocking value trapped in the current system. The team should be able to clearly identify its customer segments and support its determination with data or well-tested hypotheses about the underserved or unmet needs of one or more of these customer segments. Relevant technologies should be identified, along with an educated estimate of their developmental and adoption time lines. The team should also be able to articulate compelling reasons why the identified capabilities and resources will be a source of relative advantage over the competition. This understanding provides the basis for creating a high-level value proposition and determining capabilities that the team can bring to bear to participate successfully in the business. The examination of potential competitors enhances the team's thinking about where to participate in the identified market and what to bring to the opportunity.

There is little point in targeting a new business concept in general, or a meaningful and easy-to-reach segment specifically, if the opportunity is not attractive. The attractiveness of an opportunity is based on a performance estimate of long-term profitability in the particular industry, as well as the firm's relative competitive position within that industry. The manager can determine the character and magnitude of the opportunity through examining the following:

- Level of unmet need and the magnitude of unconstrained opportunity
- Level of interaction between major customer segments
- Likely rate of growth
- Size/volume of the market
- Level of profitability

Once we have identified the unmet customer need, assessed market readiness of technology, analyzed the resources to deliver the benefits of the offering, assessed relative advantage, and crafted the opportunity story, we next need to turn our attention to customer and market dynamics. When analyzing customer and market dynamics, five central factors must be considered: unconstrained opportunity, segment interaction, growth rate, market size, and profitability.

Unconstrained Opportunity

This is the amount of white space that is still apparent in the marketplace. Markets with a high degree of trapped or relatively untapped new-to-the-world value are particularly prized. Note the explosive growth of eBay in the online auction space. The number of goods that individuals wanted to buy and sell, combined with the relatively arcane auction system in which they found themselves trading, signaled a massive opportunity.

Segment Interaction

This level of reinforcing activity generates more purchase and usage. Companies that have member-influencing-member dynamics—in other words, viral dynamics—can quickly capture much of the opportunity. For example, through its self-serve customer feedback offering Zoomerang.com, MarketTools created a geometric viral effect. Each member can send a customer feedback survey to 30 customers, who in turn decide whether to write their own survey and send it to 30 of their customers, and so on.

Growth Rate

Growth rate refers to the percentage of annual growth of the underlying customer market. Markets with expected high growth represent significant opportunities for players. Typically, opportunities with estimated annual growth rates of 30 to 50 percent or greater are highly attractive, while those with declining or negative growth (less than 10 percent) are considered unattractive.

Market Size

This is the dollar value of all of the sales generated in a particular market. Opportunities with a large market size are very attractive, since winning even a small piece of the pie may correspond to a significant revenue flow. For example, a large number of competitors in the online pet-products industry emerged in response to the huge size of the pet food and supplies market, estimated at $23 billion.[16] Despite this large market, many of the entrants (e.g., Petopia.com and Pets.com) were unable to create successful businesses.

Profitability

This is the profit margin that can be realized in the market. Markets with high profit margins are highly attractive because they can generate high levels of profit with moderate sales volume. For example, eBay's auction market provides a highly attractive opportunity in part because it generates profit margins of nearly 80 percent.[17]

An important aspect of the assessment of market size and profitability is determining how the company will generate revenue. What are the opportunities for monetizing the value creation? Consider typical sources of revenue in the networked economy—advertising, referrals, affiliate-program fees, customer subscriptions, and the purchase of products and services.

Overall Opportunity Assessment

To assess the overall attractiveness of the opportunity, managers must not only rate each factor separately but also rate them together. Whether a particular factor helps or hinders the overall market opportunity (or does not have an effect on it at all), the manager must try to gauge the magnitude of its impact. It is important to look across all factors (technology and competition as well as the customer and market factors mentioned above) to see the overall effect, because these effects may be multiplicative and not additive. Each company must decide how to evaluate the opportunity. Exhibit 3.8 shows how Priceline.com's management team might have looked at its opportunity when the company was first conceived.

The team now must decide whether or not it is ready to define the specific value proposition and design a business model. This should be the first of several go/no-go decision gates. If it has not already done so, the team should define the criteria to be met before proceeding to the next step of the business development process.

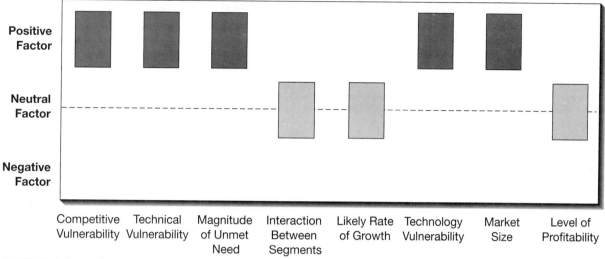

EXHIBIT 3.8   Priceline.com Overall Opportunity Assessment

MarketWatch.com Strategic Analysis for Market Opportunity

Let us now apply the market opportunity framework to MarketWatch.com. To best illustrate the framework, we turn the clock back to the early months of 2000. At that time, MarketWatch.com saw a chance to capture considerable market share and to position itself alongside the most respected online business and financial news providers. With that belief came a significant challenge: Which opportunities should be pursued, and which should be ignored? If management made the right decisions, it would be rewarded for its acumen with increased visitors as well as advertising and licensing revenue. If not, it would have to struggle for continued viability.

Step One

The first step in the market opportunity framework is to identify unmet or underserved customer needs. To do this, MarketWatch.com needed to have a clear understanding at a basic level of who its customers were. A look at its value system highlighted three sets of customers. The first and largest segment was people seeking financial and business news who had a distinct interest in global financial markets. The second segment was advertisers seeking additional and more effective venues to promote their products and services online. The final segment was licensees—companies looking to augment their products and services with financial news and information from third-party providers instead of building those capabilities internally.

With this understanding of its customers, MarketWatch.com could go through the customer decision process for each of these three customer segments. Exhibit 3.9 illustrates the customer decision process for the consumer segment and highlights its unmet and underserved needs. At the most basic level, individuals came to MarketWatch.com to keep abreast of financial markets and business news, track financial markets, and get a moderate level of

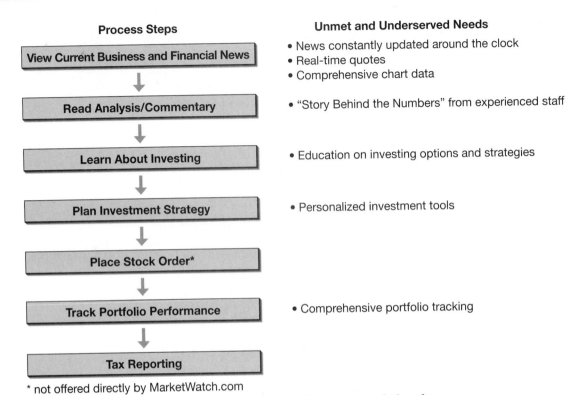

Process Steps

- View Current Business and Financial News
- Read Analysis/Commentary
- Learn About Investing
- Plan Investment Strategy
- Place Stock Order*
- Track Portfolio Performance
- Tax Reporting

Unmet and Underserved Needs

- News constantly updated around the clock
- Real-time quotes
- Comprehensive chart data
- "Story Behind the Numbers" from experienced staff
- Education on investing options and strategies
- Personalized investment tools
- Comprehensive portfolio tracking

* not offered directly by MarketWatch.com

EXHIBIT 3.9   MarketWatch.com: Unmet and Underserved Needs

analysis and commentary from respected industry sources. More involved individuals had deeper interests in financial markets and desired to learn more about investing, develop personal investing strategies, and execute against them. After outlining the customer decision process for its advertising and licensee customers as well, MarketWatch.com could come up with a list of unmet or underserved needs similar to those in Exhibit 3.10.

The customer decision process reveals three sets of interconnected unmet and underserved needs.

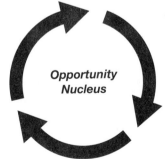

Licensee Needs

- Brand-name content
- Modularized content
- Seamless integration
- Reliable delivery

Opportunity Nucleus

Advertiser Needs

- Highly trafficked site
- Attractive demographics
- Broad ad placement options
- Multiple ad formats (e.g., banners, audio, video)
- Measurable results

Individual Needs

- High-quality reliable reporting
- Focused reporting with moderate depth
- Timely market information
- Pleasing user experience

EXHIBIT 3.10   MarketWatch.com's Customers and Needs

Step Two

The next step in the framework is to identify the specific customers to pursue. MarketWatch.com segmented each of its three customer types to identify actionable and meaningful segments within each. An expanded line of products and a strong and continuous commitment to world-class service were important goals for MarketWatch.com. However, its continued viability depended on its ability to monetize that audience, putting particular pressure on revenue-generating activities. With this pressure in mind, we look at MarketWatch.com's segmentation of its licensing customers.

MarketWatch.com wanted to expand its existing relationships with its core clients while broadening its list of new ones. It determined that these new clients needed to be consumers and distributors of financial information with complementary online offerings and deep pockets—they needed to be able to pay for MarketWatch.com's various content products, including company research, insider-trading data, and a full suite of mutual-fund data. The types of firms that fit this actionable and meaningful segment were leading brokerages, diversified financial institutions, and financial publishers looking to improve their online offerings to increase market share in a down economy. A sampling of MarketWatch.com's targeted companies is displayed in Exhibit 3.11.

Licensing Segments	Targeted Companies
Brokerages	Ameritrade Datek E*Trade
Diversified Financial Institutions	Charles Schwab Morgan Stanley UBS PaineWebber
Financial Publishers	Motley Fool The New York Times The Financial Times

EXHIBIT 3.11   MarketWatch.com Licensing Segments

Step Three

The third step in the market opportunity framework is to assess the company's advantage relative to its competitors. Three main dimensions that were meaningful given MarketWatch.com's customer segments were its reporting, technology, and branding. Exhibit 3.12 maps MarketWatch.com against three of its most successful competitors: Yahoo Finance, MSN Money, and CNNfn. MarketWatch.com held a competitive advantage in the reporting dimension due to the strength of its in-house reporters, as well as its close relationship with CBS and its ability to leverage CBS's reporting resources and outlets.

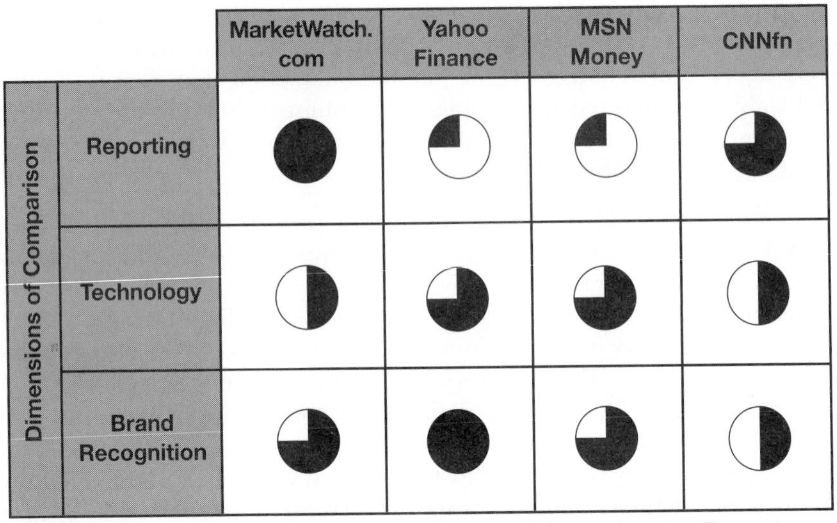

EXHIBIT 3.12   MarketWatch.com Competition: Map to Target Segments

While Yahoo Finance provided a wealth of financial information, it lacked the analysis component that was MarketWatch.com's strength. The technology dimension was led by Yahoo Finance and MSN Money. Both sites were able to leverage significant resources based on their early entry in the online space and their general expertise in technology. In branding, MarketWatch.com benefited greatly from its association with CBS and the subsequent use of its logo and name on TV and the radio. However, Yahoo was perhaps the most widely recognized online brand in the world, and Microsoft had the deepest pockets of anyone competing in the online financial news space. Both proved formidable to competitors in the branding arena.

Step Four

The fourth step in the market opportunity framework is to assess the company's resources to deliver the offering. MarketWatch.com's primary customer-facing resource was its brand name and association with CBS. "CBS MarketWatch.com" was seen on TV and in print and was heard on the radio by millions of people each day. Virtually no other competitor (perhaps excluding MSN Money, with Microsoft's near-limitless financial backing) could begin to realize that kind of brand exposure. MarketWatch.com's strongest internal asset was its corps of in-house writers. This gave it the ability to generate value-added analysis and commentary in addition to more standard and commoditized features such as stock quotes and market data. Finally, MarketWatch.com's upstream resources included both its access to CBS news outlets and its reporting resources. It was able to tap into these resources to expand the reach and breadth of its content. Its other main upstream resource was its existing relationships with its core financial institution clients.

Step Five

The next step for MarketWatch.com was to assess the market readiness of technology. On the consumer side, MarketWatch.com needed to focus on low-bandwidth services. With the majority of households still accessing the Internet through dial-up connections, and with broadband used primarily by early adopters, investments in streaming video and other broadband-friendly services had to wait for more widespread adoption. There were, however, more technology demands on the revenue-generating side of MarketWatch.com's business. Its advertisers were increasingly more receptive to alternative online advertising placements. Response rates to the traditional banner ad were approaching 1 percent, abysmal compared to a few years earlier. More attractive options included the ability to incorporate motion and sound into their ads, the ability to place ads within the body of articles or as interstitials (ads that would appear on the entire screen before an article would appear), and the ability to sponsor whole sections of the site. Each of these alternatives required MarketWatch.com to invest in the technology that would make them possible.

Finally, licensing introduced an entirely different set of technology demands. Licensees needed modularized content that could be seamlessly integrated into their sites. This required a whole suite of tools that MarketWatch.com had already invested in. MarketWatch.com needed to ensure that its technology could scale with increased licensing demands as this side of the business grew.

Step Six

The next step is to specify the opportunity in concrete terms. This involves creating the opportunity story for MarketWatch.com—a series of gating questions that would provide a rough outline of the business plan. Exhibit 3.13 illustrates MarketWatch.com's opportunity story. It outlines the benefits, needed resources, and size of the opportunity for MarketWatch.com's three target segments: consumers, advertisers, and licensees. To summarize the opportunity, MarketWatch.com needed to continue to deliver high-value content to affluent seekers of financial and investing news, and monetize that content through the effective use of advertising placements and the creation and selling of a broad suite of content modules to licensing partners.

Step Seven

The last step in the framework is to assess the attractiveness of the opportunity. Competitive intensity is just one of the seven factors to be considered when determining how attractive the opportunity was for MarketWatch.com in the early months of 2000. Exhibit 3.14 shows these factors and their effect on the opportunity attractiveness. Competitive vulnerability was a negative factor, given the intensity of the competition. The magnitude of unmet needs was a neutral factor, since many of the basic user needs were addressed—though there was room for more effective tools and more insightful analysis. The likely growth rate of the MarketWatch.com target segments and the potential size of the market (in terms of both advertising and content licensing) were very high—both positive factors in assessing the opportunity. The combination of these factors led to an attractive opportunity for MarketWatch.com, while at the same time signaling the need to closely monitor competitor moves.

The MarketWatch.com Opportunity Story							
Target Segment	**Value Proposition**	**Customer Benefits**	**Critical Resources**	**Reasons to Believe**	**Resource Sourcing**	**How to Monetize**	**Opportunity Magnitude**
Consumer — Affluent seekers of financial news and investing	Highest-quality reporting Broad set of investing tools	One-stop shopping for financial news needs	In-house reporting team CBS	Expensive-to-duplicate writing team Only one CBS	Reporters in-house CBS	Large target audience critical for advertising success	Medium
Advertiser — Auto Brokers Consumer products	Highly attractive audience Effective placements	Improved results of online advertising campaigns	Sophisticated publishing platform Strong sales team	Table stakes for continued survival	In-house	Enhanced placements and formats	Medium–large
Licensee — Brokers Financial institutions and publishers	Broad suite of products to complement own offerings	Broadened offerings on own site at reduced cost	Sophisticated publishing platform and delivery tools	Table stakes for continued survival	In-house	Develop and support multiple content modules to license	Large

EXHIBIT 3.13   MarketWatch.com Opportunity Story

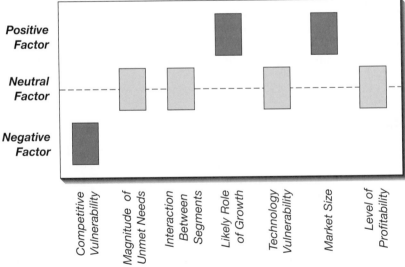

EXHIBIT 3.14   MarketWatch.com Opportunity Assessment

1. **Is market opportunity analysis unique for online firms?**

The networked economy has affected market opportunity analysis in five main ways:
   a. Networked-economy competition occurs across industry boundaries rather than within industry boundaries.
   b. Competition occurs between alliances of companies rather than between individual companies.
   c. Competitive developments and responses are occurring at unprecedented speed.
   d. Consumer behavior is still in the early stages of being defined, making it easier to influence and change.
   e. Industry value chains or value systems are rapidly being reconfigured.

2. **What are the two generic value types?**

A firm is looking for either trapped value to be liberated or new-to-the-world value to be introduced. Firms should look at the value system as a lens that yields ideas about new business possibilities.

3. **What is the framework for market opportunity analysis?**

The framework for market opportunity analysis can be thought of as the initial investigative stage of the funnel process of innovation that includes the following steps:
   a. Identify the unmet customer need.
   b. Identify the specific customers a company will pursue.
   c. Assess market readiness of technology.
   d. Assess the resources to deliver the benefits of the offering.
   e. Assess relative advantage.
   f. Specify opportunity in concrete terms.
   g. Assess opportunity attractiveness.

4. **How do you identify unmet and/or underserved needs?**

Identifying unmet and/or underserved needs requires managers to examine four key environments for opportunity analysis: customer, technology, company, and competition. The intersection of these four key environments forms the "sweet spot" for e-business innovation where an appropriate configuration of customer segment, technology platform, company resource system, and competitive advantage can create a sustainable business that provides uncommon customer value and entry into a new cycle of increased customer convenience, productivity, and satisfaction.

The customer decision process is an organizing framework that helps a company look systematically for unmet or underserved needs. The process maps the activities and the choices customers make in accessing a specific experience within a value system. The customer decision process lays out a series of steps, from awareness of the experience to the purchase experience and finally the use experience. The process of mapping the customer decision process may help in generating new ideas about unmet or underserved needs.

5. **How does a company identify the specific customers it will pursue?**

To be effective and efficient, it is essential for a company to know which customer groups are most attractive, which groups it should pursue, which groups it should de-emphasize, and what offerings to present to which target segment. Customer segmentation, or the grouping of similar customers in order to better serve their needs, must be both actionable (consistent with how the company can take action in the market) and meaningful (correlating to differences in how customers will behave). Profiling the segments will identify where the money is, how well competitors serve the segments, and where underserved customers reside.

6. **How do you assess advantage relative to competitors?**

To assess relative advantage, the manager must understand the context of competition at the industry level and specific competitors at the individual company level. Competitive advantage is based on the customer value a firm creates that exceeds the firm's cost to produce that value. There are two basic types of competitive advantage: cost leadership and differentiation. Value is not determined by the firm but rather by buyers in the amounts they are willing to pay. Firms can create value by offering lower prices than competitors for the same benefits or by providing unique benefits that more than offset the higher price.

In the online world, companies that one would not consider direct competitors can become indirect competitors. Porter defines these firms as offering products or services that are "close substitutes" for each other. Indirect competitors include two categories of companies: substitute producers and adjacent competitors.

The competitor mapping of segments can also be used to record the relative strengths and weaknesses of current competitors and their offerings at each relevant cell in the map. Ultimately, the customer seeks specific benefits. Assessing the current player performance in meeting the customer standard will provide an indication of the potential for a company to move in and win. Understanding current competitor capabilities will also give a sense of the height of competitive hurdles a company may face in its selected space.

7. What resources does the company need in order to deliver the benefits of the offering?

After the initial customer focus of the business is determined, the company should stake out the capabilities and technology needed to deliver the benefits of the offering. The management team should identify at least three or four assets of a winning resource system that it can create or provide through business partnerships. This resource system is central to delivering new benefits or unlocking trapped value—the core of the company's value story—and should hold the promise for an advantage when compared with current and prospective players in the targeted marketspace. A resource system is a discrete collection of individual and company activities and assets that, when combined, create organizational capabilities. These capabilities allow the company to serve customer needs.

On its own, a company may not be able to offer all the necessary resources to deliver value to its target segments. In opportunity assessment, a company must be realistic about any capability gaps. Partnering may be an effective alternative to building or acquiring the capability. The potential partners for a company can be grouped into two categories—complementary and capability partners.

8. How do you assess the readiness of the technology needed to deliver an offering?

The company must make a high-level judgment on the opportunity's vulnerability to technology trends, both in the penetration of enabling technologies and in the effect of new technologies on the value proposition. The management team must also make a high-level judgment on technology transfer and the rate of adoption of relevant technologies to estimate the penetration necessary to make the offering financially viable.

Several rules of thumb about technological development can guide entrepreneurs. Moore's Law forecasts that the processing power of successive generations of microchips will double every 18 months. Gilder's Law predicts that total bandwidth of communications systems will triple every 12 months for the foreseeable future. The challenge for entrepreneurs is to understand what these macro-trends will mean for their proposed businesses.

9. How do you specify opportunity in concrete terms?

The management team can compose an opportunity story, which can be thought of as the first draft of a business plan. The story should articulate the value proposition and the target customers. It should demonstrate the benefits to these customers and the way in which the company will monetize the opportunity. It should estimate the financial magnitude of the opportunity, identify the key capabilities and resources, and, finally, discuss the reasons to believe. In other words, the story should tell why the company's capabilities will create a competitive advantage for the new business in serving its target customers.

10. How do you assess the attractiveness of an opportunity?

The attractiveness of an opportunity is based on a performance estimate of long-term profitability in the particular industry, as well as the firm's relative competitive position within that industry. The manager can determine the character and magnitude of the opportunity by examining the following:

   a. Level of unmet need and the magnitude of unconstrained opportunity
   b. Level of interaction between major customer segments
   c. Likely rate of growth

    d. Size/volume of the market

    e. Level of profitability

An important aspect of the assessment of market size and profitability is determining how the company will generate revenue. Consider typical sources of revenue in the networked economy—advertising revenue, referrals, affiliate-program fees, customer subscriptions, and the purchase of products and services.

To assess the overall opportunity attractiveness, managers must not only rate each factor separately but also rate them together. Whether a particular factor helps or hinders the overall market opportunity, or is neutral, the manager must try to gauge the magnitude of its impact. It is important to look across all factors to see the overall effect, because they might be multiplicative rather than additive.

1. Visit an e-commerce website. Search the Web for competitors in the industry and market. Describe the marketspace of the company's industry, the size of the market, its growth rate, and the company's market share. Describe the customer need the company is trying to satisfy, the specific customers the company is pursuing, the technology and resources likely needed to deliver the benefits of the company's offering, the revenue model, the company's key competitors, the basis of the company's relative advantage, and the company's strategy.

2. Visit the four legal online music services: FullAudio's MusicNow (*www.fullaudio.com*), Listen.com's Rhapsody (*www.listen.com*), MusicNet (*www.musicnet.com*), and pressplay (*www.pressplay.com*). Compare and contrast the services by describing the customer need each company is trying to satisfy, the specific customers each company is pursuing, the technology and resources likely needed to deliver the benefits of each company's offering, each company's pricing and revenue model, the basis of each company's relative advantage, and each company's strategy.

3. Suppose that you are about to enter either the marketspace of Exercise 1 or the music marketspace of Exercise 2 as a new competitor. Use the market opportunity analysis framework to determine the attractiveness of your top three market opportunities.

Exercises

marketspace

co-opetition

value chain

value system

trapped value

new-to-the-world value

innovation

market opportunity analysis
  framework

four key environments

opportunity nucleus

customer decision process

segmentation

actionable segmentation

meaningful segmentation

direct competitors

indirect competitors

the offering

resource system

opportunity story

Key Terms

[1]Karen E. Klein, "The Bottom Line on Startup Failures," *BusinessWeek Online*, 4 March 2002 (URL: http://www.businessweek.com/smallbiz/content/mar2002/sb2002034_8796.htm).

[2]All stock prices at closing on April 26, 2002: Amazon at 16.91, which is 4.02 percent of historical high—High 402.25 on 4/23/1999; Autobytel at 3.53, which is 8.43 percent of historical high—High 41.88 on 3/31/1999; Drugstore.com at 2.29, which is 3.39 percent of historical high—High 67.5 on 8/27/1999; iVillage at 1.80, which is 1.58 percent of historical high—High 113.75 on 4/12/1999; Marketwatch.com at 5.01, which is 5.14 percent of historical high—High 97.5 on 1/15/1999; and TheStreet.com at 3.25, which is 5.42 percent of historical high—High 60 on 5/11/1999.

[3]Adam M. Brandenburger and Barry J. Nalebuff, *Co-opetition* (New York: Currency Doubleday, 1996).

[4]Interested readers could learn more about value chains and value systems in the following: Michael E. Porter, *Competitive Advantage: Creating and Sustaining Superior Performance* (New York: The Free Press, 1985; London: Collier Macmillan, 1985).

[5]Dell Computer Corporation, "Dell's Supply Chain," October 2000 (URL:http://www.dell.com/us/en/gen/casestudies/casestudy_dell_i2.htm).

[6]Marc van Impe, "NTT DoCoMo Set to Launch Multimedia Vending Machines," *CommerceNet Scandinavia*, 15 April 2002 (URL: http://www.mobile.commerce.net/story.php?story_id=1541).

[7]Ernest Gundling, *The 3M Way to Innovation* (Tokyo, Japan: Kondansha International Ltd.; New York: Kodansha America, Inc., 2000), 23.

[8]Andrea Hamilton, "A Bumpy Path to Palm—Handheld's Creator Had Modest Goal of Making Something New," *Special to The Mercury News*, 9 June 2002 (URL: http://www.bayarea.com/mld/bayarea/business/3433299.htm).

[9]Clayton Christensen, *The Innovator's Dilemma* (Boston: Harvard Business School Press, 1997).

Endnotes

[10]This sidebar is summarized from the following article: Dorothy Leonard and Jeffrey F. Rayport, "Spark Innovation Through Empathic Design," *Harvard Business Review* 75, no. 6 (November–December 1997): 102–13.

[11]Philip Kotler, *Marketing Management*, 10th ed. (Upper Saddle River, NJ: Prentice Hall, 2000), Chapter 9.

[12]Porter, *Competitive Strategy*, 5.

[13]Ibid.

[14]Ibid., 23.

[15]Interested persons should refer to these references for further reading: Richard N. Foster, *Innovation: The Attacker's Advantage* (New York: Summit Books, 1986); and Clayton M. Christensen, *The Innovator's Dilemma: When New Techniques Cause Great Firms to Fail* (Boston: Harvard Business School Press, 1997).

[16]Brad Stone, "Amazon's Pet Projects: Start-Ups Jump When the Online Giant Comes Calling," *Newsweek*, 21 June 1999.

[17]Russ Banham, "Sittin' on the Dock of eBay," *CFO.com*, 15 December 2000 (URL: http://www.cfo.com/printarticle/0,5317,5787|,00.html).

| Business | Models |

CASELET: VERTICALNET'S CHANGING BUSINESS MODEL

The importance of a business model is never more graphically demonstrated than when it requires an overhaul. And there has been no shortage of overhauled business models in recent years, as companies have searched—sometimes desperately—for paths to profitability in the terra incognita of the networked economy.

Take Verticalnet, a once high-flying business-to-business (B2B) exchange based in Malvern, Pennsylvania, that has radically revised its business plan not once but several times. The company started in 1995 as Water Online. In that incarnation, the company was a fledgling new-media venture looking to produce online trade magazines supported by advertising. In addition to its namesake, the firm, soon known as VerticalNet, created such titles as Food Online, Pollution Online, and Public Works Online.

When B2B became "the next big thing," VerticalNet went public and recast itself as an online exchange, attempting to parlay its vertical trade communities into online marketplaces that would bring together business buyers and sellers—and make money (a lot of money, many thought, judging by the success of the firm's IPO) by taking a small cut of each transaction. VerticalNet also charged subscription fees to companies that set up catalog-like "virtual storefronts" on its sites. This new model generated revenue but produced losses as well. When B2B exchanges began to flounder—companies and suppliers were not all that eager to abandon face-to-face interactions and preferred-provider relationships, it turned out—VerticalNet's cash reserves and stock price plummeted.

In 2002, Verticalnet (the capital "N" was jettisoned to deemphasize the firm's Internet roots) put its 59 online marketplaces up for sale and adopted a more modest core business: selling supply chain software. The new business model is relatively simple: Sell enough, and succeed. Whether it will prove a winner—or the last—for Verticalnet is anybody's guess.

This chapter was coauthored by Jeffrey Rayport, Bernie Jaworski, Geo Griffin, and Yannis Dosios.

PLEASE CONSIDER THE FOLLOWING QUESTIONS AS YOU READ THIS CHAPTER:

1. What are the four components of an online business model?

2. Do firms compete on value propositions or value clusters?

3. What are the approaches to developing an online offering, whether the business is providing a product, service, or information?

4. What is a successful, unique resource system? What are the characteristics of good resource systems?

5. What are the revenue sources available to firms?

INTRODUCTION

The previous chapter answered the question, Where will the business compete? In this chapter we turn our attention to the question, How will the business win? Certainly, winning is relative to the goals of a business. A business may choose to define victory in terms of revenue targets, gross margin, number of customers, or other criteria.

Regardless of the goals of the enterprise, a business must first specify its business model. In this chapter, we introduce the concept of a business model for an online business. An online business model requires four choices on the part of senior management. These include the specification of (1) a value proposition or value cluster for targeted customers; (2) an online offering (which could be product, service, information, or all three); (3) a unique, defendable resource system; and (4) a revenue model.

To understand the components of a business model, we apply the framework to the highly competitive, rapidly changing flower industry. The domestic retail flower business is a $16 billion industry that is highly fragmented, with no national brand, multiple layers of distribution, and uneven product quality. Given the complexity of the supply chain, flowers are typically sold 10 to 12 days after they are harvested. On the customer side, approximately 60 percent of all flower purchases are made by walk-in customers. When flowers are delivered, 80 percent are local—that is, they are ordered and delivered in the same area.

According to Forrester Research, online flower sales were approximately $760 million in 2000, almost double the sales in 1999. Forrester predicts that online sales will increase to $2.4 billion by the year 2003.

In April 2000, a *Los Angeles Times* article about the online flower industry noted that FTD.com had lost 75 percent of its value since going public in the fall of 1999.[1] Equally important, FTD.com and other major flower websites were experiencing a significant cash drain. In particular, the article made the following observations and forecasts:

- FTD.com was spending $6.1 million per month to stay in business but was taking in only $2.2 million in gross revenues, for a $3.9 million monthly deficit. Because FTD.com had $37.9 million in cash and current assets, the *Los Angeles Times* calculated that without a significant improvement in performance, the business would run out of cash by the end of 2000.

- 1-800-Flowers.com was running a monthly deficit of $22.4 million and could hold out for 8.4 months.
- Gerald Stevens was losing $17.7 million a month and would last less than two months.
- PC Flowers & Gifts was losing $326,000 a month and could hold on for 13 months.

Not surprisingly, the prediction was that the number of online flower retailers would "shrink dramatically." Indeed, FTD.com's CEO boasted that by year-end 2000 there would be only two remaining players: FTD.com and 1-800-Flowers.com.

As of June 2002, part of that prediction had come true. The number of flower retailers did shrink—Gerald Stevens and PC Flowers & Gifts were no longer industry players. Both FTD.com and 1-800-Flowers.com had seen increases in revenue—a 33 percent increase for FTD.com in fiscal year 2001 and a 16 percent increase for 1-800-Flowers.com for the same time period. FTD.com was profitable in 2002, while 1-800-Flowers.com was expected to be profitable in the near future. FTD.com was bought back by IOS Brands, its privately held parent, which planned to rename itself FTD Inc. and go public. Also, in 2000 and 2001, another competitor, Proflowers.com, became more of a presence, posting revenues of $46 million in 2001—a 70 percent increase from the previous year—and acquiring more partners.

In this chapter, we consider the components of the business models of key players in this industry (see Exhibit 4.1). Significant cross-industry competition is emerging in this product category. Flowers are sold online by conventional bricks-and-mortar flower merchants; new online flower merchants (e.g., Proflowers.com); and cross-industry players in the gift, card, and crafts markets (e.g., Hallmark.com). We examine the critical decisions companies in this industry have made in order to win in the online world.

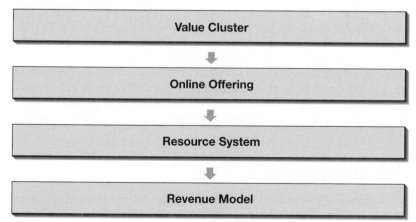

EXHIBIT 4.1   Components of a Business Model

The Four Components of an Online Business Model

To arrive at an online **business model**, senior management must define the model's four components: (1) a value proposition or value cluster for targeted customers; (2) an online offering, which could be product, service, information, or all three; (3) a unique, defendable resource system; and (4) a revenue model. While more traditional views of the business model tend to put revenue model at the center, online business models must also place importance on customer benefits, the offering, and resources. Our definition of a business model answers more than the question, How will the business make money? It also answers the question, How will the business win?

In this chapter, we consider all four business-model components. The most important message in this chapter is the need to base all online business-model decisions on the forces that are unfolding in the marketplace. All else being equal, firms that are able to understand both current and future customer needs are likely to be the long-term winners in their respective industries.

Value Propositions and Value Clusters

The first step in the articulation of an online business model is to clearly specify the value proposition for the business. Construction of a **value proposition** requires management to specify three things: (1) target segment, (2) focal customer benefits, and (3) the key resource the business has that can help it deliver the benefit package in a significantly better way than its competitors.

A value proposition can be considered the smallest (but most critical) level of benefits and resources a company offers to consumers. However, as we discussed in Chapter 3, online businesses have acquired customization capabilities that allow them to address multiple customer segments and offer a variety of benefits. Because of this, some have argued that businesses need to take a **value cluster** approach, in which the value proposition is no longer singular but a cluster composed of three parts: (1) the choice of target customer segments, (2) a particular focal combination of customer-driven benefits, and (3) the rationale for why this firm and its partners can deliver the value cluster in a significantly better way than competitors. This means the firm can serve multiple groups of customers with *different* value propositions—for example, Amazon can serve the textbook market with one value proposition, and the trade-book market with a different value proposition.

Choice of Segments

The first decision in the construction of a value cluster (or a value proposition) is the selection of target segments. A careful market opportunity analysis, as reviewed in Chapter 3, should reveal the segments in which a particular firm can be competitive. While a number of classical frameworks address

---

Point-Counterpoint

Should the Firm Deliver a Single Benefit or a Cluster of Benefits?

Should online firms focus exclusively on delivering a single benefit exceptionally well—the lowest prices, the freshest flowers, and the like—or should they attempt to deliver all of the benefits that online customers are seeking?

The argument in favor of delivering a single benefit centers largely on the alignment of the organization and its ability to easily communicate with target customers. Proponents of the single-benefit view note that this does not imply they will only deliver one benefit, but rather that they emphasize one critical benefit. Thus, while Buy.com is clearly focused on low price, it simultaneously must deliver breadth of inventory, ease of use, and order fulfillment. This strong adherence to a single critical benefit and message aligns the back-office systems of the organization and makes a clear statement to the market. Here, we define the market broadly to include target customers, potential partner firms, and potential employees.

Proponents of the multiple-benefit approach note that this emphasis on a single benefit is a legacy of the offline world. The online world enables firms to provide multiple "storefronts" to multiple segments within the context of a single URL. Moreover, it is much more customer-focused in the long run because customers *do* desire multiple benefits. For example, Yahoo.com provides a wide variety of benefits (e.g., single access point, fresh information, easy-to-use navigation tools) through its information and service offerings (e.g., information services, travel services, search, news, weather, and stock quotes).

Thus, in sharp contrast to offline business models, firms in the online world are often able to compete on multiple benefits delivered by a single, tightly conceived and implemented set of activities. But because of their multiple-benefits approach, it is difficult to evaluate any key benefit of these companies. For example, what is Amazon.com's key benefit? Is it price? Customer intimacy? Depth of the product line? Product leadership and service innovation? All of the above? Traditional business strategists would argue that the firm needs to select one critical benefit. This would miss the emergence of hybrid-benefit models such as Amazon.com.

---

the segment-choice decision, most reduce the analysis to two basic dimensions: the attractiveness of the market and the firm's ability to compete in the market. Market attractiveness is a function of many variables,[2] but the key decision variables are frequently reduced to the following:

- *Market size and growth rates.* The overall dollar size of the market and percentage growth rates of the market segments should be significant.

- *Unmet or insufficiently met customer needs.* Customers are either not being served or not being served well by existing players.

- *Weak or nonexistent competitors.* Obviously, it is best to enter markets where the competition is not evident, is performing poorly, or does not have sufficient resources to win the market.

The firm's ability to compete in a particular segment can be assessed by examining how well its business strengths (relative to competitors) match the benefits sought by a segment. For example, if a particular online flower retailer has unique strengths (such as exclusive sourcing of fresh flowers) and the target segment highly desires that strength (in this example, fresh flowers), then there would be a strong match between the relative business strength and the desires of this segment. Another important factor enters into the online segment-choice decision: degree of fit (or conflict) with existing channels. The offline businesses of 1-800-Flowers.com and

Constructing a Value Proposition

We now have a good understanding of the three components of a value proposition or cluster. The following are sample value propositions for three of the major online flower retailers.[8] Keep in mind that these are not necessarily defendable value propositions. Rather, the intent is to illustrate how a proposition can be constructed. We begin by deconstructing the value proposition of 1-800-Flowers.com, followed by those of its two major competitors.

- 1-800-Flowers.com
  - *Segment choice:* the mid- to high-end market
  - *Benefit choice:* broad gift assortment, fresh flowers, and easy access
  - *Resource choice:* strong distribution network, product and media partnerships, and multiple contact points

- FTD.com
  - *Segment choice:* the mid- to high-end market
  - *Benefit choice:* easiest way to send flowers
  - *Resource choice:* strong brand name, market communications, and supplier network

- Proflowers.com
  - *Segment choice:* price-sensitive and convenience-oriented customers
  - *Benefit choice:* freshest cut flowers at a competitive price
  - *Resource choice:* unusual sourcing and FedEx shipping arrangements

How differentiated are these value propositions? Consider not only the firm's desired position, but also its ability to "own" this position in the minds of customers. Three specific classes of criteria should be used to assess the quality of the value proposition or cluster:

- *Customer criteria.* Do target customers understand the proposition or cluster? Is it relevant to their needs? Is it believable? Is it perceived as unique, or is it indistinguishable from other propositions or clusters? Will it provoke action on the part of the target customer?
- *Company criteria.* Will the organization rally around the proposition or cluster? Does the company have the resources or capabilities to own this cluster? Will it block or facilitate the eventual move to additional vertical markets?
- *Competitive criteria.* Are other competitors attempting to hold a similar proposition or cluster? Will competitors allow the company to own the stated cluster in the market? Can current competitors match this cluster? How easy is it for future competitors to match this cluster?

A casual review of the principal flower sites shows that 1-800-Flowers.com and FTD.com are attempting to own similar segments with similar benefits (fresh flowers and a broad gift assortment). Equally significant is that neither of the sites has unique capabilities that cannot be replicated by the other. Collectively, this suggests that the market is likely to be intensely competitive, with no clear indication of who can win this segment. Proflowers.com, which targets price-sensitive consumer who are more interested in fresh flowers than gifts, has a more distinctive value proposition than the others. While the other sites may have a wider reach, Proflowers.com has positioned itself to a more targeted group of customers with different core benefits than the other companies.

The Online Offering

Once the value proposition has been articulated, the next step is to decide on the online product, service, or information offering. Keep in mind that at this stage, we are not designing the content or the look-and-feel of the website (this will be the focus of Chapter 5). Rather, we are providing a broad description of the actual product or service that will be provided online. In particular, the senior management team must complete three sequential tasks: (1) identify the scope of the offering, (2) identify the customer decision process, and (3) map the offering to the customer decision process.

Scope of the Offering

The scope refers to the number of categories of products and services that a firm offers. The scope can be anything from a firm focusing on one product category (termed a "category killer") to a firm focusing on a large number of categories. The websites SecondSpin.com, CDNow.com, and DealTime.com illustrate the various levels of scope. SecondSpin.com, at one end of the spectrum, focuses on selling used CDs, DVDs, and VHS videotapes. At the other end of the spectrum is DealTime.com, which sells a wide variety of electronics and other goods. CDNow.com, somewhere in the middle, focuses on a wide variety of CDs, DVD, and VHS videotapes, but no other products.

The following describe two specific types of scope that can be focused on:

- *Category-specific dominance.* Category-specific dominance refers to companies that focus exclusively on one product category, such as flowers. However, it is increasingly difficult to isolate firms that are focusing on only one category. Within the online flowers category, firms seem to be focusing on a combination of flowers, gifts, and complementary goods such as candy.

- *Cross-category dominance.* One of the most interesting developments in the online world is the extension of product offerings from a single category to additional product categories in order to achieve cross-category dominance. The most well-known example, of course, is Amazon's initial domination of the book market and subsequent extension to CDs, videos, toys, home improvement, and auctions. Amazon is an interesting example of supply-side cross-category dominance because it offers products that naturally group together from a logistics and distribution point of view. Amazon's products (a) are physical goods, (b) can be stored in inventory, (c) mostly cannot be digitized, and (d) are consumer-focused, as opposed to being business-to-business focused. However, the products do not naturally cluster around specific themes; in contrast to websites such as BabyCenter.com, these particular product combinations do not necessarily make sense from the customer's point of view.

The term "metamarket" has been used to refer to sites that group naturally clustering categories of goods and services. According to Northwestern University marketing professor Mohanbir Sawhney, this new breed of "metamediaries" is significant because it is based on a simple insight: Products and services are grouped according to how customers engage in activities, rather than the categorization of products and services from the physical world. Sawhney notes:

> Customers think in terms of activities, while firms think in terms of products. Activities that are logically related in "cognitive space" may be spread across very diverse providers in the marketplace. Metamarkets, then, are clusters of markets in the minds of customers. Their boundaries are derived from activities that are closely related in the minds of customers, and not from the fact that they are created or marketed by related firms in related industries.[9]

Interestingly, this observation by Sawhney has a parallel in academic literature. Consumers naturally group together products or services based upon the goals that the products help them achieve.[10] For example, consumers may classify a wide variety of disparate products in the "entertainment" category. Do consumers categorize entertainment in terms of favorite sports, clubs/organizations, food, shows, art, or dining out? Or do they categorize based on things to do with the family or things to do when the weather is problematic? The answer is that consumers categorize products and services in a variety of ways. By implication, therefore, online businesses can be organized in a variety of goal-derived ways.

If you consider Citysearch.com, you will see that consumer classification can present significant challenges. Its homepage has two broad categories of offerings—complete city guides for major cities and less extensive movie-and-entertainment guides for smaller cities. Once you choose a destination, you can search through a broad selection of activities. For Los Angeles, you can search for museums, sporting events, or restaurants. This site has search features for events by date or by categories such as arts, bars and nightlife, movies, restaurants, shopping, or traffic reports.

In effect, you can first select an activity for the evening by viewing events for that date, read reviews of shows and/or movies, search show times, purchase tickets, search for nearby restaurants, read reviews of the restaurants, make reservations, check the traffic report, choose a route, and print out directions. These activities cross a wide range of industries—entertainment, automotive, travel, literature, and so on.

Another example of a goal-derived metamarket is BabyCenter.com. BabyCenter.com offers a wide variety of products and information, and it features a support community that is based on one overarching goal—raising a healthy baby. The site is packed with reference information, links to other online destinations, helpful hints and checklists, and ways to connect with other parents. It also provides a search engine, and users can personalize the site to get information on a specific pregnancy or parenting stage. The site provides high-quality, medically reviewed information, a community of supportive fellow parents, and a store that sells baby and maternity items and offers advice on products best suited for particular lifestyles and needs.

Identify the Customer Decision Process

The second step in the construction of an online offering is articulating the **customer decision process** for the various product categories. Exhibit 4.2 provides a simplified version of the customer decision process. As discussed in Chapter 3, this process can be divided into three stages: prepurchase, purchase, and postpurchase. In the prepurchase stage, consumers go through a number of steps, including recognizing a problem or need, searching for ideas and offerings, and evaluating the alternatives. In the purchase stage, the consumer decides to purchase and goes through the process of purchasing. The postpurchase stage involves the evaluation of levels of satisfaction and, eventually, the consideration of becoming a loyal customer. When the consumer is done with the product, he or she may or may not choose to dispose of the goods.

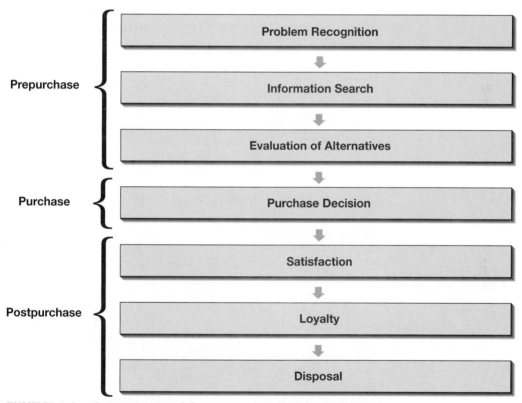

EXHIBIT 4.2   Customer Decision Process—Flower Example

The inside portion of Exhibit 4.3 shows what the customer decision process in the flower category might look like. The recognition of a need for flowers may be triggered by a holiday (e.g., Valentine's Day), a personal life event (an anniversary), or an everyday event (a first date). The consumer searches for ideas and offerings among online or offline flower vendors. After gathering gift ideas, recommendations, and advice, the consumer evaluates the options using a number of criteria, including price, appeal, availability, and convenience. At this point, the consumer may decide to make a purchase and enclose an appropriate note or message along with the flowers. After the purchase, the consumer may gain satisfaction if he or she learns that the flower order has been successfully delivered. After the transaction has been completed, the consumer may want to learn more about flowers and arrangements, and the vendor may offer some type of incentive to gain customer loyalty.

Map Products and Services onto the Customer Decision Process

The third step in the construction of the offering involves mapping products and services onto the customer decision process. The idea is that the website should walk the consumer through the entire purchase-decision cycle and encourage the consumer to continually revisit the cycle. This decision cycle should be repeated for each of the product categories on the site. Thus, for 1-800-Flowers.com, the cycle should be completed for flowers, specialty foods, garden hardware, and other gift categories.

We refer to this process as the mapping of an **egg diagram** (see Exhibit 4.3). We have enhanced Mohanbir Sawhney's metamarkets work by adding the consideration of the purchase and by mapping the product and service

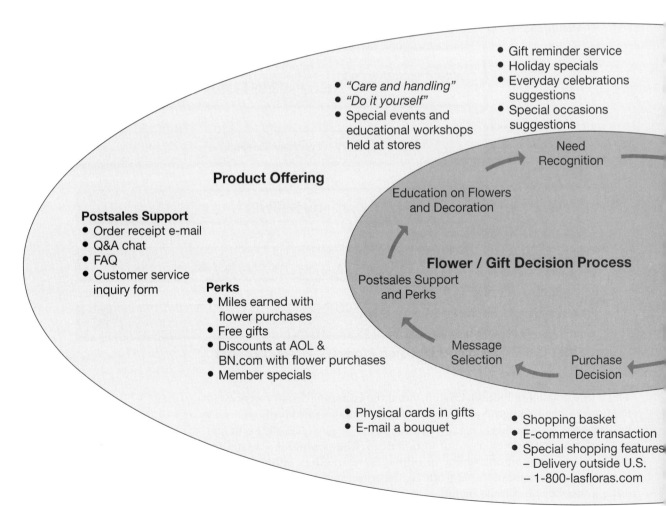

Adapted from Mohanbir Sawhney, "Making New Markets," Business 2.0

EXHIBIT 4.3   Egg Diagram for 1-800-Flowers.com

offering to this decision process. Creation of this diagram begins by articulating the steps of the decision process that the consumer passes through for a particular product category. Next, one identifies the products, services, and information that will aid the consumer in moving through these various stages.

Returning to the flower example, we can identify site activities that assist the consumer through each step of the decision process. To match need recognition, there might be a gift reminder service or holiday specials, for example. To aid in the information search, a site could provide ideas in various categories, a store locator, recommendations by budget, lists of favorite gifts, or lists of bestsellers. During the evaluation of alternatives, a site could provide product price, description, availability, and special delivery information. To support the purchase decision, the site could accept credit cards over the phone or online, provide a shopping basket, and show an assortment of cards and notes with appropriate messages to be delivered with the flowers. For customer satisfaction and loyalty, it could provide exceptional customer support, various free benefits or incentives, and special flower events and workshops to induce customers to return.

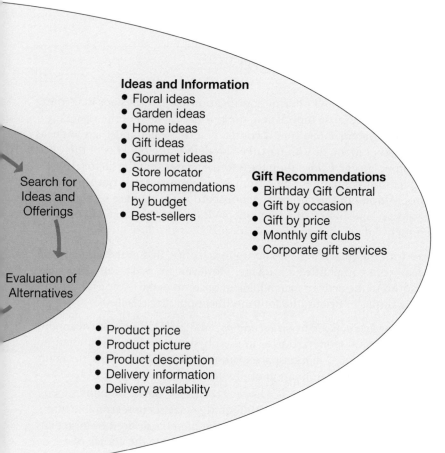

Search for Ideas and Offerings

Evaluation of Alternatives

Ideas and Information
- Floral ideas
- Garden ideas
- Home ideas
- Gift ideas
- Gourmet ideas
- Store locator
- Recommendations by budget
- Best-sellers

Gift Recommendations
- Birthday Gift Central
- Gift by occasion
- Gift by price
- Monthly gift clubs
- Corporate gift services

- Product price
- Product picture
- Product description
- Delivery information
- Delivery availability

Marketspace Interview

Rob Glaser, Founder, Chairman, and CEO RealNetworks™

When we started offering our product for free, a lot of people came to us and said, "Why don't you try to make money with every RealPlayer®?" But our view was that the value of a long-term relationship is way, way greater than the value of an initial transaction—especially if you can establish many more relationships than you ever could if you tried to thread them through immediate transactions. So we started out by just saying, "Hey, we'd like you to give us your e-mail name when you download our player." And about 90 percent of the people said, "Fine, happy to have you contact me again as long as it is a relevant communication about something I'll care about."

By taking that relationship view—which was radical at the time—we built a very broad foundation for our business. Number one, we were getting rid of the friction associated with transactions—the Internet doesn't have an easy way for you to pay 10 cents for something; you've got to fill in all the charge card information regardless of whether the price is 10 cents or $1,000. Number two, our products have a very low marginal cost; when we download a RealPlayer to you for free, the bandwidth costs may be a couple of pennies. And number three, we were establishing an ongoing relationship with our customers. I mean, restaurants don't impose a cover charge just to sit down; they give you a menu of things, and if you don't want anything, you get up and leave. Our view was, once we get people into our "restaurant," our experience, we can build up a variety of ways to make money over time. The most important thing was to get that audience, that critical mass.

The Resource System

The value proposition and offering specification are critical steps in forming a business model because they dictate the resource system of the company.[11] The **resource system** shows how a company must select and then align its resources (either alone or with partners) to deliver the benefits of the value proposition or cluster. Conventional wisdom suggests that the factor that sets highly successful companies apart from lesser companies is not simply the value proposition but the choice of actions and assets that are used to deliver the value proposition. These actions include the selection of resources that uniquely deliver the value proposition.[12]

We agree with the recent logic that unique activities, tied to the value proposition, lead to a competitive advantage. However, we make four important modifications to the activity-system logic in order to make it applicable to the online marketplace. Briefly, the four modifications are as follows:

- *Shift from physical world to virtual and physical world.*[13] The first key modification is to shift from resources in the physical world to a combination of marketplace and marketspace resources. Resource systems, for many companies, are a combination of physical and virtual assets.
- *Shift from a supply-side focus to a demand-side focus.* Many companies focus on the resources of the firm. Although this may seem reasonable, it is more appropriate to initially focus on the benefits desired by target customers. The desired benefits should largely dictate the choice of resources.
- *Shift from resources to benefits.* The resources system comprises the higher-order skills and assets of the company. Benefits are typically supported

by a cluster of resources that help to build and differentiate one or more of a company's resources. Resources may take various forms.[14] They might be physical assets such as warehouses or server farms, or intangible assets such as Yahoo's brand name or Priceline's patents on its business model.

- *Shift from single to multifirm systems.* Resource systems require capabilities that must be in place and ready to use in order to win in various markets. These resources may be resident in the firm and developed in-house, but they might also be acquired in the open market or accessed through strategic partnerships and alliances.

Specifying a Resource System

With these four modifications in mind, we turn to the construction of a resource system. While in the value proposition we selected one or two resources to provide the key benefits, the resource system includes *all* the resources that are necessary to support the offering and, therefore, the business.

Step One: Identify Core Benefits in the Value Cluster

The core benefits are identified in the construction of a value proposition or cluster. For 1-800-Flowers.com, we articulated the value proposition as follows:

> 1-800-Flowers.com serves the mid- to high-end market with a broad gift assortment, fresh flowers, and easy access because of its strong distribution network, product and media partnerships, and multiple contact points.

Thus, its cluster of benefits includes fresh flowers, a broad assortment of gifts, and easy access. Aspects of the cluster of benefits are shown in Exhibit 4.4.

Step Two: Identify Resources That Relate to Each Benefit

The second step is to link the resources that are required to deliver a particular customer benefit. At this stage, we are not concerned about whether the company has the resource; we are simply concerned about the link between the resource and the benefit. Exhibit 4.4 shows the resources that deliver each of the four benefits. For example, widespread, easy access is linked to four resources: popularity of website, wide reach to customers, multiple contact points, and brand name.

Step Three: Identify to What Degree the Firm Can Deliver Each Benefit

The third step entails a close internal look at the company. Does this particular company, 1-800-Flowers.com, contain all the necessary resources, or must the company outsource or partner with others to gain missing resources? It is clear from the resource system chart that this firm does not hold all of the needed resources on its own. In particular, both product and media partnerships are required in order to make the system operate effectively.

Step Four: Identify Partners Who Can Complete Resources

The final step is to identify key players who can complete the resource system. For 1-800-Flowers.com, this would include product partnerships with

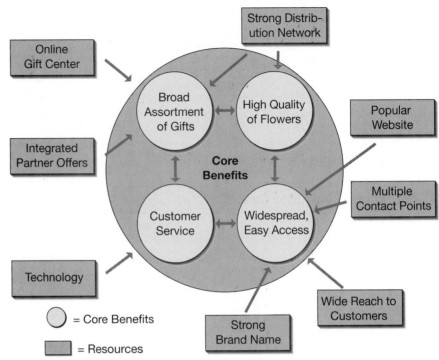

EXHIBIT 4.4   1-800-Flowers.com Resource System

Lenox, Sharper Image, Blue Mountain cards, and San Francisco Music Box Company, and media partnerships with major online sites such as AOL.

Exhibit 4.5 provides an overview of the types of offline and online products and services that are offered by 1-800-Flowers.com. Notice that many of the offline products and services integrate both telephone representatives and in-store personnel.

We would also need to adjust our resource-system model to integrate online and offline activities and assets in various combinations. For example, the benefit of "widespread, easy access" is supported by the resource of "wide reach to customers," which might need to be supported by online partnerships. The benefit of "multiple contact points" may need to be supported by three offline (telephone representatives, franchise stores, catalog) and two online (affiliates, online store) assets.

Criteria to Assess the Quality of a Resource System

A number of criteria can be used to assess the quality of the resource system.

Uniqueness of the System

Uniqueness refers to the extent to which the organization has resources that differ from those of its competitors. Is 1-800-Flowers.com's resources system unique? Which resources have not been copied by FTD.com and Proflowers.com? We could argue that the FTD.com model and 1-800-Flowers.com model differ at the resource level (e.g., only 1-800-Flowers.com partners with AOL). However, perhaps more troubling to competitors in this industry is

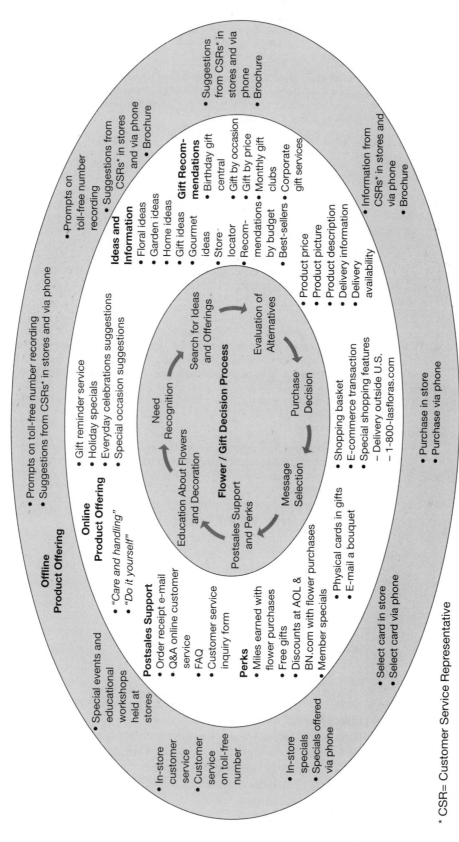

* CSR= Customer Service Representative

EXHIBIT 4.5 Online/Offline Egg Diagram for 1-800-Flowers.com

> ### Drill-Down
>
> #### An Integrated Online and Offline Business Model
>
> One of the decisions firms must confront is whether to provide both an online and offline interface to customers. The benefits of a hybrid strategy include a persistent connection with customers, new value for customers, access to new customers, and scalability. The challenges of hybridization include cannibalization, channel conflict, customer confusion, and investor confusion.
>
> The potential benefits for a company that uses both an online and offline strategy—such as Gap, Williams-Sonoma, and Wal-Mart—are many. First, there is a constant connection with customers, 24 hours a day. Also, there are new value possibilities for customers because the firm is now able to provide new-to-the-world offerings that would not be possible if they pursued an exclusively online or exclusively offline strategy. For example, a company with both online and offline strategies could allow customers to order products online but return them to the company's physical stores. Third, it is also possible to increase the size of the customer base. Wal-Mart can now reach customers who are hundreds of miles from the nearest bricks-and-mortar store. Finally, the approach is scalable in the sense that the new integrated strategy can be replicated around the world.
>
> However, firms that do not carefully manage the integration face potential difficulties. Many writers are concerned that the opening of an online store will cannibalize, or draw down sales revenues, from bricks-and-mortar stores. They frequently cite a study conducted in late 1999 that purportedly showed that online ventures did not provide significant new revenue increases. Rather, some 94 percent of sales were simply transfers of sales that normally would have occurred offline.[15] On the other hand, in the year 2000, a number of offline players went online and saw a rise in their offline sales. A good example is the well-known Zagat restaurant guide. Zagat placed the entire contents of its books online and saw its offline sales increase by 35 percent.[16]
>
> Another potential drawback is customer confusion. If a company's online and offline interfaces are not tightly linked, customers can become confused and frustrated. For example, if customers purchase products online but cannot return them to the bricks-and-mortar stores, they may decide not to frequent either the online or offline store.

that the two companies' resource systems look very similar—nationwide florist network, combined offline and online presence, clear fit between offline and online systems, strong brand names, excellent order fulfillment, and integrated technologies.

Links Between Resources and Benefits
Does each resource support the delivery of a customer benefit? Is the support strong or weak?

Links Among Resources in the System
How well do the resources complement and support one another? Are there tight linkages among the resources? Are they consistent with the overall value cluster? Are the specific resources mutually reinforcing? Are they complementary? Are they consistent with the various benefits?

Links Between Virtual-World and Physical-World Business Systems
Does the online resource system support or conflict with the offline system?

Sustainable Advantage

Is the resource system difficult to replicate? Possessing a unique but easily copied resource system will deliver only a fleeting advantage to a firm. Sustained high profits will come only from a sustainable competitive advantage. The ease with which a resource system can be imitated may depend on a number of factors.[17]

The Role of Partnerships

While partnerships are important in the offline world, they take on added significance in the online world, where firms compete with partners to lock in customer relationships. Often firms will look for exclusive partnerships to prevent competitors from accessing a customer base, a critical technology, or key competencies that are necessary to gain competitive advantage in a particular sector. In 2000, 1-800-Flowers.com seemed to have the majority of partnership agreements; other flower businesses soon realized their importance, however, and competed for them. The types of partnerships the flower companies are pursuing include portal agreements, anchor-tenant agreements, and promotion agreements.

Portal Agreements

Portals can provide significant brand exposure for online flower companies. For example, 1-800-Flowers.com will be the exclusive marketer of fresh-cut flowers across six AOL brands (AOL, AOL.com, Netscape Netcenter, CompuServe, Digital City, and ICQ) until 2005. Both 1-800-Flowers.com and FTD.com have agreements with Yahoo.

Anchor-Tenant Agreements

Anchor-tenant agreements occur when a company agrees to be the sole provider of a specific product or service for another retail site. For example, Proflowers.com is the exclusive online flower provider for Amazon.com customers.

Promotion Agreements

Promotion agreements involve either one company being promoted on another company's site or cross-promotions in which each company receives promotion. Both 1-800-Flowers.com and FTD.com have signed deals with American Airlines and Delta Airlines for promotional agreements. Customers buying flowers from 1-800-Flowers.com can earn frequent-flyer miles with American Airlines. FTD.com has an agreement with United Airlines's frequent-flyer program. 1-800-Flowers.com also has a cross-promotional agreement with Barnes & Noble.com, and FTD.com has a cross-promotional agreement with Hilton.

Revenue Models

In this section, we review the **revenue model** that follows from the resource system. During the early days of online business, it seemed that all a company needed to worry about was gaining a large customer base, and revenue would somehow follow. After many startups went bankrupt on this philosophy, online companies developed a new respect for deciding on a revenue model earlier rather than later.

While the purpose of a revenue model is relatively clear, and the ways to make money are fairly straightforward, it is often difficult to align the revenue model with the company's value proposition and offering. Many online companies now face the challenge of figuring out what their customers are willing to pay for, and how much they are willing to pay (see Drill-Down "Online Content: In Search of a Model"). To this purpose, it is even more important to consider the value proposition, offering, and resource system when deciding how the company will make money. Firms can pursue a variety of revenue models. The following are the most frequently mentioned sources of revenue:

- *Advertising.* A particular site can earn advertising revenues through the selling of ads (banner or interstitial), site sponsorships, event underwriting, or other forms of communication. While the amount spent on online advertising has certainly dropped in the last year, companies still spent more than $7.2 billion on online advertising in 2001.
- *Product, service, or information sales.* This refers to income that is generated from the sale of goods on the site; this can include sales through retail sites or pay-per-use information.
- *Transaction.* This refers to revenue that accrues from charging a fee or taking a portion of the transaction sum for facilitating a customer-seller transaction. Companies that make money this way include Charles Schwab and eBay.
- *Subscription.* This refers to subscriber fees for magazines, newspapers, or other information/service businesses. The online site for *The Wall Street Journal* charges a subscription fee.
- *License fees.* These are fees generated from the licensing of content. Software companies often generate revenue from license fees.

Online Business Models

Now that we have discussed the value proposition, online offering, resource system, and revenue model, we can start to build a business model. In this section, we identify seven alternative business models for the networked economy. There are some important differences between online and traditional business models. First of all, there has been a shift from supply-side language to demand-side language. Companies should focus more on the core benefits that customers are looking for and respond accordingly; demand comes first, supply second.

Another difference is that customers can add value to an online business. While an obvious example would be eBay, users also add value to websites with strong community features (see Chapter 5), peer-to-peer sites that rely on user content, and retail sites that allow customers to review products. Because the Internet provides users with so many tools to communicate with one another, it has created a need for companies willing to facilitate these relationships.

Drill-Down

Online Content: In Search of a Model

Advertising or subscriptions? That's *the* business-model question for online content providers. Initially, most media outlets and other online content providers chose the advertising model: Attract lots of eyeballs with free content, then sit back and cash the checks of advertisers who want to reach them. Only instead of generating profits for content sites, advertising did not even cover most sites' costs. Slow to take off during the dot-com boom, the online advertising industry lost what little momentum it had after the crash. The result was a slew of content-site deaths, near-deaths, and reconfigurations—and the inevitable swing of the pendulum toward subscription-based business models.

In 2001, for example, the highly regarded free Web publication Salon split its content into two, cable-television-like tiers: a free basic service for the masses, and premium, banner-ad-free content for readers who pay $30 a year. The following year, London's prestigious *Financial Times* put much of its previously gratis FT.com content "behind the veil."

But subscriptions are hardly a sure thing, either. The Web evolved as a largely free medium, and most of its users have shown little interest in seeing that change—or opening their wallets to pay for content. Which is why, after two years of struggling to get readers to pay a $19.95 subscription fee, the pioneering Web magazine Slate gave up and decided, in 1998, to become a free site. Slate hoped that abolishing subscriptions would dramatically boost the number of people visiting the site—and, as a result, advertising revenues. (Progress on circulation has been good; on advertising revenue, less so.)

There are hopeful examples on both advertising and subscription fronts, however. The two most respected names in American newspapering, *The New York Times* and *The Wall Street Journal*, have both managed to carve out successful online operations—the *Times* as a largely free, advertising-supported site, the *Journal* relying primarily on subscriptions. Yet each is more accurately a hybrid. The *Times* charges readers for specialized content such as archive searches, bundled collections of articles and columns, and some crossword puzzles. And the *Journal* garners advertising revenue from the widely browsed free portions of its site.

These kinds of combinations of free and fee, of subscription and advertising models, seem the likeliest future for online content. But the success of NYTimes.com, WSJ.com, and other content sites may teach a slightly different lesson: If you are an online publisher with a strong reputation, deep pockets, and/or content that people want and cannot get anywhere else, you have a shot at supporting yourself—with subscriptions, advertising, or some blend of the two. If you are not, you may have to come up with a different revenue model entirely. Assuming, that is, there is one.

Keep in mind that a company can pursue more than one model at a time. Buy.com, which follows the lowest-price business model, also has one of the widest inventories on the Web, with more than 1 million products across categories that range from electronics to magazines to wireless phone products and services. It is neither useful nor intelligent to choose an established business model and blindly follow it. Rather, companies should think carefully about each component—value proposition, online offering, resources, and revenue model—and how they will fit together to produce a successful business. The following business models are just some of those that are currently being pursued.

Point-Counterpoint

Which Would You Rather Be: A Dot-Com or a Bricks-and-Clicks Business?

Is it better to start out as a bricks-and-mortar company and then move online, or is it better to launch a purely online business?

Proponents on the pure dot-com side argue that dot-com businesses are not constrained by physical world assets because those assets do not translate into the networked economy. They argue that firms in this space need to operate differently—fast, with flat organizational structures, no functional boundaries, and a senior management team that understands the networked economy. Furthermore, dot-com proponents point to a number of successful companies that have followed this approach, such as Amazon.com, Yahoo.com, and AOL.

On the bricks-and-clicks side, proponents counter that there are basic business issues that still apply in the networked economy. Firms must be businesses—not simply customer-acquisition organizations. Furthermore, the key assets that dot-coms are attempting to build (e.g., consumer awareness, traffic, strong brands) are already possessed by the incumbent traditional businesses. Indeed, as Jack Welch recently noted, "Digitizing a company and developing e-business models is easier—not harder—than we ever imagined."[18]

Metamarket Switchboard Model

A metamarket switchboard model brings together buyers and sellers based upon the activities that customers engage in to meet particular goals (see Exhibit 4.6).[19] In the B2B world, these are often called exchanges and sometimes called Net marketplaces (if the selling price is fixed). Frequently, this model results in a few "big players" with multiple second-tier players. It is possible that niche markets could also emerge.

Example
Consider BabyCenter.com. It sells all of the standard baby-related products—maternity clothing, toys, music, videos, and books—but also provides a gift center, baby-related expert advice from preconception through toddler stages, and community bulletin boards. It aggregates many different product providers with nonexclusive arrangements. Other examples include Verticalnet, CarPoint, and FashionMall.com.

Core Benefit and Value Proposition
What is the core benefit of BabyCenter.com? The core benefit is providing a single point of access for all needs related to child development. The site offers products, services, community, news on child rearing, and advice. For the metamarkets player more generally, the key benefits are value-added services that include product information, community events, and product sales, as well as the efficiency of seeing many sellers in one area. Thus, the buyer has the luxury of one-stop shopping or information access across a wide range of sellers or content domains.

Online Offering
The scope of the offering can either be category-specific or cut across categories. For BabyCenter.com, the products are all focused on early child-

hood, although the range of product categories (e.g., education products, books, clothing, services) is quite broad. In addition to its "store partners," BabyCenter.com also provides a single point of access for community formation, medical information, developmental information, and urgent alerts related to product recalls (or other topics of interest).

Key Resources

The most critical resource for a metamarkets switchboard is a large, active customer base. Indeed, for this model to work, it must be viewed by target customers as one of the most important businesses in the category. Recently, Jag Sheth, a well-regarded Emory University professor, proposed a "rule of three," which holds that markets "shake out" until only three major players are left. Thus, from Sheth's viewpoint, there will never be 10 major metamarkets for baby care; at best, there will be three major survivors. Thus, the firm that pursues this model must become *the* destination site. This requires a significant commitment to building the brand name, with associated willingness to invest significant marketing communication dollars. The company must be able to constantly create new value-added services to sustain the customer base. Also, the ability to enhance user-to-user community formation may create switching costs for current members.

Revenue Model

The revenue model may include transactions, product sales, and advertising. In the case of BabyCenter.com, the emphasis is on affiliate deals as well as advertising from baby-focused companies such as Johnson & Johnson. Metamarkets may also provide potential transactional revenue.

Key Threats

The key threats to this model include the formation of an alternative switchboard at a higher level of aggregation (such as children of all ages for BabyCenter.com), the same level of aggregation (such as a direct competitor), or a niche market (such as a site that specializes in prenatal care). Innovative value-added services on the part of competitors who offer alternative switchboards can also threaten the profit stream.

Traditional and Reverse Auction Models

Traditional auctions such as eBay are designed to bring together large numbers of buyers and sellers. Buyers bid up to a point where no further bidding is offered. The buyer with the highest bid wins the item. Reverse auction sites such as FreeMarkets.com allow suppliers to bid prices down until no further bids are received. The supplier with the lowest bid delivers the goods to the buyer. Sites that act as hubs in these situations typically take a portion of the transaction revenue. The result is often a very high margin—for example, eBay margins are reported to be in the neighborhood of 75 percent. B2B auctions are often referred to as Net marketplaces, with one company facilitating the bidding and transactions of buyers and sellers.

Examples

The most well-known business-to-consumer (B2C) auction sites are eBay, Amazon Auctions, and Yahoo auctions. However, there are also auctions for

Business Models	Metamarkets Switchboard	Auction	Freshest Information	Highest Quality	Widest Assortment	Lowest Prices	Most Personalized
Core Benefits and Proposition	• Single point of access for all needs	• Depth and breadth of product assortment • Number of active buyers	• Timely and accurate information	• High-quality products with exclusivity	• Broadest inventory possible • Can lead to best prices	• Lowest prices	• Unique product, service, or experience
Online Offering	• Either category specific or across categories	• Usually a large number of products	• Broad or targeted audience	• Concentrates on smaller offerings for smaller markets	• Can be either category killer in one category or widest assortment across many categories	• Niche category or across wide variety of categories	• Geared toward a single buyer
Key Resources	• Large, active customer base • Commitment to building	• Large base of buyers and sellers • Good, reliable technology • Strong brand name	• Hiring best personnel	• Ability to source products • Outstanding customer service • Strong brand	• Significant brand name • Strong logistics to manage brand name	• Ability to build strong back-office systems and leverage economies of scale	• Ability to generate exceptional customer knowledge
Revenue Model	• Transaction fees • Product sales • Advertising • Affiliate deals	• Transaction fees	• Product and service sales • Subscription • Advertising	• Product, sevice, and information sales • Advertising	• Product sales	• Product sales	• Product sales • Subscriptions
Examples	• BabyCenter.com • Verticalnet • CarPoint.com • Fashion-Mall.com	• EBay • Amazon Auctions • Covisint	• NYTimes.com • Salon.com • Business 2.0 • Zagat.com	• FAO.com • Ashford.com	• Amazon.com • CDNow • Sephora.com • EBags.com	• Lowestfare.com • Allbooksforless.com • Outpost.com	• Reflect.com • Sevencycles.com • EDiets.com

EXHIBIT 4.6   Summary of Online Business Models

category-specific players. Covisint is a B2B auction site for the automotive industry, for example.

Core Benefit and Value Proposition

What is the core benefit of eBay? Billed as the world's largest flea market, eBay's core benefit for buyers is its breadth and depth of product assortment. For sellers, it is the number of active buyers. Thus, similar to the metamarkets, the key issue is the aggregation of a large number of buyers and sellers. Due to the large and deep product lines, buyers believe they will be getting the best deal through a free market exchange. Secondary benefits include the action of being part of a fun activity and subsequently winning the auction.

Online Offering

Because having a large base of buyers and sellers is critical to an auction site's success, companies need to be regarded as *the* source for the products in question. EBay is a bit unusual in that it attempts to aggregate across all product categories. The core offering is the actual transaction of a product for cash. However, eBay must make the transaction from prepurchase, purchase, and postpurchase as trustworthy and easy as possible.

Key Resources

Key success factors are similar to those of the metamarkets switchboard. The entire process begins with the building of a very large base of buyers or sellers in the particular product category. Companies need a strong brand name that signals both credibility and trust, reliable technology to facilitate bidding, an active community, and strong back-office support.

Revenue Model

Most auctions rely on transaction fees. Alternative revenue sources include selling auction software or services to run auctions in-house.

Key Threats

Alternative auctions can emerge in the market. The brand can lose credibility due to site downtime, security breaches, privacy concerns, or questionable product assortments. In the case of B2B markets, the auction site could lose a few large suppliers and the overall model could be threatened. The auction model could also be threatened by the emergence of a pure low-price player in a particular product category. Hence, a necessity for firms in this market is continued innovation on value-added services.

Freshest-Information Model

One aspect of the Internet that has influenced new business models is the ability to quickly and efficiently deliver information to users. In the past, newspapers printed only once or twice a day, and consumers would have to sit through multiple news stories told on the radio or television in order to find the news they wanted. Now, users can find information about everything and anything as soon as they are interested. Everything from international news to entertainment news to restaurant guides is now on the Internet.

Examples

Examples exist across a variety of industries including newspapers (NYTimes.com), magazines (Salon), business reporting (*Business 2.0*), and restaurant reviews (Zagat.com).

Core Benefit and Value Proposition

For firms that pursue a "freshest information" model, the key benefits are timeliness and accuracy. Online news organizations and online financial-services firms (particularly those trading equities) pursue this model with a passion. The core benefit of the website of *The New York Times*, NYTimes.com, is a combination of quality reporting and timely information. The same is true for *The Wall Street Journal*'s website, WSJ.com.

Online Offering

The offering can be directed toward either a broad audience or a small, highly targeted audience. It can be news for a specific subject matter such as entertainment (e.g., E! Online) or breaking news about weather (e.g., The Weather Channel at *www.weather.com*). For *The New York Times* online, it is local, national, and world news.

Revenue Model

Products, services, information, and advertising revenue are being pursued by firms following this business model. In the case of NYTimes.com, product sales are offered in various locations, including its online store and its "Travel Marketplace." Advertising revenue comes from a host of companies that would like to reach NYTimes.com readers. Services include news and photo archives. Subscribers can also sign up to receive a version of the website that is displayed in a format that mimics the paper version (*www.nytimes.com/ee*).

Key Resources

The key success factors for this model include hiring the best personnel, providing the most timely and accurate information, and extracting the margins from the "freshest" product lines. For MarketWatch.com, the freshest information is real-time stock quotes. For NYTimes.com, the most high-margin products are those that cannot be attained anywhere else, such as its photo archive.

Key Threats

Customers' perception that other companies have similar timeliness (e.g., others can offer real-time stock quotes as well as MarketWatch.com) is one threat to this model. Also, price sensitivity to the freshest information can become too great, and the costs associated with providing the timeliest information can grow prohibitive.

Highest-Quality Model

Companies with this business model generally charge a premium price for their products, services, or information. In all markets, there is always room for a high-quality offering. This is true across all consumer categories.

Examples

Within every product category, there is room for someone who can provide the best experience, regardless of price. Within the toys category, this could be FAO Schwarz's FAO.com; within the luxury travel category, it could be luxurytravel.com. Profit is maintained by premium prices across the entire range of products.

Consider FAO.com, whose tagline is "the ultimate toy store." In addition to the quality of its products, the company also emphasized their exclusivity. An example of this one-of-a-kind luxury is the "FAO Exclusive" product line, in which you find such products as the Barbie Sleeping Bag ($175), the Madeline Dollyhouse ($298), or Fashion Designer Barbie ($95). Again, the key issue for players in this category is the ability to charge premium prices for the quality of a product or the premium associations with the brand name. Other examples include Williams-Sonoma for cooking products and Ashford.com for luxury goods.

Core Benefit and Value Proposition

What is the core benefit of FAO.com? It is both its high-quality products and their associated exclusivity. The key idea is that the products are not available to everyone; rather, high prices automatically block their potential as mass-market products.

Online Offering

The offering can be a product, service, or information that is generally perceived to be the best. As a result, the market size for this type of offering tends to be small—a true niche market. However, the margins are often quite high. In terms of the actual offering at FAO.com, the site offers action figures, arts and crafts, collectibles, dolls, and other products in the toy category.

Key Resources

For the high-quality player to be successful, a number of resources need to be in place. These include, but are not limited to, the ability to source the products, to provide outstanding online service (in the case of FAO.com, this includes critical handoffs to the store and "live" connections to service personnel), and to ensure a customer experience that is fitting of a "best label." Furthermore, the brand has to denote exclusivity.

Revenue Model

Revenue for the players comes from a mix of sources, including products, services, information, and advertising revenue. Profit originates from the customer's perception that the particular site has the best quality information, product, or service. As noted earlier, this means that margins can be extracted for these premium products.

Key Threats

Key threats include the emergence of lower-priced offerings with similar benefits, the lack of a perceived value in higher-priced goods, and a shift in customer preferences to emergent brand labels, compared to historical favorites.

Widest-Assortment Model

Companies can also compete on the breadth and depth of product assortment, within and across product categories.

Examples

Within the music category, this could include CDNow.com, ArtistDirect.com, or SecondSpin.com. Other examples include Sephora.com (makeup selection) and eBags, which bills itself as the world's largest online retailer of bags and accessories.

Core Benefit and Value Proposition

The core benefit for users is breadth, pure and simple. Consider Second-Spin.com, which calls itself "the Internet's largest buyer and seller of used CDs, videos, and DVDs." The core proposition is that SecondSpin.com is the best place to shop because it has the best inventory. Hence, the message is quite clear: Shop here first. Often, large inventory can also translate into best prices because they are dealing in volume buying.

Online Offering

The offering can provide either the widest assortment across many categories or the widest assortment for one category. A company that offers the widest assortment for one category is often called a "category killer."

Key Resources

What resources does SecondSpin.com need to become a category killer? First, it needs a very significant brand name, one that is widely recognized by those who appreciate music or movies. Second, it need to build its user base, because inventory depends on both buyers and sellers; sellers provide SecondSpin.com with used CDs, and hence create the company's inventory. Third, it needs to have very strong logistics to manage the entire supply chain—good buyers, good quality control over used merchandise, and the ability to keep shipping costs low. Fourth, it needs to maintain the quality of additional information and services. For example, SecondSpin.com customers are automatically notified when CDs by their preferred artists are available. Using the site's "personal favorites" feature, customers can choose up to 15 of their favorite artists. Every time they visit the site, they can click on their personal favorites and see all of the titles currently in stock by those artists.

Revenue Model

Revenue is derived from product sales; however, the real source of profit lies in the selective premium pricing of the most desired products. At Second-Spin.com, for example, customers seeking used CDs by best-selling artists, rare CDs, classic CDs, or other hard-to-find music are likely to be charged premium prices. Also, SecondSpin.com acquires revenue from its dealer program whereby individuals/businesses earn revenue if sales are referred from their websites.

Key Threats

The biggest threat to this model is further specialization in the product category. For example, companies such as Amazon or Crutchfield.com could lose customers to EPC-Online, a website that specializes in digital cameras and accessories. SecondSpin.com is threatened by music sites that specialize in a particular genre of music. At the other extreme, megabrands such as Wal-Mart and Amazon could attempt to aggregate consumers at a higher level, beyond music and videos.

Lowest-Price Model

Quite simply, this model promises the customer the lowest prices online.

Examples

This model may be specific to a product category or take a broader, mall-like approach. A good example of this latter approach is Buy.com. Buy.com positions itself as the lowest-priced superstore on the Internet. It provides products in a wide range of categories, including computers, software, electronics, sporting goods, books, videos, games, and music.

Core Benefit and Value Proposition

These customers are looking for the lowest prices over product selection, good customer service, or site functionality. In August 2002, Buy.com stated on its homepage that its products were 10 percent less than those found on Amazon.com, and that it was offering free shipping for all book orders. The core benefit communicated by this message is unambiguous: You get the lowest prices at Buy.com.

Online Offering

The online offering could be a niche category or it could cut across a wide variety of categories, as in the Buy.com example.

Key Resources

While the value proposition for the lowest-price model is easy to articulate, making it work in the marketplace is much more difficult. Margins are often minimal or even nonexistent; the key is to be exceptionally strong on back-office systems and leverage economies of scale. To sustain their strategy, lowest-price sites must have outstanding supply chain management and procurement, overall operational excellence, and a culture that is exceptionally frugal.

Revenue Model

The revenue model almost always involves extracting a very small percentage of the product sales.

Key Threats

One key threat to the lowest-price model is the emergence of shop bots. Shop bots such as mySimon search the Web for the lowest-priced items in a variety of product categories. For example, a quick search for a Canon Powershot

S40 digital camera on MySimon.com produced a wide range of prices—from $449 to $719. Interestingly, several of the stores that bill themselves as low-cost leaders were not at the top of this list. Also, shop bots such as BizRate and mySimon rate the stores as well as give prices. Despite their low prices, sites with low ratings are likely to lose business to sites that appear more reliable. Other threats include the emergence of strong players that create uncertainty in the lowest-priced brand, the lack of profit imperative, shifting investor confidence in the business model, and the emergence of niche players who further specialize the market.

Most-Personalized Model

This model is based upon the ability to provide a true one-of-a-kind experience to consumers. Importantly, this is not about the level of personalization at a site like Amazon; rather, this is a business centered around providing a unique experience. One can imagine a site where physicians or consultants could provide custom diagnoses, insight, feedback, and prescriptions. In the early days of the Web, Ernst and Young launched a site called "Ernie" where small-business owners could ask key tax experts an unlimited number of questions for a nominal fee. This is an example of a most-personalized model in action.

Examples

This model is based on the best customization of the consumer experience. One recent example is Reflect.com (tagline: "true custom beauty created just for you"). Reflect.com's products are designed to give customers the power to create their own beauty care experience. Customers can create their own skin care, hair care, and makeup products. Other examples include Interactive Custom Clothes Company (*www.ic3d.com*), which allows users to customize clothes online; Seven Cycles (*www.sevencycles.com*), which allows users to customize bicycles; and eDiets.com (*www.ediets.com*), which provides customized diet and fitness information to customers.

Core Benefit and Value Proposition

The core benefit is a unique experience, a unique product, or a personalized solution to a problem. Often, the customer is the cocreator or builder of the experience. The true benefit of Ernie was functional—a short, precise answer to a particular tax problem of a specific firm. For Reflect.com, it is much more of an experiential benefit. In both cases, however, the key insight is the uniqueness of the solution.

Online Offering

The offering is built on the demands of each customer. Thus, this is not a site that is likely to have inventory. Rather, the consumer is likely to be presented with a number of choices that can be blended together for a unique solution.

Key Resources

What resources are necessary for a firm to build such a business model? The key success factors for this business model begin with the ability to generate exceptional customer knowledge. The firm must know the range of options and products that the customer might desire. Second, the firm must build a site that enables it to offer unique and original solutions. This is likely to be a combination of good personnel and technology so that customers can truly customize their experiences and control the level of personalization.

Drill-Down

Are B2B Business Models Different Than B2C?

In some ways, all business models are alike, whether they are business-to-consumer, business-to-business, or person-to-person—they must all have a well-defined value proposition, online offering, resource system, and revenue model. However, over the last several years, B2B companies have received a lot of attention, and many authors classify B2B business models differently than B2C. So, are the two categories really different?

First of all, B2B companies tend to be much more complex and generate much larger sales than B2C companies. The average order size at a typical B2B company is 1,000 times larger than at an equivalent B2C company. A B2C company such as Amazon.com receives tens of thousands of orders a day, but these orders are generally fairly small. A B2B company typically processes far fewer transactions, but the order value is much higher. An IDC report predicts that B2B will account for 83 percent of global online sales in 2002 (equaling about $830 billion) and 88 percent in 2006.

Another important area of difference is the decision-maker. B2B companies need to incorporate decision rules into their system to ensure that only those with authorization to complete a transaction are able to do so. For example, two visitors to Dell.com from the same company may have different levels of authorization. One may be able to order himself a new mouse or keyboard, while another may be authorized to spend up to $100,000 on new servers.

A further complication for many B2B companies is the challenge of digitizing, reconciling, and maintaining product catalogs from multiple suppliers. For example, esteel.com—a steel industry e-marketplace—needs to digitize and standardize the catalogs of all the participating suppliers to ensure that buyers can access consistent information and can compare multiple products across different suppliers. This can often be a very complicated task. Also, there has been a lack of industry and global standardization, which makes the B2B venture either very complicated or only capable of serving a small segment of the market.

Although we are still in the early stages of the development of B2B on the Internet, it is already clear that B2B companies are evolving very differently from B2C companies. The massive valuations achieved by many early Internet companies alerted everybody to the value creation potential of the Internet. Businesses—both suppliers and buyers—know that by participating in an exchange they are helping to create a new type of potentially valuable business, and they have been determined to share in this value creation. A significant number of B2B companies have been set up by consortia. Covisint, owned by Ford, General Motors, Nissan, and Renault, is one high-profile example of a consortium-owned B2B site. Unlike B2C startups, companies in the B2B space need to expect to offer equity to their founding members, or to face stiff competition from a consortium of industry players.

Something else that distinguishes B2B companies from other types of e-commerce is the names that are used to describe them. Sawhney uses names such as maintenance, repair, and operations (MRO) hubs (also known as e-procurement), catalog hubs (also known as consortia), yield managers (also known as e-distributors), and exchanges. While these have different names, they often can be classified as auctions, switchboards, and so forth. So, while some aspects of B2B companies are very different from B2C companies, all online companies need the same components for their business models, and these business models must answer the question, How will we win?

Revenue Model

Product sales or subscriptions are the dominate revenue model for this type of firm. While this firm is typically able to charge exceptionally high prices, the cost of serving its customers is also quite high.

Key Threats

One key threat is firms that offer a richer, more personalized experience. Other threats include the emergence of new technologies that allow other companies to match the experience.

MarketWatch.com Business Model

Let us now discuss the four components of the MarketWatch.com business model as of mid-2002. This will help us understand what MarketWatch.com offers, how it is able to deliver this offering, and how it plans to become profitable through its offering.

Value Proposition

As discussed earlier in the chapter, the value proposition (or value cluster) consists of three components: (1) the target segments, (2) the key benefits, and (3) the supporting rationale for why the company is able to deliver these benefits better than its competitors can.

In Chapter 3, we discussed MarketWatch.com's target licensing customers (brokerages, diversified financial institutions, and financial publishers). MarketWatch.com's target *consumers* are users who generate advertiser interest due to their demographics and size. MarketWatch.com's target consumers include savvy investors, "seekers," and "dabblers." We can derive the key benefits offered to these segments from the MarketWatch.com mission statement: "Our goal is to create the preeminent brand for real-time business news and financial information on the Web and other media."[20] Thus, the three elements of the MarketWatch.com value cluster are as follows:

Target segments:

- Savvy investors (frequent financial-information users, high income)
- Seekers (sporadic financial-information users, medium to high income)
- Dabblers (financial-information neophytes, all ages, moderate income, varying levels of education)

Key benefits:

- Up-to-the-minute information
- Original, in-depth, credible analysis
- Personal-finance tools
- Multiple points of access

Supportive rationale:

- Experienced editorial staff with financial expertise
- Infrastructure allowing access from multiple forms of media (Web, TV, radio, print, wireless)
- Credibility through its association with CBS News

The MarketWatch.com Online Offering

Let us now look at the MarketWatch.com online offering—the combination of products, services, and information that MarketWatch.com offers to deliver its value proposition—and map it to the customer decision process. Simply put, MarketWatch.com's goal is to be the best provider of financial information and analysis across a number of media.

Exhibit 4.7 illustrates the mapping of the MarketWatch.com offering to the customer decision process. In the inner circle, we can see the main steps of the personal-finance process. They include becoming educated on personal finance, planning an investment strategy, staying current with the latest developments, and performing and tracking investments. In the outer circle, we have displayed many of the services and information that Market-Watch.com offers users for each of these steps.

- *Learn about personal finance.* MarketWatch.com's "Getting Started" section offers primers on everything from stocks and bonds to mutual funds, options, and futures. It also provides a glossary of financial terms and a section on kids and money that helps parents teach their children about finance.
- *Planning tools.* MarketWatch.com's investing section, a subsection of its personal finance section, includes articles on investment strategy written by MarketWatch.com's in-house staff of experienced journalists. MarketWatch.com also provides a number of tools to assist consumers with their investments, including Home Price Check, which displays fair property prices for different locations.
- *Breaking news.* MarketWatch.com's news section is its real strength. Its news and commentary section keeps users updated on the latest financial news. Breaking news is broadcast over a number of different platforms: online, through real-time headlines and personalized e-mail alerts; TV, through contributions to CBS shows and through its own show, *CBS MarketWatch Weekend*; and radio, through the MarketWatch.com reports distributed by Westwood One. Market-Watch.com news is also accessible through wireless devices such as mobile phones and handheld computers.
- *Market figures.* MarketWatch.com is a data junkie's dream. Detailed domestic and global market figures are provided on the site in exhaustive depth and detail. Interactive charting enables visitors to glean information from individual stocks by adjusting multiple variables using proprietary charting technology.
- *Develop insight.* One of MarketWatch.com's greatest strengths is helping consumers manage their personal finances. The site offers a number of specialized commentary columns that are produced by

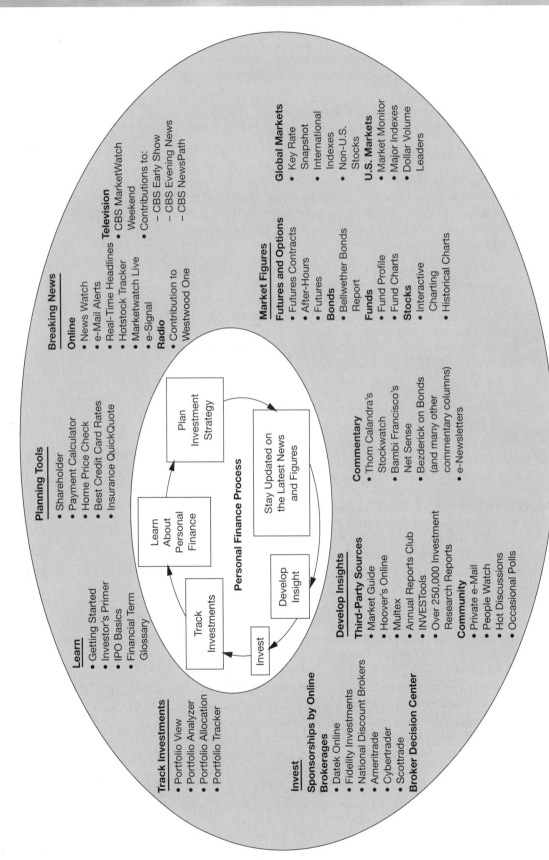

EXHIBIT 4.7   MarketWatch.com Egg Diagram

The diagram contains the following labeled content:

Planning Tools
- Shareholder
- Payment Calculator
- Home Price Check
- Best Credit Card Rates
- Insurance QuickQuote

Breaking News

Online
- News Watch
- e-Mail Alerts
- Real-Time Headlines
- Hotstock Tracker
- Marketwatch Live
- e-Signal

Radio
- Contribution to Westwood One

Television
- CBS MarketWatch Weekend
- Contributions to:
  - CBS Early Show
  - CBS Evening News
  - CBS NewsPath

Global Markets
- Key Rate Snapshot
- International Indexes
- Non-U.S. Stocks

U.S. Markets
- Market Monitor
- Major Indexes
- Dollar Volume Leaders

Market Figures

Futures and Options
- Futures Contracts
- After-Hours Futures

Bonds
- Bellwether Bonds Report

Funds
- Fund Profile
- Fund Charts

Stocks
- Interactive Charting
- Historical Charts

Learn
- Getting Started
- Investor's Primer
- IPO Basics
- Financial Term Glossary

Track Investments
- Portfolio View
- Portfolio Analyzer
- Portfolio Allocation
- Portfolio Tracker

Invest

Sponsorships by Online Brokerages
- Datek Online
- Fidelity Investments
- National Discount Brokers
- Ameritrade
- Cybertrader
- Scottrade

Broker Decision Center

Personal Finance Process
- Plan Investment Strategy
- Stay Updated on the Latest News and Figures
- Learn About Personal Finance
- Develop Insight
- Track Investments
- Invest

Commentary
- Thom Calandra's Stockwatch
- Bambi Francisco's Net Sense
- Bezderick on Bonds (and many other commentary columns)
- e-Newsletters

Develop Insights

Third-Party Sources
- Market Guide
- Hoover's Online
- Multex
- Annual Reports Club
- INVESTools
- Over 250,000 Investment Research Reports

Community
- Private e-Mail
- People Watch
- Hot Discussions
- Occasional Polls

MarketWatch.com's experienced staff of editors and journalists; it also offers access to investment reports of established third-party sources such as Hoover's Online and Multex. The perspective of financial journalists is augmented through community tools such as message boards and personalized e-mails.

- *Invest.* MarketWatch.com does not serve any online brokerage functions, so visitors to the site are not able to make or manage investments on the MarketWatch.com site. However, the site does feature a "Trading Center" that includes sponsored links to online brokerages such as Datek, Ameritrade, and Fidelity.com.

- *Track investments.* In the "My Portfolio" section of MarketWatch.com, users can create investment portfolios and view their performance in multiple formats. This section of the site is expressly focused on helping investors manage their portfolios.

The MarketWatch.com Resource System

The resource system builds on the value cluster and online offering. Exhibit 4.8 illustrates the resource system for MarketWatch.com. The three benefits that relate directly to the value proposition are (1) up-to-the-minute information; (2) original, in-depth, credible analysis and personal-finance tools; and (3) multiple points of access.

The next step is to identify the resources that allow MarketWatch.com to deliver these benefits. These include its experienced editorial staff, its association with CBS News, the technology and infrastructure to deliver content across multiple platforms, an international presence, and its content and distribution partnerships.

These resources are made possible through a number of factors. For example, leading real-time quote technology and website hosting and management were originally provided by a third-party supplier but were gradually brought in-house after MarketWatch.com acquired the investment research site BigCharts.com. MarketWatch.com developed an international presence through its connection with CBS News, as well as by opening news bureaus in places such as London, New York, and Tokyo.

It is clear from the resource system that MarketWatch.com is able to deliver its value cluster to its users by combining its internal resources with those of its partners. Exhibit 4.9 illustrates what MarketWatch.com gives and what it gets out of these partnerships. For example, what MarketWatch.com gets from CBS News includes brand credibility, access to its audience, access to its production facilities, and $30 million of rate-card promotion and advertising on CBS channels through October 2002 (MarketWatch.com's license agreement with CBS expires in October 2005). In return, MarketWatch.com gives CBS News 32 percent ownership of the company as well as reliable and in-depth coverage of world financial news generated by its experienced editorial staff.[21]

The Revenue Model

So how does MarketWatch.com make money? How is it planning to become profitable? MarketWatch.com generates revenues from the following three sources:

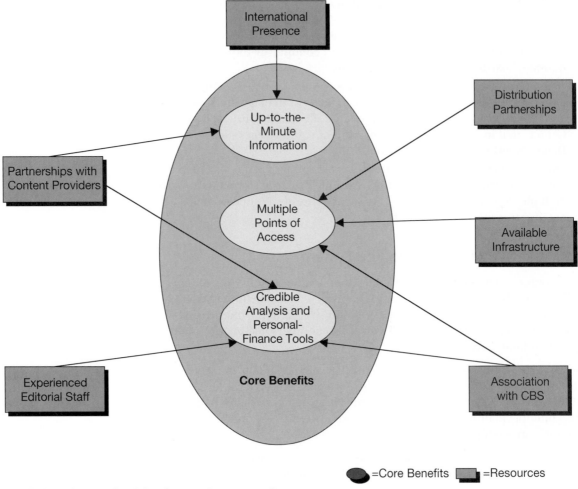

International Presence

Distribution Partnerships

Up-to-the-Minute Information

Partnerships with Content Providers

Multiple Points of Access

Available Infrastructure

Credible Analysis and Personal-Finance Tools

Core Benefits

Experienced Editorial Staff

Association with CBS

=Core Benefits   =Resources

EXHIBIT 4.8   MarketWatch.com Resource System

- *Advertising revenue.* This comes from the sale of banner ads and sponsorships on the company's website. Thirty-seven percent of MarketWatch.com's revenues in 2001 came from advertising—down from 72 percent in 1999.
- *Licensing revenue.* This comes from two sources: (a) the licensing of MarketWatch.com's content and charting technology and (b) the sale of content to third parties and a portion of subscriber payments from sites using MarketWatch.com content. Fifty-two percent of MarketWatch.com's revenues in 2001 came from licensing—up from 21 percent in 1999.
- *Other revenue.* This includes revenue generated from MarketWatch.com television shows and from paid subscriptions to the premium MarketWatch Live service. Approximately 6 percent of MarketWatch.com revenues came from this category in 1999; this figure held steady in 2000 and 2001.

Partners	Benefits to Partner: "Give"	Benefits to MarketWatch.com: "Get"
CBS News	• Experienced editorial staff • 24/7 international coverage of financial markets • Real-time financial news • 34 percent ownership of MarketWatch.com	• Credibility of CBS brand name • Access to CBS facilities • Access to CBS audience of 6.6 million homes • $30 million of rate-card promotion and advertising on CBS channels
Content Partners (e.g., Hoovers, Zacks, INVESTools)	• Access to MarketWatch.com audience	• Highest-quality analysis of financial news • Portion of revenue generated from sales to partner products
Distribution Partners (e.g., Yahoo, AOL, Quicken)	• Access to MarketWatch.com content and tools • Advertising and click-through fees	• Increase in audience reach • Increase in brand recognition

EXHIBIT 4.9   Partners Give/Get Matrix

The Online Business Model

Profits are generated by increasing advertising revenues with small incremental cost to MarketWatch.com. This is achieved by offering advertisers a wider audience for their messages, as well as a wide variety of advertising placements including traditional banners, skyscrapers, video, and interstitial formats. Profits are also generated by licensing or selling proprietary MarketWatch.com financial news and analysis content to third parties at minimal additional cost to MarketWatch.com. Exhibit 4.10 illustrates how MarketWatch.com has struck a closer balance between advertising and licensing revenue as it has matured. Looking back at the different online business models introduced earlier in this chapter, MarketWatch.com has a freshest-information value model.

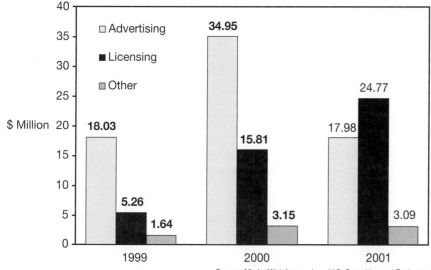

Source: MarketWatch.com, Inc., U.S. Securities and Exchange Commission, *Form 10-K* (Fiscal Year 2001), filed 1 April 2002.

EXHIBIT 4.10   MarketWatch.com's Revenue Distribution

1. What are the four components of an online business model?

A business model has four parts: (a) a value proposition or cluster of value propositions, (b) an online offering, (c) a unique and defendable resource system, and (d) a revenue model. The value proposition defines the choice of target segment, the choice of focal-customer benefits, and a rationale for why the firm can deliver the benefit package significantly better than its competitors. The offering includes a precise articulation of the products, services, and information provided by the firm. The resource system supports the specific set of capabilities and resources that will enable the firm to deliver the offerings. The revenue model details the various ways that the firm is proposing to generate revenue, enhance value, and grow.

2. Do firms compete on value propositions or value clusters?

Firms can compete on either or both. While offline firms may have difficulty competing on value clusters, their online counterparts can compete on either a value proposition or value cluster. Firms in the online world can address consumers as "segments of one." Web businesses often attract multiple segments at the same time and compete with other firms on multiple benefits that are delivered by a single tightly conceived and implemented set of capabilities. Firms can choose to focus on and primarily emphasize one critical benefit or provide multiple storefronts and clusters of benefits to multiple segments within the context of a single URL.

3. What are the approaches to developing an online offering, whether the business is providing a product, service, or information?

Development of an online offering requires completion of three sequential tasks: (a) identifying the scope of the offering, (b) identifying the customer decision process, and (c) mapping the offering (product, service, and information) to the customer decision process. The scope refers to the website's breadth, or the number of categories of products and services. The customer decision process can be divided into three broad stages: prepurchase, purchase, and postpurchase. The process of mapping the offering to the customer decision process involves the systematic matching of product, service, and information to each stage of the customer decision process.

4. What is a successful, unique resource system? What are characteristics of good resource systems?

The resource system shows how a company's value proposition is contained in a set of tailored resources that uniquely deliver the benefits of the proposition. A number of criteria can be used to assess the quality of the resource system, such as the uniqueness of a system and whether there are links between resources and benefits, and links to physical-world business systems.

5. What are the revenue sources available to firms?

Firms can draw revenue from a number of sources, including advertising; product, service, or information sales; transaction fees; and subscription fees.

1. Go to the websites of two companies in the same industry. Compare the benefits and resources for each company. Are they similar? What has each company done to distinguish itself from its competitors? Which company do you think will ultimately win in the industry? Why?

2. Find an example of a company with a lowest-price business model. What is the online offering? What companies are its key threats? Find an example of a company with a highest-quality business model. How does it compare to a widest-assortment model? How does the company present itself on its website to make customers willing to pay more for their products?

3. Go to the Seven Cycles website (*www.sevencycles.com*). Build your own bicycle. Now go to the Trek bicycle website (*www.trekbicycles.com*) and try to find a similar bike. Which experience did you prefer?

business model

value proposition

value cluster

customer decision process

egg diagram

resource system

revenue model

[1]Karen Kaplan, "DOT-GONE? An Occasional Look at Firms Struggling in the Online World: FTD.com Hoped to Flower on Web, but Prospects Are Wilting," *Los Angeles Times*, 17 April 2000, Business section, C-1, Home edition (URL: http://www.latimes.com/archives/, searchword: ftd).

[2]Market attractiveness is a function of the size of the market, growth rates of the market, weakness of competitors, strong consumer needs, supportive technology, and other forces.

[3]John G. Lynch, Jr., and Dan Ariely, "Electronic Shopping for Wine: How Search Costs Affect Consumer Price Sensitivity, Satisfaction with Merchandise, and Retention," *Marketing Science Institute Report* no. 99–104 (1999) (URL: http://www.msi.org/msi/publication_summary.cfm?publication599-104).

[4]Mitch Betts, "Brands Still Matter, Even for Shopbots," *MIT Sloan Management Review* (Winter 2001): 9.

[5]Tom Wyman, "eTailing and the Five Cs," *J.P. Morgan Industry Analysis*, 9 December 1999.

[6]Each of these terms is independent but highly related. Interested readers may wish to consider the following sources: C. K. Prahalad and Gary Hamel, "The Core Competence of the Corporation," *Strategic Management Journal* 15 (May–June, 1990): 79–91; David J. Collis and Cynthia A. Montgomery, "Competing on Resources: Strategy in the 1990s," *Harvard Business Review* 73, no. 4 (July–August 1995): 118–28; Birger Wernerfelt, "A Resource-Based View of the Firm," *Strategic Management Journal* 5 (April–June 1984): 171–80; Jay Barney, "Firm Resources and Sustained Competitive Advantage," *Journal of Management* 17 (March 1991): 99–120; Peter Reid Dickson, "Toward a General Theory of Competitive Rationality," *Journal of Marketing* 56 (January 1992): 69–83; and Shelby D. Hunt, "The Comparative Advantage Theory of Competition," *Journal of Marketing* 59 (April 1995): 1–15.

[7]See Collis and Montgomery, "Competing on Resources," 119–21.

[8]We are inferring these propositions from the websites' taglines and communications.

[9]Mohanbir Sawhney, "Making New Markets," *Business 2.0* (May 1999): 116–21.

[10]Wayne Hoyer and Deborah MacInnis, *Consumer Behavior* (Boston: Houghton Mifflin Company, 1997), 98–100.

[11]Value chains are company-specific activities that range from raw materials acquisition through to after-sale customer service [see Michael E. Porter, *Competitive Advantage* (New York: The Free Press, 1985), 37]. Activity systems are largely derived from the value chains but focus on the key "themes" and associated activities that are the most important in the delivery of a differentiated value proposition. Additionally, activity systems focus heavily on the links between activities, reflecting the need to interweave the activities as a network rather than a linear chain. This work was an important influence on the evolution of our resource system perspective.

[12]Michael E. Porter, "What Is Strategy?" *Harvard Business Review* 74, no. 6 (November–December 1996): 61–78.

[13]Jeffrey R. Rayport and John J. Sviokla, "Exploiting the Virtual Value Chain," *Harvard Business Review* 73, no. 6 (November–December 1995): 75–85.

[14]For an excellent discussion of the resource-based view of the firm, read the previously cited article by Collis and Montgomery, "Competing on Resources."

[15]Maryann J. Thompson, "Net Steals Billions from Offline Retailers," *Industry Standard*, 4 August 1999 (URL: http://www.thestandard.com/article/display/0,1151,5744,00.html).

[16]Marius Meland, "Zagat Takes a Big Byte," *Forbes.com*, 8 Februrary 2000 (URL: http://www.forbes.com/tool/html/00/feb/0208/mu2.html).

[17]Imitability of resources is discussed in Collis and Montgomery, "Competing on Resources."

[18]Pamela L Moore, "GE's Cyber Payoff," *Business Week*, 13 April 2000 (URL: http://www.businessweek.com/bwdaily/dnflash/apr2000/nf00413f.htm?scriptFramed).

[19]Sawhney, "Making New Markets," 116–21. While our metamarkets switchboard business model is based on Sawhney's, we have adapted it for this book.

[20]MarketWatch.com, Inc., U.S. Securities and Exchange Commission, *Form 10-K* (Fiscal Year 2001), filed 1 April 2002.

[21]Ibid. 33.5 percent CBS ownership as of December 31, 2001.

Strategy Formulation: Customer Interface

CASELET: HOW STAPLES DEVELOPED ITS CUSTOMER INTERFACE

When it comes to its television ads, Staples is mostly fun and games. When it comes to its online customer interface, however, the Massachusetts-based office supplies retailer is all business. From its launch in 1999, Staples's senior management has shown a deep understanding of the importance of customer experience and a firm commitment to making its website more accessible and easier to use. A prime example: the registration process.

Staples had noticed that growing numbers of its online customers were abandoning the registration process midstream—often leaving behind full shopping carts of unsold merchandise. So the company's in-house usability team (whose very existence already marked Staples as a customer-interface leader) went to work. The team conducted its own review of the registration process and immediately noticed—and rectified—several obvious impediments, such as a clunky error-message system that needlessly frustrated visitors who had made mistakes in filling out the registration form.

Staples also listened to its customers, analyzing feedback about the company posted at independent online business-ratings sites and observing and interviewing customers at in-store Web kiosks. The bottom line: The registration form was too long. To help streamline it, Staples again turned to its customers, conducting an online survey of registered customers and assessing various options via formal hands-on usability tests.

The result, after an exhaustive, three-month process, was a completely redesigned (and shorter) registration form. And the real prize: a 53 percent improvement in the registration drop-off rate. "It's all about being close to customers," Staples's director of usability Colin Hynes told eWeek. *"And not assuming that we're so smart that we can predict what customers will say and do."*

PLEASE CONSIDER THE FOLLOWING QUESTIONS AS YOU READ THIS CHAPTER:

1. What are the seven design elements of the customer interface?

2. What determines the look-and-feel of the design?

This chapter was coauthored by Jeffrey Rayport, Bernie Jaworski, Leo Griffin, and Yannis Dosios.

149

3. What are the three content classifications?

4. Why be concerned with community?

5. What are the two ways in which websites can achieve customization?

6. What types of communication can a firm maintain with its customer base?

7. How does a firm connect with other businesses?

8. What commerce features help websites perform financial transactions?

INTRODUCTION

In Chapter 4, we detailed four business-model choices: value cluster, online offering, resource system, and revenue model. These strategy decisions significantly influence the customer interface options that senior managers will face. For example, a no-frills discount retailer of functional goods, such as electronics, would have very different customer interface choices than a high-end, trend-oriented fashion site.

Consider the differing approaches of two well-regarded sports sites, Active.com (*www.active.com*) and Fogdog Sports (*www.fogdog.com*). Active.com aims to be a one-stop resource for sports participants. It has in-depth information on running, cycling, inline skating, swimming, and other individual and team sports. The site focuses on the experience that comes from competing in sports and recreation and offers tools such as training plans and customized workouts. A feeling of community is encouraged through message boards and a Web radio show. Active.com also tracks events such as marathons and other races, and makes part of its revenue by allowing users to register for thousands of events around the country. It does have a small sports store, but selling goods is not the focus of the website.

In contrast, Fogdog Sports is a shopping destination. It boasts a deep inventory that can be navigated by searching either by sport or by brand name. Much of the gear is top-of-the-line equipment, although bargain hunters can visit the Fogdog outlet. The website makes some attempt to build community by posting sports-related questions that can be answered on a message board, and there is some nonproduct information offered, such as an article in the cycling section with tips for environmentally responsible mountain biking. Yet it is clear that Fogdog's primary goal is to sell merchandise and provide superior customer service through its commerce tools.

Given their distinct value propositions and associated online offerings, it is not surprising that the interfaces of Active.com and Fogdog Sports differ in content, look-and-feel, degrees of commerce activity, emphasis on community, and connections to other sites.

This chapter introduces the 7Cs of customer interface design and discusses two higher-order design principles, fit and reinforcement. It also examines the characteristics of each "C" and gives a way to classify any website using the 7Cs Framework. The chapter concludes by applying that framework to MarketWatch.com.

The Seven Design Elements of the Customer Interface

The 7Cs Framework

Exhibit 5.1 illustrates the **7Cs Framework** for customer interface design. The interface is the virtual (and, to date, largely visual) representation of a firm's chosen value proposition. Like a retail storefront, it answers questions that prospective customers may have: Is this site worth visiting? What products or services does it sell? What messages does it communicate: Exclusivity? Low price? Ease of use? Consistent with a tightly constructed business model, an effectively designed website should both attract target segment customers and discourage others. Compelling sites communicate the core value proposition of the company and provide a rationale for visiting the site or shopping there.

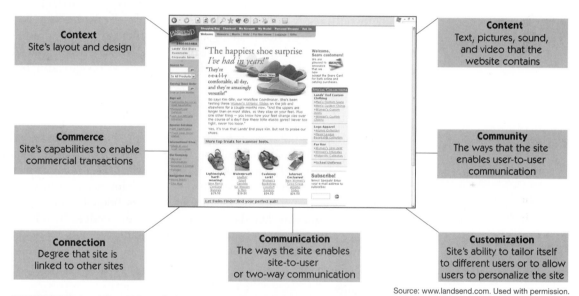

Context
Site's layout and design

Content
Text, pictures, sound, and video that the website contains

Commerce
Site's capabilities to enable commercial transactions

Community
The ways that the site enables user-to-user communication

Connection
Degree that site is linked to other sites

Communication
The ways the site enables site-to-user or two-way communication

Customization
Site's ability to tailor itself to different users or to allow users to personalize the site

Source: www.landsend.com. Used with permission.

EXHIBIT 5.1   The 7Cs of the Customer Interface

How, then, do senior managers design an effective site? Next, we briefly describe the seven choices they face. Then we provide a detailed explanation of each C.

Context

A website's **context** captures its aesthetic and functional look-and-feel. Some sites focus on bold graphics, colors, and design features, while others emphasize utilitarian goals, such as ease of navigation. Exhibit 5.1 contains a page from Landsend.com. Lands' End balances aesthetic elements (pastel colors, warm images) and functional ones (crisp, uncluttered design) to communicate its core benefits: traditional clothing, great service, and moderate prices. In contrast, the website of Lucky Brand Dungarees (*www.luckyjeans.com*) fits its hip, unconventional brand. The site is edgier than Landsend.com, with stark colors, a retro-looking Lucky Girl who says, "Hello Darlings . . . " when you ask for help, and a more focused product line. Lands' End customers might not find the Lucky Brand site appealing purely because of its look-and-feel—and that's the point. Lucky Brand aims for a young, urban, fashion-forward target customer.

Content

While context focuses on how a site is designed, **content** refers to what is presented. All the digital subject matter—text, video, audio, and graphics—on a website is considered content, and together all those forms present information about a company's products and services. Consider again the Landsend.com page in Exhibit 5.1. It uses text, photographs, and graphics to convey information about its product categories, services, and offline support (through the toll-free phone number).

Community

Community is interaction between site users. It can happen through one-on-one interactions (such as e-mail or game playing) or among many users (e.g., in chat rooms). It does not refer to site-to-user interactions. Landsend.com has an innovative community feature called "Shop with a Friend" that allows two users in separate locations to view the same webpages and browse together.

Customization

A website's ability to tailor itself to each user is called **customization**. When customization is initiated and managed by the firm, we call it *tailoring*. When it is initiated and managed by the user, we call it *personalization*. On Landsend.com, the user can personalize her shopping account by entering basic personal information, filling out an address book for potential gift purchases, and entering key dates in the reminder service. In turn, once such data are entered, the website uses the information to tailor e-mail messages, banner ads, and site content.

Communication

Communication refers to dialogue between a website and its users. It can take three forms: site-to-user communication (such as e-mail notifications), user-to-site communication (such as a customer service request), or two-way communication (such as instant messaging). Landsend.com has a feature called Lands' End Live that connects shoppers with a customer service representative. Clicking the Lands' End Live button results in two options: connection by phone (if the user has an available phone line) or connection by live text chat.

Connection

Connection refers to the degree to which a website links to other sites. Landsend.com does not host connections to other sites, but its affiliates program does allow other sites to link to Landsend.com. As part of the program, Landsend.com supplies banner ads that the affiliate can place on its site. Every time a user on the other site clicks on an ad and connects to Landsend.com, the partner earns a percentage of any sale that occurs, plus a bonus if the customer is new to Lands' End.

Commerce

A website's **commerce** capabilities allow it to sell goods, products, and services. Landsend.com obviously can perform transactions and has some extra bells and whistles, including a shopping basket that can be viewed at any time. Information about items in the shopping basket—quantity, description, size, price, and availability—is always available, as is a summary feature that displays the total price, including taxes and shipping costs. Another commerce feature is a secure server for customers' billing information and credit card numbers.

Building Fit and Reinforcement

A business's success depends not only on how well it implements each of the 7Cs, but also on how well all of the Cs work together to support the value proposition and business model. Two concepts—fit and reinforcement—are particularly helpful in understanding how to gain synergy among the 7Cs.[1]

Fit refers to how well each of the 7Cs individually supports the business model. This is illustrated in Exhibit 5.2 as links between each of the Cs and the business model. **Reinforcement** refers to the degree of consistency between each of the Cs. It is illustrated in Exhibit 5.2 as the links between each of the Cs.

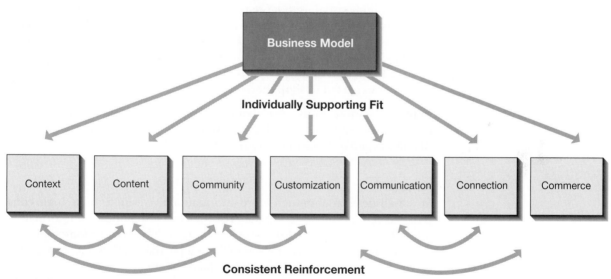

EXHIBIT 5.2   Fit and Reinforcement of the 7Cs

Consider Landsend.com again. It targets middle-class consumers who want traditional clothing, great service, and moderate prices. The content of the site "fits" this value proposition by providing mainstream and conservative fashion. Its innovative live chat "fits" with great service, and the price points of regularly priced clothing "fit" the moderate pricing strategy.

Now let's look for reinforcement. The aesthetic context—with the picture of a smiling customer service representative, the light-blue tones, and clean visual displays—conveys to the customer how easy it is to find products. In fact, the elements of context, content, customization, and commerce all work together to reinforce the value proposition.

Context: Determining a Website's Look-and-Feel

Context Features

Context, or the look-and-feel of a screen-to-face customer interface, can be categorized by both aesthetic and functional criteria. A functionally oriented site focuses on the core offering, whether that is a product, service, or information. A good example is the website CEOExpress (*www.ceoexpress.com*), an information portal that aggregates magazine, newspaper, television, and other media sites into a single destination. Its design is clean and straightforward, allowing for quick, no-nonsense access to information that is relevant to CEOs: stock quotes, business periodicals, and news articles. In contrast, Reflect.com (*www.reflect.com*) is aesthetically oriented. The site has an artistic look-and-feel with a surprising yet appealing blend of text, graphics, and photographs. This does not mean that function is unimportant, but aesthetics clearly lead the design.

The online store for J.Crew (*www.jcrew.com*) combines aesthetics and function. On the aesthetic side, the J.Crew website mirrors the J.Crew catalog in that it is highly visual, with large photographs of products and fashion models that communicate not only the product offering but also the type of people who would purchase J.Crew clothing and the kind of life they lead. Recently, the homepage of the website featured young models having fun on the beach. This photograph clearly attempted to set the tone for the type of consumer expected to shop there.

In the next two sections, we elaborate on the two key content dimensions—function and aesthetics—and give examples of how the online outlet store Bluefly (*www.bluefly.com*) uses each of them.

Function

Most websites contain much more information than can fit on a single computer screen. A well-designed site organizes this vast amount of information into sets of pages and helps customers navigate intuitively among topics. In short, function refers to a site's usability, a topic that has become recognized as a leading issue by authors including Jakob Nielsen.[2]

Function, or usability, is also affected by site-performance elements such as speed and reliability. While these may seem peripheral to a discussion on look-and-feel, slow or unreliable performance can greatly affect the user's perception of this aspect. Considering the limits of most home Internet connections, these factors also affect designers' decisions about graphics and multimedia. The following design and performance elements are critical to function:

- *Section breakdown.* This refers to a website's subcomponents. Bluefly uses a top-level tab structure that includes topics such as Search, Shopping Bag, Clearance, My Account, and Help. Beneath this are product categories, including Women, Men, Kids, House, and Gifts. The homepage also showcases links to new arrivals, top designers, and special deals.

- *Linking structure.* A website's linking structure is its way of navigating among sections. On Bluefly's homepage, shoppers can click on the Prada brand to see clothes by that brand. Once there, users see that the Prada section is framed by the top-level tab structure and general categories noted above. This linking structure keeps users from getting stranded and allows them to move easily between sections.

- *Navigation tools.* These facilitate how the user moves through the site. Bluefly's navigation tools include two search functions (by price or style number) and a feature called My Catalog.

- *Speed.* Straightforward design and limited use of complex graphics reduce the time needed to display a page on the user's screen. Bluefly's simple design contributes to its short download time.

- *Reliability.* How often a site experiences "downtime" is one indicator of reliability. Anytime users cannot get to a website, including system crashes and planned maintenance, this decreases its reliability. A second aspect is how likely the site is to load correctly on users' screens.

- *Platform independence.* Platform independence is a measure of how well the website can run on multiple platforms, including old versions of Web browsers, outdated hardware such as slow modems, and other access software.

- *Media accessibility.* As Internet-enabled devices proliferate, Web designers need to think beyond the browser-based PC—which means the issue of media accessibility (the ability of a site to download to various media platforms) becomes increasingly complex. Websites may need to be simplified or redesigned for multiple platforms until standards are established and accepted by a broad audience of users. The introduction of XML, a metalanguage for describing data, has greatly improved the Web's media accessibility. XML documents contain information about their own content that allows interface devices such as a browser to interpret how the content will be used. One example is an interface developed by Tellme Networks that uses XML to tag Web content for delivery through Tellme's voice-based portal. Users call Tellme on the telephone to access Web-based information such as stock quotes, sports news, and flight information.

Aesthetics

The **aesthetics** of a website are created by visual choices such as colors, graphics, photographs, and fonts. As bandwidth constraints ease, visual experiences on the Web will more often include interactive video and other rich-media applications. For now, however, the following two aesthetic features are the most critical to websites:

- *Color scheme.* Designers often use a consistent palette of colors throughout the site to put users in a specific mood. Bluefly, not surprisingly, uses a pastel blue as its main tone. The light color conveys softness, freshness, and youthfulness.

- *Visual themes.* Visual themes help tell a story. Lucky Brand Dungarees uses its design, motto, and retro-looking "Lucky Girl" help feature on each webpage to convey a sentiment (hip, unique) that is consistent with the brand message. Bluefly's site has the same design at the top of each of its pages—sketch-drawings that show each of its categories,

---

Drill-Down

Paying Attention to Customer Experiences?

Paying attention to customer experience is good. Paying attention to customer experiences—the full spectrum of a consumer's interactions not just with one company, but with many—is even better.

Consider an offline example: the "loyalty cards" now issued by a growing number of grocery chains and other retailers to provide their customers with automated discounts (and track their buying habits). The customer's experience of any one company's card program may be positive: Simply swipe the card at the cash register when you check out and instantly receive the store's sale prices and discounts—in other words, no more laborious coupon-clipping.

But as more and more stores jump on the loyalty-card bandwagon—each touting enhanced consumer convenience as a key feature—many consumers have begun to feel that the added convenience is undermined by the burden of carrying more and more cards on their key chains or in their wallets. Companies may look at their own card program and say, rightly, "We're making life easier for our customers." But unless they consider the broader context of their customers' experiences, including experiences with other retailers, they may miss the big picture—and wonder why their customers seem resistant to carrying their card.

There is no better online example of this principle than the user name/password problem. The need for password protection may be clear, and the implementation user-friendly, at any particular website. But multiply that website by 3, 5, 10, or 20, and you again have a recipe for consumer confusion. What in the context of one site appears to be a well-designed customer interface can turn out to be, in the context of the customer's need to interact with *many* sites, an exercise in frustration—as anyone who has ever lost the electronic record of her accumulated user names and passwords and struggled to reconstruct them from memory can attest.

The lesson? When trying to enhance its customers' experience, a company should certainly focus on its own site, products, and services. But it should also take a holistic approach to its customers, taking into account the full range of their experiences in the space—and trying to optimize its customer interactions within that context.

---

including women, men, kids, house, and gifts. These drawings act as links to each of the categories and also remind users of all the types of inventory Bluefly carries.

Context Classifications

As discussed earlier, there are two overarching dimensions of context: function and aesthetics. Some argue that designers always face the form-versus-function dilemma—that is, there is an inherent tradeoff between aesthetics and function. Others feel that with the introduction of new technological capabilities, tradeoffs are lessening and the frontier is moving. Still, we believe that most websites can be classified as one of the following: aesthetically dominant, functionally dominant, or integrated. By arranging the characteristics of function and aesthetics in a two-by-two matrix (see Exhibit 5.3), we see these classifications emerge.

Aesthetically Dominant

Aesthetically dominant websites are high on form, or aesthetics, but low on function. They emphasize look-and-feel, sometimes making heavy use of multimedia or other visual elements even though they may harm perfor-

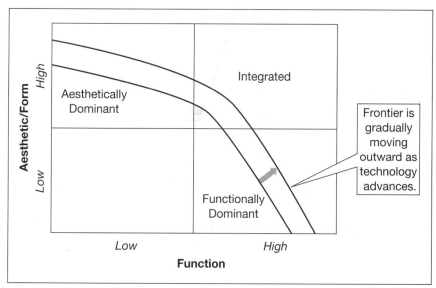

EXHIBIT 5.3   Form Vs. Function—The Design Context Frontier

mance. The goal of these websites is to use various art forms to create a pleasant escape for the user.

A good example is the website of KMGI (*www.kmgi.com;* see Exhibit 5.4), an advertising agency that specializes in online ads. It uses text, graphics, sound, and animation in its "webmercials" to create amusing, top-quality ads that look similar to television commercials. Users can view many of them from the website, a marketing plus. However, this also results in a

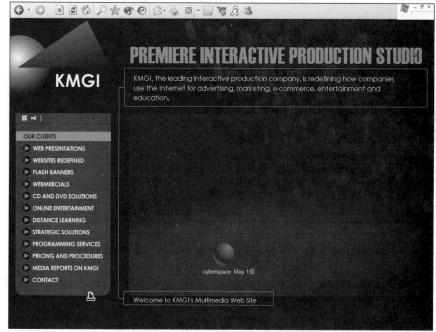

Source: www.kmgi.com. Used with permission.

EXHIBIT 5.4   Aesthetically Dominant Example—KMGI.com

website that is slow to load, limited in information, and with less evident function than most sites.

Functionally Dominant

Functionally dominant websites assume that users care more about information than visual elements. They focus on displaying textual information and limit the visual design to the bare minimum required to keep the site operational.

An example is Brint.com (*www.brint.com*), shown in Exhibit 5.5. This website, a portal for businesspeople, is all about information. The site is pure text—no graphics, sound, or animation. The homepage is organized by subject area, but looks cluttered, with an overpowering number of links; aesthetics are clearly an afterthought. This example consists of mostly text and links, but other functionally dominant websites may contain user-generated content such as chats, ratings, and reviews.

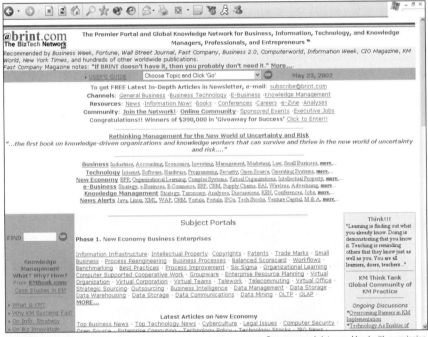

Source: www.brint.com. Used with permission.

EXHIBIT 5.5   Functionally Dominant Example—Brint.com

Integrated

The integrated classification applies to websites that balance form and function, creating an interface that is both attractive and easy to use. These sites provide navigational tools and visual cues for users and often feature clear, appealing themes that support the graphics or color schemes.

The online store of Patagonia (*www.patagonia.com*), a retailer of high-end outdoor clothing and equipment, earns a place in the integrated category (see Exhibit 5.6.) Patagonia knows its athletic customers often seek gear for a specific purpose, and so the store allows them to search by sport, to check out sales, or to browse the women's, men's, or kids department.

Courtesy of www.patagonia.com

EXHIBIT 5.6   Integrated Example—Patagonia.com

An array of magazine-quality photos makes the site visually inviting, yet they are aesthetic extras that aid navigation rather than distract from it. Each photo tells a story of outdoor adventure and imparts a sense of excitement about shopping for equipment. Product pages are similarly evocative; photos depict the beauty of the activity for which the product is designed, increasing the user's desire to participate in it. The overall design is simple, with small images that download rapidly and plenty of white space.

The site also introduces a subtle theme through its tagline, which heralds Patagonia as "environmentally conscious makers of outdoor clothing." The glorious nature shots reinforce the environmental claim.

Content: Deciding What Information to Include

Content Features

Content encompasses all digital information on a website, including audio, video, images, and text. In this section, we consider four ways of evaluating

---

Drill-Down

One Size Doesn't Fit All

Testing a website used to be simple. If all the links worked, if people could navigate it without too much stress, and if the site could stand up to a modest number of hits, it got the green light. But that was before the Internet became the place where many firms conduct much (sometimes all) of their business. Today, rigorous website testing is far more common—and far more important.

Load testing, which ensures that sites can stand up to traffic surges, became a hot topic following the rash of denial-of-service attacks that hit big-name sites in the United States and Canada in early 2000. As soon as company information technology (IT) managers saw that the victim list included Yahoo, eBay, CNN.com, Amazon.com, and Buy.com, load testing came heavily into vogue, especially with e-commerce companies that rely on websites to support their businesses.

But if a smooth-running back end is necessary for good user experience on a site, it is not sufficient. That is where usability testing comes in—the part-art, part-science of making sure that users find a site easy to navigate, logical, and predictable.

Dan Bricklin, a usability expert, software engineer, and founder of Trellix Corp., which runs a website testing laboratory, said standards are beginning to emerge, with more websites having the same basic design. In fact, Internet shoppers have expectations about the language of sites. For instance, users expect the icon that moves them to the checkout to be called a "shopping cart," and a simple variation such as "shopping basket" can confuse them. "You also have to take into account that you have different users, with different experience and comfort level on the Web," he said.

That fact was on the minds of the technical team at SaveDaily.com, a site that enables people to micro-invest in mutual funds with as little as $5 at a time and to get rebates from shopping at certain online merchants. The company recently spent several months redesigning and relaunching its site, reconfiguring the homepage to attract both experienced surfers and novice Internet users. "We found that we had all the information we needed on the site so all we had to do was change the way it was presented," said chief technology officer David LaVigna. The result is a page in which none of the main features are more than two clicks away.

After the changes were made, the company set about testing its usability by having employees, friends, and family test-drive the redesign. But when it came time to decide whether to continue testing with focus groups or additional outside consultants, LaVigna said the firm chose to trust that the early feedback was on target. Call it a different form of usability test: the leap of faith—which means hold your breath, stick to what you like, and hope for the best. Sometimes, as in SaveDaily's case, it works.

"We decided to take our chances that what we'd heard to that point would hold true," said LaVigna. "So far, what we're hearing from our customers is backing that up."

---

content—by offering mix, appeal mix, multimedia mix, and timeliness mix—and apply them to a now familiar example, Fogdog Sports.

Offering Mix

Websites can offer three types of content: products, information, and services. Often, websites feature a mix of the three, but not always. The **offering mix** refers to the weight given to each kind of content. Fogdog Sports overwhelmingly focuses on products, though it does offer some information about individual sports.

Point-Counterpoint

Can Form and Function Coexist?

Prior to our discussion of content, it is important to note that our suggested context classification is not fully representative of prevailing views of design. Jeffrey Veen, executive interface director for Wired Digital, the Web-based publisher of Hotwired, categorizes sites along two dimensions: form and function.[3] (The form dimension is similar to our aesthetic dimension.) Veen argues that there is a clear tradeoff between form and function. According to Veen, it is impossible to create a site that combines high function and elegant form. Thus, any attempt to design a site with high form and high function always results in a compromise—and therefore in a suboptimal site.

While Veen's point of view frames the context question, it does not accommodate the constant evolution toward higher function in conjunction with higher form driven by technological advances and increasing bandwidth. We would argue that designers can move sites away from a suboptimal area of low form and low function by increasing form or function or both. Hence, successful sites can be identified along a form versus function frontier. This frontier expands outward with the advent of new technology and new understandings of how to use design in the Web medium.

Appeal Mix

The appeal mix refers to the company's promotional message. (Ideally, the appeal mix is strongly linked to the value proposition.) Academic literature has identified two broad categories of appeals: cognitive and emotional. Cognitive appeals focus on functional factors such as low price, reliability, availability, breadth of offerings, customer support, and degree of personalization. Emotional appeals focus on personal ties to the product or brand and are often made through humor, novelty, or stories. One could think of the difference as appealing to the head versus the heart. Fogdog's welcome message tells visitors to "soak up the savings on popular sports gear," indicating a cognitive appeal.

Multimedia Mix

A website's multimedia mix is the designer's choice of how to combine text, audio, images, video, and graphics. Fogdog makes heavy use of images, but for the most part ignores audio, video, and graphics.

Timeliness Mix

All websites with information content need to be concerned with time sensitivity. Some information, such as stock prices or breaking news, has a shelf life of minutes or hours and is of little value when outdated. A website that offers tax information or legal advice, on the other hand, may be able to stand for months without updating. Then there is content that is virtually evergreen—historical data, reference material, or newspaper archives, for instance. A website's timeliness mix refers to its choice of time-sensitive material. Readers go to Bloomberg.com, a financial site, for up-to-the-minute stock information and daily mortgage rates as well as less time-sensitive material such as investment advice. NYTimes.com reports breaking news but also offers historical archives.

> **Point-Counterpoint**
>
> ## Is Content King?
>
> There is considerable debate concerning the role of content in the success of online businesses. There are a number of pundits who argue that content is king and that design interface and infrastructure are significantly less important. The argument has merit. Websites must have excellent content to compete in the targeted segment. Evidence suggests that even within a given product category (e.g., clothing), there are multiple strong content plays (e.g., Nordstrom versus Lands' End versus Bluelight). Users are able to discern inferior content due to negative word of mouth and network effects. This information disseminates quickly and drives out inferior content players.
>
> Opponents of this point of view argue that content is certainly important, but it is not the only game in town. First, content is necessary for success, but it is not sufficient in its own right. Second, Web businesses appear to win more often on number of users than amount of content. Hence, some large, dominant players leverage their brand names to drive out better-content competitors. Third, the freshest information websites, even if they do not have the best content, can win out over the best content providers if the content is not current. Thus, news headline sites can be dominated by content players such as *The New York Times* because NYTimes.com updates on a regular but not constant basis. However, for a segment of news junkies who want the freshest content, the Associated Press newswire may be the best source. Finally, content is a word that is misused and abused. If content means "just about everything" on the Web, then it loses precision and relevance—content will always win because "everything is content."

Content Classifications

In this section, we describe three content classifications: product-dominant, information-dominant, and service-dominant. These classifications are largely decided by the offering mix.

Product-Dominant

Online stores, or websites whose primary purpose is selling physical goods, are considered product-dominant websites. Within this category, we name three store types: the superstore, the category killer, and the specialty store. In Exhibit 5.7, we classify these stores on two dimensions: number of product categories (multiple versus single) and depth of product line (narrow versus broad).

Superstore A superstore is a one-stop shop where customers can find a wide range of goods in several product categories. These sites are usually organized by product and often compete on price. Perhaps the most well-known member of this classification is Amazon.com (*www.amazon.com*), which began as an online bookstore and gradually extended its offering until it reached superstore status. Its inventory now includes CDs, DVDs, electronics, toys, kitchen equipment, gardening tools, and more.

Category Killer Category killers concentrate exclusively on one product category. They offer a comprehensive selection of goods and services, but only within that category. Category killers often give extensive product descriptions and recommendations, along with discounts and special offers.

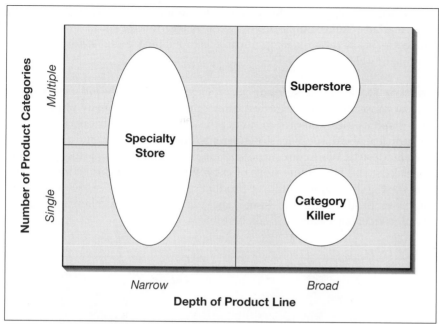

EXHIBIT 5.7   A Framework to Understand Content Classifications

PetSmart.com (see Exhibit 5.8) fits this description. It carries almost anything a pet owner could want, with subcategories for dogs, cats, birds, fish, reptiles, and small animals. As is common when shopping at a category killer, someone browsing this site probably finds himself thinking, If it's not here, it's not out there.

Source: www.petsmart.com. Used with permission.

EXHIBIT 5.8   Category Killer Example—PetSmart

PetSmart.com also has information and community content—chats with veterinarians, for example, and Q&As about vaccines and other health subjects—but because its main purpose is to sell pet products, it is a product-dominant website.

Specialty Store   These stores focus on exceptional quality and exclusivity in one or more product categories. They often pair high-quality photographs and graphics with well-written, in-depth descriptions of products. Just as in the physical world, specialty stores cater to customers who want to maintain a certain lifestyle. Wine.com (*www.wine.com*) is an example of a single-category specialty store. The online store of catalog retailer Frontgate (*www.frontgate.com*; see Exhibit 5.9) is a multiple-product specialty store. It carries a variety of high-end products for the home, including gourmet kitchen appliances, stainless-steel barbecues, and silk bedding.

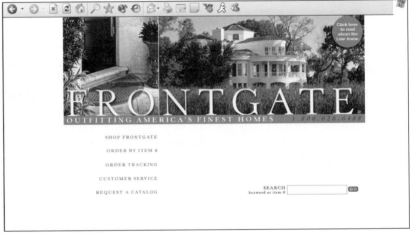

Source: www.frontgate.com. Used with permission.

EXHIBIT 5.9   Specialty Store Example—Frontgate.com

Information-Dominant

These websites house vast archives of information, along with tools for finding specific topics. These sites may generate their own content or aggregate it from other sources. Like almost all websites for magazines or newspapers, Fastcompany.com (*www.fastcompany.com*; see Exhibit 5.10) fits this category. It focuses on information for businesspeople, especially those in dynamic, fast-changing fields. Its main draw is original content by staff writers and guest columnists, although it reinforces its position as a source of business-strategy information by organizing discussion forums and occasional live events.

Service-Dominant

Service-dominant websites, as the name implies, perform a service for their users, often for a fee. Users visit these sites because they want to accomplish a task—buy an airline ticket, send flowers to a friend, or sell shares of a mutual fund, for example. Sometimes this task results in a physical product, such as the bouquet for a friend. But because the value of sites such as 1-800-Flowers.com is more closely tied to the service of sending a quick gift than it is to the sale of roses, it is considered a service-dominant interface.

Source: www.fastcompany.com. Used with permission.

EXHIBIT 5.10   Information-Dominant Example—Fast Company

Websites that provide a place for buyers and sellers to conduct transactions are also service-dominant. Called metamarkets, they act as brokers, usually taking a commission, but do not sell goods themselves. Sometimes, especially in the business-to-business sector, they provide product-comparison tools, industry information, or links to suppliers. Partner websites eBay and Half.com, which facilitate the sale of used items, are both market websites and fit in the service-dominant category. So is PlasticsNet.com (see Exhibit 5.11), which serves the plastic products industry and brings together its 90,000 monthly visitors with more than 200 suppliers.

Community: Fostering a Sense of Belonging

Community Features

Community creates a sense of membership through involvement or shared common interests. We define community as interaction among users,

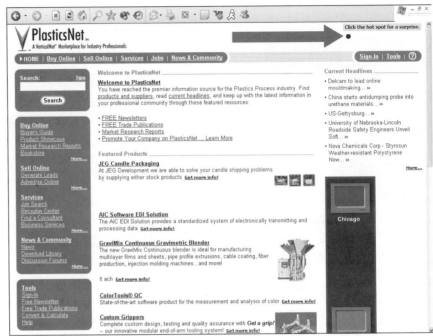

Source: www.plasticsnet.com. Used with permission.

EXHIBIT 5.11   *Service-Dominant Example—PlasticsNet*

whether it is one-to-one interaction or one-to-many interaction. Several authors have studied the formation and maintenance of online communities and developed ways to evaluate them. We discuss five aspects of communities, including characteristics, member motivation, member participation, member benefits, and interaction tools. Exhibit 5.12 illustrates how these components of a community can be integrated.

Characteristics

As communities grow and mature, certain characteristics emerge. While not every community develops all of these traits, it can be assumed that the more evolved a community and the more intense the interaction, the more likely it is to have these six characteristics:[4]

- *Cohesion.* The community develops a group identity, and individual members feel a sense of belonging.
- *Effectiveness.* The group has an impact on members' lives.
- *Help.* Members feel comfortable asking for and receiving help from other members.
- *Relationships.* Interaction between individuals leads to friendships.
- *Language.* Members develop a specialized language and/or abbreviations that have a unique meaning within the community.
- *Self-regulation.* The group sets rules for its interaction and develops a system for policing itself.

How Members Participate in the Community

Members of online communities choose their own level of participation. Mature communities will generally include members at all levels, because of a natural influx of new participants and the exit of established ones. F. Ran-

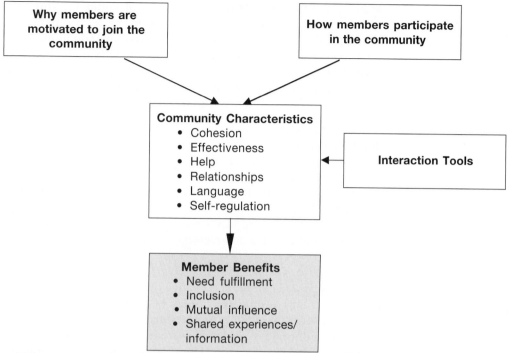

EXHIBIT 5.12   Communities–Elements, Types, and Benefits

dall Farmer describes four types of members,[5] starting with passives (those who watch or attend a community but are not actively engaged in it). Passives may become actives (those who participate in activities and take part in conversations). The two groups with the highest level of participation are called motivators (those who create conversation topics and plan activities) and caretakers (those who act as intermediaries between members).

Why Members Are Motivated to Join the Community
A member's participation is often determined by his or her motivation for joining the group. Some community members want to meet and lightly socialize with others; some share a hobby or special interest; others are looking for an emotionally intense support group. Sometimes the motivation is more specific, as in the case of those who join gaming communities, or those who join an auction website to buy and trade possessions.[6]

Member Benefits
Depending on the kind of community they join, participants receive emotional benefits. These can include one or more of the following: need fulfillment, inclusion in plans and activities, mutual influence, and shared experiences and information.[7]

Interaction Tools
A community's choice of interaction tools plays a large part in determining how the community will develop. The most significant decision is whether to use interactive or noninteractive communication.

Interactive Communication In this style of communication, community members can directly and continually converse with one another in real time (or close to it). The most common interactive communication tools are chat tools and message boards. Chat tools include both chat rooms, where several community members can type messages to the entire group, and instant messaging between two members. In both situations, participants can view messages from others within seconds of when they are sent.

On message boards, users communicate by posting messages at a specific location on a website. Others can usually view the messages quickly, although the method is not as instantaneous as chat. Message boards are also usually preserved so that users can come and go and still read and respond to all previous messages; chat is generally not archived, and only members who are present at the time can participate. Of course, members can also communicate via e-mail, although this is not likely to be organized and sponsored by the community, as chat and message boards would be.

Noninteractive Communication This style of communication does not involve direct and continual exchange of responses. Often, it is supported by a structure that gives the user a sense of permanence rather than a continuous stream of conversation. Websites that use this communication style present static information, updated periodically, and allow only unidirectional communication among users. Users can view information online, but have no way to respond.

Members make noninteractive contributions to a community by submitting content that is featured on a website or distributed through e-mail or another means. In some communities, members can craft their own webpages, which are then included in the community site.

Community Classifications

In this section, we describe three types of community classifications: nonexistent, limited, and strong. These classifications are largely determined by the type and amount of interactivity between and among members.

Nonexistent

Sites that have no community offer no way for users to interact with one another, on either a one-to-one basis or a one-to-many basis. Examples include stores such as Barnes & Noble.com and content sites such as latimes.com. Sites such as CNN.com have scheduled chats in which users can interact with guest speakers, but because they do not allow users to interact with one another, they have no community features.

Limited

Sites that offer features such as reading and posting information, stories, or opinions are limited-community sites. These sites offer mostly noninteractive community features. Exhibit 5.13 shows the Gillette Women's Cancer Connection site *(www.gillettecancerconnect.org)*, where users can post stories and read posted stories about coping with cancer but cannot interact with one another.

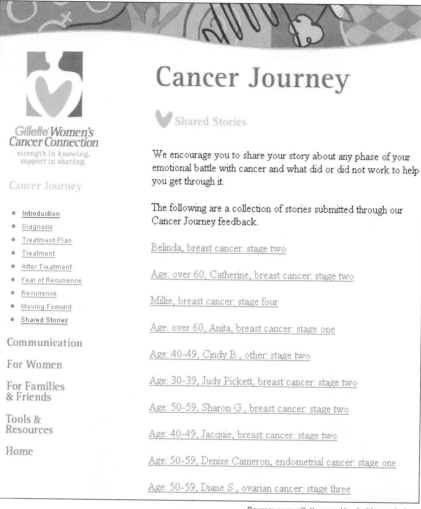

EXHIBIT 5.13   Limited-Community Example—Gillette Women's Cancer Connection

Other examples include Amazon or Circuit City, where users can post product reviews, and Zagat, which aggregates readers' reviews of restaurants for others to read. Also, fan sites such as *www.girlmore-girls.net* allow fans to post scenes and stories based on the show that other fans can read but do not allow users to interact with one another. Limited-community websites rarely allow users to form bonds with other users.

Strong

Sites with a strong community offer interactive community functions such as chat rooms and message boards. Users visit these sites with the intention of interacting with other members or to find specific information. While there are websites that offer general chat rooms, most online communities are similar to offline communities in that they revolve around a specific purpose or subject matter. One example of a strong-community website is Daily Jolt *(www.dailyjolt.com)*, which has webpages for more than 100 colleges where a student can talk to other students at his college. Sites such as Match.com offer singles the chance to get to know other singles, while *The Lord of the Rings* site *(www.lordotrings.com)*—a website created by Tolkien fans—offers users the ability to discuss anything related to *The Lord of the Rings,* as well as play games and take trivia tests. Also, the content is entirely user-created. Bolt *(www.bolt.com;* see Exhibit 5.14), a popular destination for teens and young adults, provides a variety of free interaction tools, including chat rooms, message boards, photo services, instant messaging, polls, e-mail, wireless services, and webpage hosting. Users create 95 percent of the site's content, and discussion topics range from parents to dating.

Courtesy of www.bolt.com.

EXHIBIT 5.14   Strong-Community Example—Bolt.com

Customization: Creating an Individualized Website

Customization Features

Customization is a website's ability to present individualized content for each user. A website can be designed so that it is altered by the user or by the site itself. When customization is initiated by the user, we call it **personalization**. When customization is initiated by the website, we call it **tailoring**.

Personalization

Some websites allow users to specify their preferences in a variety of areas. Once preferences have been saved, the site uses log-in registration and/or cookies to

Robert Lucky, Telecommunications Pioneer; Corporate Vice President of Applied Research Telcordia Technologies

A key thing about the Internet was that you could form spontaneous communities of people who didn't know each other before. When you use the telephone, you already have to know who you're going to call; you have to have or find their number. Mostly, you talk to them alone. But the Internet allowed you to find people who are interested in what you're interested in and form a new community. It's the formation of communities that's key here; there are a huge number of possible networks to be formed. And some companies can base their business models on that. Take eBay, for instance; it puts together communities of people who spontaneously find each other to buy and sell whatever it is that they have in common.

Here's another example: I was at a formal dinner at the World Economic Forum about three or four years ago. I was seated next to a man who owned a big bank in Germany. He was extremely stiff, and I couldn't find anything to talk to him about. So finally I asked, "What really interests you?" His eyes lit up, and he reached into his pocket and brought out these little things that he set on the table. He said, "I collect antique bottle openers. There are only 24 of us in the world who do this; we get together in various places and buy and trade antique bottle openers." All of a sudden, this formal banker turned into an effusive conversationalist. The point is, there are all these different communities out there in the world and the Internet has been able to connect them up in ways that transcend the telephone model. Now, I can go find strangers who collect antique bottle openers, and we all get together on the Internet.

match returning users with their personal settings. With log-in registration, users choose a name and password and then enter it when they return. Preferences saved with cookies, however, may not even be known to the user. Sites frequently gather data about users by quietly tracking their behavior and saving the information on the users' local disk storage in temporary files (cookies). When users return to the site, it recognizes them without the user's taking any action. Commonly used customization features include the following:

- *E-mail accounts.* Users can send and receive e-mail from the site, using a free, unique e-mail address.

- *Content and layout configuration.* Users can design their own homepage, within limits, by choosing background colors, layout design, and content sources.

- *Storage.* Users can store e-mail, URLs, favorite content, or items they want to buy.

- *Agents.* Computer programs, also known as agents, can perform simple tasks upon request, such as notifying a user via e-mail when a product is in stock.

Mylook.com (see Exhibit 5.15), which offers news and webcam images, specializes in personalization. Users can choose the kind of headlines they want to see, the locations of webcams they want to check, and one of four layouts for the resulting page.

Tailoring

Many websites dynamically publish unique versions of themselves to address a specific user's interests, habits, and needs. These sites reconfigure and

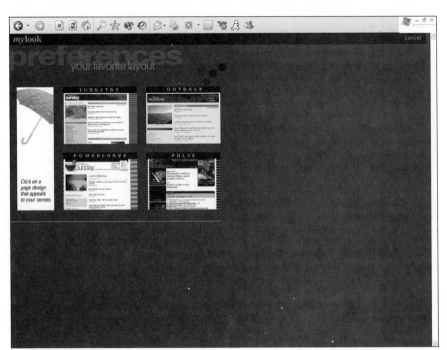

Courtesy of www.mylook.com

EXHIBIT 5.15   Personalization Example—MyLook.com

present different content with various design layouts depending on each user's responses and/or profile. A site can use a recommendation engine to adapt automatically to each user's behavior and to vary the site's offering mix of products, information, and services. The site can also recommend content or products based on the past purchases or behavior of that particular user or other users with similar profiles. Some websites have even tailored prices or payment terms based on what they think the user will spend. Marketing messages can also be developed for the individual user based on exhibited behavior or declared preferences.

Amazon tailors its site through collaborative-filtering software, which compares each user's purchases with the purchases of other users with similar preferences and creates a list of additional purchase recommendations. Amazon also makes recommendations across product categories. For example, based on a user's history of book purchases, the site recommends CDs or DVDs that others with similar book interests have bought. Exhibit 5.16 shows the Amazon homepage for two different users.

Customization Classifications

Websites can be classified according to the intensity with which they customize themselves for individual users. The style of customization—personalization by user or tailoring by site—does not affect the classification, although websites that are highly customized are likely to use both. We use three classifications: generic, moderately customized, and highly customized.

Courtesy of www.amazon.com

EXHIBIT 5.16   Tailoring Example—Amazon Homepage for Two Users

Generic

Although customization tools have become more and more sophisticated in recent years, many websites still present the same face to every user. Many of these are information-dominant, such as the websites of newspapers or government agencies, and therefore have little incentive to customize.

Moderately Customized

Most e-commerce websites fall in this classification. They are customized to some extent, often to make it easier for customers to shop there—but not so customized that the website varies wildly with each user. Best Cellars (*www.bestcellars.com*), which sells wine over the Web, is a moderately customized website. Because of restrictions on shipping wines across state lines, it must present tailored storefronts based on customers' mailing addresses. When shoppers arrive at Best Cellars, they are prompted to choose their state from a drop-down menu. This information is stored automatically by cookie, and "remembered" the next time that shopper visits. Only wines that can be legally shipped to that state—and for some states, only nonwine items such as corkscrews and other accessories—will be presented to that customer. Best Cellars also offers some personalization features such as a "wine diary" where favorites can be stored.

Highly Customized

These websites make extreme efforts to give each user an individualized experience. Often, they accomplish this by allowing users to choose their own look and content, such as portals like Yahoo, whose My Yahoo offering asks users what colors, layout, news providers, weather locations, and movie show times they want on their homepage. In other cases, the basic look-and-feel remains the same from user to user, but other content is so customized that it qualifies for this designation. Amazon.com, with its highly tailored product recommendations, is one example.

Drill-Down

Customize This!

"The customer can have any color he wants—so long as it's black," Henry Ford famously declared. Good thing Ford was not trying to peddle his Model T on the Web—he would never have made it out of Dearborn. When it comes to consumer goods and services on the Web, the customer rules, and customization is king. Consider the following businesses that have made catering to individual tastes cornerstones of their enterprises:

Interactive Custom Clothes Company

You no longer have to be rich to have your clothes custom-made—just wired. The Interactive Custom Clothes Company offers shoppers the ability to custom-design bags, dresses, jackets, pants, and other sartorial accoutrements, with the unique online benefit of try-before-you-buy visual sampling. The site guides you step-by-step through all the choices and measurements you will need to create your online ensemble. Or you can simply send in a good-fitting sample, and the company will replicate it using whatever new fabrics you have chosen from their wide-ranging catalog—including faux cow fur, metallic pink vinyl, and "living rubber," a fabric whose color changes according to your body temperature.

Thomson Learning's TextChoice

By now everyone is familiar with the custom homepage services offered by major portals and news providers (e.g., My Yahoo and myCNN). Educational publisher Thomson offers a slightly more elaborate variation on this theme through its TextChoice service, which lets instructors publish customized books comprised of content from its wide-ranging catalog. You get to mix and match the content you want and—voila—Thomson will publish and deliver to you a real book. (Actually, it takes about four weeks from creation to delivery.)

Among TextChoice's nifty features are the creation of a customized table of contents (complete with automatically generated page numbers), the ability to include one's own material in the book, and a previewing function that lets you view your creation online.

Monster

Monster, the leading online job-hunting site, offers customization features that showcase Web listings' superiority to their offline counterparts. In other words, no more eye-blearing searches through column after column of classifieds—and no forgetting where you left off when you pause for an eye-cleansing respite from four-point type. Instead, the site features the ability to post up to five different résumés, the use of search agents that continually scan Monster's job listings and e-mail users about relevant openings, and the ability to provide different levels of access to your résumé. (For example, if you want to job hunt without running the risk of alerting your boss, you can mask personally identifying details about your current job.)

Communication: Keeping in Touch with Users

Communication Features

Communication refers to dialogue between the organization and the user. The dialogue may be unidirectional (one-way from the organization to the user) or interactive. In this section, we describe and provide examples of three kinds of communication: broadcast, interactive, and hybrid.

Broadcast

Broadcast communication is one-way information sent from organization to user, with no mechanism for user response. Generally, broadcast is a one-to-many relationship between the website and its users. Here, we list some forms of broadcast communication:

- *Mass mailings.* Websites occasionally send general e-mails in large volumes, sometimes to their entire user base or to substantial numbers of potential users.
- *FAQs.* Many organizations designate a page of their website to answering frequently asked questions about the website and their goods or services.
- *E-mail newsletters.* Regular newsletters are sent by e-mail to inform subscribers about new features, changes to a site, special offers, or corporate news. Generally, recipients request the newsletter, which is mailed on a regular schedule.
- *Content-update reminders.* E-mail messages can be tailored to reflect each subscriber's interests and remind them of relevant new content.
- *Webcast events.* Events such as earnings reports or annual meetings can be broadcast from a website. Users have limited control over variables such as camera view.

Interactive

Interactive communication is two-way communication between the organization and a user. Examples include the following:

- *E-commerce dialogue.* Websites and users regularly trade e-mail messages regarding order placement, tracking, and fulfillment.
- *Customer service.* Organizations can provide customer service by swapping e-mails or through live online dialogue.
- *User input.* Interactive communication also occurs when user input is an integral part of the content of a site. Many websites showcase user-written articles, user ratings, and user feedback.

Communication Classifications

Websites can be classified by the kind of site-to-user communication they engage in, and by whether users can respond and in what way.

One-to-Many, Nonresponding User

These websites send broadcast communications to defined audiences, usually through e-mail newsletters or webcast events. The messages are usually informational, with no means (or need) for customer response. BusinessWeek Online, the Web companion to *BusinessWeek* magazine, sends out seven free e-mail newsletters on subjects ranging from the European business climate to recruiting and career tips. The newsletters are broadcast to any registered user who signs up, and they do not contain one-to-one or tailored messages.

One-to-Many, Responding User

This kind of website sends messages to registered users and invites them to submit comments and responses. BizRate.com (*www.bizrate.com*), for example, asks customers to rate their experiences with online merchants. After shoppers buy something at an online store that is a member of BizRate.com, they might see a BizRate pop-up survey that invites them to give their opinion on the shopping experience they just completed. If they participate, they are surveyed again via e-mail after the purchase's scheduled delivery date. The results are made available on BizRate.com's website.

Other websites exchange information with users in real time, often using chat tools. Accrue Software Inc. (*www.accrue.com*), a software provider for online businesses, hosts live Web seminars. Users register, dial in via phone for audio streaming, and participate in real time with chat tools.

One-to-One, Nonresponding User

This type of site sends personalized messages to address users' specific interests or needs. This information can be in the form of real-time updates or reminders, and there is no means (or need) for customers to respond. An example is found on American Greetings's website (*www.americangreetings.com*). Paying members can enter birthdays, anniversaries, or other events, and the website will send an e-mail reminder a few days before the occasion. Other than giving the information required to activate the personalized tools, however, users do not submit content to the website.

One-to-One, Responding User

This type of site also sends personalized messages such as reminders, but in this case users can respond, either by submitting information via e-mail or through live interaction. More and more sites are offering live customer service, often through a provider such as LivePerson, which sells software that facilitates real-time text dialogue. The intent is for websites to offer the same personal attention that consumers expect from traditional retailers. To start the live interaction, shoppers click a button that opens a pop-up window, where a message from a customer-service representative will appear. The user types a response, and the representative answers right away (see Exhibit 5.17). Some companies are also beginning to offer a similar service based on voice-over-IP technology rather than text messaging, a choice that will likely grow more popular as bandwidth increases.

Connection: Linking with Other Websites

Connection Features

Connection is the degree to which a website links to other sites. This often happens through hyperlinks embedded in a webpage, usually presented to the user as underlined or highlighted words, pictures, or graphics. When users click on the link, it initiates the immediate delivery of a text, graphic, or sound file, or a webpage that can be a combination of all these types of files. Files may reside on the local server or on an outside server anywhere in the world. An important concept related to these links is the pathway of con-

Source: www.liveperson.com. Used with permission.

EXHIBIT 5.17   One-to-One, Live Interaction Example—LivePerson.com

nection, or whether the link leads the user off the site. Many links do, but others will lead users to information without forcing them to formally leave the original site.

In this section, we define four kinds of connections: outside links, framed links, pop-up windows, and outsourced content.

Outside Links

These are links that take the user completely off the original site and onto another one. Many e-commerce sites try to avoid outside links because they do not provide users with an easy way to return to the original site.

Framed Links

Like outside links, framed links open in the same browser window, but they differ from outside links because the new website is literally framed in some way by the original site. When the online magazine Slate links to Barnes & Noble.com from its book reviews, for instance, a bar at the top of the browser reminds the user that he is still on Slate's site and gives him a link to return to the Slate page he left.

Pop-Up Windows

This kind of link opens up the new site in another browser window while the original site stays in the background. Users of Ditto.com, a search engine for images on the Web, can click on any thumbnail image to examine the site from which the image was retrieved. The new site opens over the Ditto.com page in a smaller frame. More and more advertisements come in the form of pop-up windows, which is attractive to websites because users can close the window after they view the ad and keep their place on the original site.

Outsourced Content

This refers to content that comes from an outside supplier. The source is usually clearly displayed, often with a link to the supplier's website, but the user does not need to leave the original site in order to view the content. Whether an organization chooses to use in-house content, outsourced content, or a combination is an important part of its content strategy. Like newspapers that print articles from wire services, many sites use content that they do not generate, own, or control. They find it too expensive to generate all content in-house; suppliers can often create content of higher quality and greater appeal.

Examples are commonly found on the many sites that use stock quotes, news feeds, or weather forecasts from outside sources such as the Associated Press or Weather.com. Another example is Real.com, an established player in streaming-media technology for the Internet. The RealSystem software (including RealPlayer®) delivers content on more than 85 percent of all streaming-media-enabled webpages. Real.com presents outsourced broadcast news content from sources such as CNN, ABCNews.com, and *The Wall Street Journal*; sports content from FoxSports.com and MLB.com; and entertainment news from sites such as E! Entertainment (see Exhibit 5.18). By outsourcing content, Real.com can focus on its core competency: developing streaming-media software.

EXHIBIT 5.18   Outsourced Content Example—Real.com, from RealNetworks™

Connection Classifications

In this section, we discuss how to classify websites based on the type of connections they feature and whether the pathway of connection generally leads users off the website or keeps them on the original site.

Destination Site

Destinations provide self-generated content almost exclusively, with very few links to other sites. These sites are often valued for their integrity and trustworthiness, and they disclose extensive information about any outside content providers. Destination sites often license their content to other sites for a fee. NYTimes.com, the website of *The New York Times*, not only includes the daily contents of the newspaper but also publishes exclusive feature stories (see Exhibit 5.19) that appear only on its site. The site updates its news every 10 minutes. As with the physical newspaper, almost all content is generated in-house.

Source: Copyright © 2002 by the New York Times Co. Reprinted by permission.

EXHIBIT 5.19   Destination Site—NYTimes.com

Hub Site

Hubs feature a combination of self-generated content and selective links to related websites. Users typically visit hub sites because they act as gateways to information on a specific industry or topic. For example, IndustryCentral (*www.industrycentral.net*; see Exhibit 5.20), a website for the motion picture and television industry, provides external links to local film commissions, production studios, film studios, a film and television résumé service, and other resources. It has self-generated information about producing and distributing film and television products, and offers industry news headlines with pop-up links to original sources such as *USA Today* or the *Chicago Sun-Times*.

Courtesy of www.industrycentral.com

EXHIBIT 5.20   Hub Example—Industry Central

Portal Site

Portals consist almost exclusively of outsourced information and links to other sites, with very little or no self-generated content. Yahoo (*www.yahoo.com;* see Exhibit 5.21) is one of the most well-known and established portals. From it, users can easily reach thousands of sites on almost any topic. Portals differ from hubs in that portals seek to be a general entryway to the Internet, suitable for any user. Their aim is to be a user's home site, the one that people go to first when they open their Internet browser. Besides providing links, portals are also heavy buyers of outsourced content. Many contract with regional news sources and weather services to provide local information to users who enter a zip code.

Commerce: Enabling Financial Transactions

Commerce Features

The commerce features of the customer interface support a website's ability to perform financial transactions. As expected, commerce features are most important to product-dominant websites, which exist for the purpose of selling products, but they are often found on information-dominant and service-dominant websites as well. (Consider the research website that charges readers to view a document, or the restaurant website that allows users to

EXHIBIT 5.21   Portal Site Example—Yahoo

place delivery orders and pay for them online.) In this section, we focus on the functional tools that enable e-commerce. They include the following:

- *Registration.* User registration allows a site to store credit card information, shipping addresses, and billing preferences.

- *Shopping cart.* When users can place items into a virtual shopping cart, it gives them the option of making the purchase immediately or storing the items until the next visit.

- *Security.* Sites attempt to guarantee the security of transactions and related data through encryption and authentication technologies.

- *Credit card approval.* Sites can have the ability to receive instant credit approval for credit card purchases through electronic links to credit card clearance houses.

- *One-click shopping.* The most well-known form of this feature is Amazon.com's patented 1-Click feature, which allows shoppers to preset credit card information and shipping addresses so they can order products almost instantly.

- *Orders through affiliates.* Websites with affiliate programs must be able to track orders that originate from affiliate sites, as well as determine the payment due for the referrals.

- *Configuration technology.* This helps users to put products and services together in a variety of ways, which allows for analysis of performance/price tradeoffs, interoperability among complex components within a system, and substitution of generic for branded products.

- *Order tracking.* Shoppers can check the delivery status of their orders.
- *Delivery options.* Most e-commerce sites give users their choice of delivery speeds, with quicker times costing more.

Commerce Classifications

After evaluating what commerce features a website has chosen to implement, it is possible to classify it as having low, medium, or high commerce abilities. In this section, we review these three classifications and provide examples of websites that fit in each.

Low

These websites have the ability to process transactions, but with few (or, as in the following example, none) of the commerce features just listed. They are likely to be owned by small businesses or those for whom the Web represents a small percentage of their sales. Gluttons' Gourmet, a fledgling business based in New Hampshire that sells homemade salsa and tortilla chips to grocery stores, has equipped its website (*www.gluttonsgourmet.com*) with rudimentary commerce features so that it can also sell directly to consumers. Shoppers who cannot find the brand in stores can fill out a Web form with their name, e-mail address, and quantity of products requested. The company then contacts the user to set up payment and shipping preferences. There is no shopping basket, credit card approval, or other typical commerce features.

Medium

Some websites have no need for all the commerce bells and whistles, simply because financial transactions are a necessary feature but not their main purpose. For example, Boston.com, the online home of *The Boston Globe*, is mainly an information source, but it also can process newspaper subscriptions, sell classified ads, and charge fees for access to archived stories. To accomplish these transactions, it has some commerce features—credit card approval, security measures, and registration—but not others, including shopping carts or affiliate ordering. Websites whose main purpose is to sell products also might fall into this classification, simply because they are not as sophisticated or established as those in the "high" category.

High

These websites are fully equipped with all or almost all of the features listed earlier. They are usually owned by large offline companies or established online companies with high sales volumes. Gap.com, the online store of the Gap clothing company, is one example. Shoppers are encouraged to register and use a shopping cart, enabling them to see what colors and sizes are in stock for the items they request. Shipping addresses and credit card numbers are stored automatically, and users can change the information in their account at any time, or view all previous and current orders. Gap.com offers several delivery options and links directly to the consumer's tracking information on the websites of UPS and other delivery companies.

Drill-Down

Online and Offline Integration of the Customer Interface

We have applied the 7Cs Framework to the online customer interface, but all the elements of the online interface also can be replicated offline. The design of mutually reinforcing online and offline interfaces provides a consistent offering and brand message to the customer. In this Drill-Down, we explore how each of the 7Cs might be implemented offline and study examples of the successful integration of online and offline interfaces.

Context in the offline world is the look-and-feel of the physical store. Context is comprised of, among other things, the store architecture, the appearance and demeanor of the store's staff, the openness of the retail environment, the lighting, the color, and the style selection. J.Crew stores provide a welcoming environment through the use of open space and abundant natural and artificial light. Store colors match store to store—and match the colors of the clothing offered in the store. The stylish and uncluttered look-and-feel of the physical store match the look-and-feel of the jcrew.com site. This look-and-feel reinforces the company's positioning as a relaxed shopping place that offers stylish and casual clothes. On the other hand, Gap stores have a consistent design to help shoppers navigate the store and to maximize sales. Customers know they can find new fashionable items at the front of the store, core lines (such as chinos and jeans) in the middle of the store, and sale items at the very back.

Content in the offline world includes all the products, services, and associated information about products and services offered at physical store locations. Barnes & Noble bookstores contain a very wide selection of books and magazines. Customers can get large discounts on some book categories, such as best-sellers. Customers get information on books by searching through catalogs or by using in-store computer terminals. Customer service is readily available through the many customer service representatives at most stores. The Barnes & Noble physical store offering of easily accessible information on a large selection of books at discount prices complements a nearly identical virtual offering at the store's website. The website provides the same easy access to information and prices but through powerful search software.

Community in the offline world is communication between customers. Community can be encouraged through store events or through store participation in and sponsoring of community activities. Borders bookstores often host author readings and book signings. At these events, readers can interact with one another and meet people with similar book tastes. Evite.com, an online event-invitation site, has hosted local gatherings to provide users an opportunity to physically meet and build relationships. Each year in Los Angeles, Revlon sponsors the Walk for Breast Cancer to increase breast cancer awareness, raise research funds, and bring together customers and noncustomers alike.

continued

Mapping the 7Cs Framework

In the business-model chapter, we discussed how a particular firm chooses to compete in the marketplace. As noted at the outset of this chapter, the 7Cs Framework is intended to provide a comprehensive road map for the management team to translate its business model into an actionable, concrete site. Exhibit 5.22 shows a summary of the options that any given firm can pursue for each of the 7Cs. Consider, for example, the content choices of a particular site. Here, the firm has three general options: product-dominant, service-dominant, or information-dominant. Which particular option makes

Customization in the offline world comes in a number of different ways. A store can personalize products and services that customers purchase. Credit card holders can have their pictures and signatures imprinted on the face of their credit cards and thus personalize the cards as well as reduce the risk of credit card fraud. Lands' End customers can order custom-tailored khakis. To some degree, stores can also customize customer experience based on exhibited customer needs. Local restaurants recognize loyal customers by automatically seating them at their favorite tables. Airlines can automatically assign customers to their preference of aisle or window seating each time they travel. Stores can also send targeted marketing messages to users based on exhibited purchase behavior. Many catalog retailers send out customized catalogs based on individual purchase history.

Communication in the offline world is the one-way (store-to-customer) or two-way interaction between store and customer. One-way store-to-customer communication can take the form of newsletters or catalogs that stores send to customers. Stores can also provide personalized alerts to customers. For example, investors using Merrill Lynch's full brokerage services can arrange for an alert by broker phone call whenever market conditions warrant it. Customers can participate in two-way communications with stores by filling out and submitting surveys generated by the store. Furthermore, customers can ask for live assistance either in person (when physically in the store) or via phone. Nordstrom is widely know for excellent customer service; its representatives have even been known to deliver purchased products directly to customer homes.

Connection in the offline world is the degree to which a store is connected to other stores. Stores in large shopping malls are closely located to a number of other stores, and customers can quickly move out of one store and into another. A retailer can rent concession space in large department stores to provide an additional sales channel, to be associated with other nearby concessions, and to allow customers to easily move back and forth between concessions. Stores can also provide links to a large number of suppliers who offer products or services of interest to customers. Travel agencies provide links to a large number of travel providers that include airlines, hotels, and cruise-line operators. Furthermore, stores can increase their number of customers through partnerships. Coca-Cola partners with McDonald's to increase sales by making Coca-Cola available at all McDonald's locations.

Commerce in the offline world refers to the transaction capabilities of a store. Stores provide transaction capabilities such as shopping carts, security, credit card and personal check verification, custom gift wrapping, and delivery options. Many clicks-and-mortar retailers are searching for ways to better integrate their online and offline commercial offerings. Grocery chain Stop and Shop has experimented with an in-store kiosk program that allows shoppers to order up to 50,000 hard-to-find items not stocked on the shelves. And Sears and Best Buy are among the growing number of firms that allow consumers to return or exchange their online purchases not only by mail, but in stores as well.

sense depends upon the business model of the firm. Moreover, the choices for each of the 7Cs should be fully integrated with one another. Thus, a product-dominant site is often classified as high on commerce. In order to see how the business model and 7Cs work together, let us consider the 7Cs decisions of three different websites.

At Foot Locker's website *(www.footlocker.com)*, it is clear that the business model is to sell athletic shoes and apparel to fitness-oriented consumers (see Exhibit 5.23). The key revenue stream is product sales. How does this business model map to the 7Cs? First, the site is largely functionally oriented with key information on products and sales. Community and customization are both minimal. These 7Cs choices work together to deliver against the promise of the business model—a revenue stream based on

Context	Aesthetically dominant		Functionally dominant		Integrated	
Content	Product-dominant		Information-dominant		Service-dominant	
Community	Nonexistent		Limited		Strong	
Customization	Generic		Moderately customized		Highly customized	
Communication	One-to-many, nonresponding user	One-to-many, responding user		One-to-one, nonresponding user		One-to-one, responding user
Connection	Destination		Hub		Portal	
Commerce	Low		Medium		High	

EXHIBIT 5.22   Map of 7Cs Framework

brand-name athletic shoes and apparel. Consumers visit the site to find information and then efficiently buy products rather than interact with other users, find resources for their respective sports, or spend large amounts of time looking at content, so the website has made choices to meet that need.

Runners might also visit Cool Running (*www.coolrunning.com*), a site that offers advice, race calendars, and community features for runners (see Exhibit 5.24). While both Cool Running and Foot Locker are sites that appeal to runners, their 7Cs maps show stark differences between their interfaces (a reflection of the stark differences between their business models). Cool Running is not a store, but a low-commerce website that is information-dominant. It has both its own content and links to other sites, so it is considered a hub. It has a newsletter, so its communication style is one-to-many, nonresponding user. Active message boards make for a strong community. While both websites attract runners, their interfaces reflect the difference in what they are offering to runners—Footlocker.com wants to sell products while Cool Running wants to provide personalized information and community.

The New Balance website *(www.newbalance.com)* is yet another variation on a theme. Though both the New Balance and Foot Locker sites are product-dominant, their purpose is very different. With its website, New Balance is trying to brand itself. It is an integrated site, providing both information and an aesthetic experience to help potential customers better understand both its products and the kind of people who use them. While it has links to stores, it has no commerce features. Community and customization are both nonexistent.

Context	Aesthetically dominant	Functionally dominant	Integrated
Content	Product-dominant	Information-dominant	Service-dominant
Community	Nonexistent	Limited	Strong
Customization	Generic	Moderately customized	Highly customized
Communication	One-to-many, nonresponding user	One-to-many, responding user	One-to-one, nonresponding user	One-to-one, responding user
Connection	Destination	Hub	Portal
Commerce	Low	Medium	High

EXHIBIT 5.23   Foot Locker (*www.footlocker.com*)

Context	Aesthetically dominant	Functionally dominant	Integrated
Content	Product-dominant	Information-dominant	Service-dominant
Community	Nonexistent	Limited	Strong
Customization	Generic	Moderately customized	Highly customized
Communication	One-to-many, nonresponding user	One-to-many, responding user	One-to-one, nonresponding user	One-to-one, responding user
Connection	Destination	Hub	Portal
Commerce	Low	Medium	High

EXHIBIT 5.24   Cool Running (*www.coolrunning.com*)

The key conclusion from these three mini-case studies is that the business model should drive the selection of each of the 7Cs elements. The elements should work together as a coherent whole. As demonstrated by each case study, the particular choice of 7C elements can vary widely—and should vary widely—depending upon the business model pursued.

Customer Interface for MarketWatch.com

In this section, we apply the 7Cs Framework to MarketWatch.com. After examining each of the interface design choices, we provide a map of the 7Cs Framework that shows where MarketWatch.com fits in each of the seven areas (see Exhibit 5.25).

Context	Aesthetically dominant	Functionally dominant	Integrated
Content	Product-dominant	Information-dominant	Service-dominant
Community	Nonexistent	Limited	Strong
Customization	Generic	Moderately customized	Highly customized
Communication	One-to-many, nonresponding user	One-to-many, responding user	One-to-one, nonresponding user / One-to-one, responding user
Connection	Destination	Hub	Portal
Commerce	Low	Medium	High

EXHIBIT 5.25 MarketWatch.com (*cbs.marketwatch.com*)

Context

Exhibit 5.26 shows the homepage for MarketWatch.com, which is more functionally oriented than aesthetically oriented. The look-and-feel is one of a newspaper, complete with story headlines and summary article descriptions. Integrated in and around the articles, charts, and graphs is a wide range of advertising and paid sponsorships. The shortcoming of the newspaper look-and-feel is that it makes it somewhat difficult for users to navigate through all of the site's information and services.

Source: © CBS MarketWatch.com. Used with permission.

EXHIBIT 5.26   MarketWatch.com Homepage

One of the most functionally dominant aspects of the site is the constantly updated headlines. The site can be accessed from a variety of platforms, including the Web, wireless telephones, pocket PCs, and handheld computers. In addition to the functional elements, the MarketWatch.com site also contains some aesthetic features, such as animated advertisements, small photos of columnists, and a number of charts.

The content-driven look-and-feel fits with the MarketWatch.com value proposition of providing "the story behind the numbers" without being slowed down by excessive graphics or other bandwidth-intensive features.

Content

MarketWatch.com is an information-dominant site. It combines around-the-clock stock quotes and related breaking news with more evergreen content, including in-depth analyses. In addition to this third-party and proprietary content, the site includes member-generated content through its message boards. The site also provides tools and services such as a stock screener and portfolio tracker. MarketWatch.com displays its content in several ways, including raw text (the news headlines), pictures and charts, sound (news transmission through MarketWatch.com Radio), and video (streaming videos of interviews with financial analysts and business executives). The content fits well with MarketWatch.com's value proposition: "providing comprehensive, real-time business news, financial programming, and analytic tools."[8]

Community

MarketWatch.com offers an array of community tools, including personalized e-mail and discussion groups. MarketWatch.com believes that "providing a place . . . to meet and share ideas about investing will increase brand awareness, motivate users to return to the MarketWatch.com site frequently, and encourage our audience to spend more time on our website."[9] Community members are enthusiastic users who are eager to share opinions on financial issues. The site provides them with the stimulus for their community interactions, which center on analyzing financial news. With the ability of users to interact with one another, the MarketWatch.com community can be classified as a "strong" community.

This fits well with the MarketWatch.com value proposition of empowering investors to make decisions, because the perspectives of other investors often prove useful and insightful.

Customization

MarketWatch.com offers a suite of personalization tools. These include a selection of 15 e-mail newsletters covering a variety of financial topics. The "Portfolio Tracker" allows users to track up to 200 stocks in their portfolios in one of three formats: basic, advanced, and an interactive Java version. It also forecasts the future value of the portfolio and adjusts the investment strategy accordingly. One of the most recent MarketWatch.com customized product offerings is its MarketWatch Alerts. Alerts allow users to sign up for instant e-mail messages tied to various market-related events, including changes in the price or volume of a stock; changes in a stock's 52-week high or low; news updates based on a stock ticker symbol, portfolio, keyword, industry, or CBS MarketWatch.com news column; and breaking news bulletins.

The site's tiered customization, which allows "power" users to receive personalized content for a fee but lets less frequent users find the information they require without significant customization, fits well with the Market-Watch.com desire to appeal to different groups of investors.

Communication

MarketWatch.com offers a number of communication tools. In the broadcast venue, it sends several free e-mail newsletters (including After the Bell, Thom Calandra's StockWatch, and Bamby Francisco's Net Sense and Net Stocks), as well as a paid subscription newsletter, The Hulbert Financial Digest, which offers rankings and profiles of more than 160 top-performing investment newsletters and the 500-plus portfolios they recommend. Also in the broadcast category is the delivery of breaking news on companies that users specify through MarketWatch.com Alerts.

MarketWatch.com tightly restricts the feedback options of its users. Users can submit feedback either through Web forms or by e-mail. No live communication options are available. Similarly, account administration is completely automated. Registered users can make adjustments to their account through a secure server, adding or removing a service or viewing their account history online only.

MarketWatch.com's broadcast nature fits well with its goal of providing reliable, current information. While that information needs to be communicated to targeted user groups, there is little need for live interaction.

Connection

MarketWatch.com connects to a number of other sites. It links to online brokerages so that investors can make transactions, and it increases the volume and quality of its financial analysis through links to content providers such as Thomson Financial Services. It maintains the MarketWatch.com look-and-feel by embedding third-party content within its page design in most instances. This third-party information notwithstanding, the overwhelming majority of the MarketWatch.com site is produced by its own staff of more than 70 journalists in nine bureaus worldwide.

MarketWatch.com has also increased its reach through partnerships and licensing agreements. Its highest-profile partnership is with America Online. MarketWatch.com entered a three-year distribution agreement with America Online to be the premier provider of business and financial news on AOL's personal finance channel. The two companies created a cobranded site where users can reach MarketWatch.com content and tools. More recently, licensing has taken on a growing importance; MarketWatch.com has had to diversify its sources of revenue in light of a pronounced advertising slump. MarketWatch.com provides its licensing clients with news from its reporters as well as portfolios, company research, insider-trading data, and a full suite of mutual-fund data. Licensing clients include leading brokerages and banks and financial publishers, including Ameritrade, UBS PaineWebber, and The Motley Fool.

These connection initiatives support the MarketWatch.com goal of being a respected source of business and financial news in the personal-finance industry.

Commerce

MarketWatch.com offers its core service for free, depending instead on advertising and license fees for revenue. As such, it does not offer commerce tools such as shopping carts, order tracking, and delivery options. It does track the revenue from advertisements associated with MarketWatch.com content on other sites, and it receives a portion of that revenue. Registered users can subscribe to The Hulbert Financial Digest for $59 a year, the only for-fee product offered on the site. The low level of commerce tools fits well with MarketWatch.com's goal of providing relevant and timely information rather than selling products or services.

Reinforcement Among the MarketWatch.com 7Cs

MarketWatch.com's context reinforces its content. By creating a site that is mostly functionally oriented, MarketWatch.com accentuates the message that it is a destination for high-quality, in-depth financial news and analysis. This message is driven home by the sparse presence of commerce tools. (A site dedicated to comprehensive news and analysis has little need for elaborate commerce features.)

Similarly, MarketWatch.com's customization reinforces its mission. By providing tiered levels of service for each of these two dimensions, the site tailors itself to its main target groups: everyday investors and highly sophisticated market players. Context further reinforces this message. The site's front page has a newspaper look-and-feel, appealing to everyday investors who want to be guided through the day's news. As users click to more sophisticated services and analyses, the look-and-feel becomes more functional and less aesthetic, appealing to sophisticated investors who are more interested in information than packaging.

1. What are the seven design elements of the customer interface?

The seven design elements are context, content, community, customization, communication, connection, and commerce. Each of the 7Cs needs to fit and reinforce the others while satisfying the business model.

2. What determines the look-and-feel of the design?

The look-and-feel of a website has two dimensions: form (or aesthetics) and function. Aesthetic designs focus on the artistic nature of the site, while function relates to usability. Some argue that these are opposing design aspects and involve unavoidable tradeoffs, while others believe that advancing technologies are leading to new techniques and fewer compromises as both aesthetic and functional dimensions continue to expand.

3. What are the three content classifications?

The three content classifications are product-dominant (which includes the subcategories of superstore, category killer, and specialty store), information-dominant, and service-dominant. The offering mix is what most often determines the classification. A product-dominant website's priority is selling goods, although it often offers information as well. Information-dominant websites exist for the purpose of providing information, generated either internally or externally. Service-dominant websites help users perform a task, such as investing money. They also include market websites, which perform the service of bringing buyers and sellers together to conduct transactions.

4. Why be concerned with community?

A sense of community encourages users to return to a website. Feelings of involvement and shared common interests can help a group of people create strong, lasting relationships. A sense of community often develops when websites create a place for engaged and extended exchanges focused on users' shared interests. However, community develops not only through common interest and group acceptance but also through individual involvement.

5. What are the two ways in which websites can achieve customization?

Websites can be customized through personalization, when the users themselves set preferences, or through tailoring, when the site adapts itself to individual users. Methods of personalization include log-in registration, personalized e-mail, content and layout configuration, storage, and agents. Websites can tailor themselves according to either the user's specific behavior or that of other users with similar preferences.

6. What types of communication can a firm maintain with its customer base?

There are two forms of communication: broadcast and interactive. Broadcast communication is one-way communication from the firm to a large group of users. Interactive communication involves back-and-forth dialogue between a firm and its users.

7. How does a firm connect with other businesses?

Connections can be divided into two basic types, depending on whether the pathway of connection leads the user off the original site or whether the user can retrieve materials from other sites without leaving the site. Outside links always cause a user's exit from the original website, while framed links, pop-up windows, and outsourced content cause the retrieval of material from the same or other sites without an exit from the current website.

8. What commerce features help websites perform financial transactions?

Tools that help enable e-commerce include registration, a shopping cart, security, credit card approval, one-click shopping, affiliate orders, configuration technology, order tracking, and delivery options. A website may have none, some, or all of these features, depending on its needs.

Exercises

1. Go to the website for the Webby Awards (*www.webbyawards.com*). Look at the nominees for "community." How have these sites excelled at creating community? How do they differ?

2. Go to a site you've never been to before (for suggestions, look at the Webby Awards site). What is the first thing that strikes you about this site? Is it functionally dominant or aesthetically dominant? Generic, moderately customized, or highly customized? What types of communication does it have? How does it use visual themes to give an impression of the company? Do you think these choices fit with the strategy of the company (or organization)? Repeat this exercise for two more sites.

3. Map the 7Cs for Salon.com. Do the same for *The New York Times* website. How do these maps differ? How are they similar? Now map the 7Cs for a retail site, such as Buy.com. Compare the three maps.

Key Terms

7Cs Framework	commerce	tailoring
context	fit	broadcast communication
content	reinforcement	interactive communication
community	function	destinations
customization	aesthetics	hubs
communication	offering mix	portals
connection	personalization	

Endnotes

[1]Choong Whan Park and Gerald Zaltman, *Marketing Management* (Chicago: Dryden Press, 1987). Park and Zaltman introduced the concepts of consistency and complementarity to refer to the degree to which various marketing management concepts resulted in synergy. Complementarity is equivalent to reinforcement, and fit is equivalent to consistency. Given the number of concepts that begin with the letter C in this chapter, we have chosen to use the terms fit and reinforcement.

[2]Interested readers should consult the following literature: Jakob Nielsen, *Designing Web Usability* (Indianapolis: New Riders Publishing, 2000).

[3]Jeffrey Veen, *Hotwired Style: Principles for Building Smart Websites* (San Francisco: Hardwired, 1997).

[4]Richard P. Adler and Anthony J. Christopher, "Virtual Communities," in Christina Ford Haylock, *Net Success* (Holbrook, MA: Adams Media, 1999), 42.

[5]F. Randall Farmer, "Social Dimensions of Habitat's Citizenry," in Carl Loeffler and Tim Anderson, eds., *The Virtual Reality* (New York: Van Nostrand Reinhold, 1994), 87–95.

[6]Myra Stark, "A Fly on the Virtual Wall: Cybercommunities Observed," *Digitrends Quarterly* (Summer 1998): 26.

[7]Adler and Christopher, "Virtual Communities," 42.

[8]MarketWatch.com, Inc., U.S. Securities and Exchange Commission, *Form 10-K* (FY 1998), filed 31 March 1999.

[9]Ibid.

Market Communications and

Branding

CASELET: GOOGLE BUILDS A BRAND

How does a graduate student's computer science project become the world's best-known search engine? For Google, as for any startup, branding was key. But not the kind of branding— TV and radio ads, splashy IPO, direct-mail blitz, and the like—that most people associate with the term. Instead, Google managed to build a top-tier brand in just a few short years by doing what successful offline companies have been doing for decades: defining its audience, understanding its customers, executing with integrity, and, once it defined its brand intent, successfully and consistently executing it.

In 1998, Stanford PhD candidates Larry Page and Sergey Brin addressed the difficulty of finding information on the fast-expanding Web with an innovative new algorithm for conducting Web searches, one that took into consideration not only the presence of keywords on a site but the number of links to it from other sites. The technology worked so well that Google soon became the talk of the digerati, generating a growing buzz (much of it electronic) that boosted its daily search count from 10,000 to half a million in just six months. And all with virtually no traditional marketing or advertising.

How did it manage such a feat? With its stark, uncluttered homepage and clear disinterest in any portal-like aspiration beyond the performance of its core mission—fast and accurate searching—Google's medium is its message. And if "a brand is the promise of an experience," as the old saying goes, the experience that the Google brand promises—efficiency with a dash of fun and irreverence (playful name, colorful-but-spare graphics, whimsical "holiday logos")—is tightly aligned with the experience that it actually delivers. It is the single-minded execution of a brand intent that resonates with customers—not glitzy Super Bowl ads—that has made Google one of the top Internet brands.

PLEASE CONSIDER THE FOLLOWING QUESTIONS AS YOU READ THIS CHAPTER:

1. What are the four categories of market communications?

2. What constitutes a good brand?

This chapter was coauthored by Jeffrey Rayport, Bernie Jaworski, Nancy Michels, Ellie Kyung, Jennifer Barron, Marco Smit, and Rafi Mohammed.

193

3. What is the 10-Step Branding Process?

4. How does online branding compare between American Airlines and Continental Airlines?

5. What are the arguments for and against leveraging an offline brand into the online environment?

INTRODUCTION

Chapter 5 focused on the types of interface design choices that confront the senior management team. Once these choices are made, the managers must turn their attention to building customer traffic, strengthening the brand, and locking in target customers. In this chapter, we consider how the online company communicates with its target customers and attempts to build a strong brand.

We begin this chapter by introducing the link between communications and branding. Next, we introduce a simple marketing communications framework. This framework considers both online and offline media approaches as well as individualized and broad audiences. We review a number of new online approaches and traditional media approaches; we also consider how to build superior, lasting brands. This requires some basic discussion of brand equity as well as a methodology for the branding processes. After introducing this methodology, we apply it to two well-known businesses: American Airlines (*www.aa.com*) and the career website Monster (*www.monster.com*). Early pundits thought the Internet would lead to pure commoditization of products. However, these case studies reveal the potential for highly differentiated, unique brands.

As in prior chapters, we conclude our discussion with an application of the market communications and branding concepts to MarketWatch.com.

Integrating Communications and Branding

Regardless of the source of differentiation, **branding** is about the consumer's perception of the offering—how it performs, how it looks, how it makes one feel, and what messages it sends. These perceptions are nurtured by a combination of market communications in the marketplace—one's interaction with the brand, others' experiences with the brand, and, more generally, mass-marketing approaches. In the offline world, these communications tend to be one-way, from the firm to the customer. In the online world, communications are much more interactive and two-way.

Communications and brands are actually the media of which the Web is made. Old marketing notions such as "shelf space equals market share" in retail or "mind share leads to market share" in entertainment apply with a vengeance to the Internet. Mental space is marketspace, so it should come as no surprise that e-commerce or networked-economy markets are realms in which there has been an explosion of innovation in business communications techniques—as well as in the power of brands.

If brands are real estate owned by companies in the minds of consumers, then communications and brands on the Web represent real estate competing to attract the scarcest resource in the networked economy—consumer attention. This is the critical challenge for businesses on the Web, and it links the two themes of this chapter.

Finally, approaches to claiming the real estate of the mind are varied and must take place in both the offline and online worlds. The opportunity to reinforce online with offline and vice versa is a profound value-creation machine for business. The Internet has created a completely new channel, which, when combined with offline marketing tools, can create a completely new and unique experience. This back-and-forth experience between the two worlds is what we are talking about when we introduce the hybrid approaches to marketing communications involving both offline and online worlds.

Four Categories of Market Communications

Market communications refers to all the points of contact that a firm has with its customers. These include obvious offline communications such as television advertising, promotions, and sales calls, as well as emergent advertising approaches on the Internet. It is important to stress that any chapter on marketing communications in the networked economy must include a blended discussion of offline and online approaches.

Consider the case of Amazon.com. In its quest to develop—and retain—its customer base, Amazon has been losing large sums of money. In 2001, Amazon lost $157 million (although its fourth quarter was its first profitable quarter ever), compared with losses of $417 million in 2000 and $390 million in 1999. However, its marketing investments (broadly defined) have been paying off. In 1999, sales surpassed $1 billion for the first time; in 2001, sales surpassed $3.1 billion. In addition, Amazon now has about 25 million active customer accounts, compared with 14 million in 1999.[1] Amazon is a good example of a company that has invested significantly in all four types of marketing communications: (1) general online communications, (2) personalized online communications, (3) traditional mass media communications, and, to a much more limited extent, (4) direct communications.

The Customer Decision Process and Market Communications

Prior to our discussion of these four communications types, we reflect on the objectives of the marketing communications effort and examine the so-called hierarchy-of-effects communications model. It is difficult to think about the choice of marketing communications without first considering the objectives that one wants to accomplish (e.g., increase brand awareness, increase sales). At the same time, we also need to consider a structured approach to moving the customer through the decision process—from early awareness of the brand through purchase.

In Exhibit 6.1, we illustrate the customer buying process, which mirrors the hierarchy of effects. In traditional "big ticket" product categories, consumers are thought to pass through multiple decision stages. Each stage is a prerequisite for the next stage—for example, you cannot move through the decision process to purchase without first forming a preference for the brand. It should be noted that this buying process is a simple illustration of the egg diagram in Chapter 4.

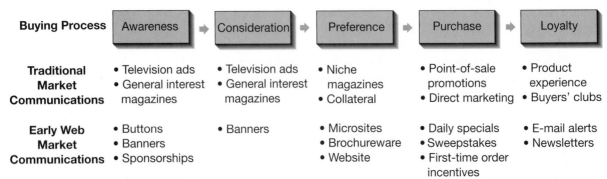

EXHIBIT 6.1   Evolution of Customer Buying Process

Source: Forrester Research, Monitor Analysis.

In the middle portion of Exhibit 6.1, we show the types of traditional marketing communications that are used to move the customer through the buying process. For example, television ads may create brand awareness, while point-of-sale promotions tend to trigger purchase. The lower portion of Exhibit 6.1 shows Web market communications that can be linked to the buying process. For example, banner ads can make target customers aware of the product or service, while "daily specials" tend to be most associated with purchase.

It is important to reflect on how the marketing communications process changes as we move from traditional to online communications. Perhaps the most important shift is from the acquisition mindset of the traditional world to the experience, retention, and interactive (two-way) mindset of the networked economy. In the next section, we introduce a simple framework for marketing communications that provides a backdrop to our more detailed explanation of both offline and online communications tools.

A Framework for Online Marketing Communications

This section describes marketing communications that online companies use to attract new customers. These marketing strategies are clustered into four major categories: (1) **general online communications**, (2) **personalized online communications**, (3) **traditional mass marketing**, and (4) **direct communications** (see Exhibit 6.2). In Exhibit 6.3, we list some of the communications options in each category.

The Four Categories of Communications

General Online Communications
The following are nonpersonalized approaches that companies take to communicate with users.

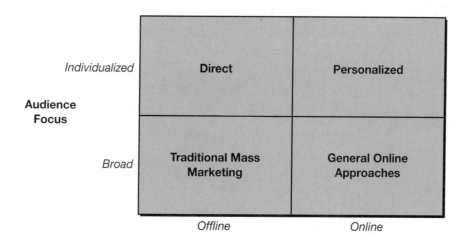

Communications Media

EXHIBIT 6.2   Framework for Marketing Communications

Direct
• Salesforce
• Direct mail
• Telemarketing
• Customer service representatives

Personalized
• Personalized permission e-mail
• Personalized recommendations
• Personalized advertisements
• Personalized webpages
• Personalized e-commerce stores

Traditional Mass Marketing
• Television
• Radio
• Print
• Billboards

General Approaches
• Banner ads
• E-mail
• Viral marketing
• Portal sponsorship/exclusive agreements
• Associate programs
• Online and offline partnerships
• Customer information
• Online transactions

EXHIBIT 6.3   The Four Categories of Communications

Banner Ads   **Banner advertisements** exemplify the application of old offline advertising techniques to the Internet. They are essentially electronic billboards and come in a variety of types and sizes; standard formats have been developed by the Interactive Advertising Bureau (*www.iab.net*). A single webpage will often simultaneously display multiple banners. A page could display one across the top, for example, and one or two smaller ones running vertically down each side. These ads usually display a simple message that is designed to entice viewers to click the ad. In general, this click-through leads to a company's website. Buttons and hypertext links have similar capabilities. The fact that such ads can serve as gateways to the advertiser's own website is one great advantage to advertising on the Web.[2]

Ad space is often sold on the basis of what is called cost per thousand impressions (CPMs). According to a 2001 Morgan Stanley report, the average CPM for a website with broad general appeal is about $3.50. Depending on the popularity and reach of the website, however, CPMs can be 10 or 20 times higher for very desirable audiences.[3] On high-traffic sites such as Yahoo.com, which may be seen by more than a million people in a day, advertising may be charged as a flat weekly or monthly fee. Another pricing structure is based on the click-through rate, or the number of times viewers go to the advertiser's website by clicking on the banner ad.

The differing pricing structures indicate that the industry is still unsure about whether banners ads must deliver clicks on the advertiser's website to be worth the cost. The Morgan Stanley report shows that banner ads are extremely effective at generating brand recall, even surpassing TV or radio ads. It also found that streaming media ads, which feature animation or offer some kind of interaction, were five times as effective as traditional banner ads. This kind of evidence gives credence to the CPM pricing model.[4]

E-commerce players continually try to improve upon the banner ad. Currently, there is a trend toward using larger formats for banner ads, including the vertical skyscraper ad.[5] Larger banners that allow interaction within the banner box without leaving the original site are another example.

e-Mail   E-mail is an attractive marketing vehicle to e-commerce players because of its low production costs and simplicity. In 2001, spending on e-mail marketing was about $1 billion (with about $580 million going toward customer retention). It is expected to jump to $9.4 billion by 2006.[6]

As more and more e-mails flow into mailboxes, however, it becomes harder to convince the intended readers to open them. Already, e-mail users say they are becoming less likely to research or buy products that they learn about through e-mail. Especially harmful to online marketers' efforts is the increasing volume of junk e-mail, or spam. (The nickname comes from a Monty Python sketch in which the canned luncheon meat Spam was pushed onto every diner regardless of whether he or she wanted it.) By 2006, the average e-mail user will receive 1,400 spam messages annually.[7]

To cut through the clutter, marketers are turning to opt-in messages, which help ensure that their offers or newsletters are reaching an audience that is interested in their products. Also, they are making sure that messages are relevant to customers and that the frequency of e-mails is not burdensome. One study of online users found that 88 percent reported having made a purchase as a result of receiving an opt-in e-mail; 80 percent prefer to receive such e-mail on a weekly or monthly basis.[8]

Seth Godin coined the term **permission marketing** to describe how successful e-mail campaigns can result from creating relationships with customers. Permission marketing presumes successful marketing campaigns can be created by establishing a mutually beneficial and trusting relationship between the firm and its customers. In exchange for some offered benefit, customers volunteer information about themselves and, in essence, ask to be marketing

Community

MarketWatch.com offers an array of community tools, including personalized e-mail and discussion groups. MarketWatch.com believes that "providing a place . . . to meet and share ideas about investing will increase brand awareness, motivate users to return to the MarketWatch.com site frequently, and encourage our audience to spend more time on our website."[9] Community members are enthusiastic users who are eager to share opinions on financial issues. The site provides them with the stimulus for their community interactions, which center on analyzing financial news. With the ability of users to interact with one another, the MarketWatch.com community can be classified as a "strong" community.

This fits well with the MarketWatch.com value proposition of empowering investors to make decisions, because the perspectives of other investors often prove useful and insightful.

Customization

MarketWatch.com offers a suite of personalization tools. These include a selection of 15 e-mail newsletters covering a variety of financial topics. The "Portfolio Tracker" allows users to track up to 200 stocks in their portfolios in one of three formats: basic, advanced, and an interactive Java version. It also forecasts the future value of the portfolio and adjusts the investment strategy accordingly. One of the most recent MarketWatch.com customized product offerings is its MarketWatch Alerts. Alerts allow users to sign up for instant e-mail messages tied to various market-related events, including changes in the price or volume of a stock; changes in a stock's 52-week high or low; news updates based on a stock ticker symbol, portfolio, keyword, industry, or CBS MarketWatch.com news column; and breaking news bulletins.

The site's tiered customization, which allows "power" users to receive personalized content for a fee but lets less frequent users find the information they require without significant customization, fits well with the Market-Watch.com desire to appeal to different groups of investors.

Communication

MarketWatch.com offers a number of communication tools. In the broadcast venue, it sends several free e-mail newsletters (including After the Bell, Thom Calandra's StockWatch, and Bamby Francisco's Net Sense and Net Stocks), as well as a paid subscription newsletter, The Hulbert Financial Digest, which offers rankings and profiles of more than 160 top-performing investment newsletters and the 500-plus portfolios they recommend. Also in the broadcast category is the delivery of breaking news on companies that users specify through MarketWatch.com Alerts.

MarketWatch.com tightly restricts the feedback options of its users. Users can submit feedback either through Web forms or by e-mail. No live communication options are available. Similarly, account administration is completely automated. Registered users can make adjustments to their account through a secure server, adding or removing a service or viewing their account history online only.

MarketWatch.com's broadcast nature fits well with its goal of providing reliable, current information. While that information needs to be communicated to targeted user groups, there is little need for live interaction.

Connection

MarketWatch.com connects to a number of other sites. It links to online brokerages so that investors can make transactions, and it increases the volume and quality of its financial analysis through links to content providers such as Thomson Financial Services. It maintains the MarketWatch.com look-and-feel by embedding third-party content within its page design in most instances. This third-party information notwithstanding, the overwhelming majority of the MarketWatch.com site is produced by its own staff of more than 70 journalists in nine bureaus worldwide.

MarketWatch.com has also increased its reach through partnerships and licensing agreements. Its highest-profile partnership is with America Online. MarketWatch.com entered a three-year distribution agreement with America Online to be the premier provider of business and financial news on AOL's personal finance channel. The two companies created a cobranded site where users can reach MarketWatch.com content and tools. More recently, licensing has taken on a growing importance; MarketWatch.com has had to diversify its sources of revenue in light of a pronounced advertising slump. MarketWatch.com provides its licensing clients with news from its reporters as well as portfolios, company research, insider-trading data, and a full suite of mutual-fund data. Licensing clients include leading brokerages and banks and financial publishers, including Ameritrade, UBS PaineWebber, and The Motley Fool.

These connection initiatives support the MarketWatch.com goal of being a respected source of business and financial news in the personal-finance industry.

Commerce

MarketWatch.com offers its core service for free, depending instead on advertising and license fees for revenue. As such, it does not offer commerce tools such as shopping carts, order tracking, and delivery options. It does track the revenue from advertisements associated with MarketWatch.com content on other sites, and it receives a portion of that revenue. Registered users can subscribe to The Hulbert Financial Digest for $59 a year, the only for-fee product offered on the site. The low level of commerce tools fits well with MarketWatch.com's goal of providing relevant and timely information rather than selling products or services.

Reinforcement Among the MarketWatch.com 7Cs

MarketWatch.com's context reinforces its content. By creating a site that is mostly functionally oriented, MarketWatch.com accentuates the message that it is a destination for high-quality, in-depth financial news and analysis. This message is driven home by the sparse presence of commerce tools. (A site dedicated to comprehensive news and analysis has little need for elaborate commerce features.)

and Sony through a combination of traditional advertising and product innovation.[29]

Priceline believes that radio is the most effective medium through which to reach potential customers. In 1999, Priceline allocated two-thirds of its $60 million marketing budget to radio. Jay Walker, Priceline's founder, claimed that the radio campaign helped Priceline increase sales by 5 percent a week.[30] In 2002, Priceline renewed a contract with celebrity spokesperson William Shatner to continue appearing in radio and television advertisements. According to the company's chief marketing officer, the Shatner campaign "focuses squarely on what differentiates Priceline in today's travel industry."[31]

EToys's initial success illustrates both the effectiveness of TV advertising and the folly of overspending. Launched in 1997, eToys cleared $2 million in revenues in its first year. During the 1998 holiday season, Visa U.S.A. ran a cobranded TV ad that featured parents using the eToys website to purchase holiday presents for their children. Due in large part to the effectiveness of these TV ads, eToys's fourth-quarter revenues skyrocketed to $23 million.[32] Not surprisingly, the company was unable to sustain a business that spent more than a third of its budget on advertising; eToys declared bankruptcy in 2001. Nevertheless, when KB Toys purchased the remains of eToys, one of the main assets it acquired was an established household name with a decent reputation among consumers.[33]

Monster also found that using traditional TV marketing fueled explosive growth in its business. In its quest to establish itself as the best place for job-seekers to post their résumé, as well as the easiest place for employers to find people online, Monster invested heavily in TV advertising. Its 1999 and 2001 advertising campaigns were named the most effective in the Internet services category. Monster supported the campaign with outdoor advertising and street teams showing off Internet kiosks connected to the Monster website.[34]

Direct Communications

Direct communications can take many forms, from the use of the classic business-to-business sales representatives, retail sales clerks, and telephone customer sales representatives to direct marketing and telemarketing.

Sales Representatives   One of the most interesting developments on the Web is the reemergence of the traditional sales representative. When properly managed, the Web can paradoxically lead to the increased effectiveness of sales representative, rather than make sales representatives obsolete. Dell found that sales leads increased in quality because of its website. Sales representatives became more efficient, and their satisfaction increased after the online channel was added.

Direct Marketing   A second form of offline marketing communication is **direct marketing** through the postal system. Of course, a key difference is that with the new information gained online, firms are able to target and customize the mailings to a much more significant degree. Firms such as Amazon.com send coupons through the mail to select customer groups. For instance, people who purchase a DVD at Amazon may receive a discount voucher for DVDs through the mail, followed by a reminder e-mail a few days later.

Telemarketing   A third option is the use of a **telemarketing** salesforce. We have all received those wonderful sales pitches near the dinner hour. The aim of telemarketing is clearly to increase sales—not to strengthen brand awareness or image.

What Is a "Good" Brand?

According to the American Marketing Association, a brand is a "name, term, sign, symbol, or design, or a combination of them, intended to identify the goods and services of one seller or group of sellers and to differentiate them from those of the competition." The brand (e.g., Amazon.com) signifies both the product and the additional "wrap-arounds" (e.g., easy customer interface, one-click shopping, collaborative filtering) that differentiate it from other products in the category.

Drill-Down

Quotes on Online Branding

"E-branding is more important [than e-commerce]. And it must come first. Because few people will buy your stuff—online or off—unless you are top-of-mind." —Annette Hamilton, Executive Producer, ZDNet

"Brand is the price of entry [to the Internet], not the winning strategy." —Dylan Tweney, InfoNet

"By the time your potential customers log on, they already know what they're looking for, and they often know from whom they want to buy it. . . . They're just not listening to branding messages anymore." —Michael Fischler, Principal, Markitek Consulting

"Brands stand as comfort anchors in the sea of confusion, fear, and doubt. In dynamic markets, strong brands have more value than ever, precisely because of the speed with which these markets move." —Chuck Pettis, BrandSolutions, Inc.

"A company's website *is* the brand. It's the hub of consumer experience, the place where all aspects of a company, from its annual report to its products to its support, intersect. It's the company in a nutshell, all there in a way that just is not possible in the analog world." —Sean Carton, Chief Experience Officer and Managing Partner, Carton Donofrio Partners

Perhaps due to the limited "real estate" that a screen-to-customer interface provides, or to a desire to build consumer-goods companies quickly, or to the perception that this is a winner-take-all environment, it is abundantly clear that branding in the e-commerce arena is receiving a great deal of management attention.

Several key concerns are apparent in these quotes:

- Branding is a necessary but not sufficient condition for success.
- Branding may be more important in the online than the offline environment.
- Brands serve to add value in each step of the decision process—at prepurchase (e.g., driving traffic to the site), purchase (e.g., erasing doubt), and postpurchase (e.g., assurance).

Do Strong Online Brands Matter?

As the discussion in the previous section implies, a strong brand can be viewed as essential to the growth of an online business. In particular, with the introduction of so many brands, a strong brand name provides a clear presence in the market. Furthermore, strong brands attract customers. In the long run, firms may be able to decrease marketing expenditures once the brand is established. In effect, a strong brand is an instant message that contains a wide variety of associations on the part of target customers. Clear brands are also associated with higher conversion rates. Finally, and most importantly, all current online "winners" have strong brands.

Opponents of the strong-brand line of reasoning argue that history will prove this assumption to be limited. They believe that alliances are the key to locking up a market—and these alliances can be accomplished with strong venture backing. Second, third-party evaluators such as Gomez and BizRate will increasingly influence consumption—much like *Consumer Reports* does today. However, unlike *Consumer Reports*, the BizRate data are easily available, easy to access, and, hence, can drive consumption behavior during the purchase process. Third, speed to market may be more important than branding. Also, the meaning of brands is changing. Because all experiences are increasingly becoming customized, "mega-brands" are no longer relevant. Finally, while it is true that all winners have strong brands, a number of "big losers" also have strong brand names.

Branding Basics

Exhibit 6.4 provides a few key insights into what constitutes good online branding. At the center of the exhibit is the core product or service. In the case of American Airlines (*www.aa.com*), this means safe, on-time transportation from location A to location B. The wrap-arounds for American Airlines include superior service, the AAdvantage frequent-flier club, in-flight service, and the comfort of the environment. Its market communications emphasize the benefits of membership, which can be functional (e.g., mileage points), symbolic (e.g., communicates your social status versus Southwest Airlines), or experiential (e.g., comfort of seating).[35]

Good brands provide a clear message to the market about the core offering, the wrap-arounds, and the communications. All not only provide a signal about the functional offering, but are simultaneously differentiated by their emotional, symbolic, and experiential benefits—for both the firm and target customers.

A Simple Conceptual Model of Brand Equity

Exhibit 6.5 provides a simple framework for understanding the effects of the brand (core, wrap-around, and communications) and brand equity. The exhibit has three basic parts: the brand, customer responses, and benefits (both to the firm and the customer). **Brand equity** has a wide variety of definitions in the academic literature.[36] According to David Aaker, brand equity is a combination of assets that can be viewed from both the firm's and the customer's perspectives. In other words, Aaker views brand equity as a combination of consumer responses and benefits. In particular, he notes that brand equity is "a set of assets [and liabilities] linked to a brand's name and symbol that add to [or subtract from] the value provided by a product or service to a firm and/or that firm's customers."[37]

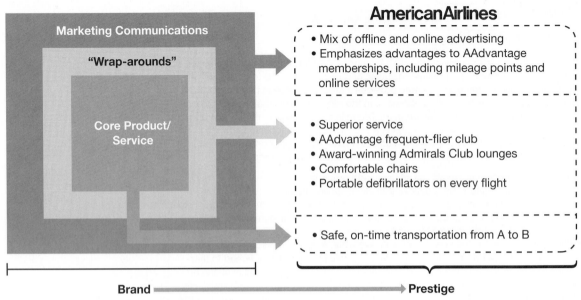

EXHIBIT 6.4   What Is a Good Brand?

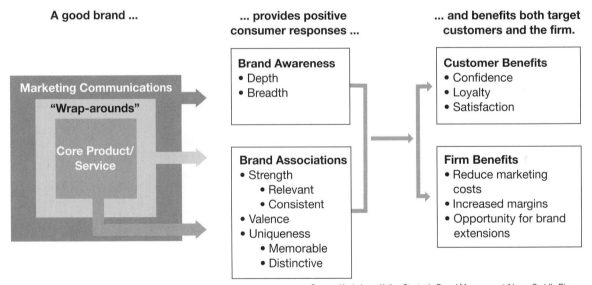

Source: Kevin Lane Keller, *Strategic Brand Management* (Upper Saddle River, NJ: Prentice-Hall, Inc., 1998); David Aaker, *Building Strong Brands* (New York: The Free Press, 1996); market2customer Analysis, Marketspace Analysis

EXHIBIT 6.5   A Simple Conceptual Model of Brand Equity

Other authors tend to focus heavily on the customer responses only: "Customer-based brand equity is defined as the differential effect that brand knowledge has on consumer response to the marketing of that brand." Still others focus only on financial criteria, such as the dollar value of the brand. Like Aaker, we tend to divide brand equity into two key components: (1) intermediate customer responses and (2) the benefits to both the customer and the firm. Thus, the framework has three basic parts: the brand, customer responses to the brand (awareness and associations), and benefits (to both the firm and the target customers).

Consumer Responses Consumer responses can take two broad forms: brand awareness and brand associations. Brand awareness refers to the strength of a brand's presence in the consumer's mind. A brand with high brand awareness (e.g., Monster) is more likely to be recalled—either prompted by an advertisement or unaided.

Brand associations refer to the connections that consumers make to the brand. These associations can be categorized in terms of strength, valence, and uniqueness.

Consider the Amazon brand. **Strength of association** refers to the intensity with which the target consumer links a particular word, phrase, or meaning to a particular brand. Thus, if one were to cue the customer to reflect on the meaning of Amazon, the customer might say "big company," "Jeff Bezos," "They sell books," "It was my first Internet purchasing experience," "It is easy to use," or "unprofitable." Strong associations tend to be those that are "top of mind" for the customer. Measures of strength include the number of times an association is mentioned, the ranking of the association, and speed of recall.

Valence refers to the degree to which the association is positive or negative. Again, consider the Amazon associations above. "Easy to use" is a positive association, "unprofitable" is a negative association, and "They sell books" is a neutral association. **Uniqueness** captures the degree to which the association is distinct, relative to other brands. "Jeff Bezos" is an association that is unique to the Amazon brand.

Consider the American Airlines example again. A customer may strongly associate certain words or features with the brand name. The strength of the association is often divided between two criteria: relevance and consistency. *Relevance* is defined as the degree to which the brand is perceived as meeting the needs of the target customer. Is the tagline relevant to the needs of the airline's key target segment—the business traveler? *Consistency* is the degree to which each element of the brand reinforces the brand intent. Does the AA symbol reinforce the airline's positioning as an airline for the business traveler? This is, of course, debatable. All else being equal, brands that are highly relevant and highly consistent tend to produce strong associations. Companies hope these associations will be positive ("I had a great time flying American Airlines" versus "That is the airline that always is late"). Hence, associations can be rated on the degree to which they produce positive or negative associations—that is, their valence.

Finally, associations can be rated on their uniqueness, which can be further subdivided into distinctiveness and memorability. *Distinctiveness* captures the degree to which the brand is differentiated from its competitors (e.g., Jeff Bezos is distinctive), while *memorability* captures the brand's ability to provide a lasting communications effect (e.g., customers remember the tagline). A memorable brand association leaves an impression in the mind of the customer, which enables easy recall.

Firm and Consumer Benefits As seen in Exhibit 6.5, positive consumer responses produce benefits for both customers and the firm. Customer benefits include increased confidence in the purchase decision, loyalty to

---

Marketspace Interview

Bob Davis, Venture Capitalist; ex-CEO Terra Lycos

We [at Lycos] quickly saw that because online content isn't highly differentiated, the quality of the brand becomes so important. Eventually, you get to a point where brand is everything. Brand is consuming; brand drives the success of one property versus another.

But when you're online, you've got to do much more than traditional branding and advertising. There's a crucial grassroots component of branding on the Internet that allows you to put the community of the Web, the users, to work for you. Smart branding online uses community; it uses chat, message boards, and e-mail systems. It builds those into its online activities in a way that retains the user. On the Internet, I can develop a relationship with a consumer the way a traditional media company cannot. I can develop a one-on-one relationship. Just think about the words we use to describe the different media: We *watch* TV. We *listen* to the radio. But we *use* the Internet. This is an interactive medium, and a strong brand takes advantage of that.

---

the brand, and satisfaction with the experience. Firm benefits translate into top-line revenue growth, increased margins, and lower marketing costs. The firm also has the opportunity to extend the brand into new categories, such as Amazon's expansion into home improvement.

Types of Brands

Pure Offline and Online Brands

In the early days of the Internet, brands were categorized as pure offline or pure online brands. Exhibit 6.6 provides a sampling of these brands. Classic offline brands included Gap, UPS, Office Depot, and Disney. New-to-the-world online brands include Amazon, Yahoo, and Priceline. However, as the Internet expanded, we observed the crossover of offline brands into the online world, and the transition of online brands into the offline world.

Traditional Brands	Online Brands
The product/service with which the brand is associated was established offline in the bricks-and-mortar world.	The product/service with which the brand is associated was established in the online world.
Examples: – Gap – UPS – Dell – J.Crew – McDonald's – Office Depot – Ragu – Coca-Cola – Disney	*Examples:* – Amazon – Yahoo – ZDNet – AOL – Priceline – CDNow – Excite – E*Trade

EXHIBIT 6.6   Types of Brands

Blurring of the Distinction

The end result is a blurring of the distinction between pure offline and pure online brands. Consider the following developments:

- Yahoo was established online but used offline promotional activities to grow brand awareness.
- E*Trade is a traditional brand in the sense that its products are established in the physical world but are extensions of the online brand—and thus a mixture of the two.
- Egghead.com completely shifted from an offline brand to a purely online brand.
- Wingspan Bank was established in the virtual world but by a traditional brand. (Subsequently the offline brand, Bank One, replaced the online brand.)
- Charles Schwab successfully bridged the gap between online and offline activities.
- Ragu was established offline but used online promotional activities to grow brand awareness and loyalty.

Exhibit 6.7 provides a simple diagram to capture the movement of brands. The figure has two basic dimensions: mix of promotion (online versus offline) and initial product establishment (online brand versus offline brand). This figure illustrates that Schwab was initially a traditional brand—and has now moved toward the center of the figure to reflect its hybrid nature. Also, Schwab is doing both online and offline promotion—hence, the circle is quite wide. Egghead.com initially was a traditional offline brand but moved to an online brand with online promotion activities.

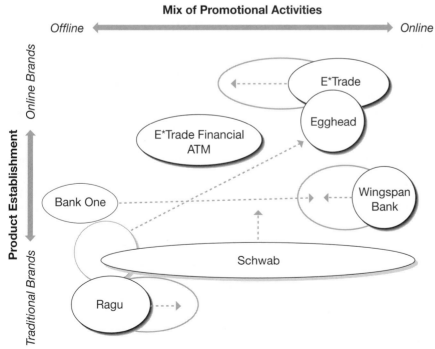

Source: Forrester Research, Monitor Analysis.

EXHIBIT 6.7   Brand Presence

The 10-Step Branding Process

There are a number of well-known frameworks that can be used to build brands. In this section, we provide a simple **10-Step Branding Process** (see Exhibit 6.8). In addition to the broad review of each step, we also discuss how the branding process may differ in the online environment.

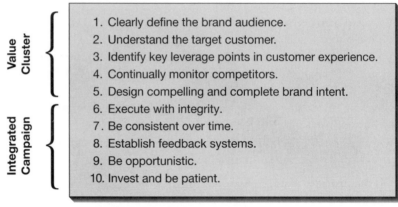

EXHIBIT 6.8   Building an Online Brand

Step 1: Clearly Define the Brand Audience

In Chapter 3, we discussed the need to specify the target audience for the offering. A clear picture of the target customer segment is critically important. As noted in Chapter 3 and Chapter 4, it could be argued that a larger number of segments can be effectively addressed in the online environment than in the offline environment. This is due to a number of factors, including the firm's ability to reconfigure its storefront in a real-time fashion for each customer.

Step 2: Understand the Target Customer

After defining the brand audience, it is frequently useful to describe a typical customer who can bring the target segment to life. Both online and offline environments require deep understanding of customer behavior. Indeed, firms building brands exclusively in one environment still need to be aware of consumer behavior in the other environment. It is clear that a great deal of information can be collected online through click-stream data. However, this information is not sufficient to infer the process of consumption (e.g., attitudes, knowledge, brand image). Hence, a blending of traditional and online research is often necessary.

Step 3: Identify Key Leverage Points in Customer Experience

While target customers may share many of the same behavioral characteristics, this step forces the firm to consider the key organizational levers—product prices, customer interface, mix of online versus offline communications—that will activate the customer to behave in a manner that is consistent with the objectives of the firm. Consumer research should focus heavily on these key organizational levers that can motivate consumption.

The customer decision process involves prepurchase, purchase, and post-purchase decisions in both the online and offline environments. In the offline environment, it is the retail salesperson or the telephone customer service representative who guides the customer through the buying process. In the online environment, the store can be reconfigured to guide or direct consumers. It is a more subtle form of selling.

Step 4: Continually Monitor Competitors
Building a brand is tough even when there are no competitors in the space. However, competition in the online world is incredibly intense. It is not unusual for a firm to develop a clear business plan only to have competitors emerge before the launch date. Hence, it is critical that emerging and existing competitors are constantly monitored. Competitors must be monitored in both online and offline environments, but the online environment is distinctive in two respects. First, the degree of competitive intensity is different. Numerous new firms can emerge both within the product category and across product categories. Second, it is much easier to analyze competitors given the emergence of sources such as Hoover's Online (*www.hoovers.com*), the Securities and Exchange Commission (*www.sec.gov*), and financial-news sites (MarketWatch.com).

Step 5: Design Compelling and Complete Brand Intent
The brand intent brings to life the value proposition. Value propositions, or clusters, tend to focus on the high-level customer benefits. The goal is a customer-friendly description of how the brand should be interpreted from the customer's viewpoint. The intent should be both compelling (i.e., provide the positive brand associations) and comprehensive.

While the brand intent is important in both environments, there is more opportunity for customization in the online environment. In general, the brand intent tends to be more segment focused in the offline environment, while the online environment allows individuals within the segment to customize the offering.

Step 6: Execute with Integrity
This step refers to the quality of the implementation choices and the extent to which the firm provides a clear, trustworthy message. Historically, in the offline environment, building a brand took consistent, long-term investment. Most well-known Internet brands were introduced after 1995.

Step 7: Be Consistent over Time
Strong brands take time to develop. Of course, on Internet time, this may be months or years rather than decades. Regardless of the time line, the key is a consistent message. It is also clear that, given the interactive nature of the Internet, each consumer can have a slightly modified experience with the brand; the Internet allows customers to experience the brand in unique ways.

Step 8: Establish Feedback Systems
Market communications and reactions in the marketplace rarely work out exactly as planned. Hence, it is important to have regular feedback systems in place. The effects of branding can be measured more quickly and

more precisely in the online environment. Sophisticated tools exist to track customer responses to the brand and marketing communications.

Step 9: Be Opportunistic

Brand-building opportunities present themselves in unexpected ways. For example, Monster has always attempted to be one of the first in its category to try communicating in new ways, including through Super Bowl commercials and blimp advertising. Opportunism typically occurs at the segment level in the offline environment and at the individual level in the online environment.

Step 10: Invest and Be Patient

While the stock market's valuation of dot-coms may vary considerably, it is also evident that brands need to be nurtured and managed over time. Careful investment, long-term patience, and the ability to focus on the long run are critical. Both environments require long-term investments in a consistent, compelling message. While it could be argued that online brands have the potential to generate loyalty more quickly—due principally to the newness of the experience for many consumers—both environments require significant long-term investment (Exhibit 6.9 illustrates the ten steps).

A Framework for Branding

Exhibit 6.10 illustrates a simple categorization scheme for brands. On the top row, we divide brands into two categories according to whether they were established as traditional or online brands. We subdivide the traditional category into "branding online" and "branding and selling online." We place online brands in two categories: intermediaries and e-commerce sites. We also note that these categorizations can apply to both business-to-business and business-to-consumer sites.

Branding Choices

A firm's online branding choices depend on its communications objectives. Exhibit 6.11 illustrates the types of decisions that influence the ultimate choice of communications elements. In the middle of Exhibit 6.11, we note that a firm can have at least six communications objectives.

Brand Creation

The objective may be to build a new-to-the-world brand name. Under such a scenario, it is likely that the firm will focus on brand awareness rather than brand loyalty. This choice, in turn, would lead to a mix of choices that emphasize brand-name awareness rather than communications that provide detailed information on the brand, such as comparative advertising.

Sales Leads

The company may decide that the Internet will be used to facilitate the sales-lead process. Dell and others have found that their Web presence actually

Key Elements	Offline	Online
1. Clearly define the brand audience	• Limited to manageable number of segments to prevent inconsistent messaging	• Could include larger number of segments, with customer-driven messages
2. Understand the target customer	• Requires understanding of environment and desired purchase and usage experience	• Requires more thorough understanding of desired purchase and usage experience in an interactive environment
3. Identify key leverage points in customer experience	• Buying process is typically a simplified representation of customer segment behavior with static leverage points	• Buying process tends to be more dynamic and flexible
4. Continually monitor competitors	• Requires monitoring of competitor advertisements and activities	• Competitor advertisements and activities can be monitored online
5. Design compelling and complete brand intent	• Brand intent (desired positioning) is designed to address the needs and beliefs of target segments	• Greater opportunity for customization of key messages
6. Execute with integrity	• Strong, positive brands are built up over time	• Online interactions bring in added concerns of security and privacy • Limited familiarity with online brands makes fostering trust more difficult
7. Be consistent over time	• Brand intent guides marketing communication • Image reinforced through variety of offline media	• Brand intent guides marketing communications • With the ability to customize, one customer's brand image may be different from another customer's brand image
8. Establish feedback systems	• Collecting and analyzing customer feedback is more time-consuming	• Sophisticated tools exist for tracking online; allows for anonymous, interactive, and quick feedback
9. Be opportunistic	• Marketing strategy includes plan for sequenced growth and adjustment of brand based on changing customer needs	• Customization for multiple segments and opportunity for early recognition of changing customer needs • Corresponding tailoring of brand intent
10. Invest and be patient	• Building brand awareness requires significant investment • Building brand loyalty takes time offline, especially because early customer receptivity to brands is difficult to assess (and usually involves market research)	• Building brand awareness requires significant investment, especially for competitors who are not first in their category online • Brands have the potential to generate loyalty more quickly, especially if customers are targeted effectively

EXHIBIT 6.9   Similarities and Differences Between Offline and Online Branding

builds qualified leads more quickly and effectively than traditional sales approaches. Hence, in sharp contrast to the view that the salesforce will decrease as the Web expands, this finding suggests that the focus of the salesforce will change from lead generation to "closing the sale."

	Established as Traditional Brand		Established as Online Brand	
	Branding Online	**Branding and Selling Online**	**Intermediary / Vertical Portal**	**e-Commerce**
Business to Consumer	Ragu	American Airlines	Monster.com	CDNow
Business to Business	FedEx	Cisco Systems	WebMD	eRoom

EXHIBIT 6.10   Cases of Successful Online Branding Efforts

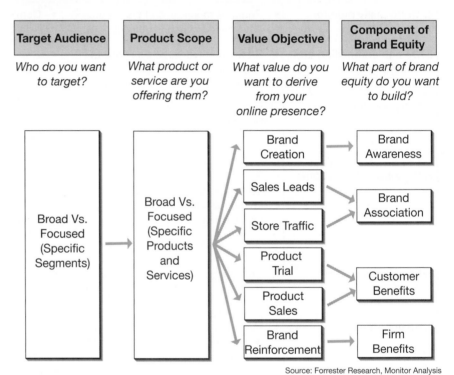

EXHIBIT 6.11   Online Branding Choices

Source: Forrester Research, Monitor Analysis

Store Traffic

The principal objective for some websites is store traffic. That means the effectiveness of the campaign will be judged by the increase in unique visitors.

Product Trial

A fourth objective may be trial usage of the product. For example, *The Wall Street Journal*'s interactive edition provided two weeks of free access to Palm VII users to encourage trial adoption of the newspaper.

Product Sales

The company can also measure the success of a campaign based upon the actual increase in product or service sales.

Brand Reinforcement

Finally, the communications effort might be focused largely on reinforcing a brand image that is already widely accepted in the marketplace. These communications objectives, in turn, can affect brand awareness, brand recognition, and firm/customer benefits. Finally, the particular choice of brand equity that is targeted will naturally lead to the selection of certain communications elements.

Point-Counterpoint

Should Offline Firms Create New Brands or Use Their Existing Brands?

There is considerable debate in the business community on the value of leveraging an existing brand name in the online environment. Simply put, should companies such as Lands' End, Wal-Mart, American Airlines, and Kmart use their existing brand name online, or should they create a new-to-the-world brand name? Consider the following examples:

Wal-Mart Vs. Kmart

Wal-Mart decided to use its existing brand name to launch its website (*www.walmart.com*). Kmart, a top competitor, decided to use a new brand name, BlueLight.com (*www.bluelight.com*). In June 2002, Kmart reversed this decision and changed BlueLight.com to Kmart.com even though the Kmart brand was tarnished by the company's bankruptcy filing earlier in the year. According to a company spokesperson, "One of our new goals is to strengthen ties with our parent company. . . . People still have affection for Kmart and the Kmart name. It's more recognizable than the BlueLight name."[38]

American Airlines Vs. Travelocity

Until 2000, American Airlines's parent, AMR, owned 83 percent of Sabre, a company that provides technology and marketing services for the travel industry. Sabre, in turn, owned more than 80 percent of Travelocity. American saw a clear advantage to using a different brand name in its attempt to become the dominant company in the entire category of travel.

Proponents of the "keep the same brand" school argue that it takes an enormous amount of time and money to build a strong brand name. People in the venture-capital community claim that it costs $50 million to $100 million to launch a new consumer brand on the Web. Hence, it makes a great deal of sense to continue using the offline brand name for the online brand. Second, customers who decide to purchase online can sometimes be assured that services can occur offline (e.g., they can return a product to a physical store, or make a phone call to service centers). Third, it is difficult to uncover interesting new brand names. Fourth, the online and offline brands can have a synergistic effect—one that is greater than either brand operating alone. Finally, target customers will not be confused by brand offerings that appear on new sites (e.g., Kmart brands appearing on BlueLight.com).

Opponents argue that using an existing brand limits the growth of the user base. That is, it is easier for customers to believe that Travelocity or Expedia is the most comprehensive travel site versus their majority stockholders (American Airlines and Microsoft, respectively). Second, it is possible to sign up more partners—potential competitors, collaborators, and others—when a third-party name is used. For example, General Motors, Ford, and DaimlerChrysler selected a new brand name, Covisint, for their B2B exchange. Later, they brought on Renault/Nissan and Delphi. Finally, at one time it was argued that existing offline brands "don't get the Net." Their user interfaces are likely to be less usable, hip, and interesting than those of true dot-com brands.

Comparing Online Branding: American Airlines and Monster

In the following section, we consider two online branding cases—American Airlines and Monster. In order to understand the branding process and show how branding can be differentiated on the Internet (an equally important topic), these companies are compared to average performers in their product categories.

Case Study: American Airlines

American Airlines is an excellent example of a bricks-and-mortar company that increased brand recognition and cemented customer loyalty by successfully taking its brand online. American had been a pioneer in the industry since developing the Sabre computer-reservation system in the 1960s and initiating the first frequent-flier program in the 1980s.

Overview of Online Branding Efforts

On May 17, 1995, American Airlines became the first airline to establish a website. It is now one of the top airline sites in terms of unique visitors and awards. By March 2002, it was logging more than 4 million unique visitors per month and was one of the top 10 online travel destinations. On peak days, it receives upward of 375,000 visits, and the site boasts more than 2.5 million active users. In May 2002, American was ranked among the top three airline carriers, according to an index based on five dimensions of online consumer behavior: number of unique visitors, usage frequency, customer loyalty, online sales, and online growth.[39] Also that month, American redesigned and relaunched its website to expand personalization options.

A key to American's success in creating an online brand has been its ability to differentiate itself from competitors by consistently being first (see Exhibit 6.12). Among the airlines, American was:

- First to have a service-oriented website (May 1995)
- First to launch an e-mail service of discounted fares (March 1996)
- First to offer real-time flight information (spring 1996)
- First to offer flight information on competitors (spring 1996)
- First to offer airline reservations online (June 1996)
- First to offer paperless upgrade coupons and stickers (spring 1997)
- First to send e-mail confirmation of itinerary and ticket purchase (fall 1997)
- First to offer high personalization for consumers (June 1998)
- First to receive a BBB privacy seal validating the way it handles customer data (October 1999)
- First airline to partner with AOL to create a rewards program (fall 2000)

American's online strategy and brand are tightly aligned with its offline objectives: to provide the best possible product to the consumer and, in

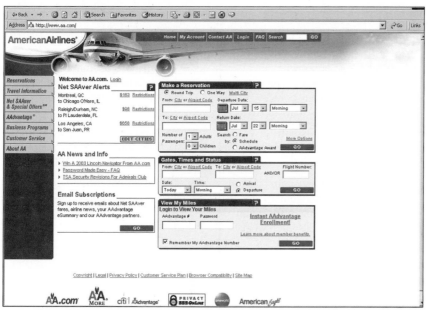

Courtesy of www.americanairlines.com

EXHIBIT 6.12   American Airlines Website

turn, increase the profitability of the company. Online resources not only provide an additional customer base and an additional medium for branding, but also reduce the need for costly phone transactions.

Several other features of the American effort are worth noting. In addition to the American website at *www.aa.com*, American's parent company, AMR Corp., set up Travelocity as a separate online initiative with its own profit-and-loss statement to allow for flexibility and speed of responsiveness. Travelocity constantly attempts to anticipate and fulfill the needs of customers by offering competitive information and fares. It develops and adopts new technologies to respond to customers' needs, including the creation of a single, integrated consumer database and new design features for an interactive, visual appearance. In 2001, by which time it had been spun off from AMR, Travelocity's revenues exceeded $300 million, up 50 percent from the previous year.

Comparison to Average Performer

Exhibit 6.13 compares the American Airlines site to the website of Continental Airlines, using the 10-Step Branding Process. Keep in mind that Continental is by no means the worst performer in the category. Indeed, Forrester Research ranked the site 18th in terms of reach, tickets booked, and revenue—and first in its travel-category ratings. Jupiter Media Metrix (now a part of comScore Networks) ranked Continental 10th in its May 2002 ranking of airlines.

To interpret this exhibit, it is necessary to understand the key at the bottom. The circles are a visual way to express a five-point scale in which a clear circle indicates poor performance (one-point score) and a completely black circle is the highest rating (five-point score).

A quick visual scan of the exhibit reveals that American Airlines systematically outperforms Continental on almost all of the relevant elements. On seven

	American Airlines		Continental	
Key Elements	**Rating**	**Rationale**	**Rating**	**Rationale**
1. *Clearly define the brand audience*	◕	• Targets AAdvantage members—highly profitable and loyal customers familar with travel (and thus more likely to buy tickets online) as well as low-fare seekers	◑	• Targets high-spending business customers, as well as OnePass members and non-OnePass members
2. *Understand the target customer*	●	• Constantly anticipates and innovates to meet the needs of the customer	◕	• Tends to be a "follower" in the industry; late in launching its website (June 1997)
3. *Identify key leverage points in customer experience*	●	• Net SAAvers and new customization program leverage consumers' desire to find cheap fares into transaction by sending out e-mails each week; site features section for current travelers, prospective travelers	◑	• Does not promote e-mail subscriptions on the site
4. *Continually monitor competitors*	●	• If a competitor adopted a technology before American, it was quick to follow	◑	• Tends to follow what competitors are doing at a slower pace, launching "copy cat" initiatives many months after competitor rollout
5. *Design compelling and complete brand intent*	◕	• Focus, streamlining, and ease of use of website all convey American's message of customer needs first	◑	• Unclear target segment (business travelers? OnePass members?) causes lack of clarity with brand intent
6. *Execute with integrity*	◕	• Trust fostered in the offline world carries over into the online world	◕	• Trust fostered in the offline world carries over into the online world, with extensive information for members on privacy and use of provided information
7. *Be consistent over time*	●	• Although constantly innovating new technologies and features, stays true to "something special online"	◕	• Consistent over time but does not stand out
8. *Establish feedback systems*	●	• Customer contact offered as a service at the top of each page and customer service offered as a specific menu item	●	• Very easy to access, prominent feature for obtaining customer feedback on the website
9. *Be opportunistic*	●	• Leader in its industry in innovation and development	◔	• Follower in the industry
10. *Invest and be patient*	●	• Invests significantly in technology for the future	◑	• Has a tendency to wait too long to make changes competitors make to their sites

○ = Very Low   ◔ = Low   ◑ = Moderate   ◕ = High   ● = Very High

EXHIBIT 6.13   American Airlines—Assessment of Key Branding Elements

of the elements, American has a "very high" score, while Continental received this score for only one element. A few particular elements are worth examining in depth. With respect to the target audience, American's website clearly targets its frequent-flier group; Continental's target client base is less clear. While American tends to be an innovator, Continental is a consistent laggard. One key leverage point for American is the Net SAAver Fares program. American's early debut of an e-mail newsletter for last-minute fare discounts enabled it to grow a user base very quickly. While Continental eventually followed with a similar e-mail discount program, the late entry led to significantly lower subscription rates.

Overall, American has projected a more consistent brand image over time. It prominently brands its frequent-flier program and its e-mail newsletter. It has invested in its key constituent base—the business traveler. It has provided consistent technology and customer-facing innovation. Finally, with respect to brand recognition, the American website receives high marks for relevancy, distinctiveness, consistency, and memorability (see Exhibit 6.14).

Case Study: Monster

Monster is a good example of an online company that has succeeded by branding itself in both online and offline environments (see Exhibit 6.15). Monster is a metamarket switchboard that offers employment services to jobseekers and employers. For jobseekers, Monster aims to serve as a "lifelong career network," offering not only job and résumé postings but also chats,

Online Branding Best-in-Class

Comparison

American Airlines

Continental

Key Attributes	Rating	Rationale	Rating	Rationale
1. Relevant	●	• Up-to-date flight and gate-check information • Personalized information based on AAdvantage profiles • PDA applications with flight information	◕	• Offers only information for Continental Airlines, but does not offer bookings for rental cars and hotels • Allows travel preferences to be saved in profiles
2. Distinct	●	• Offers highly personalized experience • First to offer tie-in with PDA applications	◕	• Offers extensive online customer service options • Offers customized services for the business traveler
3. Consistent	●	• Portrays an image of "something special online," consistent with its image of offering "something special in the air"	◔	• No key messages online associated closely with the offline campaign
4. Memorable	●	• Provides a unique service others cannot offer (in terms of personalization) • Net SAAver Fares™ is a well-known and effective e-mail marketing tool	◑	• Low use of branding on the site and lack of online/offline message association fail to create a cohesively memorable brand for the consumer

○ = Very Low　　◔ = Low　　◑ = Moderate　　◕ = High　　● = Very High

EXHIBIT 6.14　Assessment of Key Brand Attributes

message boards, and expert advice on career management. For employers, Monster provides value-added solutions such as résumé-skills screening, résumé routing, and real-time recruiting, in addition to access to its database of more than 21 million jobseekers.

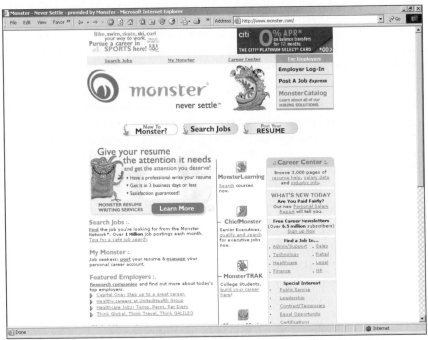

EXHIBIT 6.15   Monster's Homepage

Overview of Branding Efforts

Launched in 1994 as the 454th website in the world, Monster was a true early entrant in the commercial world of the Internet. It boasts more than 50 percent of the "career eyeball minutes" (unique visitors multiplied by average minutes per user per month) on the Web. Its revenues increased from $6.9 million in 1996 to $535.8 million in 2001. The site's traffic—more than 14 million unique visitors in June 2002—puts it among the top 30 most visited sites and translates into a reach of 13.5 percent of all U.S. Internet users. By the first quarter of 2002, Monster had 16.5 million résumés on file and more than 800,000 job listings.[40]

Some have argued that a large part of Monster's early success was its ability to brand itself both online and offline. Its offline advertising and associated Monster logo provided a distinctive branding message. Its first Super Bowl ad showed young children discussing their desired futures: "I want to file all day," "I want to claw my way up to middle management," and "I want to have a brown nose." These provided a clear message of what Monster could deliver—good jobs, challenging careers, and rapid advancement.

These somewhat risky ads produced immediate results. In the 24 hours following the campaign's debut, 2.2 million job searches were conducted on Monster—a 450 percent increase in traffic from the previous week. A considerable jump in job searches also followed the 2000, 2001, and 2002 Super Bowl ads. In the 24 hours following the 2002 Super Bowl ad blitz, the number of jobseekers visiting Monster increased by 93 percent; the number of résumé submissions increased by 84 percent, and the number of page visits increased by 167 percent.

The jobs posted on Monster cover a wide range of industries and all levels of experience. To further its branding efforts, Monster formed an alliance with MSN and a $100 million four-year agreement with AOL to be the online service provider's exclusive career-information provider.

Comparison to Average Performer

Exhibit 6.16 compares Monster to HotJobs on the 10 steps of branding. At first glance, it is apparent that Monster is outperforming HotJobs on a number of elements—although the gaps in performance are not as wide as the gaps between American and Continental. Indeed, HotJobs is strong in a number of areas, including customer focus, specialization by entry-level positions, and privacy screens/policy. It is comparatively weaker on interactivity, the compelling nature of its brand intent, and opportunity for feedback. Similar to Monster, it is clearly willing to take advertising risks—both with Super Bowl ad placement and with its ad copy (e.g., "all the hottest jobs at all the hottest companies").

Exhibit 6.17 shows a comparison of Monster and HotJobs on four brand-recognition criteria. The brands are similar on relevancy and distinctiveness, but Monster outperforms HotJobs on consistency and memorability.

MarketWatch.com Market Communications and Branding

As discussed in earlier chapters, MarketWatch.com tries to appeal to a broad audience interested in financial information. In order to reach that audience and to communicate its marketing and branding messages, it uses a number of methods.

Market Communications for MarketWatch.com

Exhibit 6.18 uses the marketing communications framework to classify the marketing methods into four categories: general approaches, traditional mass marketing, personalized marketing, and direct marketing.

In terms of general online approaches, MarketWatch.com aggressively advertises on sites with broad reach, such as Yahoo and AOL. In addition, it is a recommended link on the CBS site and the sites of CBS partners. More significantly, an increasingly successful way of communicating its message online is through licensing its content to other sites, generating both revenue and increased brand exposure. Licensing revenue grew from 21 percent of total revenue in 1999 to 53 percent in 2001. Licensing partners include industry-leading financial organizations such as E*Trade, Fidelity, and Morgan Stanley. Additionally, MarketWatch.com has a number of strategic distribution relationships. One example is AOL. MarketWatch.com is the premier provider of business and financial news for AOL's Personal Finance channel, with links on the AOL site leading to MarketWatch.com. In addition to agreements with

Online Branding Best-in-Class

Monster.com

Comparison

HotJobs.com

Key Elements	Rating	Rationale	Rating	Rationale
1. Clearly define the brand audience	◕	• Within the employer market, targets all types of companies, from startups to large corporations	◕	• Appeals to a wide range of job-seekers, but specializes in intern and entry-level positions
2. Understand the target customer	●	• Offers highly personalized services for jobseekers, addresses security concerns, and offers value-added services (résumé help, advice, interactive communication with other jobseekers)	●	• First to offer privacy feature that allows jobseekers to select which companies have access to their résumés
3. Identify key leverage points in customer experience	●	• Provides interactive career information for customers who are not necessarily "looking," thus increasing the probability that they will become jobseekers	●	• Allows recruiting process to become internal through HotJobs.com and its proprietary Softshoe technology, eliminating concerns about adding an additional venue for recruiting
4. Continually monitor competitors	◔	• Currently a leader in providing unique services to its consumers, but lacks some features that competitors have	◐	• Adopts successful features of the Monster.com site, but usually on a lesser scale
5. Design compelling and complete brand intent	●	• Message of "there's a better job out there" combined with diversified strategic alliances and "intern-to-CEO" strategy to convey the idea that Monster.com can find you that better job	◐	• Message of "all the hottest jobs at all the hottest companies" evolved to message of "onward, upward"
6. Execute with integrity	◔	• Offers password and ID protection, as well as some ability to selectively decide when and where your résumé can be seen	◐	• Offers most specialized security measures for individual users (prevents current employers from viewing résumé)
7. Be consistent over time	◔	• "There's a better job out there" message evolved to "job good, life good" to "never settle"; consistently uses humor; backs up television advertising with consistent approaches in other media	◐	• Recent "Hottest Hand on the Web" campaign different from past branding messages
8. Establish feedback systems	●	• Offers extensive feedback system for users, allowing users to even select categories of information/feedback	◕	• Also offers feedback mechanism for users, although less specialized
9. Be opportunistic	●	• Partners with firms that could potentially be competitors rather than trying to eliminate competition	◕	• Took a risk with Super Bowl advertising, even without a compelling ad campaign, to raise brand awareness
10. Invest and be patient	◔	• Willing to invest heavily in the off-line world to gain brand recognition	◔	• Also willing to invest in the offline world to gain brand recognition

○ = Very Low   ◔ = Low   ◐ = Moderate   ◕ = High   ● = Very High

EXHIBIT 6.16   Assessment of Key Branding Elements

		Online Branding Best-in-Class *Monster.com*		Comparison *HotJobs.com*
Key Attributes	**Rating**	**Rationale**	**Rating**	**Rationale**
1. Relevant	●	• For jobseekers: Provides information for individuals regardless of whether they are actively pursuing a new position, including career information and chats with other members on various career topics	●	• For jobseekers: Provides information geared more specifically for those individuals who are seeking positions
2. Distinct	●	• For jobseekers: Aids in résumé building, personalization with "My Monster" pages, and enhanced privacy options; also offers opportunity for interactive communication with other members	●	• For jobseekers: Allows selection of companies that view posted résumés
3. Consistent	●	• Recent partnerships have been consistent with Monster.com's aim to provide the most diverse set of individuals with the most diverse set of employment opportunities	◐	• Campaigns have not been consistent since the company's beginning
4. Memorable	●	• Witty and award-winning offline advertising has allowed Monster.com to cement itself as the best-known career site on the Web	◐	• Although also one of the most well-known career services on the Web, has not been as successful as Monster.com in creating a uniquely memorable advertising campaign and message

EXHIBIT 6.17   Assessment of Key Brand Attributes

other parties, MarketWatch.com offers the majority of its content and tools for free, encouraging users to explore the site and to return to it regularly.

MarketWatch.com also uses a variety of traditional mass-marketing media to promote its brand. In connection with its formation in 1997, MarketWatch.com entered into a license agreement with CBS, under which the website was renamed CBS MarketWatch.com. MarketWatch.com reporting, logo, and domain name have been included on the *CBS Evening News* with Dan Rather, *CBS This Morning, The Early Show,* and on the news programming of the CBS Television Network and its affiliated television stations. Additionally, Market-Watch.com has its own weekly show, *CBS MarketWatch Weekend,* which reaches 85 percent of all U.S. households. It also provides financial content to CBS News-Path, a CBS news service that supplies CBS News video to more than 200 CBS-affiliated television stations for use in their news programs. This exposure to the MarketWatch.com brand gives it a huge credibility boost and invaluable brand exposure compared to that of its competitors. In radio, MarketWatch.com contributes content that is aired through the Westwood One syndication company across the country (208 stations, including the top 25 markets in the nation, reaching about 650,000 listeners in an average quarter-hour).

In addition to placing ads in business trade journals, MarketWatch.com communicates through the print medium by providing financial content to newspapers, such as the *Daily News Express.* This allows MarketWatch.com to

Drill-Down

Brand Loyalty

Shot in gritty black and white, the scene is bleak: A young child, his expression blank and humorless, stares into the camera and declares, "I want to be forced into early retirement."

Remember the ad? Even though it aired during the 1999 Super Bowl, many do. Like other Internet players, Monster is betting that memorable ads like this one and the ones it ran during the next three Super Bowls will translate into page hits, revenue, and, ultimately, staying power as an online brand. But despite the success of the Monster Super Bowl ads—each seen by some 100 million people and each triggering a sharp rise in traffic to the Monster.com website—Monster is hardly home free. When it comes to establishing and maintaining dominant brands on the Web or offline, even companies that break fast out of the branding gate face tough competition.

The first problem: battling for consumer mind share against successful established brands with deep pockets for spending on advertising. The *Advertising Age* list of 100 leading national advertisers in 2001 starts off with powerhouses such as General Motors, Procter & Gamble, Ford, PepsiCo, and Pfizer. No Internet-only company even makes the list. A 2002 Harris Interactive poll also shows the power of superbrands. In the eight years that Harris has been surveying consumers on the "best brand," Sony has occupied the top spot five times and has never been lower than third. Ford has always been in the top four brands. Others on the list are giants Dell, Coca-Cola, General Electric, and Pepsi-Cola. Tide, Honda, and General Motors made the list of top 10 for the first time.[41] In an earlier Harris survey of online brands, consumers were well acquainted with a few online stars—Amazon, eBay, and Egghead topped the name-recognition list—but were unable to name a single Web retailer in the insurance, fitness, or online electronics categories, despite a slew of advertising for companies that fit the bill.

The 2002 Harris poll underlined a strong link between corporate reputation and brand image; the majority of respondents said that reputation and what they knew about the company behind the brand was very important. An earlier Harris poll in 2001 found that respondents' experience with a company's products, management reputation, and customer service website or department explained why people were willing to trust some brands and not others.[42] No wonder that new brands find it hard to establish recognition and esteem.

If a company establishes its brand successfully, that means it has conquered the branding problem and is here to stay for the indefinite future, right? Maybe not. A study done by Peter Golder, a marketing professor at New York University's Stern School of Business, reexamined a 1923 benchmark NYU study of top brands in 100 product groups and showed that only 23 were still leaders in 1997.

"I'm not here to bash brands. I certainly agree that they're important," Golder said. "What my study suggests is that the staying power of brands is a lot less than what people may believe." In the dot-com world, he said, the lack of staying power is particularly relevant as Internet companies try to build brand awareness quickly in a busy marketplace. Golder suggested an alternative tack: "In the Internet environment, there's confusion over brand awareness versus brand equity. I think the primary emphasis of too many Internet companies is on just getting people to be aware of their name. But it's the equity that resides in the brand that ensures success."

So, if you can get consumers to your site, but have difficulty filling orders or providing customer service, you can kiss those branding dollars goodbye. Golder said, "If the customer's experience at the site is consistent with your advertising message, then branding works. But if it's inconsistent, it'll ruin whatever efforts you've made." If awareness is bolstered with equity, it's time and money well spent. "With branding, people build associations. If the entire usage experience for the customer reinforces those good associations, then you'll have staying power in an Internet environment that's constantly evolving."

Audience Focus

	Direct (Offline)	**Personalized** (Online)
Individualized		■ Permission marketing e-mails sent to groups from opt-in lists
Broad	**Traditional Mass Marketing** **Television** – Advertising on CBS – Mentions and scrolls during CBS shows – *CBS MarketWatch Weekend* – Contributions to CBS NewsPath **Outdoor Advertising** – Outdoor placards – Bus advertisements in target cities **Radio** – Contributions to Westwood One Network – Spots during NFL radio broadcasts – Mentions on CBS-owned and operated radio stations **Print** – Limited ads in trade journals **Conferences** – Participation in online finance, online journalism, and Internet-related conferences	**General Approaches** ■ Advertising on heavily trafficked websites (e.g., Yahoo, AOL) ■ Licensing content to industry-leading financial organizations (e.g., E*Trade) ■ Strategic distribution relationships (e.g., Yahoo, AOL, Quicken.com) ■ Advertising on CBS site and other CBS Internet partners (e.g., CBS SportsLine, CBS HealthWatch) ■ Advertisements on targeted sites (e.g., other online financial sites) ■ Free information on site
	Offline	Online

Communication Needs

EXHIBIT 6.18   MarketWatch.com Market Communications

target people interested in financial news and who have varying degrees of knowledge of financial concepts. MarketWatch.com also markets itself offline through bus advertisements in target cities and by participating in conferences related to online finance issues.

MarketWatch.com does not personalize its marketing communications, online or offline. It does, however, perform online permission marketing using opt-in e-mail lists. As it collects more information on its users, it is likely that it will be able to better target its marketing communications to individual users.

Key Branding Elements and Brand Attributes for MarketWatch.com

Earlier in this chapter, we introduced a 10-step process for building a successful brand. In Exhibit 6.19, we assess the performance of MarketWatch.com using these steps. We can make some interesting conclusions by looking at areas in which MarketWatch.com performs very strongly and in which there seems to be the most room for improvement. MarketWatch.com's ability to execute its branding message of providing "the story behind the numbers" with integrity, through its staff of experienced journalists and its association with CBS News, makes the MarketWatch.com brand stand out from its competitors, many of which do not have the staff to generate their own financial content. The opportunistic nature of its marketing strategy—communicating its branding message across multiple media—has allowed MarketWatch.com to broaden its reach and appeal to new target groups, such as people who are not as knowledgeable but are still interested in financial news and analysis ("seekers" and "dabblers" segments). Furthermore, the close monitoring of its competitors allows MarketWatch.com to tailor its branding message so that it remains unique and memorable in a very competitive market.

There are also some branding elements that MarketWatch.com might be able to improve. By trying to appeal to a very wide audience (including savvy investors, people interested in financial news and analysis, and people new to financial concepts), MarketWatch.com may be trying to satisfy the needs of too many types of users, leading to a potential loss of focus. Also, even though the decision to change its brand message to "get the story behind the numbers" from "your eye on the market" was successful in expanding the target audience, it may have been confusing to savvy investors who were used to a site that focused on providing breaking news. MarketWatch.com may need to evaluate which of the two groups (savvy investors versus people marginally interested in financial news) it needs to target and focus its efforts on that group.

In terms of key brand attributes, the MarketWatch.com brand message is both distinct and memorable compared to those of its competitors. Early TV ads, which began with the announcement of a market result then explained the unlikely events that led to that result, bolstered the memorability of the MarketWatch.com brand. Competitor sites did not communicate messages that were nearly as catchy or as clear.

Finally, the MarketWatch.com brand is highly relevant. It determines the needs of distinct user groups for financial information and guidance, and addresses them with different levels of sophistication. Exhibit 6.20 includes a detailed assessment of the MarketWatch.com brand, along with the key brand attributes, and helps explain its popularity and success.

MarketWatch.com

Key Elements	Rating	Rationale
1. Clearly define the brand audience	(Moderate)	• Three target groups cover a wide range of the population: savvy investors, financial information seekers, and "dabblers" (users with little financial knowledge)
2. Understand the target customer	(High)	• Understands the different needs of savvy investors versus less sophisticated investors and provides offerings accordingly
3. Identify customer leverage points in customer experience	(High)	• Focuses primarily on providing breaking news and analysis, rather than enabling investors to make transactions • Has developed a community that shares knowledge and encourages frequent returns to the site
4. Continually monitor competitors	(Very High)	• Continuously tracks studies on demographics, behavior, and brand awareness of its users versus competition
5. Design compelling and complete brand intent	(High)	• Message of "get the story behind the numbers" captures most of the value offered to users—relevant and in-depth financial information and analysis; it does not fully capture the tools and education that the site offers
6. Execute with integrity	(Very High)	• The message of the CBS MarketWatch.com brand is trustworthiness; its credibility is enhanced by the association with CBS News and its staff of over 70 experienced journalists and editors
7. Be consistent over time	(High)	• Initial branding message was "your eye on the market"; switched to "get the story behind the numbers" in 1999; the new message was designed to appeal to a broader user group
8. Establish feedback systems	(High)	• Rigorously tested site and message effectiveness with focus groups halfway through the new marketing message campaign, at a time when the market was in turmoil; results were highly positive
9. Be opportunistic	(Very High)	• Establishing CBS MarketWatch.com brand over a number of different media, including Web TV, Radio, print, and wireless
10. Invest and be patient	(High)	• Investing a large percentage of the company budget in sales and marketing activities—patiently waiting to become profitable, even with a market that currently demands profitability

○ = Very Low   ◔ = Low   ◑ = Moderate   ◕ = High   ● = Very High

EXHIBIT 6.19   Assessment of Key Branding Elements for MarketWatch.com

Key Attributes	Rating	MarketWatch.com
		Rationale
1. Relevant	●	• Directly addresses the needs of different user groups for savvy investors, providing real-time quotes, in-depth analysis and tools; for financial information seekers and users new to financial concepts, provides headline news and analysis as well as education tools
2. Distinct	●	• Brand message "get the story behind the numbers" is distinct from competitor messages; it focuses on the unique MarketWatch.com capability of providing new-to-the-world, relevant, in-depth content
3. Consistent	◖	• The initial brand message was "your eye on the market," which changed to "get the story behind the numbers" in mid-1999; the intent was to appeal to a wider group of users, shifting the focus toward less sophisticated investors and people new to financial information • The main offering message of providing quality market analysis has remained relatively consistent
4. Memorable	●	• The Marketwatch.com brand message is highly memorable • Early on, this was aided by appealing and memorable TV advertisements, which started with the end market result and traced it back to the unlikely events that led to it • As a result, the CBS MarketWatch.com brand rose 10 points in aided awareness in one year

○ = Very Low   ◔ = Low   ◐ = Moderate   ◕ = High   ● = Very High

EXHIBIT 6.20   Assessment of Key Brand Attributes for MarketWatch.com

Summary

1. What are the four categories of market communications?

Market communications can be categorized into a simple two-by-two framework based upon the audience focus (broad versus individual) and communication media (offline versus online). The four categories of communications are direct, personalized, traditional mass marketing, and general online approaches.

2. What constitutes a "good" brand?

Good brands provide a clear message to the market about the core offering, the wrap-arounds, and communications. All provide a signal about the functional offering and are simultaneously differentiated by their emotional, symbolic, and experiential benefits. Good brands provide benefits for both the firm and target customers.

3. What is the 10-Step Branding Process?

The 10-Step Branding Process can be broken down into two general stages: building the value cluster and the integrated campaign (see Exhibit 6.8). The steps are as follows:
a.   Clearly define the brand audience.
b.   Understand the target customer.
c.   Identify key leverage points in target customer experience.
d.   Continually monitor competitors.
e.   Design compelling and complete brand intent.
f.   Execute with integrity.
g.   Be consistent over time.
h.   Establish feedback systems.

i. Be opportunistic.

j. Invest and be patient.

4. How does online branding compare between American Airlines and Continental Airlines?

Exhibit 6.13 illustrates that American Airlines systematically outperforms Continental Airlines on almost all of the relevant elements. On seven of the elements, American Airlines received a "very high" score, while Continental received this score for only one element. American consistently innovates in e-commerce.

5. What are the arguments for and against leveraging an offline brand into the online environment?

Arguments for the use of existing brands are that they (a) are known, (b) are less costly to develop, (c) provide assurance to the target segment, and (d) provide an integrated online and offline experience. Opponents argue that using an existing brand limits the growth of the user base. Second, it is possible to sign up more partners—potential competitors, collaborators, and others—when a third-party name is used. Additionally, with a new brand it may be easier to develop an innovative, up-to-date image.

1. Go to the finance page on Yahoo (finance.yahoo.com). How are companies using the page to advertise themselves? When you click on "Home Loans," what companies are advertising? Which are sponsoring the site? Now go to Google. Search for the word "mortgage." Which companies are at the top of the list? Have any of the same companies from the Yahoo page sponsored links on Google?

2. Go to Nike.com. Has Nike kept its website branding efforts consistent with its offline branding efforts?

3. Go to the websites for BMW and Saturn. Evaluate them both on the four key brand attributes. Does one of them have a stronger brand than the other? If so, on what attributes?

Exercises

branding	banner advertisement	brand equity
market communications	permission marketing	strength of association
general online communications	viral marketing	valence
personalized online communications	affiliate programs	uniqueness
traditional mass marketing	direct marketing	10-Step Branding Process
direct communications	telemarketing	

Key Terms

[1]Amazon.com Inc. SEC Form 10-K, filed 24 January 2002.

[2]Rex Briggs and Nigel Hollis, "Advertising on the Web: Is There Response Before Click-Through?" *Journal of Advertising Research* 37, no. 2 (1997): 33.

[3]Jane Black, "Online Advertising: It's Just the Beginning," *BusinessWeek Online*, 12 July 2001 (URL: http://www.businessweek.com/technology/content/jul2001/tc20010712_790.htm).

[4]Ibid.

[5]Michael Pastore and Christopher Saunders, "Ad Spending Down, Use of Larger Ads Increases," *CyberAtlas*, 8 March 2002. (URL: http://cyberatlas.internet.com/markets/advertising/article/0,,5941_987871,00.html).

[6]JupiterResearch, "Email Marketing: Redefining Communication Tactics to Increase Customer Value," *Jupiter Media Metrix Study*, 16 October 2001.

[7]Ibid.

[8]"DoubleClick 2001 Consumer Email Study: Executive Summary," *DoubleClick.com*, October 2001 (URL: http://www.doubleclick.com/us/knowledge/documents/research/dc_consumer_email_0111.pdf).

[9]"Case Study: Email Campaign Generates More Revenue Than Forecasted!" *DoubleClick*, 2002 (URL: http://www.doubleclick.com/us/knowledge/documents/case_studies/cs_sony_style_0204.pdf).

[10]Jeffrey Rayport, "The Virus of Marketing," *Fast Company*, no. 6, December 1996/January 1997: 68.

[11]Joseph L. Butt, Jr., "Universal Escape Webcams Turn Images into Marketing," *The Forrester Report* (October 1999): 18.

Endnotes

[12]"Yahoo and SBC Expand Alliance to Include Strategic Sales Relationship for Yahoo! Yellow Pages," Press Release, 8 July 2002 (URL: http://docs.yahoo.com/docs/pr/release994.html).

[13]Rich Thomaselli, "Internet Ad Revenue Declined 12% in 2001," *AdAge.com*, 24 May 2002 (URL: http://www.adage.com/news.cms?newsId=34893).

[14]Christopher Saunders, "Web Ad Industry Facing Down Problems," *CyberAtlas*, 22 March 2002 (URL: http://cyberatlas.internet.com/markets/advertising/article/0,,5941_996401,00.html).

[15]J. Segrich, "Analyst Report: L90 Inc.: Initiating Coverage,"CIBC Worldmarkets Corporation (25 February 2000): 5.

[16]Alex Salkever, "Growing Pains for E-mail Marketers," *BusinessWeek Online*, 1 March 2002 (URL: http://www.businessweek.com/technology/content/mar2002/tc2002031_2745.htm).

[17]Cisco Systems Inc., "Cisco Realizes Significant Productivity Gains for FY 2001," *News@Cisco*, 6 December, 2001 (URL: http://newsroom.cisco.com/dlls/ts_120601.html).

[18]"Amazon's Amazing Ambition," *Economist*, 26 February 2000, 24.

[19]"Case Study: DARTMail Personalization Increases Email Efficiency for FedEx," *DoubleClick.com*, 2002 (URL: http://www.doubleclick.com/us/knowledge/documents/case_studies/cs_fedex_0203.pdf).

[20]"NetP™ Increases Musician's Friend Web and Catalog Sales by 60%," *Net Perceptions Case Studies & Interviews*, 2002. (URL: http://www.netperceptions.com/case-mf.php).

[21]Net Perceptions, "Net Perceptions to Provide Realtime Ad Targeting to ZDNET," Press Release, 4 January 2000 (URL: http://www.corporate-ir.net/ireye/ir_site.zhtml?ticker=netp&script=413&layout=-6&item_id=67053).

[22]CMGI Inc., "MyWeather Selects Engage Ad Management Technology for Delivery of Personalized Ads into MyWeathers Online Weather Service," Press Release, 7 May 2002 (URL: www.cmgi.com/news/prdata/MyWeatherselectsEngage.shtml).

[23]Robert Hof, Heather Green, and Linda Himelstein, "Now It's Your Web," *BusinessWeek*, 5 October 1998.

[24]Heather Green, "The Information Gold Mine," *Business Week*, 26 July 1999.

[25]Hof, Green, and Himelstein, "Now It's Your Web."

[26]Michael Pastore, "Ad Spending to Rebound, Digital Marketing to Soar," *CyberAtlas*, 8 August 2001 (URL: http://cyberatlas.internet.com/markets/advertising/print/0,,5941_862241,00.html).

[27]Leslie Kaufman, "Web Retailers Empty Wallets on Advertising," *The New York Times*, 2 November 1999.

[28]Alice Z. Cuneo, "Amazon.com Returns to TV Advertising," *AdAge.com*, 1 July 2002 (URL: www.adage.com/news.cms?newsId=35247).

[29]Moon Ihlwan and Gerry Khermouch, "Samsung: No Longer Unsung," *BusinessWeek*, 6 August 2001 (URL: http://businessweek.com:/print/magazine/content/01_32/b3744015.htm?mainwindow).

[30]Andrea Petersen, "Getting Noticed: You Can Have the Greatest E-Commerce Site on the Web. The Trick Is to Get People to Come to It," *The Wall Street Journal*, 12 July 1999.

[31]"William Shatner Takes Center Stage in New Priceline.com Advertising Campaign Launching," *Newstream.com*, February 2002 (URL: http://www.newstream.com/us/story_pub.shtml?story_id=5183).

[32]Leslie Kaufman, "Web Retailers Empty Wallets," *The New York Times*, 2 November 1999.

[33]Joanna Glasner, "Rising from the eToys Ashes," *Wired*, 22 October 2001 (URL: http://wired.com/news/print/0,1294,47745,00.html).

[34]TMP Worldwide Inc., "Monster's 'Job Good. Life Good.' Advertising Campaign Awarded Gold EFFIE; Monster Receives Second Golden EFFIE," Press Release, 6 June 2002.

[35]Functional benefits capture the intrinsic advantages of the product. They tend to be correlated with the features or attributes of the product. Symbolic benefits relate to social approval and personal expression. Experiential benefits relate to what the product feels like to use, and tends to capture various sensory pleasures. See the following article for further elaboration: Choong W. Park, Bernard J. Jaworski, and Deborah J. MacInnis, "Strategic Brand Concept-Image Management," *Journal of Marketing* 50, no. 4 (October 1986): 135–45.

[36]Kevin Lane Keller, *Strategic Brand Management* (Upper Saddle River, NJ: Prentice-Hall, Inc., 1998), 43.

[37]David Aaker, *Building Strong Brands* (New York: The Free Press, 1996), 7–8.

[38]Michael Singer, "ISP: Bluelight Fades to Favor Kmart," *Internetnews.com*, June 19, 2002 (URL: http://www.internetnews.com/isp-news/article.php/1367911).

[39]JupiterResearch, "Southwest Leads First-Ever Commercial Airline Index Based on Online Consumer Behavior," Press Release, 30 May 2002 (URL: http://www.jmm.com/xp/jmm/press/2002/pr_053002.xml).

[40]This information can be found in two press releases from TMP Worldwide Inc.: "TMP Worldwide Announces Fourth Quarter and Full-Year 2001 Results," Press Release, 19 February 2002 (URL: http://pr.tmp.com/ireye/ir_site.zhtml?ticker=PR_131001&script=410&layout=-6&item_id=269284); and "Monster Leads Career Category During Month of June; Monster Garners 52.8 Percent of Career Eyeball Minutes According to Nielsen//NetRatings," 17 July 2002 (URL: http://pr.tmp.com/ireye/ir_site.zhtml?ticker=PR_131001&script=410&layout=-6&item_id=315828).

[41]Humphrey Taylor, "Sony Retains Number One Position in The Harris Poll Annual "Best Brand" Survey for Third Year in Row," *HarrisInteractive*, 17 July 2002 (URL: http://www.harrisinteractive.com/harris_poll/index.asp?PID=311).

[42]Harris Interactive, "Why Some Companies Are Trusted and Others Are Not: Personal Experience and Knowledge of Company More Important Than Glitz," Press Release, 20 June 2001 (URL: www.harrisinteractive.com/news/index.asp?NewsID=319).

Implementation

CASELET: CISCO'S HUMAN ASSETS

In the high-tech hothouse that was Silicon Valley in the late 1990s, new companies, technologies, and business plans proliferated. Not quite so plentiful, however, was the talent to implement those grand designs—the people needed to actually lead the companies, build the machines, write the code.

As a result, many would-be worldbeaters struggled. One exception: Cisco Systems. The San Jose–based Internet-infrastructure giant seemed to understand better than most the importance of building an effective organization. What's more, it proved unusually adept at doing it.

Among Cisco's hiring tactics: recruiting at nontraditional events such as art fairs and microbrewery festivals; linking to websites frequented by restless or disaffected techies, such as Travelocity and Dilbert.com; and pairing online jobseekers with a volunteer "friend" from within Cisco. Once hired, new employees were immediately funneled into a "Fast Start" program that did everything from ensuring their phones and e-mail were up and running when they arrived to pairing them with an experienced peer "buddy." And the company worked to create an employee-friendly, results-oriented culture—for instance, making all offices the same size and reserving windowed offices for nonsenior staff. (Senior management got the interior cubicles.)

Cisco was also noted for acquiring smaller companies, not only for their technologies but for their engineering talent. And once that talent was on board, Cisco went to great lengths to help it fit in: Once again, integration teams and one-on-one "buddies" were mobilized to smooth the transition, both structurally and culturally.

As a result of its efforts, Cisco emerged as a leader in both hiring and retaining talent. In one of the hottest job markets on the planet, the company was able to bring on upward of 1,000 new employees every three months. And employee turnover—including employees from acquired companies—was less than 10 percent in a region where the average was three times that.

With the recent tech-sector meltdown, Cisco has suffered its share of underwater stock options and employee layoffs. Still, the company remains a fixture on Fortune *magazine's annual list of the "100 Best Companies to Work For." At a time when many e-commerce companies are struggling to keep both morale and productivity up, Cisco offers a lesson in how to treat employees.*

This chapter was coauthored by Jeffrey Rayport and Bernie Jaworski, with contributions by Katherine Jocz and JoAnn Kienzle.

235

PLEASE CONSIDER THE FOLLOWING QUESTIONS AS YOU READ THIS CHAPTER:

1. What factors are involved in successful strategy implementation?

2. What are the implementation challenges for online firms?

3. What human-assets issues must firms be concerned with?

4. What are the different types of processes that firms must develop?

5. What are the advantages of the two types of hybrid organizational structures?

6. What systems might online firms be concerned with?

7. What kind of culture is best for e-commerce companies?

8. How has the role of leadership changed for online companies?

9. Why are partnerships so prevalent for online firms?

INTRODUCTION

Once a company has attracted customers to its website, it must deliver the total customer experience that the brand communication has promised. Not only must the customer interface work as expected, but the company must also be able to correctly execute transactions initiated through the customer interface.

For example, if a customer orders flowers through the company's website to be delivered to a certain address on Valentine's Day, then the company cannot make any mistake with the delivery of the flowers. Potential execution mistakes could include incorrectly processing the credit card payment, delivering to the wrong person or on the wrong date, delivering the flowers without the correct accompanying note, or delivering the wrong sort of bouquet. In short, how the firm implements its strategy has a direct bearing on the customer's total experience and his or her beliefs about the brand. It also has a major effect on customer retention and, therefore, on the lifetime value of the customer base.

This chapter reviews how a firm implements its online strategy. Recall that in Chapter 4 we introduced the concept of a resource system. In Chapter 5, we considered the Web interface choices that brought the firm's business model to life, and in Chapter 6 we discussed the market communications and branding decisions that would draw customers to the website. However, a usable interface and strong brand are not sufficient to deliver the brand to target customers; rather, the firm must build the resource system defined in the business model. It must hire and train the right talent and build systems that will move the physical (or digital) products from suppliers to the end customer.

The purpose of this chapter is to introduce the firm-specific infrastructure that must be created and configured to achieve the firm's strategic goals. There are many ways to think of the ingredients of this implementation or resource system. In this chapter, we introduce a resource system with seven parts: human assets, processes, organizational structure, systems, culture, leadership, and partnerships.

We begin our discussion by introducing the general implementation framework. We consider why implementation is important and the consequences of poor implementation. We then describe each of the resource system's seven key components. We conclude with an application of these concepts to Market-Watch.com.

A Framework for Implementation: The Resource System

Exhibit 7.1 provides an implementation framework that includes the seven factors needed to build a strong and enduring resource system: human assets, processes, organizational structure, systems, culture, leadership, and partnerships. Although we discuss those components in detail later in the chapter, we begin with a short overview of each one.

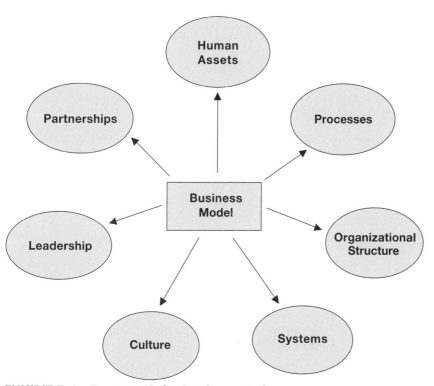

EXHIBIT 7.1   Framework for Implementation

The term **human assets** refers to how employees are developed, managed, and retained. More attention has been paid to human resources management since the collapse of Internet stocks and the associated recent uncertainty by employees regarding stock options. These forces placed enormous pressure on organizations to nurture their most important resource—people.

Processes outline how particular tasks are accomplished in organizations. Certainly, firms have the option of telling employees to do the work however they think best. However, this would be enormously inefficient and would decrease the possibility of continuous improvement (because the processes are not institutionalized in the organization). Rather, it makes most sense for organizations to identify and rigorously enforce clear processes to direct workers and provide an opportunity for continuous improvement.

Organizational structure is perhaps best understood as the way the firm devises both horizontal and vertical reporting responsibilities. In this section, we focus on whether online operations should be part of a separate organization or whether a company should attempt to integrate all online and offline activities in a single organization.

Next, we turn to the systems that a firm puts in place. We emphasize supply chain management because this area is often very different for online companies. We also discuss compensation systems and technology systems.

The final three components of the framework are culture, leadership, and partnerships. All firms have distinct cultures. The best cultures are ones that provide a sense of meaning to employees and drive the organization toward productivity. Moreover, the best company cultures are often those that are different from others in their industry. Leadership is one of the most well researched but least understood areas of management. In this short section, we review several characteristics of well-managed leadership teams. Finally, we review the importance of partnerships and explain why they are so common in the online environment. Indeed, we argue that partnerships are much more significant for online companies because network effects can be multiplied more easily online.

We conclude this chapter with a discussion of six principles that guide effective implementation. These principles are based on research as well as contemporary writings by well-known CEOs. While these are certainly not the only principles, they do begin to identify the most important areas for senior management to watch as they attempt to win in the market.

The Importance of Successful Implementation

Exhibit 7.2 provides a simple illustration of the importance of successful implementation. On the horizontal axis, we observe two conditions: appropriate and inappropriate strategy. On the vertical axis, we consider both good and poor implementation. When crossed, we can view the following four conditions that can be experienced by firms in the marketplace: success, roulette, trouble, and failure.

In this chapter, we are particularly concerned with conditions that steer firms into the trouble quadrant. A firm in this quadrant has made all the right strategy choices related to the business model, interface, brand, and marketing communications, but its implementation is poor. As a result, the firm will likely perform poorly in the marketplace. The takeaway lesson is obvious—high-performing companies maximize both the core strategy and its implementation.

Implementation Challenges for Online Firms

Exhibit 7.3 provides an overview of the implementation challenges that confront online businesses. In particular, the complete transparency of the

Strategy

	Appropriate	Inappropriate
Good	**Success** • All that can be done to ensure success has been done	**Roulette** • Good execution can mitigate poor strategy or hasten failure
Poor	**Trouble** • Poor execution hampers good strategy • Management may never become aware of strategic soundness because of execution inadequacies	**Failure** • Bad strategy is difficult to diagnose because it is masked by poor execution • Since two things are wrong, problems are more difficult to fix

*(Left axis label: **Implementation**)*

Source: Modified version of materials in Thomas V. Bonoma, *The Marketing Edge* (New York: The Free Press, 1985)

EXHIBIT 7.2 Why Does Implementation Matter?

online storefront—to both customers and competitors—can mean that implementation mistakes will be punished much more severely and quickly than in the offline world. For example, if competitors are able to monitor a firm's prices immediately, they can respond with price adjustments in a real-time fashion. On the customer side, if the customer finds that a particular book is not available on Amazon.com, it would only take a few minutes to order the book at Barnes & Noble.com. In the following section, we articulate five implementation challenges for online firms.

Higher Visibility of Errors   The Web offers consumers a wide variety of easily accessible sources of information on e-commerce companies, and many ratings services have been established to help shoppers choose reputable companies. In addition, some websites and online bulletin boards (such as PlanetFeedback) give disgruntled customers the opportunity to vent their feelings and experiences to a large audience. Some consumers become so frustrated by failed implementation that they create their own websites to share (and invite others to share) their experiences. Yahoo, Amazon, and eBay are all subjects of websites created by shoppers who have had bad experiences with those companies. Bricks-and-mortar companies are not exempt from the criticism—many banks, credit card companies, and utilities have similar websites directed at them.

Lower Switching Costs   It can be argued that **switching costs** for consumers who shop on the Internet are significantly lower than for consumers who shop at bricks-and-mortar firms. Should a consumer have an unsatisfactory experience shopping at a physical store and decide to shop elsewhere, switching costs could include additional driving, new constraints on method of payment, and time spent learning about a new retailer. Consider two pieces of data: One study revealed that 34 percent of online U.S. customers use shop bots and 50 percent shop website-to-website most of the time when making

Essential Challenges of Online Implementation

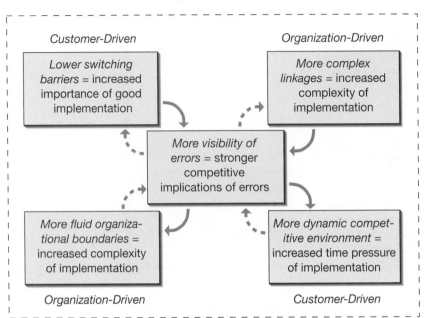

EXHIBIT 7.3   Challenges of Online Implementation

online purchases,[1] but (as we discussed in Chapter 4) users are willing to spend 6.8 percent more to buy from a store where they have shopped before.[2] If customers are satisfied with their experience with an e-commerce store, they will spend a certain amount more to continue to shop there. If they become unsatisfied, they will quickly look at competitors. Because switching costs involve only a simple click of the mouse, companies are under constant pressure to make their current customers want to return to their stores.

More Fluid Organizational Boundaries   The lack of clear dividing lines between partnering and collaborating parties creates fluid organizational boundaries. While this fluidity increases contact and community between partners, it also increases the complexity of interactions.

More Dynamic Competitive Environment   The speed of change in the market places a significant burden on firms to respond quickly. Netscape went from being the absolute dominator of Web browsers to a struggling also-ran in the market over a period of barely three years. The speed of evolution and its implications for strategy implementation are clear. Even the best company cannot afford to implement changes too slowly or in a fashion that will inhibit it from adjusting to changing marketspace conditions.

More Complex Linkages   Complexity of linkages refers to the number of linkages among various partners. The more linkages, the more likely it is that decisions will become slowed, prone to miscommunication, or more bureaucratic. In *The Mythical Man-Month*, Fred Brooks illustrates the effects that an increase in the number of communication linkages can have on an organization. He uses this example of a team writing software: "If each part of the task must be separately coordinated with each other part, the effort increases as $n(n-1)/2$. Three workers require three times as much pairwise intercommunications as two; four require six times as much as two." In the online world, the number and nature of the linkages frequently change, adding another layer of complexity.[3]

Implementation Mistakes Made by Companies

While the Internet has exposed some implementation mistakes, managers often do not realize they are not executing their strategy well until the company is failing. Companies can hobble along, not meeting their potential. Michael Beer and Russell Eisenstat studied more than 150 units from 12 companies and analyzed the factors that most often blocked successful strategy implementation.[4] They found six "silent killers" of implementation:

1. Top-down or laissez-faire senior management style

2. Unclear strategy and conflicting priorities

3. Ineffective senior management team

4. Poor vertical communication

5. Poor coordination across functions, business, or borders

6. Inadequate down-the-line leadership skills and development

While these problems occur in bricks-and-mortar companies, they are especially troublesome for Internet companies. Online companies are often encouraged to do as much as possible as soon as possible, creating an environment of conflicting priorities that uses resources ineffectively and causes confusion for employees. Senior managers may be so busy getting the company off the ground and profitable that they can neglect to give employees the information they need. Many companies that were started in the late 1990s on an interesting idea instead of a solid business plan often had young, inexperienced leaders at the helm. Regardless of whether the company is offline, online, or a combination, it will need good management, clear strategy, good processes, and solid leadership.

Along with these issues, there is a special complication for bricks-and-mortar companies that have an online presence: integrating online strategy with offline strategy. As we discuss later in this chapter, these hybrid organizations must have clear customer communications and internal coordination processes in order to provide a consistent customer experience.

Human Assets

Recruit, Select, Develop, and Retain Employees

Many authors have noted that a firm's most important resource is its people. Hence, a quick scan of the most successful firms in the world—General Electric, General Motors, Microsoft, and others—demonstrates a dedicated, sustained, almost maniacal focus on developing managerial talent that fits the performance goals of the organization. As Jerry Porras and James Collins

Built to Last or Built to Rebuild?

In 1995, James Collins and Jerry Porras published *Built to Last*, an analysis of visionary companies that were more successful than their competitors over a period of more than a century. This book drew a number of very strong conclusions about the key factors that differentiate visionary companies from their peers. It is interesting to see that the current online population of companies is marked by characteristics that are opposites of those that Collins and Porras identified. Debate continues about whether these characteristics are temporary or sustainable phenomena.[5]

For advocates of "built to last," the argument is that growth is largely organic—it comes from careful and systematic analysis of chosen markets. The firm scales up over a period of years and repeatedly leverages its brand in the marketplace. Brand assets and equity take many years to build and must be carefully nurtured over a long period of time. Finally, these companies are often not led by visionary leaders with strong personalities.

In sharp contrast, there is no time for elaborate planning and analysis in the online world. Rather, firms act very quickly. While growth can be organic, it is just as likely to be from acquisitions of competitors and complementors. The challenge is not finding opportunity—it is having a leader who can choose the right opportunity.

point out in *Built to Last,* winning companies often develop an approach to people development that is unique to that particular firm. Certainly, every firm wants the appropriate talent for the tasks at hand; however, how a firm hires, nurtures, and develops that talent varies markedly, even for the most successful ones. Some firms build exceptionally strong mentoring programs; and others have corporate universities, while still others focus on meticulous performance reviews that prune away the bottom 10 percent of employees. Regardless of which approach is used, there are four basic tasks that are common to all firms:

- *Recruitment.* Recruitment refers to the formal task of searching for the right employees. Recruitment involves a host of activities, including establishing criteria for particular positions, crafting clear job descriptions, deciding the right mix of hiring channels (e.g., universities, job fairs, online websites, and company websites), and setting up particular performance metrics (e.g., how many undergraduate hires to aim for this year).

- *Selection.* Selection is the process of making hiring decisions and formal job offers. A host of factors may influence the selection choice, including characteristics of the potential employee and work experience, as well as needs of the firm (e.g., shortage of personnel in a particular area). Increasingly, firms are balancing the opinions of multiple employees in making the final choice.

- *Development.* Once hired, the employee is typically provided a professional development plan to accentuate individual strengths and improve weaknesses. Working closely with the human resources staff and his or her direct managers, the individual often follows a yearly development path that includes specific areas of on-the-job training, off-site training, and other activities to build individual skills. As job markets tighten, candidates often look at management development programs as a key factor in their selection of a firm.

- *Retention.* Retaining the best talent is a constant challenge. The best talent is highly sought after even in difficult job markets. Well-run companies are constantly evaluating and "ranking" their employees to ensure that they provide the best work environment and the best total compensation packages. Much as some of the best firms constantly prune the bottom 10 percent of their workforce, they pay equal attention to adequately compensating high performers.

Human Resources Trends for Online Firms

More Stringent Requirements

After the Internet bubble burst and online companies started going through series of layoffs, many potential recruits began looking at more established, secure companies.[6] Online companies went from being a hip, desirable alternative to being seen as unstable and undesirable to many top recruits. While younger workers are still willing to take a chance on an unstable environment, many older, experienced workers are more interested in stability. As a result, online companies are taking a more traditional recruiting approach and focusing on base salary and benefits instead of stock options. They are also using multiple interviews, another traditional hiring technique, so the company understands what it is getting and the recruit can get a good idea of the management team, the company's chance of profitability, and its commitment to long-term goals.[7]

Managing Human Resources Uncertainty

In the short time that the Internet has given companies a new sales channel, the stock market has risen and crashed, and companies have gone from desperately searching for new employees to receiving hundreds of résumés for positions that do not exist. Human resources directors for online companies must deal with a very high level of business uncertainty, which translates into employee perceptions of unsure futures within the firm. While all firms face uncertainty, online firms (and online divisions of offline firms) are under increasing pressure to show returns on investment. The result of this shift toward showing clear sales, profits, and returns is that senior managers must keep the workforce motivated and on task even while they may be unable to guarantee long-term job prospects.

Processes

Processes are defined as the patterns of interaction, coordination, communication, and decision-making that employees use to standardize how work is done. For example, consider the process of developing a marketing plan. It makes a great deal of sense for organizations to develop one standard process for developing a marketing plan. The rationale is that it facilitates organizational communication (e.g., same vocabulary, same analyses) and organizational learning (e.g., given that the organization follows the same process, it is easier to practice the principle of continuous improvement). The following processes must be configured by online firms during implementation:

- *Resource-allocation processes.* There are often more opportunities available than a company can pursue in a sustainable manner. The **resource-allocation processes** are the formalization of the tradeoffs and prioritizations that the company takes into account when making choices about which opportunities to pursue. If the firm can develop a standard approach to resource allocation, it will reduce the extent of organizational politicking and provide a common framework to make critical choices for the firm.

- *Human resources management processes.* Online companies need to scale up and adjust quickly to keep growing with the market. Upgrading the **human resources management processes** to focus on the recruitment, selection, development, and succession of employees is a critical activity for any firm.

- *Manufacturing and distribution processes.* The **manufacturing and distribution processes** are defined as the supply chain and are the subject of a later section in this chapter.

- *Payment and billing processes.* It is clear that without proper functioning of the **payment and billing processes**, an online company will have difficulty producing anything other than virtual profits. However, billing processes are not equally important for all online companies. For Internet service providers (ISPs), it can be a strong strategic advantage to produce one integrated bill for the customer's telecom, cable television, and online services. For most online companies, however, these processes are simply a minimum performance requirement and have a negative effect if they are not performed properly. For example, payment processes for B2C (business-to-consumer) companies are typically credit card–based and, as discussed in Chapter 2, have different procedures than cash or credit card payments in which the purchaser is present. B2B (business-to-business) payments are more complex, and enabler companies have launched new billing products specifically for this market.

- *Customer support/handling processes.* The customer may have questions when he or she is on the website, as well as after a transaction has been completed. Questions may arise about how to track the delivery of an order, how to change an order in process, or how to resolve a problem once the product has been received. The **customer support/handling processes** should address these questions.

Organizational Structures for Hybrid Organizations

Traditional strategy textbooks typically review the types of organizational structures (e.g., by function, by strategic business unit, by geography) and rationale for those structures (e.g., pros and cons of a geographic structure). We do not review those debates here. Rather, we turn our attention to two other types of structures: a single organization (one that combines offline and online activities) and a dual organization (where online and offline organizations are separate). As noted earlier, many companies in the online environment have significant difficulty not only creating a smooth integration between the front end of the customer experience and the resource system but also integrating their online and offline front ends (e.g., retail outlets and websites). This integration is most complex for hybrid companies.

Exhibit 7.4 provides a simple illustration of the formation of hybrid companies as either one organization or two separate organizations in one company. A pure online or pure offline company is not considered a hybrid; hybrid companies combine both online and offline systems, whether it be customer interface, fulfillment, or both. Sephora is an example of a hybrid; it has more than 150 stores in Europe and the United States and in 1999 launched its website, Sephora.com., which carries more than 11,000 products.

Single Organization

Company CEO
• Company strategy
• Human assets
• Operations
• IT infrastructure
• Processes
• Culture
• Online and offline partnerships

Dual Organization

Company CEO	
Online CEO	Offline CEO
• Online strategy	• Offline strategy
• Human assets	• Human assets
• Operations	• Operations
• IT infrastructure	• IT infrastructure
• Processes	• Processes
• Culture	• Culture
• Partnerships	• Partnerships

EXHIBIT 7.4   Single Organization Vs. Dual Organization

For the websites of bricks-and-mortar companies, the mix of products offered on the Web may significantly differ from the selection offered at retail stores. Consider drugstores, for example. Many of the items bought at a physical drugstore are impulse or convenience items. Therefore, retail stores stock many items targeted toward convenience-related demand. Because shopping over the Web is not very conducive to the purchase of impulse items, drugstore websites stock items that are not normally sold at drugstores but are nonetheless important to their customers. In addition, the economics of shopping on the Web versus shopping in a retail store are very different due to the low prices of many items in drugstores and the costs of delivering Web-ordered goods. Also, offline-based companies must consider the demographics of their online customers; they may have significantly different motives or purchase patterns than their offline customers. Online and offline product mixes, as well as selling approaches, need to reflect the differences among customer bases.

Because of their dual-interface nature, hybrid firms face issues that do not concern pure online firms. One key decision the hybrid firm must make is how the company should be organized: Should the online part of the business be housed in the same organization as the offline business, or should it be organized as a separate firm or operating unit?

Single Organization

We first consider the advantages associated with a fully integrated business—that is, one in which the online and offline activities are part of the same business unit. Examples include Office Depot and Texas Instruments. In the case of Texas Instruments, its online component (TI.com) is part of the worldwide marketing and sales organization. While it has its own management team, it is not a separate organization with its own profit and loss statement.

There are a number of advantages to having online and offline operations be two parts of one organization:

- *Flexibility between channels.* Tightly coupled online/offline back-office support systems benefit the customer as well as the firm. The more integrated the two interfaces, the more likely customers will be able to migrate back and forth between the online and offline platforms during their interactions with the company. For instance, The Home Depot's website tries to make it easy for customers to interact with the company however they want, whenever they want. Website visitors can browse online listings of The Home Depot's products, assemble a shopping list, pay for their purchases online, and have the merchandise shipped to their home. Alternatively, they can choose to send the order to their nearest Home Depot store, where it will be packaged and left for them at a checkout station.

  Contrast the flexibility offered by The Home Depot to that offered by the department store Nordstrom. Customers who purchase goods on the Nordstrom website cannot pick up their purchases at a Nordstrom store—they must have them shipped to them. They cannot return the purchases to the store, either—returns must be sent back to the online operation.

  A recent study found that 39 percent of customers who planned on buying electronic products researched the products online but bought them at a bricks-and-mortar store.[8] Businesses such as Circuit City exploit this tendency by allowing customers to choose how to receive their product: Customers can research products on the website (which includes general information about the category, product specifications, and customer reviews) and then buy the product at the store; buy the product online and pick it up at the store; or buy it online and have it shipped to them. This integration of information, purchasing, and pickup options gives customers the greatest flexibility and, therefore, the most benefits.

- *Consistent integration of online and offline customer service.* Good customer service can build customer trust in the company managing the website. Single-organization structure can help create seamless online and offline customer service since all customer service is done by the same organization. Companies such as Lands' End have one set of merchandise and one phone number for customer service. This helps alleviate customer confusion and keeps the customer from feeling that he or she must make a choice between shopping on one channel or another. It also helps make sure that Lands' End customers are treated the same whether they decide to order through the mail, on the phone, or through the Internet. Companies such as Nordstrom, which have different merchandise for catalog, online, and in-store shoppers, can create confusion for the customer.

- *Managing a consistent brand.* As with customer service, it is easier for single-organization companies to maintain a consistent brand. Maintaining a consistent brand image across multiple organizations requires a large amount of cooperation and communication between managers of the online and offline channels. Together, managers must answer questions such as the following: How similar should the look-and-feel of the two channels be? How much consistency should there be between the online and offline versions of customer activities such as product selection, purchase, and returns? Coming to an agreement on these decisions is enough of a challenge when online and offline managers are part of a single organization; it is especially difficult in dual-organization hybrids, in which managers may have less contact with colleagues, less mutual trust, and fewer incentives to cooperate. Even when managers of the two stores share a common vision, their ability to execute it may be hampered by separate back-office systems with differing capabilities and limitations.

- *People.* The single-organization structure can be a recruiting advantage for firms that begin offline and expand to the online platform. In this environment, the personnel have the option of learning a much broader set of skills and capabilities.

- *Taxes.* In cases in which one interface is operating at a loss and the other is profitable, combining the operations into a single entity can provide significant tax benefits. The profit of one venture is reduced by the loss of the second, immediately lowering the tax liability of the profitable venture. As a separate organization, the unprofitable venture would amass its losses for application against future profits, in effect postponing the benefit that could be gained immediately in a single organization.

- *Valuation.* Some have argued that single organizations have greater value than dual organizations. Also, in comparison to pure online companies, companies that have both online and offline operations are valued more highly.

- *Systems.* The ability of any interface, online or offline, to deliver value to a customer depends in large part on the back-office infrastructure that supports it (e.g., IT infrastructure, order-processing and fulfillment systems, inventory control). Online and offline interfaces that are housed in a single organization can potentially rely on a single set of back-office systems. This is particularly true for firms that start out as hybrids and therefore can design their back-office systems specifically to support two different types of channels.

  When the online and offline interfaces are housed in different organizations, it is unlikely that they will be supported by a single set of back-office systems. At best, the two organizations may attempt to link their systems at critical points—an endeavor that can be costly and not always successful.

Dual Organization

A dual-organization structure has its own advantages:

- *Coordination and cooperation processes.* Trying to manage one set of back-office systems for online and offline operation is difficult and requires considerable coordination and cooperation between the two entities. Also, online and offline entities often evolve and require people with different types of skills to run them. Keeping the two sets of operations separate can help the firm realize the most benefits from each channel.

- *License to cannibalize.* A cannibalistic strategy is easier to execute when the new interface is housed in a separate organization. Few organizations have the will or strength of leadership to cannibalize themselves.

- *People.* Housing the interfaces in two separate organizations can be a recruiting advantage for both organizations.

- *Allocations.* Unlike the single organization, when the two interfaces are housed in separate organizations, they do not have to fight with each other for senior management time, funding, or staff.

- Sales *Tax.* As this book went to press, most online sales were exempt from sales tax. If the online and offline interfaces are legally separate entities, offline sales are subject to sales tax, but online sales are exempt. If the two stores are housed in a single corporation, both online and offline sales are taxed.

Systems

Systems are defined as routines or established procedures for the organization and can be related to any aspect of the organization. In this section, we focus on three types of systems: information technology systems (including enterprise resource planning and customer relationship management), evaluation and compensation systems, and supply chain management. In the current context, there is an obvious emphasis on technology systems. These include database systems, website support systems, management information systems, and other digital data-based approaches. All systems are important, though, as they set a structure for how the organization works.

Information Technology Systems

Proper and relevant implementation of **information technology** (IT) systems is critical to business. As with all areas of implementation, it is important that the IT systems of a company are aligned with the company's strategy. While it may be more interesting to think about interfaces, culture, or leadership, technology systems are the backbone of most of today's companies. One company, Clarica Life Insurance, has committed itself to promoting IT employees to business areas within the firm (and hiring employees with liberal-arts degrees to work in the technology department) to help integrate the company's business and technology functions.[9]

IT systems allow employees to share information with one another. These systems can include groupware such as Lotus Notes, where employees can post information on bulletin boards, or management information systems, which allow users to reach out across the enterprise and collect data and then present that data. There has been a change over the past 8 to 10 years, where information that used to be collected and controlled by the IT staff can now be accessed by many employees across different levels of the company. Also, systems such as enterprise information portals (not to be confused with enterprise resource planning, discussed later) provide an interface for users to post and find information.

Difficulties of Information Technology Implementation IT departments face a conundrum—they are expected to build and maintain the technology infrastructure but are rarely given enough money to do so; they are often the first to have their budgets slashed. Also, in today's environment, companies are expected to be dynamic and innovative, while many IT systems have been built to be stable and reliable. There is a fundamental tradeoff between systems that are efficient and systems that are receptive to innovation.[10] IT and business managers must weigh all the factors—including cost, reliability, and adaptability—when choosing and implementing technology systems.

Enterprise Resource Planning

IDC defines an **enterprise resource planning (ERP)** product as "one that helps automate a company's business process by employing an integrated user interface, an integrated data set, and an integrated code set." Basically, it allows a company the ability to integrate the systems from different departments and allows the different departments to talk to one another and share data. Companies can implement ERP systems that integrate all of their departments, or they can implement ERP systems on just a few. The types of software that ERP systems can be set up for include manufacturing, order entry, accounts receivable and payable, general ledger, purchasing, warehousing, transportation, and human resources.[11]

There are many benefits to ERP. Because the departments share data, there are fewer errors, faster performance and efficiency, and better access to information.[12] Since it serves as one system for many departments, the data tend to be "cleaner"—older data are weeded out, and the most recent data are kept. In 2002, Meta Group estimated that the average total cost of implementing an ERP system was $15 million, and the median annual savings was $1.6 million per year.[13]

Future of ERP There are currently many vendors of ERP systems; the largest are SAP, Oracle, and PeopleSoft. It is expected that there will soon be consolidation among many of the medium and small-sized companies.

As the Internet has grown, new e-business applications have been developed. ERP vendors have faced the challenge of making their products more flexible overall and also able to integrate these new applications, which include categories such as salesforce automation, customer relationship management (CRM), e-procurement, and supply chain management. ERP systems are also becoming accessible to all employees, not just managers. While the Internet has brought a host of potential improvements for ERP systems (allowing different users to work on the same data at the same time), it has also meant that ERP systems have had to adapt to the Internet as a platform.[14]

Customer Relationship Management (CRM)

The phrase **customer relationship management (CRM)** is used in many different ways, but it usually refers to technology systems that help the company serve, satisfy, and retain customers. CRM systems help companies store data about their customers (including who they are and in what ways they've interacted with the company), and they help employees to better communicate and serve customers. As the Internet has developed and customer satisfaction has become more important, a lot has been written about CRM. The Internet itself has changed CRM: There are more data collected by companies, the data collected are more immediate and dynamic, and these data, when analyzed correctly, give better insight into the way customers behave.[15] The actual benefit of a CRM system, however, has been questioned by some. As with other IT systems, CRM systems can be extremely complex, so it can take significant energy to implement and use them correctly. Also, CRM systems are only as good as the data they store—if the customer data are out of date or incorrect, the CRM system cannot help the company.

Difficulties of Implementing CRM Systems   CRM systems are usually not set up solely for customer service representatives. They are integrated throughout the company and can be put in almost all departments, including sales, human resources, and marketing. While CRM programs can positively affect a company's relationship with its customers, it is essential that the application is implemented properly for the company to realize the full potential of the system. Gartner predicts that the number of unsuccessful CRM projects will increase from 65 percent in 2001 to 80 percent by the middle of 2003.[16]

To make sure they get the most from their CRM initiatives, companies should do the following:[17]

1. Create a customer strategy first. Then choose a CRM system that fits that strategy.

2. Make sure that the organizational structure fits the customer strategy.

3. Choose only the technology elements necessary for the customer strategy. Not only is more not necessarily better, but too much technology can make the system too expensive to implement and too complicated for employees to use.

4. Use the system to benefit customers without compromising their privacy or making them feel as if they are being harassed by the company.

Future of CRM   CRM functions are being integrated into ERP systems so that companies can use just one system. Financially, some believe the potential for CRM is huge. Accenture estimates that if a company with sales of $1 billion implements a CRM system correctly, it can add $40 million to $50 million to its profits.[18] This profit would come from improving customer service, motivating and rewarding people, turning customer data into insight, attracting and keeping people, and developing selling and service skills.[19]

Evaluation and Compensation Systems

While employees can feel apathetic toward information systems, **evaluation and compensation systems** are near and dear to their hearts. As discussed before, employees are one of a company's most important assets. Evaluation and compensation systems not only help companies hold onto their employees but also increase those employees' satisfaction with their jobs. Because many e-commerce companies are struggling to show profits and must make every dollar count, evaluation and compensation systems are even more important because they help a company use its human assets as efficiently as possible. They help valuable employees to be at their most productive and can identify those who are not helping the company reach its goals. These systems also benefit the company by identifying those with specific skills that benefit the company's strategy.

Companies should think about the following when designing an evaluation and compensation system:

- *The system must link closely to the company's strategy and reward employees for outcomes that promote that strategy.* Employees who do not produce what is expected of them serve no purpose to the company, no matter how many hours they work or how talented they are. Often, companies give rewards to employees for trying or doing work that isn't necessary. This not only wastes company resources but causes confusion among employees about what is expected of them.

- *The system should expose both the strengths and weaknesses of the employees.* While the system should not make employees fear for their jobs, a system should be able to show if an employee is suited for his or her job. Successful systems can also reveal skills that may make the employee more suitable for a different job.

- *Rewards should be both monetary and nonmonetary.* While many employees are driven solely by financial rewards, others are motivated by flexible hours, vacation time, or the ability to become autonomous or to manage their own project.[20] In fact, some studies suggest that individual incentive pay causes employees to think more about short-term productivity and getting along with managers than about meeting the long-term goals of the company. While monetary rewards are a necessary part of compensation, companies, especially those with lean budgets, should be aware of other benefits they can give employees.

- *The system should apply to the specific types of employees in the company.* What motivates investment bankers can be very different than what motivates secretaries or those in creative jobs. The company must understand what motivates its employees, and the system must be flexible enough to reward them appropriately.

- *Performance judgment should be consistent.* One study found that, while most managers judge three variables—task performance, citizen performance, and counterproductive performance—they weighed the criteria very differently. Some weighed task performance far more than the other two, while others weighed counterproductive performance more heavily.[21] Often, frequent reviews are better than one or two big reviews a year, because smaller ones help managers review employees more thoroughly.

- *Feedback should go both ways.* As much as employees need feedback to improve, they should be given the ability to evaluate those they work for and the company's systems and practices. There should be systems in place to act on this feedback. Asking employees what they want to change and then ignoring those suggestions is worse than not asking.

Supply Chain Management

The online environment has changed the structure of business **supply chains** and the options available to retailers and manufacturers. We first focus on B2C supply chains and several different supply chain models that have arisen to serve B2C companies. Next, we review B2B supply chains and reveal how the online environment is creating significant efficiencies and opportunities in the B2B market. Finally, we discuss developments in the peer-to-peer (P2P) and consumer-to-business (C2B) markets (see Exhibit 7.5).

B2C—Business-to-Consumer	B2B—Business-to-Business
• Stock-it-yourself • Outsource warehousing • Drop shipping • Fulfillment intermediaries	• Customer-centric • Vertical hubs

C2C—Consumer-to-Consumer	C2B—Consumer-to-Business
• Much like a vertical hub (many sites have created consumer-to-consumer sales) • Provides a forum for buyers and sellers to meet and trade directly • A global marketplace with a large and interested trading company	• Individual consumers place bids with businesses (e.g., Priceline) and businesses decide whether to sell

EXHIBIT 7.5   Four Types of Supply Chains Found Online

Business-to-Consumer Supply Chains

One reason for the many supply chain options in the B2C market is that online retailers do not need to have products physically in stock in a network of retail outlets to sell directly to consumers. Unlike bricks-and-mortar retailers, which must maintain stock on hand, as long as the online retailer fulfills its promise to deliver goods in a specified time period, consumers do not care how the order is fulfilled. This provides the retailer significant flexibility in designing its supply chains.[22] On the other hand, the B2C supply chain for online companies is significantly more complex than for offline companies. Web-based deliveries are often small, time-sensitive deliveries to individuals about whom the company might have very limited information. This is very different from periodically delivering to an established network of shops with which the company has long-term relationships. In addition, a physical outlet network provides the outlet supplier with a predictable expectation of needed routes and volumes. Such predictability is certainly absent when it comes to delivering goods to a changing volume of new and existing consumers every day.

One of the weakest links in the B2C implementation chain has been fulfillment. The cost of handling a return is generally three to four times the cost of shipping a product. In addition to refining fulfillment processes to satisfy customers, many firms are beginning to use expedited fulfillment as a means to product differentiation. For example, in December, many stores will guarantee delivery by Christmas if the item is ordered by a certain date. Also, many companies have distanced themselves from guaranteeing delivery—they instead guarantee that an item will be shipped within a certain amount of time.

In today's B2C market, there are four primary supply chain models: stock-it-yourself, outsource warehousing, drop shipping, and fulfillment intermediaries:

- *Stock-it-yourself.* For a bricks-and-mortar company that also sells online, this model typically involves maintaining an integrated warehouse that is able to handle shipments to stores as well as shipments to Web customers. This is often very difficult, if not impossible, to implement. Systems and processes must handle both large deliveries to physical stores and small, individual orders to online customers.

  For purely online companies, the stock-it-yourself model generally involves an automated warehouse that can directly fulfill online orders. A primary benefit of this model is that it gives the online firm control over its fulfillment process. Control over fulfillment is a major concern for online companies. The only disadvantage of this model is that the whole supply chain is no longer likely to be a strategic asset that the firm can shape in a proprietary way. Hence, it could be argued that such a structure commoditizes the supply chain.

- *Outsource warehousing.* Outsourcing warehousing generally involves the use of logistics specialists such as Federal Express (FedEx) or UPS to stockpile and ship Web orders. Hewlett-Packard (HP) uses FedEx to fulfill all of its orders from its retail website. FedEx warehouses HP inventory in Memphis, Tennessee (one of its hubs). Once an order comes in through HP's site, it is automatically transmitted to FedEx's Memphis facility. Orders are packaged at its warehouse and directly shipped to the customer via FedEx.[23] HP has another very efficient distribution system to handle fulfillment to its distributors. However, that distribution system is simply not configured to handle small, individual shipments. It is not a trivial task to reconfigure its system to be able to handle both distributor and individual order fulfillment.

- *Drop shipping.* Drop shipping requires an e-commerce company to depend on its manufacturers or distributors to pack and ship its retail Web orders. Drop-shipping specialists even go as far as placing the retailer's name and logo on all shipped orders. Direct-mail catalog companies are benefiting greatly from the growth of retail drop shipping; they are experienced in fulfilling individual mail-order catalog purchases and are applying this experience to e-commerce fulfillment. The general design of a drop-shipping fulfillment warehouse is one in which shipments from manufacturers are unloaded at one end, merchandise is organized throughout the warehouse, and individual customer orders are shipped out via the U.S. Postal Service or an overnight service through the other end of the warehouse.

- *Fulfillment intermediaries.* Fulfillment intermediaries take care of all back-office operations for e-commerce companies. They process orders, direct orders to suppliers, keep customers updated on their order progress, and handle cancellations and product returns. These types of systems reduce setup costs for e-commerce entrepreneurs and give them the opportunity to focus on developing their businesses. Outsourcing order fulfillment also minimizes risk. In the rapidly changing online environment, e-commerce companies that outsource do not have to commit to a specific type of supply chain.

Business-to-Business Supply Chains

Buyers reduce costs by creating an environment in which sellers are more competitive. Sellers can use B2B websites to instantly advertise their products to potential customers. B2B activity accounted for $433 billion in online sales in 2000, and Gartner predicts it will reach $8.5 trillion by 2005.[24] IDC estimates that B2B sales will account for 83 percent of online sales in 2002, and 88 percent in 2006.[25]

B2B supply chains in the online space are somewhat different than other supply chains. Whereas other supply chains are truly new to the industry, B2B supply chains are rooted in more than a decade of enterprise-level expenditures in various technologies, including computing, networking, and client servers.[26] Thus, companies may have had existing supplier relationships, and the parties simply converted the relationship into an electronic format.

There are five main reasons that big buyers (such as automobile companies) push such systems on their suppliers:

- Lower costs compared to offline management of suppliers and transactions
- Improved transaction speed and control (e.g., allowing for dependable global production of cars)
- High security of the system (it is purely proprietary and often supervised by the buyer)
- Proprietary nature of the system creates a strong switching barrier for participating suppliers
- Good reliability of capacity to process the transaction volume (the buyer is the key driver behind capacity management of the system)

Benefits of B2B Supply Chains on Business   B2B sites are revolutionizing manufacturers' supply chains by allowing manufacturers the opportunity to realize lower input prices, reduced inventory and transaction costs, faster delivery, and improved customer service.

- *Lower input prices.* Manufacturers use B2B sites to conduct auctions from prequalified bidders for their supply chain inputs. The ease of bidding expands the universe of potential supplier bidders and takes favoritism out of the buying equation. Increased competition coupled with decreased supplier overhead pushes suppliers to offer lower prices. One negative effect of using the auction process for procurement is that suppliers may become less inclined to invest in customizing products for a manufacturer if they have to bid against others for contracts at purchase time.

- *Reduced inventory.* B2B supply chains establish a closer communication process with suppliers regarding input needs and procurement time frames. This allows manufacturers to reduce their warehousing and inventory costs and to increase returns on assets. At 3Com, in an effort to make its inventory process more efficient, expanded product production automatically triggers additional orders for input supplies such as cardboard boxes.

- *Reduced transaction costs.* By using the Internet to announce order requests and to receive bids, both manufacturers and suppliers reduce the transaction costs associated with supply procurement.

- *Faster delivery.* Because procurement transactions are no longer processed through multiple internal departments or entered in several different data systems, the time between supply request and supply delivery can be greatly reduced.

- *Better customer service.* General Motors is trying to use B2B supply chains to provide better service to its customers (the current wait from order to delivery of a new car is up to eight weeks) by connecting its factories and suppliers via the Internet. This connection will provide suppliers with real-time notification of needed materials and delivery deadlines. Prequalified suppliers can instantly submit a bid to provide supplies. GM hopes the system will reduce the order-to-delivery time of new cars to four or five days.[27]

GM began to move its purchasing process to the Web by establishing its TradeXchange website and announcing its intent to do all purchasing (some $500 billion per year) over this website by the end of 2001. In February 2000, GM and Ford merged their online purchasing efforts with those of Daimler-Chrysler, Renault, and Nissan to form Covisint, a B2B exchange whose partners include Oracle and Commerce One.[28]

Consumer-to-Business Supply Chain

The C2B concept was illustrated by the business model of Mercata (*www. mercata.com*). Mercata tried to organize consumers and harness their group buying power when dealing with suppliers. The company aggregated customers who were interested in buying in volume and reaping lower prices; it then negotiated with suppliers to provide discounts on their merchandise based on the volume of goods sold. Mercata offered goods for sale on its website with a group-buying incentive—as more purchases were made, the selling price would decrease. By creating an online group of customers interested in gaining group-buying power, Mercata aimed to create a "win/win" for consumers and suppliers. Consumers benefited by receiving lower prices, and sellers could move a large amount of merchandise with low transaction costs.

While group buying is common in the bricks-and-mortar world, it is often very cumbersome to organize online. Mercata tried to eliminate many of the obstacles associated with old-economy group buying. By establishing a large and varied group of buyers interested in participating in group deals, suppliers offered their merchandise to Mercata's price-conscious group-buying crowd, and the crowd participated without costly negotiations. In return, Mercata received a small fee for each product sold over its website. Ultimately, the C2B company was unable to aggregate enough consumer demand to allow it to negotiate meaningful discounts with manufacturers before its $90 million of funding ran out. In January 2001, Mercata announced that it would cease trading due to a lack of funds.

Consumer-to-Consumer Supply Chain

The eBay business model clearly illustrates a C2C supply chain. The auction website's mission is to help people sell practically anything—it is a platform to facilitate person-to-person trading. EBay allows sellers to place individual items up for sale; interested buyers can bid for them. EBay has created the largest online community of individual buyers and sellers in the world, as well as an efficient platform on which members of this community can interact and complete business. The platform provides a forum for buyers and sellers to meet and trade directly (as opposed to hiring an intermediary), uses the Internet to create a global marketplace, and offers convenience to the community. EBay has about 50 million registered users. It receives about 5 percent of the final auction price of each item.

Culture

Organizational culture is the social context that shapes how things get done and the way people work in an organization. It can be defined as the pattern of shared values, beliefs, and assumptions that influence opinions and actions. Consisting of ingrained beliefs, behaviors, and thought patterns, culture is largely invisible. However, culture manifests itself in observable behaviors, stated values, and the "folklore" of a company. When culture is consistent with strategic intent, it can be a powerful force in implementation. But when culture is inconsistent with a firm's direction, it can hinder or undermine strategy implementation.[29]

Consider a company, whether an airline, bank, or hospital, that decides to compete on the basis of superior customer service. If the existing culture conveys to employees that paying attention to customers is unimportant or counterproductive to getting work accomplished efficiently, then employees will not care enough about customers to deliver high-quality service. Implementation of the new strategy will require changing the culture. Likewise, implementing a strategy based on producing highly innovative products will likely founder when the company culture is averse to change.

In addition to shaping actions, culture influences how decisions are made and what is valued. For example, in some corporate cultures the only outcome that matters for calculating returns on investments is financial improvement. Softer, intangible benefits such as better customer relationships, strong branding, or the ability of a team to work more productively are discounted.[30]

Along with an organization's formal reporting structures and human resources systems, cultural norms and values govern work performance. When organizational culture is aligned with structures and systems, culture serves as an informal basis for coordination and control of employees that can lessen the need for bureaucracy and detailed procedures. When the informal and formal systems are misaligned, employees will be unclear about which signals to respond to. One system will need to be changed.

Culture Types

Understanding a company's culture is complicated by the fact that culture resides in the background; members of an organization tend not to be consciously aware of it. A further complication is that many elements of culture, including underlying values and assumptions, are not directly observable but rather must be inferred from the "feel" of an organization and its patterns of actions, communications, relationships, and so forth. For these reasons, deciphering and interpreting a particular culture is perhaps most easily accomplished by referring to generic culture types.

A number of models of organizational culture propose four or five generic culture types.[31] One such model differentiates cultures along two dimensions: the degree to which the organization is outwardly versus inwardly focused and the degree to which the organization relies on highly specified roles, processes, and routines (see Exhibit 7.6). The four resulting culture types are called adaptive, committed, bureaucratic, and entrepreneurial. Keep in mind that an organization may not fit precisely in any one category; although one generic type is likely to best describe the culture, elements of each of the other cultural types are also likely to be found.

	Entrepreneurial	Adaptive
External	- Unbounded by rules and precedents - Willing to take risks - Flexible - Innovative	- Proactively identifies issues - Good at planning and setting goals - Responsive to market changes - Outcome-oriented
Orientation	**Committed**	**Bureaucratic**
Internal	- Emphasizes internal cohesion, participation, teamwork, and loyalty	- Emphasizes stability, established routines, and formal authority
	Low — Specificity — **High**	

EXHIBIT 7.6   Generic Organizational Culture Types

Best Culture for e-Commerce Companies

In the 1990s, an entrepreneurial organizational culture clearly prevailed among dot-coms. Such mantras as "overturn the status quo," "move at Internet speed," "new rules for the new economy," and "24-7 availability" all signified the entrepreneurial culture. Not surprisingly, the rapid downturn in the fortunes of these dot-coms called into question whether other cultural types might suit e-commerce companies. In particular, adaptive cultures, which share the opportunity-focused mindset of entrepreneurial cultures, combined with a focus on specified outcomes, appear to be well-suited to e-commerce companies.

A Stanford study that followed 200 Silicon Valley startups from their founding assessed which organizational blueprints (a combination of organizational design and culture) allowed companies to survive and prosper. Many of these startups were online ventures. On most measures, bureaucratic organizations performed poorly. Blueprints that emphasized fostering a strong culture based on enduring employee attachment to the company (containing elements of adaptive and commitment cultures) were associated with strategies emphasizing superior marketing, service, or customer relationships. Moreover, the study pointed to the importance for startups of anticipating and managing cultural and organizational issues early in the company's history, rather than leaving them to chance.[32]

Creating Culture

Culture originates with the founding of the firm. It reflects the founders' underlying values and assumptions about how organizations should work, even if these values and assumptions are not explicit. Culture becomes part of the "genetic material" of the firm and, in turn, gives rise to explicit values and operating norms. This is not to say that all firms have strong, consistent cultures. Weak or inconsistent cultures can arise when leaders do not pay attention to organization-building activities, when they let competing cultures arise in different parts of the firm, or when they try to radically alter culture to match a new strategy.[33] A strong culture that is compatible with the firm's strategy will help implementation, while a weak or incompatible culture will not help or may even hurt implementation. One sign of a strong culture is that organization members "indoctrinate" new members into appropriate ways of thinking and behaving.

Emphasizing values is one of the ways companies develop and maintain culture. Many firms include values in their mission statements. For example, JetBlue's values are safety, caring, integrity, fun, and passion.[34] Cisco describes its culture on a badge handed out to every employee that lists terms including customer success, empowerment, teamwork, frugality, and open communication.[35]

Symbolic activities such as informal storytelling that highlights events and people that exemplify the culture can be a powerful means of instilling culture. Both the words and actions of senior managers are cultural cues, and employees quickly notice and absorb any disparities.

Management can deliberately shape culture through formal systems including hiring and assignment of employees, organization charts, and compensations and rewards. Other mechanisms include formal and informal training systems and recognition of culturally consistent behaviors with ceremonies and rewards. JetBlue hires employees based on cultural fit (it assesses their fit with values translated into specific actions) and provides new hires an orientation on culture. The company's coordination and control system depends on having employees make decisions guided by values, with managers acting as coaches.

Changing Organizational Culture

Sometimes a company will need to change its culture in order to implement strategy successfully. This can be the case when there is no strong existing culture, when the strategy has changed in a way that is incompatible with the culture, when mergers and acquisition of culturally different organizations occur, or when growth requires transitioning to a different culture.

Hewlett-Packard is famous for its strong organizational culture, termed "the HP way." This culture fits the committed type described earlier, along with elements of the adaptive type. It fosters collaborative work by semiautonomous groups of employees to produce innovative high-tech products and reflects the founders' respect for individual professional achievement. In this egalitarian culture, employees feel attached to the company through their individual contributions to noble goals. However, when HP spun off the scientific instrument parts of its business in 1999 to form Agilent Technologies, the executive appointed to lead Agilent decided to create an adaptive culture for the new entity. Why the culture change? The new company quickly needed to demonstrate its viability through excellent performance in its product markets. The CEO believed a downside of the HP way was employees' sense of entitlement and a reluctance to hold people accountable for performance. The new adaptive culture would emphasize high performance, accountability, and monetary rewards. It turned out that Agilent was able to develop a new culture, but not as quickly or completely as initially envisioned because of the enduring strength of the original HP culture.[36]

During HP's 2002 acquisition of Compaq, industry analysts raised concerns about its ability to absorb a company with a very different corporate culture. Experts disagree on the best solution, but most agree that the new company will have to opt for one culture aligned with the revised business strategy, and that transforming the culture will be a tough process that consumes significant resources.[37]

Leadership

The quality of leadership affects all aspects of an organization's performance. With respect to implementation, leaders play a crucial role in clarifying strategic intent. They communicate the strategy to stakeholders, including employees, shareholders, suppliers, and key customers. Talented leaders rally the organization around a compelling purpose. They ensure that strategy is translated into action plans and performance targets.

A company's leadership is responsible for building the capacities needed for strategy implementation. Designing structures and systems, setting roles and responsibilities, allocating resources, and assigning managers are essential activities in firms ranging from small startups to members of the Fortune 100. Leaders must be forward-looking and prepare the organization for dealing with complexity and change that may arise in the future. They encourage subordinates to anticipate the need for change and to respond with innovative approaches.

As noted in the previous section, leadership plays a primary role in establishing and maintaining organizational culture. Leaders shape culture both by example, through their words and actions, and by deliberate efforts to ensure that organizational culture and strategy remain aligned. When strategy and culture are aligned, leaders have less need of policies, rules, and procedures to enforce implementation and greater ability to see and respond to new opportunities for the organization.

The Role of Top Leadership

Excellent leadership is particularly important at the top levels of an organization. Ultimately, CEOs are the ones held responsible for the organization's performance and reputation. According to professor of management Michael Useem, CEOs need to "think strategically, communicate persuasively, act decisively, demonstrate ethical behavior and strong character, and build a sense of momentum for their firm."[38] Notice that these requirements do not imply a particular leadership style: A top manager who works behind the scenes can be just as effective as one with a take-charge style.

Without exception, the success of major organizational initiatives depends on effective guidance and support from the company's top leadership. Implementing successful mergers and acquisitions, new-to-the-world innovations, alliances and partnerships, new IT systems, and supply chain reengineering requires continuing involvement from chief executives. In addition, very few bottom-up efforts to change the organization even on a more modest scale will succeed without eventually attaining support from the top. Without such support, lower-level managers have trouble establishing legitimacy, finding sufficient resources, and overcoming internal politics.

Marketspace Interview

Rob Glaser, Founder, Chairman, and CEO RealNetworks

I realized early on as the CEO of a fast-growing company that if I have a choice of working 2 or 3 percent harder versus being 2 or 3 percent more lucid, I'll take the latter—because the success of our organization is dependent on the work of hundreds of people, be it the technology they develop, the marketing plans they put together, the way they work with customers, or the way they build financial systems or legal practices or build out new sales territories.

So as your company grows, that's probably the biggest challenge: staying hands-on enough to keep in touch with the underlying trends and changes and nuances of your industry, yet at the same time realizing that it's the quality of your team that will ultimately determine how successfully you scale to the next level. One guy who met that challenge pretty well is Bill Gates. Bill went from being a 19-year-old with no CEO experience to being CEO of a company that scaled up. I was fortunate enough to work closely with him [in my previous job at Microsoft] and watch him and see how he changed the way he interacted with his teams and organization over time. And I hope I learned well from him, because I think that's one talent of his that's underappreciated.

Building a Strong Management Team

In Chapter 11, we talk about the specific roles that must be filled for each management team and the importance of the management team to an e-commerce startup. For established e-commerce companies, a good management team is still critical to success. Abilities that are important for management teams of online companies include the ability to keep the CEO in check; the ability to communicate the vision of the company; experience in startups, online businesses, or catalog businesses; and experience in technology roles.

The Shifting Role of Leadership for e-Commerce Companies

While most principles of sound leadership are universal, some environments may demand higher levels of leadership than others. According to Kotter, excellent basic management is sufficient when a firm operates in an environment of little change or continuous improvement; visionary leadership is needed when a firm faces nonincremental change; and energy-unleashing leadership is required when a firm is developing a new business or new business model.[39] Initially, e-commerce businesses face either between nonincremental change or a new business model, thus according to Kotter they would need visionary and possibly energy-unleashing leadership.

This view is consistent with the widely accepted thinking about leadership of e-commerce ventures during the dot-com boom. It was commonly held that new-economy leaders needed to operate as high-energy visionaries—racing to bring investors on board, attracting employees willing to work around the clock, sealing strategic partnerships in hours or days—with no need to think about traditional management structures.

Currently, however, successful e-commerce companies are more like established businesses, and new e-commerce ventures are often part of existing companies. To be sure, leaders still need to function in an environment of nonincremental change. It is generally agreed that they need the ability to create flexible, fast-moving, adaptive, results-oriented organizations. They need to foster innovation and develop new intellectual capital. At the same time, leadership entails more traditional responsibilities. In addition to rallying support, leaders need to listen and respond to employees and external stakeholders; nurture middle and lower managers; and employ traditional management tools for planning, budgeting, and coordination and control.

Partnerships

In Chapter 4, we discussed the importance of partnerships in defining the resource system for the online business model. In the online space, partnerships take on added significance. We define partnerships very broadly: Partnerships are agreements between two or more companies that are created to benefit each company—either strategically or economically or both. Partnerships include formal strategic alliances, affiliations, joint product offerings, marketing agreements (such as cross-promotion, portal agreements, and link exchanges), product licensing, fulfillment outsourcing, vendors, and research and development partnerships. Companies have used partnerships to support research and development efforts, to develop joint products, and to help with globalization efforts.

Companies enter into partnerships for many reasons, though ultimately all partnerships are created with the hope of building value and, eventually, revenue for the company. One study found that the stock price for a company rose 1 percent every time a strategic alliance was announced.[40]

Partnership Attributes

Partnerships tend to vary on two attributes: purpose and strength. On the first attribute, partnerships range from strategic to functional. Strategic partnerships are often alliances between two companies in which they both invest resources in order to achieve something that they could not do on their own. Research and development partnerships are mostly strategic. Functional partnerships tend to simply fill a function, and often one company pays the other company for the partnership—outsourcing and licensing agreements are largely functional partnerships. Partnerships can also be strong, where the two companies are heavily invested, or weak, where the companies have a more casual relationship. Exhibit 7.7 shows where some types of partnerships fall with respect to the purpose and strength attributes.

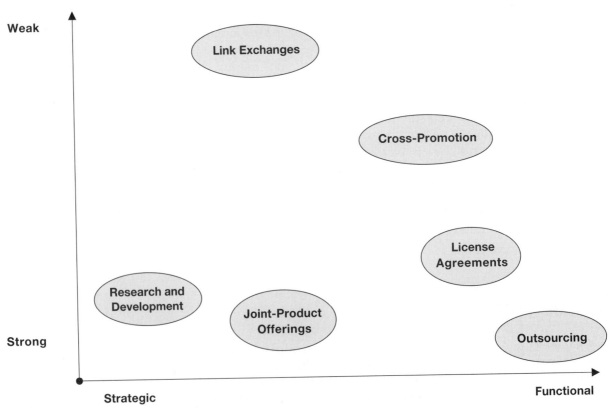

EXHIBIT 7.7   Partnership Attributes

Online Partnerships

Online businesses depend heavily on partnerships for three reasons. First, because of the complex technology and fulfillment issues involved with starting an e-commerce business, most companies cannot afford to do everything on their own—it would be a waste of their money to build warehouses and hire all the technology experts they need. Often, technology and operation functions get outsourced, either completely or partially. Even though Office Depot, Toys "R" Us, and Target are established companies, they have all partnered with Amazon.com to deliver their wares through Amazon's website. While Office Depot and Target have their own websites as well, Toys "R" Us delivers its merchandise only through Amazon.

Another reason is that online companies often need to find exposure quickly and create a presence on the Web. In Chapter 6, we discussed the different ways that firms can advertise through both online and offline methods. Partnerships give companies another way to build both awareness and their brand. Because customers cannot see the actual operations, online companies benefit from building trust through agreements with established online entities. Companies that trust AOL will trust 1-800-Flowers.com when they associate it with the AOL service.

The last reason that online companies enter into so many partnerships is simply because they can. Casual relationships have proliferated in the online environment because they are much easier than in the offline world. While it is relatively easy for a company to put links to another business on its website, it is quite difficult for a bricks-and-mortar store to carry another store's merchandise. Also, signs in a bookstore directing users to a toy store one state away wouldn't do much good—a link on a website that takes the book buyer to a toy store is relatively easy and effective.

In the future, we expect to see partnerships in the online world become more formal and strategic. Amazon's deal with Office Depot and other bricks-and-mortar stores is a sign of this. As established companies become more convinced that companies such as Amazon, Yahoo, and eBay will still be here in 10 years, they will become more willing to establish long-term relationships that they need to invest in. This is not to say that casual and functional relationships will disappear but only that online managers must understand how to manage many types of partnerships.

Managing Partnerships

As difficult as it can be to create partnerships, managing them is often much harder. Each company must constantly judge whether the partnership is worth the resources it is investing. For companies that are receiving money for their cooperation—outsourcing or licensing companies—as long as the amount they are getting paid more than covers their cost, the partnership is usually worth it. For companies that are giving up human or financial resources for intangible benefits—higher visibility, important research—they must even more carefully monitor how the partnership is benefiting their companies and if the gains are justifying the losses.

Jeffrey Dyer, Prashant Kale, and Harbir Singh found that companies that had a specific team within the organization dedicated to coordinating a partnership with another company had a 25 percent higher long-term success rate with that partner than if there were no team. Why? They found several reasons. First, there was increased external visibility of the partnership—marketing managers were able to tell others outside the company about the partnership. Internally, the team was able to coordinate efforts throughout the company, as well as intervene more quickly when they saw problems with the partnership. Also, the team was able to keep more of an eye on accountability, providing internal coordination and facilitating intervention and accountability.[41]

Another way to make sure a partnership is successful is to insist that it make money. While it is important to invest in strategic partnerships, those partnerships need to be kept to financial goals. Often, companies become reluctant to dissolve partnerships, even when they consistently lose money, because of the effort and money already invested in them. Sometimes companies are so overwhelmed with the current workload that they don't take the time to even evaluate the partnership. It seems easier to continue doing the same thing instead of stepping back and analyzing whether or not a partnership is succeeding at its original purpose.

Getting Things Done: Integrative Resource System

In the previous sections, we reviewed the seven parts of an integrative resource system. In order to keep the discussion manageable, we focused on each of the seven parts of the system in isolation. However, as Michael Porter of Harvard Business School has noted,[42] an important aspect of an integrated system is the degree to which the components work together in the marketplace. Hence, when the human assets are combined with great processes around human asset management as well as timely information systems, the overall effect can be magnified many times in the marketplace. Significant sustainable competitive advantage can arise as much for the choice of parts as from the blending of the parts—thus, the senior management team needs to consider how best to make this blending work.

In addition to the blending or mixing of the seven parts, the senior management team must also keep in mind six major principles of strong execution. The six major principles are based on our observation of great execution in practice combined with recent academic and managerial publications. These six principles are not the only principles, but they can be considered "best practice" observations of winning firms.

Principle 1: Execution Is Led by Senior Management—Not the Troops

Larry Bossidy, in his recent book, *Execution*, notes that senior management must take hands-on responsibility for making the organization run. Too frequently, he observes, senior management helps craft the overall strategic plan and then assigns middle managers the responsibility of executing the plan. Bossidy says that this approach is seriously flawed because the senior management team will be too far removed from the operations of the marketplace to understand subtle changes in customer behavior, competitor responses, and, perhaps most important, employee evaluation. The most effective senior managers are personally involved in the day-to-day operations. They know what employees do each day, who is performing well (and who is not), and the subtle interpersonal dynamics that often have to be managed as the firm attempts to win in the marketplace.[43]

Principle 2: Hold People Accountable for Meeting the Numbers

Employees must be held accountable for meeting specific, concrete targets. Virtually all writings on human motivation point to the need to have clear, unambiguous targets of performance. In addition to these performance quotas, individuals must also be held responsible for meeting those targets. To say that a particular website must have easy navigation is not very helpful guidance for the front-line manager. Thus, the first step in the evaluation process is to agree on the key metrics that reflect overall performance of the business and the levels of performance for those chosen metrics. Once these are set, individuals must be held accountable for meeting the numbers. If numbers are not met, senior management has every right to reduce variable compensation—or perhaps even stricter actions—to get the business back on course.

Principle 3: It Is Not Just About the Numbers; It Is Also About the Process

Bossidy also makes the point that it is not solely about the numbers. Rather, individuals must also have a clear idea of the guidelines, processes, rules, and generally acceptable ways to attain goals within an organization. Thus, while it is important to hit the targets, employees must also be responsible for how the goals are accomplished. Yes, winning firms always pay close attention to the numbers. However, the entire culture cannot simply be about achieving financial targets. In the long run, firms must also be able to replicate the process for achieving the targets. Why? Because the firm must be able to trust that employees are working in ways that are ethical, within the cultural boundaries of the firm, and scaleable or repeatable by other parts of the organization.

Principle 4: Continuous Improvement Is Still Relevant and Important

One of the interesting concepts of the total quality management era is the concept of continuous improvement. As we discussed in Chapter 3, innovation is important for online firms. Consider the following situation: If a particular firm is known as the market leader for customer satisfaction or ease of use, is it satisfactory to conclude that a certain level of performance is good enough? Very often, the answer is no. The reason is that competitors are constantly improving their level of service and ease of navigation. Thus, one key point of the total quality management movement was the importance of quantifying the critical processes and outputs of the firm to both document performance and set a baseline for continuous improvement.

Principle 5: The Customer Is the Starting Point

In the course of building a sustainable resource system, it is absolutely essential to state the most important benefits desired by the target market. Recall that in Chapter 4, we began the process of building a resource system by first specifying the three or four most important desired benefits. From this cluster of benefits, we then asked the question, What resources must the firm build to deliver against these desired benefits? Thus, when authors raise the issue of the importance of core resources and competencies, the most critical test of their importance is the firm's ability to tie each competence to specific customer benefits. Resources are only important if they can be tied to customer benefits.

Principle 6: Hire and Develop the "Doers"

We have all worked for companies in which a small number of employees produce a disproportionate share of the sales of the company. What would happen if you were able to work for a firm in which *all* employees were so productive? The best companies focus a great deal of attention on hiring people who get things done. This is in sharp contrast to a workforce that confuses mere activity with productivity. Highly motivated, task-driven employees who are given clear performance targets can make things happen.

In summary, these six principles are meant to serve as guidelines in helping firms go to market. These principles are based on the observations of leading practitioners as well as academic research. In addition to these principles, it may be useful for you to consider what other principles of great execution you can recall from your work experiences or from other courses you have completed.

MarketWatch.com Resource System

As we discussed earlier in the chapter, our implementation framework is divided into seven components, three of which we examine in this section within the context of MarketWatch.com: human assets, IT systems, and partnerships.

Human Assets

MarketWatch.com's head count was 201 at the end of 2001, down from 259 at the end of 2000. MarketWatch.com's CEO, Larry Kramer, was formerly the executive editor of *The San Francisco Examiner*, and metro editor and assistant managing editor of *The Washington Post*. Other members of the MarketWatch.com editorial staff previously worked for companies such as Bloomberg News, Associated Press, UPI, CBS Radio News, and Dow Jones Television. Based on his prior experience, Kramer believes that the ideal newsroom should have no more than 100 journalists, regardless of the audience it caters to. This allows for a highly scalable people model that can lead to increasing levels of profitability as the site's audience grows. The content-generating nucleus of MarketWatch.com, comprised of 72 professional journalists and editors in nine bureaus worldwide, sets it apart from its online competitors. It is also one of the main reasons that CBS News found MarketWatch.com such an appealing partner. Most members of MarketWatch.com's news staff specialize in particular financial topics, such as IPOs or investment conferences.

A group of 24 people working on product and content development complement the journalists. They devise new features to deliver on the site and products to license through their licensing program. Their website operations team of 33 people is responsible for publishing the content to the site and maintaining its servers and related site infrastructure.

At the end of 2001, MarketWatch.com had 45 people in sales and marketing, including a direct salesforce of more than 20 specialists to help understand and meet advertisers' needs. The company's salespeople had considerable experience in Internet sales and traditional media and developed and implemented advertising strategies for existing and new advertisers. Rounding out the MarketWatch.com team were 27 people in administration.[44]

Systems

The current MarketWatch.com technology infrastructure is centralized in a primary data center in Minneapolis, Minnesota; two additional data centers are located in New York and California. The three data centers are networked through Virtual Private Network connections, and all of the MarketWatch.com offices are connected to the central Minneapolis data center through a direct line. The MarketWatch.com system could comfortably run on just one-and-a-half data centers, but having multiple data centers allows the systems to continue to function properly in the event of a localized malfunction and allows the company to turn off one of the centers independently for maintenance work.

Within each data center, there is a four-tier infrastructure with multiple points of redundancy. Each data center has 60 Web servers, and there are systems in place to balance the information load between them. Internet access in the California area is maintained through multiple connections with three different ISPs, and the computer equipment used to operate the MarketWatch.com website is powered by multiple uninterruptible power supplies. This configuration further ensures against system failures and site malfunctions. Any content generated by journalists in any office gets submitted to the data centers and from there can be distributed to any interested party, including users, content licensees, and other partners.

Partnerships

The most significant partnership to MarketWatch.com is with CBS. In connection with its formation in 1997, MarketWatch.com entered into a license agreement under which its website was renamed "CBS Marketwatch.com." The site was granted the right to use the CBS name and logo, as well as CBS Television Network news content. Its agreement with CBS expires on October 29, 2005. Under the terms of an amended and restated license agreement, MarketWatch.com pays CBS a percentage of its gross revenues, excluding certain revenue. The agreement is subject to termination if competitors of CBS acquire specified amounts of Market-Watch.com common stock.

Under this partnership agreement, CBS agreed to place $30 million in advertising and on-air promotions for MarketWatch.com during the period from October 29, 1997, through October 29, 2002. The $30 million contribution was delivered in full by June 30, 2000. Other benefits of the partnership include the sharing of news resources. MarketWatch.com's New York City–based bureau is located in CBS facilities, and its staff frequently works with CBS News staff to generate stories for distribution over the CBS broadcast network. The staff files three market reports each day on CBS Newspath, which supplies CBS News video to more than 200 CBS-affiliated television stations for use in their news programs. Their correspondents also file customized daily reports to major CBS affiliates via satellite links, produce periodic reports for the CBS Evening News weekend broadcasts, and contribute a daily report to *The Early Show* on the CBS network. While MarketWatch.com does not receive any cash payments from CBS for its reporting, it does receive significant brand awareness benefits.

Summary

1. What factors are involved in successful strategy implementation?

A successful company needs to correctly manage seven factors to have a successful resource system: (a) human assets, (b) processes, (c) organizational structure, (d) systems, (e) culture, (f) leadership, and (g) partnerships.

2. What are the implementation challenges for online firms?

It has been argued that increased speed and intensity of competition in the online environment means implementation mistakes are punished much more severely and quickly than in the offline world. Online firms face five primary implementation challenges: (a) higher visibility to errors, (b) lower switching costs, (c) more dynamic competitive environment, (d) more fluid organizational boundaries, and (e) more complex linkages.

3. What human-assets issues must online firms be concerned with?

Online firms must worry about recruitment, selection, development, and retention of employees. Also, in the current environment, online companies are stressing stability to attract employees, and offering better pay and benefits over stock options. With so many online companies going out of business amid market uncertainty, managers must also deal with employees' concerns about job security.

4. What are the different types of processes that firms must develop?

The types of processes a firm must develop include resource-allocation processes, human resource management processes, manufacturing and distribution processes, payment and billing processes, and customer support/handling processes.

5. What are the advantages of the two types of hybrid organizational structures?

Single-organization firms are able to make it easier for customers to use different platforms to interact with the company. Because online and offline customer service is integrated, they have an easier time managing a consistent brand. Their employees are able to work across platforms, gaining a broader set of skills and capabilities. Also, because they are taxed on the entire organization, if the online unit is losing money but the offline unit is making money, they are able to pay less in taxes. They are often valued higher than pure online or offline companies. Finally, they have only one set of systems to worry about.

Dual-organization structures also have advantages. They do not have to coordinate their processes, so each unit can make decisions based on what is best for it. The units are able to cannibalize each other, and people who want to work in one type of unit can choose their work environment. The two units don't have to fight with each other for human resources. Finally, the customers of separate online units often don't have to pay sales tax.

6. What systems might online firms be concerned with?

Systems are important for companies because they establish procedures for the organization. Systems that online firms might concern themselves with include information technology, ERP, CRM, evaluation and compensation, and supply chain management.

7. What kind of culture is best for e-commerce companies?

While there is no one culture that is best for any type of company, the type of culture that would work best for e-commerce firms is one that is based on enduring employee attachment to the company. This happens when there are strategies that emphasize marketing, service, or customer relationships.

8. How has the role of leadership changed for online companies?

E-commerce leaders still need to create flexible, fast-moving, adaptive, results-oriented organizations as well as foster innovations and develop new intellectual capital. However, now they must also embrace more traditional responsibilities, such as rallying support. Leaders need to listen, respond to employees and external stakeholders, nurture middle and lower managers, and employ traditional management tools for planning, budgeting, and coordination and control.

9. Why are partnerships so prevalent for online firms?

Partnerships are important to online firms for several reasons. They help new companies create complex technical and fulfillment infrastructures, and they help provide important marketing and branding functions. Also, the nature of online companies makes it easier to create partnerships. For example, it's a relatively simple matter to place a link to another company on a website.

Exercises

1. Go to QVC.com. How is the website integrated with the television channel? Do you see any differences? Now go to Barnes & Noble.com. How is it integrated with Barnes & Noble retail stores? How is it separate?

2. Go to the Google search engine (*www.google.com*). Find the "All About Google" page and look at the descriptions of the company, its culture, its available jobs, etc. How is the culture aligned with the strategy of the company? Look at the "Reasons to Work at Google" page. What kind of nontraditional benefits does it offer? Does it make an effort to present itself as a stable company?

3. Find articles about Meg Whitman (CEO of eBay), Jeff Bezos (CEO of Amazon), or Steve Case (former chairman of AOL Time Warner). What qualities does that person possess that helped him or her lead an online company to success? What qualities might make him or her unable to sustain the success?

Key Terms

human assets
switching costs
processes
resource-allocation processes
human resources management
   processes
manufacturing and distribution
   processes

payment and billing processes
customer support/handling
   processes
systems
information technology (IT)
enterprise resource planning (ERP)
customer relationship management
   (CRM)

evaluation and compensation
   systems
supply chains
organizational culture

[1]"Comparison Shoppers Let Their Fingers Do the Walking," *eMarketer*, 19 March 2002, citing data from Bizrate.com.

[2]Mitch Betts, "Brands Still Matter, Even for Shopbots," *MIT Sloan Management Review* 42, no. 2 (Winter 2001):9.

[3]Fred Brooks, *The Mythical Man-Month* (Reading, MA: Addison-Wesley Publishing, 1995), 18.

[4]Michael Beer and Russell A. Eisenstat, "The Silent Killers of Strategy Implementation and Learning." *MIT Sloan Management Review* 41, no. 4 (Summer 2000):29–40.

[5]James Collins, "Built to Flip," *Fast Company*, March 2000, 131–43.

[6]Elaine X. Grant, "Can Dot-Coms Still Attract the Best and the Brightest?" e-*Commerce Times*, 11 March 2002 (URL: http://www.ecommercetimes.com/perl/story/16682.html).

[7]Ibid.

[8]"Multi-Channel Shopping for Home Electronics," *eMarketer*, 31 July 2002, citing Marshall Marketing and Communication for Vertis, July 2002.

[9]Kate Sweetman, "Spreading IT Expertise Throughout the Company" *MIT Sloan Management Review* 42, no. 4 (Summer 2001):13.

[10]C. K. Prahalad and M. S. Krishnan, "Synchronizing Strategy and Information Technology," *MIT Sloan Management Review* 43, no. 4 (Summer 2002):24–33.

[11]"ERP Overview," *Information Technology Toolbox, Inc.* (URL: http://www.erpassist.com/pub/erp_overview.htm).

[12]Adrian Mello, "ERP Fundamentals," *ZDNet*, 7 February 2002 (URL: http://www.zdnet.com/filters/0,6061,2844319-92,00.html).

[13]Ibid.

[14]Adrian Mello, "4 Trends Shaping ERP," *ZDNet*, 7 February 2002 (URL: http://zdnet.com/filters/printerfriendly/0,6061,2844338-92,00.html).

[15]Philip Manchester, "Understanding CRM 2001: Secret Surprises," *FT.com*, 26 November 2001, updated 28 November 2001 (URL: http://specials.ft.com/understanding crm/FT3TIDVEIUC.html).

[16]Kim Benjamin, "Building a Strategy," *FT.com*, 26 November 2001, updated 28 November 2001 (URL: http://specials.ft.com/understanding crm/FT3M2ROFIUC.html).

[17]Darrell K. Rigby, Frederick F. Reichheld, and Phil Schefter, "Avoid the Four Perils of CRM," *Harvard Business Review* (February 2002):5–11.

[18]Andrew Fisher, "Customer Relationship Management—The Personal Touch," *Financial Times*, 26 November 2001, updated 7 December 2001.

[19]Ibid.

[20]Jeffrey Pfeffer, "Six Dangerous Myths About Pay," *Harvard Business Review* (May–June 1998):109–119.

[21]Peter Gwynne, "How Consistent Are Performance Review Criteria?" *MIT Sloan Management Review* 43, no. 4 (Summer 2002):15. This article discusses the work of Maria Rotundo, assistant professor of human resources management and organizational behavior at the University of Toronto's Joseph L. Rotman School of Management.

[22]Technically, many of these retailers, such as Amazon, do have large warehouses with stock on hand. However, companies such as Amazon are able to take advantage of significant cost differences relative to other retailers since they do not need to maintain expensive retail locations.

[23]Abigail Goldman, "e-Commerce Gets an F Without the 'D' Word Retailing," *Los Angeles Times*, 25 July 1999, Home edition, Business section.

[24]Elaine X. Grant, "Why B2B Has Been a Bust—So Far," e-*Commerce Times*, 7 March 2002 (URL: www.ecommercetimes.com/perl/story/16657.html).

[25]Elaine X. Grant, "Study: E-Commerce to Top $1 Trillion in 2002," e-*Commerce Times*, 13 February 2002 (URL: http://www.ecommercetimes.com/perl/story/16314.html).

[26]Goldman, Sachs and Co., "B2B: 2B or Not 2B? Version 1.1," 12 November 1999.

[27]Thomas W. Gerdel, "Industry Takes to the Web; Internet Fast Reshaping Traditional Supply Chain," *Cleveland Plain Dealer*, 27 February 2000, final edition.

[28]Nikki Tait, Louise Kehoe, and Tim Burt, "U.S. Car Monoliths Muscle In on the Internet Revolution: Ford and GM Plans to Buy from Suppliers Online May Reduce Costs Further," *Financial Times*, 8 November 1999, International Companies & Finance section.

[29]For a comprehensive discussion of organizational culture, see E.H. Schein, *Organizational Culture and Leadership* (San Francisco: Jossey-Bass, 1985).

[30]"Measuring Returns on IT Investments: Some Tools and Techniques," *Knowledge@Wharton*, n.d. (URL: http://knowledge.wharton.upenn.edu/articles.cfm?catid=14&articleid=396).

[31]See, for example, T. Deal and A. Kennedy, *Corporate Culture: The Rites and Rituals of Corporate Life* (Reading, MA: Addison-Wesley, 1982); R. Quinn and M. McGrath, "Transformation of Organizational Culture: A Competing Values Perspective." In *Organizational Culture*, ed. Peter First et al. (Beverly Hills, CA: Sage Publishing, 1985); R. Deshpande, J. Farley, and R. Webster, "Organizational Culture and Marketing: Defining the Research Agenda," *Journal of Marketing* 53 (January 1989); and R. Deshpande, J. Farley, and F. Webster, "Corporate Culture, Customer Orientation, and Innovativeness in Japanese Firms: A Quadrad Analysis," *Journal of Marketing* 57, no. 3 (1993).

[32]J. N. Baron and M. T. Hannan, "Organizational Blueprints for Success in High-Tech Start-Ups: Lessons from the Stanford Project on Emerging Companies," *California Management Review* 44, no. 3 (Spring 2002).

[33]Ibid.

[34]Jody Hoffer Gittell and Charles O'Reilly, "JetBlue Airways: Starting from Scratch," Case no. 9-801-354, October 29, 2001 (Boston: Harvard Business School Publishing, 2001).

[35]Stephanie L. Woerner, "Networked at Cisco," Center for eBusiness, Sloan School of Management, Massachusetts Institute of Technology, Teaching Case no. 1, 20 July 2001 (Cambridge: Massachusetts Institute of Technology, 2001).

[36]Grace Yokoi and Charles O'Reilly III, "Building the Culture at Agilent Technologies: Back to the Future," Case (Field), no. HR20, 1 September 2001, revised 6 December 2001 (Stanford: Stanford Graduate School of Business, 2001), 14. Case distributed through Harvard Business School Publishing.

[37]"Corporate Culture Can Break (or Make) a Merger," *Knowledge@Wharton*, n.d. (URL: http://knowledge.wharton.upenn.edu/ articles.cfm?catid=10&articleid=429); and Meta Group, "Commentary: Merger Requires Patience," *CNET News.com*, 5 September 2001 (URL:http://news.com.com/2102-10010272651.html).

[38]"As CEOs Fall Off Their Pedestals, Is a Leadership Crisis Looming?" *Knowledge@Wharton*, n.d. (URL: http://knowledge.wharton. upenn.edu/print_version.cfm?articleid=564&catid=2).

[39]"Kotter's Point of View: 5 Degrees of Change," *HBSWorking Knowledge*, 17 August 2002 (URL: http://hbsworkingknowledge.hbs.edu/ kotter/5degreesprint.htm).

[40]Jeffrey J. Dyer, Prashant Kale, and Harbir Singh, "How to Make Strategic Alliances Work," *MIT Sloan Management Review* 42, no. 4 (Summer 2001):37.

[41]*Ibid.*

[42]Michael Porter, "What Is Strategy?" *Harvard Business Review* 74, no. 6 (November–December, 1996):61–78.

[43]Larry Bossidy and Ram Charan, *Execution: The Discipline of Getting Things Done* (New York: Crown Business, 2002).

[44]MarketWatch.com, *Annual Report 2001.*

Metrics

CASELET: WELLS FARGO WATCHES ITS METRICS

Metrics matter. Just ask Wells Fargo.

Though more than 150 years old, the San Francisco–based, multi-billion-dollar regional bank holding company was able to reinvent itself as an online-banking powerhouse—in no small part because it thought carefully and strategically about both its online goals and how to gauge its progress in meeting them.

The company entered the online banking field in 1995. Within a few years, it had invested hundreds of millions of dollars to become the leading U.S. Internet bank. But it faced the same question as all companies pursuing aggressive Internet strategies: How should it measure the success—or lack of success—of its online investments?

From the start, Wells Fargo was committed to finding the answers to that question, monitoring the relative costs of providing services online and offline. And it found that it was, in fact, saving money on products such as wire transfers and services such as call centers when customers moved online.

But Wells Fargo also thought carefully about why it wanted to be on the Web. It concluded that, while cost-savings was a valuable metric, it wasn't the most valuable metric. The bottom line, the company decided, was customers: getting them, keeping them, and ensuring that they bought Wells Fargo products. And by using sophisticated analysis—for instance, comparing its online customers not to its overall customer base but to a carefully selected control group of demographically and financially similar offline customers—it found that its online initiatives were doing just that.

Research showed that the bank's online channel was generating more new customers than its branches. Once on board, the online customers were twice as likely to stay put. (Online bill-payers, the bank found, were the most loyal segment of all.) What's more, the online customers were twice as likely as their offline counterparts to purchase additional banking products.

"Our feeling is that you must have some kind of feel for benefit," Webb Edwards, executive vice president of Wells Fargo's technology and operations group, *told* Banking Wire. *"And it must be in some kind of quantifiable or measurable terms."*

This chapter was coauthored by Jeffrey Rayport, Bernie Jaworski, Leo Griffin, and Yannis Dosios.

PLEASE CONSIDER THE FOLLOWING QUESTIONS AS YOU READ THIS CHAPTER:

1. Why should senior managers be concerned about metrics?

2. How can the health of online firms be assessed?

3. What are the steps to implementing the Performance Dashboard?

4. What external sources of metrics information can firms use to chart their progress?

INTRODUCTION

In Chapter 7, we analyzed the key components of strategy implementation. In this chapter, we turn our attention to the **metrics** that senior managers can use to evaluate the progress of their businesses. Because senior and stock-market analysts tend to have a bias toward financial metrics, this is not a straightforward issue. Though important, financial metrics are limited in two respects. First, financial results are essentially a measure of the success of past strategies. While they reflect the performance history of the company in the marketplace, they do not provide managers with a warning system by which to take corrective action before disappointing returns are realized.[1] Second, financial measures are only output measures; to assess the true progress of an online company, a company needs to develop company-specific metrics that precisely track its strategy.[2] To return for a moment to our flower example from Chapter 4, the value proposition of 1-800-Flowers.com focused on freshness of flowers and reasonable prices. Hence, one of its early warning metrics would be the degree to which customers in the company's target segment perceive that competitors of 1-800-Flowers.com are outperforming it on freshness and reasonable prices. Because the value proposition is only one component of the overall strategy, other metrics would also need to be developed for each strategy component, such as the offering, resource system, and implementation.

The purpose of this chapter is to provide a framework by which one can assess the health of an online business. The framework is composed of five categories of metrics: market opportunity, business model, marketing and branding, implementation, and customer. Market opportunity metrics focus on the conditions in the customer and competitor environments. Business-model metrics include topics related to the value cluster, marketspace offering, resource system and capabilities, partnerships, and the financial model. Marketing and branding metrics focus on relationship stages (awareness, exploration, commitment, dissolution) and market levers (product, price, communication, community, distribution). Implementation metrics focus on human resources, processes, organizational structure, systems (including information, incentives, and rewards), coordination mechanisms, culture and management style, and technology systems. Customer metrics focus on output measures that relate to the customer experience (overall satisfaction, average dollar amount of purchases, stickiness) as well as metrics that relate to the customer interface.

In this chapter, we first answer the question, Why do metrics matter? Then we introduce the Balanced Scorecard as a reference framework, discuss its limitations, and introduce the Performance Dashboard. We then focus on a five-step process for implementing the Performance Dashboard. Because most of the chapter discusses only online businesses, we then turn to integrating metrics of online and offline businesses. We also provide an overview of the sources of information that firms can use as inputs to the metrics process. Finally, we apply the five-step implementation process to MarketWatch.com.

Why Senior Managers Should Be Concerned About Metrics

Before we discuss **metrics** frameworks, it is important to consider whether metrics are significant to online managers. In the past, many people doubted the usefulness of metrics for e-businesses for many reasons. Here are some of their arguments and the reasons those arguments are now invalid.

- *Companies' strategies change rapidly, so the metrics needed to evaluate them will have to change too often to be useful.* Now that online initiatives—and the companies that fund them—realize that it is costly to change business models, they are more apt to commit to a long-term strategy and, therefore, they can devise and stick with metrics that will assess it.

- *Measurement is resource-intensive, and no one has time to analyze and implement what is learned.* Though it is true that online tracking systems have given managers the ability to collect far more data than they will ever have time to analyze, many companies are finding it more useful to track a few key metrics than to try to track everything. For example, Dell tracks just three metrics: order fulfillment, product performance, and postsale service and support. By making sure that what is measured is closely aligned with strategy, the data collected are more relevant and better understood.

- *Results of online measurements could be exaggerated so companies look better to investors.* A company hoping to raise money could compromise data, artificially boosting its number of unique users or submitting false demographic data. But because the financial community no longer solely uses these types of metrics to judge an investment, companies no longer have a reason to inflate their numbers. They are better off being realistic with their data so they have a true picture of how they are doing.

- *Meaningful metrics change on Internet time.* Metrics considered relevant and appropriate in tracking a site's success often change. Less than four years ago, companies used "hits" as the basic metric of success. Then it was page views. Now, conversion rates are considered the appropriate measure. As companies track metrics to determine how well they are executing against the company's strategy, it only follows that companies with different strategies should track different metrics.

Choosing metrics carefully and acting on the data are crucial if measurements are to be useful. When used correctly, metrics are a necessary addition to support the strategy of any online initiative.

Tracking and acting on the data from metrics can produce very important results for an organization. We now isolate five ways in which metrics can help a company's growth and vitality.[3]

Better Definition of Business Model

The act of specifying concrete goals with precise measurement can help senior managers define the business model of a company. Companies often struggle with their choice of value proposition or cluster. Focusing attention on measurement can help increase the precision of the value proposition.

A good example is a service offered by Dell Computer Corp. called Premier Dell.com. Businesses that have large accounts with Dell can access their own customized portal to manage their PC purchases and service. On this password-protected website, users can search, select, buy, track shipping, and receive service.

Should Premier Dell.com's value cluster focus on price, speed of delivery, level of custom configuration of the PC, customer service, or assurance of reliability? The answer depends on which attributes the particular customer segment (in this case, medium and large businesses) values most. How can Dell know this? It can ask its customers and then track the areas that customers use most frequently to refine the offering. Do the vast percentage of customers log on to receive service? If so, it may make sense to track metrics such as the speed of response from the customer service center, the ability of the customer to receive the answers they seek from online Q&A sections, and the ability to reach an online customer service representative at the point on the site where the user has questions. Dell can track all of these items by using a variety of methods, including online questionnaires, followup calls from customer service representatives, and online tracking. It is important to track the metrics that matter most to the customer segment, which then influences what is critical to the business model.

Strategy Communication

Clearly documented performance targets can go a long way toward communicating the goals and strategy of a company. Once performance metrics are specified, they should be communicated as widely as possible within the organization. Communicating the strategy to the workforce helps employees understand and appreciate the metrics-setting process.

Performance Tracking

One of the unique features of the online world is the availability of instantaneous site-performance feedback. Metrics concerning usage, types of visitors, length of time spent on site by occasion, average sales, most frequent pages or sections viewed, and the like, are constantly available. Thus, in sharp contrast to traditional offline models, firms are able to track performance in real time and make appropriate modifications in tactics or strategy.

Increased Accountability

Metrics need to be linked to the reward system, in order to have weight behind them. Individual performance appraisals can be tied to company-wide, team-specific, and individual metrics. General performance measures such as sales growth and amount of sales are likely to have companywide accountability. Furthermore, specific measures related to site usability can be tied to the interactive design department, while customer service metrics can be tied directly to the customer service department.

Alignment of Objectives

Clear, precise metrics can help align individual objectives, departmental functional goals, and companywide strategic activities. For example, understanding that a firm has made it a priority to increase its look-to-book ratio (the number of customers who buy relative to the number who visit) enables various departments and individual employees to adjust their daily activities to execute against this goal.

Assessing the Health of Online Firms

In this section, we introduce the Performance Dashboard, a framework for judging the progress and health of an online business. We use the dashboard metaphor to describe the real-time management tasks that confront the leaders of an online enterprise. Analogous to an automotive dashboard, the framework provides vital performance feedback to the firm, either confirming success or identifying problems that should be corrected. We begin our discussion by reviewing Robert Kaplan and David Norton's seminal work on the Balanced Scorecard.

The Balanced Scorecard

Kaplan and Norton introduced the **Balanced Scorecard** in response to their perception that managers overwhelmingly focus on short-term financial performance. They argued that firms must balance their financial perspective by analyzing other domains of the business, including internal business processes and customer responses. In particular, they introduced four categories of metrics they believed more accurately captured companies' performance: financial, customer, internal business process, and learning and growth (see Exhibit 8.1). This approach not only added perspective to a restricted financial focus but also provided managers with an early warning system that allowed for corrective measures to be taken before poor financial results were realized. A key feature of the Kaplan and Norton approach is to start with the firm's strategy and then derive the metrics in the four areas. In the following paragraphs, we describe each of the four areas in detail.

Financial Metrics
Financial metrics are designed to assess the financial performance of the company. Typical financial measures include revenue, revenue growth, gross margins, operating income, net margin, earnings per share, and cash flow. Financial measures reflect strategic choices from the most recent planning period and, to some degree, an accumulation of all previous planning periods. Hence, Amazon's financial performance in 2003 is a result not just of the choices of those 12 months but of all the decisions since its 1995 launch.

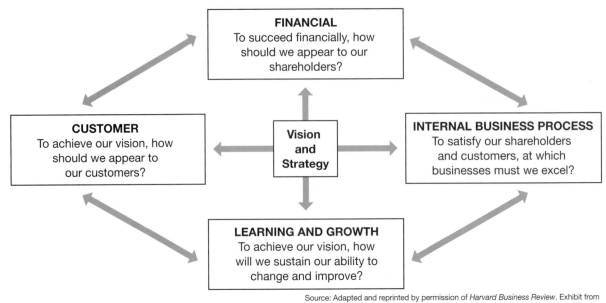

EXHIBIT 8.1   The Balanced Scorecard Strategy in Operational Terms

Finally, financial measures are used by all stakeholders of the company, including employees, customers, and partners, and are the metrics most heavily weighed and analyzed by the investment community.

Customer Metrics

Customer metrics are intended to assess the management of customer relationships by the firm. With the Kaplan and Norton scheme, these metrics typically focus on a set of core measurements, including market share and customer acquisition, satisfaction, and profitability. Basically, they reflect the overall health of the customer base. Kaplan and Norton also point out that these measures need to be customized to the target segment. To return to our Dell example, a large client such as Boeing Co. would probably have fairly large customer acquisition costs but high profitability if the relationship is solidified. In contrast, smaller clients may have lower acquisition costs for Dell but also a lower total lifetime customer value.

Internal Business Process Metrics

Internal business process metrics focus on operations inside the company. In particular, this set of metrics focuses on the critical value-adding activities that lead to customer satisfaction and enhanced shareholder value. Kaplan and Norton divide these metrics into three broad groups: innovation, operations, and postsale service:

- *Innovation.* Innovation metrics measure how well the company identifies customer needs and either changes or adds new offerings. These measures could include customers' perceptions of the innovativeness of the company or quantitative measures of innovativeness (e.g., percent of product sales from new products, percent of new products versus competitors).

- *Operations.* Operations metrics measure the quality of the entire supply chain process through to delivery of products to the customer. This could include measures that reflect customer order processing, order cycle time, delivery time, and order error percent.

- *Postsale service.* Postsale service metrics measure the quality of the service the company offers to customers. This includes return processing, warranty processing, turnaround time for e-mail questions, and payment processing.

Learning and Growth Metrics

Learning and growth metrics broadly cover employee, information systems, and motivation metrics. Employee metrics relate to selection, training, retention, and satisfaction. Information system metrics capture the quality of the infrastructure that must be built to create long-term growth and improvement; measures would include timeliness, accuracy, and utility of data. Motivation encompasses employee motivation, empowerment, and alignment. Metrics would relate to alignment of company goals and incentives with personal employee goals.

Limitations of the Balanced Scorecard

The Balanced Scorecard has become a classic management tool. However, it becomes less useful when we attempt to apply it to the online world. The following are some of its shortcomings:

- *No clear definition of strategy or business models.* A key theme of the Balanced Scorecard is that it is based on the strategy of the firm. However, Kaplan and Norton do not clearly define the components of the strategy or business model. Without this definition, it is difficult to assess whether the four categories of metrics accurately capture the critical aspects of the business strategy or the business model.

- *Unclear location of organizational capabilities or resources in the framework.* Organizational capabilities and resources span a variety of domains, including internal business processes, customer relationships, and the unique selection of markets (e.g., market-sensing capabilities).[4] Thus, capabilities often extend beyond internal business processes. This is especially true in an online model, where suppliers are often integrated into the system (as with Cisco Systems). In this case, organizational boundaries become fuzzy, and it is unclear where capabilities are located in the framework.

- *Unclear location of partnerships in the framework.* Strategic partnerships are a critical measure of a firm's ability to compete in today's networked economy. However, partnerships are not addressed in the Balanced Scorecard framework.

In sum, the Balanced Scorecard has taken the important first step toward the development of a set of metrics to assess the effectiveness and efficiency of businesses. In the next section, we introduce a framework that accounts for the issues not addressed by the Balanced Scorecard.

The Performance Dashboard

Similar to the Balanced Scorecard, the **Performance Dashboard** is intended to reflect the health of a business. We now address each of the Balanced Scorecard's limitations through features of the Performance Dashboard. We

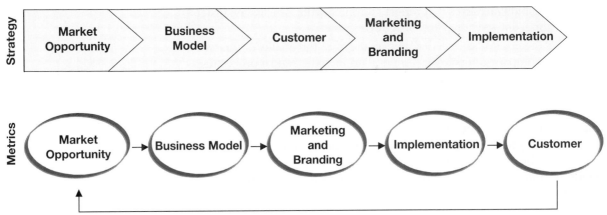

EXHIBIT 8.2 The Performance Dashboard

also review the five categories of metrics that reflect the strategy framework of this book.

The Strategy Framework Drives the Necessary Metrics

While the Balanced Scorecard offers no clear definition of strategy or business model, the Performance Dashboard uses the strategy framework to drive the necessary metrics. In Chapters 3 through 7, we articulated a strategy process that is captured in an organizing framework for the textbook (see Exhibit 1.5). In the proposed framework, there are five critical steps to the strategy process: (1) strategic analysis, (2) business model specification, (3) customer interface design, (4) marketing, and (5) strategy implementation.

These five steps represent a strategy process for online businesses and can be used to identify the categories that map onto and directly link to the strategy. Relevant metrics categories include (1) market opportunity metrics, (2) business model metrics, (3) marketing and branding metrics, (4) implementation metrics, (5) and customer metrics (see Exhibit 8.2). In the Performance Dashboard, as in building a strategy, each metric category leads to another one. Market opportunity metrics lead to business model metrics, which lead to marketing and branding metrics, and so on. The steps to define a strategy are different than the steps to define metrics because, while customers need to be considered while building a strategy, they cannot really be measured until the strategy has been implemented.

Resources Are Featured in the Business Model

While the Balanced Scorecard does not specify the location of organizational resources, the Performance Dashboard identifies the resources featured in the resource system of the business model. Firm-level resources are defined during the third step of the business model. Hence, resources of the firm are highlighted and integrated into the Performance Dashboard metrics. Recall that the isolation of these resources is essential to determining the drivers of the customer benefits.

Partnerships Are Featured in the Resource System of the Business Model

While the Balanced Scorecard is unclear about where partnerships reside in its framework, partnerships are featured in the resource system of the business model in the Performance Dashboard. Recall that in Chapter 4 we isolated the firm-level resources that related to the various benefits. We also noted that it is at this step that partnerships need to be considered to fill in where the firm does not have the requisite resources. Hence, partnerships are explicitly considered in the Performance Dashboard measures.

Components of the Performance Dashboard

The Performance Dashboard is composed of five categories of metrics: strategic analysis, business model, marketing, implementation, and customer. As stated before, each strategy category corresponds to a metrics category.

Market Opportunity Metrics

Recall that we defined market opportunity as the firm's ability to discern an unfulfilled need in the marketplace, a critical part of the strategy process. This is not a one-time event but rather a continual process, because market conditions ceaselessly evolve. For example, by constantly expanding its offerings to include complementary gifts, 1-800-Flowers.com extended its segment focus beyond the core offerings.

Market opportunity metrics assess the degree to which the firm can accurately gauge the conditions in its competitive environment as well as the conditions underlying market opportunities. Generic indicators include the ability of the firm to target the most attractive segments, to understand and map competitors' strategy, and to track the evolution of target-segment needs.

Business-Model Metrics

Business-model metrics capture the subcomponents of the business model: the value proposition, egg diagram, resource system, and financial metrics. We review each of these metrics below.

Value Proposition or Cluster Benefits Metrics   The value proposition is composed of three parts: target segment, core benefits offered, and resources that drive the core benefits. Metrics for this assessment would focus on customer perceptions of the benefits that a given site offers relative to competitors. Resources in the value proposition will be addressed in our discussion of the resource system.

Thus, to return to 1-800-Flowers.com, the key customer benefits are low prices, fresh flowers, a broad assortment of gifts, and widespread access. Its managers would be concerned about how customers judge the firm's performance relative to its competitors' on these four benefits.

Online Offering Metrics   This phase of the business model is captured in the egg diagram reviewed in Chapter 4. Metrics should capture all phases of the customer decision process as well as the features and attributes of the offering.

Offering metrics focus more on the website's nuts and bolts—in other words, its basic attributes and functionality. Thus, to return to our egg diagram, the offering metrics would capture performance on the products and services ring of the diagram. For 1-800-Flowers.com, this would include customer evaluations of the gift recommendations section, FAQs, the ease of commerce transaction, and member specials.

Resource System Metrics   The resource system is based on all the benefits offered to consumers. From these benefits, the firm would analyze the resources that are necessary to supply the benefits. These benefits can be offered by the firm or its partners.

In this phase of metrics building, the firm should track its performance on the most critical resources and associated activities. In the context of 1-800-Flowers.com, those resources include logistics, sourcing, brand name, multiple contact points, media partnerships, product partnerships, and an online gift center. Also, recall that resources are provided by both the firm and partners and, therefore, the firm would also want to consider performance metrics for these critical partnerships.

Financial Metrics   Financial metrics capture the revenues, costs, profits, and balance-sheet metrics of the firm. These are the most critical metrics for the long-term success of the firm. However, as noted earlier, these results are a function of the accumulated strategy decisions of the firm. Hence, while they focus management attention on what results need to be corrected, they offer no guidance to factors that can influence their correction.

Marketing and Branding Metrics
Marketing and branding metrics focus on marketing communication and branding effectiveness. In Chapter 6, we introduced approaches to developing branding. Fulfillment of the brand promise could include metrics related to the brand's strength—widespread customer awareness of the brand, for example.

Implementation Metrics
Implementation metrics focus on the effectiveness of a company's human resources program as well as its processes, organizational structure, systems (including information, incentives, and rewards), coordination mechanisms, culture and management style, and technology systems.

Customer Metrics
While the market opportunity metrics determine customers' potential needs, **customer metrics** measure how customers relate to the website. To do this, they capture two forms of metrics. The first class of metrics measures the customer's experience with the technology interface—that is, the customer's response to the 7Cs of the interface. The second class captures output metrics such as overall levels of satisfaction, average order size, and customer profitability. Although customer interface is designed before marketing and implementation in the strategy formulation process, measuring how customers react to the website, both aesthetically and practically, can happen only after it has been marketed and implemented. Therefore, in the Performance Dashboard, marketing and implementation metrics are considered before the customer metrics.

Customer Interface Metrics   In Chapter 5, we provided a detailed description of the 7Cs of the customer interface. In this chapter, we are concerned with customer perceptions of the firm's performance on each of the seven characteristics. For example, how would customers rate the level of customization on the firm's site versus competitors' sites? Is the content adequate? Is the level of community adequate? Obviously, a host of specific measures could be created for each C. The challenge for managers is to select a subset of the most critical interface metrics. A starting point for this winnowing exercise is the value proposition of the firm.

Customer Outcome Metrics   The customer interface metrics just described capture the process measures that the firm believes will produce favorable customer responses such as satisfaction and loyalty. Thus, a great community section will lead to more favorable overall levels of satisfaction with the website. Here, we focus attention on both the subjective and objective customer outcome metrics. Subjective measures include customer satisfaction and, in regards to the website, an overall evaluation of the customer's experience. Objective, quantitative measures include customer acquisition costs, average order size, customer profitability, and number of visits per month. These latter metrics can be aggregated into a measure of the overall lifetime value of the customer.

Drill-Down

Are Financial Metrics Objective?

While much weight has been given to financial metrics, we only need to look at financial reporting in Europe to see how financial results can vary. Currently in the European Union, accounting and financial reporting methods vary greatly among member countries due to differences in countries' legal systems, finance providers, and taxation policies. Another reason for the variations is that because most companies are private, the accounting methods are often designed to determine tax liabilities, not necessarily to provide investors with a window into the financial workings of a company.[5]

As we just mentioned, varying legal systems also contribute to the discrepancies. In the Netherlands, accounting law is contained in the civil code; in Germany, accounting rules are detailed in the commercial codes, with supplements found in company law; and in France, a government-controlled agency provides an accounting plan in addition to the rules described in the commercial codes. The United Kingdom and Ireland rely on a limited amount of statute law to provide answers to particular cases rather than create a general rule. In those systems, accounting and financial reporting systems are controlled by the accounting profession and are not dependent on statutory law, which is slow to change.

Another contributing factor is differing business and ownership structures, which dictate the needs and uses of financial reporting. In France and Italy, capital is predominately provided by the state or banks. In Germany, the banks are significant owners and the providers of corporate debt. Because the majority owners of these companies nominate directors, rapid access to detailed companies' financial information is available to this constituency. In the United Kingdom and the Netherlands, companies are funded by shares that are held primarily by institutional investors or by individuals. This ownership structure calls for the availability of unbiased information because the majority of owners are outside owners.

One last major difference is in tax structures. Treatment of deferred taxation, depreciation, and asset valuation affects accounting valuations and the way information is reported. In countries where accounting and financial reporting are mandated and prescribed by the legal codes, depreciation schedules are generally fixed, deferred taxation is not an issue, and the treatment of asset valuation and bad loans, for example, is also mandated by legal code. In the United Kingdom, these issues are a matter of practice and not prescribed by law. Treatment of these matters is

continued

focused on minimizing tax liability and taking advantage of investment incentives, resulting in a difference between tax and financial reporting. This reporting difference does not arise in countries with statutory laws governing corporations.

To unite the European Union into one commercial market, steps have been taken to unify the practices of member countries. Recently, the European Commission welcomed the positive opinions adopted by the European Parliament's plenary session in Strasbourg, France, on a proposal concerning the adoption of international accounting standards (IAS) for European companies.[6] The Parliament's March 12, 2002, opinion proposes that IAS be applied to all listed companies in the European Union from 2005 onward. Member states will also have the option of extending this requirement to unlisted companies. The regulation, although it still needs to be ratified by EU ministers, will help eliminate barriers to cross-border trading in securities by using a common reporting language, making it easier to compare company accounts and thus improving the efficiency of European capital markets and reducing the cost of capital.

Life Cycle of a Company

Exhibit 8.3 illustrates that online firms pass through four stages of development in the **life cycle of a company**. These stages are called *startup, customer acquisition, monetization,* and *maturity*. The relative weight of the metrics varies by the stage of the business. For example, in the startup phase, the market opportunity metrics and the articulation of the business model are critical. In the customer acquisition stage, customer acquisition is crucial and financial metrics are not as vital. However, at the maturity stage, customer retention and cost control become as important as customer acquisition costs.

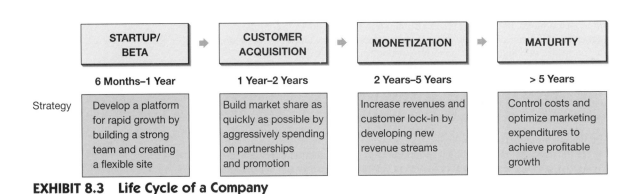

EXHIBIT 8.3   Life Cycle of a Company

Implementing the Performance Dashboard

In this section, we provide an overview of how a company would implement the Performance Dashboard. As noted earlier, it is important to develop these metrics based on the strategy of the firm. The strategy, however, is likely to be influenced by the life cycle of the company.

Exhibit 8.4 provides a road map for the metrics development process. The five steps of the process are illustrated on the top row of the figure. Next, we show a more detailed flow of the sample metrics, leading indicators, and specific performance targets. Keep in mind that this is simply an illustration; any metrics that followed would need to be tied specifically to the strategy.

Step One: Articulate Business Strategy

The first step in the process is to articulate the business strategy. The business strategy has six stages: market opportunity analysis, business model, customer interface design, branding, implementation, and evaluation. The business strategy was the focus of Chapters 3 through 7.

Step Two: Translate Strategy into Desired Outcomes

The second step in the process is to specify key actions and desired outcomes in specific performance areas. For example, we identified five areas where desired outcomes can be targeted. Consider the customer interface design and the outcomes areas. Here we may target increased levels of customer conversion, retention, and customer profitability. However, we are not setting the performance target levels (e.g., increase conversion rates from 2 to 4 percent); rather, we are simply specifying the outcome that we want to affect.

Step Three: Choose Metrics

This step takes the outcomes areas and identifies specific metrics that reflect the desired outcomes. Thus, we would specify the exact measurement (or, often, a set of metrics) used to track the desired outcome. Again, we are not specifying the exact level of the metric that we desire (that will occur in the fifth step) but rather isolating the metrics that can be gathered, measured, and tracked over time.

Take, for example, the conversion rate. We noted earlier that the conversion rate is typically measured in terms of look-to-book ratios—that is, the ratio of paying customers to entire number of visitors. At first glance, this seems straightforward, simply requiring a website to track its log files and find out how many shoppers conducted e-commerce transactions.

However, this conversion-rate metric can be complicated in several ways. Should the firm separate new users from returning buyers? A reasonable look-to-book ratio for completely new visitors may be lower than one that includes previous shoppers. Should this look-to-book vary by sections of the website or by product category? Does the firm need to target different look-to-book ratios depending on the level of site traffic?

It gets more complicated when we look at qualitative measures, such as employee or customer satisfaction. Say a company wants to increase its customer satisfaction from 80 to 95 percent. How does the firm translate this desired outcome into metrics that everyone in the organization buys into? Should it be a general measure derived from the question, How satisfied are you with the site? Or should the website ask a series of questions about satisfaction with usability, content, products, ease of use, and related topics, and then aggregate these measures into a customer satisfaction index?

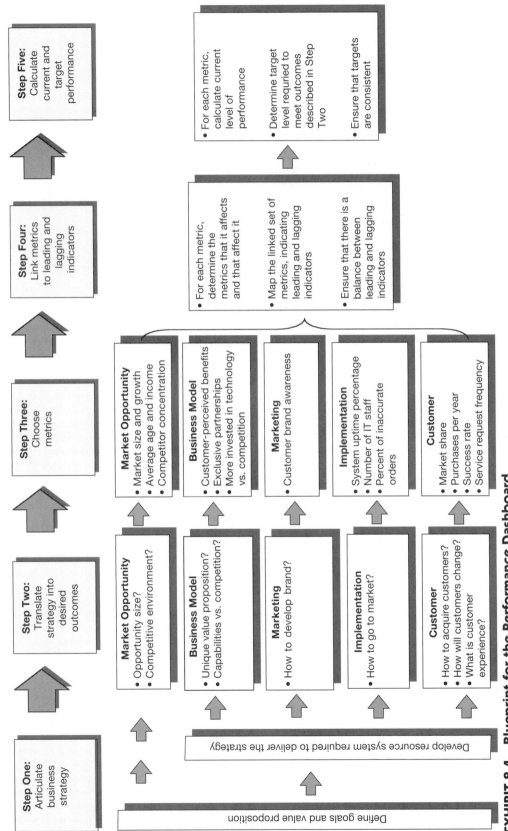

Step One: Articulate business strategy

Step Two: Translate strategy into desired outcomes

Step Three: Choose metrics

Step Four: Link metrics to leading and lagging indicators

Step Five: Calculate current and target performance

Define goals and value proposition

Develop resource system required to deliver the strategy

Market Opportunity
- Opportunity size?
- Competitive environment?

Business Model
- Unique value proposition?
- Capabilities vs. competition?

Marketing
- How to develop brand?

Implementation
- How to go to market?

Customer
- How to acquire customers?
- How will customers change?
- What is customer experience?

Market Opportunity
- Market size and growth
- Average age and income
- Competitor concentration

Business Model
- Customer-perceived benefits
- Exclusive partnerships
- More invested in technology vs. competition

Marketing
- Customer brand awareness

Implementation
- System uptime percentage
- Number of IT staff
- Percent of inaccurate orders

Customer
- Market share
- Purchases per year
- Success rate
- Service request frequency

- For each metric, determine the metrics that it affects and that affect it
- Map the linked set of metrics, indicating leading and lagging indicators
- Ensure that there is a balance between leading and lagging indicators

- For each metric, calculate current level of performance
- Determine target level required to meet outcomes described in Step Two
- Ensure that targets are consistent

EXHIBIT 8.4   Blueprint for the Performance Dashboard

Another important issue to consider is the usage occasion (the reason a user comes to the website) and the specific pages being measured. Consider the concept of duration (total time spent viewing all pages divided by total number of visits in a certain time). High duration is a great measure of success on pages that users tend to browse, such as the Vacation Expert section on the travel website Travelocity.com. There, users can find packages based on whether they are a "sun worshipper" or a "thrill seeker," look for packages based on region, or read traveler reviews. A high measure of duration, however, would be problematic if the user is a business traveler who wants to quickly find a specific flight, buy the ticket, book a hotel, and then return on the day of his flight to check arrival and departure times. Of course, the vacation dreamer and the business traveler could be the same person on different days, so websites must consider why the customer is there more than who the customer is.

Thus, linking outcomes with desired metrics is an intricate, involved process that requires a great deal of management attention. Metrics must be established for all the desired outcomes targeted across the stages of business strategy.

Step Four: Link Metrics to Leading and Lagging Indicators

The fourth step is to determine the leading indicators (factors that change ahead of the economy) and lagging indicators (factors that change behind the economy) of a particular metric and to map the entire set of metrics, including focal and leading indicators. Thus, if conversion rate is the target metric, managers also need to identify leading indicators such as levels of advertising expenditure and the degree of positive (or negative) word of mouth. More often than not, the financial metrics are lagging measures of business performance.

Step Five: Calculate Current and Target Performance

The fifth step is to calculate the current level and the target level of performance for selected metrics. Thus, the firm identifies the current conversion rate, advertising expenditures, and word-of-mouth levels. It then attaches specific numeric levels to each of the desired outcomes. For example, it might state that the customer conversion rate should move from 2 to 4 percent, that customer retention should increase from 15 to 20 percent, and that the firm should move from 10 to 30 percent in customer profitability in the allotted time period.

Online and Offline Integration Metrics

The metrics described so far refer primarily to a firm's online strategy and operations. We can also use the Performance Dashboard, with its five areas (market opportunity, business model, marketing and branding, implementation, and customer), to determine appropriate measures of performance for offline operations. Obviously, metrics must be adjusted to reflect a change of focus from the digital to the physical world. An extensive body of literature exists on the subject. In particular, Kaplan and Norton's Balanced Scorecard provides a comprehensive approach for offline companies. Here, we focus on metrics that measure the successful integration of online and offline operations.

A well-integrated operation exhibits two major attributes: a seamless customer experience (front end) and a seamless set of internal business processes and operations (back end). We now examine each of these in greater detail.

Seamless Customer Experience

A seamless customer experience refers to the firm's ability to deliver consistency as its customers move between online and offline channels. The customer decision process framework (introduced in Chapter 3) is useful in identifying metrics that measure this ability.

Exhibit 8.5 outlines steps in the customer purchase process and lists associated metrics to measure the consistency between the online and offline channels at each step. As discussed in Chapter 3, the customer decision process has three stages: the prepurchase stage (includes brand awareness, knowledge, and evaluation of alternatives), the purchase stage, and the postpurchase stage (includes satisfaction, loyalty, and disposal).

In the first step, when alternatives are evaluated, customers will notice whether the online and offline channels provide the same pool of product offerings. Wal-Mart, the world's leading retailer, offers nearly the same selection of products and services in its offline stores and on its website, Walmart.com. However, differences exist. For example, travel planning services are available through the website but not at offline stores.

Point-Counterpoint

Which Is Better? Online or Offline Data Sources?

With the emergence of online metrics, an interesting debate is unfolding on the advantages and disadvantages of online data collection compared with the older, more traditional forms of market research.

Traditional market research allows for richer real-time interaction with respondents, deviations from planned scripts, and a rigorous sampling plan. For example, consider the real-time, one-to-one interview process that many market research firms use. Here, the interviewer can adjust the script as needed to delve deeper into issues, watch the interviewee's body language, and listen to his tone of voice, all of which helps to provide a richer interpretation of the interviewee's responses. As a result, the interviewer can give a true "thick description" of the phenomena of interest.

At the same time, the traditional research approach has several drawbacks. The sampling process is typically lengthy and resource-intensive. Data collection is very costly, and there are few economies of scale. Once the data are collected, there is an additional step of data entry and storage. This approach is quite good for assessing attitudes, preferences, viewpoints, and purchase intent, but it is not as strong for measuring actual behavior. In general, traditional market research is very human-resource intensive at each step in the process.

Interestingly, online research reverses many of the advantages and disadvantages of traditional market research. It is less time-intensive, allows for automatic data capture, and, most importantly, allows for real-time data tracking. Its disadvantages relate to potential sampling biases, issues of privacy, and more difficult real-time adjustments to unexpected responses.

EXHIBIT 8.5   Metrics for Seamless Online/Offline Customer Purchase Process

In the second step (purchase), consistent security and privacy standards in offline and online stores allow users to feel equally comfortable when providing sensitive information. Toys "R" Us, one of the largest toy retailers, offers a consistent level of security through its stores and on its site. Toysrus.com uses "secure socket layers" technology to encrypt all order-related information in transit to the company server. If a user's browser does not support this encryption technology or if the user does not want to send credit card information over the Web, the website urges customers to call its guest relations department to complete the order by phone.

In the third step, which includes satisfaction, customers should experience consistent response time to customer service requests whether they use online or offline channels. AT&T Wireless allows customers to look up their accounts on the Web and then send an e-mail to a customer representative, call a toll-free number to talk to a representative, or go to a physical store. How well the requests are handled at each of these locations needs to be measured. Companies such as BizRate.com can do online and offline surveys that measure customer satisfaction with various methods of customer service.

Seamless Internal Business Processes and Operations

Seamless internal business processes and operations refer to a company's ability to perform all internal processes and operations, regardless of whether a customer is interacting with the company through its online or offline channel.

Exhibit 8.6 outlines metrics that can be used to assess internal business processes and operations. Most metrics refer to capabilities that are clearly "available" or "not available." Therefore, the metric value will be either a "yes" or a "no." We can group these metrics into two categories: information sharing and fulfillment systems.

Information-sharing metrics measure the website's ability to collect and analyze information on customers or products seamlessly between online and offline channels. For example, allowing customers to access their accounts online and offline is essential to a company's integrated back-office operations. Merrill Lynch customers can open and access their accounts through the Merrill Lynch website, by calling a customer service representative, or by visiting a Merrill Lynch branch office.

Fulfillment systems metrics refer to a company's ability to deliver on a customer's order, regardless of whether that order was placed online or offline. For example, a company that provides seamless tracking will allow customers to check their order status online or offline, regardless of which channel they used to place the order. Federal Express customers can get information about the delivery status of a package by going to FedEx.com and entering the package delivery confirmation code. Alternatively, they can call a Federal Express customer service representative and get the same information over the phone.

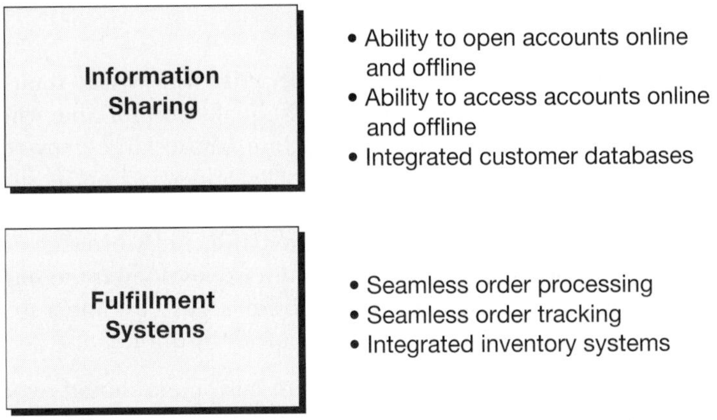

Information Sharing	• Ability to open accounts online and offline • Ability to access accounts online and offline • Integrated customer databases
Fulfillment Systems	• Seamless order processing • Seamless order tracking • Integrated inventory systems

EXHIBIT 8.6   Metrics for Seamless Internal Business Processes and Operations

External Sources of Metrics Information

We now discuss sources of industry-standard metrics and benchmark values. As noted earlier, traditional financial metrics are common and easy to acquire, but more qualitative metrics can be difficult to obtain. Firms are likely to track their value proposition versus competition, customer satisfaction with the site, site usability, and financial outcomes. However, it is also useful for the firm to complement these internal data sources with market-level data from outside sources in order to compare its performance to that of other websites. For example, Forrester publishes ratings of the top three travel websites: Expedia, Travelocity, and Orbitz. Not only can these three companies use the data to see how they compare with one another, but other travel websites can see what does and does not work on these websites.

In this section, we review three types of data sources for the metrics assessment. We then map the available Internet research sources to the various metric categories.

Online Information

Market Research

Online **market research** firms collect primary customer data through online surveys or customer submissions. Their research tends to emphasize site usability, customer satisfaction, and traffic level. BizRate.com bills itself as the "people's portal" to e-commerce and rates businesses by asking tens of thousands of customers about their shopping experiences. BizRate.com asks every customer at participating online stores to take part in a survey immediately after completing a purchase, or after exiting the website without purchasing something. Followup queries ensure that the customer received the order as scheduled and that the overall experience met expectations.

In particular, BizRate.com asks consumers to rate the performance of an online store on its "10 dimensions of service." Some of these are briefly noted in Exhibit 8.7 and include ease of ordering, product selection, product information, and website performance.

Other online market research firms include Planet Feedback (*www.planetfeedback.com*) and AC Nielsen (*www.acnielsen.com*). ComScore (*www.comscore.com*), which bought the market research arm of Jupiter Media Metrix, provides reports on the most visited sites and Internet usage.

Analyst Reports

Analyst reports are data sources that blend primary market data on a particular topic with an analyst's view of the market. Forrester Research (*www.forrester.com*) provides some of the most well-regarded reports on the e-commerce industry (see Exhibit 8.8). Its research tends to cover the competitors, consumers,

---

Point-Counterpoint

Which Is Better? User-Based or Expert-Based Research Content?

A second interesting debate in this area concerns the sources of research information. Of the sources noted earlier in the chapter, some focus on user responses while others focus on analysts' viewpoints.

User-based data sources rely on the input of consumers. Consumer-oriented data sources are often very up-to-date, may have a large customer base for input, and tend to be viewed as trustworthy by other users. In contrast, when experts rate a site, they tend to be more episodic in their reviews, can offer the input of only one expert, and provide information often viewed as objective. On the other hand, expert sites typically are reviewed by people whose responsibility is to know how to evaluate the features and functionality of a site, who have deep knowledge of competitor sites, and whose annual performance reviews are based on the soundness of their analysis. Hence, they have an enormous incentive to provide the best information to their customer base.

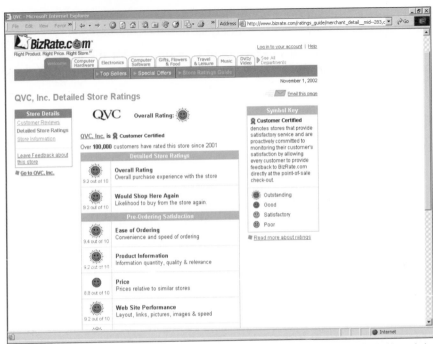

Source: www.bizrate.com. Used with permission

EXHIBIT 8.7   BizRate.com—QVC Ratings

and technology evolution in a particular segment of the industry. Forrester's ratings are based on expert reviews and customer surveys, as opposed to the pure user reviews of BizRate.com. Other firms in this space include the Aberdeen Group, Frost & Sullivan, IDC, and Jupiter Research.

Financial Information

These data sources provide statutory filings of **financial information** on particular companies or aggregated financial data across industries. Reports may appear with or without analyst commentary. The data collected generally include an income statement, balance sheet, and statement of cash flow information. Hoover's Online, one of the leading providers of financial and market information, prepares company profiles, financials, and industry research for all major online and offline companies. Hoover's company profiles include company overviews, history, press releases, products and operations, competitors, financial information, and research reports. Company financial data include annual and quarterly financial data, Securities and Exchange Commission filings, stock-market data, and comparison data by industry and market. Finally, industrywide information puts the entire analysis in proper context.

Other providers include Edgar Online (*www.edgar-online.com*) and brokerage houses such as DLJ Direct (*www.dljdirect.co.uk*).

Mapping Internet Research onto the Performance Dashboard

In Exhibit 8.9, we map Internet research sources onto the business strategy framework for this book. This analysis reveals that each data source special-

Courtesy of www.forester.com

EXHIBIT 8.8   Forrester Homepage

izes in a different type of data. For example, Jupiter Media Metrix and AC Nielsen tend to emphasize market information and traffic, while Hoover's Online specializes in financial information. It is rare that a single source covers all types of data. (The closest is Forrester Research.)

MarketWatch.com Metrics

We will now look at the metrics selection process that MarketWatch.com would go through to implement the Performance Dashboard (see Exhibit 8.10). As we discussed, an Internet company's strategy can change rapidly depending on the stage of the business. Hence, it is important that we apply the process to a particular stage in the MarketWatch.com life cycle. By the fourth quarter of 2001, the company had delivered on its year-old promise of having a positive cash flow, finishing December with $1.3 million more than it had at the end of September. However, it still faced challenges. With the worst media recession in memory not far behind, it was unclear whether the economy would turn for the better or if difficult times would continue to affect its performance and that of its suppliers and customers in the financial services industry. MarketWatch.com needed to defend itself against competitors and maintain and extend its lead in the online financial

		Market Research			Analyst		Financial Information
	AC Nielsen	BizRate	ComScore Media Metrix	Jupiter Research	Forrester	Gomez	Hoover's
Market — Market Info		●	●	●	●		●
Market — Traffic		●	●				
Implementation — Fulfillment	●				●		
Implementation — Implementation				●	●		
Implementation — Privacy	●						
Customer — Usability	●			●	●	●	
Customer — Content	●			●	●	●	
Customer — Customer Satisfaction	●				●	●	
Customer — Customer Service	●				●		
Financial — Financial Performance					●		●

EXHIBIT 8.9   Mapping Internet Research onto the Performance Dashboard

news market. It also needed to maintain profitability and fend off concerns that it was mired in a money-losing business.

The metrics selection process is the third step in implementing the Performance Dashboard. By this stage, MarketWatch.com has already articulated its strategy—"Our goal is to create the preeminent brand for real-time business news and financial information on the Web and other media"[7] —and translated the strategy into desired outcomes.

Market Opportunity

In the market opportunity category, we establish metrics for the attractiveness of the market opportunity for MarketWatch.com and the degree of competitive intensity.

Is the Opportunity Significant?

Desired Outcome 1: Identify a significant market opportunity in the financial services industry.   MarketWatch.com chose to play in the financial media industry. With financial services accounting for 20 percent of the online advertising market and projections calling for strong growth in that sector, MarketWatch.com and its advertising-based business model initially seemed to fit in a significant market. Four years later, with the online advertising

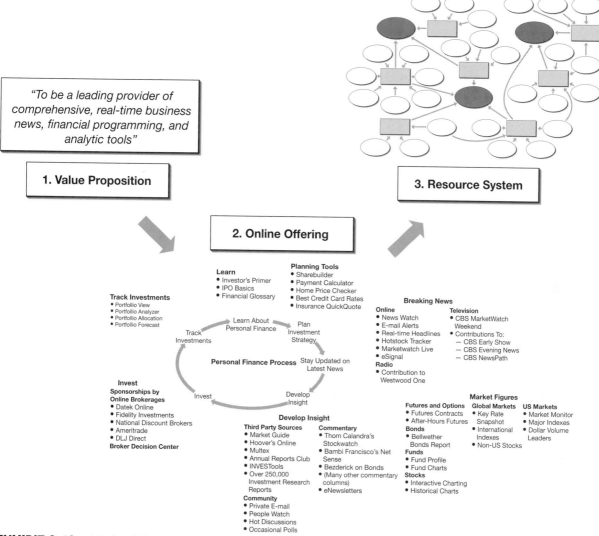

EXHIBIT 8.10   MarketWatch.com Strategy

market not meeting analysts' projections, MarketWatch.com shifted its business model and put more emphasis on licensing content to partners in the financial services industry. This shift paid off, with the company's revenues growing from $5.2 million in 1999 to $24.8 million in 2001. As it continues to refine and adjust its business model with the realities of the marketspace, MarketWatch.com can look at several metrics to understand how it is meeting its targeted market opportunity.

Metrics to Track:

- Size of the online advertising market
- Percentage of online advertising that is related to financial content
- MarketWatch.com's share of that market versus the competition
- CPM (cost per thousand impressions) of online financial advertisements
- Size of the content-licensing market in the financial services industry
- Quarterly growth of content-licensing revenue and number of clients

How Intense Is the Competition?

Desired Outcome 2: Serve segments where competition is not very intense. MarketWatch.com competes in a crowded market that includes Web portals (such as Yahoo and AOL), traditional media companies (such as CNN and NBC), online brokers (such as Fidelity and Schwab), and niche sites (such as Motley Fool and TheStreet.com).

Metrics to Track:

- MarketWatch.com's Media Metrix rating versus competition
- Daily/weekly/monthly unique visitors
- Daily/weekly/monthly page views
- Average time spent on website per user
- Rate of competitor entry and exit in the market
- Number of mergers or acquisitions within the market
- Advertising expenditures versus competition

Business Model

In the business-model category, we establish metrics for the uniqueness of the MarketWatch.com value proposition, the strength of the company's capabilities compared with competitors, and the sustainability of the value proposition over time. Additionally, we establish metrics for the financial performance of the company in terms of revenue, profit, and cost.

How Unique Is the MarketWatch.com Value Proposition Relative to Competitors?

Desired Outcome 3: MarketWatch.com value proposition is unique relative to competitors. MarketWatch.com was one of the leading online financial news sources, mostly because of its in-house staff of experienced journalists. However, competitors were slowly trying to develop similar capabilities through partnerships.

Metric to Track:

- Customer perceptions of MarketWatch.com's key benefits versus competition

Are MarketWatch.com's Resources and Partnerships Significantly Better Than the Competition's?

Desired Outcome 4: Market perceives MarketWatch.com resources and partnerships are superior to those of the competition. Analyst reports cited the experienced editorial staff of MarketWatch.com and the credibility associated with its relationship to CBS News as two key reasons MarketWatch.com was better positioned to deliver on its value proposition than the competition.

Metrics to Track:

- MarketWatch.com versus the competition for the following:
  - Number of journalists on staff

- Average journalist's experience
- Number of markets where the company has operations
- Cumulative reach of distribution partnerships
- Percentage of outsourced content
- Production capacity

How Sustainable Is the MarketWatch.com Value Proposition Relative to the Competition's?

Desired Outcome 5: Key resources are well maintained. Factors such as an experienced staff of journalists are highly sustainable over time. However, factors such as an exclusive relationship to CBS News or to distribution portals are more likely to change and introduce uncertainty.

Metrics to Track:

- Exclusivity and length of MarketWatch.com partnership agreements versus competition
- Number of MarketWatch.com patents on tools and services

Will MarketWatch.com Be Able to Maintain Profitability?

Desired Outcome 6: MarketWatch.com will continue an unbroken string of profitable quarters. Following the technology market slump during the spring of 2000, investors became increasingly cautious, looking for profitability as quickly as possible. Even though MarketWatch.com was on a clear path to profitability, its stock still dropped significantly. However, the company's strong fundamentals, its shift from an advertising emphasis to a more balanced model (including content licensing), and its profitable fourth quarter in 2001 provide optimistic indications for the company's future financial performance.

Metrics to Track:

- **Revenue**
  - Revenue breakdown by advertising, licensing, subscription, etc.
  - Total revenue per employee
- **Profit**
  - Total gain/loss and percentage increase/decrease over time
  - Number of sequential profitable quarters
- **Cost**
  - Total cost
  - Customer acquisition cost
  - Percentage of revenues spent on marketing and sales
- **Other**
  - Balance sheet
  - Stock price
  - Available funds in liquid assets
  - Cash burn rate
  - Average day's receivables

Marketing and Branding

In the marketing and branding category, we establish the metrics that measure the effectiveness of MarketWatch.com's marketing and brand building efforts. These metrics include measuring recognition and loyalty.

How Effective and Efficient Are MarketWatch.com's Marketing Efforts at Attracting New Users?

Desired Outcome 7: MarketWatch.com has a lower user acquisition cost than the competition.   MarketWatch.com has a large number of unique visitors. However, that achievement requires a large marketing budget.

Metrics to Track:

- User acquisition cost
- Number of unique visitors versus competition
- Percentage of revenues spent on marketing versus competition
- Percentage of visitors who purchase services on the website
- Percentage of visitors who return to the website
- Frequency of user visits

How Is the MarketWatch.com Brand Perceived in the Market?

Desired Outcome 8: Users are aware of the MarketWatch.com brand and make positive associations with it.   MarketWatch.com's association to CBS News and its strong marketing led to strong brand recognition among users.

Metrics to Track:

- Percentage of users who believe MarketWatch.com and CBS MarketWatch.com are different brands
- Aided user awareness of MarketWatch.com brand name
- User associations with MarketWatch.com brand versus competition
- Percentage of MarketWatch.com users that fit in the company's target segments

Implementation

In the implementation category, we establish the metrics that measure MarketWatch.com's ability to seamlessly support its product and services in the marketplace.

Does MarketWatch.com Have an Infrastructure That Enables It to Reliably Distribute Financial Content Across Multiple Platforms?

Desired Outcome 9: The MarketWatch.com infrastructure enables reliable content distribution across multiple platforms.   MarketWatch.com's innovative IT infrastructure allowed it to seamlessly communicate financial information both internally and externally.

Metrics to Track:

- Website's uptime/downtime percentage

- Average download time
- Maximum number of concurrent users
- Maximum response time
- Maximum information volume
- Number of articles produced each day
- Percentage of website that gets updated each day

Customer

In this category, we determine the metrics that measure users' perception of the usability and effectiveness of MarketWatch.com, as well as their usage behavior, satisfaction, and loyalty.

What Is the Perception of the Online User Experience?

Desired Outcome 10: The MarketWatch.com site is usable and attractive. One way to measure MarketWatch.com's effectiveness is to evaluate its performance in the 7Cs (see Chapter 5). Another way is to study users' online behavior.

Metrics to Track:

- Users' evaluation of the 7Cs versus competition
- Number of subscribers to various product offerings (such as news alerts)
- Average time spent on website per user
- Popularity of individual articles
- Average time to complete a task
- Amount of negative feedback

How Satisfied and Loyal Is the User Base?

Desired Outcome 11: MarketWatch.com has the highest user satisfaction and loyalty in the industry. Satisfied and loyal users are a significant source of long-term profitability. MarketWatch.com regularly tracked user loyalty.

Metrics to Track:

- User loyalty
- Overall user satisfaction with the website versus the competition, as well as user satisfaction key attributes such as tool effectiveness and information relevance and timeliness
- User churn rate

MarketWatch.com Summary

Exhibit 8.11 provides a summary of the desired outcomes. For each desired outcome, we identify a number of metrics in the preceding analysis. While it may seem large at first glance, managers must be able to track all relevant metrics in order to recognize early signs of problems with the company's strategy or its implementation.

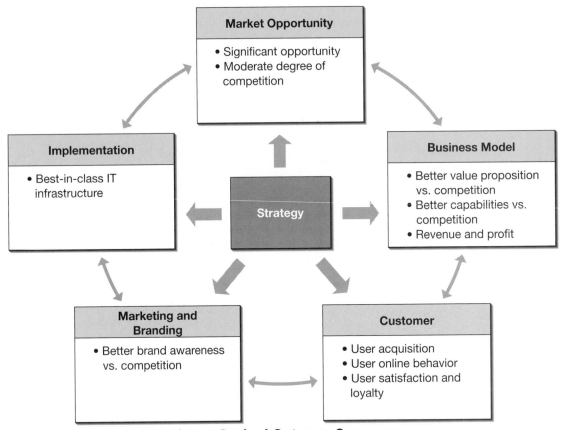

EXHIBIT 8.11   MarketWatch.com Desired Outcome Summary

Exhibit 8.12 shows the leading and lagging indicators for MarketWatch.com. We trace just one flow in this exhibit. Metrics tracking competitive intensity and the degree to which competitors are underserving the market help determine a value proposition that is unique. A unique value proposition that is marketed successfully leads to the creation of a strong brand and high brand awareness among users. This stimulates usage, which leads to an increase in ad revenue because there are more users viewing more pages. Such an increase in ad revenue, associated with marginal incremental cost, leads to an increase in profitability.

Finally, Exhibit 8.13 puts some of the metrics into context by mapping MarketWatch.com's performance to its competitors. By mid-2002, MarketWatch.com was in the top-performing group of business and financial news providers in terms of unique users and reach. This is important, given its reliance on advertising revenue and the higher rates that can be charged with a large audience. In time spent on the website and unique page views, however, MarketWatch.com lagged behind some of its competitors, including Hoovers and Morningstar, because visitors to those websites conduct exhaustive research on individual companies. It also lagged behind others with broad brand recognition, including Motley Fool and Yahoo Finance. To maximize its advertising revenue, MarketWatch.com needed to maintain its near-leadership position in its number of unique visitors while increasing the

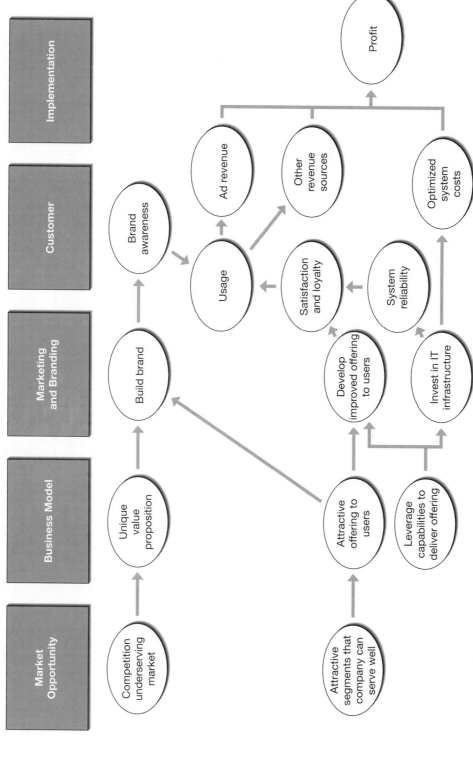

EXHIBIT 8.12   Leading/Lagging Indicators for MarketWatch.com

	June 2002		
	MarketWatch.com Value	Market Position	Best Performer
Unique visitors (in thousands)	5,080	4	Yahoo Finance
Average daily unique visitors (in thousands)	520	4	Yahoo Finance
Reach	4.3%	4	Yahoo Finance
Average minutes spent per visitor per day	4.1	17	Hoover's websites
Average unique pages per visitor per day	3.3	15	Hoover's websites

EXHIBIT 8.13   MarketWatch.com Best-in-Class Metrics

number of pages viewed per visit. It could achieve this by increasing its brand awareness with a stronger brand and a clearer, more appealing value. This summary could help managers by pointing to the levers they need to pull to achieve the desired results.

Summary

1. **Why should senior managers be concerned with metrics?**

Managers need to consider metrics because they drive organizational behavior in a number of ways. They help to define the business model, communicate the firm's strategy, track performance, increase accountability, and align objectives.

2. **How can the health of online firms be assessed?**

The Balanced Scorecard assesses the health of a business by using four categories of metrics: financial, customer, internal business process, and learning and growth. While this framework may be appropriate for some firms, it is also limited in three respects: It does not offer a definition of strategy; it does not clearly articulate the capabilities of the firm (instead, the focus is on internal business processes not linked to customer benefits); and it does not explicitly include partnerships.

3. What are the steps to implementing the Performance Dashboard?

There are five steps in the Performance Dashboard: (1) articulate the strategy, (2) translate strategy into actions, (3) choose metrics, (4) link metrics to leading and lagging indicators, and (5) calculate current and target performance levels.

4. What external sources of metrics information can firms use to chart their progress?

Market-research data sources tend to focus on website performance and customers' perceptions of websites. Analyst reports often combine primary data collection with an analyst's strong point of view on the industry. Financial sources focus on the investment community and tend to include in-depth financial information. Each approach has its strengths and limitations, but each complements the others. Firms often need to acquire data from all three areas to obtain a complete picture of their markets.

Exercises

1. Go to the website for Salon magazine (*www.salon.com*). If Salon could choose only three customer metrics to track its success, what should they be? Why? Do the same for PetSmart.com (*www.petsmart.com*). How do the metrics that you have chosen for these websites differ?

2. Go to comScore's website (*www.comscore.com*). Compare the number of unique visitors for Yahoo and eBay. Now go to Hoover's Online (*www.hoovers.com*). Compare the financial information for these two companies. Which company would you rather be? Why?

3. There is a general rule that 80 percent of customers look at only 20 percent of a website's pages. Go to the Citysearch city guide (*www.citysearch.com*) that covers your area. Which pages do you think are used most often? Are these the pages that best serve Citysearch, or should it try to move users toward other parts of its website?

Key Terms

metrics	Performance Dashboard	life cycle of a company
Balanced Scorecard	market opportunity metrics	market research
financial metrics	business-model metrics	analyst reports
customer metrics	market and branding metrics	financial information
internal business process metrics	implementation metrics	
learning and growth metrics	customer metrics	

Endnotes

[1]Robert Kaplan and David Norton, *The Balanced Scorecard* (Boston: Harvard Business School Press, 1996). Readers are encouraged to review this seminal work of Robert Kaplan and David Norton on the Balanced Scorecard.

[2]Ibid, Chap. 2.

[3]Ibid, 10–19.

[4]George Day, "The Capabilities of Market-Driven Organizations," *Journal of Marketing* 58, no. 4 (October 1994): 37–52.

[5]Christopher Nobes, *Interpreting European Financial Statements: Towards 1992* (London and Edinburgh: Butterworths, 1989).

[6]"Financial Services, Securities: Commission Welcomes Significant Progress in European Parliament on Financial Services Action Plan," *The European Commission*, 14 March 2002 (URL: http://europa.eu.int/comm/internal_market/en/finances/mobil/02-417.htm).

[7]MarketWatch.com, Inc., U.S. Securities and Exchange Commission, *Form 10-K* (Fiscal Year 2001), filed 1 April 2002.

Website Development Process

CASELET: SCHWAB BUILDS ITS WEBSITE

Schwab Learning, a service of the Charles and Helen Schwab Foundation, provides support and resources for children with learning disabilities and their families. In 1999, the organization decided it was time to radically expand its Web presence and began the process of building a brand-new website.

Schwab Learning's first step was to hire an outside agency to help it research its target audience's needs, develop a Web strategy to meet those needs, and then build the site. The agency started by conducting focus group and individual interviews with mothers of learning-disabled children. From these interviews, the various stages of managing a learning-disabled child were identified and mapped, as were the needs associated with each stage. After digesting the research, Schwab Learning and its partner agency determined that the website ought to focus primarily on the "novice mom" who is just beginning to learn about her child's disability and the tools and strategies available to cope with it.

Next, the team began to work on the site's design, branding, and information architecture (with, as is not uncommon, a new agency). They created a pair of "wire frames," or schematics, each featuring a different means of organizing the site's 200 pages of information. One was domain based (schools, family, community, and work). The other was based on life cycle (initial symptoms, identifying a learning disability, managing a learning-disabled child, and sharing knowledge). Next, they did two rounds of user testing to determine which structure mothers preferred—the life-cycle approach won out—and refined the chosen model. As a result of this second round, the number of information "buckets" was reduced from four to three.

In December 2000, Schwab Learning launched its new website. By all measures, it was a success: Both visitors and page views soon rose dramatically. But that hardly marked the end of Schwab Learning's efforts to connect with its customers; ongoing usability testing resulted in a further wave of architecture and design refinements in February 2002. The lesson, according to Schwab Learning.org's Web director Jeanene Landers Steinberg, is clear: "User research and usability testing will always put you on the right track."[1]

This chapter was written by Ian Findlay. Drill-Downs were written by Ryan Jones and Blair Hotchkies.

305

PLEASE CONSIDER THE FOLLOWING QUESTIONS AS YOU READ THE CHAPTER:

1. What are the steps involved in building a website?

2. How is the user experience definition created?

3. What is the architecture design process?

4. What is the implementation process?

5. What is involved in the test process?

6. What factors are involved in launching a website?

INTRODUCTION

When the Internet emerged as an important new channel for business in the late 1990s, companies raced to build websites—and to build them as quickly as possible. Being second or third on the Web in your industry seemed like a death warrant, and companies that did not utilize the Web were considered archaic.

By mid-2002, the landscape had changed. Now, so many companies are on the Internet that the notion of "first-mover advantage" seems obsolete. Also, most existing companies already have a Web presence, so there is less of an urgency to simply get on the Web. Companies are focusing on building an Internet presence that reflects their strategy rather than developing a Web strategy separate from their bricks-and-mortar business.

In the late 1990s, few companies had the in-house expertise to build their own websites; most hired third-party Web development companies such as Razorfish, Sapient, and Scient to do the job. Today, many companies have their own in-house personnel who specialize in the creation and maintenance of websites. As a result of this shift to in-house development, companies such as marchFirst and Scient have filed for bankruptcy, and Razorfish and Sapient have scaled down their businesses.

This chapter examines the website-building process. Whether a website is big or small, and whether it is outsourced or created in-house, the steps for building a website are basically the same (see Exhibit 9.1). First, the company must develop a strategy. If it is decided that a website should be part of the strategy, the user experience must be defined. This information is then carried into the architecture design process, where it is translated into functionality and screen representation. In the implementation phase, the website is actually built. The website is then tested—and tested again—until it is considered acceptable. Only then is the website ready to launch.

Considerations Before Planning a Website

Website development is a game of tradeoffs, and the team responsible for implementing the website must be willing and skilled enough to make those tradeoffs—otherwise, the development process will become derailed and

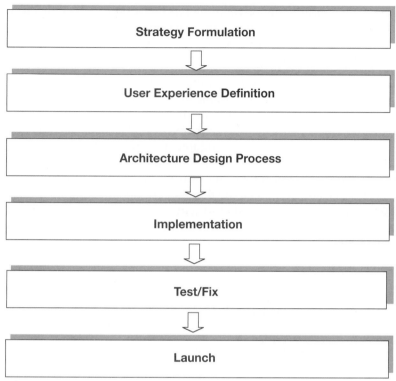

EXHIBIT 9.1   Process for Building a Website

delayed. The goal of website development is to present functionality and content through some type of visual interface. While this goal seems straightforward, it is shaped by external forces, the most important of which are time, budget, and resources.

Time is fairly simple to define: What is the deadline for this project? Is the deadline flexible or nonnegotiable? Can the site be phased in over time, or do all of the desired features have to be built immediately? Budget can be one of the biggest constraints when it comes to building a website: How much money has been allocated to the project, and how was that number derived? Is there enough in the budget to hire additional staff if the deadline is too tight? Can the project be outsourced in part or entirely? Resource questions include these: Does the organization have the right mix of skills internally to deliver the project as specified? Does it have enough of each type of skill given the timetable that has been laid out? Are these resources available, or could the resources needed be pulled off another project—and what is the relative importance of this project to the organization versus the other project?

In addition to tradeoffs that must be made about the size and scope of the project, additional compromises must be made throughout the process. These compromises might include the type of hardware and software to use when developing and running the site, the types of audiences the site will serve (and which audience types are the most important), the visual design of the site, and what measurements will be used to decide whether the team has been successful. Some of these compromises are brokered internally within the team; some are brokered externally with the website's various stakeholders (individual business owners within the organization, the management team, suppliers, etc.).

Ideally, any negotiations about the scope and functionality of the website should take place at the very beginning of the development process, because it is critical that the team have a static definition of *what* they are building and for whom by the time they begin the process of actually building it. Most importantly, it is crucial that throughout the process of negotiation and development the team stay *focused*—on who the website's customers are; on continually refining and tuning the team's understanding of the needs of those customers; on building a site that reflects those needs, rather than the company's internal organizational structure. This focused approach should manifest itself in website structure and page design that actively move customers forward in achieving their goals.

Process for Building a Site from Scratch

In many ways, building a website is like putting together a puzzle. However, the process of solving the puzzle cannot begin until several important pieces (in some sense, the biggest pieces of the puzzle) are in place. These include the following:

- A well-defined set of business objectives for the site
- Executive support
- A general definition of the audience segments to be served by the site
- A clearly articulated project plan with checkpoints and milestones
- A succinct definition and description of the relevant branding systems (for the organization, the product, and the website)
- A competitive analysis for the industry and for the product/service to be offered on the site
- A budget
- Development resources
- A steering committee made up of senior stakeholders and executives

Of these pieces, the two most critical are the set of business objectives for the site and the identification of the audience segments that the site will serve. These two pieces of information will direct the development of a site that is user-experience driven. How a user perceives and interprets the website is the **user experience**; for the user experience to be positive, and the user to benefit from that interaction, the site design must combine content, features, and functions in a meaningful way. Great content, features, or functions by themselves will not make for a successful website—these items must work together in concert, and they must be made available to users at a time and place that is meaningful to them given the task that they are trying to complete at that particular time. Hence, it is critical to understand the business objectives that have been defined for the site and for each of the site's discrete user types. Only by understanding the two can you begin to understand what combination of content, features, and functions is going to be relevant and beneficial to a given user at a given time.

The simplest example of this principle in action is the search engine Google (*www.google.com*). Google's homepage offers one main feature—a box into which users can type terms they would like to search for on the Web—because Google knows that that is its users' primary goal. Another example is ESPN's website (*www.espn.com*). ESPN has clearly identified that its largest group of visitors are sports fans who are primarily interested in breaking sports news, well-written original articles, and game summaries. To meet their interest, ESPN designed its homepage to provide direct, easy access to this content while still providing an easily navigable interface for visitors whose interests might differ from those of the site's core user group.

Additional components of the site development process include a well-defined functional specification. The **functional specification** (also called the func spec) provides a highly detailed guide to what every page on the website does. This document is much like a blueprint for the development phase of the project; it tells developers what pieces of information and functionality go on which page, where the information comes from, where the information should go, and what rules apply to how the page and its functions are used. Additionally, the func spec defines all actions that can be undertaken on the page, such as "add to shopping cart" and "recalculate shipping."

Another important component is the **change-management process**. This is a framework for identifying problems within the project (e.g., software bugs or a change in site requirements), prioritizing these problems, assigning the task of resolving these problems to an individual or team, and tracking the progress of these efforts until all problems are resolved. Because e-commerce website development is typically a complex affair with many minute, interrelated parts, having a process in place to handle problems and changes as they occur significantly increases the quality of the end-product.

Another component is the **project plan**, which lays out the checkpoints, milestones, and resources that are expected to be required to move the project forward to completion (see Exhibit 9.2). The project manager uses this plan to proactively manage the expectations of stakeholders, interested parties, and the development team, as well as to identify project bottlenecks, flag resource constraints, and spot project dependencies. Perhaps most importantly, the project plan allows the manager to break down a large task ("Build me a website!") into small, discrete components, which means that progress on the project can be easily measured.

The development of a website is additionally challenged by its multidisciplinary nature. Successful site development requires a multitude of employees to cover different areas, often ones that are frequently exclusive to one another. Such areas include the following:

1. Business strategy
2. Functional/subject-matter expertise
3. Information architecture
4. Content development/writing
5. Visual design

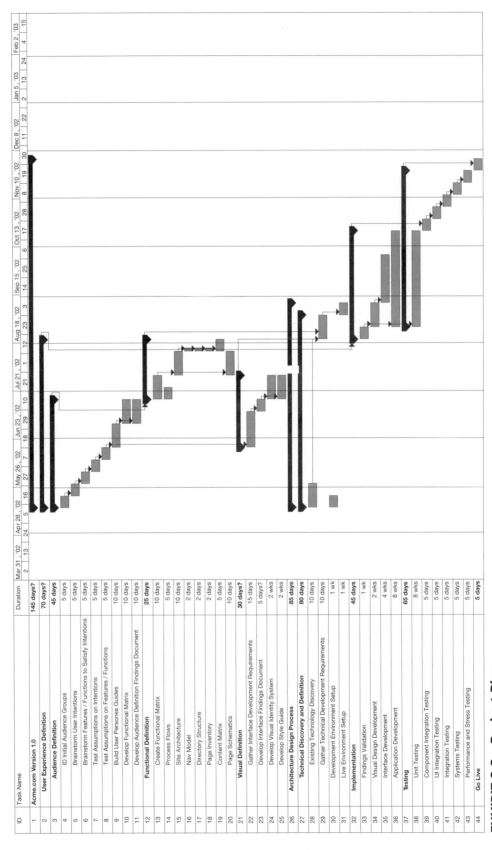

ID	Task Name	Duration
1	**Acme.com Version 1.0**	**145 days?**
2	**User Experience Definition**	**70 days?**
3	**Audience Definition**	**45 days**
4	ID Initial Audience Groups	5 days
5	Brainstorm User Intentions	5 days
6	Brainstorm Features / Functions to Satisfy Intentions	5 days
7	Test Assumptions on Intentions	5 days
8	Test Assumptions on Features / Functions	5 days
9	Build User Personea Guides	10 days
10	Develop Functional Matrix	10 days
11	Develop Audience Definition Findings Document	10 days
12	**Functional Definition**	**25 days**
13	Create Functional Matrix	10 days
14	Process Flows	5 days
15	Site Architecture	10 days
16	Nav Model	2 days
17	Directory Structure	2 days
18	Page Inventory	2 days
19	Content Matrix	5 days
20	Page Schematics	10 days
21	**Visual Definition**	**30 days?**
22	Gather Interface Development Requirements	15 days
23	Develop Interface Findings Document	5 days?
24	Develop Visual Identity System	2 wks
25	Develop Style Guide	2 wks
26	**Architecture Design Process**	**85 days**
27	**Technical Discovery and Definition**	**80 days**
28	Existing Technology Discovery	10 days
29	Gather Technical Development Requirements	10 days
30	Development Environment Setup	1 wk
31	Live Environment Setup	1 wk
32	**Implementation**	**45 days**
33	Findings Validation	1 wk
34	Visual Design Development	2 wks
35	Interface Development	4 wks
36	Application Development	8 wks
37	**Testing**	**65 days**
38	Unit Testing	8 wks
39	Component Integration Testing	5 days
40	UI Integration Testing	5 days
41	Integration Testing	5 days
42	Systems Testing	5 days
43	Performance and Stress Testing	5 days
44	**Go Live**	**5 days**

EXHIBIT 9.2 Project Plan

6. Interface design

7. Technical architecture

8. Database administration

9. Data modeling

10. Technical development

11. Quality assurance team lead

12. Quality assurance testing

The challenge is to harness the people who have the skills needed for each of these areas so that their individual skills and knowledge inform and shape the output of one another's tasks. The integration of these skills, leveraged against discrete site development tasks, provides the best possibility for delivering an integrated website. Some of these team members are capable of performing more than one skill, as some skills are naturally similar to others. However, it is important to understand what these skill sets are before tasks are assigned to individual team members. For example, a technical developer may not know anything about how to create a webpage, even though both skills are "technical." It is also important that the team members have relevant previous experience in their assigned tasks and that they work well together. If the team is unfamiliar with the systems that it is developing, or if turf wars exist between members of the team, the project is unlikely to proceed smoothly.

User Experience Identification

Before the website building process begins, the project team must know the website's business objectives. In Chapter 4, we discussed the various components of an online business model: the value proposition or value cluster, the offering, the resource system, and the financial model. Also in Chapter 4, we learned that an online offering is developed by (1) identifying the scope of the offering, (2) identifying the customer decision process, and (3) mapping the offering to this decision process. These activities will have provided the basic information needed to define a representative set of **user types** (the discrete types of users who will use the site, sometimes also referred to as user occasions) and the specific **user intentions** (what tasks users want to accomplish when they visit the site, sometimes also referred to as user occasions) for each of these user types. Defining the user types and usage occasions allows us to identify and define the functions that are required on the site, as well as what information and content will be required to support those functions.

The easiest way to understand the relationship between user type, user intentions, and function is through an example. Let's say that you are asked to build an e-commerce website for Acme Computer, a company that sells computer equipment, software, and peripherals. The business objectives for this site are simple:

1. Increase the ease of doing business with Acme Computer for customers, partners, and suppliers

2. Increase the overall revenue of Acme Computer by increasing the purchase frequency and quantity of its customers

3. Increase customer satisfaction and loyalty

4. Lower the cost per transaction for goods purchased

Given these business objectives, the development team must identify the initial set of target audiences for the site—who will be coming to the site, and why.

User Types

The process of identifying the potential users for a website is iterative. However, the first step is to conduct a series of brainstorming sessions that will identify as many user types as possible. Since it is not practical to construct a website that satisfies the needs of every imaginable customer, the team needs to examine its list of user types and consolidate those users into groups. This consolidation is based on the similarities of their needs, as well as Acme Computer's business intentions for each of them.

The team consolidates its list into six major groups of users:

1. Customers

2. Prospects

3. Partners

4. Vendors

5. Interested parties (media, jobseekers)

6. Employees

This list of user groups might be very different if the team were building a marketing site for the company, or a site that provided news and content.

Now that these user groups have been identified, the development team must gain an intimate understanding of who those users are and what they expect to accomplish through their interaction(s) with the site. The result of this process is a series of **user personas**—fictitious, archetypal examples of real users that allow the development team to focus on the collective core needs of the users within a group (versus the peripheral or unique needs of individual users).

User Persona

The first step in creating a persona is to build a user profile. Exhibit 9.3 shows the user profile for Cindy the College Student, who represents the largest identified group of customers for Acme Computer—young college students purchasing a computer. The user profile helps build the human representation of the user, placing that user in a situational, educational, and demographic representation that ideally allows the team to uncover the *personality* of the user.

The development team must identify the relevant general attributes of the customer. If there are clearly distinct sets of customer groups, the team may decide

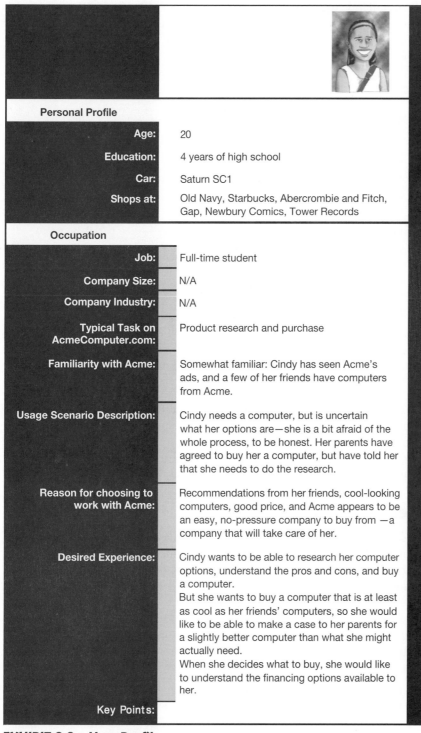

Personal Profile	
Age:	20
Education:	4 years of high school
Car:	Saturn SC1
Shops at:	Old Navy, Starbucks, Abercrombie and Fitch, Gap, Newbury Comics, Tower Records

Occupation	
Job:	Full-time student
Company Size:	N/A
Company Industry:	N/A
Typical Task on AcmeComputer.com:	Product research and purchase
Familiarity with Acme:	Somewhat familiar: Cindy has seen Acme's ads, and a few of her friends have computers from Acme.
Usage Scenario Description:	Cindy needs a computer, but is uncertain what her options are—she is a bit afraid of the whole process, to be honest. Her parents have agreed to buy her a computer, but have told her that she needs to do the research.
Reason for choosing to work with Acme:	Recommendations from her friends, cool-looking computers, good price, and Acme appears to be an easy, no-pressure company to buy from —a company that will take care of her.
Desired Experience:	Cindy wants to be able to research her computer options, understand the pros and cons, and buy a computer. But she wants to buy a computer that is at least as cool as her friends' computers, so she would like to be able to make a case to her parents for a slightly better computer than what she might actually need. When she decides what to buy, she would like to understand the financing options available to her.
Key Points:	

EXHIBIT 9.3   User Profile

to build unique user profiles for each. In our case, the Acme Computer team believes that the relevant information for the customer group might include:

- Age
- Education level
- Job title and company
- Company size
- Daily tasks at work
- Primary task on AcmeComputer.com
- Brief usage description
- Primary benefit to using AcmeComputer.com
- Overall desired experience from using AcmeComputer.com
- Type of car
- Stores shopped at
- Household income
- Education level
- Type of computer at home and work
- Frequency of Web usage
- Reasons for Web usage
- Favorite websites
- Whether they typically purchase products on the Internet
- Buying for home or for work

This information, which sets the groundwork for the user profile, will need to be culled from a variety of sources, such as interviews with existing Acme Computer customers, past purchase records, interviews with Acme Computer customer service representatives and sales associates, and competitive benchmarks.

User Intentions

Once the user profile is completed, the team can move to figuring out user intentions. User intentions describe, in specific terms, each task the user is trying to accomplish, and what process she expects to go through in order to be successful. It also answers the questions: What information or service does the site have to deliver in order for the user to achieve success? What does Acme Computer get in return for providing the user with a successful visit? Does the user want to accomplish multiple tasks that may or may not be related?

The output of this investigation is a descriptive list of each of the user's intentions, a list that more than likely contains several discrete intentions per user type. Let us continue to build out the example of Cindy the College Student. Through its research, the team has discovered that Cindy would most likely want to do five primary things on AcmeComputer.com:

1. Research and purchase a computer
2. Check on the status of a previous purchase
3. Get technical support information

4. Work with customer service

5. Obtain general contact information

For the first activity—researching and purchasing a computer—what steps would Cindy need to undertake to be successful in making a purchase? Through its research, the team finds that she is most likely to (1) research her options, (2) narrow her selection, (3) gain feedback from parents and friends, and (4) purchase the system. Given that this is the process that Cindy expects to follow during her purchase, the team builds out this process (in its user intentions matrix—see Exhibit 9.4) as the general set of needs that must be met if Cindy is to make a successful transaction. The user intentions matrix, combined with the user profile, creates the user persona. The user persona ties together the attributes defined in the user profile with the goals that the user is trying to achieve, the needs that must be met for the user to achieve his or her goal, and the benefit that Acme Computer expects in return for satisfying those needs.

It is highly likely that across each of the user types, there will be groupings of very similar if not identical intentions. This is important, because as the team builds out the profiles for the other user groups, and identifies the list of intentions for those groups, a consolidation process happens—the team will want to bring together user groups that share intentions. The resulting consolidated list represents the discrete set of usage occasions that the website will need to satisfy and the set of functionality it will require in order to do so.

Functionality and Content Matrix

The benefits of spending time up front to consider and define the specific audiences for a website become apparent in the next step of development. As a result of defining who the users are, the team can define the goals for each of those users when they visit the site—and, consequently, what functions the site has to be able to perform and when. Thus begins the first phase of clearly articulating the scope of the project—what components of the website have to be developed by the development team, how they interrelate, and what their dependencies are.

Take a closer look at the computer purchase scenario briefly described earlier. What type of information does Cindy need to obtain from Acme Computer (and Acme Computer from Cindy) in order to decide which computer she wants and get that computer shipped to her at school? Think of how Cindy might have bought a computer in the past, at a store on campus. Here is how her shopping experience might have gone:

1. Find the store location

2. Travel to the store

3. Find the location in the store that has computers on display

4. Pick up the "specials flyer" to see what the store is currently discounting

5. Peruse the selections and read the description cards for the computers

Intentions	Needs (Features and Functions)	Actions (User Objectives)	Acme's Business Objectives
Research and Buy a Computer *Cindy needs a computer, but is uncertain what her options are. She needs to be able to show her parents the options and ideally have them purchase the computer for her.*	**Look Up Products** - General product information - Quick comparison of products - Upgrade and accessory information **Research the Technology** - System to explain what the system pieces are and how they compare to each other - Have products suggested based on needs **Pick the System** - Pick a solution(s) - Configure/customize the system - Store picked solutions for viewing later/sharing to parents/friends - Allow friends/parents to vote on system if she can't make up her mind **Buy the System** - Send parents to her customized computer to have them buy it on her behalf	Get product information Learn the differences between products and product options Have a product suggested to her based on her needs Show friends what system she is getting Show parents 2 to 3 systems and have them buy one—persuade them to buy the better machine Buy the best system she can get	Increase customer base Educate customer to better understand benefits of the technology Up-sell/cross-sell customers into new products/peripherals Leverage user's circle of community to advertise Acme
Check purchase status			
Knowledge base, documentation, troubleshooting wizard, live CSR			
Contact information			
Customer service—RMA, swap parts			

EXHIBIT 9.4 Intentions Matrix

6. Find a salesperson to explain the features/benefits of one computer versus another

7. Take the literature and recommendations home to get the opinions of friends

8. Take one of these friends to the store to help choose a computer

9. Provide salesperson with credit card information

10. Load computer into car and drive home

Cindy walked away from the purchasing experience happy because she bought a computer that she thought was great. However, the process took a significant amount of time, and it was difficult to include her family and friends in the decision. Additionally, she felt that she was under significant pressure by the salespeople to make a decision on the spot. She would have appreciated being able to better understand the options that she had available to her before she purchased the computer. Clearly, the proposed Acme Computer website has the potential of delivering significant benefit to both Cindy and Acme Computer if it can improve the shopping experience described above.

But how? If Cindy were using the website to research and purchase the computer instead of visiting the physical store, she would want and need at least the same level of information, just not necessarily the way it was presented at the store.

1. To purchase the computer, Cindy must be able to:
   a. Browse products sold by Acme Computer
   b. Read literature to better inform her on what computer will be appropriate
   c. Read information on the specials that are currently being offered
   d. Request more information from a customer service representative to clarify a question not answered in the literature
   e. Possibly use a system to match her needs with the capabilities of a computer
   f. Select and store several potential systems to be compared feature by feature (this would also allow her parents and friends to see what systems Cindy was contemplating)
   g. Poll/collect feedback on systems from parents and friends, including the ability to have a ranking of each potential computer system
   h. Have a notification system that friends and relatives link to the potential computers
   i. View comments/rankings from friends and family
   j. Select a system to purchase
   k. Select the options to go with the system
   l. Create an account if this is the first purchase at AcmeComputer. com, or log in to an existing account
   m. Select payment and shipping properties

2. To check on the status of her purchase, Cindy must be able to:
   a. Be notified when the computer is shipped
   b. Log in to her account to check the status of the order

By thinking through a given task or usage occasion—in this case, shopping for a computer—we can see that it is possible to derive (1) a process flow for how the task is most likely to unfold from start to finish, (2) a description of each screen that the user would see, and (3) the content and functions that should be available at any given time. Doing so allows us to build a "use case" for the scenario. At its simplest, a **use case** describes how a user and a system interact to accomplish a specific goal. This is typically a step-by-step guide describing all of the actions that the user takes, and what the system does in return. The process of developing each of the use cases for each usage occasion allows the development team to clearly identify all of the discrete sets of functionality and content that will be required to deliver the site. Additionally, the team will be able to see sections of the site in which functionality and content are shared, allowing it to take into account any unique requirements that a particular section might have of a function. Together, these discrete sets of functions represent the **functional matrix** for the website (see Exhibit 9.5 for the distinction between functional matrix and functional specification).

Functional Matrix Purpose:
- Define project scope, used to build project plan
- Communicate with executives, project team, any external contractors
- Track enhancements as they are discovered during development
- Plan future release functionality—by priority

Functional Specification Purpose:
- Provide detailed design of system processes and pages
- Provide details of the life cycle of different objects (search, payments, etc.)
- Define the details of each page (list of fields on a page, their validation requirements, their data sources)
- Define all actions on each page (save shopping cart, send e-mail, update account, checkout)

EXHIBIT 9.5   Functional Matrix Vs. Functional Specification

Additionally, because the team is now able to define what *screens* will be required in order to satisfy the use case, it can go a step further and define what *content* will be required on each screen. Together, these sets of content are referred to as the **content matrix**. The content matrix allows the team to clearly understand the depth, breadth, and types of content that will need to be generated for the site. Because content development frequently involves significant executive input and signoff (with multiple revisions), it is imperative to get this process started as early as possible. Together, the use cases, functional matrix, and content matrix provide information critical to the development of the functional specification.

Architecture Design Process

Now that we have defined the user experience, it is time to design both the look and function of the website. The architecture design process allows the development team to translate what was learned during the user experience definition process into what functions the site needs and how those functions will be represented on the screen.

Site Map and Page Schematics

At this point, the team is well positioned to generate the next set of important documents that it will need: the site map and the page schematics.

The Site Map

The **site map** is typically a hierarchical view of the proposed website and encompasses all of the primary pages, or templates, to be developed (see Exhibit 9.6). The site map allows the development team to logically group content into content areas and to understand how different content types relate and link to one another. Aside from providing a visual representation of the website, the site map performs a very important function: It allows the team to identify the full scope of the website, including future phases of development, and to develop the website's navigational system.

The challenge is to develop a navigation system that is meaningful to the user and also fits within the visual design of the site. If the site is small, then the job is an easy one. However, if the site is large, with many discrete content areas, each of which has multiple layers, then the team must work significantly harder. Additionally, by providing a clear view of the breadth and depth of the site, the site map allows the team to build the navigation system beginning with the most deeply nested page or area of the site and ending with the homepage. Doing so helps to ensure that the navigation system will be flexible enough to accommodate every other page and function within the site.

Page Schematics

Sometimes referred to as "wire frames," **page schematics** are simple drawings or diagrams that serve as a conceptual layout for what each page on the site will look like (see Exhibit 9.7). The schematic provides the team with a way to brainstorm how and where certain functionality and content will appear on a particular page. The focus is on function rather than appearance. This is important, because once the visual design team begins to apply color and images to the design, it is very easy for the team to focus on visual problems (I don't like that color) rather than functional problems (if you put the search button in that location, the user won't see it).

It is expected that the team will generate page schematics for each primary page type, but not necessarily for every page. For example, if the site AcmeComputer.com is going to have a "press releases" section, a page schematic will need to be created for that section—but not for each press release that is going to be placed on the site. In other words, the press

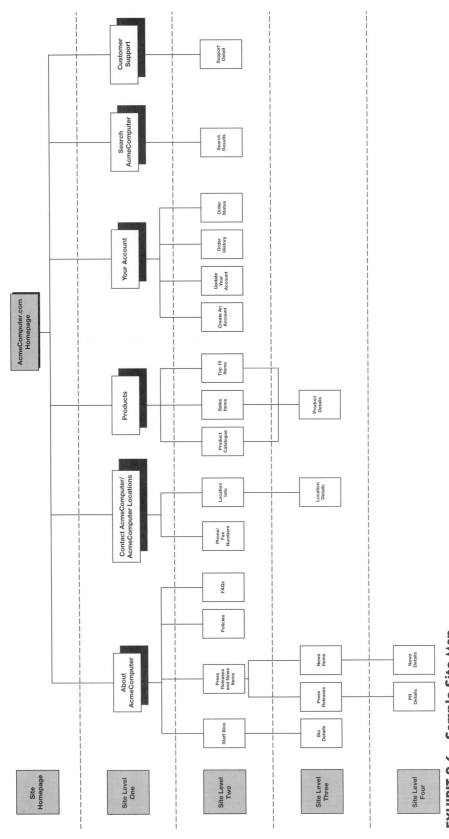

EXHIBIT 9.6 Sample Site Map

release schematic becomes the template for all press releases. Some page schematics will define the layout of templates; others will define the layout for primary pages that do not function as templates, such as the homepage.

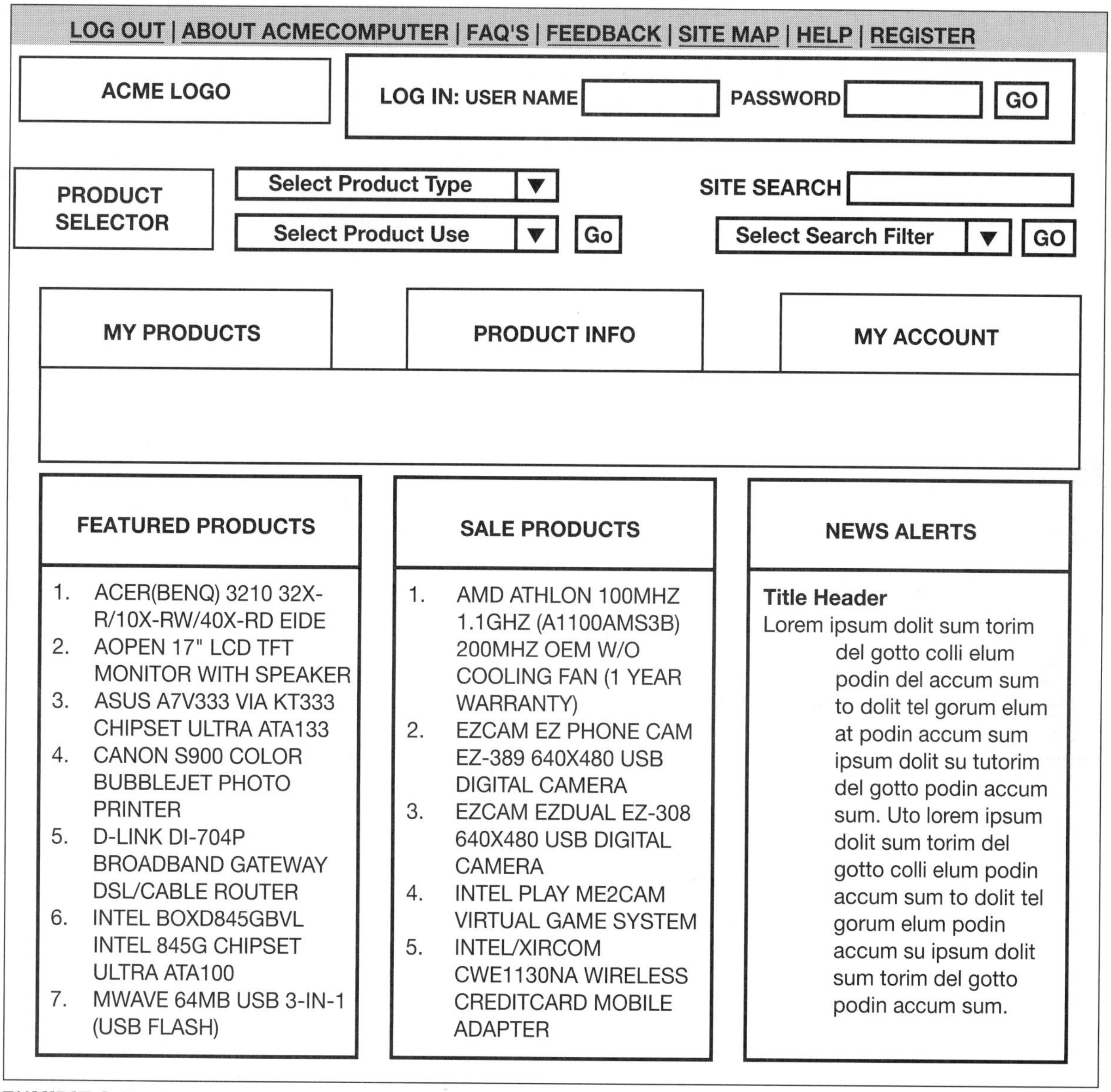

```
| LOG OUT | ABOUT ACMECOMPUTER | FAQ'S | FEEDBACK | SITE MAP | HELP | REGISTER |

+----------------+    LOG IN: USER NAME [        ]  PASSWORD [        ]  [GO]
|   ACME LOGO    |
+----------------+

+----------------+  Select Product Type  [▼]        SITE SEARCH [              ]
|   PRODUCT      |
|   SELECTOR     |  Select Product Use   [▼]  [Go]  Select Search Filter [▼] [GO]
+----------------+

   MY PRODUCTS            PRODUCT INFO              MY ACCOUNT
```

FEATURED PRODUCTS	SALE PRODUCTS	NEWS ALERTS
1. ACER(BENQ) 3210 32X-R/10X-RW/40X-RD EIDE 2. AOPEN 17" LCD TFT MONITOR WITH SPEAKER 3. ASUS A7V333 VIA KT333 CHIPSET ULTRA ATA133 4. CANON S900 COLOR BUBBLEJET PHOTO PRINTER 5. D-LINK DI-704P BROADBAND GATEWAY DSL/CABLE ROUTER 6. INTEL BOXD845GBVL INTEL 845G CHIPSET ULTRA ATA100 7. MWAVE 64MB USB 3-IN-1 (USB FLASH)	1. AMD ATHLON 100MHZ 1.1GHZ (A1100AMS3B) 200MHZ OEM W/O COOLING FAN (1 YEAR WARRANTY) 2. EZCAM EZ PHONE CAM EZ-389 640X480 USB DIGITAL CAMERA 3. EZCAM EZDUAL EZ-308 640X480 USB DIGITAL CAMERA 4. INTEL PLAY ME2CAM VIRTUAL GAME SYSTEM 5. INTEL/XIRCOM CWE1130NA WIRELESS CREDITCARD MOBILE ADAPTER	**Title Header** Lorem ipsum dolit sum torim del gotto colli elum podin del accum sum to dolit tel gorum elum at podin accum sum ipsum dolit su tutorim del gotto podin accum sum. Uto lorem ipsum dolit sum torim del gotto colli elum podin accum sum to dolit tel gorum elum podin accum su ipsum dolit sum torim del gotto podin accum sum.

EXHIBIT 9.7   Page Schematic

Technical Discovery

While one part of the development team performs the experience discovery and definition function, a core technical team begins to define the technical environment, goals, and vision for the project. This process involves talking with technical stakeholders within the organization (such as the database administrator or company CIO) as well as outside partners (such as the warehousing partner that will provide real-time inventory information and shipping status). The technology vision is not created in a vacuum, however—it is strongly informed and structured by many elements, including the following:

- *The business objectives for the site.* What kind of website will it be? There can be a vast difference in the technical requirements of a small corporate brochure website versus an e-commerce site.

- *User persona.* Who are your users, and what is their level of technical sophistication? Are they using a dial-up modem to access the website, or do they use a high-speed connection from work? Do they use modern software? Do they all use a single operating system—all Macintosh, or all Windows, or all Linux?

- *Existing technology.* What type of technology exists in the organization today, what can be leveraged, and what will pose a roadblock to development? Existing systems could include warehousing systems, inventory control, human resources, customer relationship management systems, and fulfillment systems, to name a few.

  — Where do the data that the system needs to access reside today? If it is in a mainframe or other legacy system, extra effort may be needed to access and manipulate the information so that it is useful to the user.

  — How clean are the data? When publishing corporate information on a public system, it is crucial to ensure that the data you are publishing are what you think they are.

  — How fast is the system that the data sit on today? Depending on what the information is and how the site will use it, you may need to build a replica of those data just for the website to use, in order to ensure that the data do not create a bottleneck in site performance.

- *Internal skill set.* What technical skills does your staff have today? If you build the website entirely in Java, but your staff has mostly C++/COBOL development skills, who will maintain the code for the system? Do you have the skills to manage the complex set of servers and software required to keep the site up?

- *User intentions.* What does the user need to accomplish, and what type of data does that user need to access in order to achieve that goal?

- *Time and budget.* How long does the team have to build the systems, and how much money can it spend to do so?

- *Traffic.* The greater the amount of traffic that the site is expected to handle, the more sophisticated the systems will need to be to manage the load that the traffic will place on the servers. How best to mitigate the effects of increased load will be informed by the decisions that the team makes about site performance metrics.

- *Uptime requirements.* The more critical a website is to a company, the more reliable that site must be. A decision by the business that the site is of significant importance, and must therefore be available for use 99.999 percent of the time ("five nines"), can place significant additional architectural requirements on the site. In real terms, 99.999 percent availability translates into a system that is offline for a total of five minutes per year. The problem with trying to achieve this goal with a full e-commerce system is that there are a tremendous number of interrelated components that make up the system—if one component breaks, it is likely that some part of the site will go down. Five nines is a goal that is very difficult (and expensive) to achieve. The team will have to design a self-healing, highly redundant architecture to try and ensure that, if some part of the site fails, another takes over in its place. The team should investigate if a more realistic goal of "three nines" (8.76 hours of downtime per year) is satisfactory, as it will have a significant effect on the infrastructure required.

- *Security requirements.* Security issues start with the security of the site itself (its ability to protect itself from illicit attack) and end with the data that the site either contains or collects from its users. To address these security issues, the technology plan will need to specify:

  — Security requirements for the network. Which servers are directly exposed to the Internet? Which protocols are allowed to access the servers? Do systems need to be in place to deal with large-scale attacks? How will the servers communicate with one another?

  — Security requirements for the hardware and software. This could detail which individuals physically have access to what equipment, and under what conditions; the type (and versions) of software installed on the servers; and which services are enabled. Additionally, this set of requirements could detail a policy on how and when software patches are applied to the servers and equipment.

  — Security requirements for information. If the website contains sensitive information, the plan might specify where this information is stored, whether it is encrypted, who has or what parts of the system have access to it and under what conditions, whether the information can be cached and for how long, and whether the information needs to be destroyed after a specific time period. A similar set of restrictions might be placed on information obtained from the users of the system, especially in countries that have strictly regulated policies on the types of information that websites can track and store about individuals.

This initial vision for the website helps to establish an early direction for the technology plan. This direction, in turn, gives the development team a greater sense of the level of sophistication that the technical underpinnings for the site will require. However, it is really through the functionality matrix that the team gets its deepest understanding of what type of systems will need to be built. Fortunately, that process comes later. At this point, the team should be able to deliver a technical summary document, detailing:

- Existing corporate systems, including all relevant back-end systems and databases
- How the proposed site differs from those of the company's competitors
- Conceptual technical architecture to support the website
- An analysis of and recommendations for the software components to be used during the development process, such as applications servers, product configuration, order management, personalization, supply chain management, B2B e-commerce, and legacy integration

Experience Definition and Architecture Design Outputs

By this point, the development team should be able to create the following outputs:

- User experience and functional definition document
- User type definition document
- User intentions definition document
- User persona definition document
- Functionality matrix
- Content matrix
- Use cases
- Site map
- Page schematics

Drill-Down

Rapid Site Design

Any site can be developed rapidly. Many should not be. However, there are times when even a relatively sophisticated website can be built rapidly, in three to four weeks. When is this reasonable?

When Rapid Site Design Is Realistic

Websites that can be designed rapidly share four characteristics:

- *They are relatively small.* "Relatively small" means less than 30 total webpages. It is often very difficult to predetermine the number of pages that will go into one website before it is actually built. Companies should estimate based on what they know. If a separate profile page is needed for 10 people, the website is already 10 pages.

- *They can be quickly visually designed with minimal constraint.* If the team insists that many contributors give feedback on the visual design, then the site cannot be developed rapidly. The visual design cycles will take up too much time.

- *Their content is relatively static.* Being relatively static helps a great deal when it comes time to testing the site. With more dynamic sites, testing is much more involved because the output is dependent on user input data.

- *They have a limited audience.* The bigger a site's projected audience, the more technical development it requires. The amount of development required for a site with 10 users per month is much different from that required for the same site serving 1 million users per month.

When Rapid Site Design Is Not Realistic

Websites that should not be developed rapidly have the following characteristics:

- *They are dynamic and/or database-driven.* In general, any site with a great deal of dynamic content (i.e., content that changes based on user input) takes longer to develop. Often, dynamic sites require a connection with a database for simple content updating. Database-driven sites are extremely powerful but do not lend themselves to rapid development. Variables added to the system, such as dynamic content exchanged with a database, add considerable time to the development cycle. Not only do the functional areas need to be built, but all of the moving pieces need to be tested extensively.

continued

- *They have e-commerce capabilities.* E-commerce sites present many of the same problems as dynamic/database-driven sites. There are too many moving parts involved with e-commerce (e.g., purchasing, fulfillment, product/inventory management, customer relationship management, content management, user registration, search engine) that can go wrong if not tested extensively. It would be similar to attempting to build a car from scratch in four weeks with four people: You might be able to do it, but you would be amazingly lucky if it worked properly. Both are very intricate systems with many potential points of failure.

- *There is sophisticated visual design.* Visual design is a difficult, time-consuming process. Extensive visual design cannot be rushed. If the site calls for a spectacular design, then you simply cannot do it rapidly. That is not to say, however, that the site cannot look good. In fact, simpler site designs often can be much more compelling than complicated ones. Think about Yahoo, eBay, Google, and Amazon. None of them have a very complicated visual design. Instead, they have very simple designs that allow users to navigate quickly and easily. If you need to make a lot of visual design iteration cycles between the visual design team and the rest of the team, then you will lose a lot of time. So if the site absolutely needs to be done quickly, plan on early sign-off on a relatively simple visual design.

- *They contain extensive content.* Content can take a very long time to develop. If there is a lot of content that needs to be written to fill all of the proposed pages of the site, then the writers may not be able to finish the work in just a few weeks. Oftentimes, companies that have to create content for their sites are not aware that (1) they are responsible for the content, (2) it can often take a long time to write, and (3) once finished, it takes a technologist time to put that content into the webpage. The technologists will always finish last, of course, because the final draft of the content always needs to be put into the website and thoroughly tested.

- *A large audience is expected for the site.* When there is a large audience hitting a website for information or making transactions, systems need to be in place to handle that load. Building those systems requires infrastructure planning, budgeting, and implementation that need to happen even before there is a website to place into that infrastructure. CNN (*www.cnn.com*) ran headfirst into that very problem on September 11, 2001, when millions of users flocked to CNN.com—and crippled its systems. While having a link posted on Slashdot (*www.slashdot.org*), a "news for nerds" website, can be good exposure for a site, it can often be a problem for smaller sites that will immediately have millions of Slashdot readers click on the link, creating so much traffic it brings the site to a standstill. The moral of the story: If you expect that kind of traffic, you need to plan for it, and that planning takes time.

Implementation

Validation

Up to this point, the team has focused on identifying the needs of the user segments that the website is going to serve, and figuring out how the website satisfies those needs. From the types of computers that users use to their personal demographic backgrounds, the team has painted a sophisticated picture of how the website can provide a compelling experience for its visitors. This investigation has, in turn, allowed the team to very clearly articulate the functionality and content that the site must provide to its users in order to satisfy those needs.

The last step before building begins is to finalize the visual design of the site and to test the design and navigation system in a limited fashion by building a functioning prototype. No doubt, the site's visual design has been incubating since the project's inception. Since the development of the initial creative brief, the team has been immersed in the elements of the project—the company and product brand, the audience, and the offering of the site. For each team member, these elements have combined to create a very personal point of view about how the site should look. It is the job of the lead designer and his or her team to turn these collective visions into a visual design that accomplishes the site's specific business goals. A site that is visually stunning and interactive is a failure if it does not fulfill the business mission.

For example, when Cindy goes to research her computer options on AcmeComputer.com, she is likely to want to print out the specifications for each computer that interests her so that she can compare them. However, if the designers elected to build an interface that does not easily accommodate printing, or only partially prints the content, Cindy may opt to buy nothing out of frustration. The visual design of the site should be decided only after the user persona, functionality matrix, content matrix, and site map are completed.

Developing a website's visual design is an iterative process. It is also a subjective process. After collecting and absorbing its own research, plus the research generated by the other team members, the design team will typically produce three design themes, each of which usually includes a top-level page and designs for two or three lower-level pages. For example, a design might include the AcmeComputer.com homepage, a "Products" page, a "Product Detail" page, and a "Shopping Cart" page. At this stage, the various design themes might be radically different. Once these design themes have been presented, the feedback team (including internal Web team members and outside stakeholders) is asked to provide feedback: What do they like about the designs? What do they dislike? Which design is their preference? The design team may wish to collect this feedback offline or within an interactive brainstorming session. Regardless of the method, the goal is to achieve signoff on a particular design direction. This could mean one of the designs, or a combination of elements from two or all of the design concepts.

Once the initial design direction is determined, the team will begin an iterative process of refinement and feedback collection—preferably with no more than four iterations—before getting signoff on the final design concept. When the final design concept has been approved, the team at last has a design system that can be applied to the rest of the website.

The final step of the validation segment of the development process is to actually take a small section of the website and build a functioning prototype. This does not mean that all of the functionality has to be built; in fact, the prototype is often entirely mocked up. The idea is to see whether the combination of visual design, navigation elements, and content satisfies customer needs. The team selects a representative use case, builds a functioning prototype that reflects the chosen visual design, and tests it. The testing process can involve team members and interested outside parties, but most importantly the prototype should be tested by a real set of users from the target audience. For example, the team might take the prototype to Cindy's college and ask her and several of her friends to try it out and give feedback.

More sophisticated testing can be conducted within a "usability lab" environment, which typically features multiple cameras and software that monitor exactly how users interact with the site—what they look at first on a page, which links/buttons they click on, and what confuses them. Feedback and observations from these sessions are then incorporated into the visual design and navigation system.

Build Phase

At this point, the development team can start to build the website. The development typically takes place in multiple, simultaneous streams of activity: (1) application, or back-end, development; (2) interface development, including production of HTML pages and other interface technologies such as Macromedia Flash; (3) interactive development, which includes the production of imagery, artwork, sound, and video (if required); and (4) content development.

It is important to note that once the previous work has been finalized, it is very, very costly to make changes to these specifications (such as adding functionality or content, defining a new user type, or changing the visual design system). These changes require new sets of iterative design and may have significant effect on other, seemingly far removed parts of the system. Thus, changes to the specifications at this late phase in the project delay the delivery of the working system (unless other parts of the system are sacrificed to add the new functionality), increase the complexity of the final system, and possibly demoralize the development team.

Generally speaking, the building process boils down to some very simple steps:

1. Design the technical infrastructure (e.g., security, persistence, transaction management, auditing, logging)

2. Design the technical components so that they will be both flexible and extensible

3. Build the components (both visual and functional) that will make up the website

4. Integrate those components so that they work together as expected

5. Test those components, both individually and after they have been integrated with one another, to ensure that they work as expected and perform up to par

6. Refine the system and components based on the results of these tests

7. Launch the website

Before any development can begin, however, the team must first set up an appropriate development environment. The development environment is a combination of software and hardware that defines how the code that is developed runs and helps to manage and coordinate the development of the code by multiple people. Some software is placed on developers' workstations; other software runs on servers. The developer software can consist of one or many code-writing tools, frequently referred to as the integrated development environment (IDE). These tools are usually meant to be used with a specific computer language (the computer language is the way a programmer interacts and communicates with a computer, allowing him or her to build the functionality required by the website) and include packages such as Microsoft Visual Studio, Macromedia ColdFusion Studio, Borland JBuilder, or Sun's Sun One Studio. The tools typically include functionality designed to reduce development time such as debuggers, fast compilers, and prebuilt code components. Deciding which language should be used is guided by a number of factors:

1. *Available skills.* If the majority of in-house developers are skilled in one particular language (say, Perl), it may not make sense to develop the website in another language (say, Java). While the company may be able to hire external consultants to develop the initial application in that language, the internal team will be stuck with it after the consultants have finished their work. Remember, the initial development is just the beginning of the effort required; most likely, the internal team is responsible for the ongoing maintenance, enhancement, and support of the application.

2. *Portability.* The decision of which development language the team chooses is framed by whether the chosen language and or development environment is "open" (open source) or proprietary. Interestingly, most of the languages that are commonly referred to as "open" (such as Java and Perl) in fact are not. These languages are actually owned by a particular person or company (Java by Sun Microsystems and Perl by Larry Wall), but the specifications for the languages are made available to the public. By making the specifications available, the owners allow other companies to write "runtime environments"—basically, the engines that run the specification for their language—thereby allowing for more than one company to provide an application server for that language. On the other hand, other languages do not have published specifications, or only partially publish the specification and do not guarantee them to be accurate. Because these specifications are only partially published and subject to change, it becomes nearly impossible for companies to develop runtime environments for the language. A good example of this is Microsoft, which partially publishes the specifications for its programming languages. Because the specifications for their languages are highly likely to change, without documentation, almost no company has been willing to develop a runtime environment for their languages, leaving developers with only one viable choice of runtime environment—Microsoft's Windows Server. These languages require that the runtime environment be present. However, in this case, the runtime environment can only be sourced from one vendor. Importantly, the Windows Server Operating System (OS) only runs on computers that use Intel microprocessors, and not on equipment from Sun or on large-scale mainframe equipment from companies such as IBM and Hewlett-Packard. On the other hand, if a developer chooses to use Java as the development language, a Java runtime environment (JRE) is required and can be acquired from a variety

of companies, including IBM and Sun. Typically, these JREs are augmented by an application server that provides a framework of functionality on top of the JRE. The JRE and application servers typically run under a variety of server operating systems, including Windows, Sun Solaris, and Linux, and consequentially run on a variety of different hardware platforms.

3. *Scalability/enterprise features.* The website being developed may be simple or complex and may or may not need to connect to back-end database systems and scale to handle a very heavy traffic load. Depending on the level of complexity and scalability required by the website, the team may choose one language over another. Some languages are known for their ability to support rapid development but sacrifice some enterprise sophistication along the way. Others have significant levels of complexity that add to their flexibility and enterprise appeal, while at the same time sacrificing ease of development. Additionally, some languages have significant performance advantages but have the drawback of being significantly more difficult to develop in (C++, for example).

4. *Cost.* The cost of the actual language is nothing—except, of course, in the time it takes to learn and become proficient in the language. However, the cost to set up the appropriate environment in which to develop software in that language varies to a great degree. As mentioned earlier, the Microsoft solution bundles most (not all) of the software needed to run a Microsoft solution within the server operating system. On the other hand, the cost of Java application environments varies significantly, ranging from free to hundreds of thousands of dollars. Additional cost considerations include the amount of staff training that is required on the selected platform, the type of hardware required, and the cost of ongoing support.

The development language is just one of the environment decisions that need to be made. Next, the architecture of the hardware and software environment must be laid out. This decision is complicated by the fact that you most likely are making the decision not for one environment, but for three. Web development environments typically include a maximum of three "zones" for development:

- *Zone 1—The live site.* These are the servers and website code from which a website is currently being published to the Internet. This zone contains the latest "published" version of the website and is located within the site's hosting facility. Careful control of what code is published to this zone ensures that only approved/published code is running.

- *Zone 2—The staging environment.* These are the servers and website code that have a "ready to be published" version of the site. This is an isolated area in which the development team can post a new version of the site for review and testing while at the same time not interfering with ongoing development or threatening the live site. A decision might be made to make the servers within the staging environment at least as powerful as those within the live environment so that (a) the staging system accurately represents the performance of the live site for load testing and (b) the staging environment can substitute for the live environment in case of catastrophic failure of the live systems.

- *Zone 3—The development environment.* These are the servers and website code that are actively being worked on by developers. The actual environment depends on whether or not the team elects to use a code management tool (known as "source control" software) to manage check-in/check-out of the code being developed, but typically each developer keeps a full copy of the code in an isolated "sandbox." This allows the developer to write sections of code in isolation so that when a problem arises with one developer's code, it does not affect the productivity of the other developers. When a developer has finished a set of code, it can be published to the master set residing on the stage server.

Within each of these zones, there may or may not be multiple servers (Web servers, application servers, and database servers), depending on the size and complexity of the website. The more servers that exist within each zone, the more complicated the task of ensuring that the proper set of code and data exists in the proper place.

Page Design

Now that the visual design system has been finalized and approved by the team, it can be applied to the actual pages on the site. Website pages can typically be divided into two groups—**unique pages** and **template pages**. Unique pages are pages that have a design that is different from any other page on the site. The design and layout of template pages, on the other hand, is repeated more than once, usually on a section of the site that has multiple pages of similar content (e.g., press releases).

Whether the page is unique or a template, the designers must go through a process for each page that is similar to the process they went through to create the design system itself. In this case, however, they are not working from scratch. The design system allows the designers to leverage a common framework and approach for each page design, providing a consistent look-and-feel across the site. Depending on the complexity of the page, the designers may elect to submit multiple concepts for each page (or perhaps just for the most complex pages), have a selection committee identify the best concepts, and then provide three or four iterations of that concept before the page is approved.

Once the pages are approved, the design team works with the interface development team to transform the design into actual webpages. The interface team needs to translate the design and intended functionality of the pages into an interface that is usable on the Web. This interface might make use of a number of Internet technologies, including HTML, Flash, Java, JavaScript, Cascading Style Sheets (CSS), and others, depending on which are deemed appropriate. Additionally, if the design includes imagery from a stock photography house or other copyrighted materials, the design team is responsible for obtaining the licenses and rights to reuse these materials on the site.

After (or even before) the design team hands off the project to the interface team, it should develop a design style guide. The style guide is an effective tool for identifying and maintaining the visual design of the site after it is released. The style guide clearly illustrates the exact color palate for the website along with font styles and types, image standards, and rules on where any particular element is used on any particular page.

Interface Development

The choice of which technologies to implement within an interface is a tricky one. Not all pages require the same set of functionality or deliver the same type of information and therefore require different technologies within them. For instance, a website's homepage may require nothing more than plain HTML to deliver the design. However, the team may have also decided that the site needs a sophisticated, highly flexible search interface for its products and that this might be done most effectively through DHTML, for example. As a result, DHTML might be used extensively on the search page, but very little (or not at all) elsewhere on the site.

Ultimately, the success of an interface, and of a website as a whole, is determined by whether its users are successful in getting the information they need and understanding the information that is presented to them. The same information, when presented one way, could confuse the user, but when presented another could be perfectly clear. It depends on *how* the information is presented.

Before the team gets started on the development of the interfaces, it must come to an agreement with the application development team and the visual design team on how they will combine the results of their efforts—the integration process. This agreement involves setting rules about common naming conventions for files and application code, revision control, file locations, and external links. Once a plan has been hammered out, the interface team can define the set of technologies that are used on the site, as well as a general approach to how to build the pages. This approach most likely has some commonality across all of the pages on the site, with some sections requiring unique capabilities given the needs of the audiences for that particular set of features and content. As the pages and templates are being developed and tested by the team, the exact approach for delivering unique functionality or content may be modified depending on the success of one approach versus another.

While it is relatively straightforward for the interface team to build and complete webpages that are static with little or no dynamic functionality, these types of pages are rarely used. More common are webpages that contain content that is actually stored in a database or other external systems (rather than in the page itself) and functionality that does something based on a user's request. The development of an interface to accommodate this type of functionality and content requires a tight interaction with the application development team. Some of this functionality is performed by the interface itself—especially functionality that manipulates the *display* of information or the manipulation of information on the screen. The majority of this functionality, however, is developed by the application team.

Application Development

The application development effort begins with the functionality matrix and functional specification. These documents, at their core, define generally (the functionality matrix) and very specifically (the func spec) what the website does. These functions can range from the simple (If I click on this link, I expect to be taken to this other page) to the more complex (how do I search for a product?). Through the functionality matrix, the team received a concrete list of all the capabilities the website needs to have, plus a prioritization of each function and an indication of where on the site these functions are located. They also now understand the relative complexity of the function and what kind of information is needed in order to make it work properly.

For example, a search function definitely needs information about what the user is searching for but may also use other information to narrow the search, such as which area of the site the user is searching from. Some of the functions may also interact with and depend on one another. Take, for example, the shopping cart function on AcmeComputer.com. The shopping cart will not be useful unless users have the ability to fill it with items and then "steer" it to the virtual checkout counter. However, by knowing in advance through the func spec exactly what information each function will need, how it is supposed to manipulate that information, and what to do with the information when it is finished, it is possible to very clearly define and build functional modules that work with one another. It is these modules that are the heart of application development. Typically, a development team is divided up to tackle these modules, with one developer being assigned to work on each module. If the modules are large enough, they may be broken up into smaller modules to make the work more manageable.

Once a module has been assigned, however, the process for developing the module is reasonably straightforward. Based on the information provided by the func spec, the developer first needs to locate the information required by the module for it to function. Some of this information may be passed to the function when the function is activated by the user, but it may also be information that is stored in another location (e.g., a database). Additionally, the function may need to store some information of its own—perhaps in a database, perhaps elsewhere—and the developer would need to get this storage facility ready. Once the sources and the repository of information are ready, the module can be developed and tested. In this phase, the testing process is known as **unit testing**. The module, by itself, is made to do exactly what is expected of it—when handed a specific set of information, it manipulates the information in an expected manner and delivers an expected result.

Additionally, unit testing might include a test to see whether the module handles errors as expected or a test to see that the module meets specific performance requirements. Errors that occur can be entered into a bug-tracking system, allowing the developer to concentrate on finding bugs, documenting them, and fixing them later. Depending on the structure of the application development team, this testing may actually be performed by a developer assigned solely to test code or by an entire team. In either case, the developer will review the bugs outstanding in the module, address the bugs, and resubmit the module for testing.

The development team continues in this mode of module development and unit testing until all of the functionality called for by the functional specification is developed. Typically, the team is working to develop this complete set of functionality against a deadline, which, for the project manager, is the milestone marking the end of the development phase of the project and the beginning of the testing phase. At this point, a "code-freeze" is implemented, which dictates that no new functionality will be developed by the team.

This is important, because whenever new functionality is added to the system, it can significantly affect other areas of the system, introducing new bugs or other site performance problems.

Drill-Down

Development Methodologies

In today's fluid development environment, a team must determine the most suitable approach to attacking a particular project. Different methodologies make different assumptions about the business and work environments of the project, and knowing each of their pros and cons will allow the team to pick the most efficient methodology for that particular project. Three methodologies are outlined below to give a taste of the different tradeoffs that exist.

Traditional Approach

The traditional waterfall methodology is most commonly used in large development projects with well-known deliverables and deadlines. It has the advantage of only needing heavy involvement from the business team during the beginning design stage, during key milestones, and during acceptance testing. Early deliverables often include very detailed technical and functional specifications. This allows a team to allocate resources efficiently to avoid roadblocks, but it also makes introducing change requests a potentially difficult affair. The business team needs to be minimally allocated to the project during the development phase, and the development work could potentially be outsourced once the design stages are complete, freeing up internal resources.

Rapid Application Development (RAD)

RAD is a methodology that was developed to provide a greater degree of efficiency in an environment of rapidly changing or loosely defined requirements. RAD can best be described as an iterative approach to development in which cycles of requirements gathering, mockup creation, and client testing take place. Feedback is then gathered, and the process is repeated until the requirements stabilize and the project is launched. This can be less efficient than the waterfall approach, because much work is discarded, but it allows the requirements to change without a drastic reworking of a finished design. RAD projects are traditionally hard to budget, require tight project management to control the scope of the project, and involve the business team throughout the entire project.

Extreme Programming (XP)

XP has been developed to attempt as an attempt to combat the chaotic tendencies of RAD while still maintaining the flexibility to respond to changing business needs. XP advocates rigorous and automated testing and simplicity of code. The development team should never make assumptions about future requirements and should constantly reevaluate old code in light of new requirements.

XP's goal is to release software as often as possible in order to test it with real users. Whereas the waterfall methodology often has one large testing phase near the end of the project, XP strives to release versions of the project as early and as often as possible. This creates a "one feature at a time" mentality that slowly grows the software and reduces risk by ensuring that a project will have a degree of stable functionality at any given date.

The development methodology for a given project is chosen by examining both the needs of the project and the knowledge and temperament of the development team. Some methodologies emphasize testing, some documentation; others stress code reusability. Certain methodologies are better suited for projects with tight deadlines or unclear and changing requirements. Executing against a methodology takes knowledge and experience on the part of a development team. The team needs to learn the rules and practices of a specific methodology. As with anything else, the more familiar they are with it, the more efficient they will be.

Test/Fix

The two aspects of code development that developers probably loathe the most are (1) properly documenting their code and (2) testing their code. Both are time-consuming, tedious processes. However, good developers recognize the value in both. Preproduction testing identifies and rectifies problems *before* the site goes live (when it is least expensive to do so), and can discover how much real-world load the site can handle.

Proper testing of applications begins with the creation of test scripts. Test scripts are similar to the scripts that actors follow. In this case, the test script guides the tester exacitely through a "scene." These scenes are based on the use cases and the functional specifications that have already been developed during the project. Use cases describe the tasks that users need to perform on the website, and test scripts describe how the module, page, or process that lets the user perform that task must be tested (i.e., what information goes into the module and what is expected as a result). Interestingly, the test script itself can be very simple—it is often just a word-processing document that describes the scene, and it can be printed out and handed to the person conducting the tests. It can also be complex, especially if the scene needs to be entered into a software program that performs the test automatically. Test scripts are applied to all phases of testing—unit testing, integration testing, systems testing, and load testing—with the simplest test script being applied to an individual module for unit testing. The code is tested in isolation and in highly ideal conditions. If the code does what is expected of it, the test is a success. If not, problems with the code are isolated and fixed.

However, the test scenario becomes more complex when applied to a test that integrates the functionality of multiple code modules, a process that is aptly called integration testing. Integration testing tests how individual functionality modules work with one another and with the modules within the visual interface system. However, when multiple modules work together and depend on one another, it becomes significantly more complicated to isolate what set of code is causing any particular bug. Developers might first try to identify which module is to blame, whether the problem is with the original data that the module was provided, or whether the module handed information to the next module in an improper way.

Once the offending module has been identified, it may turn out that it is actually doing its job correctly but is masking a problem that exists deeper in another module. As layers of interdependent functionality are added to the site, the system tends to become exponentially more fragile. This is why rigorous testing is necessary. An e-commerce website that is unreliable, appears to mishandle user information, or has functions that simply do not work is going to deter visitors, not draw them in.

The process of unit and integration testing is by nature a highly iterative one. As bugs are discovered, the bugs are logged in the bug-tracking system (see Exhibit 9.8) and addressed by the developer. After fixing a bug or multiple bugs, the developer resubmits the code for testing.

One of the benefits of bug testing is that the development team is able to see very clearly what bugs are *open,* or not yet fixed, in what modules (and their

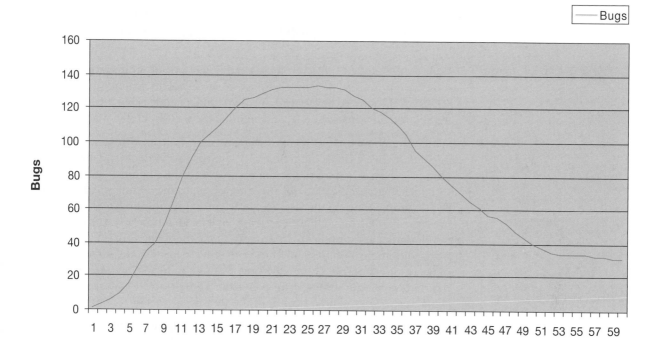

Bugs

EXHIBIT 9.8   Number of Bugs over Testing Days

level of severity). and what bugs have been *closed*. It is conceivable that a module may be released or published even though some of its bugs have yet to be fixed. Often, these are minor or noncritical bugs that can be addressed later in the project. Because many of these modules are interdependent, other developers may be waiting to test their module's ability to integrate with a module that is still being debugged. Getting a module published allows this integration testing to proceed quickly.

While nothing replaces the human element of software testing, many products are available that automate at least some of the testing. These software products allow the team to define test scripts within software and perform module testing and load testing using these scripts. The advantage to this approach is that these scripts are then automated and are highly repeatable. In fact, the test scripts can be scheduled to run repeatedly throughout the testing phase (and after) to ensure that fixing one module does not cause a test script that had previously passed to fail. The automation process is especially useful in testing the capacity of the site, as the software is capable of simulating hundreds or thousands of simultaneous users. One of the companies best known for testing software is Mercury Interactive (*www.mercury-interactive.com*), which also provides an outsourced resource for testing.

Launch

Once the testing phase is over, final steps are taken to make the website "go live." The rollout process, in its simplest form, involves taking the approved version of the site and publishing it to the servers within the hosting environment. Typically, this publishing process happens from the staging environment.

Prior to this rollout, however, a reasonable amount of groundwork must be done to ensure that the launch will be a success. This groundwork includes selecting a hosting facility to serve the site, building and testing the servers, testing the connectivity of the site, and auditing the security of the overall system.

Where and how to host a website is an important issue that needs to be decided before a site is launched. (We discuss this in detail in Chapter 10.) However the site is hosted, the servers that host the site must be configured to match the specifications of the development and testing environments. For example, they should use the same software; different versions of software can cause strange, hard-to-trace problems that do not occur within the development and testing environments. Once the servers are set up, the network communication between the servers, the security of the servers and the network, the Internet connectivity, and any monitoring/support processes that have been put in place can be tested. These tests should be conducted using as close to the final version of the website as possible.

If all of the tests meet the developers' expectations, it is time for the site to go live. Publishing a website can be complicated, depending on the sophistication and complexity of the site and the systems required to support it. Regardless, launching a site is always an exciting moment, as the team savors the satisfaction of releasing the result of so much effort to the world.

Summary

1. **What are the steps involved in building a website?**

First, the company must decide its strategy. Next, the user experience must be defined so that the development team understands who will use the site and what tasks those users want to accomplish. Then the architecture design process starts, which determines how the functions of the site work and how the site looks. Next, the implementation phase begins, during which the site is actually built. The site then undergoes testing and, when testing is done, the site launches.

2. **How is the user experience definition created?**

First, the user type must be defined, as well as the usage occasions for each of the user types. From there, a user profile is developed, which is then combined with the user intentions to create a user persona. From the user persona, the team can think through a specific user task to determine (a) a process flow for how the task is most likely to unfold from start to finish, (b) a description of each screen that the user would see, and (c) the content and functions that would be available to the user at any given time. By thinking through this task, the team can develop a functional matrix and content matrix for the site.

3. **What is the architecture design process?**

The architecture design process determines how the website functions and looks. In this process, the team develops a site map, which is a hierarchical view of the proposed website, and page schematics, which are simple drawings or diagrams that show a conceptual layout for what each page on the site looks like. During this phase, the team also starts to define the technical environment for the project. Some issues that are discussed during the technical phase are (a) objectives of the site, (b) user persona, (c) existing technology, (d) internal skill set, (e) user occasion, (f) time and budget, (g) traffic, (h) uptime requirements, and (i) security requirements.

4. What is the implementation process?

The first part of the implementation process is to finalize the visual design of the site and build a functioning prototype. The next part is to build a site based on the functionality matrix, content matrix, use cases, site map, page schematics, and visual design. The steps involved in the design process are (a) design the technical infrastructure, (b) design the technical components so that they will be both flexible and extensible, (c) build the components, (d) integrate these components so that they work together as expected, (e) test the components, and (f) refine the system. Also during this process, the visual design system is applied to the actual pages on the site and the interfaces and application(s) are developed. The page design phase creates both template and unique pages. Interface development ensures that the website is presented in a way that the user can understand. Finally, the modules for the site are developed during the application development phase.

5. What is involved in the test process?

During the test process, test scripts are created for the modules of the site and are applied to all phases of testing: unit testing, integration testing, systems testing, and load testing. Once the modules are tested, integration testing, which tests how the modules work with one another, begins. Throughout the process, bugs that are found are fixed, though it is very difficult to get rid of all the bugs. Testing can involve both human testing and software testing.

6. What factors are involved in launching a website?

While it is a complicated task to launch a website, and every case is different, some basic issues must be solved. A hosting facility/ISP must be selected; the servers must be built and tested; the connectivity of the site must be tested; and the security of the overall system must be audited.

1. Go to ChannelOne.com (*www.channelone.com*). Who would be the user types for this website? What would be the user intentions? Now go to TheStreet.com (*www.thestreet.com*). What would be their user types and user intentions?

2. Go to your favorite website. Look at the different pages. Which are unique pages and which are template pages? Sketch what you think the site map would be. Sketch a page schematic for one of the pages.

3. Think of an idea for an online business. Who would be the user types? What are the user intentions? What functions and content are needed for each page? Draw a site map and page schematics for a few of the pages.

user experience	user personas	unique pages
functional specification	use case	template pages
change-management process	functional matrix	unit testing
project plan	content matrix	
user types	site map	
user intentions	page schematics	

Exercises

Key Terms

[1]Material in this section adapted from Jeanene Landers Steinberg, "SchwabLearning.org: A Case Study," *Boxes and Arrows*, 1 April 2002.

Endnotes

Site Architecture

CASELET: VICTORIA'S SECRET LEARNS THE IMPORTANCE OF GOOD ARCHITECTURE

Sex sells, but architecture rules. That's what Victoria's Secret found out on February 3, 1999, in what still stands as one of the most infamous and compelling examples of why site architecture is so crucial to any e-commerce endeavor.

It all started with Victoria's Secret's Super Bowl ad touting an hour-long "fashion show" to be broadcast live on the Web later that week. The lingerie retailer seriously underestimated gridiron fans' (and others') appetite for jerky, postage-stamp-size video of scantily clad models. Instead of the expected half a million viewers, it was deluged by three times that many. As a result, its website teetered, then crashed. Only about 2 percent of the page requests sent to the site actually reached it, and those users who actually could get through waited nearly three minutes on average to get any kind of response—even an error message. "Unless it's a fashion show in a snowstorm, I'm not seeing anything," one frustrated viewer told USA Today. Despite being the most-viewed Internet broadcast of its time, the webcast became the butt of jokes and was widely panned in the press.

So when the company decided to mount a second fashion show webcast the following year, it completely re-architected its site, working with partners such as IBM Global Services, Microsoft, Yahoo, and Akamai to anticipate and meet the host of complex demands, from traffic flow to transaction management, generated by millions of viewers from around the world attempting to simultaneously access the same high-bandwidth, streaming video. The company, now all too familiar with the intimate connection between site performance, customer experience, and brand integrity, spent countless hours and $9 million to avoid the previous year's debacle. And in large part, it succeeded: This time, glitches were few and far between as some 2 million viewers successfully logged on and watched. Their average wait to access the site: five seconds.

"It's clear Victoria's Secret learned from its first webcasting experience," said NetRatings's Timothy Sean Kelly, "and succeeded in beefing up its website capacity to accommodate all the traffic."

This chapter was written by Pete Giorgio.

PLEASE CONSIDER THE FOLLOWING QUESTIONS AS YOU READ THIS CHAPTER:

1. What is logical architecture?

2. What are the factors involved in choosing a logical architecture?

3. What is the presentation layer?

4. What is the business logic layer?

5. What is the data layer?

6. What are the factors involved in choosing a physical architecture?

INTRODUCTION

In Chapter 9, we discussed how a website gets built, from developing the strategy to launching the site. In this chapter, we discuss the logical and physical architecture behind the website. As e-commerce sites have grown in complexity over the years, so too has the underlying hardware and software of these sites—and at an even faster rate. Today's e-commerce site not only has to look good but must also provide the user and the company with information and services that can only be delivered through extremely complex systems. This often involves collating information from multiple systems, business units, and geographic locations. The combination of hardware, software, and external systems that makes up a site is commonly referred to as the site's architecture.

Site architecture has become important not only to the technical staff of a business, but to almost every other division as well. Understanding a site's architecture, and especially the tradeoffs made to implement it, can affect the viability and success of everything from a company's marketing campaigns to its year-end reporting capabilities.

Logical Vs. Physical Architecture

At the highest level, site architecture can be divided into two parts: logical architecture and physical architecture. **Logical architecture** attempts to define the system in terms of its software components and the desired functionality of those components. These software components include everything from existing systems to systems purchased to use in building the site. When designing a site, logical architecture is typically created first and helps to define the requirements of the physical architecture. **Physical architecture** defines the hardware and third-party software needed to host and maintain a website. This includes the computers on which the software will run, the network on which those machines will run, and other site-specific hardware needed to implement the design. Often, multiple logical components will run on a single physical component, but one-to-one logical to physical mappings are possible as well.

It is important to consider both parts of the architecture—logical and physical—when designing a website. Each offers points of view that drive the decisions and tradeoffs that need to be made. These high-level views help frame the approach taken to building the website. They also become extremely important in documenting the decisions that have been made and communicating them to both technical and nontechnical players in the process. They are a common point of reference between the people defining the business requirements of the website and the people implementing the website.

Logical Architecture

Logical architecture includes software components and the desired functionality of those components. It takes all the functions that a site must perform and breaks them into smaller modules. As discussed in Chapter 9, modules are functionalities such as a shopping cart or a search box. The logical architecture defines which modules are present, which modules interact with which other modules, and by what means those interactions occur; modules must not only perform their specific task but must also be able to talk to one another so that the user has a seamless experience. Typically, there is a core set of modules that deliver the main functionality of the site and a number of peripheral modules that provide ancillary services or information needed by the main modules.

Over the years, a number of different models for logical architectures have been defined. Choosing between the various models depends on the business requirements defined for the site. While some models provide greater security, others allow for easier maintenance or reliability. Choosing the appropriate architecture is both a skill and an art, and it is typically handled by the most experienced members of a technical staff.

Four main logical models have evolved over the years: mainframe architecture, client/server architecture, n-tier architecture, and distributed architecture.

Mainframe Architecture

Mainframe architecture systems are built around a single, monolithic computer that is shared by all users on the system. This lone computer is responsible for all functions of the system—from data storage through display to the user. There are several advantages to mainframe architecture, including ease of maintenance (if there is a problem, there is only one place where it can be occurring) and reliability. However, these systems are usually lacking in GUI (graphical user interface) capabilities and are extremely costly. Exhibit 10.1 illustrates the mainframe architecture.

Client/Server Architecture

In response to the limitations of mainframe architectures, developers began creating systems based on a **client/server architecture**. In this model, a central server is used to store information that is accessed and acted upon by any number of client machines connected to the server through a network. The

Drill-Down

Talking to Your Techies

One of the largest obstacles facing a website development team is the communication gap that often exists between the people who know the business processes that the website needs to support and the people whose job it is to build the website—a dynamic often referred to as "suits versus T-shirts." However, bridging this gap can often mean the difference between the success and failure of a website—which is why understanding and addressing the underlying issues is paramount.

The problem can have numerous roots. There is often a large age difference between "suits" and techies; the latter tend to be younger and more junior in the organization. In addition, preexisting tensions from previous projects can be brought into new projects, and it is not unusual for each group to misunderstand the nature of the work that the other group does—not to mention the importance of that group to the company.

The first step toward bridging this gap is to acknowledge that it exists. An open dialogue about the challenges a project faces, from both technical and personnel angles, can go a long way toward creating an atmosphere of communication. Resolving other common issues can produce good results as well.

Jargon

The No. 1 obstacle facing smooth communication on website projects is jargon. Each group has an extensive and specific set of terms that it uses frequently in its communications. Each group often has enough of a grasp of the other group's jargon to be dangerous; one group might throw around the other group's terms without completely understanding their meaning, or use its own terms to intimidate the other group and make its members uncomfortable with asking questions. It is important to establish an environment that makes each group comfortable asking the other for clarification.

Pictures

As the saying goes, "A picture is worth a thousand words." This is especially true in communications between these groups. Both suits and techies have a predilection for presenting their points through pictures and diagrams. Diagrams, especially of intricate processes or procedures, create a common ground of understanding and a basis for additional discussions; they also serve as an excellent record of information and decisions that can be used extensively once development of the site begins. Whether it is something as formal as PowerPoint or as casual as a drawing on a piece of paper, pictures can be universally understood.

Shared Goal/Shared Adversity

Nothing helps gel a team more than a shared goal or shared adversity. By focusing the entire team the same way and in the same direction, you can create a shared focus that propels the team through the adversity toward the goal.

Patience

You can never spend too much time ensuring that the technical team understands the business processes that the website will be asked to support. Once the project moves into full development mode, innumerable, detailed questions will be raised about how the site should behave in given situations. By ensuring that the technical team has a good grasp of the underlying business processes, the team becomes equipped with the tools it needs to accurately answer questions as they occur.

Clear Expectations

Even though techies are often the driving force behind the building of a website, they also rely on input—site content, design approval, and so forth—from people on the business side. It is important for the business folks to understand what they need to contribute to the project, and contribute it on time, for the website to launch as planned. Not communicating with the Web developers about possible delays or changes (no matter how legitimate) risks a delay in launching and also fosters ill feelings from the developers.

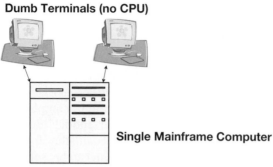

Dumb Terminals (no CPU)

Single Mainframe Computer

EXHIBIT 10.1   Mainframe Architecture

server is responsible for storing and disseminating data, while each client is responsible for collecting the data needed by the user, presenting those data to the user, and communicating any changes back to the server. Because the work of the system is distributed across multiple machines, each machine bears only a part of the burden and can therefore be a less powerful (and therefore less expensive) computer. In addition, when problems occur in one client system, it does not affect other clients using the system, although problems with the central server affect all clients. Also, with the advent of the personal computer and GUI operating systems such as Windows, more complex and intuitive interfaces could be created on these systems. Exhibit 10.2 illustrates the client/server architecture.

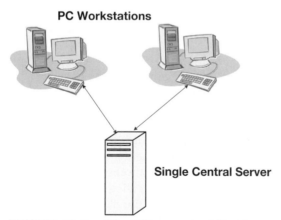

PC Workstations

Single Central Server

EXHIBIT 10.2   Client/Server Architecture

N-Tier Architecture

As client/server architectures matured and grew more complex, it became necessary to further delineate the functions of a system and spread the burden over even more machines. Complexity is one of the biggest problems with modern computer systems. It is *the* major factor not only in missed deadlines during development but also in maintaining websites once they are functional. Therefore, managing this complexity is paramount when creating a system. One of the cleanest ways to do this is to compartmentalize different functions of a system into modules that interact with one another and clearly define how these interactions occur. Once these functions have been compartmentalized, they can be designed and developed in relative isolation from one another. Thus, a very complex system is disaggregated into smaller, more manageable chunks.

This type of architecture (one in which there are more than two discrete modules) is referred to as an **n-tier architecture** (see Exhibit 10.3). The main advantage of this architecture is the reduction in complexity, but it also has the same advantages as the client/server model: decreased costs and increased reliability. In addition, this model can allow for increases in scalability; individual bottlenecks within the system can be isolated and addressed independently, whether through hardware or software upgrades.

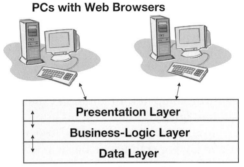

EXHIBIT 10.3 N-Tier Architecture

Distributed Architecture

All of the previous architecture models make some basic assumptions about ownership and the locations of the various parts of the architecture—namely, the components are most often all owned and operated by a single division within the company and are located in close proximity to one another. With the advent of faster networks and more open and recognized internetworking standards such as Web services, it has become possible and even practical to locate and operate modules across dispersed networks, as well as to lease modules from third-party organizations. A **distributed architecture** is a system of servers, loosely coupled across these dispersed networks, that work together to deliver a website. Distributing the modules in this way not only saves money, but also allows the most appropriate group or company to manage the module and the data within it. However, decentralized control of the modules has obvious drawbacks—including loss of control over maintenance, which leaves users at the mercy of the backup and security procedures of the supplier. In addition, as more and more modules become dispersed, management and monitoring of the various parties involved can become quite complex. Exhibit 10.4 illustrates a distributed architecture.

Choosing an Architecture

Choosing the appropriate architecture is one of the most fundamental and critical steps in the development process. A number of factors can influence this decision, many of which originate with the required functionality of the system but can extend as far as the skill sets of a company's technical staff.

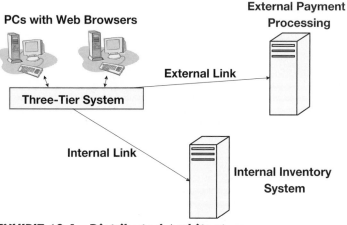

EXHIBIT 10.4   Distributed Architecture

Functionality

Functionality refers to the functions that a system must implement. This is usually the most fluid of all the factors involved in design. When tradeoffs are made, functionality is most often decreased in order to accommodate other factors.

Flexibility and Adaptability

Flexibility and **adaptability** refer to the ability of a system to adapt to changes in its function. Sometimes the functional requirements for a system are clear from the beginning of its development, while in other instances it might be clear that the requirements will change quite often over the life of a system. Planning to accommodate these changes is necessary to the success of the system.

To understand the importance of this issue, let's draw an analogy about how building a website is like building a house. While it is easier and cheaper to design a house with just the necessary elements—only as many electric plugs as needed, the minimal number of rooms, a hot water heater just big enough for the occupants—the needs of the occupants must stay the same for a long time for the money to be well saved. If the needs of the occupants change in a year or two, then it will be much more costly to upgrade the house. It is the same for website design. If there is a chance the site may undergo changes in the future, it is easier to adjust for those possible changes in the beginning than redesign the site a year later.

Scalability

Scalability refers to the ability of a system to be extended to handle a greater load, usually as a result of an increase in the user base. It is often hard to predict the popularity of a system, especially a website. If the goal of the system is to increase the use of the system, it needs to be designed from the beginning to be extended as the load increases.

In general, two types of scalability need to be addressed. New sites will typically start with a small amount of traffic but will need to be able to accommodate the full expected load. Also, there are times when some websites

Drill-Down

Clustering

As n-tier systems have evolved over the years, the focus has been on making each physical machine perform better and, therefore, achieve greater overall increases in speed and load capacity. This is done by increasing the speed of the processors in the machine, the speed of memory and disk access, and the speed with which the machine accesses the network. In addition, a lot of work has been done to make these machines more resilient and reliable. You can buy machines these days that have redundant components for every part of the system, including two electrical plugs so that you can plug the machine into two different power sources from two different companies. The result of all this work is that machines today are extremely reliable, extremely fast—and extremely expensive. In step with this increase in hardware complexity and cost has been an equal increase in the complexity and cost of the software that runs on these machines. Many of today's enterprise server products cost well into six figures.

In response to the growing complexity and cost of these systems, many companies have sought ways to build websites that are just as fast and reliable, only less expensive. One way is by clustering. **Clustering** involves building a system that relies not on a few large, complicated, and expensive machines, but rather on a system of smaller, less expensive machines. In this system, the machines are configured to share the load for the website, often with each machine handling a few requests at a time. However, for this system to work, websites need to be built from the ground up with clustering in mind. From the very beginning of the architecture, modules need to be created or altered to allow for the extra communications and data sharing necessary to distribute the processing. Though doing so can involve extra work up front in the design process, the payoff in the end is often well worth the effort. Clustered systems typically have the following advantages over more conventional systems:

Cost

As stated earlier, the machines that make up a clustering system are considerably less expensive—it is not uncommon to be able to buy 30 to 40 smaller machines for the price of a larger server. The savings in software can be just as impressive. As the open source movement and other similar enterprises have matured over the years, the stability and capability of many free software packages have increased dramatically. These packages are not foolproof and often do not come with any attached support; however, a good architecture can overcome these flaws through redundancy.

Scalability

One of the most intriguing advantages of a clustered architecture is the ability to quickly scale the capability of the architecture by adding new machines to the cluster. This is usually relatively easy because of the cost of the machines involved. Rather than asking for a huge sum of money to update a server, you end up asking for a relatively small amount of money to buy a number of new machines to add into the cluster. If the cluster and the architecture have been designed correctly, it can often be as simple as buying the machine, installing the software from CD, and plugging the machine into the network. The cluster then recognizes the arrival of the new machine or machines and balances the load accordingly. If you are running a site that has seasonal or unexpected increases in traffic, you can even rent machines for a short period, add them to the cluster, and then remove them once the demand wanes.

Maintenance

In a cluster, there are typically more machines to administer to than there are in more monolithic systems. However, these machines can be easier to maintain because of the reduced necessity for ensuring that any one machine is constantly powered up. In more monolithic systems that do not have redundant servers, powering down a machine for maintenance or upgrades can have a severe effect on the performance of the website that it runs, even taking the site down for the time it takes to do the upgrade. With clusters of computers, individual computers can be removed from the cluster, updated, and then put back online with little or no performance degradation or effect on the users. Typically, all the machines in a cluster are very similar, so bulk updates can be achieved for little extra effort.

bear extreme amounts of traffic. For example, on September 11, 2001, CNN.com took all of the stories off its website except for those about the terrorist attacks in order to be able to handle the overwhelming number of users flocking to its site (see Exhibit 10.5). Some companies, such as Akamai, specialize in helping companies cope with large amounts of traffic to their websites.

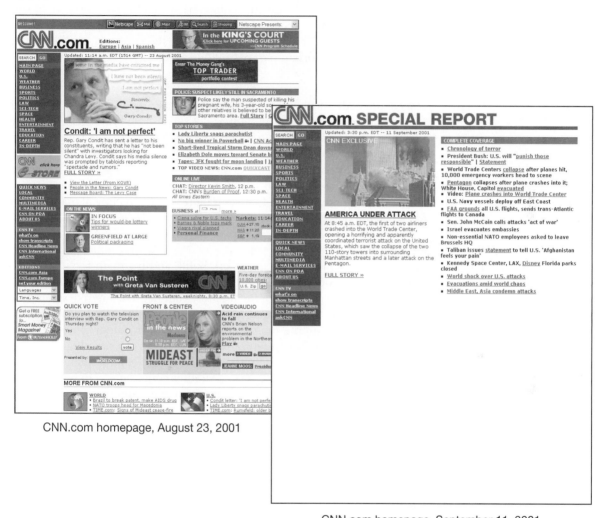

CNN.com homepage, August 23, 2001

CNN.com homepage, September 11, 2001

Courtesy of www.cnn.com.

EXHIBIT 10.5   Changes in CNN's Homepage

Performance

Performance is the perceived speed of a system, often measured by the user as response time. Making a system fast is most often a requirement, and it is relatively easy to do for a small user base. However, making a site *very* fast, especially for a larger user base, is a very complex task. It often involves adding tremendous complexities to the design and maintenance of the system.

Performance is not just an objective perception but an emotional one as well. While one second may not seem like a lot, there is a big difference in customers' minds between websites that take one second to load and sites that take two seconds. Companies must ask themselves whether it is important to have their sites run as quickly as possible; they must also consider how customers will judge a company if they perceive its website to be slow. Also, customers do not always expect sites to be fast. When sending credit card information to make a purchase, for instance, customers can get nervous if the process goes too quickly, thinking that the transaction may not have taken place. This is not to say that companies should make transactions slow on purpose, but simply that not every function needs to be as fast as possible, as often as possible. This is why understanding the customer, as discussed in Chapter 9, is an important part of building a website.

Maintenance

Once launched, a system must be monitored and updated. This is true both at the technical level (e.g., upgrading the servers) and at the content level (e.g., keeping the information in the database up-to-date). A balance needs to be struck between how much can be automated and how much requires human involvement. If there is a dedicated staff available to enter new information into the system, then automatic data feeds are not as necessary. In addition, as the complexity of a system increases, the technical maintenance of the site increases proportionally, necessitating a larger technical staff.

Required Skills

These are the skills needed to design, build, and maintain a system. Many systems are developed in-house by full-time employees of the company. It is important to keep the skills of the in-house staff in mind when designing the architecture. The easiest way to ensure the failure of a system is to ask a group of mainframe programmers to build an n-tier system when they have had no exposure to that type of architecture. This can be mitigated somewhat through training; however, the majority of the team implementing the site should have relevant experience. Another common way to build a site is to outsource the development but maintain the system internally once it launches. Again, it is important to keep in mind the skills of the people being asked to maintain the system when planning the project with the outsource partner. This ensures that the system is built on an architecture that can be supported and extended by the internal team.

Security

Security refers to the ability of a system to prevent illegal or inappropriate use of its data and to deter hackers. As discussed in Chapter 2, security is critical for e-commerce sites. This factor becomes more and more important with every passing day, especially on the Web. The media is constantly filled with stories of hacker intrusions, security flaws, and lost data. An entire industry has emerged to address these problems at both the system and corporate level. By planning for the appropriate amount of security in the architecture from the beginning of a project, many of the risks can be mitigated; on the other hand, overlooking security when designing an architecture almost ensures that serious issues with the final system will emerge.

Reliability

Reliability refers to the amount of time a system can be expected to be available to users. This is most often measured in terms of percentage of uptime. A goal of 99.999 percent uptime (often referred to as "five nines") means that over the

Drill-Down

Security

In today's world of e-commerce, security is one of the biggest concerns that a company with a website must face. The term security has grown to mean a lot of different things, but fundamentally it refers to protecting a site and its data against malicious or accidental damage and loss. Security must be factored into all phases of the building of a site—including the site's architecture.

Much has been published about cybercriminals, hackers, and viruses, but these are only part of the problem. As the importance of a company's site and data increases, so too do the measures taken to protect them. No site is ever 100 percent safe, but by addressing and limiting vulnerabilities as early as possible in the design process, these risks can be decreased dramatically. The three most common types of attacks that most websites face are denial-of-service attacks, vandalism, and information theft.

- *Denial-of-service attacks.* Denial-of-service attacks attempt to overwhelm a website's servers to the point that they can no longer handle legitimate requests or users. This is typically done by flooding the site with an overwhelming number of "virtual" users until the site crashes, or until it is so busy responding to spurious requests that it cannot answer legitimate ones in a timely fashion.

- *Vandalism.* An increasingly popular activity on the Web is to deface or vandalize a website by replacing its content with offensive or inappropriate material. These types of attacks are typically targeted at high-traffic or high-profile sites but can be disruptive and embarrassing to any site—especially if they are not caught quickly.

- *Information theft.* This is by far the most frightening form of website sabotage. In this type of attack, a cybercriminal gains access to part or all of a system and is able to download sensitive data from the site. Such data could be anything from customers' personal information (including credit card numbers) to internal corporate data. What makes this type of attack even scarier is that it can occur without anyone in the company even noticing—the data can just be downloaded and then distributed. Typically, companies only learn of these types of attacks after the damage has already been done.

Preventing these types of attacks involves good planning from the beginning of the architecture design process. For vandalism and information theft to occur, a cybercriminal must first gain privileged access to the system. This usually means obtaining a user name and password that allow them to access the information they are seeking. There are a number of ways to prevent this type of intrusion when designing a system. Limiting access to servers and the services those servers provide is first on the list. Most servers are set up to handle not just Web requests but internal connections and connections from other external systems. There are a number of ways in which these connections can be made, and some methods are more inherently secure than others. Typically, the more secure a method is, the more cumbersome it is to operate. In addition, these services should only be made available to the people who need them. One of the most common ways to do this is through a firewall. A firewall restricts access to certain services so that only people internal to the network (i.e., employees) can get to them; users outside the firewall have no way to gain access.

There are monitoring software solutions as well. A number of companies offer intrusion detection software and services that monitor systems for suspicious activity; they either report the activity or take actions to prevent the activity. You can also design the system to produce reports that can be analyzed for suspicious activity. For instance, if a login report shows that a user is logging on to the system an inordinate number of times in a day, you might check to see if that user has been distributing his or her password to unauthorized people. The login report might also show someone who has tried multiple times to log in without success—sometimes a sign that he or she is trying to guess passwords.

continued

Indeed, passwords are one of the primary things that websites need to protect. The main way to do this is through proper use of encryption and database access control. When passwords are stored in a database, they should be stored so that only the system has access to them, and they should be encrypted with a strong, one-way encryption scheme that will prevent anyone from de-encrypting the password. If a hacker or cybercriminal does get access to the list of passwords in the database and the passwords are encrypted, he or she must use a brute-force approach to determine the real passwords. This involves trying every word in the dictionary, as well as combinations of words, to see if the encrypted version matches. It is always a good idea to force users to choose passwords that include combinations of numbers, letters, and other symbols. This will help to thwart brute-force attacks.

One of the best ways to keep a system safe is to establish and enforce security procedures. This can be done by tracking published security flaws and ensuring that the system is not vulnerable to them. Often this involves installing a patch or security update, but it can also involve more basic changes to the system. Organizations such as CERT/CC (Computer Emergency Response Team/Coordination Center) track vulnerabilities and potential computer threats and publish notices explaining them. A working knowledge of common vulnerabilities on this list is important when designing a website. Other procedures are important as well, including auditing access to systems and reviewing usage logs. Some companies even go so far as to stage mock attacks on their site, either by having employees try to crack the system or by hiring outside firms to attempt break-ins.

Finally, it is important to have known, predetermined procedures for changing system administration passwords. Often, there are a number of different passwords that need to be changed, including administration passwords to all of the machines that support the functioning of a website. Knowing ahead of time which machines and systems need to be addressed allows you to respond more quickly to any threats that occur.

Potential Threats

When most people think of the need for security on a website, they picture protection from anonymous cybercriminals who are working in a basement somewhere, trying to access credit card numbers. In truth, some of the most frightening threats come from a company's own employees—especially those who have deep access to the system and can do the greatest amount of damage. This includes purposeful, malicious attacks by disgruntled current or former employees, as well as accidental (but no less disastrous) situations as well. The Internet is full of stories of employees accidentally deleting a website's entire user database.

It is also important to note that there is a distinction between cybercriminals and hackers. Cybercriminals are usually intent on malicious attacks, while hackers enjoy the thrill of breaking into a system. Oftentimes, when hackers discover a vulnerability in a site, they will notify the company of its existence rather than exploit it to some nefarious end.

course of an entire year, a system can be expected to be unavailable to users for only five minutes. Obviously, the higher the reliability number, the harder it is to achieve. Sound site architecture is critical to achieving such reliability goals; however, physical architecture is equally important and will be discussed later in this chapter.

Metrics

Metrics are the measurements and data needed by the company to understand the operation of a system. These often include such measures as frequency of use, uptime, user actions, and frequently used pages or sections. Metrics help measure the successfulness (or unsuccessfulness) of a system. It is important to decide which metrics will be tracked before the architecture is designed, because retrofitting a system to accommodate new metrics after development is complete is often quite expensive—or even impossible.

Cost

This is the amount of money spent to design, build, and maintain a system. Oftentimes this is the most limiting factor in a design.

Time

This refers to the number of people/hours, as well as the total time period, needed to develop a system. Time is another limiting factor in designing a system and is often closely associated with cost. Most projects do not begin until a budget and launch date are decided.

In an ideal world, all of these factors could be maximized; however, many of them come into direct conflict during the design process. For instance, increasing the security inherent in a design often causes a degradation in performance. In addition, cost often limits the extent to which many of these factors can be pursued. Striking a balance between all of these factors is both an art and a science, but it is also the key to a successful architecture. To do so correctly takes a lot of time, often up to a quarter of the total project time. It also requires patience; those involved in the project must resist the urge to produce tangible results too quickly.

Today's Websites

Most of today's websites are built on some variant of the n-tier logical architecture model. Most follow the three-tier model, consisting of a data tier, a business-logic tier, and a presentation tier. In this model, the data tier is responsible for storing and retrieving data, the business-logic tier is responsible for implementing business rules, and the presentation tier is responsible for communicating with the user. Exhibit 10.6 illustrates the three-tier model.

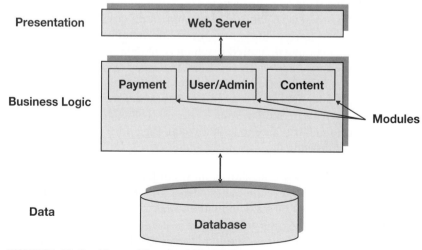

EXHIBIT 10.6   Three-Tier Architecture

Dividing up responsibilities for different functions of the site in this way allows the appropriate technologies and products to be used for each segment. Although many vendors offer integrated products that address all three of these layers, typically a single product is used for one or two layers and needs to be combined with a product from a different vendor to produce the optimal solution.

It is also important to consider the manner of communication between layers. Most of these communications occur within standard, well-understood parameters called protocols. These open protocols allow different pieces of software from different vendors to communicate with one another. However, there are systems built on proprietary protocols that are not shared throughout the industry. Typically, you would only use a proprietary protocol if it were significantly faster than the available standard protocols, or if it were the only one available to communicate with the system.

The Data Layer

The job of the **data layer** is relatively straightforward. Its main function is to provide fast, reliable access to the data needed to run a system. Although that sounds quite simple, it can get very complex—especially in today's systems, where terabyte-size (1,000-gigabyte) databases are not unheard of. In addition, the data layer is responsible for maintaining information about the relationships between data. For instance, it not only needs to store the name and address of a customer of the company, but also must link that customer to his or her purchase history, which might be stored in a completely different part of the database. Throw in a customer relationship management (CRM) system that needs to tie all of that information to the marketing and sales databases, and you start to get an idea of the demands of today's databases.

Types of Databases

Choosing the appropriate product to use to implement your data layer is a very important step in the design process. There are many types of databases to choose from and many different vendor implementations of each. The following are the most common types of databases used today.

Flat-File   **Flat-file databases** are single computer files that store all of the information for a system. A single system can run off either a single file or a series of files, each storing different types of information. Flat-file databases are usually either comma delimited (each piece of data is separated from the next by a comma) or fixed width (each field takes up a specified number of characters in the file). They are most often used with legacy mainframe databases but still find some use today in modern systems. The problem with these files is that they are hard to scan; if you are looking for a specific record for a single customer, you have to look through the entire file to find it, reading each record individually.

Relational   In response to the shortcomings of flat-files, a new type of database was created called a relational database. In a **relational database**, data are stored in a series of tables. Each table stores a discrete piece of data for the system; for example, user information is stored in one table, while purchase information is stored in another. Tables can be linked, which erases the need to store redundant data in different places.

The majority of systems built today rely on relational databases. Because of their popularity, a number of standards have emerged to make database software from different vendors relatively interchangeable. For instance, a common language is used to interact with the database called SQL (structured query language). This language defines common ways to create data, update data, and query data, and is recognized by the vast majority of relational databases. SQL provides the language to use when talking to a database, but it does not define the method of communication. Indeed, nonstandard, vendor-specific communication methods can often be faster and more reliable. However, using a vendor-specific communication method does tie a system more closely to a specific vendor, thus making it more difficult to switch to a different database in the future.

Object-Oriented   Both flat-file and relational databases are very good at storing text and numbers. However, today's multimedia systems make it necessary to store other types of data as well, such as image and video data. Most relational databases have rudimentary means to store this type of data, but a new type of database, called an object-oriented database, handles these different types of data much better. Since the way a user interacts with the data is no longer limited to alphanumeric data, an **object-oriented database** encapsulates all data into different types of objects. These types of databases are much less common, mostly due to their large price tags, their complexity, and a lack of interoperability standards.

Choosing a Database

Different vendors offer different database solutions. To choose the right database, you must weigh several factors.

Load/Storage Capacity   This refers to the amount of data (usually measured in gigabytes or terabytes) that need to be stored in the database. Some databases are optimized to handle large amounts of data, while others have limitations that would prevent their use in a very large system. When choosing, it is important to have an understanding of the amount of data that will be stored at the launch of a system as well as throughout that system's life. Updating at a later date can be a complex process.

Type of Data   Different databases (and database types) are best at storing different types of data. For simple alphanumeric data, a relational database is usually the best bet. However, for systems that need to store more complex types of data, such as audio or video, object-oriented databases should also be considered.

Speed   Speed is one of the most important factors to consider when evaluating a database, but it is often the hardest to ascertain. Vendors typically offer a list of reasons their database is the fastest available—and it probably is the fastest, within a narrow scope of measurement—but it is nearly impossible to claim that a particular database is truly the fastest, due to the complexities of the actions that databases perform. One database might be very fast at complex queries, while another might be faster at updating information. To choose the right database for your system, you need to understand the manner in which the database will be used. You can typically then get evaluation copies of the different products and perform the tests yourself to determine which one best suits your needs.

Cost   This is another major area of consideration for most companies. Databases can easily become the most costly single purchase item in building a system; however, they can also be had for free. There are a number of free, open source, relational database products available on the Internet. The price of a database is usually driven by how reliable and fast a database is (or is perceived to be). The fastest and most reliable systems command the highest prices.

Reliability   Computer systems have become an integral part of companies today. As a result, it is vital that these system be reliable, from both an availability perspective (is the system there when I need it?) and a backup perspective (is our data safe?). As the repository for information in a computer system, the database must address both of these areas. If the database goes down, the entire system goes down; therefore, it is imperative for a good database to be extremely robust. In addition, the data stored in the system must be safe from both malfunction and intruders. This requires a database to have easy methods for the storage and recovery of data, and strong security systems to protect the data.

The Business-Logic Layer

The main consumer of the services that the data layer provides is the business-logic layer. The **business-logic layer** is responsible for implementing the basic rules of the system according the operating rules of the business. Its main function is to take requests from the presentation layer, determine what actions the request requires, implement those actions (usually by manipulating the data in the data layer), and return response data to the presentation layer.

Typically, this layer is divided into a number of submodules, each handling different aspects of the system. You may have a scheduling module that handles all calendar requests. You could also have a CRM module that either implements CRM functionality within the system or interfaces with an external CRM system. Again, this division of labor allows the team building the system to divide and conquer. It also allows you to test individual components before testing the system as a whole, which makes it much easier to isolate problems.

The market for servers that offer ways to implement business logic for a system is maturing rapidly. Such servers range from targeted, prebuilt systems that already implement a number of preset rules specific to a task or industry to systems that just give you the tools to implement your own rules. The generic term most often used to refer to this class of servers is *application server*, but the class is also referred to as middleware or business servers. Choosing an application server is one of the hardest parts of system design because of the vast number of solutions on the market—ranging from out-of-the-box implementations that just need customization before they start running to basic shells that have to be built up by a dedicated team of programmers. To make the choice even more difficult, there are competing technologies used to implement these servers. The two primary technologies are the Java platform pioneered by Sun and the Microsoft platform. However, there are also a number of smaller niche players in the market who use their own proprietary standards and methodologies.

Choosing a platform involves weighing the factors discussed earlier (functionality, scalability, performance, etc.). However, some of these factors tend to be more important than others. The skills required to install, extend, and maintain the server are very important because incorrect installation, implementation, or maintenance can seriously affect the viability of the system over time. Also very important is cost: The prices for different servers vary greatly, with some costing well into six figures. In the end, you want to make sure you choose one that fulfills your business requirements but allows for flexibility in the future. The one thing constant about computer systems is their need to change and adapt to new business rules.

The Presentation Layer

The **presentation layer** is responsible for all communications with the user's computer. For a website, this typically means getting information from and sending information to the user's Web browser. The presentation layer is typically implemented by the Web server. Each time a user clicks on a new page of the website, the Web server must run through a process of determining what to do with the request. If no business rules need to be invoked and no information is needed from the database, the Web server may just return a static page to the user. If a more complex request is made, the presentation layer communicates with the business-logic layer to fulfill the request.

One very important job of the presentation layer is to reply to the user in a format that the user can understand. This is where elements of visual design come into play. When communicating with Web browsers, this mostly involves retrieving data from the business-logic layer, then wrapping HTML code around the data so that it displays correctly in the user's browser.

There are many ways to present a website to a user, and choosing a method involves weighing a number of factors. First and foremost, it is important to understand the technological abilities and requirements of the users that the website is trying to attract. What technologies are they most comfortable with? What software are they likely to have installed on their computer? The following is a list of some of the most common ways to present data to site users, and the benefits and drawbacks of each.

- *HTML.* As already discussed, HTML is the most common way to communicate with a user's browser. At its heart, HTML is quite simple: Each page includes text as well as formatting information that tells the browser how to display that text. There are several advantages to HTML. First, it is universally understood by all browsers—there is no need to worry about whether it will work in Netscape or Internet Explorer. Second, HTML is easy to create; just about anyone can create a page after receiving a small amount of instruction. HTML's simplicity, however, is also a drawback. By itself, HTML can only construct relatively rudimentary interfaces, which stand in strong contrast to the more sophisticated Windows and Apple GUI interfaces that we are used to seeing today.

- *Third-party plug-ins.* Because of the relatively limited capabilities of HTML, some standard third-party browser plug-ins have become readily available. A plug-in is a program that gives the website more control over how its pages look and function. Because HTML cannot play video, sites often require Real Player or Windows Media plug-ins. Probably the most universally used plug-in is Macromedia's Flash. This plug-in allows you to make more media-rich, animated, and interactive interfaces show up in a user's browser. However, this enhanced functionality comes at a price—flash files tend to be larger than HTML files and can extend download times for users, especially users on dial-up connections. Also, when using plug-ins, you are relying on the user to have the plug-in installed. (Most browsers come with Flash preinstalled, but there are other plug-ins that the user would have to self-install.) Other common plug-ins include QuickTime, which allows users to play video clips, and Adobe Acrobat Reader, which is used to view PDF-formatted documents. E! Online (see Exhibit 10.7) incorporates Flash, Real Player, and Windows Media into its site in order to show scrolling headlines and television and film clips.

Macromedia Flash Plug-In

Microsoft Media Player Plug-In

Courtesy of www.eonline.com.

EXHIBIT 10.7   E! Online Plug-Ins

- *Homegrown plug-ins.* You do not have to rely on a third party to create a plug-in. Companies can write their own. Typically, these plug-ins are written in one of two ways: as either an ActiveX component or a Java applet. ActiveX components are basically Windows programs that run within the confines of the user's Web browser. They have all the functionality of a regular Windows program, including all the common interfaces that are expected on a PC. However, they can only be viewed on a PC (not an Apple) running Windows (not Linux) and running Internet Explorer (not Netscape). In contrast, Java applets work across all platforms, operating systems, and browsers. However, they tend to be less functionally rich and can operate more slowly than a comparable ActiveX component. In some cases, companies create both an

ActiveX component and a Java applet, then use the appropriate one based on the user visiting the site. However, this has some obvious drawbacks, including doubling the effort required to create the site.

How the Three Layers Work

To understand how each layer works, it is helpful to walk through an example. Consider Acme Computer, introduced in the previous chapter. A typical interaction with a user of Acme's website might go something like this:

1. A user types *http://www.acmecomputer.com* into his browser and gets the homepage for the site.

2. The user clicks on a link to see Acme's latest line of Pentium-based servers and gets a list of computers with prices.

3. The user chooses a computer from the list and reconfigures the computer to meet his needs.

4. The user purchases the computer.

Step One

When the user types *http://www.acmecomputer.com* into his browser, a few things happen. First, his computer sends a request to the presentation layer for the homepage of the site. In this case, it is a static page that gets updated each morning with that day's specials. The presentation layer grabs the static file and returns it to the user's browser as HTML. The browser then interprets the HTML and displays it on the user's screen.

Step Two

When the user clicks on the link to see the list of servers, the user's browser sends another request to the presentation layer—this time for a dynamic, database-driven page. The presentation layer receives the request, determines that the page being requested is a dynamic one, determines the type of data needed to fulfill the request, and forwards a request for those data to the business-logic layer. In this case, the request is for a list of Pentium-based servers and their prices. The business-logic layer sends a request to the database for the list of servers, and then stores the result temporarily in memory.

In a simple system, the business-logic layer might just send that list back to the presentation layer. However, Acme has some pretty complex rules about discounting servers based on factors such as the day of the week and inventories. It is the job of the business-logic layer to implement these rules and adjust the prices of the servers on the list accordingly. Once this has been done, the business-logic layer sends the list to the presentation layer. Once the presentation layer receives the information, it produces the necessary HTML to display the list correctly and returns it to the user's browser.

Step Three

Now things get interesting. The user wants to configure the server to meet his needs. Again, the request will be sent to the presentation layer, which in turn sends a request to the business-logic layer to determine what options are available. The business-logic layer then sends a request to the database to determine the available options and to receive those data. Following that, depending on the complexity of the configuration, the business-logic layer has to determine if there are any combinations of options that are incompatible (e.g., you need to get more memory if you want to include a DVD player) and then determine the price of the specific configuration. These data are then returned to the presentation layer for formatting and transmission to the user.

Step Four

This step is very similar to the previous two steps, except for an important addition: security and access control. On most Web systems today, any personal or financial information entered by a user is transmitted over what is called an SSL (Secure Sockets Layer) protocol. This simply means that the information that is sent from the user to the presentation layer is encrypted, and that the information sent from the presentation layer to the user is encrypted as well. This encryption prevents anyone who shares network lines with a system from eavesdropping on the transaction. Access control serves as a gate that either prevents or allows certain users from gaining access to site information or functionality. This access control is typically handled by the business-logic layer (although, as in other cases, the data needed to determine the level of access are stored in the data layer).

Also, in this step information is actually *written* to the data layer, not just read by it. Information such as name, address, and credit card number will be sent to the data layer for storage and eventual use by the fulfillment system.

External Systems

In these days of integrated systems and seamless delivery of services, it is not just enough for a site to operate smoothly by itself: It must integrate and communicate with other systems in the organization to keep the organization as a whole running smoothly. Specifically, the business-logic layer and the data layer have to communicate with other systems in the organization. This sometimes occurs on a real-time, as-needed basis. For example, when a user wants to connect to a website to get tracking information for a package, the site's business-logic layer would make an external connection to the fulfillment system to get the status of the package and perhaps return tracking information. In other instances, this interaction occurs as a batch update, in which timed updates of information across the systems occur. A nightly download of the inventory in a retail company's various warehouses would be one example of a batch update.

Determining which type of interaction the system will implement is driven by two things: necessity and ability. It is typically easier and quicker to perform batch updates on an infrequent basis. However, it could be that day-old or even hour-old information will not meet the needs of a site's users. It is often impossible, or impractical, to do real-time integration, in which case batch updates are the only option.

It may also be necessary to integrate with systems outside of the organization, perhaps in another division of the company or in another company altogether. Often, a company will need to implement special measures in order to connect with external system, because normal connections over the Internet with other companies are relatively slow. In such circumstances, a company must rely on other companies' infrastructures to make the connection—both the infrastructure of the network provider and the internal network at the external site.

In addition, there can often be a blurry line between where one system stops and another system begins. This delineation can sometimes be relatively arbitrary and can often be based on political aspects of the system's operation rather than on any technical demarcations. The following is a partial list of the kinds of systems that are most often connected and the kinds of services they provide.

CRM

Typically, this integration involves keeping the CRM database up-to-date about how customers are using the site, as well as keeping information on the site current. By integrating the two, the salesforce can be better informed about a customer's site usage and make appropriate adjustments to what and how they sell to that customer. It also helps keep contact information current and makes sure that updates to one system propagate to the other.

Payment Processing

In many instances, companies have separate invoice and payment processing systems that need to be informed about activity on the website. For a content-heavy, subscription-based site, the integration would involve keeping the site up-to-date on the current status of an account. If the account is past due, then perhaps access to the site needs to be revoked. In the case of an e-commerce site, the site needs to let the invoice system know about a purchase so that the customer can be billed accordingly.

Shipping

If an e-commerce company's products need to be shipped to customers after purchase, integration with the shipping system needs to occur. Sometimes, real-time information about shipping costs needs to be accessed at the time of payment, so that customers can see the total cost of their purchase. In addition, most sites these days send tracking numbers to their customers so that they can follow the progress of their shipments. These sites must integrate with the shipper's software in order to get that information.

Fulfillment

Once an item has been ordered from a site, information must be passed to the company's fulfillment system. In many instances, this is done through e-mail. At the time of purchase, an e-mail is sent to the person responsible for fulfillment to let them know what item to send and where to send it. For larger volume sites, there is often a completely separate system to handle this process, especially if fulfillment can happen from a number of different geographic locations. This could also be an interface with a third-party fulfillment house to whom fulfillment is outsourced.

Inventory

Fulfillment and inventory are usually one system, but they can be separated. It is important to integrate the site with the inventory system to ensure the site does not oversell products that the company does not have in stock. In the early days of e-commerce, especially during holiday seasons, this was one of the largest shortcomings of most sites.

Financial

It may be necessary to integrate a site into a company's internal financial systems in order to facilitate tasks such as financial reporting. This is most often done on a batch basis, but it becomes extremely important as a company tries to understand how well it is doing against its financial goals or to help close the books on a quarter or year.

Human Resources

In some cases, integration with an internal human resources (HR) system becomes necessary. For extremely large companies, the corporate website usually contains a list of job postings that are available at the company. Rather than keep two copies of the postings, a batch process can be created to keep the site up-to-date with the latest job requisitions in the HR system. Integration can also be used in internal intranets to give people access to information about health plans or vacation status.

B2B Exchanges

Some companies need to tie internal systems and intranets into B2B exchanges to give people access to the services and products provided by those exchanges. An example would be a company intranet that allows divisions to order office supplies, but does it by presenting the orders to an exchange for competitive bid submission.

Outside Suppliers

Similarly, an intranet may need to connect employees to outside providers, such as a travel company that helps employees arrange business travel. This could be done through an interface from the company's intranet to the systems of the travel agency.

Physical Architecture

The physical architecture of a site refers to the actual hardware and software used to run the site. Developing a physical architecture is usually done in parallel with the logical architecture and is driven by the needs of the logical architecture. However, there needs to be a balance between cost, complexity, and functionality. In general, the more complex and functional a site is, the more it will cost and the longer it will take to develop. Physical architecture breaks down into the areas of software and hardware.

Software

As discussed earlier, choosing the software to run the site is a very important step and involves weighing a number of different factors.

continued

Drill-Down

Build Vs. Buy

Before building a website, a company must decide who should build the site and who should maintain it. There are typically three different scenarios:

1. The company builds and maintains the site.
2. The company hires a third party to build the site, but maintains it internally after launch.
3. The company hires a third party to both build the site and maintain the site after launch.

Deciding which route to take requires weighing a number of different options.

Cost

This is typically the No. 1 factor when making the build-versus-buy decision. Most outside firms charge a lot of money to build websites; prices can easily reach the seven-figure range for even a modest site. Typically, using internal resources has a much more palatable price tag since the employment costs of existing workers can be discounted.

Required Skills

It is hard to ask employees to build a website if they have no experience doing so. In this situation, you have two choices: Either hire new people who do have the experience, or hire an outside firm. However, with the former, it sometimes takes a long time to find the people, hire them, and get them oriented. Many times, companies will hire an outside firm, but require it to train existing employees so that maintenance and upgrades of the site can be handled internally.

Time

Typically, an experienced third party can build a website more quickly than a less experienced internal team. However, you also need to factor in the amount of time it will take to get a third party up-to-speed on your business and your requirements. If the internal technical team already knows these, then it has a huge jump on the external team.

Resource Management

It could be that you have all the right skills in-house and it would be very easy to tackle the project internally, but all of your internal resources are busy maintaining current systems. Sometimes these resources can be freed to work on a new site, but often they need to keep performing their business-critical functions. In these situations, a company will most often hire an outside firm to build the site and, depending on resource availability, switch internal resources to support of the new site after launch.

continued

Hardware

Hardware includes the physical computers and networking equipment on which the website runs. When choosing hardware, a number of factors must be considered.

Platform

In the past, large websites have always run on large UNIX-based systems from companies such as Sun, Hewlett-Packard, and IBM. However, with the increased stability and reliability of Microsoft Windows servers and the advent

Quality

One of the drawbacks to third-party firms is that they do not have as much invested in the success of the site as the company itself. As a result, in many situations an internal team will work much harder and better than an outside, uninterested firm. This problem can be mitigated through incentive-laden contracts with the third party, but it is very hard to instill an external team with the same motivation.

Fun

If you do have technologists available within the company, it is almost guaranteed that they will want to work on a new site rather than maintain an old one. If a third party is hired to do the development, this can alienate internal staff, send a message of mistrust, and lead to problems in morale. Managing the communication of a "buy" decision to an internal team can be very tricky.

Intellectual Property Protection

Often, companies try to keep the development of sites as secret as possible, especially if the company is trying to protect or increase its competitive advantage in its industry. By including a third party in the development effort, a company increases the risk that its competitors will not only find out that the development is occurring but also learn details of any innovations being introduced.

of the Linux operating system, more and more sites are turning to Intel-based servers. These servers are typically less expensive to both buy and maintain. In addition, the operating software for the machines tends to be less expensive—or even free. Choosing between the different platforms can be a challenge and is most often decided by outside factors such as a company's familiarity with the platform or the type of software chosen for the logical architecture.

Power

Different types of machines can be used for different roles within the system. Typically, the largest, most powerful computers are used as database servers, especially in situations in which multiple applications connect to one database server. In addition, large storage capacities and fast disk access are necessary in database machines because of the intense writing and reading of data. For application servers, there is often not as high a requirement on storage capacity or disk access speed; the code that runs on the application server is most often loaded into memory at the time the machine starts, and very little reading or writing to the disk occurs. What is at a premium, however, is CPU speed and memory capacity. Because the application server loads the program into memory upon startup, the more memory that is available, the bigger the program that can be loaded, resulting in a faster system. CPU speed also plays a major role. The logic involved in implementing the business rules can at times be convoluted and can require a fair amount of processing power to determine. Multiply that by the number of users on the system at any one time, and you can begin to understand the requirements of these machines.

Finally, machines used in the presentation layer (typically, Web servers) can have a range of requirements depending on how they are used. For a site that has very few static pages and relies mostly on business logic to generate pages, the Web server's job is fairly easy—just pass the request through. However, if large amounts of static data (e.g., lots of documents) need to be stored on the server, then the machine needs the disk space to accommodate them all. CPU speed is a little less important, since typically there is not a lot of processing of the data that occurs, just formatting of data produced by the application server.

Hosting

As discussed in Chapter 9, where a site will be hosted—in other words, where the servers that run the site will be located—is an important issue. A **Web host** serves as a website's secure, high-bandwidth, professionally maintained connection to the Internet. Professional Web hosting works in a variety of ways, depending on the company's need. Most Web hosts have a high-bandwidth, dedicated connection to the Internet that they lease out to customers. All of a customer's website content resides at the Web host's location, and customers manage their content from a remote location. Any changes made to the website are uploaded to the host's servers by the customer. In essence, the Web host does two things: (1) It provides the website owner with a high-bandwidth connection to the Internet, and (2) it stores all of the website's content on its servers, which process all of the information traveling to and from the website.

Hosting Alternatives   There are a variety of Web hosting alternatives available, including free, shared server, dedicated server, co-located server, and in-house hosting.

- *Free hosting.* For very simple websites, such as personal homepages, free hosting is often a good choice. A variety of hosts offer free service, including Yahoo GeoCities (*geocities.yahoo.com*), Homestead (*www.homestead.com*), and Tripod (*tripod.lycos.com*). While these hosts can provide space on the Web, they are limited in the amount of data they allow you to store with them, the amount of bandwidth that you receive, and the kind of content you are allowed to host.

- *Shared server hosting.* For companies that want to do business on the Web, shared server hosting—where many websites are placed on the same Web server—is often a better alternative than free hosting. Shared server hosting is the cheapest alternative for small businesses looking for options such as increased bandwidth, more storage space, increased security, electronic payment software, and database software. While a sufficient alternative for small businesses that do not need a large amount of bandwidth or processing power, this is not a reasonable choice for larger websites.

- *Dedicated server hosting.* For larger websites, dedicated server hosting—in which a website is allocated its own dedicated server—is often a suitable alternative. Dedicated servers are the next step up from shared servers and provide additional bandwidth and processing power. In addition, the servers are often monitored constantly and most simple problems with the server can be dealt with by the hosting facility.

- *Co-located server hosting.* Of any outsourcing option, this one offers companies the most control over the hardware running their website. With co-location, the customer actually owns the server—he or she is paying only for bandwidth and a physical space for the server. The customer makes all hardware decisions and has complete control over the configuration of the server. However, resource-constrained organizations might not want to choose this option because they would be responsible for most hardware and software maintenance.

- *In-house hosting.* The previous alternatives are all examples of outsourced hosting solutions. For companies with adequate resources, another alternative is in-house hosting. Typically, only large firms (e.g., Global 1000 companies) are successfully able to host their own websites, given the demanding resource needs. These needs include 24-hour dedicated personnel, power backup, security, maintenance, and redundancy (redundant systems such as multiple servers, server locations, Internet connections, and power supplies). For example, the hosting provider NaviSite offers services and resources that include a full-time security team, biometric locks (locks that recognize a person based on unique physiological identifiers such as retina patterns, fingerprints, or the density of the bones in one's hand), redundant network architecture, multiple connections to the Internet backbone in physically different locations, seismic bracing, and backup power supplies including 50,000-gallon diesel fuel tanks.

Hosting for Large Websites   Most large websites are hosted by a third party. Third-party facilities offer a wide range of services, from allowing companies to co-locate computers at the site to the full management and maintenance of servers. The main service offered by all of these companies is reliability: They decrease the amount of time that a website is unavailable by removing some risks and managing the rest. Typical offerings from these companies include the following:

- *Redundant Internet connections.* Many facilities offer redundant connections to the Internet to decrease the likelihood of Internet failure. **Redundancy** itself refers to having two or more of an essential component configured so that if one fails, the other can take over. Redundant Internet connections require a few main fiber connections to the Internet owned by different providers so that an outage by one provider does not bring down the connection. Also, many companies have redundant connections through different physical means. They might have a few "wired" connections such as T1 lines, but will also have a satellite connection or other type of wireless connection to use in case the physical connections fail.

- *Backup power.* Most facilities protect against power failures through either generating capacity or battery backup. Battery backup is usually used for short outages or to bridge gaps while the generating capacity comes online. In addition, redundant power connections to the facility, as well as to each machine, are often provided.

- *Physical security.* Most facilities provide physical protection for the machines that they host. This includes theft prevention as well as restricted access to the machines.

- *Server management services.* Servers typically require a fair amount of maintenance to keep them running optimally. Many facilities perform mundane maintenance on the servers they host, including disk backup and recovery, operating system updates and patches, and security and intrusion monitoring. In addition, some facilities offer crisis response services, which attempt to fix server crashes or software crashes when they occur.

- *Offsite backup storage.* To mitigate the damage caused by environmental disasters such as fire, earthquakes, and floods, third-party hosting facilities typically store the backup tapes of websites at a secure offsite location.

Performance Optimization

There are a number of relatively simple, inexpensive ways to optimize site performance. Performance can be addressed at the single-machine level by optimizing machines to their tasks, as discussed earlier. If a company is using multiple machines, or "clusters" of machines, to perform the same function, each machine can be made to handle different requests, thus boosting the speed with which those requests are answered. However, the company must be using software that supports clustering, and clustering must be factored into the logical architecture design. One of the easiest machines to cluster is often the Web server. Many websites use a "load balancer," which is simply a separate machine in between the user and the Web servers that forwards each request for a webpage to the least busy Web server.

Redundancy These clusters can also help to increase reliability, because they are often engineered to transfer connections between machines in the event that one of the machines fails. One of the biggest pitfalls to avoid in physical architecture design is a "single point of failure." A single point of failure is any single piece of hardware or software in the system whose failure would cause the entire system to fail. An ideal system has enough redundancies and backup systems to prevent any single points of failure.

Summary

1. What is logical architecture?

The logical architecture of a site is its software components and desired functionality of those components. Logical architecture takes all the functions that a site must perform and breaks them into smaller modules—such as a shopping cart or a searchbox. The logical architecture defines both the modules and how the modules interact.

2. What are the factors involved in choosing a logical architecture?

There are many factors involved in choosing a logical architecture. Among them are functionality, flexibility and adaptability, scalability, performance, maintenance, skills required, security, reliability, metrics, cost, and time.

3. What is the presentation layer?

The presentation layer is responsible for communicating with the user. This layer can either answer a simple request or communicate with the business-logic layer for more complicated requests. The presentation layer is also responsible for formatting all replies to the user in a format that the user can use and understand by following the visual design of the site.

4. What is the business-logic layer?

The business-logic layer is responsible for implementing business rules. This layer takes requests from the presentation layer, determines what actions the request requires, implements those actions (usually by manipulating the data in the data layer), and returns response data to the presentation layer.

5. What is the data layer?

The main function of the data layer is to provide fast, reliable access to the data needed to run a system. The types of databases used include flat-file, relational, and object-oriented. The factors involved in choosing a database include load-storage capacity, type of data, speed, cost, and reliability.

6. What are the factors involved in choosing a physical architecture?

The factors involved in choosing a physical architecture include platform, power, hosting, and performance optimization.

Exercises

1. Take your business idea from Chapter 9. Evaluate what kind of requirements you would need for the website based on the 11 factors involved in choosing an architecture—functionality, flexibility and adaptability, scalability, performance, maintenance, required skills, security, reliability, metrics, cost, and time. Is this a site that collects a lot of personal data and therefore needs to be very secure? Is it a site that will need to change a lot in the next few years? Will there be a large increase in users?

2. Go to Kazaa (*www.kazaa.com*). Now, think about the factors for choosing an architecture. Of functionality, scalability, performance, reliability, and security, which factor do you think is the most important for this site? The second most important? Do the same for Salon.com (*www.salon.com*) and E*Trade (*www.etrade.com*).

3. Go to the IFilm website (*www.IFILM.com*) and to ESPN's website (*www.espn.com*). What third-party plug-ins do you see?

Key Terms

logical architecture	functionality	flat-file database
physical architecture	flexibility	relational database
mainframe architecture	adaptability	object-oriented database
client/server architecture	scalability	business-logic layer
n-tier architecture	security	presentation layer
distributed architecture	reliability	Web host
clustering	data layer	redundancy

Human and Financial Capital

CASELET: MILITARY.COM BUILDS ITS MANAGEMENT TEAM

Like countless would-be entrepreneurs, Naval reservist and freshly minted Harvard MBA Chris Michel had a great idea: Why not create a website to serve as a virtual hub for the nation's 70 million active-duty military personnel, reservists, veterans, and family members?

But during the enthusiastic days of 1999–2000, Michel knew that a great idea was not enough. He needed a great team.

"It was important that I could share the burden," Michel recalled. "There's a lot of burden early on when you start these businesses, because there's a lot of risk every day."

So Michel began looking for a few good men (and women). He immediately hired one of the senior partners from a consulting firm he had been working with—someone he knew well and could trust—and a classmate from Harvard Business School with experience developing and assessing startups' business plans. Then he cast the net wider, for advisors who would help him gain credibility in both the capital and consumer markets. Among his recruits: two former members of the Joint Chiefs of Staff and prominent military historian Stephen Ambrose. Finally, he assembled a heavy-hitting board of directors that included Xerox PARC veteran David Liddle and Mayfield Fund general partner Michael Levinthal.

Only then did he approach the venture capitalists. When he did, the combination of strong idea and solid team proved irresistible to Sand Hill Road: Michel secured about $5 million in first-round financing, then another $18 million more in second-round financing from the Mayfield Fund, U.S. Venture Partners, and Broadview International. The funding—and the team, which soon numbered several dozen, including many passionately committed veterans and military buffs—enabled Military.com to weather the dot-com debacle and become the leading website of its kind.

So Michel's chief admonition to budding entrepreneurs is hardly surprising: "Find some smart people to work with. Very quickly."

This chapter was coauthored by Jeffrey Rayport, Bernie Jaworski, Ellie Kyung, and Dorsey McGlone.

PLEASE CONSIDER THE FOLLOWING QUESTIONS AS YOU READ THIS CHAPTER:

1. What is a startup?

2. What are the different sources of human capital that can play a role in a startup business?

3. What are the typical sources of funding for early-stage startup businesses?

4. What elements are needed for a successful pitch to investors?

5. How is the value of a startup determined?

6. What are the factors involved in negotiating with investors?

7. What is an initial public offering? What process must an entrepreneur undertake to successfully complete an IPO?

INTRODUCTION

Capital is crucial to developing companies, and so understanding capital is important for business managers. While much has been made of the dot-com boom and bust, the truth is, funders are still investing large amounts of capital in young companies each year. Exhibit 11.1 shows the amount of money that venture-capital firms invested between 1995 and 2001. Note that even though investments dropped significantly from 2000 to 2001, the amount remained higher than in 1998, signaling that investment companies and individuals are still finding attractive opportunities in this market. Yet because of heightened competition, it is more important than ever for business managers to understand how money is invested and how to present themselves as an attractive opportunity.

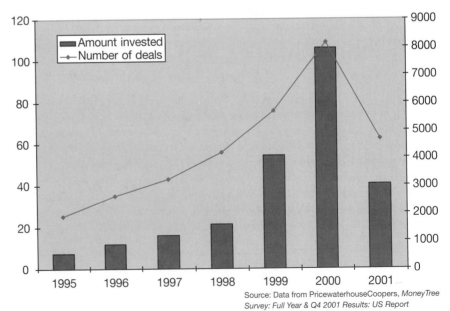

Source: Data from PricewaterhouseCoopers, *MoneyTree Survey: Full Year & Q4 2001 Results: US Report*

EXHIBIT 11.1   Venture Capital—Market Size, 1995–2001

This chapter examines how the right people and the right funding help bring an e-commerce startup to life. First, we introduce business planning as a dynamic process of testing a business's current resources against what it hopes to achieve tomorrow. Next, we detail the human capital that the entrepreneur can leverage to attract the financial capital needed to make the business come alive. We also overview common sources of funding for startups and the pitch entrepreneurs must make to investors to receive financial capital. Finally, we look at the valuation process and the various liquidity events that a company might choose to pursue.

While many of the principles discussed in this chapter apply to all categories of startups, we focus specifically on online startups—companies that need to grow quickly and require relatively large amounts of initial capital to achieve market success. For that reason, we spend more time discussing equity sources of financing than debt financing (because equity sources are more likely to grant funding to online businesses) and focus largely on the early stage of the company's development. By early stage, we are referring to both the seed phase of financing, in which small amounts of money are given to the company to fund preliminary research and development, and the startup phase of financing, in which the company begins to build its team and its business. Exhibit 11.2 provides an overview of the various financing stages through which a startup progresses and the types of financing required during each life stage of a new company.

Building a Business

There are myriad schools of thought and personal opinions about the best way to build a business. However, one point is rarely refuted: Building a business is hard work. For a time, the Internet boom of the 1990s seemed to flout this conventional wisdom. Companies went public mere months after being founded, and more than a few enjoyed multi-billion-dollar market capitalizations. Founders made fortunes overnight. Not to trivialize the blood, sweat, and tears of those startups' employees, but building a business almost seemed easy—that is, until the Nasdaq crash in April 2000 and the subsequent return of the "rational" markets.

At the height of the Internet boom, more emphasis was placed on *starting*—rather than *building*—a business. Launching quickly to gain first-mover advantage was valued over thoughtful business strategy. However, laying a good foundation during the early stages of a business is critical for sustained future success—even in the networked economy—and many of the Internet startups that rushed toward initial public offering (IPO) were not prepared to be operational.

There is no single formula or step-by-step process for assured success, whether success is defined as obtaining funding, going public, or building a business that lasts through the next millennium. Factors both internal and external to the business—as well as luck—play a role. The business components outlined in this chapter are necessary ingredients of entrepreneurial success, but by no means guarantee it.

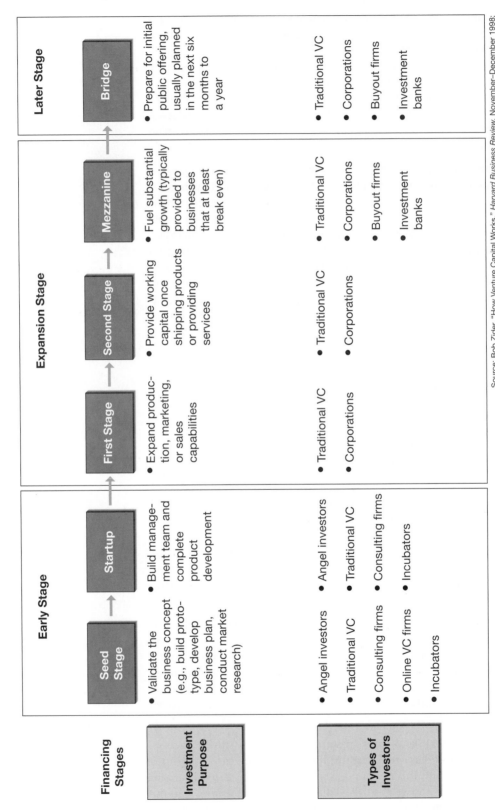

Financing Stages

Early Stage

Seed Stage	→	Startup

Expansion Stage

First Stage	→	Second Stage	→	Mezzanine

Later Stage

Bridge

Investment Purpose

- **Seed Stage:** Validate the business concept (e.g., build prototype, develop business plan, conduct market research)
- **Startup:** Build management team and complete product development
- **First Stage:** Expand production, marketing, or sales capabilities
- **Second Stage:** Provide working capital once shipping products or providing services
- **Mezzanine:** Fuel substantial growth (typically provided to businesses that at least break even)
- **Bridge:** Prepare for initial public offering, usually planned in the next six months to a year

Types of Investors

- **Seed Stage:**
  - Angel investors
  - Traditional VC
  - Consulting firms
  - Online VC firms
  - Incubators
- **Startup:**
  - Angel investors
  - Traditional VC
  - Consulting firms
  - Incubators
- **First Stage:**
  - Traditional VC
  - Corporations
- **Second Stage:**
  - Traditional VC
  - Corporations
- **Mezzanine:**
  - Traditional VC
  - Corporations
  - Buyout firms
  - Investment banks
- **Bridge:**
  - Traditional VC
  - Corporations
  - Buyout firms
  - Investment banks

Source: Bob Zider, "How Venture Capital Works," *Harvard Business Review*, November–December 1998; and *The Gold Book of Venture Capital Firms* (New Hampshire; Kennedy Information), vii

EXHIBIT 11.2 Startup Business Investment Stages

Defining a Startup

Startup seems like a word of modern origin, but the term was actually coined back in 1845 to describe any business enterprise in the early stages of development.[1] As this definition suggests, there is no precise moment at which an entrepreneur can say that his company is no longer a startup. In general, startups are in the process of developing the underlying infrastructure needed to support their future growth. We define a startup as a business engaging in these three basic processes:

1. Developing and refining the offering and strategy

2. Obtaining initial funding to begin operations

3. Building a capable management team to handle those operations

In theory, a startup should be structured to adapt to change—to foresee and maneuver through difficult external circumstances such as a shift in market conditions, inflation, and newly imposed government regulations. Still, even for a sound startup, the risk of failure remains quite high: Only six out of every 1 million business ideas hatched by entrepreneurs go all the way to IPO.[2]

However, two observations should give the entrepreneur some hope. One is that putting together a business plan increases the chance of success dramatically. The other is that obtaining funding increases that likelihood even further. To do both, entrepreneurs must begin by figuring out exactly which people, and what kind of money, they will need in order build their businesses intelligently.

Understanding the Relationship Between Human and Financial Capital

Human capital and financial capital are critical ingredients in the business planning process. Indeed, they are the primary assets over which the entrepreneur has some measure of control during the early stages of the business. **Human capital** refers to the individuals who fill important roles in the growth of the business. **Financial capital** refers to the funding that an entrepreneur needs to attract in order to run the business.

Exhibit 11.3 shows the relationships among human capital, financial capital, and the business planning process. Human resources that are usually present during the planning stage, listed on the left side of the diagram, include the following:

1. *Entrepreneur.* The entrepreneur is the person with the "big idea," the one who puts the startup in motion. The idea can be a piece of technology, the identification of a market inefficiency, or a concept about unmet customer needs.

2. *Management team.* This is the group of people (possibly including the founding entrepreneur) that maps the strategic direction and operations of the startup.

3. *Strategic advisers and partners.* These include members of the advisory board, the board of directors, and companies with which the

startup forms strategic alliances. Strategic advisers and partners provide expertise and advice for the entrepreneur and the management team, especially in areas in which they might be lacking. With the right names, they can attract potential investors to the fledgling company.

4. *Logistical advisers and partners.* Similar in profile and function to strategic advisers and partners, these outsourced parties—paid through either fees or equity—are more involved in the day-to-day operations of the firm. They include lawyers, accountants, consultants, intermediaries, and incubators.

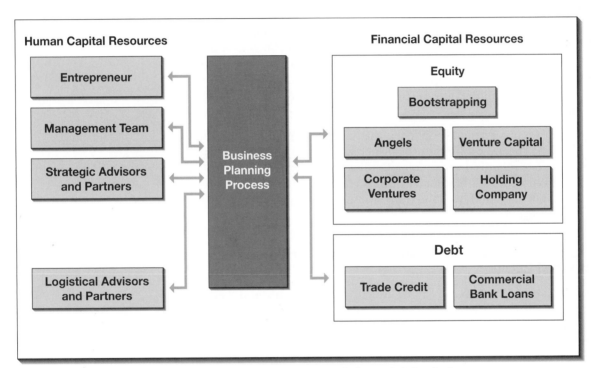

EXHIBIT 11.3   The Relationship Between Human and Financial Capital

On the right side of Exhibit 11.3 is a list of the most common sources of financial capital for early-stage businesses. These sources fall into two categories: debt financing, in which a startup might borrow a certain amount of money for a specified time period and repay the principal plus interest, and equity financing, in which a startup exchanges a portion of ownership for cash, with the investor expecting financial return in the future as the value of the business increases. These two forms of financing are discussed in greater detail later in this chapter.

As suggested by the arrows between the business planning process and financial capital sources, good business plans attract financial capital, and those who provide that financial capital are instrumental in aiding the start-up in its planning stage. The same is true of the dynamic arrows pointing back and forth between human capital and the business planning process. Furthermore, the fact that each arrow in the diagram is two-directional illustrates a critical fact about early-stage business planning: It is a constant, iterative progression.

Elements of a Solid Business Planning Process

Solid business planning begins with the plan itself. The business plan of any startup has two primary objectives: (1) to serve as a "résumé" for potential investors, and (2) to provide a framework for testing the business from conception through early development. Because of the first objective, entrepreneurs tend to focus the business planning process on what the investor wants to see rather than fleshing out strategy, which is a dangerous mistake. To borrow the words of Harvard Business School professor William A. Sahlman, the entrepreneur or management team should evaluate whether they have the means to "just do it" and, if not, have the sense to "just say no."[3]

If it is determined that the means—and the idea—are there, the next step is to create an overall picture of the business venture's feasibility by formulating a business plan. In that plan, the entrepreneur and management team must do the following:

- *Define the value proposition.* What is the product or service the business proposes to provide for customers, and why would customers want it?
- *Frame the market opportunity.* Is there a need for what the company is offering? If so, who needs it? Potential customers should be identified, segmented, and numbered to determine their attractiveness. (See Chapter 3 for more detail.)
- *Detail how to reach customers.* How do you bring your offering to the market? What marketing plan or strategy will the business employ to attract and keep customers in the noisy online world? How much will this cost? Solid marketing, sales, and customer relationship strategies are essential.
- *Develop an implementation plan.* For a product-oriented business, how will the product be designed and manufactured? For an e-commerce website, how will the website be structured and built? What aspects of the business will be pursued in-house, and what will be outsourced to other parties? What type of facilities will be needed to house the operation?
- *Evaluate potential external influences.* Market conditions, inflation, exchange rates, interest rates, and government regulations are just a few of the outside forces that can affect a business. Determining the forces most likely to touch the company, for better or for worse, prepares the company for possible future scenarios.
- *Articulate the revenue model.* How will the business make money? As many dot-coms painfully learned, the strategy of acquiring customers first and addressing profitability later is generally not rewarded in the long term.

- *Identify needed people.* These parties are the human capital previously identified as well as strategic alliances that help provide a sustainable advantage for the business. As the company continues to expand, long-term staffing plans and compensation must also be sorted out.

- *Calculate preliminary financial projections.* These numbers are necessary for the funding process, but they should also be seen as a way to check the financial viability of the business. How much money is needed? At what intervals? What types of returns might investors expect? Projections should include a list of underlying assumptions, five-year forecasts, an income statement, a balance sheet, and cash flow statements—and should be as realistic as possible.

- *Establish milestones.* Although predicting a startup's exact development path is impossible, milestones provide a documented benchmark for future progress evaluations. These milestones can include an estimated time line for product or website launch and projections for future head count or revenues. Many investors require some evidence of success to continue funding, and establishing and passing milestones can provide it.

- *Summarize the advantage.* Some combination of the previous elements should constitute the startup's advantage over current and potential players. What are the driving principles that make this organization different? What is the startup's vision for the future, and what will it do to reach it? Most importantly, what is the organization's core competency or competitive advantage, and how will it be maintained?

Human Capital

While human capital is necessary for any business, its role in a startup business is especially critical because, for a time, it is the only resource available. A true startup has no assets to speak of, so when funders consider investing in an early-stage company, they look closely at its human capital. Who is the entrepreneur? Does he or she have the drive to see this business through? Who is on the management team? Human capital attracts financial capital, and each person on the team makes an important contribution to the business.

The Entrepreneur

Every company in existence today was once a startup. Coca-Cola, Hewlett-Packard, and FedEx all began in the same place: with an entrepreneur and an idea that evolves into a vision for a business. E-commerce startups are no different.

Of course, an entrepreneur alone does not make a business. In fact, some think that a charismatic entrepreneur with far-reaching ideas is not necessarily a critical player in a startup's success. (See Point-Counterpoint, "Does the Entrepreneur Matter?") As Amazon's Jeff Bezos once said: "Ideas are easy. It's execution that's hard."[4] Whether they are considered central to a startup's success or just daydreamers sitting in the corner office, entrepreneurs tend to have in common the following characteristics:

- *Keenly observant.* The best entrepreneurs are those who are able to make observations about industries, markets, and everyday life and find the best way to meet customer needs—or create them. In 1994, Amazon's Jeff Bezos read a report claiming that access to the Web was growing 2,000 percent annually. Recognizing the audience potential, he drew up a list of 20 items he could sell online and decided the most promising was books.[5]

- *Willing to take risks.* In the early stages, this can mean not only leaving a stable job, but also risking the savings of family and friends to pursue a hunch—even if they've tried and failed at other hunches before. Before his success with the Internet instant-messaging service ICQ, Arik Vardi unsuccessfully tried his hand at creating ISP software and selling T-shirts.[6]

- *Driven.* Entrepreneurs typically put in long hours and make sacrifices in their personal lives to bring a business to life. This is especially critical in the early stages, when the entrepreneur's enthusiasm spurs on employees. Yahoo founders Jerry Yang and David Filo famously forewent corner offices for standard cubicles and labored through long nights side by side with their staff.

- *Flexible.* The ability to react and adapt quickly is especially important in the networked economy, where the market changes in extra-speedy Internet time. If the next round of funding is smaller than expected, adjustments need to be made. If a key person in management decamps for the nearest competitor, contingencies must be in place. Flexibility and ingenuity are critical in an environment that will likely throw a few curveballs.

- *Visionary.* History has shown that the most successful entrepreneurs were not driven solely by money but by a vision or a passion consistently pursued. "Money is not the motivator or even the measure of my success," said entrepreneur Marc Andreessen.[7] Rather, it was his desire for a better way to access information on the Internet that led to the development of his first Internet interface, Mosaic, and later to Netscape.

From the outset, the entrepreneur is faced with reconciling several difficult paradoxes. This is especially true for the e-commerce entrepreneur who requires equity funding to quickly scale the business:

- *Being visionary versus being realistic.* While investors are looking for "the next big thing," they are also looking for ideas grounded in reality. The entrepreneur is faced with the challenge of coming up with unique ideas that are also practical and actionable.

- *Generating quick returns versus investing in the future.* Building an organization that will last takes time. In an almost contradictory fashion, investors are looking for companies that will last as investment prospects, but they require a return on their investment in three to five years. Keeping the business on course and on pace while meeting the demands of the investors is challenging.

- *Optimism versus pragmatism.* The entrepreneur's enthusiastic belief in the startup motivates employees in these early stages. However, this optimism must be balanced with the pragmatism to evaluate potential weaknesses and pitfalls. The excitement of "Yes, we can do it!" must be balanced with "But, really, can we do it?"

The Entrepreneur and the Idea

Although we mentioned that the entrepreneur may not be driven primarily by a desire for personal financial gain, the idea itself must make money in some way. Some ideas are applications, or a way of doing business; others create or meet new market needs. Either way, the idea should embody the competitive advantage the startup hopes to gain. Below are some common business approaches of startups:

- *Introduce a new product.* New products can be classified by how they affect existing products. *Products that enhance* increase the functionality or lengthen the life cycle of existing technology, such as software upgrades. *Products providing alternatives* compete head to head with existing products. *Products that displace* provide an entirely new means of doing something. Finally, *products that transform* fundamentally change the way people do business or the way they live—think of the invention of the PC or the advent of the Internet.

- *Introduce a new service.* Ideas for new services can come either through identifying previously unmet needs in an existing market or as the result of new technology.

- *Improve an existing model of business.* This is the classic "faster, better, cheaper" improvement to existing industry paradigms. Startups can sometimes gain an advantage over large, established players because they can react more nimbly to market changes.

The Management Team

A solid management team is critical to a startup's success. In the early stages of a company, these are the people who shape the entrepreneur's idea into a functional business. They can also be the ones who make or break investors' decisions about financing. Well-seasoned management teams are difficult to come by, and investors place a premium on experience. Startups that are able to secure quality managers have a significant advantage.

A startup is seldom able to begin operations with a full management team in place, however. The management team evolves, and the right people are brought on board as needed. In some instances, investors help pinpoint the right individuals for the jobs. But if management teams are needed to attract investors, and investors and the promise of financing are needed to attract the right managers, it raises the question: Which comes first, the management team or the financing? The exact sequence depends on each startup's capabilities and weaknesses, rather than a strict set of rules. In most instances, this ends up being a somewhat simultaneous process. The management team coalesces as the funding process is finalized, oftentimes consisting of individuals recommended by investors.

Regardless of whether the management team comes together before or after funding, an incomplete team will slow a startup's development. Certain individuals are necessary at critical developmental milestones.

The Core Team

The core team comprises those individuals essential to the formative days of the startup. Their exact titles or positions are not as critical as their roles. The entrepreneur usually fills one of these roles, according to his or her

Point-Counterpoint

Which Is More Important—the Idea or the Management Team?

This is a question that became especially relevant in the late 1990s, when it seemed (at least for a time) that any twenty-something with a bright idea could obtain funding and set up shop online. What was more important to investors—the idea or the management team? The entrepreneur's idea has always been the driving impetus behind an organization without which there would be no business venture at all. In the online environment, where speed to market can make or break an organization, investors were willing to take risks on the business ideas of inexperienced entrepreneurs. Some of the most novel concepts brought to the Web were those of young entrepreneurs. Shawn Fanning was 18 years old when he founded Napster—the music exchange that threatened old recording industry giants. Twenty-somethings Jerry Yang and David Filo built Yahoo into one of the Internet's most recognized brands. These young entrepreneurs and their ideas seemed to be the investor's key to finding "the next big thing." However, these were also entrepreneurs who were unlikely to attract the expertise of skilled management teams on their own, and in many instances, investors had to be willing to take a risk on an idea alone.

On the other hand, the collapse of the Internet economy (including the downfall of Napster) has shown the importance of execution and solid business experience, even in operating e-commerce startups. The collapse of a host of retail sites, from eToys to Pets.com, demonstrated the importance of managers with the financial and strategic experience to operate a company within its financial means. The management team description is one of the first sections read in a business plan, and the makeup of this team can make or break a deal. Investors are comfortable betting their money on people who have experience because they are more likely to build organizations that are operationally sound.

So in the end, which is a better bet—banking on the idea or on the management? The answer, in most instances, is probably both, but it largely depends on the taste of the individual investor.

area of expertise, and may be replaced if more experienced management can be brought onboard when funding is secured. Early on, three roles need to be filled:

1. *Technology specialist.* In a product-oriented business, this person understands how the product works, how it is manufactured, and how it can be utilized. For e-commerce businesses, this is the person who determines the technology platforms that will be used or developed. He or she knows what is technologically feasible and understands how to develop what is lacking. This individual is often called the chief technology officer (CTO) or chief intelligence officer (CIO).

2. *Sales and marketing specialist.* This person has an in-depth understanding of the startup's customers. The marketing specialist's expertise lies in segmenting the potential customers, selecting the most attractive targets, understanding their wants and needs, and figuring out how to best position the company to capture the customer's attention. His or her primary responsibility is successful customer acquisition and retention. This individual can be the vice president of sales, marketing, or business development, often holding several of these titles at once in the early stages of the business.

3. *Execution specialist.* This person is responsible for turning the vision for the business into a reality. He or she oversees all aspects of the startup's development, from ensuring the connection between the technology and the market to securing funding for continued operations. This individual is typically the chief executive officer (CEO).

The Extended Management Team

Once the core management team is in place, other members of the management team can be added as needed, depending on how quickly the startup is growing and how far along product and business-model development have come. Some of these "extended" jobs will already be covered by the core management team:

1. *Chief operating officer.* This person takes care of the day-to-day business operations.

2. *Chief financial officer.* It is this person's job to ensure that the company remains financially solvent. Having an internal team member intimately familiar with the startup's financials is extremely helpful when the startup enters into investor negotiations.

3. *VP of marketing.* This person is responsible for creating and maintaining the company's brand image and creating its positioning strategy.

4. *VP of sales.* This person is responsible for generating revenues and creating and maintaining a network of direct sales channels for the organization.

5. *VP of business development.* It is this person's responsibility to further expand both the customer base and the business and also to develop strategic partnerships and seek potential acquisition targets.

6. *Chief people officer.* In an environment in which exceptional employees can be scarce, creating a company culture that fosters learning, growth, and appreciation for the individual is central to retaining talent. The chief people officer handles recruiting and promotes a consistent culture in the company.

Marketspace Interview

Bob Metcalfe, Venture Capitalist; Inventor of Ethernet; Founder of 3Com

For a couple of years, I asked venture capitalists for the reasons that companies fail, and I got three of them: ego of the founder, failure to focus, and lack of capital. So when it came my turn to start a company, I decided to make different mistakes from those. I decided to try not to let my ego get in the way, which meant that running the company couldn't be as important to me as making the company successful—which, in turn, meant recruiting people who knew what they were doing, so that every job in the company was filled by someone who was excellent at it.

Then there was focus. When you're a little company, you can't do everything well; you have to do one thing really well and go from there. And then, of course, you have to have the resources to do it, which means raising capital. Now, all of this was complicated, and there was pain and suffering and learning involved. But I have no doubt that it was worth it.

However, given the difficulty of hiring competent and experienced management and the uncertain timing of obtaining funding, it is entirely feasible that key areas of the business plan remain weak even with a preliminary management team in place. These weaknesses can be strengthened through strategic advisers and partners, discussed in the following section.

Strategic Advisers and Partners

Even with a strong management team in place, a startup can always benefit from the expertise of industry veterans. Strategic advisers and partners provide the startup with direction and advice, not to mention credibility. They are usually involved with the startup through the advisory board, the board of directors, or partnerships—all of which are disclosed to investors in the business plan. If the entrepreneur is new to a particular industry, finding a reputable industry player to sit on the advisory board can strengthen the startup's position.

Advisory Board

Advisory board members typically receive stock options in exchange for their expertise. There is no specific number of individuals needed or recommended for an advisory board; selection should be based purely on necessity. The need for an advisory board wanes as the company grows. Few public companies have advisory boards.

Board of Directors

The board of directors is responsible for the well-being of the company, as well as for holding the management team accountable for its actions when the business formalizes its operations. In a public company, shareholders vote for these individuals; in a startup, board members are selected by the management team and entrepreneur and later by investors. Members of the board of directors usually hold an equity stake in the company. Like advisory board members, they provide strategic expertise and advice, but they also have voting power of approval over key decisions, such as investments, mergers, acquisitions, offerings, and management team selection or replacement.

Once the startup becomes incorporated, the board of directors is legally responsible for the financial health of the company. Unlike the role of the advisory board, which tends to diminish as the startup develops, the power of the board of directors increases when and if the company goes public.

Strategic Partnerships

Strategic partnerships take several forms. A *strategic association* is the partnership with the least commitment and can consist of a verbal or written agreement for two entities to mutually exchange expertise. In a *strategic alliance*, the parties draw up a legally binding contract to share resources on a project for a particular timeframe. As we learned in Chapter 4, 1-800-Flowers.com has created many partnerships, including ones with AOL, Barnes & Noble.com, and American Airlines. The most dedicated strategic partnership is a *strategic joint venture*, in which different businesses contribute resources to create an entirely separate business.

Logistical Advisers and Partners

Logistical advisers and partners assist the startup on a more operational level than strategic advisers and partners. They too can be involved in strategy formulation, but are more involved in the down-and-dirty, day-to-day operations of the business.

- *Certified public accountant.* The CPA is responsible for compiling the financial history of the business, verifying assumptions made for financial projections, and preparing all tax and finance-related documents. Once the funding processes become more formalized, venture-capital firms and investment banks require CPAs.

- *Legal counsel.* The startup's attorney handles everything from preparing incorporation documents to defending the company's intellectual property rights. A reputable attorney with experience in the startup's field can provide credibility, and even contacts, with investors.

- *Intermediaries.* Intermediaries are well-connected people in the investment community who match a startup with the right investors and, in some instances, acquisition targets—for a fee. They are positioned between startups seeking funding and funding sources seeking good investments. In return for their service, the intermediary receives a percentage of the funding it brings in, typically between 2 and 10 percent, and sometimes has the right to purchase an investment stake in the startup.

- *Consultants.* "Consultant" is an umbrella term for a number of types of outsourced advisers—from corporate financial advisers to valuation experts to traditional strategy consultants. Well-connected consulting firms with experience in the startup's industry often provide investor leads and sometimes have corporate venture funds themselves.

Financial Capital

To get up and running, startups need money—and, generally, lots of it. Funders provide e-commerce companies with several key assets: the large amounts of cash needed to move the business quickly, the networks needed to form management teams and partnerships, and the publicity needed to attract attention in a noisy online market. In this section, we provide an overview of factors that can influence an entrepreneur's decision to pursue a particular type of financial capital: (1) what the source is and why they are in the game, (2) criteria for investment selection, and (3) general advantages and disadvantages to turning to this source for financial capital. Exhibit 11.4 provides a quick overview of each source discussed in this chapter.

Each category of funders discussed in this chapter has different objectives when evaluating an investment opportunity. For the entrepreneur, knowing a potential funder's objectives is critical. For example, an entrepreneur developing a product with a lengthy research and development cycle should not seek financing from funders who want a quick return on their investment. Similarly, entrepreneurs should know whether the sources they are approaching are *financial* or *strategic* investors. The former are primarily concerned with seeing a return on their investment; the latter are primarily

	Source	What Is It?	Primary Criteria for Investment Selection	Key Advantages and Disadvantages	
				Pros	**Cons**
Debt Financing	**Trade Credit**	Credit extended to a business by its suppliers	• A track record of prompt payment	• Provides an interest-free loan	• Certain terms could carry a costly implied interest rate • Difficult for e-commerce startups to obtain
	Commercial Bank Loan	Installment loans in which a business borrows a specific amount for a specified length of time, to be repaid in installments (with interest)	• Likelihood of loan repayment • Cash on hand • Positive cash flow • Acceptable burn rate	• Provides cash without losing equity	• Difficult for e-commerce startups to obtain criteria for investment
Equity Financing	**Bootstrapping**	Using personal resources to finance the early stages of a startup	• Entrepreneur's belief in his own business	• Provides cash without losing equity • Entrepreneur gains valuable operational experience	• Unlikely to provide enough cash to sustain extended growth
	Angels	Wealthy individuals who invest personal capital in startups	• Referral through network connections • Business in early stage of development • Personal objectives • *Market potential* • *Nature of the business concept* • *Quality of management team (if any)* • *Track record of the entrepreneur*	• Can provide expertise, networks, and credibility to help the entrepreneur build the business • Can provide referral to additional funding sources • Angels tend to negotiate terms more favorable for entrepreneurs than VCs	• Difficult to locate • Investors can decide to get very operationally involved with the startup, creating potential conflicts with the entrepreneur • One angel alone is unlikely to provide enough capital for operations • Dealings with multiple angels can cause operational and logistical complications
	Venture Capital	Private partnerships or closely held corporations that raise money from investors that is then invested in companies that hold promise for a liquidity event	• Referral through network connections • Potential return on investment in three to five years • Firm's strategic objectives • Existence of proprietary technology or concept for sustainable advantage • *Plus items italicized for angels*	• Can provide large amounts of cash to sustain growth • Coaching, expertise, and industry contacts • Name-brand recognition and publicity	• Objectives are primarily financial, which can create conflicts with the entrepreneur's vision for the company • Requires high equity stake • Entrepreneur must give up a certain degree of control • Difficult to locate and obtain
	Incubator	Organizations that support new companies, primarily through services rather than cash, in exchange for a piece of the business	• Firm's strategic objectives • *Plus items italicized for angels*	• Allows entrepreneur to focus on strategic rather than operational issues • Coaching, expertise, and industry contacts	• Requires high equity stake
	Corporate Venture	Venture funds set up by large corporations	• Degree to which business complements corporation's current strategic objectives • Right to utilize technology developed in the venture • *Plus items italicized for angels*	• Provides operational expertise • Provides credibility and visibility for the business through corporation's brand name • Provides large amounts of cash • Financing terms tend to be more favorable than those of VCs • Patient capital	• Potential conflict of interest with parent company can cause problems • Complicated discussion of intellectual property rights if business later seeks VC funding • Slow to make investment decisions
	Holding Company	Company that offers cash in exchange for equity in companies with an operational rather than financial focus; equity stakes typically range from 25 to 50 percent	• Usually defined by particular focus of the holding company • *Plus items italicized for angels*	• Patient capital due to operational focus • Ability to learn from other portfolio companies • Investors usually very experienced in specific industry	• Requires a large equity stake, and thus control

Note: Items italicized for angels are those criteria common to multiple sources of funding.

EXHIBIT 11.4 Summary of Primary Financial Capital Resources

concerned with how the business complements their current activities. Understanding whether investors are primarily financial or strategic will help the entrepreneur decide which ones to avoid and which to approach.

Debt Financing

Simply put, **debt financing** is a loan—money that you borrow and agree to pay back, with interest, at a future date. Debt financing is a purely financial transaction; once the debt is paid, the relationship between lender and borrower ends. The two most common sources of debt financing for startup companies are trade credit and commercial bank loans, which together account for about 70 percent of the debt financing extended to new businesses.[8]

Trade Credit

Simply put, **trade credit** is an interest-free loan extended to a business by a supplier. When a business orders goods from a supplier, instead of demanding payment for those goods upon delivery, the supplier extends the payment due date for an agreed-upon period of time. For example, a business might receive a shipment of goods and start using them today but not have to pay for those goods for 30 more days. This is effectively an interest-free 30-day loan.

Criteria for Selection   Suppliers typically offer trade credit to buyers with a track record of prompt payment. Early-stage startups lack such track records and therefore are usually not offered trade credit. Established firms stand a much better chance of getting trade credit, as well as beneficial terms for financing.

Commercial Bank Loan

A **commercial bank loan** typically takes the form of an installment loan in which the business borrows a certain amount of money for a specified length of time—usually one to five years—at either a fixed or variable interest rate. Monthly payments are made until the loan is paid in full. The bank makes money on the interest when the loan is repaid.

Criteria for Selection   Commercial banks evaluate a loan application by assessing the likelihood of loan repayment. This involves determining how much cash the business has available through equity financings or positive cash flow. In the absence of these indicators, the bank also looks at the amount of cash the business uses on a monthly basis (its "burn rate"), its current cash balance, planned amounts of equity financing in the future, and level of investor support.

Because e-commerce startups tend to have no positive cash flows and few tangible assets to offer creditors as collateral, trade credit and commercial bank loans are rarely extended. However, there are ways in which entrepreneurs can boost their chances. One way is to offer personal assets as collateral as a display of commitment to the business; another way is to apply for a small loan—even if the business does not require it at the time—and repay the loan on schedule to establish a reputation as a safe loan candidate with the bank. With an established relationship at a commercial bank, the entrepreneur can gain access to a host of other loan products, such as capital-equipment leasing programs or revolving credit.

Although both trade credit and commercial bank loans are helpful sources of financial capital, an e-commerce startup that does manage to secure them will have difficulty surviving on these sources alone. The dollar value of loans offered by these sources—seldom more than $250,000—is too small to be helpful to the startup beyond the very early stage, which also happens to be the stage when they are least likely to qualify.

Equity Financing

Roughly half of all startup funding comes from **equity financing**, in which the entrepreneur gives up a portion of the ownership of his company in exchange for capital. In contrast to debt financiers, who are largely risk averse, equity financing sources are willing to take a gamble, hoping for significant returns on their share of the company at some point in the future.

In some instances, the logistical advisers and partners discussed in the human capital section might exchange their services for equity rather than cash. However, the most common sources of equity financing are bootstrapping, venture-capital firms, angel investors, corporate ventures, incubators, and holding companies. Below is a summary of each of these equity sources, along with a brief run-through of their selection criteria and their pros and cons.

Bootstrapping

Bootstrapping is the art of using personal resources to finance the early stages of a startup. For the entrepreneur, this may include taking out a personal loan, mortgaging a home, using credit cards, or draining a savings account—essentially, taking on personal debt financing. If these personal sources are not enough to get the company started, the entrepreneur may turn to friends and family for additional cash, keeping the ownership of the business among himself and the friends and family members who contribute.

While this may seem like a piecemeal process, it is often necessary and, more important, successful. More than 40 percent of all financing used to start businesses comes from bootstrapping. According to the venture-capital investment bank Garage Technology Ventures, 80 percent of the top 500 fastest-growing companies were initially bankrolled solely by bootstrap financing.[9]

Criteria for Selection   Bootstrapping is the most viable financing option for the entrepreneur when the startup is in its earliest stages—especially while proving the business concept—because embryonic companies are rarely able to attract significant amounts of outside funding.

Pros and Cons   In addition to allowing the entrepreneur to retain full ownership of the company, bootstrapping forces the entrepreneur to become intimately involved with the finances and the mechanics of running the company. Bootstrapping also allows the entrepreneur to refine his business strategy without pressure from outside investors seeking quick financial returns.

One disadvantage of bootstrapping is that it is unlikely to provide sufficient cash beyond the earliest stages; the startup will need to turn to additional sources of equity to maintain growth.

Venture Capital

Venture capital is perhaps the most widely known and publicized funding source, even though it accounts for less than 3 percent of all startup financing.[10] Venture-capital firms are in the business of finding companies with the potential for great economic return, nurturing them, then "cashing out" to make a return on their investment. VC firms are usually private partnerships or closely held corporations that invest the money of a group of private investors ranging from corporate pension funds to governments to private individuals.

A VC firm typically invests between $250,000 and $10 million in a business in exchange for a 30 to 40 percent equity stake and a seat on the board of directors.[11] In general, it seeks opportunities that will return 5 to 20 times its original investment within five years, but realistically expects only 10 percent of the companies it invests in to succeed. For a typical venture capitalist, the success of that one investment should outweigh the failure of the other nine.[12]

Venture-capital investment reached unprecedented heights during the Internet boom, soaring from $13 billion in 1998 to $105 billion in 2000.[13] But when the Nasdaq crashed, the amount of venture-capital money dropped; in 2001, VC firms' investments were $36.5 billion.[14] In 2001, only 28 percent of companies that had already won venture backing were able to drum up follow-on venture-capital funding, and the number of first-time fundings was the lowest in six years.[15]

Drill-Down

SBICs—Government-Backed Private Equity

In addition to private venture-capital funding, more than $5 billion is available annually through small-business investment companies, also called SBICs. SBICs are privately owned and managed firms that use their own capital, as well as funds borrowed from the government's Small Business Administration, to invest in small companies in early stages of growth.

Congress created the Small Business Investment Company program in 1958 to encourage private, venture-capital investments in small-business startups. Since then, the program has provided more than 90,000 small U.S. companies with $32.7 billion in long-term debt and equity capital. Among the many major U.S. companies that have received early financing from SBICs: America Online, Apple Computer, Staples, and Federal Express. In 2001 alone, investments in small businesses through SBICs totaled $4.5 billion.

All SBICs are licensed and regulated by the SBA. The only requirements are a management team with some venture-capital expertise and at least $5 million in private capital. An SBIC can be organized as a corporation, limited partnership, or limited-liability company, depending on the investors, which are typically small groups of local financiers or bank-owned entities. The SBA licensed 51 new SBICs in 2001, bringing the total number operating in the United States and Puerto Rico to 430.

continued

Like venture-capital firms, SBICs offer cash in exchange for equity, but they also offer long-term loans, which would otherwise be difficult for startups to obtain. Loans can have a maturity of up to 20 years, and the SBA dictates that they can be used for "financing, growth, modernization, and expansion." The average loan size in 2001 was $1.3 million.

Eligibility for SBIC financing, as defined by the SBA, is generally restricted to businesses with a net worth of less than $18 million and an average after-tax income of less than $6 million for the preceding two years. There are no industry-specific criteria or restrictions, and SBICs tend to invest in a broad range of industries, depending on the expertise of the management team.

Why does the government invest in such programs? Every new business, no matter how small, expands the U.S. economy and increases the number of new jobs. In terms of cost, the program more than pays for itself through tax dollars collected from the new businesses. Often overlooked for the glitz and glamour of venture-capital funding, the SBIC program provides a significant capital source for small startups that would otherwise have to bootstrap until they could approach traditional VCs.[16]

Criteria for Selection   As Exhibit 11.5 illustrates, the vast majority of VC investments are in companies in their expansion phase—companies with developed business concepts that are in the process of assembling their management team, but not yet at the point of product launch. An ideal investment candidate would have the following characteristics: (1) a large and growing market potential, (2) some proprietary or revolutionary product or strategy to sustain competitive advantage, and (3) an experienced and driven management team. Each VC firm also has different strategic objectives and areas of focus, whether by industry, technology, or geography.

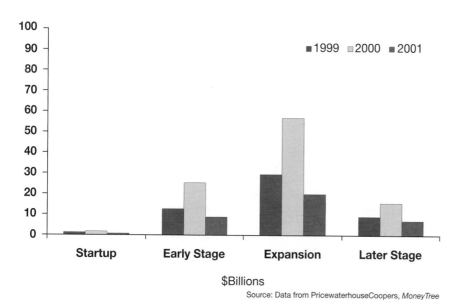

Source: Data from PricewaterhouseCoopers, *MoneyTree Survey: Full Year & Q4 2001 Results: US Report*

EXHIBIT 11.5   Venture-Capital Investments—Breakdown by Stage

Investment criteria can sometimes depend on the market climate and trends; the Internet boom saw a great deal of this trendlike investing, with VC dollars moving from B2C to B2B to P2P—whatever area seemed hot at the time. Venture capitalists seldom review unsolicited business plans. The entrepreneur must use network connections to gain access to a venture capitalist, even to get a business plan read. If a business plan catches the eye of an investor, the entrepreneur may be invited to pitch his business to the firm. Venture capitalists generally invest in only about 1 percent of the opportunities presented to them.[17]

Pros and Cons   Venture-capital firms are able to provide startups with large amounts of cash that cannot be obtained from sources unwilling to take the associated risk. Venture capitalists are normally very active investors. In addition to receiving cash, the entrepreneur receives guidance for building the startup, which could include industry expertise, contacts with potential management team members, and further strategy development. Obtaining funding from a high-profile, reputable venture-capital firm will also give the startup credibility, publicity, and industry networks. The biggest disadvantage is a VC firm's concern with the bottom line. VC firms are looking for a certain return on investment, and when strategic imperatives clash with financial constraints, the entrepreneur often cannot exercise total control—especially when a VC representative sits on the board of directors. If a venture capitalist believes that his investment is in danger of failing, he can choose to replace the management team and take over the company.

Venture-capital firms also require a relatively large equity stake in exchange for cash, with financing terms that are often not favorable to the entrepreneur. However, owning a small share of a business valued at several hundred million dollars might look more attractive to the entrepreneur than retaining full control of a business worth only a few million dollars. Exhibit 11.6 lists the 10 most active venture-capital firms in 2001.

Company	Location	Deals
New Enterprise Associates	Baltimore, MD	82
Intel Capital	Chandler, AZ	72
J.P. Morgan Partners	New York, NY	69
Bessemer Venture Partners	Wellesley Hills, MA	68
Austin Ventures	Austin, TX	62
U.S. Venture Partners	Menlo Park, CA	61
Warburg Pincus	New York, NY	53
St. Paul Venture Capital	Eden Prairie, MN	52
Technology Crossover Ventures (TCV)	Palo Alto, CA	49
Mobius Venture Capital	Mountain View, CA	47

Source: Data from PricewaterhouseCoopers, *MoneyTree Survey: Full Year & Q4 2001 Results: US Report*

EXHIBIT 11.6   Top 10 Venture-Capital Deal Makers in 2001

Drill-Down

Recent Developments in the European Capital Markets

Over the past several years, the European capital markets have grown and changed in fundamental ways. One of the changes has been the adoption of a common currency—the euro. The euro has been a major catalyst leading to changes in the way Europeans and European companies and financial institutions conduct business. The common currency eliminates currency exchange transactions. Direct access to capital markets through technology channels has enabled growing numbers of investors access to financial markets directly, leading to the disintermediation of the broker. These developments have resulted in lower capital costs and more efficient access.

To facilitate further market development, Europe's more than 30 segmented stock exchanges are beginning to merge, although this is not without its problems. For example, an unofficial bargaining game is being played between financial centers—London, Frankfurt, and Paris. The French, Dutch, and Belgian exchanges are merging to form EuroNext, and there has been some integration of the Scandinavian exchanges, to name just a few examples. Fewer exchanges coupled with the adoption of a single International Accounting System (IAS) for listed companies by 2005 will result in greater market transparency and enable more mobile capital at a lower cost.

With the progress already made to unite the financial markets across Europe, there are still significant barriers. There is no common regulation in Europe regarding takeovers, mergers and acquisitions (M&A), and bankruptcy, and there is not a unified settlement system. These barriers are largely the result of conflicting legal systems and result in inefficient markets. Initiatives to improve M&A activity face continued delays. Banking and investor settlement systems are numerous, and they vary in terms of legal and tax systems, further impeding the pan-European market functionality and raising transaction costs. Finally, bankruptcy law dictates the rights of creditors and debtors and differs between countries. Differences in country legislation regarding collateral and a creditor's claim to that collateral in the event of a bankruptcy can lead to concern about cross-border agreements, thus exposing a creditor to uncertain risks that are accounted for by more expensive credit terms or inefficient transactions.

Even though Europe has taken steps to create a pan-European financial market, considerable work is needed to make the existing markets competitive in the international capital arena. With continued progress toward developing common financial accounting procedures and the establishment of common legal structures to govern corporate systems, the capital markets in Europe should continue to reform and grow. Many of these changes are still being negotiated in European Union committees while others are already in place. An EU-wide securities market is expected by 2003, while an integrated retail financial market is not expected until 2005.

Angels

About 5 percent of startup funding comes from angel investors. **Angels** are wealthy individuals who invest personal capital in startups in exchange for equity—and sometimes a seat on the board of directors. Angels fulfill the important role of closing the "capital gap" that exists between an entrepreneur who is bootstrapping her company and one who needs a larger investment (more than $5 million) from a venture-capital firm. Angel investments range from a few thousand dollars to a few million; few angels disclose figures, so it is difficult to get a sense of the average size of their investments.

According to a Genesis Technology Partners study, angels fall into four categories: guardian angels (industry veterans), professional-entrepreneur angels (angels who are less experienced), operational-expertise angels (large-company senior executives), and financial-return angels (wealthy individuals).[18] Individual angels sometimes come together to form "angel firms," making it possible for entrepreneurs to receive larger amounts of capital without having to go through the logistics of dealing with multiple angel investors.

Angels are primarily interested in early-stage companies that are not yet ready to seek venture-capital financing. It is estimated that angels invest twice as much as venture capitalists do in seed-stage companies in the United States. While the exact dollar amount of angel investments is unknown, estimates run from $20 billion[19] to $50 billion[20] per year. On average, angels will take ownership of 4 to 5 percent of a company in which they invest.

There is a symbiotic relationship between angels and venture capitalists because the structure of a venture-capital firm makes it less likely that the two groups will compete for the same deals. Most angels are savvy enough to construct deals that will be attractive to future financing from VC firms. After all, if a VC firm invests in the deal, the company has a greater chance of success, and therefore the angel has a greater opportunity to increase the value of his initial investment. It is a goal of angels to get top-tier VC firms to invest in their companies.[21]

Criteria for Selection   Each angel has his or her own reasons for investing in certain enterprises, and thus slightly different criteria for investment. Like venture capitalists and other prominent sources of equity financing, angels seldom look at unsolicited business plans. Like most investors, angels are interested in the quality (or existence) of the management team, the market potential for the business idea, and the track record of the entrepreneur. However, angels do tend to be less interested in scrutinizing balance sheets than in whether they find the business intriguing. They are inclined to be more emotional investors than venture-capital firms, which seek specific returns.

Pros and Cons   A well-connected angel has friends or associates that he or she can interest in a business—either as investors or as members of the management team—and also has contacts at venture-capital firms. As individuals, angels have the flexibility to be "patient capital" if everything does not go according to plan; they also typically possess deep industry knowledge and expertise. Perhaps most important, angels tend to work in financial terms that are more favorable to the entrepreneur than those of venture capitalists.

The disadvantages of angel investment include the fact that angels can be difficult to locate and often make relatively small investments. Depending on the amount of capital required, a startup might require investments by multiple angels, which can significantly complicate logistics for the entrepreneur. Angels tend to involve themselves in the day-to-day operations of startups because of the riskiness of their investment. This could cause problems if the angel(s) and entrepreneur have different visions for the company.

Corporate Ventures

Large corporations sometimes set up venture funds as a subsidiary that can make investments on behalf of the parent company, referred to as either **corporate ventures** or "direct investors." While venture-capital firms invest primarily for financial reasons, corporate venture funds invest primarily for strategic reasons. In exchange for cash, they seek an equity stake in the startup and access to its technology or product; in some instances, corporate venture investment leads to acquisition.

In 1999, corporate venture funds invested almost $8 billion in more than 900 companies in various stages of development; in 2000, investments in the third quarter alone topped $4 billion.[22] However, like all investors, corporations with venture funds grew more cautious with their money after the Nasdaq crash, and by late 2001, roughly 1 in 10 companies with corporate venture arms shut them down. As CFO.com's Joseph McCafferty put it, "The economic downturn has shown many companies just how risky their VC units truly are." Among the companies that decided that venture investment might be better left to pure venture-capital firms were Compaq and Commerce One.[23]

Criteria for Selection   The criteria used by a corporate venture fund to evaluate an investment opportunity depend on the strategic objectives of the firm. In addition to a solid business idea, qualified management team, and driven entrepreneur, investors look for a startup that bolsters the parent organization through complementary technologies, customer bases, distribution systems, or services.

Pros and Cons   Established corporations can offer both operational expertise and the credibility and visibility that come from associating with an established high-profile parent. Because the investments are strategic rather than financial, deals with corporations tend to favor the entrepreneur more than deals with venture-capital firms. Corporations are also more patient than venture-capital firms because they are more interested in the business and its products succeeding than immediate financial returns.

However, there are a number of challenges associated with working with a corporate venture fund. Large corporations tend to be slow to make investment decisions. Changes in the financial situation of the parent can affect the amount of money in the fund, and funding can be curtailed if revenue numbers need to be met. Corporate funding can also cause complications if the startup later needs to seek venture-capital funding. Also, conflicts of interest can arise if the startup develops technology that could compete with the parent firm's products.

Incubator

Incubators are organizations that nurture new companies through the startup phase, supporting fledgling businesses in exchange for a share of returns. In some instances, they also offer a small amount of seed capital, but primarily they aid startups through services. Incubators take care of many of the operational issues that typically plague startups; common incubator perks include free office space, technical infrastructure, coaching, and recruiting assistance. Reputable incubators also offer opportunities for networking, as well as pooled purchasing power with other portfolio companies. For-profit hatcheries typically take between 30 and 70 percent equity in the startups they incubate. The startup is expected to leave the incubator in two to three years, when it is financially viable.

Selection Criteria   Most incubators have established guidelines that determine the types of companies in which they might invest. They typically choose to incubate companies in one particular industry.

Drill-Down

Real-Life Funders

Venture-Capital Firm: Charles River Ventures

One of the top-rated venture-capital firms in the country, Waltham, Massachusetts–based Charles River Ventures has invested in more than 200 early-stage companies since its founding in 1970. Most of its investments are in the software and information-services sectors, but it has also funded businesses in the nonprofit sector, including medical foundations and universities. Charles River Ventures's average initial investment in a startup is $3 million, with typical lifelong company investments ranging from $10 million to $25 million. In May 2000, Charles River Ventures founded CRVelocity, a provider of incubator-type services such as recruiting, law advice, IT, and other operations services. It has invested in Excite, Sybase, Ciena, and Be Free. In 2001, the company closed 28 financing deals and also closed its 11th venture fund, worth $1.2 billion. In May 2002, though, it cut this fund to just $450 million.

Angel: Band of Angels

Formed in 1995, Band of Angels is a firm of angel investors. It consists of 150 former and current high-tech executives from companies such as Hewlett-Packard, Intel, and 3Com. Band of Angels invests in startups seeking seed-stage or early-round financing; the group meets each month to consider three startups that have been vetted by its members. The individual angels' diverse backgrounds means the group can provide entrepreneurs with expert advice and a diverse set of contacts, in addition to financial capital. As of January 2002, Band of Angels had invested nearly $100 million in 148 early-stage companies, including GlobalCast, NetBuy, and Wit Capital.

Corporate Venture: Intel Capital

In 1991, Intel founded Intel Capital primarily as an investment source for companies involved in chip manufacturing. In 1996, it began to diversify its investments into a range of companies, from content to technology to telecommunications. Intel Capital's investments are made in companies at all stages of development, both in the United States and internationally, ranging from $1 million to $10 million per transaction. In 2001, Intel Capital was the second most active venture investor in the United States, closing 72 deals. Past investments include CNet, Inktomi, Stamps.com, and Micron Technology.

Incubator: Cambridge Innovations

By the end of 2000, more than half of all incubators had either shut down or completely changed their business models. One of the survivors of the dot-com fallout was Cambridge, Massachusetts–based Cambridge Innovations, formerly Cambridge Incubator, which learned that incubators could not survive on equity stakes alone. Cambridge Innovations provides seed-stage startups with office space, recruiting support, product development advice, and network operations. After the Nasdaq crash, Cambridge Innovations began charging startups for these services in addition to receiving an equity stake. Since its founding in 1999, Cambridge Innovations has launched five startups: Veritas Medicine, Peoplestreet, BrandStamp, Job Rewards, and the nonprofit Secure Sponsorship.[24]

continued

Pros and Cons With incubators focusing on the mundane needs of the startup, entrepreneurs and employees are free to focus on developing their ideas into a business. Also, most incubators have established relationships with venture-capital firms as well as other categories of investors, and these connections can help startups gain access to later rounds of financing. One downside of incubators is the relatively high share of equity they take in a company. Because much of what an incubator gives is services, not money, incubated companies essentially give away more equity for less funding.[25]

> **Holding Company: Sand Hill Capital**
>
> In 1996, frustrated with the difficulty of lending to startups, William Del Biaggio cofounded Sand Hill Capital. He wanted Sand Hill to serve as a "venture lender," somewhat of a cross between a bank and a venture-capital firm. Like VC firms, it has a general partnership and limited partners and receives about 20 percent of profits and a 2 percent management fee from the companies to which it lends money. But, because it is not a charter bank, it is not subject to federal regulations. It makes most of its money from fees on loans and discounted warrants to buy stock in the companies to which it lends. The money for the loans is obtained through limited partners.
>
> Since the market downturn in April 2000, Sand Hill has focused on bridge loans— lending money to startups that need short-term cash to keep operations going while they seek additional funding. Sand Hill finds its investments from among the 20 venture-capital firms it works with; it reviews 40 to 50 deals and makes six to eight loans each month. To date, Sand Hill has offered loans or lines of credit to more than 125 companies, and it manages more than $200 million from multiple funds.

Holding Company

As with all equity sources, a holding company offers cash to a startup in exchange for equity. The distinction between a **holding company** and a venture-capital firm is the nature of the investment as defined by the U.S. Securities and Exchange Commission. Venture-capital firms have more of an investment focus, while holding companies have an operational focus. A holding company usually owns 25 to 50 percent of its portfolio company— often becoming the majority stakeholder—for an extended period of time.

Criteria for Selection Holding companies have criteria similar to those of other investors. They look at the quality of the idea, the business plan, the management team, and the entrepreneur. However, holding companies usually have a particular area of expertise that dictates the kinds of investments they select.

Pros and Cons Because holding companies are operational rather than financial investors, they are more patient with their capital than venture-capital firms, which expect returns in a specified timeframe. The startup can also benefit from the experience of the individuals running the holding company and from the experiences of other businesses in the portfolio. The biggest downside to receiving capital from a holding company is the substantial amount of equity taken by the holding company, which often results in a loss of control for the entrepreneur.

Hybrid Sources of Funding

The dot-com era brought attention not only to new types of business but also to new sources of funding. In truth, many sources of funding are a hybrid of the types just described. For example, although Andover, Massachusetts–based CMGI is, by definition, a holding company, it has occasionally acted as an incubator and also has a venture-capital arm, @Ventures. Many top-notch venture-capital firms, such as Softbank and Benchmark Capital, also provide incubating services; so do many corporate venture firms. Some equity financing sources also offer debt financing. Another example is a firm that is set up similar to venture-capital businesses but offers debt financing. (See the section on Sand Hill Capital in the Drill-Down, "Real-Life Funders.") As the financial needs of startups continue to evolve, other sources of hybrid financing are likely to develop.

Packaging Your Offering: Preparing the Pitch

The Business Plan

Once familiarized with his various funding options, the entrepreneur must then approach one or more of these sources with his business idea. To do so, he or she needs a **business plan**—basically, a few pages that succinctly summarize the vision and strategy of the business. The objective of the business plan is to pique the interest of investors. Like a résumé, it should make investors curious enough to want the entrepreneur to present the business plan in person. And, as with résumés, unsolicited business plans are largely ignored by investors; only networking on the part of the entrepreneur will get the business plan read.

When investors read a business plan, they are looking for a concise justification of the startup's business opportunity and its advantage over other players that are pursuing similar opportunities—and they want to find it within three or four minutes of reading. While the plan should be tailored according to its intended audience, the required elements of a business plan are more or less the same:

- Description of the product or service offered and the value it holds for the customer
- Summary of the size and nature of the market opportunity
- Explanation of the revenue model
- Profiles of members of the management team, advisory board, and board of directors (the first section most investors read)
- Clear articulation of the startup's core competencies and sustainable competitive advantage
- Summary of financials and financing needs

Visual presentation and writing style are also important elements of a business plan. Graphic design does not need to be complex, but it should be neat and clear. Straightforward writing ensures that it is the business, rather than the composition, that attracts attention. Honesty is also crucial. The plan can be enthusiastic, but investors are rightly skeptical of entrepreneurs who believe that they will easily conquer a new market with unprecedented returns. Unsubstantiated or exaggerated claims detract from the entire business plan and will most likely turn away investors.

The Pitch

With a solid business plan in hand, the entrepreneur should launch a campaign to reach her target investors. However, before embarking on this quest, the entrepreneur should decide on a reasonable timeframe to pursue funding sources (after which the business may fold or need to look for alternative means) and how much time she will devote to the process. Although it is essential for the entrepreneur to participate, she should not lose sight of running the business and making sure it moves forward while funding is being sought.

If interested in a particular business plan, the investor arranges an hour-long personal meeting with the entrepreneur to determine if the business is worth researching. At this point, the entrepreneur should prepare a concise PowerPoint presentation that summarizes the key aspects of the business, making sure to address competitive advantage and realistic estimates of return on investment. The presentation should not bore or confuse the investor, but provide enough information to interest him or her in another meeting. The second meeting usually runs at least two hours and should again involve a professional-quality presentation.

At both meetings, the entrepreneur should be prepared to answer difficult questions about her business plan, particularly questions about any proclaimed sustainable advantage that distinguishes the startup from other players and any assumptions made to determine return on investment. The entrepreneur also needs to play the role of salesperson and advocate for the business, but not in an overly aggressive fashion.

Know the Audience

Knowing what investors want helps the entrepreneur hone his pitch. Before ever approaching investors, the entrepreneur should know the following: What is the average deal size? Does the investor prefer to invest in early- or later-stage companies? What type of return do these investors normally seek? Are they hands-on investors, or do they prefer to keep a low profile, stepping in only when the company misses a predetermined milestone? How can the specific investor complement the company and management team? The answers to these questions will not only help customize the pitch but also help determine if the investor should even be a target.

Talk About the Management Team

Especially in an early-stage company, investors are as interested in the management team as the idea itself. They have to be convinced that the management team assembled will make the company successful. To accomplish this, the background of each of the key members of the team should be highlighted, focusing on how the team members complement one another and explaining how their experience is relevant to the industry in which the company will compete.

More often than not, the quest for cash results in rejection. However, these experiences help the entrepreneur learn what aspects of the business plan and pitch need to be tweaked for the next investor. If, on the other hand, the investors decide they are interested, they will most likely engage in some form of due diligence, depending on the type of funding source and the resources available. **Due diligence** is a careful process on the part of the investor to check on the validity of the business plan and the expertise of any individuals involved. References are checked, management team individuals interviewed, and business ideas tested. Potential customers may be interviewed about the likelihood of purchasing or using the product or service. If and when investors are satisfied with what they find, they will agree to fund the business enterprise. However, nothing is final until the documents are signed and the cash is in the bank, and this comes only after a valuation for the firm is determined.

Drill-Down

When Going Online, Sometimes Established Companies Act Like Startups

It's not just startups that must scramble for managers and money to launch their e-business initiatives. Bricks-and-mortar businesses often need to be aware of management teams and sources of capital as well.

Take Wal-Mart. When the world's largest retailer decided to venture into cyberspace in 1996, it bankrolled and ran the venture entirely in-house. (It was the first major discount chain to set up an e-commerce website.) But a series of problems—from disappointing traffic to poor design to inconsistent fulfillment—forced Wal-Mart to rethink its strategy.

The result, announced in early 2000, was the recasting of Walmart.com as a "carve-out," or a separate company that, though closely allied with the corporate parent, would function much like an Internet startup—right down to its Silicon Valley locale, a long way both geographically and culturally from Wal-Mart's Bentonville, Arkansas, headquarters. And, just like any fledgling dot-com in search of money and expertise, Wal-Mart made the rounds of venture capitalists. Its choice was Accel Partners, a well-connected Valley firm that agreed to a joint partnership with Wal-Mart, taking a 20 percent equity stake in the new company. (The amount of Accel's investment in Walmart.com was not disclosed; Wal-Mart itself was believed to have kicked in $100 million.) The joint venture's board included Wal-Mart's chairman, its CEO, and one of Accel's managing partners.

Even more valuable to Wal-Mart than Accel's cash was its cachet: its knowledge of and connections in a high-tech, dot-com world that was largely new and strange to the big-box discounter. Particularly attractive was Accel's ability to attract and retain top-drawer talent—the kind of people who would rather work at a nimble 180-person startup (and gamble on its then-promising prospect for lucrative stock options) than an old-school corporate behemoth. Indeed, Accel persuaded e-commerce veteran Jeanne Jackson to leave her post overseeing online initiatives for Gap, Banana Republic, and Old Navy to become CEO of Walmart.com.

Jackson set about assembling a retail- and tech-savvy management team; among the perks she could dangle in front of candidates was an equity stake in the new company. The site was relaunched in the fall of 2000.

Did Wal-Mart's carve-out strategy pay off? Yes and no. Website traffic and sales did improve. But the dot-com crash and fading hopes for a big IPO prompted both Wal-Mart and Accel to reconsider their joint venture. In July 2001, Wal-Mart announced it was buying out Accel's minority interest in Walmart.com, ending the fledgling company's independent run. It was folded back into the corporation as a Wal-Mart business unit.

Valuation

Valuation is the act of trying to determine a company's worth, and it is as much an art as it is a science. The goal of valuation is to determine a reasonable range of values for the company as a starting point in negotiations. Many methods can be used to value a company, and each may produce a different result. We do not attempt to discuss all of the intricacies of valuation in this chapter; indeed, that would take several books. Rather, we quickly describe the most commonly used methods of valuing a company and point out the strengths and weaknesses inherent to each technique. The three most common methods for determining the value of a startup company are the comparables method, the financial performance method, and the venture-capital method.

The Comparables Method

The **comparables method** of valuation estimates a company's value by comparing it with similar companies, both private and public. The comparison companies should be similar to the startup in as many respects as possible, but especially in the following areas: industry, customer base, income statement ratios, relationship with suppliers, growth rate, and capital structure (the percentage of debt and equity in the company). Obviously, no two companies will be identical, but it is the management team's job to look for the best matches, find out the valuations, and then intelligently adjust those valuations to calculate the value of its company.

One of the weaknesses of the comparables method is that it can be extremely difficult to gain information on private companies, which are more likely to resemble the startup than a public company. Whenever a public company is used as a basis for comparison, the amount of the valuation must be discounted to compensate for illiquidity. The startup's shares are not traded publicly yet (they are "illiquid") and, therefore, are worth less than shares that can be sold easily in the public market—normally, 25 to 30 percent less.[26] So if a public company is worth $10 million, the startup might be valued at only $7.5 million, even if the two companies are identical. Also, a public company has a different capital structure, and adjustments have to be made for this as well.

Generally, the comparables method values comparison companies by looking at their basic accounting ratios, including the price-to-earnings, or P/E, ratio (the relationship between the company's trading price and its earnings), market-to-book ratio (the market value of the company's equity divided by the book value of shareholders' equity), and EBIT (earnings before interest and taxes). However, accounting metrics are not as useful when attempting to value an early-stage company, because the company has not yet posted a profit and is experiencing rapid growth. For an e-commerce company, it makes sense to look for other points of comparison. For instance, what are the key drivers of success in the startup's industry: Conversion rate? Number of registered users? Relationship with suppliers? Whatever the key metrics are, they should be the measurements used when attempting to create a valuation based on comparables.

The Financial Performance Method

The **financial performance method** of valuation uses projections of future cash flows to estimate what a company is worth today, or its "present value." A company's present value is determined by first figuring out what sort of cash flows the company is expected to generate in the future, then applying a "discount rate" to those cash flows. A discount rate does just what it says: It discounts future earnings to determine an appropriate present value for those earnings. The discount rate reflects the risk of the returns. Because a company can only make an educated guess about what it will be making in five years, a good deal of risk and uncertainty are inherent in the calculation of future cash flows. That risk and uncertainty are factored into the valuation by applying a discount rate. The higher the discount rate, the lower the present value of the earnings and, thus, the lower the present value of the company.

Most discounted cash flow analyses are projected for at least a five-year period, roughly corresponding to the projected date of a liquidity event such as an IPO or a merger. To figure out a company's discounted cash flow, three projections must be made: pro forma income, free cash flow, and terminal value.

Pro Forma Income Statement

The first step is to estimate the company's expected profit over the next five years, also known as preparing a pro forma income statement. To make this estimate, two factors need to be considered: (1) the revenue that the company expects to generate, and (2) the expenses the company will incur while doing so. Projections are based on these cost/revenue growth assumptions, as well as the growth rates of similar companies in the same industry. If no similar companies or products exist, growth rates are based on the foreseeable market in which the company will play and the size of the market that the company expects to own (which will result in projections for sales figures). Above all, assumptions must be made explicit; they will serve as the basis for negotiations with the financier.

Drill-Down

Present Value

The concept of present value can seem complex, but it is really simple. Essentially, cash today is worth more than cash tomorrow. For instance, if someone were offered $50 today in exchange for paying $100 five years from now, should they take the deal? First, they would have to determine an appropriate rate of return on their money (how much could they get for the $50 over five years if they invested it?) and perform a present-value calculation. Assume that someone determined that they could invest the $50 and receive a compounded return of 15 percent over five years. They would take the $100 and divide it by the total of 1 plus the rate of return, raised to the power of the number of years over which they would invest, to determine what that $100 is worth today:

$$100/(1.15^5) = \$49.71$$

In this case, the $100 that they would have to pay out in five years is only equal to $49.71 today. So they should take the offer, because the $50 is "worth" more than the present value of the $100. In other words, the offer has a positive NPV.

Free Cash Flow

Once the company's future income has been calculated, the next step is to determine how much of that income will be converted into actual cash profits, or free cash flow. Free cash flow can be determined by applying a relatively simple formula:

$$
\begin{array}{ll}
 & \text{EBIAT (earnings before interest but after taxes)} \\
+ & \text{Depreciation} \\
- & \text{Change in operating working capital} \\
- & \text{Capital expenditures} \\
\hline
= & \text{Free cash flow}
\end{array}
$$

Terminal Value

The third step in calculating the company's discounted cash flow is to arrive at a terminal value (sometimes called a "residual" or "continuing" value) for the company. The terminal value is the expected value of the company at the end of the projected period (usually three to five years). Essentially, it is the likely selling price for the company at the time of a liquidity event.

Using free cash flow in the last year of the projection as a starting point, an assumption must be made about the terminal growth rate: If the company were to continue to grow forever, at what rate would it grow? A good rule of thumb is to use 3 percent as a terminal growth rate. In this case, the terminal value is equal to the free cash flow in the last year of the projection, divided by the total of the discount rate used minus the terminal growth rate.

Once these steps are complete, the entrepreneur has all of the information needed to calculate the company's value.

The Venture-Capital Method

When venture-capital firms calculate the value of a company, they rarely use the methods just described. Rather, they use somewhat of a hybrid method, looking at both comparables and future free cash flows. Essentially, the **venture-capital method** sets a terminal value for a potential investment by (1) multiplying the P/E ratio (market price per share divided by earnings per share) by the earnings in the last year of the projection and then discounting the resulting terminal value to the present using a very high discount rate, or (2) using the terminal-value technique just described, but with a much larger discount rate. The discount rate that venture capitalists use in valuations depends on what rate of return they desire on their investments. While the most desirable rate of return varies, most VC firms are looking for companies that will multiply their investment by either 5 times in three years or 10 times in five years.[27]

The discount rates applied by venture capitalists are very high—they typically range from 30 to 70 percent—and vary according to a host of factors, including the development stage of the company, the industry in which the company plans to operate, and the profile of the management team. Early-stage companies are extremely difficult to value because there are so many variables to consider and the value of the company can take a sudden downturn.

To try to compensate for some of this increased risk, a venture capitalist applies an enormous discount rate to the terminal value of an early-stage company to determine its present value (see Exhibit 11.7).

Startup	50% to 70%
First Stage	40% to 60%
Second Stage	35% to 50%
Third Stage	30% to 50%
Fourth Stage	30% to 40%
IPO	25% to 35%

Source: Data from James L. Plummer, *QED Report on Venture Capital Financial Analysis* (QED Research, Palo Alto, CA), 1987

EXHIBIT 11.7   Typical Discount Rates by Funding Stage

Consider an example. Say that a company is projecting that its earnings will be $20 million in five years. Similar companies are trading at 10 times earnings, so the terminal value for the company is calculated to be $200 million ($20 million $\times$ 10). Because the company is a startup, the VC decides he should use a 60 percent discount rate on the terminal value to calculate the present value. The discounted terminal value equals the terminal value in year five divided by 1 plus the discount rate (which is also the VC's target rate of return on the investment) raised to the power of the year of the projection. In this case, the discounted terminal value equals $200 million$/(1 + 60\%)^5$, which in turn equals $19 million.

Now say that the VC plans on investing $5 million. The required percent ownership for this investment would be 26 percent (the $5 million investment divided by the $19 million value of the company). However, the 26 percent ownership stake that the VC demands now only yields the target rate of return (60 percent) if the company does not raise any more money. If the company does participate in future rounds of financing, which it almost certainly will, the VC will demand a higher percentage of ownership to compensate for the dilutive effect of future financing rounds.

The valuations produced by the preceding methods, however mathematical, are necessarily subjective. Changing the underlying assumptions in any method changes the company's valuation. The smart entrepreneur will develop several valuations based upon best-case, worst-case, and average scenarios, and use these valuations to assess the range of possible values for the company. Keep in mind, however, that if a company is truly in its early stage, the numbers and the projections are not going to be very important to a venture capitalist because these numbers simply cannot be trusted. There are too many variables in the model for it to be reliable.

Negotiations

Term Sheet

If the pitch is successful, the parties will produce a **term sheet**—a nonbinding description of the proposed deal between the funder and the entrepreneur. In his book *The Fundamentals of Venture Capital*, Joseph Bartlett writes, "The term sheet is analogous to a letter of intent, a nonbinding outline of the principal points that the stock purchase agreement and related agreements will cover in detail."[28] Term sheets are fairly short documents that can be produced quickly and provide both parties with a baseline to begin further negotiations.

First and foremost, the term sheet states the amount of money the investor is offering and the type of security that will be used in the transaction. Essentially, a **security** is an IOU from the company to the investor and offers investors a share of ownership. The security chosen by the company and the investor will reflect the risk/reward appetite of each. The basic types of securities that investors might choose include the following:

- *Zero coupon bonds.* These securities afford investors the most protection. Upon maturity, the investor redeems the initial investment, as well as predetermined interest on that investment. Also attached to zero coupon bonds are warrants—a form of stock option that gives the investor the right to purchase future shares at a fixed price.

- *Convertible debentures.* Investors ask for this type of security if the company is perceived to be extremely risky. Convertible debentures are loans that can be converted into equity. The investor is considered to be a creditor until the company is past its risky stage; if the company goes bankrupt, the investor is paid before other stockholders. The convertible debentures are "converted" (thus the name) into common stock based on the conversion rights associated with the security.

- *Preferred stock.* This is the security most commonly used in a transaction with a venture capitalist. The three common forms of preferred stock are *convertible preferred*, in which the shareholder has the right to convert his or her shares into common stock; *redeemable preferred*, in which the investor receives the face value of the stock, plus a dividend; and *participating convertible preferred*, which, for investors, is the most prized. Participating convertible preferred is also known as "double dipping" because investors not only get their original investment back (as in the case of redeemable preferred) but also get to convert their securities into common stock (as is the case with convertible preferred) to share in the company's upside. VC firms use common stock to structure a deal only in rare circumstances because this security does not provide investors with any of the protections of the other securities.

The term sheet also includes a list of the rights, preferences, and privileges that the investor wishes to be granted. Investors can demand a range of rights and privileges designed to safeguard their money and establish the level of control they wish to have in the company, and all of them are spelled out in the term sheet. Some of the most common rights and privileges that investors ask for are listed here:

- *Right of first refusal.* First-refusal rights give investors the opportunity, but not the obligation, to invest in future financing rounds. They tend to be favorable to investors and unfavorable to the companies they invest in because they do not guarantee the company any additional funding and increase the investor's ability to gain further ownership and control of the company.

- *Preemptive rights.* Preemptive rights require that company shares be offered to current shareholders before they are offered to outside investors.

- *Redemption rights.* These give the investor the right to achieve liquidity if the company has not been sold or undergone a public offering within a predetermined time period. Upon redemption, the investor generally receives the original investment plus any dividends that have accrued.

- *Registration rights.* Registered shares can be freely traded on the market, whereas unregistered shares cannot. Investors with registration rights will have their shares registered automatically any time the venture registers its shares. Demand registration rights give the investor the power to force the registration of shares, thereby forcing the company into a liquidity event.

- *Covenants.* There are both affirmative and negative covenants, and both are designed to make sure that the money provided by the investor is used in a manner that is consistent with the agreement between the investor and the company. Affirmative covenants are actions that the entrepreneur promises to take in exchange for the investment, such as maintaining certain financial ratios and sending financial statements to investors at predetermined times. Negative covenants are actions that the entrepreneur promises not to take without consent of the investor, such as changing the nature of the business or altering the company's compensation structure.

- *Antidilution provisions.* Of all of these rights, antidilution provisions can be the most vexing to the entrepreneur. Antidilution provisions protect the investor—but not the entrepreneur—from the weakening effects of the sale of lower-priced company stock by granting him or her additional equity in a company without additional cost. If the company is forced to raise additional funds by issuing new shares at the same or a lower valuation, not only would the investor's percentage ownership of the company decrease, but the value of that percentage ownership would decrease as well. Clearly, a wise investor wants protection from this type of dilution.

Keep in mind that having a term sheet does not mean that a deal is imminent. Investors will still be conducting due diligence even after the term sheet is signed, and since it is nonbinding, they can pull out if they uncover something that they find unacceptable, or if the two parties fail to reach a compromise.

Stages of Investment

A venture capitalist will invest in stages, rather than giving the entrepreneur all of the necessary cash up front. This is because an investor wants to give a little bit of cash, see how the company does, and then invest more if the company performs well. By staging the investments, the investor retains his "option to abandon" the investment if the company does not perform up to expectations. The investor may decide not to invest any additional funds in the company, or might invest additional funds but only at a renegotiated, lower company valuation.

Venture capitalists look at their investments in terms of pre- and postmoney valuations. A **premoney valuation** is the value that the investor puts on the company before his investment, and a **postmoney valuation** is the premoney valuation plus the amount of the investor's contribution. For example, if a company is determined to be worth $3 million immediately before an investor puts in $2 million, the premoney valuation is $3 million and the postmoney valuation is $5 million.

At each round of financing, the entrepreneur must give up a percentage of equity in the company to the investor in exchange for the cash investment, thereby diluting his ownership share of the company. Exhibit 11.8 illustrates this dilution process. The entrepreneur starts with 100 percent of the company. After the first round, the entrepreneur's 60 percent stake is worth $1.5 million (60 percent of the postmoney valuation). After the third round of financing, the entrepreneur owns only 38 percent of the company, but his stake is worth $28.5 million (38 percent of the postmoney valuation). Even though the entrepreneur's stake has been diluted on a percentage basis, its worth has still increased. Remember that at every stage, the entrepreneur has to renegotiate the company's valuation with the investors, and the higher the valuation of the company, the more the diluted percentage of ownership is worth.

Round of Financing	Amount Invested This Round	% Received This Round	Cumulative		Implied Valuation (Postmoney)
			VC's Share	Founder's Share	
Seed Round	$1,000,000	40%	40%	60%	$2,500,000
First Round	$4,000,000	20%	52%	48%	$20,000,000
Second Round	$15,000,000	20%	62%	38%	$75,000,000

EXHIBIT 11.8   Pre- and Postmoney Valuations Made Easy

Exit (The Path to Liquidity)

After an entrepreneur secures the funding to finance the growth of his business, the next step is to have some sort of liquidity event through which he, his employees, and the company's outside financiers will see a return on their investment. Normally, venture capitalists expect a liquidity event in three to five years. While there are many ways to obtain liquidity—including management buyouts, which normally take place in later-stage companies, and selling equity to an employee stock option plan—we focus on the two liquidity events most common for e-commerce companies: initial public offerings (IPOs) and mergers and acquisitions (M&A).

The Initial Public Offering

Initial public offerings (IPOs) received much attention during the dot-com boom, as entrepreneurs took their companies to market to tap into the vast wealth of a new shareholder: the public. Venture capitalists who backed these companies were ecstatic; investment bankers were desperate to get in on the hottest deals; and the public swallowed up shares at an alarming rate—never mind that most of these companies posted no profits and had no plans to be profitable in the near future. It seemed as if the market for IPOs would exist forever and that if a company could go public, then by all means it should. Then the walls came crashing down, and the market experienced a correction.

As of mid-2002, the public has not regained its once voracious appetite for Internet-related offerings. In the first quarter of 2002, only four companies completed IPOs, raising $345.3 million.[29] Compare that with the 70 IPOs and $6.6 billion raised during the third quarter of 2000.[30] Exhibit 11.9 shows the drop in venture-backed IPOs from 2000 to 2001.

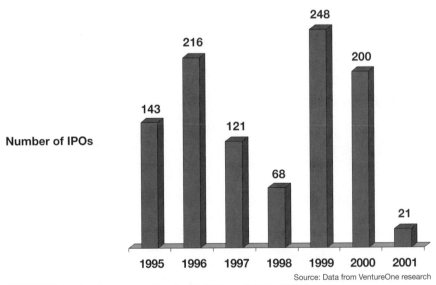

Source: Data from VentureOne research

EXHIBIT 11.9   Venture-Backed IPOs, 1995–2001

An **initial public offering** is the sale of shares of a company that has never before been traded on a public stock exchange. It is a way of tapping the greater public for investment dollars when either (1) the original investors are pushing toward a liquidity event or (2) the company is about to experience rapid growth and needs more money than the original investors or new investors are willing to provide. However, before rushing headlong into an IPO, the entrepreneur and management team must decide if their company is a good candidate for a public offering. In order to do so, they need to understand the positives and negatives of becoming a public company (see Exhibit 11.10) as well as how the IPO process works.

Pro	Con
Provides founders and shareholders with liquidity (although not immediate liquidity because of lock out periods, signals to the market, etc.)	IPOs are expensive and time-consuming; an unfavorable market (something that the company cannot control or predict) might necessitate pulling the IPO at the last second
Provides capital to fuel expansion and growth within the company	Strict SEC reporting requirements
Possibility of attracting and retaining employees at lower-than-market rates because of granting of stock options and promise of eventual liquidity	Pressure to produce quarterly numbers for analysts
The price of the company's shares should increase dramatically with an IPO, providing (at least on paper) wealth to the founders and other shareholders	Increased officer and director liability
As long as the company is performing well, it can return to the market to raise additional cash	Hostile takeover is possible
The ability to use stock as currency	Doesn't necessarily provide a liquid market for all shareholders because of restrictions on trading the stock

EXHIBIT 11.10   IPO Pros and Cons

The IPO Process

Will there be a better valuation from the public markets if the company waits for a year? Does the company need cash right now to fuel the expansion needed to crush its nearest competitor? Should the company wait until it has launched its next killer product? These are important questions that the CEO and board need to ask and answer when assessing whether the timing is right for an IPO. If the timing is right both internally and externally, the company enters into the 10- to 14-week process necessary to complete an IPO. There are seven major steps in the IPO process, all of which have many components.[31]

Selection of the Underwriters

This is one of the most important decisions of the IPO process. The underwriters are investment bankers who arrange the purchase of stock for a commission. The underwriters are responsible not only for taking a company public but also for making sure that, once public, the company has the analyst coverage it needs to receive favorable attention from the market.

Many entrepreneurs actually ask investment bankers to compete for the chance to take their company public. In this competition, often referred to as a "bake-off" or "beauty contest," each prepares an evaluation of the company and explains why they would be best suited to become the lead underwriter. In most cases, the lead underwriter works with one or more additional investment banks in a syndicate to spread risk and increase sales and distribution capabilities. When choosing an underwriter, companies should ask the following questions:

1. *Will this investment bank give a firm commitment to sell the newly issued securities, or will it just employ a "best efforts" approach?* A firm commitment means that the investment bank will actually buy the securities from a company and then make its money by reselling them. "Best efforts" means that the investment bank will try to sell all of the securities, but if it does not, the company has no recourse.

2. *Does the investment bank have the ability to syndicate with other top banks?*

3. *What kind of analyst coverage will the company have after it is public, and which investment bank has the best analyst in the company's field?* When the management team chooses an investment bank, it also chooses an analyst—the person who will be most responsible for providing coverage to the firm long after it has become public and the investment bank has forgotten its name.

4. *Has the investment bank worked with other companies in that industry, and what were the results?* The investment bank will be largely responsible for explaining the company's fundamentals to potential investors and convincing these investors that a company has the right business model, technology, and management team to succeed in the marketplace.

5. *What is the investment bank's reputation?* The management team needs to know the bank's strengths and weaknesses, as well as how it is perceived by the investment community.

6. *Do I like this bank?* If all other things are equal, the management team should ask itself whether it likes the people it will be working with. After all, the team is going to have to work closely with the bank for several months.

Preparation of the Registration Statement for the SEC

The next step is to register the startup with the Securities and Exchange Commission. As part of preparing the registration statement, the company must write a prospectus, which is a document that outlines the company's business and financial fundamentals. It is extremely important that the prospectus is truthful and accurate; directors, managers, and underwriters are liable for any errors in the prospectus and are usually named as defendants in any lawsuits that might ensue. The company submits its preliminary prospectus to the SEC for review at the same time that it distributes the preliminary prospectus to its underwriters, who can then pass it on to potential investors.

The preliminary prospectus is also known as the **red herring** because of the red marks on the front of the prospectus warning investors that it has not yet been approved by the SEC. Every prospectus contains the following main sections:

- *Box summary.* The box summary is a one-page summary of the offering, which includes a description of the business and an overview of the most recent financials.

- *Risk factors.* This section lists all of the possible challenges and risks that the company may face. All risks, even outside market risks that the company cannot control, are listed. This section is meant to make every potential risk explicit to the investor and can protect the company from lawsuits.

- *Use of proceeds.* This section describes how the company plans to use the money raised by the IPO.

- *Management's discussion and analysis of financial conditions and results of operations.* This section includes an analysis of the financial state of the company for the past three years on an annual and period-to-period basis. All material changes in the company's statements must be discussed and explained.

- *Business.* This is a description of the business that addresses its strategies, goals, R&D, marketing, and anything else that is material to the business. The company must make sure that this section clearly states all of the threats that could hinder its success, while still showing the company in a favorable light.

- *Management.* This section describes the key members of the management team.

- *Audited financial statements.* These statements include income statements from the last three years and balance sheets from the last two.

Distribution of the Preliminary Prospectus

After the prospectus has been written and the registration statement has been filed, the red herring is distributed to potential investors by the underwriters chosen to represent the company. With any luck, the red herring drums up interest among investors.

The Road Show

The road show is when a company presents its offering directly to potential investors, and it is one of the most time-consuming activities of the IPO process. It usually lasts for two or three weeks, involves traveling from city to city, and demands a huge time commitment from top managers. This is a critical opportunity for management team members to present themselves to investors. No matter how adept the chosen underwriters are, many potential investors want to meet and feel comfortable with the management team before they invest. The only material that can be presented during the road show is material from the red herring, and the red herring is the only document that can be distributed to potential investors.

Incorporation of Comments from the SEC into the Registration Statement

While the road show is occurring, the SEC reviews the red herring. If the underwriters have timed the event well, the company should receive comments from the SEC as the road show is entering its final stages. Once the SEC's comments have been received, they must be incorporated into the red herring. These "pre-effective" amendments address any issues flagged by the SEC and should be filed within a week of receiving the SEC comments. If the

SEC is satisfied with the pre-effective amendments, the company then files an acceleration request to make the registration statement effective. Once the SEC has declared the registration effective, the company is allowed to trade its shares on the stock market.

Agreement on a Final Share Price and Number of Shares for the Offering

The company and the underwriters must agree on the number of shares to offer to the public, as well as the price per share. The share price, typically set between $10 and $20, is determined by previous valuation discussions between management and the underwriters, but it could be adjusted before the offering depending on market conditions, the success of the road show, and myriad other external factors. This final negotiation typically takes place the night before trading commences.

Close of the Offering and Distribution of the Final Prospectus

The close of the offering normally takes place three days after trading has begun. Closing involves delivering the stock certificates to investors and receiving the funds from the offering.

Mergers and Acquisitions

If an IPO is not the right path for a company, there are certainly other options. One of the easiest routes to quick growth is to buy the assets of, or combine assets with, another company. Mergers and acquisitions can accomplish the same goals as an IPO—namely, liquidity and increased valuation—but with less risk. The major difference between a merger and an acquisition boils down to who is in control of the resulting company. In a merger, two companies combine to achieve a financial and/or strategic objective, usually through an exchange of shares. In an acquisition, one company buys another, usually with cash and/or stock. In certain industries or markets where only a few public companies can be supported, companies can often achieve 80 percent of an IPO valuation by being acquired.[32]

While mergers and acquisitions might be logical approaches to growth, the process is far from easy. Entrepreneurs must consider the potential downside of combining with another company, including the structure of the deal and the often-overlooked cultural disconnects. Also, the dot-com fallout had a profound effect on the M&A market. During the boom, buyers snatched up e-commerce companies at a frenzied pace. Since the market crash, the pace—and profitability—of mergers and acquisitions have declined. By 2002, deals were still being signed in large numbers, but the amount of money exchanged during those deals was considerably less than it had been. In early 2001, the average deal size was $32 million. In early 2002, it had shrunk to $17 million.[33] Exhibit 11.11 shows the total amounts of merger and acquisition deals in 2001. More than half of that spending was on Internet infrastructure companies, with traditional technology companies stocking up on tools and software. As one Webmergers.com report put it, "The dot-com boom was a veritable Manhattan Project of infrastructure development that left an array of valuable tools in its wake. Far-sighted acquirers are snapping up this technology at bargain prices to create a new and more profound second wave of Internet applications."[34]

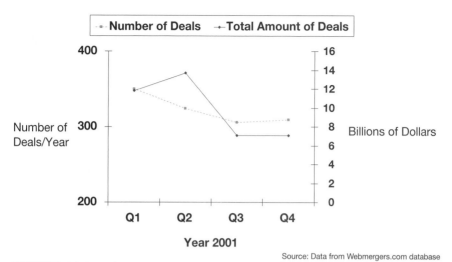

EXHIBIT 11.11   Internet Mergers and Acquisitions in 2001

Source: Data from Webmergers.com database

1. What is a startup?

A startup is a business in the process of developing the underlying infrastructures needed to sustain future growth, specifically (a) developing and refining its offering and strategy to go to market, (b) obtaining initial funding to begin operations, and (c) building a capable management team to handle operations.

2. What are the different sources of human capital that can play a role in a startup business?

There are four key sources of human capital that can play a critical role in building an early-stage business: (a) the entrepreneur with the idea who begins the business; (b) the management team that transforms the entrepreneur's idea into an operational reality; (c) the strategic advisers and partners who provide direction, advice, and strategic advantage through their own experiences; and (d) the logistical advisers and partners, consisting of individuals and organizations that can fill missing skill sets within the nascent startup. Each plays a role in developing the business plan and/or attracting financial capital.

3. What are the typical sources of funding for early-stage startup businesses?

The most typical sources of debt financing for startup businesses are trade credit and commercial bank loans. On the equity side, bootstrapping, angels, incubators, venture-capital firms, corporate ventures, and holding companies are the most common sources of financing.

4. What elements are needed for a successful pitch to investors?

A successful pitch requires a solid business plan based on reality, but even more important, it requires that the entrepreneur make the right contacts in the industry so that his business plan is read. The business plan should be brief, with a short and compelling executive summary. The pitch itself should be concise and clear, and it should convey the business's sustainable competitive advantage and financing needs, piquing the investor's interest in further meetings. Both the business plan and the pitch should be truthful and honest, so as not to cloud the message and mission of the startup.

5. How is the value of a startup determined?

The major methods of determining valuation for a startup are the comparables method, the financial performance method, and the venture-capital method. The comparables method requires a startup to find companies that are comparable to it and use them as the basis from which to extrapolate its own value. The financial performance method uses a company's earnings to project future cash flows and then applies a discount rate to determine the present value. The venture-capital method values a company by determining the terminal value (usually by looking at comparables) and then applying a larger discounted rate to the terminal value than the free cash flow method.

6. What are the factors involved in negotiating with investors?

When negotiations begin, the startup's management team and the investors must agree upon the terms. Those terms include the amount being invested, the valuation of the company, the type of security they will use in the transaction, the rights and privileges that the investors will have, and the antidilution provisions for the investors. The basic types of securities include zero coupon bonds, convertible debentures, preferred stock, and common stock. The rights of the investors include right of first refusal, preemptive right, redemption right, registration right, covenants, and antidilution provisions.

7. What is an initial public offering? What process must an entrepreneur undertake to successfully complete an IPO?

An IPO is the public sale of shares of a company that has never been traded on a public stock exchange. To complete an IPO, the company must choose underwriters, prepare the registration statement for the SEC, distribute the preliminary prospectus, prepare for and complete the road show, incorporate the comments from the SEC into the registration statement, agree on a final share price and number of shares for the offering, and close the offering and distribute the final prospectus.

Exercises

1. Go to your favorite website. Think about what the business plan for the company would have looked like and answer the following questions: What is the value proposition? What is the market opportunity? How does the company reach customers? How does it implement its strategy? What are the external influences that act on the business? How does the company generate revenue? What kind of people need to be hired to make the business plan work? What would the milestones have been? What is the advantage? Now, think of your own online business idea. Answer the same questions.

2. Go to *www.pwcmoneytree.com*. Find the PricewaterhouseCoopers/Venture Economics/National Venture Capital Association MoneyTree Survey for the most recent quarter. Compare the amount of venture capital invested for that quarter versus that quarter the year before. Compare both total amounts and amounts by stage of development. Has there been an increase or decrease from the previous year? Has more venture-capital money gone to startups or later-stage companies?

3. In the above survey, look at the most active venture investors. Who were the top five? Look up one of the investor companies on Hoovers (*www.hoovers.com*). What industries does it concentrate in? How much money does it invest? Look at one of its competitors. How are they different?

Key Terms

startup	angels	venture-capital method
human capital	corporate ventures	term sheet
financial capital	incubator	security
debt financing	holding company	premoney valuation
trade credit	business plan	postmoney valuation
commercial bank loan	due diligence	initial public offering
equity financing	valuation	red herring
bootstrapping	comparables method	
venture capital	financial performance method	

[1]"Start-up," *Merriam-Webster Online: Collegiate Dictionary* (URL: http://www.m-w.com/cgi-bin/dictionary?va=start-up).

[2]John L. Nesheim, *High Tech Start Up* (New York: Free Press, 2000), 8.

[3]William A. Sahlman, "Some Thoughts on Business Plans," Note no. 9-897-101 (Boston: Harvard Business School Publishing, 1996).

[4]Lesley Hazelton, "Profile: Jeff Bezos," *Success* (July 1998), 60.

[5]Joseph H. Boyett and Jimmie T. Boyett, *The Guru Guide to Entrepreneurship* (New York: John Wiley & Sons, 2001).

[6]Daniel Akst, "Mirabilis Dictu," *Industry Standard*, 17 January 2000.

[7]Steve Hamm, "The Education of Marc Andreessen," *BusinessWeek*, Industrial/Technology Ed., 13 April 1998, 92.

[8]"Venture Capital and Angels Provide Just Over 7% of Funding for Private Companies," *Business Wire*, 23 April 1999.

[9]"Q&A Archive: What Is Bootstrapping," *Garage Technology Ventures* (URL: http://www.garage.com/forums/commercialBanking/qandaArchive.shtml#Q7).

[10]"Venture Capital and Angels Provide Just Over 7% of Funding for Private Companies."

[11]"Venture Capital," *American Express Small Business Network: Finding Money* (URL: http://home3.americanexpress.com/smallbusiness/resources/expanding/financing/venture_cap.shtml).

[12]Nesheim, *High Tech Start Up.*

[13]"Venture Capital Backed Companies Raise $35 Billion in 2001," *VentureWire*, Press Release, 21 December 2001 (URL: http://www.venturewire.com/release.asp?rid=MJJQILKOJI); and Penelope Patsuris, "There's Still Too Much Venture Investing," *Forbes.com*, 4 February 2002. (URL: http://www.forbes.com/2002/02/04/0204vc.html).

[14]*MoneyTree Survey: Full Year & Q4 2001 Results: US Report*, PricewaterhouseCoopers LLP (URL: http://www.pwcmoneytree.com/PDFS/MT_Q4_01_Report.pdf).

[15]Tamar Zemel, "Sea-Change in Venture Capital Investment Allocation," *VentureOne*, Press Release, 19 March 2002.

[16]For further information see: U.S. Small Business Association (URL: http://www.sbaonline.sba.gov) and National Association of Small Business Investment Companies (URL: http://www.nasbic.com).

[17]Jeffrey D. Nuechterlein, "International Venture Capital: The Role of Startup Financing in the United States, Europe and Asia," *Global Venture Investors Association: Global Venture Capital Overview* (URL: http://www.gvia.org/gvia_vc_outlook.doc). Reprinted from Nuechterlein, "International Venture Capital," in Patrick J. DeSouza, ed., *Economic Strategy and National Security: A Next Generation Approach* (Boulder, CO: Westview Press, 2000).

[18]Stephani Gates, "Angels Are, Increasingly, Among Us," *Red Herring*, 17 June 1999.

[19]Center for Venture Research at the University of New Hampshire.

[20]Tom Ehrenfeld. "The Angel's Share," *Industry Standard*, 19 June 2000.

[21]Lawrence Aragon, "Bankrolled by an Angel: Part 2," *Red Herring*, 18 December 1999 (URL: http://www.redherring.com/insider/1999/1218/vc-vcps.html).

[22]Jonathan Rabinovitz, "Venture Capital, Inc," *Industry Standard*, 10 April 2000.

[23]Joseph McCafferty, "Corporate Venture Capital in Decline," *CFO.com*, 26 November 2001 (URL: http://www.cfo.com/article/1,5309,5888,00.html).

[24]Lawrence Aragon, "Getting into Debt," *Red Herring*, 17 January, 2001.

[25]"Incubator FAQs," *American Express Small Business Network: Articles and Tools—Starting a Business* (URL: http://home3.americanexpress.com/smallbusiness/tool/dotcom/faqs.asp).

[26]Shannon P. Pratt et al., *Valuing a Business: The Analysis and Appraisal of Closely-Held Companies*, 3rd ed. (Chicago: Irwin Professional Publishers, 1996).

[27]Mark Cameron White, "Business Valuation Techniques and Negotiation," *White and Lee LP*, 2000 (URL: http://www.whiteandlee.com/papers_transactions_bvtn.html).

[28]Joseph W. Bartlett, *The Fundamentals of Venture Capital* (New York: Madison Books, 1999).

[29]Tamar Zemel, "Venture-Backed Liquidity Market Continues Decline in 1Q," *VentureOne*, Press Release, 2 April 2002 (URL: http://www.ventureone.com/ii/liquidity1Q02.pdf).

[30]Tamar Zemel, "Venture-Backed IPOs Scarce in 4Q'00," *VentureOne*, Press Release, 8 January 2001 (URL: http://www.ventureone.com/press/4Q00Liquidity.pdf).

[31]On the process of going public we are deeply indebted to the outline provided in William A. Sahlman, Howard H. Stevenson, Michael J. Roberts, and Amar V. Bhide, eds., *Entrepreneurial Venture*, 2nd ed. (Cambridge: Harvard Business Press, 1999). Please refer to this work for a more comprehensive overview of the IPO process.

[32]Zemel, "Venture-Backed IPOs Scarce in 4Q'00."

[33]"Q1 Report: Volume Up, Values Down," *Webmergers.com* (URL: http://www.webmergers.com/editorial/article.php?id=56).

[34]Ibid.

CHAPTER

12

Media Transformation

CASELET: REALNETWORKS

Rob Glaser says he became fascinated by the intersection of technology and media when cable television burst onto the American scene while he was in college in the late 1970s. "I always thought, if there is going to be another one of these revolutions, I'd love to be at the center of it," he recalls.

Well, there was. And he is.

Glaser's company, RealNetworks, has been at the forefront of bringing multimedia to the Internet—and vice versa—since he left Microsoft to found it in 1995. Back then, aside from a few sound clips that required considerable savvy—and patience—to download, the nascent Web was basically a text and still-picture medium. But as soon as Glaser navigated his first hyperlinks, he was struck by the multimedia possibilities.

"I thought, If we could deliver audio and video this way, it would be a pretty powerful concept," he says. He started with audio, debuting his RealAudio player, the first mass-market software that allowed "streaming," or real-time feeds, with content from two radio partners, ABC and NPR. On the first day it was available, more than 100,000 people logged on. RealVideo followed in 1997; RealJukebox, for music, in 1999. Now, as any of the fast-growing number of people who have watched a video clip online, e-mailed a music file to a friend, or used a set-top digital video recorder like TiVo can attest, the convergence of multimedia and the Internet is well under way.

It's a transformation whose scope and speed have surprised even Rob Glaser. "I was certainly optimistic that in the long term we'd be able to do something that would have a huge impact," he notes. "But if you told me that all of this would happen in just a few years, I wouldn't have believed it."

PLEASE CONSIDER THE FOLLOWING QUESTIONS AS YOU READ THIS CHAPTER:

1. What is media convergence?

2. What conditions make technological convergence possible?

3. How have companies attempted to realize organizational convergence?

411

4. How do new-media companies leverage traditional media channels?

5. What are the barriers to organizational convergence?

INTRODUCTION

The purpose of this chapter is to provide an understanding of media convergence, a process that has both technological and organizational components. The increasing fragmentation of media usage in American households, recent shifts in federal telecommunications laws, and advances in digital technologies (especially broadband) suggest that the evolution of a single digital-media platform will usher in a future of widespread, convenient access to new and innovative media services.

As the multiplicity of media channels converges to a digital platform, businesses have seen an opportunity to gain economies of scale and scope. The megamergers in the media industry—including the marriages of AOL and Time Warner, Viacom and CBS, The Walt Disney Company and Capital Cities/ABC, and Vivendi and Universal—represent an attempt to exploit cross-platform synergy.

Media convergence describes the migration of the various analog media channels and businesses to a common digital platform, with the Internet as its primary driver (see Exhibit 12.1). In Chapter 2, we reviewed the market infrastructure, which showed how the Internet is evolving to become the digital platform of the networked economy. Since the Internet has grown, businesses now use the Web as a single digital-media base to create an electronic architecture for commercial applications. As discussed, the infrastructure convergence from analog to digital technology involves the conversion of all data streams into bits of 0s and 1s—the binary language of computers.

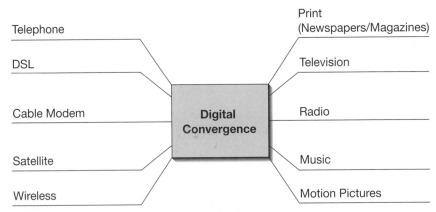

EXHIBIT 12.1   Network and Media Convergence

Many companies believe that this convergence requires a new organizational model for media businesses, one that includes businesses from the mostly single-channel industries that delivered analog media content: broadcasting (radio and television), publishing (books, newspapers, and magazines), and movies. Many media companies have banded together to form megacompanies in an attempt to exploit cross-platform synergies and efficiencies. These businesses represent new levels of both horizontal and vertical integration in the media industry, but their emergence has not taken place without regulatory and consumer scrutiny and criticism.

In this chapter, we begin by discussing technological convergence and reviewing both the proliferation of media and the fragmentation of media usage for news, information, and entertainment. We explore the current effects and potential long-term effect of media convergence across an array of old- and new-economy media, with special attention to public policy. We then turn to the organizational aspects of media convergence and look at how Internet companies are leveraging the media of the old economy to build brand awareness and usage for their products and services in the networked economy. We examine how synergy, propelled by technological convergence, has been a driving force for several recent media megamergers. We review the potential effect of media convergence on various media platforms and their current revenue models. Finally, we look at the public policy issues that govern media convergence.

Conditions of Technological Convergence

There are many factors that make **technological convergence** possible. Along with the shift from **analog** to **digital** technology, other reasons include continued advances in and the decreasing cost of digital technology, low-cost digital network infrastructure, current and potential media proliferation and media usage fragmentation in American households, advances in new digital technologies, and media economics.

Continued Advances in and Decreasing Cost of Digital Technology

Advances in computing, along with the decreased cost of PCs and related digital technology, have led to the creation of a cost-effective common platform for placing all types of media content into binary form. Most media content now begins in digital form. Once text, audio, video, and graphics are in the digital domain, that content is easily manipulated, combined, stored, and transmitted across the Internet and onto digital devices such as PCs, digital television sets, or any other type of Internet-enabled device.

Low-Cost Digital Network Infrastructure

The development of nonproprietary Internet standards, including Internet Protocol (IP), Hypertext Transfer Protocol (HTTP), HyperText Markup Language (HTML), and Extensible Markup Language (XML), has allowed Internet hardware and software development to occur in a relatively unencumbered environment. The standardization of HTTP and HTML led to the development of a universal graphical user interface for the Internet browser, which reduced navigation to a click of the mouse.

Drill-Down

What Is the Difference Between Analog and Digital Information?

We live in an analog physical world—that is, analog is continuously variable in quality. When we speak, our mouths create air-pressure changes that are continuously variable and are then captured by our ears. Our eardrums convert air-pressure changes to mechanical changes, and then through nerve-cell stimulation and transmission to the brain we hear and perceive sounds as speech. Continuously variable light is reflected off objects in our field of vision, focused by the lens of our eyes onto our retina, converted to nerve-cell stimulation by the eyes' internal rods and cones, and transmitted to the brain so that we see the varying light as patterns.

With the use of a coder-decoder (codec), analog signals can be digitized through an analog-to-digital (A-to-D) conversion process, and digital signals can be put into analog through a digital-to-analog (D-to-A) conversion process. A-to-D and D-to-A conversions are performed routinely to bring all types of signals in and out of the digital domain for fast, inexpensive, and precise processing and/or mixing with other digital signals, which are then returned to the analog physical world for our consumption.

Until the recent availability of inexpensive digital-signal processing components and subsystems, analog technology was the only way to process and transmit electronic information. Analog technology uses a continuously varied amplitude, frequency, or phase of an electronic signal and/or carrier to transmit information. We continue to use analog technology to transmit voices (and now data) over telephone wires and to broadcast AM and FM radio and TV (digital TV transmission is now possible but not yet widely available). However, because of the nature of analog signal processing and its requisite use of various signal-filtering techniques to isolate and process the signal, the ability to accurately carry and process multiple types of analog signals through multiple generations becomes greatly limited. The analog signal becomes mixed with background noise until it is no longer intelligible. Also, analog technology does not allow easy compression of signals—we cannot easily transform and pack more signals through a given amount of bandwidth. For example, it could not permit efficient videoconferencing or other emerging forms of telephone traffic, which by 1999 was mostly computer-to-computer, not voice-to-voice.

Digital information is a series of discrete bits represented by 0 or 1 (or any pair of symbols that represent "on" or "off"). This binary language of computers allows for easy generation, processing, and transmission of signals with the assistance of microprocessors. Eight bits make up a "byte," usually a letter or numeric character, which is the smallest accessible unit in a computer's memory.[1] With the increased volume of electronic signals and a physical limit of bandwidth to all transmission media, data requirements in the late 1990s strained the usefulness of analog technology and pushed for the convergence and increased use of digital technology across a variety of information products and platforms.[2] Digital technology has become a means to convert analog electronic signals to the digital domain and to process and compress more signals into a given bandwidth while maintaining an acceptable level of signal quality.

With the lifting of commercial-use restrictions, the Internet fast became the backbone of digital communications—and the low-cost digital network infrastructure of the World Wide Web began its explosive growth. And, with XML as the emerging standard for data interchange on the Web, development of the next-generation data-rich Semantic Web will produce languages for expressing information (rather than data) in a form that is able to be processed by machines. Therefore, users will not be the only ones manipulating a website—the computer will, as well.

Media Proliferation

At the start of the 20th century, newspapers were the only form of mass media. In the 1920s, radio and magazines emerged as additional sources for news, information, and entertainment. After World War II, in the late 1940s and throughout the 1950s, broadcast television emerged, and TV sets became the primary media source in many American households.

In the 1960s, most Americans had just three networks to choose from. By the 1970s, cable television had arrived, with channels such as HBO and Turner Broadcasting's TBS Superstation picking up viewer traffic. Cable television expanded further in the 1980s. That decade saw the birth of CNN, ESPN, and MTV, as well as the emergence of the videocassette recorder (VCR). In the 1990s, direct-broadcast satellite services found their way into American homes, and the number of cable television channels continued to grow. Exhibit 12.2 illustrates the increase in **media proliferation** and the resulting fragmentation over the years, including the potential for the early part of this century.

TV faces the worst audience fragmentation of all. Here, News Corp. tracks and forecasts the explosion of TV viewing choices available in any given hour. Once there were three options; soon there will be 1,000.

1960s	**1970s**	**1980s**	**1990s**	**2000s**	**2010s**
Most Americans watch the Big Three networks every night.	UHF stations bring more choices, and the fledgling cable industry introduces a few new channels like HBO and Turner's TBS Superstation.	The VCR becomes commonplace, letting consumers watch recorded shows and movies whenever they want. Cable explodes with new networks such as CNN and MTV.	Direct-broadcast satellites are introduced, offering hundreds of channels. Cable systems are slowly upgraded with more channels.	Digital compression and two-way networks allow cable companies to offer even more channels and services. DBS services grow more entrenched. As TVs are linked to the Internet, new programming delivered via the Internet takes hold. Result: 300 choices at any moment.	Broadcasters may use the high-definition TV spectrum to launch more channels. Internet chat evolves into networked virtual-reality games, interactive movies, and other activities being hatched by MIT's Media Lab and others. News Corp. forecasts 1,000 channels, now called "context windows."

Source: Data from Elizabeth Lesly Stevens, "The Entertainment Age" *BusinessWeek*, February 16, 1998

EXHIBIT 12.2   Media Fragmentation (1960s–2010s)

Media-Usage Fragmentation in American Households

In the spring of 2002, the Pew Research Center in Washington, D.C., conducted a survey on the increasing **media-usage fragmentation**. The results showed that while broadcast television news, both network and local, remained the primary media source (newspapers were second), its total audience penetration had declined. The decline was most obvious for the nightly network news, where viewership dropped from 60 percent in 1993 to 42 percent in 1996, 38 percent in 1998, and 30 percent in 2000. In 2002, it made a slight recovery, to 32 percent.[3]

The Pew Research study noted that the declining size of the audience for television news was apparent in all demographic groups, but particularly younger people. This is consistent with an overall lack of interest in news among young Americans. Since 1994, the percentage of people younger than 25 who said they received no news the previous day from newspapers, television, or the radio rose from 14 to 37 percent. Only 26 percent of those under age 30 had read a newspaper the day before they were surveyed, and only 19 percent said they regularly watched the nightly network news.[4]

Despite the decline in the viewership of network news programs, the Pew Research study reported that more Americans are regularly turning to websites for news and information. The increase was marked from 1998 to 2000 (from 13 to 23 percent) and then tapered off in 2002 (25 percent). Such a leveling of growth tempers the notion that the Internet will become the dominant medium for news, as does the Pew statistic that 73 percent of online readers say their Web surfing does not affect their use of other media.[5]

The audience for television entertainment shows has also declined, largely due to the increased penetration of cable television. For example, during the 1985–1986 television season, approximately 93 percent of the prime-time audience in the United States was for network affiliates, independent television stations, or public stations, with only 7 percent for cable television. During the 1999–2000 season, however, traditional television channels captured only 59 percent of the prime-time audience, while cable television's share grew to 41 percent.[6] The number of subscribers to basic cable increased from 39.8 million (or 46.2 percent of all households) in 1985 to 69.5 million (or 68 percent of all households) in 2001.[7] Although the amount of time that members of all age groups spend watching network television has steadily declined over the past two decades, the percentage of households with alternative forms of media entertainment and information has dramatically increased—contributing to the fragmentation of media usage. Exhibit 12.3 compares media penetration in U.S. households in 1990 and 2001.

With the wide range of media devices now available in the typical American household, it is no surprise that children spend a large percentage of their time immersed in multimedia. A November 1999 study by the Kaiser Family Foundation showed that American children spent, on average, 5.5 hours per day—or more than 38 hours per week—using media. Television viewing accounted for almost half of that usage, followed by listening to music, reading, watching videos, and using a computer. The study also found that the typical American household had three television sets, three radios, two VCRs, two compact (CD) players, and a video-game console.[8]

Forecasted Continued Media Proliferation and Media Usage Fragmentation

The continued proliferation of television channels and services, as well as other media outlets, has led to a considerable increase in audience fragmentation. Furthermore, experts predict that over the next 10 years, consumers

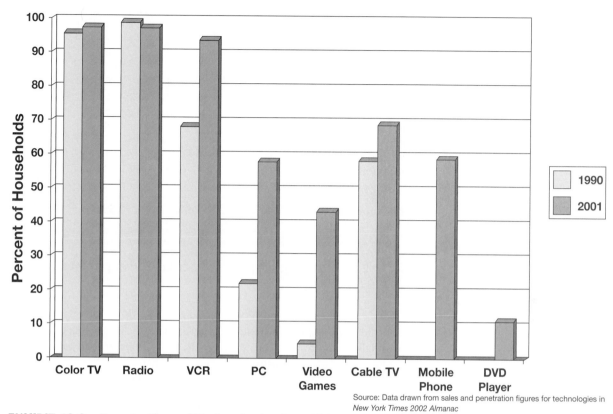

EXHIBIT 12.3   Penetration of Technologies into U.S. Households, 1990 and 2001

Source: Data drawn from sales and penetration figures for technologies in *New York Times 2002 Almanac*

will be presented with an even more diverse range of media choices. Advances in wireless technology, digital compression, two-way networks, and digital and high-definition television—not to mention advances in the technology that powers the Internet—certainly support this prediction.[9]

Exhibit 12.4 provides a breakdown of the number of hours per year that consumers were exposed to media, tracked from 1992 to 2002. Television viewing accounts for almost half of the typical consumer's annual media usage, with the average American watching about 1,575 hours of television in 2002 (with an increasing percentage of those hours spent watching cable). In addition, the time spent listening to music, watching videos, playing video games, and surfing the Internet has also increased significantly since 1992.[10] Internet activity is perhaps the most notable, as the United States currently adds 2 million new Internet users per month.[11]

Advances in New Technologies

Because of the rapid advances in new digital technologies, media companies can now put their content online in various forms. Options range from the current streaming-media technology to playing short audio and video clips over a narrowband feed. The future promises the possibility of delivering movies on demand via broadband.

	1992	1997	2002
Total television (broadcast and cable)	1,510	1,561	1,575
Radio	1,150	1,082	1,040
Recorded music	233	265	289
Daily newspapers	172	159	152
Consumer books	100	92	97
Consumer magazines	85	82	79
Home video	42	50	58
Movies in theaters	11	13	13
Video games	19	36	46
Consumer online	2	28	49
Total hours per person	**3,324**	**3,368**	**3,398**

Sources: Veronis, Suhler & Associates, Wilkofsky Gruen Associates, Nielsen Media Research, Simmons Market Research, Interactive Digital Software Association Paul Kagan Associates, Motion Picture Association of America, Book Industry Study Group, Magazine Publishers of America, Software Publishers Association

EXHIBIT 12.4   Hours Spent per Year per Customer per Media, 1992–2002

An example of media convergence on the Internet is ABCNews.com, which The Walt Disney Company owns through the ABC Television and Radio Network. On ABCNews.com, visitors can read, listen to, or view content from ABC's television or radio programs. For example, digital technology allows video clips from the television network's branded shows—*Good Morning America, 20/20*, and *ABC World News Tonight*—to appear on any of its 215 affiliate television stations and on the Web at ABCNews.com. Hourly audio clips of news and sports reports from ABC Radio are also available on ABCNews.com through audio-streaming.

With increased digitization of content and the promise of widespread broadband delivery in the near future, the personal computer (PC) will not necessarily be the prime receiver of Internet content. Currently, other Internet receivers include digital telephones, handheld computers, and video-game consoles. In fact, Sony touts the ability of its PlayStation 2 gaming system to become a DVD player, a CD player, and an Internet connection. While the console has not yet become a primary household appliance for converging media, the potential is there. As Howard Stringer, CEO of Sony Corporation of America, observed, "Synergy was forced in the analog world, but in the digital world, people can't get out of the way of each other."[12]

Media Economics

As stated previously, over the last five years media companies have been merging as a way to develop vertical integration for content and distribution across all types of media. For today's media company, the strategy is to collect formerly disparate media and—through organizational convergence and technological convergence—create a synergistic combination that produces a direct bottom-line benefit. Each form of media has its own economics and, therefore, its own business model. The types of media most commonly discussed in connection to convergence include newspapers, magazines, books, broadcast television, cable television, radio, film, videos, DVDs, CDs, and MP3s.

Newspapers

At the end of 2000, there were 1,480 daily newspapers in the United States, with a cumulative daily circulation (the number of copies sold) of 55.8 million on weekdays and 59.4 million on Sundays. Although only half of those were morning newspapers, the morning publications accounted for 82 percent of the total circulation, or about 47 million copies.[13] The top four newspapers in the United States were *The Wall Street Journal, USA Today, The New York Times,* and the *Los Angeles Times,* all of which had a daily circulation of 1 million or more.[14]

After reaching a peak of 62.8 million in 1987, total daily newspaper circulation began to decline. There were several reasons for this drop-off, including the closing of several evening newspapers, an increase in alternative weekly newspapers, and the emergence of electronic news sources. In 1987, the number of evening newspapers being published was 1,166; in 2000, that number had slipped to 760. Over that same time period, however, the number of weekly newspapers increased from 7,600 to 8,138, with total circulation growing from 47.5 million to 74.4 million.[15]

Paralleling the overall decline in daily newspaper circulation was a decline in the percentage of adults who read them. In 2000, 55.1 percent of people said they read a daily paper, down from 56.9 percent in 1999 and 62.4 percent in 1990.[16] The drop-off in Sunday readership was similar—it declined from 72.6 percent in 1995, to 66.9 percent in 1999, to 65.1 percent in 2000.[17]

The average newspaper reader is older, well educated, and earns a relatively high income; 60 percent of daily newspaper readers have college degrees, and 64 percent have household incomes of $75,000 or more. (The median household income in the United States in 2001 was $42,148.[18])

Newspaper sales account for only a portion of a daily newspaper's revenue—approximately 75 percent comes from advertisers, who covet access to that well-educated, high-income audience. In 2000, newspaper advertising accounted for $49 billion, or 20.2 percent of advertising expenditures in the United States.[19] The bulk of this was retail and classified advertising, which, respectively, accounted for an estimated 45 percent (or $21.5 billion) and 40 percent (or $19.4 billion) of newspaper advertising in 2000. The balance comes from national advertising accounts for industries such as financial services, airlines, and hotels.[20]

As of July 2002, AOL reported that it had 26.5 million subscribers[21]—approximately the combined circulation of the top 100 daily newspapers in the United States.[22] With the increasing usage of the Internet, newspapers have rushed to create a Web presence and win a share of this audience. By 2001, more than 1,200 newspapers in North America (including all of the top 100 in circulation) had online products of some kind, ranging from classified ads to reproductions of the entire newspaper.[23]

Magazines

As of 2000, there were more than 500 consumer magazines and 2,700 trade publications in the United States. The top 100 consumer magazines had a combined circulation of approximately 248 million. The top four magazines by circulation were *NRTA/AARP Bulletin, Modern Maturity, Reader's Digest,* and *TV Guide*—each with a circulation base greater than 10 million.[24]

Unlike newspapers, consumer magazines range from the very specialized, such as *Cooking Light* or *Runner's World*, to those of general interest, such as *Newsweek* or *People Weekly*. Approximately 82 percent of consumer magazines are sold through subscriptions; the remaining 18 percent are sold through retail outlets such as supermarkets and newsstands. Trade publications focus on a particular business sector, such as restaurants and computers, and most are free or sold by subscription.

Like newspapers, almost all magazines make money through a combination of circulation and advertising revenue. Magazines usually guarantee their advertisers a base circulation of readers. The top six magazines by advertising revenue in 2000 were *People Weekly* ($724 million), *Time* ($661 million), *Sports Illustrated* ($650 million), *BusinessWeek* ($572 million), *Fortune* ($477 million), and *Better Homes and Gardens* ($471 million).[25]

Although magazines do not face the direct threat from the Internet that newspapers do, more and more magazines have recognized the importance of online content. Many have begun attempts at symbiosis. *CosmoGirl, ESPN The Magazine*, and *inCite*, to name a few, launched eponymous websites simultaneously with the print launch of their magazines. Research has shown that a magazine can spike interest in the related website and that a partnership with a similarly named website can drive subscriptions for the magazine.[26]

Books

According to the Book Industry Study Group, which tracks the reading habits of American households, U.S. book sales increased for the ninth straight year in 1999. Approximately 119,000 book titles were published in the United States that year, more than twice the number published in 1990. However that number crept downward in 2000, to 96,000 titles.[27] The most popular book subjects were sociology, fiction, juvenile, and technology.[28] Part of the reason for the growing popularity of books is the increase in education among Americans over the past two decades. In 1998, 83 percent of the U.S. adult population had completed high school, compared with 68 percent in 1990. Twenty-four percent had attained a college degree, compared with only 17 percent in 1980.[29] In the year 2000, the average American consumer spent an estimated $87.94 on books.[30]

In the year 2000, many pundits predicted a seismic shift for the book industry with the advent of the electronic platform. Some foresaw a change from a "print and distribute" model to an Internet "distribute and print" model. Consumers can download a book's content over the Internet or a dedicated phone line and read it off an e-book device. Stephen King's 66-page e-book, *Riding the Bullet*, released in March 2000, was the first mass-market trial and was available for downloading from Amazon.com, Barnes & Noble.com, and PalmPilot websites.[31]

However, the dream of conquering the print world has come about more slowly than many expected. Many e-book publishing businesses or divisions have closed, and the only dependable profits seem to come from highly specialized niche markets such as engineering trade books (serviced by Knovel Corporation).[32] In 2000, the consulting firm Accenture predicted that by 2005, e-books would be a $2.3 billion business, or 10 percent of the $23 billion consumer book market.[33] That number is considered unattainable now, but the e-book industry still has a valid general concept and interested software players, including Microsoft and Adobe. So while the e-book market has a slower growth curve than initially expected, it has not been abandoned.[34]

While many doomsayers predicted that increased PC usage would bring the demise of books, it has actually been a key reason for the increase in book production since 1990. Computers reduce publishers' production costs and enable the publication of many more titles. The computer has also made possible book superstores such as Borders and Barnes & Noble, where computer indexes, rather than humans, track inventory and local buying patterns.[35]

Broadcast Television

Unlike most businesses that produce or sell tangible products and services, TV network broadcasting is essentially a programming service. The three largest U.S. networks—ABC, CBS, and NBC—each have approximately 200 local affiliates and generate revenues by creating and delivering audiences to advertisers. Each network airs an average of 90 hours of programming a week. The amount of money that a network or a station charges advertisers for commercial time depends on the size and composition of the program audience. Because advertising is sold on a cost per thousand (CPM) basis, the larger the audience for a particular show, the higher the advertising rates. CPM rates do, however, vary considerably depending on audience demographics. In contrast with other media, such as newspapers, magazines, cable television, and a few websites, broadcast television is fully supported by advertising revenue.[36]

Cable has changed the television landscape, drawing up to 40 percent of the total viewing audience. With so many channels available and the increasingly fractured nature of today's television audience, no single broadcast program will likely reach the kind of viewership numbers achieved during the 1960s and 1970s, when viewers had only three or four choices. For example, the final episode of *Seinfeld* in May 1998 drew fewer viewers than regular episodes of *The Beverly Hillbillies* during the 1960s.[37]

The widespread introduction of digital television (DTV) will increase the number of channels—and therefore, the number of programs—offered in the future; while this change will bring an increase in quality, it will do so at a bandwidth cost. Digital compression techniques permit the transmission of several DTV channels over the same bandwidth currently required for a single analog standard-definition television (SDTV) channel, but the transmission of a single digital high-definition television (HDTV) channel will require even more bandwidth than is used currently for conventional television. Broadcasters and policymakers need to determine what is in the public interest.

Digital television, which offers a lifelike picture and CD-quality sound, has been called the biggest broadcast innovation since color television was introduced in the 1950s. All commercial stations will be required to broadcast a digital signal by the summer of 2003, and all analog broadcasts are scheduled to stop by the spring of 2006. Each of the three networks currently broadcasts select programs, such as *ER* or *Judging Amy*, using high-definition digital technology.[38]

Cable Television

Cable television was originally introduced to improve television reception in rural areas. In the 1960s, cable operators realized that viewers were willing to pay for commercial-free programming, but their efforts to offer it were hampered by Federal Communications Commission (FCC) restrictions. The industry began to boom when RCA launched its first communication satellite into orbit in 1975. Under the name Home Box Office (HBO)—which was later sold to Time Warner—RCA began to transmit programming to independent cable operators around the country, who then relayed the programming to subscribers for a small fee. With the 1977 federal court dismissal of most of the FCC's regulations governing cable television, the door opened for what has become a $50 billion industry. The number of cable television subscribers grew from 9.2 million in 1975 to 69.5 million in 2001.[39]

The cable channels make their revenue through a combination of advertising and subscription fees. In 2001, the top six cable channels in the United States were TBS Superstation, The Discovery Channel, TNT, ESPN, USA Network, and Fox Family Channel—all available to 80 million or more cable subscribers. The top five premium cable services were The Disney Channel, HBO/Cinemax, Showtime, Encore, and Spice.[40]

With the changes brought forth by the Telecommunications Act of 1996, cable companies can now compete directly with telephone and utility companies to provide cable, telephone, and electrical services to homes. Because of this increased competition and the anticipation of broadband delivery and media convergence, there have been several megamergers involving cable television systems and regional telephone companies, including AT&T's acquisition of TCI in 1998 and US West's acquisition of MediaOne in 1999.

Radio

In 2001, there were 576.5 million radios in the United States, with 98 percent of households owning at least one. They were distributed as follows: 367.4 million (or 63 percent) in homes; 142.8 million (or 24.7 percent) in cars; 43.7 million (or 7.5 percent) in trucks, vans, and RVs; and the remaining 22.6 million (or 6.1 percent) in the workplace.[41] Ninety-five percent of listeners over the age of 12 listened to the radio for an average of three hours and 20 minutes each workday.

Like broadcast television, radio generates nearly all of its revenue by delivering a select audience to advertisers. Radio channels are more specific in their audience targeting, however. In 2001, the three most popular radio formats were country, news/talk, and adult contemporary, and there were 13,058 radio stations on the air, approximately 78 percent of which were commercial stations.[42]

Radio and audio programs are now offered on the Internet; however, they do not fall under the authority of the Federal Communications Commissions. Anyone, from relative unknowns to celebrities such as Robin Williams (on Audible.com), can host a radio program and broadcast it to the public through the Internet.[43]

Film

The motion-picture industry earned an estimated $8.35 billion in box-office receipts in 2001,[44] and the various studios together now release an average of 700 films per year.[45] The cost of making movies has escalated dramatically in recent years. In 1988, the average price tag for a motion picture was $18.1 million, according to the Motion Picture Association of America. By 2000, that had nearly tripled, to $54.8 million, largely due to spiraling actor salaries and increased demand for special effects. On average, studios spent $27.3 million per film—or almost half of total production costs—on publicity and advertising in 1998.[46]

One threat to the studio system is the advent of digital filming technology, which delivers high quality at a relatively low cost. Directors can more easily make films without the assistance of the major studios (although distribution of those films is another matter). "It's too late for the studios to panic. They've already lost," said director Francis Ford Coppola, whose Zoetrope.com allows filmmakers to read scripts, get feedback, hire directors, and show their work. "The minute artists don't need studios, they'll abandon them."[47]

Videos

In the decades since its introduction in the late 1970s, the videocassette recorder (VCR) has become a household staple—94 percent of American households own at least one. Despite studios' initial resistance, video releases are now the largest part of a motion picture's revenue stream. In 1995, a film's theatrical release accounted for almost 30 percent of its total revenue; the video release accounted for over 40 percent.[48]

DVDs

Digital video disks (DVDs) have become a popular format for viewing movies since their introduction in the mid-1990s. In 2001, nearly 13 million DVD players were sold in the United States—an increase of 49.5 percent over the previous year. The growth gave the DVD player an approximate household penetration of 33 percent. Sales are expected to grow an additional 25 percent in 2002, according to the Consumer Electronics Association.[49]

A DVD's storage capacity is 4.7 gigabytes (a CD's is 680 megabytes), which allows DVD producers not only to provide a much higher resolution video image than with VHS tape (up to 720 horizontal line resolution using MPEG-2 compression versus less than 400 horizontal line resolution with VHS), but also to offer many more features. For example, the special-edition DVD of *Ocean's Eleven* includes interviews with the film's stars, storyboards from the original Rat Pack version of the film, deleted scenes, and commentary from director Steven Soderbergh.

In February 2001, there were an estimated 11,000 movie titles available on DVD.[50] The average cost of a DVD movie ranges from $15 to $25, with special-edition DVDs priced slightly higher.[51] A number of DVD variants exist, including DVD-Audio, an additional prerecorded application format for consumer players introduced in mid-year 2000; DVD-ROM, a prerecorded data format; and DVD-R, a recordable data format (Apple Computer recently made this an option in the Power Mac G4).

Music CDs

Since its introduction in 1982, the digital audio compact disk, developed jointly by Sony and Philips Electronics, has become the most popular music format among consumers. Fewer than 100,000 CDs were sold in 1983—the first full year they were available—but CD sales overtook album sales by 1988 and topped cassette sales in 1992.[52] In 2000, CDs accounted for 89.3 percent of all music sold, followed by cassettes (4.9 percent) and singles (2.5 percent).[53] The total U.S. dollar value of all music sold was $14.3 billion in 2000 (and the top four genres were rock, rap, pop, and country). About one-third of all consumers of musical devices were 24 years old or younger.[54] Although CDs cost no more than albums or cassettes to produce, consumers are still willing to pay a premium for the digital format's superior sound quality and compact format.[55]

More and more, however, consumers would rather get their music free, as evidenced by the huge jump in the downloading of music from the Internet. Worldwide sales of music in all formats fell 6.5 percent in 2001, equating to a revenue drop of more than $3 billion for the recording industry. And the world's top 10 best-selling English language albums sold a combined 40 million copies worldwide in 2001, or 20 million fewer than 2000's top 10.[56]

MP3

The music industry has been thrown into turmoil by the recent emergence and mainstreaming of digital music technologies. At the center of the firestorm is MP3.com and similar websites that offer free downloading of digital music. MP3 technology is revolutionizing the way that music is consumed. Members of MP3.com (and BearShare, AudioGalaxy, and the other approximately 38,000 other websites where music can be downloaded) gain online access to thousands of CDs. They can copy music files free of charge to their computers' hard drives and listen to those recordings whenever they like. Because digital music quality does not decrease with copying, a 50th-generation copy is as clear as a 2nd-generation copy.[57]

Adding more fire to the MP3 controversy is the use of Napster software. The "sharing" website, started in 1999 and shut down in mid-2001, allowed music fans to easily search and swap MP3 musical files. At one time boasting 80 million registered users, Napster was sued by Metallica, Dr. Dre, and the Recording Industry Association of America for "operating a haven for music piracy on an unprecedented scale."[58] In October 2000, Napster appeared to be on the path to legitimacy with an $85 million infusion from recording giant BMG, a division of Bertelsmann. As part of BMG, Napster was to charge users and pay royalties to recording companies. However, that subscription model has not come to fruition yet, and the ousting of Bertelsmann CEO Richard Middlehoff (a proponent of the deal) in July 2002 could spell the end for the bankrupt Napster.[59] The downloadable-music business, however, shows no signs of abating and will likely be the dominant issue in music for the foreseeable future.

Video-Game Consoles

One of the fastest growing forms of home entertainment, the $5.5 billion video-game market is dominated by three companies: Sony, Nintendo, and Sega. The first home video games were introduced in 1966 by Magnavox,

---

Drill-Down

What Is MP3?

MP3 is the most popular format for audio compression on the Internet. The acronym stands for MPEG Layer-3, and MPEG itself is an acronym for Moving Picture Experts Group, though MPEG is most often used to refer to the set of digital video compression standards developed by the group. The two most important MPEG standards are MPEG-1 and MPEG-2; the first produces VCR-quality video resolution, and the second is used for DVD-ROMs and produces CD-quality audio. MPEG is not to be confused with JPEG (Joint Photographic Experts Group), which is a computer file format and compression specification for photographs. MP3 is one in a series of audio encoding standards developed under MPEG and formalized by the International Organization for Standardization (ISO).

For "hi-fi" quality sound reproduction, the frequency response to human hearing ranges from 20 Hz to 20 kHz; in other words, humans can typically hear sounds with frequencies between 20 cycles per second and 20,000 cycles per second. Nyquist's Theorem states that to accurately capture an analog signal digitally, a sample rate of at least twice the highest frequency desired is needed. Therefore, to capture 20-kHz sounds as well as a few harmonics above, standard CD-quality digital audio is typically created by taking 16-bit samples of the analog sound signal at 44.1 kHz. This means that CD-quality stereo sound requires two channels × 16 bits × 44,100 times per second—some 180 kilo bytes of data for one second of stereo audio.

MP3 includes a compression algorithm that reduces the "noise" around sounds that listeners cannot perceive. MP3 allows the compression of any sound sequence into a small file (typically a 10:1 compression ratio) while mostly preserving the original sound quality. MP3 files are usually downloaded and played with free MP3 player software.

---

which had developed a game that could be played on a color television set.[60] In 1972, Atari entered the market, followed by Nintendo, with its 8-bit console, in 1986.

In 1990, Sega launched a 16-bit console called Genesis; Nintendo quickly matched it in 1991 with Super Nintendo—and established an industry standard of rapid one-upmanship. In 1994, Sony introduced PlayStation. Nintendo countered with its Nintendo 64, and then Sega released its Saturn in 1996. Sony pulled ahead in video-game console sales with the 2000 launch of PlayStation 2.[61] Given that, plus the expected launch of Microsoft's Xbox in November 2001, Sega decided to stop manufacturing consoles and focus on producing video-game software in January 2000. As video games become increasingly sophisticated, the average time that American consumers spend playing them increases. In 1992, the average consumer spent 19 hours per year playing video games; by 2000, that number had risen to 43.[62]

The Digital Lifestyle

The Digital Home of the Future

What will media consumption be like in the digital home of the future? Experts predict that as media-based household appliances—from television sets to cameras to video-game consoles—become digitally based and interconnected, they will fulfill a vision foreseen almost 20 years ago by Nicholas Negroponte, the cofounder of the Media Lab at the Massachusetts Institute of Technology. Negroponte observed that as bits become "the DNA of information"—replacing atoms as the basic commodity of human interaction—"commingled bits and bits-about-bits" will "change the media landscape so thoroughly that concepts like video-on-demand and shipping electronic games down your local cable are just trivial applications—the tip of a much more profound iceberg."[63]

As more household appliances convert from analog to digital platforms, it becomes easier to imagine the digital lifestyle that Negroponte wrote about 20 years ago, one in which we can access media with one touch of a button. For example, through basic interactive television services such as Microsoft's UltimateTV and AOL Time Warner's AOLTV, consumers can now access e-mail, chat with others, surf the Web, and watch their favorite shows, all on the same television set, by using a set-top box and telephone modem. With increased adoption of broadband technology (usually defined as having a connectivity speed exceeding 128 kilobits per second, significantly faster than the narrowband speeds of 40 to 53 kilobits per second achieved over regular telephone lines), they will also have access to a wider range of media services over the Web, from downloading books to videoconferencing to exchanging video clips with family members.

The Digital Lifestyle

Several CEOs have envisioned this **digital lifestyle** (see Exhibit 12.5 for a comparison of life in 2000 with what it might be like in 2010). For example, Bill Gates, the chairman, cofounder, and chief software architect of Microsoft Corp., believes that the personal computer, the set-top box for interactive television, and the video-game console will all be important household devices. In a recent speech, Gates observed:

> The PC is going to be . . . the center of control. . . . But it won't just be the PC, it will be all these things connected up to the PC, both in wired and wireless fashion. . . .
>
>   The set-top boxes that connect up to the satellite world, they're changing and changing very rapidly. That's where the cutting edge is right now. But it won't stay that way; it won't just be satellites. It will also be the entire cable infrastructure, and this year we'll see the first significant rollout of digital set-top boxes. . . . Last, but not least, there's a revolution about to take place in game consoles. . . .
>
>   As it comes together, all these things happening at once are about a digital lifestyle.[64]

At the end of 2000, Microsoft began to develop a wide range of digital platforms that can serve as home Internet portals. In addition to improving the interface of its Windows platform for personal computers, Microsoft is developing several products: a Pocket PC version of the Windows CE platform in wireless handheld devices, which competes directly with the Palm platform; the Windows Reader for electronic books, which will compete with Adobe's Acrobat Reader; the Xbox, a video-game console with Internet access that launched in November 2001 and competes directly with Sony and Nintendo consoles; and the UltimateTV set-top box, which will connect to cable and satellite television and will compete with AOLTV and direct-recording services such as TiVo and ReplayTV.[65]

2000—Media Services to the American Household

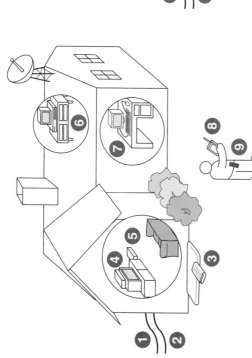

1. Subscribes to cable television: 68%
2. Access to broadband: 5%
3. Daily newspapers read: 57%;
   Sunday newspapers read: 67%
4. Owns a VCR: 91%
5. Owns a CD player: 55%; Owns DVD
   player: 22%
6. Owns a video-game console: 44%
7. Owns a home computer: 53%; has
   online service: 31%
8. Owns a PDA/smart phone: 20%

2010—Media Services to the American Household

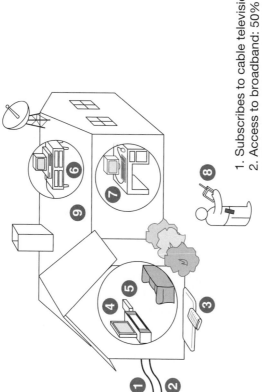

1. Subscribes to cable television: 80%
2. Access to broadband: 50%
3. Daily newspapers read: 50%;
   Sunday newspapers read: 60%
4. Owns a digital television: 100%
5. Owns DVD and CD players: 95%
6. Owns a video-game console: 90%
7. Owns a home computer: 75%
8. Owns a PDA/smart phone: 80%;
   e-books: 40%

EXHIBIT 12.5 The Digital Lifestyle in 2000 and 2010

While Microsoft has invested broadly in a wide range of Internet platforms, several CEOs believe that the PC will remain the home's command center. Craig Barrett, CEO of Intel Corp., talks about an "extended PC era," with consumers adopting PC accessories such as the digital camera, personal digital assistants (PDAs), and digital sound morphers. In a recent speech, Barrett said:

> The world is digitizing, whether it is communication or information or the Internet. . . . And if you look at the center of that digital universe, the central focal point for the big bang, it really is the core of the PC. . . . The PC is really at the center of the Internet, the main client. But what we are seeing today is more and more devices attached around the PC, extending the PC's influence.
>
> Whether it is audio or video or still images or animation . . . more and more of these devices are going digital, and more and more of them are getting connected to the PC. . . . If you add up all of these devices, you are seeing the center of each one of these activities is the PC. . . . But these other devices extend the range, extend the user interface.[66]

Steve Jobs, founder and chairman of Apple Computer Inc., shared Barrett's sentiment about the personal computer as command center. In addition to seeing the PC as the home's Internet portal, Jobs envisioned it as the digital hub, where consumers could edit their own movies or create customized CDs with easy-to-use interfaces. In fact, 320 million writable CDs were sold in the United States in 2000,[67] many of which were then burned with audio content that had been downloaded free on the Internet. By June 2002, 41 million Internet users had downloaded more than 1 billion free music files,[68] indicating a trend toward customized digitized media. In a recent *New York Times* article, Jobs observed:

> We believe that the PC or Mac can become the digital hub of our new digital lifestyle . . . . The Internet is a wonderful thing, and for a while it was such a blinding bright light that it obscured other bright lights. It's a wonderful thing. It's a magical thing. Music is a wonderful thing, movies are wonderful things.[69]

Other CEOs, including Nobuyuki Idei of Sony Corp., take a countering view, believing that personal electronic devices—such as the PlayStation 2 video-game console, which could at some point serve as a portal to services including online banking, online gaming, and music and video downloading—will be the home's digital command centers. At its introduction at Comdex in 1999, Kazuo Hirai, president of Sony Computer Entertainment of America, called PlayStation 2 "the first mass-market product for the broadband world," and asserted, "We believe that PlayStation 2 will actually accelerate the deployment of broadband networking into consumers' homes. We are poised to take this to the next level of entertainment." Idei himself envisioned a much broader role for Sony: "Some call Sony a hardware company. Some call it a media company. What we are and what we will be is a broadband entertainment company."[70] Howard Stringer, chairman and chief executive officer of Sony Corp. of America, the U.S. subsidiary of Sony, echoed Idei's thoughts:

> Video-on-demand is around the corner. Digital channels will put interactivity at your fingertips. Furthermore, delivery systems are multiplying. Soon, wireless-electronic delivery of customized content to home networks may bypass traditional gatekeepers. . . . PlayStation 2 . . . is a super PC or an advanced set-top box with a 128-bit processor more powerful than the Pentium III. It's another independent delivery system, a Trojan horse into the home for all kinds of digital content.[71]

It is clear that opinions differ on whether the personal computer will be the home's digital hub. Still, Michael Dell, chairman, founder, and CEO of Dell Computer Corp., notes that four key trends will drive the personal computing market over the next few years: increased consumer migration to high-speed broadband connections, increased demand for data storage through servers, an expanding number of new computer-powered devices, and a continued shift to mobile computing.[72]

With an increasing number of digital platforms being introduced by both hardware and software makers, media content providers such as AOL Time Warner and The Walt Disney Company will seek to have their content and services available on as many platforms as possible. Steve Case, then chairman of AOL Time Warner, reflected in 2000 on how new technologies in the household would affect content-based media companies and their consumers:

> *If the last five years have been about leveraging the PC and modem, the next five years will be about cellphones and wireless devices across a range of platforms designed to bring all the benefits of the Internet to consumers in a seamless, easy way that really improves their lives. . . .*
>
> *The companies that will lead in this new world will be those that . . . are able to make sense of this world of dizzying complexity both by building on trusted brands that people can count on and by creating new services to collect and package products and services. . . .*
>
> *[They will] utilize multiple delivery platforms, giving consumers multiple access options . . . and using interfaces that give consumers the simplicity, functionality, and personalized services they desire.[73]*

Effect of Broadband on Internet Usage

Applications of Broadband

The increased use of **broadband** technology allows for widespread adoption of more Internet applications, such as video-on-demand, multiplayer games, streaming of audio and video, and software distribution. Motion-picture companies, video-game makers, streaming-media companies (such as Real-Networks), and software companies all benefit.

At the beginning of 2002, there were over 7 million cable modem subscribers and 4.6 million DSL subscribers in the United States[74] (see Exhibit 12.6). The 2002 Telecommunications Market Review and Forecast predicted that cable and DSL services will grow by an average 24.2 percent annually through 2005.[75] This figure meshes with the projections of the Yankee Group, which hold that by the end of 2005, more than 30 million Americans will have access to broadband, with 15 million American households accessing it through a cable modem, 10 million through DSL, and 5 million through satellite.[76] Adoption of broadband technology could happen faster in the workplace; Jupiter Communications projects that the number of workers with access to broadband will increase from 24.4 million, or 22 percent of the workforce, in 2000 to 54.6 million, or 47 percent of the workforce, in 2005. Consequently, it predicts, the number of individuals who access the Internet through dial-up service will decrease from 18.5 million in 2000 to 8.1 million in 2005.[77]

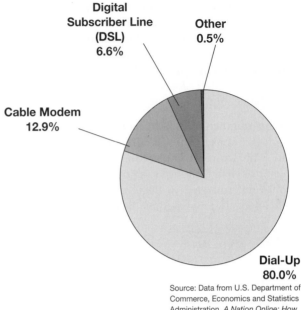

Source: Data from U.S. Department of
Commerce, Economics and Statistics
Administration, *A Nation Online: How
Americans Are Expanding Their Use
of the Internet*, February 2002

**EXHIBIT 12.6   Connection Type Among Those
with Home Internet Access in 2001**

Internet Service Providers

In September 2001, only 10.8 percent of all individuals (and 20.0 percent of home Internet users) claimed to have something faster than dial-up service in their homes.[78] The rest of Internet users still accessed the Internet primarily by dialing a telephone number provided by an Internet service provider (ISP).[79] These ISPs ranged from well-known services (America Online, EarthLink, and the Microsoft Network) to regional telecoms (BellSouth, Nynex, and Pacific Bell) to local firms (Access Internet Communications in Cupertino, California, and Montana Communications Network in Bozeman, Montana). By the middle of July 1999, there were an estimated 6,000 ISPs in North America.[80] In December 2000, AOL was the largest ISP in the United States with more than 29 million members, followed by EarthLink/Mind-Spring, the Microsoft Network, AT&T, and NetZero. However, AOL's dominance in this arena is clearly shrinking. In July 2002, the company claimed only 4 percent of the 12 million broadband subscribers in the United States, as opposed to its 40 percent share of dial-up subscribers. "The number of U.S. households with dial-up has peaked," said Jed Kolko, an analyst with Forrester Research. "U.S. consumers are switching from dial-up to broadband faster than new households are getting dial-up."[81]

Prior to the increase in Internet usage during the mid-1990s, online commercial services such as AOL, CompuServe, and Prodigy were often closed-end, proprietary systems. Registered members usually paid an hourly fee for proprietary features, such as sending e-mail, reading online content, or participating in chat rooms. With the increase in Web popularity—made possible by the development of Web browsers—many Internet users began seeking direct access to the Internet through independent ISPs. In 1992, Delphi became the first national commercial online service to offer Internet access, including e-mail, to its subscribers.[82] By 1997, almost all commercial online services offered a direct connection to the Internet as part of their online services packages.

In November 2001, 46 million Internet subscribers in the United States connected to the Internet through a telephone line and an analog modem.[83] At the time of this writing, analog modems had a theoretical maximum speed of 56 kilobits per second[84] (for illustrative purposes, one page of text is roughly 2.7 kilobytes and one webpage is 30 kilobytes), although most run at top speeds of 40 to 53 kilobits per second, depending on line quality and the distance from the telephone company's central office.[85] Bits of data are transmitted from a PC through a modem, which converts (or modulates) the digital bits into analog signals and sends them over the phone lines. When the modem receives analog signals, it converts (or demodulates) the analog signals into digital form before transferring them into the receiving computer. The word modem (*mo*dulate/*dem*odulate) comes from this behavior.

The Telecommunications Act of 1996 allowed regional telephone companies and cable companies to compete with each other for the first time. Telephone companies can offer cable TV services, and cable companies can offer telephone services (and both offer broadband). With the growing demand for broadband Internet service, the competition between telephone and cable companies has never been more fierce. Each wants to become the premier provider of home broadband service. The primary types of broadband services are digital subscriber lines (DSL), cable modems, and satellites. A discussion of each type of broadband connection follows.

Differences Among High-Speed Internet Delivery Services

Digital Subscriber Line

Also known as **DSL**, a **digital subscriber line** allows for high-speed connections over existing copper telephone wires. The service requires DSL modems on each end of the connection, in the user's home and at the telephone company's central office. DSL modems are different from traditional modems because they send and receive all data as digital data—no translation to analog signal ever takes place—allowing for faster data transmission.

One advantage of DSL is that it enables people to talk on the telephone and use the Internet simultaneously over a single phone line. DSL divides the phone lines into three channels: one for receiving data, one for sending data, and one for talking on the telephone. To work properly, a DSL modem must be within a certain distance—usually 18,000 feet, or about three miles—from the phone company's answering DSL modem. The exact distance varies according to the DSL service, the speed being offered, and even the gauge of the copper telephone wire. DSL speeds range from 128 kilobits per second to over 1 megabit per second.

There are several variations of DSL, but the most common versions are the data rate digital subscriber line (HDSL or T1) and the asymmetric digital subscriber line (ASDL). HDSL uses four transceivers: two at the subscriber's end and two at the telephone company's central office. Data, both downloaded and uploaded, can be transmitted across an HSDL at a speed of 1.5 megabits per second. ASDL is more common than HDSL because it is less expensive. ADSL uses only two transceivers and is capable of uploading and downloading at different maximum prescribed speeds. Downloading speed through an ADSL is usually between 1 and 12 megabits per second, while uploading is typically between 160 kilobits and 1.5 megabits per second. The uneven speeds for uploading and downloading are why ASDL is labeled asymmetric.

Another form of DSL is the ISDN (integrated services digital network) line. It can dial the Internet at higher speeds than regular nondigital phone lines, usually between 64,000 and 128,000 bits per second. Special ISDN modems must be used at both a subscriber's location and the telephone company's central office. ISDN lines cost more than normal phone lines, so users' telephone rates are usually higher. ISDN requires the installation of a second line because it cannot run over the same line as regular telephone lines and, like DSL, must be within 18,000 feet of a central office. ISDN subscribers accounted for only 0.5 percent of Internet users in 2001.[86]

Cable Modem

With the use of a special modem, the Internet can be accessed over some cable TV systems through the existing coaxial cable that carries TV signals. Starting around 1996, most cable companies began upgrading their plants by installing fiber-optic transmission technology. By replacing the coaxial copper with fiber-optic lines, cable operators could improve signal reliability and reception quality, increase channel capacity, and support the introduction of two-way interactive services.[87] To date, cable operations in the United States have spent $10 billion to transform their aging phone lines from coaxial to fiber optic. Another $20 billion is projected to be spent over the next few years.[88] **Cable modems** send and receive data at speeds of 2 to 3 megabits per second, or 35 to 52 times faster than conventional analog modems of 56 kilobits. Exhibit 12.7 illustrates the speed differences from the different types of connections.

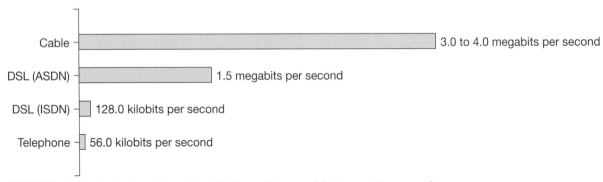

EXHIBIT 12.7   Relative Speed of Various Types of Internet Connections

Satellite Transmission

Three types of systems—geostationary, medium earth orbit (MEO), and low earth orbit (LEO)—have been proposed for satellite Internet access. Geostationary satellites would orbit 22,000 miles above the equator at the same speed as the earth's rotation, appearing stationary from the ground. They would communicate with fixed-orientation dish antennas attached to customer homes and use advanced-signal processing to compensate for transmission delays caused by the great distances their signals must travel. MEO and LEO satellites, on the other hand, would circle the globe once every two hours at altitudes of between 500 and 10,000 miles, reducing the time needed to beam signals to and from the earth's surface. Both MEO and LEO satellite methods, however, would require sophisticated subscriber antennas that can track and communicate with fast-moving MEO and LEO satellites.

The advantages of satellite transmission include ubiquity, economics, and performance.[89] However, dozens of satellites are required to service a single downlink station with continuous transmission, and handoffs from one satellite to the next could be technically complex.[90] Direct PC from Hughes Electronics currently offers satellite-based Internet access and data delivery downstream at 400 kilobits per second. Upstream access is available only by modem or other landline connections through ISPs.[91] Hughes merged with EchoStar Communications in February 2002 and pledged to further "bridge the digital divide" by providing satellite Internet connections to all of its 210 television markets. The company is hoping that satellite Internet will be particularly attractive to rural consumers, who often do not have affordable access to high-speed cable lines.[92]

Advocating an "Open System"

Freestanding ISPs such as EarthLink or NetZero do not believe that cable companies or telecoms will automatically become the leading ISPs of the future because of their dominance of the channels for broadband technology. These independent ISPs advocate an "open system" in which telephone

---

Point-Counterpoint

Which Is Better—Cable or DSL?

The battle for "the last mile" of broadband transmission into the home has largely been between telecoms that provide DSL services and cable companies that provide cable-ready modems. While the monthly costs of $40 to $50 are comparable, cable modems have lower installation costs and can download data from the Internet at much faster speeds than DSL.

With the expected increase in services such as video-on-demand and multiplayer games, which require downloading speeds of at least 3 megabits per second, advocates of cable modems say DSL may become outdated. Supporters of DSL, however, say it is more reliable and secure than cable-modem service because additional subscribers in a neighborhood hub do not dilute the quality of the connection. Also, there is less risk of an outsider hacking into an individual's personal computer system when using DSL. Some observers, such as the Yankee Group, see potential for satellite transmission to gain a significant portion of the market; an estimated one-fourth of U.S. homes will still not have access to DSL or cable modems by 2004.[93]

or cable subscribers still choose an ISP. These ISPs believe that they can differentiate themselves through price or superior customer service. As one of the conditions for the $105 billion merger of AOL and Time Warner, completed in January 2001, the Federal Communications Commission mandated that AOL Time Warner keep Time Warner's cable systems open (or available for lease) to freestanding ISPs.

Gateway to the Internet: Digital Household Devices of the Future

Just as it is unknown whether DSL, cable, or satellite transmission will become the ultimate pipeline for broadband technology, a parallel debate is taking place at the receiving end. The question is whether the personal computer, video-game console, or interactive TV set-top box will dominate as the household command center.

At the end of 2000, approximately 55 million U.S. households, or 53 percent, had personal computers.[94] In 2001, of these households with computers, 41.7 million, or 39.4 percent of all households in the United States, had Internet access. Adding those users who use the Internet outside their own home, the number of total individual Internet users in the United States rises to 138 million.[95] In 2001, 72.3 percent of all Americans used the Internet, up from 66.9 percent in 2000.[96] In 2001, 17.5 billion computers were sold, at an average price of $949.[97] At the end of 1999, there were an estimated 200 million personal computers in use,[98] with most running the Windows/MS-DOS operating system (see Exhibit 12.8).

Despite the fact that the PC is the primary Internet gateway for most Americans, many consumers say they would prefer an easier Web interface at home. According to a survey conducted by AOL and the research firm Roper Starch Worldwide in September 2000, almost half of all American adults who are currently online said they would be interested in checking their e-mail on a television, and two-thirds said they would be interested in checking a website on a television instead of a PC.[99] Sixty percent said they believed that in 10 years, every room in the house would be Internet-ready, and 54 percent said they would be interested in using a small device to access the Internet from any room in their house.[100]

As a result, many experts believe that the video-game console—such as Sony's PlayStation 2, Microsoft's Xbox, or Nintendo's GameCube—or the interactive television set-top box could emerge as the preferred "gateway entry," over the personal computer, for accessing the Web at home.

Video-Game Consoles

Launched in the United States on October 26, 2000, PlayStation 2 had sold over 30 million units worldwide by May 2002.[101] The console is the sequel to the original PlayStation system, which launched in December 1994 and was considered the first **video-game console** with the potential to access a wide range of broadband services on the Internet.[102] Like its predecessor,

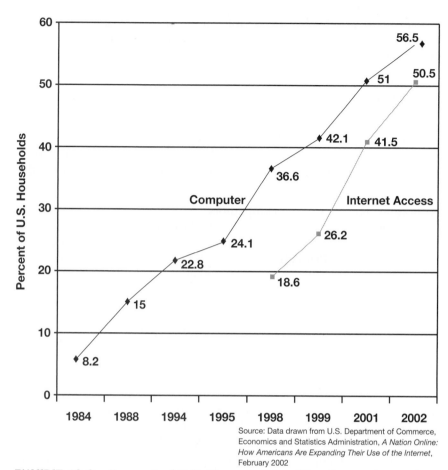

Source: Data drawn from U.S. Department of Commerce, Economics and Statistics Administration, *A Nation Online: How Americans Are Expanding Their Use of the Internet*, February 2002

EXHIBIT 12.8 Percent of U.S. Households with a Computer and Internet Access, 1984–2002

PlayStation 2 is a video-game console, but a more powerful version that can generate 66 million polygons per second—220 times faster than the 300,000 polygons-per-second speed of the original. The increased polygon usage allows for more realistic—almost lifelike—three-dimensional images. To develop 3-D images for video games, the polygons are the basic building blocks. Graphic artists then take thousands of these polygons and cover them with textures to represent a single color or multiple colors to create objects, shadows, and characters.[103]

In addition to being a video-game player, PlayStation 2—with 32 megabytes of random access memory and powered by a 128-bit central processor—could function as a CD and DVD player. In 2001, Sony added to the console a hard-drive adapter device that allows either broadband or dial-up Internet access for a fee of $40. Conceivably, with this device, a consumer could use the PlayStation 2 to bank, shop, and e-mail through a television set,[104] as well as download, store, and replay digital music and video from the Web.[105] (In January 2001, Sony announced plans to create an Internet bank in a joint venture with Sakura Bank and J.P. Morgan as the first step in providing Web-based services.[106]) In addition to a hard drive, the PlayStation 2 has built-in "firewire" ports, which allow it to transfer data seamlessly from camcorders, digital cameras, and other PC peripheral devices in the future.[107] Jeremy Schwartz, a senior analyst at Forrester Research, commented on the impact of using game consoles to access the Web:

> *Certainly the arrival of these new game consoles coming online represents a signifi-cant shift from what we have had in the past—being tied to a living room and crowd-ing around a television set playing to friends and family across town and country.*[108]

The PlayStation 2 system, which is sold at a near-cost-of-production price (profits come from video-game sales),[109] is considered one of the corner-stones of Sony's strategy to create digital-based products for the entire household.

Meanwhile, Sony's two key competitors—Nintendo and Microsoft—have constructed their own game consoles. In October 2001, Nintendo intro-duced the GameCube, which features a 405-megahertz chip that is 33 per-cent faster than the PlayStation 2, although the video-game console will not be able to play CDs or DVDs. As of May 2002, there were between 4 million and 5 million GameCubes in use.[111]

Microsoft introduced its Xbox game console in November 2001. The Xbox can access the Internet and play CDs/DVDs like the PlayStation 2 and has a chip that is twice as fast.[112] Still, Microsoft said the Xbox accounted for $750 million in losses in fiscal 2002 (with projections of losses up to $1.1 billion for 2003).[113] Such losses have prompted Microsoft to try to challenge the PlayStation 2's hold on console multitasking. An upcoming version of the Xbox will be able to record TV programs on the device's built-in hard disk, the same way that TiVo does now. The new console would retail for $500 and could be on store shelves in 2003.[114] The Xbox also plans to implement an *Xbox Live* online component that will allow video-game players to compete head-to-head over the Internet for an additional monthly fee.[115]

Interactive Television

Another potential Internet gateway is the set-top box for **interactive televi-sion**. Currently, AOL and Microsoft offer basic interactive TV services—through AOLTV and UltimateTV, respectively—that allow users to access e-mail, chat, and surf the Internet with a set-top box and dial-up modem while watching TV. Additional features that cable companies may someday offer as premium services include a choice of camera angles for sporting events, local entertainment guides during the airing of local news shows, and online purchases (such as CDs from an artist giving a televised concert).[116] Forrester Research projected that by 2005, 40 million households will have access to digital set-top boxes, almost an eightfold increase from 4.9 million households at the end of 1999.[117] This growth has not yet been realized, though; the percentage of Internet users who gained access through a televi-sion actually dropped from 3.9 percent in 2000 to 1.7 percent in 2001.[118] Nevertheless, Michael Willner, president of Insight Communications, the nation's ninth-largest cable company, observed, "I think the implications of being able to do things between television shows without having to get off your sofa, without turning on the computer, are enormous."[119]

Interactive television was tried before the widespread usage of the Internet, most notably with Warner Cable's Qube System in the late 1970s in Columbus, Ohio, and Time Warner's Full Service Network in the mid-1990s in Orlando, Florida.[120] Both experiments failed due to the high cost to the consumer and inadequate technology.[121] Experts believe that the cost of interactive television is no longer as prohibitive as it was almost a decade ago because of recent improvements to its delivery infrastructure by cable companies, which will finally make interactive features a possibility.[122] The recent testing of Enhanced TV—which lets television viewers log on to their computers for interactive features while watching TV—by ABC-TV during *Who Wants to Be a Millionaire* and *Monday Night Football*—indicates that there is widespread interest in interactive TV. Although TV viewers log on to a separate computer while using Enhanced TV, ABC says that an estimated 20,000 of the 20 million viewers of *Millionaire* play along on the Web, while between 50,000 and 100,000 of the 18 million viewers of *Monday Night Football* log on for additional player statistics. Once the demand for interactive set-top boxes increases, ABC plans to move Enhanced TV from the Web to interactive television systems,[123] where the network thinks the interactive audience would be larger.[124]

Another service that will become more widely available through interactive television is video-on-demand, which allows consumers to watch any movie or television show at any time and even pause in the middle of it. In July 2002, some 2.5 million homes already had video-on-demand, and in the next five years, that number could reach 51 million, according to Kagan World Media.[125] This service would be similar to the digital video-recording (DVR) services currently offered by TiVo and ReplayTV—potential competitors to the interactive services offered by cable companies—which allow consumers to record television shows and then pause or fast-forward while viewing.[126] The DVR services could signal a significant change in the entire structure of "free" television. Because 70 percent of viewers fast-forward through the commercials on their recorded program, DVR has the potential to render television advertising obsolete. If DVR viewership ever reached critical mass (there are currently only 400,000 subscribers), it is estimated that every TV household might have to pay $250 annually on top of its current cable or satellite bill to pay for programming.[127]

Whether through WebTV or a form of video-on-demand, according to a survey conducted by Jupiter Communications, the six features that online viewers want most in interactive television are (1) the ability to pause live television shows, (2) television program reminders, (3) more program information, (4) a program feature, (5) e-mail, and (6) the capability to view websites.[128]

In-House Wireless Technology

One near-term application is Bluetooth, an in-house wireless technology named after the Scandinavian monarch Harold Bluetooth, who sought to unite the countries of Norway and Denmark during the 10th century. Bluetooth would allow ubiquitous Web access throughout the home without the need for a modem or other accessories. It is being developed by a consortium of companies, including Ericsson, IBM, Intel, Nokia, and Toshiba.[129] With Bluetooth-enabled devices—which use short-range radio frequency to transmit data—users can connect their PCs, personal digital assistants, digital cameras, and other devices to the Web and to one another within 30 feet, without the use of connecting cables.[130] Merrill Lynch estimated that the number of Bluetooth chipsets—now being used in select IBM and Toshiba laptops, as well as by Nokia phones in Europe and Asia—will grow from 9.2 million in 2000 to 2.1 billion in 2005. Over the same period, the average price of a Bluetooth chipset is expected to fall from $15 to $2.02.[131] Beginning in 2001, Palm will begin to build Bluetooth transmitters into its Palmtops.[132] The projection might have to be curtailed a bit; the user interface was reviewed in 2002 as costing too much "in dollars and aggravation."[133] Nevertheless, analysts are extremely optimistic. Martin Reynolds of Gartner Group's Dataquest said, "It really will ship in the billions of units once it gains momentum. It's really a multibillion-dollar market."[134]

An alternative wireless technology is a networking system called 802.11, which is already being used by Apple Computer in its AirPort wireless system. The 802.11 system differs from Bluetooth because it functions more like a wireless Ethernet system that would allow two or more computers to interact with one another, instead of merely connecting devices with a personal computer. It can operate computers within a distance of 100 feet and at speeds equivalent to the low end of today's Ethernet systems.[135]

Home RF is a third home wireless technology and is being developed by a consortium that comprises Microsoft, Intel, Motorola, and Hewlett-Packard. Like Bluetooth, Home RF is intended to create a wireless network for the home market and operates on a similar 2.4 GHz frequency band.[136]

Fragmenting Media Usage Through Expanding Media Content Services

Forecasters see mobile wireless technology as one of the fastest-growing alternatives to PCs for accessing the Web, especially when it is used as an "electronic wallet" or to check stock quotes, services that require relatively low bandwidth. Projections estimate that the number of installed wireless Web devices—whether they are Qualcomm PDQs (a combination of a Palm organizer and a cellular phone), National SemiConductor Web Pads, or Nokia WAP phones—will grow almost 20-fold, from 3.4 million to 67.4 million, between 1999 and 2004.[137]

Palm-size computers are now enabled to receive wireless data through the Internet as well. These computers do everything from serving as electronic appointment calendars to acting as MP3 players and digital cameras. While Palm dominates the market, its market share in the United States dipped from 76 percent in 1999 to 72 percent in 2000 to 58 percent in 2001. Handspring, which licenses the Palm operating system, increased its market share in 2001 to 15 percent from 2000's 14 percent.[138] Sales of palm-size computers in 2000 more than doubled in the United States from a year earlier, and unit growth almost tripled in the same period. However the growth from 2000 to 2001 was only 25 percent.[139] In the future, the mantra will be to "give [users] what they want when they need it," observed Alan Kessler, general manager of Palm's platform solutions group. "That's a lot different than the PC era, when everyone said, 'Give me more memory. Give me more power. Give me more complex software.' "[140]

Another popular wireless device is the BlackBerry, which originally allowed users to receive and send e-mail from their regular accounts and which now allows an integrated wireless communications service—including voice, data, and calendaring. It features a miniature, built-in QWERTY keyboard. As of September 2000, there were 200,000 BlackBerrys in use, compared to 4 million Palm devices.[141] However, users of the BlackBerry, which is manufactured by the Canadian firm Research in Motion, pay about $400 to $500 for the device and a monthly service fee of $40. For large companies, the software to connect the BlackBerry to a company's e-mail system costs roughly $5,000 (for 20 users). The device itself weighs about 5 ounces, is powered by a 32-bit Intel 386 chip, and can run up to three weeks on a AA battery.[142]

One technology that enables other wireless communications is WAP, an open system (originally advocated by Finnish mobile-phone manufacturer Nokia) that allows Internet users to access information from the Web on their cellphones. The key to WAP is a language called Extensible Markup Language (XML), another open standard. This language tags all the data being distributed wirelessly and makes sure that it is displayed in a comprehensible way on the user's device.[143]

Another emerging wireless communications service is i-mode, which was introduced in Japan in February 1999 by the mobile-phone company NTT DoCoMo. In less than two years, i-mode added more than 17 million subscribers in Japan who access the Internet through their digital phones at an average cost of $20 per month, making DoCoMo the fastest-growing ISP in the world and the corporation with the third-highest market capitalization, behind Microsoft and General Electric. Subscribers to i-mode—which offers 24-hour Internet access, unlike WAP-based phones, which require dialing an ISP—can send e-mail, watch cartoons, search the Web, or check stock quotes. In addition, i-mode provides Web services through third-party agreements and adds the costs to subscribers' monthly phone bills. Long-term plans call for DoCoMo to launch the next generation of broadband wireless Internet services, which it claims "can be 100 times faster than existing speeds and make the mobile phone the all-purpose communication, entertainment, and information device, where users can also read e-books, play MP3 music, and watch television shows."[144] DoCoMo has already purchased minority stakes in wireless carriers in Asia, South America, Europe, and, most recently, AT&T Wireless in the United States. Kei-Ichi Enoki, managing director of i-mode, said this about the future of wireless phones:

> We will all eventually have our own wireless phone. The PDA and PCs will be secondary. We humans, it does not matter whether we're Americans or Japanese, we are all lazy in nature. It's just too much to carry two devices around.[145]

Just around the corner is the widespread debut of 3G—short for third-generation—networks, which will allow for increased broadband wireless usage on telephones. Currently, wireless phone connections, such as those for i-mode, operate at a top speed of between 9.6 and 19.2 kilobits per second.[146] With 3G, information can be sent across the wireless network at a speed of 64 kilobits per second, which would be a bit faster than existing dial-up modems for personal computers.[147] Third-generation technology will also enable increased multitasking, allowing users to send e-mail, utilize videoconferencing, surf the Web, take digital photos, and listen to MP3 music—all on a single mobile phone.[148] While the operating speed for 3G is technically slower than that of broadband home service, fewer bits are needed to fill up the tiny screens of mobile phones compared with PC screens.[149] NTT DoCoMo introduced 3G technology in Japan on a limited basis in May 2001—in addition to i-mode usage—and has steadily added subscribers, services, and coverage in cities throughout 2002.[150]

Even so, some experts believe that wireless Web technology will be less likely to take off in the United States, where 55 percent of the population accesses the Internet through desktop computers, compared with 25 percent in Japan.[151] As a result of a more established telecommunications infrastructure, in 2000, only 32 percent of all Americans had mobile phones (109.5 million total subscribers), compared with 45 percent in Japan, 59 percent in Sweden, and 65 percent in Finland.[152] In addition, the United States lacks both Europe's and Asia's uniform standard for digital communications—a standard responsible for improved signals and easier technological innovation across wireless Web products.[153] Nevertheless, American mobile-phone ownership grew to 49 percent (128 million total subscribers) in 2001.[154]

Amanda McCarthy, an analyst with Forrester Research, said this about the importance of an easy-to-use interface for these small wireless devices:

> *Nothing is going to happen through these devices if it isn't relatively simple, involving a small sum of money, and suited to real-time transactions. . . . You're not going to have a relationship with a handset that you aren't first going to have with a PC screen.*[155]

Defining Organizational Convergence

Organizational convergence describes the increasing ability of a business to deploy multiple digital platforms (consisting of both human and technological assets) against tactical or strategic goals. While the convergence of digital technologies continues apace, the end goal—to create an organization

---

Marketspace Interview

Walter Mossberg, Personal Technology Columnist, The Wall Street Journal

The Internet is like the electrical grid; it's a massive grid that contains power. Now, think about the electrical grid. There are plugs in all the buildings we're in. And you can plug anything in; you know, lights, your toaster, a CD player, an electric lawn mower. They all plug in, yet they're all different. Each takes something from that grid and creates an experience that is unique to the task that it's supposed to be performing.

That's how I think of the Internet. There will be plugs all over every building and there will be wireless "plugs" in the sky that you can connect to. And there will be 10,000 devices that will, in whole or in part, depend on a certain discrete subset of stuff that's out there on the Internet: commerce, content, entertainment, services. And they will take that "stuff" and display it in an appropriate way for the moment you're in, the task you're doing, the room you're in, the size and shape of the device you're using. That's where we're heading: the Internet as the enabling backbone for a world full of digital appliances ranging from mobile ones you hold in your hand to things that might resemble the PC (in the sense that they sit on a table and have a relatively bigger screen) to things in your kitchen or your house that will just have a little Internet intelligence behind them to do what they need to do.

that can consistently and profitably leverage these converged technologies—remains elusive. At the core of these aspirations lies the concept of synergy: that the organizational and technological "whole" is greater than the sum of each of the individual parts. Some media businesses have assembled an impressive portfolio of platforms and have shown they can, for example, release a movie; promote it on other, complementary channels (Web, cable, TV, magazines); and realize additional revenue from related products (books, music CDs, video and interactive games).

For businesses to combine these assets, a number of factors had to fall into place, including changes in government regulations, the availability of capital to fund acquisitions, and the receptivity of public markets to mergers of a scale far beyond what had occurred before in the media industry. Even with this alignment, the organizational strategy and the human assets necessary to sustain that strategy also need to fit.

Achieving Organizational Convergence

Perhaps the most visible attempts to gain the advantages of organizational and technological convergence have been the many megamergers that have taken place since 1995. The increased fragmentation in the use of media and the promise of broadband technology have sent media companies searching for new ways to capture wider audiences. One strategy has been to vertically integrate for content and distribution across the three core media types—print, video, and audio. Media megamergers include the following:

- Time Warner and Turner Broadcasting (1995)
- The Walt Disney Company and Capital Cities/ABC (1995)
- Westinghouse and CBS (1995)
- Viacom and CBS (1999)
- AOL and Time Warner (2000)
- Tribune Company and Times Mirror (2000)
- Vivendi, Universal, and Canal Plus (2000)
- Vivendi, MP3.com, and Houghton Mifflin (2001)
- Vivendi and USA Networks (2002)

With the continued fragmentation of media usage, mergers of content-based media companies will continue to be seen as a way to reach different segments of consumers. For example, the $105 billion merger of AOL and Time Warner allows the company to reach an estimated 60 percent of all American households through its magazines, cable television, movies, books, or online service. AOL Time Warner reaches 29 million households through its online service and 14 million through its cable systems, owns 40 magazines through Time Inc., has 37 million subscribers to its HBO channel, and reaches 12 percent of all moviegoers through Warner Bros. Studios.[156] With multiple media channels, increased digitalization allows AOL Time Warner to feed its content across different platforms, such as delivering Warner Bros. motion pictures on demand over its cable channel and on the Web, or distributing music from its Warner Music Group over the Internet.[157] Observed Robert Pittman, then vice chairman of AOL Time Warner:

> *With all its copyrights, Time Warner is in a marvelous position to take advantage of the Net and not be frightened by it. AOL's mindset, assets, and expertise help them in that path.*[158]

Renetta McCann, chief executive of Starcom North America, a Chicago-based media services agency, said this about the merger of AOL and Time Warner and its benefit for advertisers, the main source of revenue for many media companies:

> *In this world of fragmentation, what this does is re-aggregate some of the media vehicles, so you can get an Internet presence, a TV presence, [and] a cable presence packaged for a particular demographic.*[159]

With no geographic barriers to the distribution of digitized content on the Internet, many media companies have sought to create global markets for their content through mergers. Brand names that have expanded into overseas markets include CNN International, MTV Overseas, ESPN, and The Disney Channel. Exhibit 12.9 shows AOL Time Warner synergies.

Broadband

Digital Music

X Cross-Promotion

e-Books

Wireless

The AOL Time Warner Empire	2001 Revenues	Synergies
America Online — Including both AOL and CompuServe, provides service to a total of 37 million members	$8.7 billion	Broadband X Wireless
Cable — Time Warner Cable has 100,000 subscribers and is rolling out advanced services such as digital and high-definition television programming, high-speed Internet service, video-on-demand, and telephony	$6.9 billion	Broadband X
Publishing — Time Inc., publisher of 139 magazines, including *Time*, *Sports Illustrated*, *People*, and *Fortune*; also AOL Time Warner Book Group Inc., which includes Warner Books, Little, Brown and Company, and Time Warner Books UK	$4.8 billion	e-Books X
Networks — Includes HBO, Turner Broadcasting System (TBS), and the WB Television Network	$7 billion	Broadband X
Filmed Entertainment — Warner Bros. Pictures (both film and television), New Line Cinema Corp., and Warner Home Video	$8.7 billion	X
Warner Music Group — Includes artists such as Staind, Enya, Faith Hill, and Missy Elliot; The AOL-TW deal will allow digital distribution of music over the Web	$3.9 billion	Digital Music X Broadband

Source: AOL Time Warner, *2001 Annual Report*. URL: *http://www.AOL.com*

EXHIBIT 12.9   AOL Time Warner Synergies

Even as media companies continue to merge so they can distribute content across multiple media channels, Nobuyuki Idei, chairman and CEO of Sony, foresees a day when the companies that create the network infrastructure will also dominate the media infrastructure. Sony itself acquired CBS Records—originally a joint venture between CBS and Sony—and Columbia Studios in the late 1980s. In the late 1990s, Microsoft developed the MSN

Network and the online newsmagazine Slate.com and took joint ownership with General Electric of the MSNBC news channel. Some observers note that Sony's interest in CBS/Sony Records helped the company set the standard for compact disks in 1982, whereas its failure to own a major Hollywood studio or movie library allowed JVC's Video Home System (VHS) to be selected over Betamax as the operating standard for videocassette recorders in the late 1970s.[160] Interestingly, Sony's Nobuyuki Idei noted in 1998 that hardware would at some point be deprived of its stand-alone value:

> In the Age of Networks . . . it won't matter whether TV screens are bright and have beautiful resolutions. What matters will be the content: who creates it and who controls the networks that distribute it.[161]

Forces Enabling Organizational Convergence

Several forces contributed to these megamergers, including changes in telecommunications laws, vertical integration of both content and distribution channels, pursuit of multiple revenue streams, advances in new digital technologies, and entry into global markets.

Telecommunications Act of 1996

The Telecommunications Act of 1996, signed into law by President Clinton on February 8, 1996, was the first major overhaul of federal laws regulating the communications industry since 1934. The act increased competition by fostering a shift from a regulation-based telecommunications industry to a market-based one. The act also allowed for increased ownership of television stations by a single entity (up to 25 percent of the total U.S. market) and, more important, for media convergence. In 1999, the FCC followed up the act by allowing ownership of multiple TV stations in a given market under certain restrictive conditions.[162] As a result of subsequent court rulings, telephone service providers, cable television companies, and utility companies could now directly compete with one another to provide telephone, cable, and utility services to American homes.

The media industry is eagerly awaiting further FCC review of nearly all of its media ownership regulations—with the process expected to be completed by the spring of 2003. At present, no broadcaster's stations can reach more than 35 percent of U.S. viewers, nor can any one company own more than one of the four major networks. In addition, current rules control the number of stations a company can own in any particular market and the cross-ownership of newspapers, TV, and radio in any single market.[163]

Vertical Integration

While the Telecommunications Act of 1996 allowed for increased competition among regulated media-distribution channels, media companies were often at the center of the media megamergers because of a common overall strategy that called for vertical integration of media content with media distribution. For example, the Disney–Capital Cities/ABC and Viacom–CBS mergers saw traditional providers of movie and television content linking up with a television network as a way to distribute content into households through broadcast television.

The most common reason given for such media mergers was "synergy." As Michael Eisner, Disney chairman and CEO, explained to a gathering of Chicago executives in 1996:

> At Disney, it is our conviction that synergy can be the single most important contributor to profit and growth in a creativity-driven company. . . . [The goal is for] every segment of the business [to] promote or exploit its potential in every other possible market, product or context.
>
> [For example, if a film] does well in its initial domestic run, it almost ensures later success on home video, network television, pay-per-view, cable, and internationally. At Disney, a well-received film will also provide profitable opportunities in our theme parks . . . and in consumer products for Disney stores, for Sears, and for others.[164]

Pursuit of Multiple Revenue Streams

The consolidation of media companies—and also of advertising agencies—provides an opportunity to seek increased advertising revenue through increased cross-selling, niche media buys, and advertising sales packages. When AOL and Time Warner merged, advertising executives promised increased cross-selling opportunities for the advertisers of *Time* (print), CNN (cable television), and AOL (online) as a way to deliver upon the additional $1 billion in pretax earnings promised by management.[165] As a result, AOL Time Warner created an internal advertising council, comprising executives from its various media divisions, to promote cross–media advertising sales.

Constraints on Organizational Convergence

As we have seen, the assembly of multiple media platforms presents a number of related organizational challenges. First, the capital required to acquire or to develop multiple synergistic platforms can strain the normal operational machinery of the core businesses. Second, the architects of these new entities face challenges from internal constituencies and from external investors and regulators. These challenges have included the ability to manage disparate—and often global—business cultures, the resistance of board members or majority stakeholders with more traditional viewpoints, and the expectations of the investment community in general. Finally, these entities have been especially susceptible to fluctuations in the global business environment.

The capital benefits of the turbo-charged 1990s economy allowed some organizations to begin a rapid, record-breaking series of acquisitions. Most notable among those listed earlier, perhaps, was AOL's acquisition of Time Warner in 2000 for $165 billion. Vivendi followed its acquisition of Seagrams (including Universal Pictures) for $34 billion in 2000, with additional media acquisitions and transactions of similar scale and complexity (it obtained Houghton Mifflin, a stake in EchoStar, and USA Networks).

The combination of the large amounts of capital involved in these transfers (often in the form of equities) and the investment community's equally large earnings expectations placed great pressure on each subsequent strategic venture. Ultimately, after the softening of media markets and accounting scandals in nonrelated industries, the accounting practices of some companies attracted the attention of government regulators. At stake (and under examination) were the metrics for success or failure of these ventures: how well or poorly they worked often depended upon how the counting was done and who was doing it.

In addition to these financial hurdles, attempts at corporate convergence have faced basic operational challenges. Having assembled a number of platforms, what organizational mechanics hold them together and encourage or enforce the goal of synergy? Three areas have proven especially problematic as companies struggle to maintain organizational convergence and reap the benefits of synergy: corporate governance, alignment of corporate goals and cultures, and maintaining the confidence of the general public in the viability of such extensive organizations.

Attempts at organizational convergence demand strong corporate leadership. Nearly all of the megamergers we discussed were engineered by one strong senior executive (including Steve Case at AOL, Jean-Marie Messier at Vivendi, Sumner Redstone at Viacom, and Thomas Middlehoff at Bertelsmann). Often, these leaders found themselves struggling with a corporate board. At Bertelsmann, for example, CEO Middlehoff's strategic goals—to expand the number of media platforms under the corporate umbrella and to raise additional cash by taking the company public—conflicted with the more conservative goals of members of the founding family who sat on the corporate board and favored a return to the company's core businesses. Although Middlehoff was considered a visionary only a year previously, his struggles with the board and the company's lackluster performance led to his dismissal in the spring of 2002.[166]

In other instances, the attempt to fully merge two successful leadership teams led to problems. The initial partnership between AOL's governing team, led by Steve Case, and Time Warner's team, led by Gerald Levin, broke apart amid claims of clashing cultures and differing strategic goals. Levin resigned in 2001, and his departure was followed by a number of changes at the top level of the new entity, culminating in the resignation of COO Robert Pittman (also interim chief executive of its America Online unit) in the summer of 2002 and the restructuring of the senior leadership team of AOL Time Warner by its CEO, Richard Parsons, with more traditional executives from Time Warner. In January 2002, Steve Case decided to resign.

For some initially successful mergers, things seem to fall apart after the deal is signed. Jean-Marie Messier of Vivendi Universal attempted to radically transform the core business of his company, even going so far as to literally "Americanize" it by moving the corporate operations from Paris to the United States, only to resign after widespread resistance in France from within the company and from the French public. In addition, Vivendi has struggled to integrate its wide-ranging media acquisitions while facing a crushing $26 billion debt.[167]

Challenges to organizational convergence have existed at lower levels as well. Merely articulating a vision of synergy does not necessarily lead to success, particularly for a vast organization that is scattered across industries and locations. While there have been a handful of bright spots in the AOL Time Warner merger (Warner Bros.'s seismically lucrative movie *Harry Potter and the Sorcerer's Stone* benefited greatly from generous promotions on AOL websites), the disparate factions in the conglomerate feud more often than they mesh. The resulting cross-marketing underperformance was one of the many causes of AOL Time Warner's stock dive in mid-2002. Thus, the theoretical benefits of multiple revenue streams must be tempered by practical limitations.

AOL Time Warner's postmerger difficulties extend beyond limited cross-marketing. The combined company's shares have fallen more than 75 percent since the merger. While the potential for synergy was, and still is, present, the supposed fruits of the combination of old and new media have failed to materialize.[168] AOL Time Warner posted a record $54.2 billion loss on the value of its assets in the first quarter of 2002 while struggling with a steep decline in advertising revenues.[169]

The Future of Synergy

Since the collapse of the dot-com sector, we have seen an adjustment of the initial high expectations for achieving synergy through technological and organizational convergence. In the 1990s, there was a dramatic technological convergence of media assets to a single digital platform. Separate streams of media content—newspapers, radio, music, books—began to find an additional outlet on the Internet. The increase in the sheer number of devices and the decline in the cost of those devices led to expectations by media companies and the investment community that efficiencies of scale (economic benefits from combining assets of a single type) and of scope (economic benefits from combing assets of several different types) could be easily achieved through mergers. A series of mergers and acquisitions followed in short order, all based on the hopes of a rapid achievement of organizational convergence.

If the pendulum had swung to an extreme optimism for the realization of these goals during and after this period of consolidation, then the climate in the middle of 2002 reflects an equally extreme backward swing, to pessimism and skepticism about the possibility of realizing the benefits of synergy in the media industry. Several architects of notable megamergers have lost their jobs, a number of highly visible attempts to capture synergy have failed, and the investment community waits with increasing impatience for sustainable returns on the enormous capital outlays to create the new media giants. Indeed, the very size of these ventures has raised concerns about their accounting practices—part of a broader backlash against 2002's corporate accounting scandals.

Such an extreme reaction overlooks some very tangible successes and the possible rewards for the company that overcomes the difficulties of organizational convergence. The seemingly universal reach of the *Harry Potter* and *The Lord of the Rings* film franchises—not only on movie screens, but also in additional products such as DVDs, CD soundtracks, books, and action figures—certainly illustrates compelling and effective cross-platform leverage by AOL Time Warner. In fact, Wall Street's true concerns about technological and organizational convergence seem to be more about *when* synergistic benefits will emerge and the size of those benefits, not whether any such benefits will ever be realized. A balanced view of media convergence—one that recognizes its challenges while embracing its possibilities—appears to be the most likely outcome of the dot-com turmoil.

Summary

1. What is media convergence?

Media convergence describes a combined technological and organizational process in which content from various media platforms—print, audio, and video—will ultimately become available through a single Internet platform, with organizations ultimately realizing the synergistic benefits of such a platform. As broadband Internet access becomes widespread, that one platform will support not only traditional graphics, streaming video, and streaming audio, but also video-on-demand, software distribution, books-on-demand, and multiplayer games.

2. What conditions make technological convergence possible?

The following conditions have contributed to the merging of various forms of media: continued advances in digital technology, a low-cost digital network infrastructure, growing media-usage fragmentation in American households, and the forecasted continued proliferation of new media types. Together, these conditions encourage digital convergence and make the media environment attractive for consolidation and vertical integration.

3. How have companies attempted to realize organizational convergence?

The Telecommunications Act of 1996 allowed for both the increased ownership of television stations by a single entity and direct competition among telephone companies, cable television companies, and utility companies. Mergers became part of an overall strategy of media companies to vertically integrate media content with media distribution. With no geographic barriers to the distribution of digitized content on the Internet, many media companies seek to create global markets for their content through mergers. With increased digitization of content and the promise of widespread broadband delivery in the near future, the personal computer will not be the only receiver of information over the Internet. For today's media company, the strategy is to collect and, through media convergence and digital convergence, create a synergistic combination of what were once disparate media to produce a direct bottom-line benefit.

4. How do new-media companies leverage traditional media channels?

While the Internet is an increasingly important source for news, information, and commerce, the networked economy is still dependent on traditional old-economy news outlets. In fact, online media outlets have attempted to build their audiences through traditional media channels. Dot-coms advertised in newspapers and magazines and on broadcast television during the first stage of attracting early adopters and into the secondary stage of attracting mainstream users. To build brand awareness for a rapidly growing mainstream audience of Internet users, dot-com companies spent an estimated $3 billion to $4 billion in advertising in 1999; some 90 percent of those dollars were spent in traditional media outlets, such as network television, national newspapers, and network radio.

5. What are the barriers to organizational convergence?

Attempts at organizational convergence have struggled with the difficulty of executing corporate and business-unit strategies across the breadth of these newly formed media companies. In addition, the expectations set during the creation of new-media companies—internally among board members and business-unit heads, and externally in the investment community—have created increased pressure when synergies have not been immediately realized.

1. Visit the corporate website of one or more of the following companies. For each one, construct a map of the mergers or acquisitions it has been involved in over the last four years.

   - AOL/Time Warner (*http://www.aoltimewarner.com*)
   - Vivendi Universal (*http://www.vivendiuniversal.com*)
   - The Walt Disney Co. (*http://www.disney.com*)
   - Viacom (*http://www.viacom.com*)
   - Sony (*http://www.sony.com*)
   - Bertelsmann (*http://www.bertelsmann.com*)

2. Choose one of the companies listed in Exercise 1, and outline its attempts at organizational convergence. Has it developed any unique ways to achieve synergy?

3. For one of the companies listed in Exercise 1, choose an initiative it has introduced and trace the number of platforms that the initiative includes.

4. Choose one of the companies listed in Exercise 1. Does it provide metrics for the success or failure of its synergy efforts?

technological convergence	media-usage fragmentation	cable modem
analog	digital lifestyle	video-game console
digital	broadband	interactive television
media proliferation	digital subscriber line (DSL)	organizational convergence

[1] *New York Times 2002 Almanac*, s.v. "Computers: A Glossary of Computer Terms—Bits and Bytes: Quantifying Data," 798.

[2] Jeffrey F. Rayport, George C. Lodge, and Thomas Gerace, "National Information Infrastructure (A): The United States in Perspective," Note no. 9-396-111, Revised 20 March 1997 (Boston: Harvard Business School Publishing, 1997), 4.

[3] "Public's News Habits Little Changed by September 11," *Pew Research Center for the People & the Press: Survey Reports*, 9 June 2002 (URL: http://people-press.org/reports/print.php3?ReportID=156).

[4] Ibid.

[5] Ibid.

[6] *New York Times 2002 Almanac*, s.v. "Primetime Viewing Shares of Free and Cable TV Networks, 1995–2000," 396. Almanac data cites Nielsen Media Research.

[7] Ibid., s.v. "Basic and Pay Cable TV Systems and Subscribers, 1952 to 2001," 397. Almanac data cites National Cable Television Association, Cable TV Developments, Nielsen Media Research.

[8] Vicki Haddock, "How Media Saturates American Kids' Lives," *San Francisco Examiner*, 17 November 1999.

[9] Elizabeth Lesly Stevens, "The Entertainment Glut," *BusinessWeek*, 16 February 1998.

[10] Veronis, Suhler & Associates. "Veronis, Suhler & Associates Communications Industry Forecast," October 1998.

[11] U.S. Department of Commerce, Economics and Statistics Administration, *A Nation Online: How Americans Are Expanding Their Use of the Internet*, February 2002 (URL: http://www.esa.doc.gov/508/esa/nationonline.htm).

[12] Steve Levy, "Here Comes Playstation 2," *Newsweek*, 6 March 2000, 57.

[13] *New York Times 2002 Almanac*, s.v. "Daily Newspapers, Number and Circulation, 1900–00," 388. Almanac data cites Newspaper Association of America, *Facts about Newspapers, 2001*.

[14] Ibid., s.v. "Top 100 US Daily Newspapers by Circulation, 2000," 389. Almanac data cites *Editor and Publisher Yearbook, 2001*.

[15] "Facts About Newspapers 1999: Number of U.S. Daily Newspapers," *Newspaper Association of America* (URL: http://www.naa.org/info/facts99/11.html). Data was drawn from *Editor and Publisher Yearbook, 1999*.

[16] *New York Times 2002 Almanac*, s.v. "The Media: The Print Media—Newspapers," 388.

[17] "Facts About Newspapers 1999: U.S. Daily and Sunday/Weekend Newspaper Reading Audience," *Newspaper Association of America* (URL: http://www.naa.org/info/facts99/02.html). The NAA cites data from NAA; W.R. Simmons & Associates Research, Inc. 1970–1977; Simmons Market Research Bureau Inc. 1980–1994; Scarborough Research—Top 50 DMA Market Report, 1995–1998.

[18]Newspaper Association of America, For statistics about who reads newspapers, see "Facts About Newspapers 2002: U.S. Daily and Sunday Newspaper Readership Demographics" (URL: http://www.naa.org/info/facts02/5_facts2002.html). For income figures see U.S. Bureau of the Census, *Current Population Survey*, 25 September 2001 (URL: http://www.bls.census.gov/cps/cpsmain.htm).

[19]*New York Times 2002 Almanac*, s.v. "Total U.S. Advertising Volume by Medium, 1998–99," 353. Almanac cites data from *Advertising Age*, 22 May 2000.

[20]James M. Marsh, Brian Shipman, and William Lerner, "Media Monthly," Prudential Securities, June 2000.

[21]Saul Hansell, "Can AOL Keep Its Subscribers in New World of Broadband?" *New York Times*, 29 July 2002.

[22]*New York Times 2002 Almanac*, s.v. "Top 100 U.S. Daily Newspapers by Circulation," 389. Almanac cites *Editor and Publisher Yearbook*, 2001.

[23]Ibid., s.v. "The Media: The Print Media— Newspapers," 389.

[24]Ibid., s.v. "Top 100 U.S. Magazines by Circulation, 2000," 390. Almanac cites Magazine Publishers of America, 2001.

[25]Ibid., s.v. "Top 50 Magazines by Advertising Revenue," 391. Almanac cites Magazine Publishers of America, *Publisher's Information Bureau Publications Ranked by Revenue, 2000* (2001).

[26]Jennifer Steil, "The New Realities of New Launches," *Folio*, 30 January 2001.

[27]*New York Times 2002 Almanac*, s.v. "New Books and Editions Published, by Subject, 1980-2000," 394. Almanac cites data from R.R. Bowker Co., *The Bowker Annual: Library and Book Trade Almanac* (2001).

[28]Ibid.

[29]Ibid., s.v. "The Media: The Print Media—Books," 391.

[30]Veronis, Suhler & Associates, "Veronis, Suhler & Associates Communications Industry Forecast," October 1998.

[31]Romesh Ratnesar and Joel Stein, "Everyone's a Star.com," *Time*, 27 March 2000.

[32]Donald T. Hawkins, "Electronic Books: Reports of Their Death Have Been Exaggerated," *Online*, 26, no. 4 (July/August 2002) (URL: http://www.onlinemag.net/jul02/hawkins.htm).

[33]"The New Digital Content Consumer: Large and in Charge," *Accenture: Research and Insights*, 6 June 2002 (URL: http://www.accenture.com/xd/xd.asp?it=enWeb&xd=industries/communications/media/medi_thought10.xml).

[34]Hawkins, "Electronic Books."

[35]*New York Times 2002 Almanac*, s.v. "The Media: Print Media—Books," 391.

[36]Dickson Louie, "CBS Evening News," Case no. 9-898-086, Rev. 11 March 1999 (Boston: Harvard Business School Publishing, 1999).

[37]*New York Times 2002 Almanac*, s.v. "Electronic Media: Cable Television," 397.

[38]"Change the Way You Look at TV," Best Buy Co. Brochure, 1999.

[39]Details and statistics on cable television are drawn from *New York Times 2002 Almanac*, s.v. "Electronic Media: Cable Television," 396–398.

[40]Ibid.

[41]*New York Times 2002 Almanac*, s.v. "The Electronic Media: Radio," 398.

[42]Ibid. The almanac cites data from M. Street Corporation, 1999.

[43]Rebecca Winters, "Live from Your Basement," *Time*, 27 March 2000 (URL: http://www.time.com/time/everyone/magazine/sidebar_dj.html).

[44]Sharon Waxman, "Hollywood's Great Escapism," *The Washington Post*, 4 January 2002.

[45]*New York Times 2002 Almanac*, s.v. "The Electronic Media: Film," 400.

[46]Ibid., s.v. "The Electronic Media: Film—Movie Budgets," 400.

[47]Ratnesar and Stein, "Everyone's a Star.com."

[48]Harold Vogel, *Entertainment Industry Economics*, 4th ed. (New York: Cambridge University Press, 1998).

[49]Richard Shim, "DVD Players Ready for a Makeover," *ZDNet*, 21 January 2002.

[50]Michelle Slatalla, "Get Movie Popcorn, Then Check the Mail," *New York Times*, 22 February 2001.

[51]*New York Times 2002 Almanac*, s.v. "The Electronic Media: Video—DVD (Digital Video Discs)," 400.

[52]Ibid., s.v. "The Electronic Media: The Recording Industry," 398.

[53]Ibid., s.v. "Recorded Music Sales by Genre, Format and Age Group, 1987–2000," 399. Almanac cites the Recording Industry Association of America, 2000 Consumer Profile.

[54]*New York Times 2002 Almanac*, s.v. "Recorded Music Sales by Genre, Format and Age Group, 1987–2000," 399. Almanac cites Recording Industry Association of America, 2000 Consumer Profile.

[55]Ibid., s.v. "The Recording Industry," 398.

[56]"Burn Baby Burn," *Straits Times*, 14 July 2002. The article cites data from the International Federation of the Phonographic Industries.

[57]Chris Tucker, "Online Pirates Beware," *Southwest Spirit Magazine*, April 2000.

[58]Karl Taro Greenfield, "The Free Juke Box," *Time*, 27 March 2000.

[59]Matt Richtel, "Upheaval at Bertelsmann May End Plans for Acquisition of Napster," *New York Times*, 31 July 2002.

[60]Adam Brandenburger, Julia Kou, and Monique Burnett, "Power Play (A): Nintendo in 8-bit Video Games," Case no. 9-795-102, Revised 12 July 1995 (Boston: Harvard Business School Publishing, 1995).

[61]Stephanie Storm, "Why PlayStation 2 Isn't Children's Play," *New York Times*, 10 October 2000.

[62]Veronis, Suhler & Associates, "Veronis, Suhler & Associates Communications Industry Forecast," October 1998.

[63]Nicholas Negroponte, *Being Digital* (New York: Knopf, 1995).

[64]Bill Gates, "Remarks CES 2001," *Microsoft.com*, 6 January 2001 (URL: www.microsoft.com/billgates/speeches/2001/01-06ces.asp). Portions reprinted with permission from Microsoft Corporation.

[65]John Markoff, "For Microsoft, a Shift Toward New Vistas," *New York Times*, 18 December 2000, C-25.

[66]Craig Barrett, "Executive Speeches: 2001 CES Pre-Event Kickoff Keynote," *Intel.com*, 5 January 2001 (URL: www.intel.com/pressroom/archive/speeches/crb20010105ces.htm).

[67]John Markoff, "Thinking Revolution, Talking Evolution at Apple," *New York Times*, 21 January 2001.

[68]"File Sharing and CD Burners Proliferate," Ipsos-Reid Polls and Research, *Ipsos/Reid*, 12 June 2002 (URL: http://www.angusreid.com/media/dsp_displaypr_us.cfm?id_to_view=1542).

[69]Markoff, "Thinking Revolution, Talking Evolution at Apple."

[70]"PlayStation: News—Story: Comdex: Sony Aims High with PlayStation 2," *IGN.com*, 16 November 1999 (URL: http://psx.ign.com/articles/072/072207p1.html).

[71]Howard Stringer, "Digital or Die: Broadcasting in the 21st Century," Speech before the National Association of Broadcasters, *Hollywood Reporter.com*, 19 April 1999 (URL: www.hollywoodreporter.com/inwords/speeches/HowardSt.asp).

[72]Michael Dell, "Comdex 2000: 'PC Goes Wireless,' Michael Dell Keynote Address, " *Dell Computer Corporation*, 13 November 2000 (URL: http://www.euro.dell.com/countries/uk/enu/gen/corporate/speech/speech_2000-11-13-lv-000.htm).

[73]Steve Case, "Speeches: Goldman Sachs Communicopeia Conference," *AOL.com*, 28 September 2000 (URL: http://corp.aol.com/press/speeches/092800communicopeia.html).

[74]ISP-Planet Staff. "Market Research: Worldwide Broadband Trends," *ISP-Planet.com*, 25 July 2002 (URL: http://www.isp-planet.com/research/2002/broadband_020725.html).

[75]Matthew Flanigan, "Long Live Broadband," *Telecommunications America*, 1 July 2002.

[76]Seth Schiesel, "Rules for AOL Time Warner May Have Only a Narrow Impact," *New York Times*, 18 December 2000.

[77]Michael Pastore, "Broadband Access to Increase in Workplace," *Cyberatlas.com*, 25 January 2001 (URL: http://cyberatlas.internet.com/markets/broadband/article/0,,10099_570571,00.html).

[78]U.S. Department of Commerce, *A Nation Online*.

[79]Ibid.

[80]Matt Richel, "Small Internet Service Providers Survive Among the Giants," *New York Times*, 16 August 1999.

[81]Hansell, "Can AOL Keep Its Subscribers in a New World of Broadband."

[82]"Timeline of the Internet," *Sunday Contra Costa Times*, 19 December 1999.

[83]Michael Pastore, "Life in the Slow Lane Is Just Fine," *Cyberatlas.com*, 12 November 2001 (URL: http://cyberatlas.internet.com/markets/broadband/article/0,1323,10099_922121,00.html).

[84]"Westell Technologies Develops Next Generation of WireSpeed Products," *Business Wire*, 11 April 2002.

[85]Jay O. Light, Lynda M. Applegate, and Dan J. Green, "The Last Mile of Broadband Access, Technical Note," Note no. 9-800-076, 14 September 1999 (Boston: Harvard Business School Publishing, 1999).

[86]*The UCLA Internet Report 2001, Surveying the Digital Future: Year Two* (Los Angeles: UCLA Center for Communimcation Policy, 2001), 25.

[87]Thomas R. Eisenmann, "Telecommunications Inc.: Accelerating Digital Deployment," Case no. N9-899-141, 3 December, 1998 (Boston: Harvard Business School Publishing, 1998), 2.

[88]Todd Wallack, "The Need for Speed," *The San Francisco Chronicle*, 28 March 2000.

[89]Robert P. Norcross, "Satellites: The Strategic High Ground," *Scientific American*, October 1999.

[90]Light, Applegate, Green, "The Last Mile of Broadband Access: Technical Note," 15.

[91]PriceWaterhouseCoopers, *e-Business Technology Forecast* (Menlo Park, CA: PriceWaterhouseCoopers Technology Centre, 1999), 217.

[92]Hughes Electronics Corp., "The EchoStar-Hughes Merger Benefits: Merger Benefits," *Hughes.com* (URL: http://mergerinfo.hughes.com/5060/wrapper.jsp?PID=5060-3).

[93]Andrew Pollock, "Coming Soon, Downloads from Up Above," *New York Times*, 27 February 2000.

[94]*New York Times 2002 Almanac*, s.v. "Personal Computer Households, 1995–2000," 798. Almanac cites U.S. Department of Commerce and Jupiter Media Metrix.

[95]Ibid., s.v. "U.S. Online Households and Internet Users, 1996–2001," 808. Almanac cites U.S. Department of Commerce.

[96]*The UCLA Internet Report 2001*, 5.

[97]*New York Times 2002 Almanac*, s.v. "Personal Computer Sales, 1985–2001," 798. Almanac cites Consumer Electronics Manufacturers Association.

[98]John Markoff, "A Strange Brew's Buzz Lingers in Silicon Valley," *New York Times*, 26 March 2000.

[99]*America Online/Roper Starch Worldwide Adult 2000 Cyberstudy*, Roper No. CNT375 (October 2000).

[100]Ibid.

[101]John Markoff, "Microsoft's $1 Billion Bet on Xbox Network," *New York Times*, 20 May 2002.

[102]The Sega Dreamcast, launched in September 1999, had the capability for dial-up Internet access, but not broadband Internet access.

[103]Steven L. Kent, "PlayStation 2: The Wait Is Over," *Sony Style*, Holiday 2000.

[104]Ibid.

[105]Jeffrey F. Rayport and Bernard J. Jaworski, *e-Commerce* (New York: marketspaceU/McGraw-Hill/Irwin, 2000), 377.

[106]Bill Clifford, "Sony Applies for Net Banking License," *CBS MarketWatch.com*, 31 January 2001.

[107]*Official U.S. PlayStation Magazine*, Issue 38 (November 2000).

[108]Michel Marriott, "PlayStation 2: Game Console as Trojan Horse," *New York Times*, 26 October 2000.

[109]Storm, "Why PlayStation 2 Isn't Child's Play."

[110]Reiji Asakura, *Revolutionaries at Sony: The Making of Sony Playstation and the Visionaries Who Conquered the World of Video Games* (New York: McGraw-Hill, 2000).

[111]Markoff, "Microsoft's $1 Billion Bet on Xbox Network."

[112]Marriott, "PlayStation2: Game Console as Trojan Horse."

[113]Marc Saltzman, "Xbox That Records TV Shows Forecast," *Gannett New Service*, 9 July 2002.

[114]Ibid.

[115]Markoff, "Microsoft's $1 Billion Bet on Xbox Network."

[116]Bill Syken, "Do Touch That Dial," *Time Digital*, September 2000.

[117]Ibid.

[118]*The UCLA Internet Report, 2001*, 25.

[119]Syken, "Do Touch That Dial."

[120]Ibid.

[121]Ibid. For an excellent article on the launch of the Full Service Network, see also Ken Auletta, "The Magic Box," *New Yorker*, 11 April 1994.

[122]Syken, "Do Touch That Dial."

[123]Saul Hansell, "Clicking Outside the Box," *New York Times*, 20 September 2000.

[124]Syken, "Do Touch That Dial."

[125]Stephen Battaglio, "Coming to a Couch Near You," *New York Daily News*, 21 July 2002.

[126]Hansell, "Clicking Outside the Box."

[127]Battaglio, "Coming to a Couch Near You."

[128]Syken, "Do Touch That Dial."

[129]Kevin McLaughlin, "Bluetooth Reality Check," *Business 2.0*, 20 December 2000 (URL: http://www.business2.com/articles/web/0,1653,16125,FF.html).

[130]"A Techpilgrimage: Bluetooth," *www.techpilgrim.com*, n.d. (URL: http://www.techpilgrim.com/technews.htm).

[131]McLaughlin, "Bluetooth Reality Check."

[132]David Pogue, "New Palms Will Use Bluetooth to Cast a Much Wider Net," *New York Times*, 15 February 2001.

[133]Rob Pegoraro, "The Bluetooth Blues Play On," *Washington Post*, 28 July 2002.

[134]McLaughlin, "Bluetooth Reality Check."

[135]Lee Gomes, "E-Commerce (A Special Report): Overview—The Wireless World—in English," *The Wall Street Journal*, 11 December 2000.

[136]"A Primer on Bluetooth Technology," *123jump.com*, 15 December 2000.

[137]David Lake, "Worldwide Information Appliance Installed Forecast," *Industry Standard*, 3 April 2000.

[138]Tam, Pui-wing. *The Wall Street Journal Europe*, "Technology Journal: Hand-Held Devices Sold 25% Better Last Year in U.S.," 1 February 2002.

[139]Ibid.

[140]William Holstein, "Moving Beyond the PC," *U.S. News and World Report*, 12 December 1999.

[141]Michael Newman, "BlackBerry Preserve," *e-Company*, September 2000.

[142]Ibid.

[143]Holstein, "Moving Beyond the PC."

[144]Information on DoCoMo has been drawn from Joe Ashbrook Nickell and Michele Yamada, "Exporting Japan's Revolution," *Industry Standard*, 5 February 2001.

[145]Ibid.

[146]Tim Larimer, "Internet a la i-Mode," *Time*, 5 March 2001.

[147]Gomes, "The Wireless World—in English."

[148]Larimer, "Internet a la i-Mode."

[149]Gomes, "The Wireless World—in English."

[150]"NTT DoCoMo to Invite Monitors for 'FOMA' Introductory Service," NTT DoCoMo, Press release, 8 May 2001 (URL: http://www.nttdocomo.com), May 2001; "NTT DoCoMo to Introduce FOMA P2002 Phone," NTT DoCoMo Press release, 5 June 2002 (URL: http://www.nttdocomo.com).

[151]Simon Romeo, "Weak Reception," *New York Times*, 29 January 2001.

[152]Ibid.

[153]John Ellis, "Digital Matters," *Fast Company*, July 2000.

[154]Ben Macklin, "Who's a U.S. Wireless Subscriber," *eMarketer*, 25 July 2002.

[155]David Hamilton, "Going Places," *The Wall Street Journal*, 11 December 2000.

[156]Catherine Yang, Ronald Glover, and Ann Therese Palmer, "AOL Time Warner: Showtime!" *BusinessWeek*, 15 January 2001, 57–64.

[157]Ibid.

[158]Ibid., 57.

[159]Stuart Elliott, "Ready or Not, the Future Is Big and Bundled," *New York Times*, 13 November 2000.

[160]John Nathan, *Sony: The Private Life* (Boston: Houghton Mifflin, 1999), 106, 144, 183.

[161]Ibid., 321.

[162]For an overview of the media ownership issue see the summary in the most recent court opinion, *Fox Television Stations Inc., v. FCC* (which required the FCC to reconsider its opposition to relaxing ownership rules), *Fox Television Stations, Inc. v. FCC*, 280 F. 3d 1027 (D.C. Cir. 2002),(URL: http://www.fcc.gov/ogc/2002opin.html).

[163]For a summary of U.S. Federal Communications Commission rulings on ownership see "Guide to FCC Rules on Media Ownership," *Center for Digital Democracy*, n.d. (URL: http://www.democraticmedia.org/issues/mediaownership/chart.html).

[164]Michael Eisner, "Speech to Chicago Executives Club," 19 April 1996. Used by permission from Disney Enterprises, Inc.

[165]Susan Orenstein, "Carving Out an Empire," *Industry Standard*, 5 February 2001.

[166]Mark Landler with David Kirkpatrick, "Bertelsmann Chief Fired in Top-Level Clash," *New York Times*, 29 July 2002.

[167]Richard Verrier, "Vivendi CEO Has Explaining to Do" *Los Angeles Times*, April 29 2002.

[168]David Kirkpatrick, "AOL Profits Under Scrutiny from S.E.C.," *New York Times*, 25 July 2002.

[169]James Bates, "AOL Posts Record $54.2-Billion Loss," *Los Angeles Times*, April 25 2002.

CHAPTER

13

Public Policy

CASELET: AMAZON'S 1-CLICK PATENT

It takes two mouse clicks for a returning customer to buy a book or CD at Barnes & Noble.com. The first click is for the transaction itself. The second is for the U.S. Patent and Trademark Office.

Barnes & Noble.com's chief competitor, Amazon.com, had already pioneered what it calls "1-Click" shopping, a process that allows repeat customers to make purchases without reentering their billing and shipping information. In 1998, Amazon applied for and was granted U.S. Patent No. 5,960,411, "Method and System for Placing a Purchase Order via a Communications Network."

So when Barnes & Noble.com constructed and launched its own single-click shopping system— dubbed "Express Lane"—Amazon sued for patent infringement. Just as the 1999 holiday was getting under way, a federal judge issued a preliminary injunction ordering Barnes & Noble.com to shut down its single-click service. That's when the site's second—superfluous—click was born.

The suit and ruling spawned immediate controversy. Critics charged that the patent office, in granting patent protection not just to concrete inventions but to conceptual "business methods," was turning a system designed to promote innovation into one that was stifling it—especially in the warp-speed-evolving, one-innovation-builds-on-another worlds of Internet technology and e-commerce. "Patents such as yours are the first step in vitiating the Web, in raising the barriers to entry, not just for your competitors but for the technological innovators who might otherwise come up with great new ideas that you could put to use in your own business," technical publisher Tim O'Reilly wrote to Amazon CEO Jeff Bezos in January 2000, voicing a common criticism. "We spent thousands of hours to develop our 1-Click process," Bezos countered in a company statement. "And the reason we have a patent system in this country is to encourage people to take these kinds of risks and make these kinds of investments for customers."

Even Bezos, however, eventually suggested that business-method patents should last only three to five years, not the standard 20 years. And in 2001, a U.S. appeals court overturned the preliminary injunction against Express Lane. Finally, a year later, Amazon and Barnes & Noble.com settled their legal dispute. Terms were not disclosed. As of late 2002, however, buying on Barnes & Noble.com remained a two-click affair.

This chapter was coauthored by Jeffrey Rayport, Bernie Jaworski, JoAnn Kienzle, and Steve Szaraz.

PLEASE CONSIDER THE FOLLOWING QUESTIONS AS YOU READ THIS CHAPTER:

1. How is the Internet currently regulated?

2. What are the challenges the Internet has brought to regulation?

3. What are the main regulation issues affecting the Internet today?

INTRODUCTION

Governmental regulation can have a major effect on both the strategy and the financial survival of an e-commerce business. For example, companies such as Napster and MP3.com have lost millions of dollars because of rulings against them in the courts and accompanying legislation; many content sites could have their sole current revenue source—personalized advertising—threatened if strict privacy laws are passed in Congress; and many commerce sites could lose valuable customers if U.S. states decide customers must pay sales tax on their online purchases.

Existing laws governing the ways businesses operate often prove ill-equipped to handle the Internet's swiftly changing technology and its lack of physical borders. Throughout the world, countries must decide not only how to regulate but how much to regulate and at what level. Plus, they must decide who should regulate the Internet within their own boundaries and how to regulate Internet activities with other countries as well.

The main focus of this chapter is regulation within the United States; however, relevant regulations in the European Union (EU) and elsewhere are also considered. Although different countries have different laws regarding the Internet, the underlying issues are essentially the same—how to regulate the Internet and its activities in a way that balances the concerns of the state (as different governments define them) with the concerns of businesses and individuals. In some countries, the balance tends toward the state; government regulations control physical access to the Internet, how individuals and businesses may use the Internet, and what content they may distribute or encounter on the Internet. Other countries and regions have tended to favor the rights of businesses and individuals over state concerns.

When reviewing the role of public policy in this area, bear in mind the complexity of the issues and the quickly shifting course of developments in the Internet environment. Confronted with the tangled currents of legal precedent, legislative action, and public opinion, even those responsible for overseeing regulations are often daunted. Judge Sidney Thomas of the Ninth Circuit U.S. Court of Appeals, facing requests to broaden the court's ruling on *AT&T v. City of Portland* and thereby shape a national broadband access policy, decided against it:

> *That is not our task, and in our quicksilver technological environment it doubtless would be an idle exercise. The history of the Internet is a chronicle of innovation by improvisation, from its genesis as a national defense research network, to a medium of academic exchange, to a hacker cyber-subculture, to the commercial engine for the so-called new economy. Like Heraclitus at the river, we*

address the Internet aware that courts are ill-suited to fix its flow; instead, we draw our bearings from the legal landscape, and chart a course by the law's words.[1]

Implications of Internet Regulation

Views on the extent to which the Internet should be regulated fall along a spectrum. At one end of the spectrum are those who regard the Internet as a new kind of public or common space that has grown organically from its scientific origins to accommodate the varied needs of individuals, governments, and businesses and that should be available to all and subject to minimal regulation. Those who hold this view point to the Internet's origins to defend their views: The Internet was born without regulation and has thrived with little regulation, they say, and the innovation and economic growth that has characterized Internet business would be stifled if governmental oversight increased. Noting that the Internet has transcended geographical boundaries, those in favor of little or no regulation point out the impracticality—and perhaps even impossibility—of managing the many contradictory laws and cultures of the offline world. Finally, they contrast the slow and measured pace of determining and testing such regulations with the pace at which the Internet is changing. Interestingly, some in this camp also believe that market forces set by businesses should guide the development and operation of the Internet in place of established governments, while others take a more populist view and tend toward a more free-for-all and individualistic approach.

At the opposite end of the spectrum are those who believe that while the Internet has brought great changes to business and society, those changes are no different from—and no less able to be regulated than—those brought by previous technological changes (for example, the telephone). This group believes that the Internet needs more extensive regulation in order to ensure the ongoing and efficient operation of commerce and communications. Its members argue for the extension and enforcement of existing laws that either apply to or have been greatly affected by the Internet, particularly those concerning patents, copyrights, and forms of speech or behavior regulated in the offline world. They note that without government intervention to update and extend regulations, online business practices will be stifled by the application of outmoded codes and laws—the primacy of paper documents and physical signatures, for example. They note that the Internet can provide a "Wild West" atmosphere for those threatening public safety and that law enforcement needs new tools in order to combat new forms of criminal action. Finally, they argue that the Internet provides an ideal way for countries to begin to standardize laws regarding online business in order to transcend the physical barriers of geography and culture and create a global online business community.

Adding to the complexity of the subject is that there is often no single governing body within a country, and certainly no governing body globally, that oversees the Internet. There are as many different departments and commissions as there are issues. In the United States, for example, the Federal Trade Commission (FTC) handles privacy issues, the U.S. Copyright Office enforces copyright laws, and free speech (First Amendment) issues have been fought out in the courts. Moreover, issues such as online gambling and sales taxes are decided at the state level. The European Union, in its Directive on e-Commerce (2000),[2] made an attempt to standardize Internet practices and regulations among all of its member nations. However, getting those individual nations to ratify the directive proved complicated.

Businesses have alternately suffered under and exploited this complexity. Yahoo found itself subject to content laws in Europe that were different from those in the United States. American companies, their European counterparts argue, possess an unfair advantage in cyberspace because they do not have to pay taxes on the products and services they sell outside their borders. Faced with increased regulation of gaming activities in the United States, many gaming sites have moved to countries less opposed to online gambling.

Challenges of Internet Regulation

The new technology and lack of physical borders associated with the Internet are changing the way societies look at existing laws. While new technology allows businesses and consumers new freedoms, it also poses problems to regulation. Should governments ensure equal access for all to the Internet? Should governments have access to private e-mails and records of Internet use? How should copyright laws, originally written for offline materials, be applied to the Internet and digitized content? The Internet's lack of physical borders raises the question of whose laws should be applied to certain transactions. If a consumer is sitting at a computer in California, connected to a server in Massachusetts, buying something from a business in Iowa, where does the transaction take place? Whose sales tax should that person pay? Which state laws govern the transaction? If an American goes to a French website, which country's free-speech laws should she follow? How much of her identity must she reveal, and to whom? And what can companies do with the information they have about her?

As we discussed in Chapter 10, there are three layers to the Internet: presentation, business logic, and database. There are parallel layers regarding regulation: physical (presentation), business logic, and content (database) (see Exhibit 13.1). In this chapter, we discuss five important regulatory issues affecting each layer of the Internet:

1. Access (physical layer)

2. Taxation (business-logic layer)

3. Privacy/security (business-logic layer)

4. Copyright (content layer)

5. Free speech (content layer)

We discuss each issue in three parts. First, we give an overview of the issue. Then we discuss the current status of Internet regulation. Finally, we end by discussing the effect that this issue has on the future of e-business.

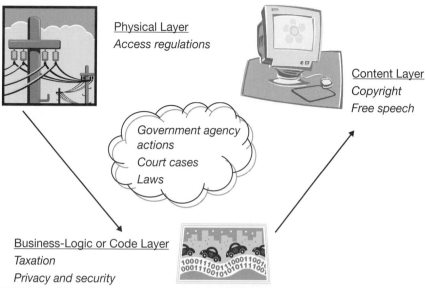

Physical Layer
Access regulations

Content Layer
Copyright
Free speech

Government agency
actions
Court cases
Laws

Business-Logic or Code Layer
Taxation
Privacy and security

EXHIBIT 13.1   Elements of Internet Regulation

Marketspace Interview

William Kennard, The Carlyle Group, ex-Chairman U.S. Federal Communications Commission

We have to make sure that as new technologies develop, they don't become saddled with legacy regulations. This is really the lesson of the Internet. The Internet grew so quickly—faster than any communications technology in the history of the world—because government made a decision early-on that we were not going to regulate it. We allowed the application layer, which became the layer for the IP protocol, to basically develop in an unregulated environment. And these decisions were made long before the Internet was really conceived of in its current form. But you continue to see these conflicts in Washington, where a new technology gets a little foothold in the economy and the powerful entrenched interests that are threatened by it try to quash it, regulate it, confine it. We always have to be vigilant.

Physical: Internet Access

The dramatic growth in the number of Internet users over the past decade is largely the result of three factors falling into place. First, users had to have a relatively unfettered way to access the Internet over the existing narrowband telecommunications infrastructure. Second, computers with the appropriate speed and memory needed to become affordable for home use. Third, the software—both to manage the link from the computer at one end of the network to the other and to manage content and functionality on the sites themselves—had to become readily available.

In this section, we concentrate on how government regulation of the telecommunications industry has made the Internet more widely available to the public. In the United States, two regulatory acts of the Federal Communications Commission (FCC) were particularly important: the *Carterfone* decision in 1968,[3] which rejected an attempt by AT&T to prevent customers from connecting their own equipment to AT&T's network (thus allowing the development and use of modems); and the *First Computer Inquiry* (1971),[4] which concluded that data service companies should be exempt from common carrier regulations (later allowing the growth of ISPs independent from telecom providers).

Roughly speaking, since 1971 the government has chosen to regulate the so-called narrowband services and functions that are under the local telephone service providers. Other aspects of Internet communication have remained unregulated—for example, actions of the ISP and of the ISP's backbone provider to complete the user's "click" to the Internet.[5]

As we move into the 21st century, the most important access issue for businesses, individuals, and governments is the development of broadband connections to the Internet, which are many times faster than narrowband connections (for more on broadband, see Chapter 12). Because of the increased competition fostered by the Telecommunications Act of 1996, a number of companies—including existing cable TV providers and local telephone access providers—have invested heavily in broadband connections such as cable and DSL technologies and wish to remain free from most, if not all, governmental control. At the same time, traditional telecom providers accuse these new broadband providers of unfair advantage, and the general public has raised concerns over the amount of control wielded by these providers.

On another front, the government has controlled the wireless spectrum, another broadband connection, since the 1930s, and increased calls for opening portions of this spectrum to Internet uses have unleashed a furious debate over whether (and, if so, how) portions of the spectrum should be apportioned. Finally, there has been rising concern that those who cannot easily or inexpensively get access to the Internet will be unfairly disadvantaged in a society increasingly dependent upon it. The fear of this so-called **digital divide** has led to governmental pressure on Internet access providers to find ways to serve poor or rural communities that might be underserved or overlooked entirely in their plans for expansion.

The FCC, which has oversight of the telecommunications and wireless sectors, has taken an active interest to promote, in the words of current FCC chair Michael Powell, "the ubiquitous availability of broadband-capable infrastructure to all Americans." According to Powell, "This is Congress's vision, and it is universally recognized that the promise and potentials of broadband are ones that every American [and world] citizen should enjoy." At the same time, Powell was quick to caution against overregulation and to stress the importance of regulation as both a policy and a business issue: "At this stage in the development, any broadband regulatory environment must serve to promote *investment* and *innovation*. Substantial risk investment is needed to either upgrade legacy networks or develop new networks to support broadband capabilities and applications. Broadband-capable networks must, whether through market forces or government mandate, reserve a proper climate for innovation."[6]

In the United States, historically, access-related regulatory issues have fallen into three broad and linked categories: (1) competition among broadband service providers, (2) conditions of access by end-users, and (3) the allocation of the wireless spectrum. Generally speaking, ambiguity concerning the

Drill-Down

The Global Digital Divide

Take an already yawning disparity between haves and have-nots. Then add a powerful new information technology that can facilitate social and economic development—but apportion it almost exclusively to the haves. The result? Greater, more intractable inequity.

That, in a nutshell, describes the digital divide: a phenomenon that exists not only within countries but among countries, as well. This latter issue—the *global* digital divide—may be less familiar to many than the technology gaps within their own country's population. But it is no less (and, in some cases, far more) acute. Consider the following:

- The United States has more computers than all other countries combined.

- The total international bandwidth for all of Africa is less than that for the city of Sao Paulo, Brazil. The total bandwidth for all of Latin America is roughly equal to that of Seoul, Korea. The combined bandwidth of the eight Arab nations is equal to that of 518 cable modem subscribers in the United States.

- In Nepal, the cost of Internet access is almost three times its citizens' average income.

- The 49 least-developed countries account for more than 10 percent of the world's population but less than three-tenths of 1 percent of world Internet users.

- About 55 percent of Americans and 28 percent of other first-world denizens use the Internet. The numbers for the rest of the world: Eastern Europe and Commonwealth of Independent States, 4 percent; Latin America and the Caribbean: 3 percent; East Asia and the Pacific, 2 percent; Arab States, 0.6 percent; and Sub-Saharan Africa and South Asia, 0.4 percent.

Alarmed by the prospect that the ongoing digital revolution may be exacerbating rather than easing the gap between developed and developing nations, a number of public and private international organizations have begun to address the global digital divide. Among the most significant recent initiatives are these:

- In 2000, the Group of Eight (G8) summit established the Digital Opportunity Task Force. A year later, it approved an action plan focused on improving Internet connectivity and lowering information technology costs, helping to develop national Internet strategies, deploying information technology in healthcare and development aid, and facilitating entrepreneurship.

- Stemming from the G8's task force is the Digital Opportunity Initiative, a public-private partnership spearheaded by the Markle Foundation and the United Nations Development Programme that will deploy private-sector expertise to spur e-development in some dozen nations.

- In 2001, the United Nations launched a new initiative to facilitate global interconnectivity. Dubbed the Information and Communication Technologies (ICT) Task Force, its mission, in the words of Secretary General Kofi Annan, is "to help build digital bridges to the billions of people who are now trapped in extreme poverty, untouched by the digital revolution and beyond the reach of the global economy."[7]

Of course, not everyone agrees that bridging the global digital divide is an important, or even desirable, goal. Antiglobalization protesters have been known to burn computers at their demonstrations, arguing that initiatives to wire the developing world will simply facilitate its economic exploitation. Others question whether money should be spent on technology when so many lack basic necessities such as food, water, sanitation, and healthcare.

Leaders such as Annan, however, believe that the Internet and other digital technologies can be powerful tools to help deliver those necessities—as well as to foster democratic governments and greater social equality. "The digital revolution holds great promise for prosperity and progress," Annan said. "Let us act urgently so that all the world's people can benefit from the potential of the ICT revolution."[8]

classification of broadband services and the regulatory implications of that classification has tied these issues into a complicated knot that has only recently begun to unravel—largely as the result of judicial decisions rather than government initiatives. Exhibit 13.2 lists some notable regulatory events. Simultaneously, and with additional implications for competition and for end-users, conflict among local and long-distance telephone service providers and new DSL providers has been tangled in the ongoing battle over access to local exchanges and physical networks and wires.

Outside of the United States, access-related issues depend upon the degree of government control of the telecommunications industry in a particular country or region.

- Communications Act (1934)
- Carterfone Decision (1968)
- FCC First Computer Inquiry (1971)
- Breakup of AT&T (1981–84)
- European Memo of Understanding on Unified Wireless Standard (1987)
- Telecommunications Act (1996)
- *AT&T v. Portland* (1998)

EXHIBIT 13.2   Access—Notable Regulatory Events

Competition Among Broadband Service Providers

Taking a long view, the growth of the Internet in the United States can be seen as only the latest—albeit perhaps the most significant—development in the continuing evolution of the U.S. telecommunications industry. The issue of a competitive market for telephone (and now data) services proved one of the most complex public policy issues of the 20th century. Underlying all discussions of increased competition are the enormous fixed costs of the physical infrastructure to support increased use of a telecommunications system. The struggle has been to balance the belief that a competitive market provides better and more innovative services with the tendency of the industry to consolidate in order to run these systems most efficiently.

The regulatory rules governing the telecommunications industry in the United States were initially set forth in the Communications Act of 1934, which provided guidelines for both telecommunications services (Title II) and cable services (Title VI), which it considered separate categories. The Telecommunications Act of 1996 was designed to update this earlier act. Such an update was considered necessary because of the growth of computing, network, and Internet services. However, the 1996 act provided more confusion than clarification about the degree to which cable television providers, who had by then begun to expand their services to include broadband access, should be considered a telecommunications service (Title II) or a cable service (Title VI). For example, providers of DSL—broadband access over existing or new copper wires—have always been classified under Title II and considered their relatively unregulated cable competitors to have an unfair advantage.

It is interesting to note that other countries have struggled less with these issues. For example, in 1996 the Canadian Radiotelevision and Telecommunications Commission (CRTC) determined that providers of Internet and data services should be classed and regulated as telecommunications services. Brazil has made similar regulatory changes.[9]

The realization that the infrastructure for cable television could be used for other purposes—not only for broadband connection to the Internet but also for competitive local and long-distance telephone services—made cable companies unforeseen and, to an extent, unregulated competitors with the established players. As the cable industry has consolidated (following a pattern of increasing consolidation in the media industry generally) and as giants such as AT&T and Time Warner entered the cable and broadband markets and began to acquire local cable companies, the fear of noncompetitive actions by these companies increased.

With the FCC unable, or at times unwilling, to resolve the issue of whether cable broadband services should fall under telecommunications or cable regulations, the decision fell upon the U.S. judiciary. In June 2000, in a landmark decision overturning a ruling by a lower federal court in the matter of *AT&T v. City of Portland*, the Ninth Circuit Court of Appeals determined that AT&T's cable Internet service should be defined as a telecommunications service.[10]

With one eye on their cable competitors, DSL service providers have waged their own wars over access to local lines and exchanges. Reinforced by the Telecommunications Act of 1996, new providers of local telephone services and startup DSL providers, or CLECs (competing local exchange carriers), have struggled with existing providers, called ILECs (incumbent local exchange carriers), to obtain the requisite access to offices and switches, to provide the copper wire necessary to deliver their services, and to allow shared access over the same wires to customers for their services. Although these shared services are mandated by the Act and by FCC regulation, final resolution of these conflicts depends on federal court rulings.[11]

Interestingly enough, DSL providers began their own process of consolidation in 1999. However, this process was not greeted with approval by either the FCC or state regulatory bodies, both of which are very cautious of mergers in this industry.[12] These newly consolidated entities are calling for regulatory parity with cable providers.[13]

Conditions of Access by End-Users

As of the writing of this text, the majority of users connect to the Internet over telephone lines with modems. On the user side, access to data across telephone lines has, for the most part, received the same regulatory treatment as access to voice services, and most governments have instituted mechanisms to ensure that telephone access is widely available. In the United States, the Communications Act of 1934 instituted methods to bring affordable telephone services to all Americans, the so-called universal service provisions. The provisions for ensuring that high-cost areas, low-income consumers, and schools and libraries received affordable access were extended to data services in the Telecommunications Act of 1996. While there has been some consolidation among providers of late, a relatively open and competitive market prevails.

With the rise of alternative access to the Internet via cable broadband services, as well as the ongoing consolidation of broadband providers into a few large players, came increased concern that unregulated broadband providers were limiting users' access to certain Internet services. Critics alleged that some of these companies were restricting third-party ISP providers from access to their customers across cable lines, limiting customer access to services and to content, and engaging in unfair pricing practices. Proponents of **open access** argue that cable ISPs, in particular, were in danger of becoming a monopoly and threatened the very existence of an open Internet. Unfettered by competition or regulation, they could raise prices without opposition. Unlike dial-up connections (where ISPs were provided equal access to the customer and vice versa), some cable providers limited customers to their own proprietary ISPs—leading to concerns that these ISPs could filter unfavorable or sensitive content and direct customers to preferred advertisers and vendors and slow down or block access to "outsiders." The cable ISPs responded that overregulation by the FCC would stifle innovation and lead to endless litigation, that competitive services (such as DSL and others) existed, and that they should reap the benefits of their investment in cable networks. Finally, they contended that requiring third-party ISP access would violate their free speech rights under the First Amendment.[14] Although *AT&T v. Portland* specifically avoided resolving the open-access issue, the classification of cable providers as telecommunications services has increased pressure on the FCC to make a decision.

There are three arguments against the contention by cable providers that DSL provides a competitive alternative. First, the physical limitations of DSL (namely, proximity to the local exchange) impose some limitation on it as a widely distributed broadband service outside of major urban areas. Second, regulations by the FCC have restricted the entry of large numbers of new DSL players into this market. Third, any continued resistance by ILECs to access to their equipment threatens access by larger DSL players to customers in smaller communities.

Allocation of the Wireless Spectrum

Interest in wireless access to the Internet, by businesses and consumers, has grown considerably over the past five years, raising a host of issues related to how devices can use the spectrum and which parts of this spectrum can and should be made available for wireless access. Since the early 1930s, the FCC has possessed ultimate control of the spectrum. Development of broadband Internet applications has taken place in the unallocated or unlicensed portion of that spectrum. Additional uses of the wireless spectrum include wireless application protocol (WAP) enabled devices such as mobile phones, pagers, and PDAs.

Critics of the FCC's control over the spectrum argue that unlike other natural resources, the spectrum cannot be depleted by increased use, and that the concern over radio interference—one of the primary issues in this debate—has more to do with the limitations of increasingly outmoded technology than with the properties of the spectrum itself. In addition, they argue that treatment of the spectrum as an open-market item where bands can be "owned" will further constrain innovation and community-building on the Internet.[15]

The European Union tackled the spectrum issue earlier than the United States, beginning with the selection of the GSM (global system for mobile communications) standard in the early 1980s. While Europe has identified particular blocks of spectrum for 3G use, the FCC—under pressure from private business, other federal agencies, and the Department of Defense—has been slower to comply with President Clinton's executive order (issued in late 2000) to identify and make available new spectrum to meet the demands of new devices. The Asia-Pacific region, perhaps because of fewer competing demands for spectrum, has had a much smoother experience in allocating spectrum and utilizing wireless services. In Europe, spectrum is allocated either by auction or by "beauty contests" that attempt to award spectrum on the basis of merit. License fees remain the standard in the Asia-Pacific region.[16]

Current Status

Regulatory attention has continued to focus on oversight of the consolidation of the media and communications industries, on increasing the availability of high-speed Internet services, and on the standardization of appropriate regulatory supervision across Internet delivery platforms. The pattern has continued to be a mix of FCC oversight, court action (often undertaken to enforce or to sustain FCC actions or regulations), and congressional action.

The FCC began a more vigorous course of regulatory action after the *AT&T v. Portland* decision in 2000. In a series of communications over the spring of 2002, the FCC outlined "a comprehensive and consistent national broadband policy" to facilitate increased access to "advanced services," by which it means data-delivery services greater than 200 kilobits per second. According to the FCC, its activities in this arena will be guided by four goals and principles: (1) the encouragement of "ubiquitous availability" of broadband access to all Americans; (2) promotion of competition across different access platforms; (3) commitment to a "minimal regulatory environment that promotes investment and innovation"; and (4) the development of "an analytical framework that is consistent . . . across multiple platforms."[17] In combination with the Department of Commerce, an effort to select an appropriate spectrum for 3G wireless systems also began.[18]

While the FCC has pursued an integrative course in its broadband rulings, the courts have undercut its authority in other arenas, most notably in the FCC's attempts to slow the pace of mergers. In February 2002, the U.S. District Court of Appeals, D.C. Circuit, struck down the FCC's continued curb against the ownership of cable and broadcast stations in the same market. This ruling opens the door to further consolidation across the media and communications industries.[19] In May 2002, the same court ordered the FCC to redraw regulations that required the ILECs to provide access to their networks—which may have significant cost implications for smaller DSL and competitive local phone services providers trying to compete against the incumbents.[20]

Recent activity in the U.S. House and Senate has focused on similar initiatives to extend and ensure broadband access. Most notable among these efforts have been the Broadband Internet Access Act of 2001 and the Internet Freedom and Broadband Deployment Act of 2001. The first, introduced in both the House and the Senate, proposes tax incentives to users in rural and underserved areas "to provide an incentive to ensure that all Americans gain timely and equitable access to the Internet over current and future generations" so that those areas do not lag in obtaining current and next-generation broadband services. The second, introduced in the House, also identifies the current regulatory climate as providing a barrier to increased access to the Internet and proposes deregulation of the local telecommunications access providers.

Business Impact

From a business standpoint, the regulatory aspects of high-speed Internet access are still very much in flux, although the trends in the United States seem to be toward some deregulation under the banner of cross-platform standardization. The FCC's commitment to the minimum amount of regulation necessary to foster innovation and economic growth seems to favor large cable companies (increasingly composed of media conglomerates such as AOL Time Warner and growing cable operators such as AT&T), existing broadcasting companies that may now enter the market (such as Viacom and Fox), and local telephone services providers (such as Verizon in the U.S. Atlantic region).

The final chapter of the open-access debate has yet to be written. In March 2002, the FCC ruled out requiring cable companies to provide access to third-party ISPs.[21] The FCC has also continued to enforce a more narrow-band-focused ruling that shifts the burden of paying local incumbent providers for Internet access from CLECs to ISPs.[22] In addition, the growing alignment between the FCC and the courts toward a level playing field, created by removing regulatory advantages conferred on competitive entrants, may result in concentration similar to that taking place in the cable industry. On the wireless front, the 3G Initiative of the FCC, the Department of Commerce, and the National Telecommunications and Information Administration (NTIA) has the potential to foster innovation as more of the spectrum is opened to access. However, questions about how access will be granted and what portions of the spectrum will be available to such access remain unresolved.

What this evolving situation holds for companies that will need high-speed access to reach customers, deliver content, and transact business remains unclear. While seemingly taking place at a distance—in Washington or in a courtroom—the outcome of the access battle will have real and immediate business implications for everyday users who wish to take advantage of the opportunities of the broadband world. The potential for commercial employment and customer adoption of wireless devices, for example, is great—"anytime, anywhere" is a phenomenon, the foreshadowing of which can be seen in airports with temporary wireless Internet access for travelers to check e-mail, make purchases, or surf the Internet.

Business Logic: Taxation

Sales and use tax laws present a daunting complexity offline; when applied to the virtual world they inspire fear, frustration, and even greater bureaucratic confusion. For example, there are currently more than 36,000 state and local taxing jurisdictions in the United States, with approximately 7,000 of these jurisdictions imposing sales and use taxes. To add to the confusion, these taxes change from year to year. The current taxing structure requires the company to understand sales tax, nexus, use tax, and tax exemptions (which include knowledge of tax holidays, certain tax-exempt merchandise, or buyers who are tax-exempt through government or nonprofit affiliation). Once the Internet is added to the equation, there can be up to 15 possible locations where taxes may or may not be required: variables include the location of the business, the location of the consumer, the location of the consumer's ISP, and the location of the company's server.[23]

While e-commerce companies benefit from being able to attract consumers who do not want to pay taxes (see Exhibit 13.3), they also benefit from not having to pay the high costs associated with collecting sales tax in this current complicated system. In an attempt to simplify the U.S. tax system and make it more Internet-friendly, a coalition of states has begun work on the Streamline Sales Tax Project. At the same time, frustrated by what they perceive is an unfair competitive advantage, companies in EU member states have forced the European Union to extend collection of value-added taxes (VAT) to all companies doing business with customers in the European Union—including U.S. companies exempt from their own government's taxes.

Current Status

In October 1998, the Internet Tax Freedom Act was enacted. Despite its name, this law does not free Internet companies from taxes. Rather, it restricts changes to current laws and limits new taxes from being imposed on e-commerce purchases and Internet access. For now, Internet companies must impose the current sales taxes that apply to remote sales—a law that catalog companies have been adhering to for years. According to a precedent set in the Supreme Court's 1992 decision in *Quill Corp. v. North Dakota*, catalog or remote sellers do not have to collect sales tax from purchasers living in states where the sellers do not have a physical presence. As of June 2002, the law was up for renewal in Congress. If the law is renewed, the tax moratorium will be extended until 2006.

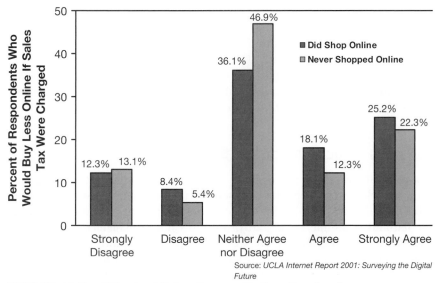

Source: *UCLA Internet Report 2001: Surveying the Digital Future*

EXHIBIT 13.3   Effect of Sales Tax on Online Purchasing

In the spring of 2002, the European Union announced that it would impose a tax on sales of digitally downloadable products—including software, videos, and music—citing the competitive disadvantage of European Internet businesses compared to U.S. Internet businesses not facing similar tax issues. Non-European-based Internet companies providing digital goods must register in one of the European Union's 15 member countries and pay periodic sales taxes to that country. The amount of tax collected depends on the country of the customer.[24]

While purchasers enjoy being able to buy online without having to pay the same sales tax they would have to pay at their local store, offline stores have begun to protest. One of the biggest issues is that many bricks-and-mortar stores have started separate online companies, so their online counterparts do not have to charge sales tax in the same states where they—and their offline competitors—have stores. A bill that went before California Governor Gray Davis would have required businesses that had both bricks-and-mortar stores in California and Internet counterparts to charge sales tax for online purchases sent to residents in California. One of the lobbyists for the bill was the Northern California Bookseller's Association, which viewed it as a necessary means of redress against what they perceived as the unfair competitive advantage of companies such as Borders.com and Barnes & Noble.com. The bill was vetoed by Governor Davis in September 2000.[25]

While almost all online corporations support the tax moratorium, state and local governments are mostly against extending the moratorium because of the lost revenue. State governments are, however, wary of enacting laws that would push online companies out of their states and therefore take money away from the local economy.

Business Impact

As far as consumption is concerned, the effect of an Internet sales tax remains to be seen. Preliminary evidence suggests it would be minimal. Exhibit 13.4 shows the effect that sales tax would have on users' online purchases. Basically, the higher the item's price tag, the more likely the user is to decide not to purchase the item online.

An Internet tax would have a greater impact on states, which stand to lose considerable amounts of money if a sales tax law is not passed. As much as $12 billion may go uncollected if taxes on Internet transactions continue to be suspended. It is estimated that, by 2003, states such as California, New York, and Texas may each lose $1 billion in e-commerce sales tax each year (see Exhibit 13.5). Exhibit 13.6 summarizes the notable regulatory events of taxation and commerce.

Business Logic: Privacy and Security

Concerns about privacy and security came late to the Internet, although the groundwork for regulating this issue was laid much earlier in discussions about database security. The initial purpose of the Internet was to support governmental and academic work, and privacy was not an issue. However, as the Internet and its user base grew, so too did concerns about privacy. **Privacy issues** fall into three categories: (1) security and privacy of sensitive consumer information related to online sales and services transactions (business-to-

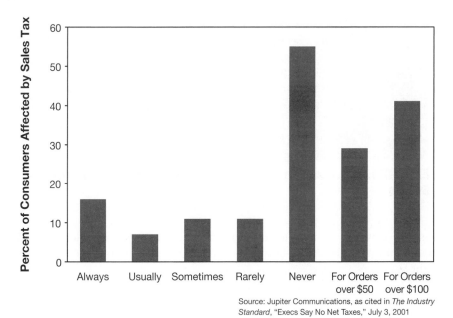

Source: Jupiter Communications, as cited in *The Industry Standard*, "Execs Say No Net Taxes," July 3, 2001

EXHIBIT 13.4   Effect of Sales Tax on Consumers

Remote and Internet Sales Tax Loss Forecast for State and Local Governments				
	2000		2003	
	All Remote Sales	Internet Sales	All Remote Sales	Internet Sales
California	$298–$1,446	$23–$533	$686–$3,650	$86–$1,720
New York	$196–$889	$22–$357	$521–$2,339	$81–$1,155
Texas	$252–$992	$26–$342	$655–$2,446	$96–$1,125
Illinois	$117–$545	$13–$212	$298–$1,389	$44–$671
Florida	$120–$503	$13–$179	$321–$1,279	$48–$595
Pennsylvania	$102–$381	$12–$156	$281–$1,012	$45–$505
Ohio	$108–$357	$11–$141	$286–$955	$43–$454
New Jersey	$101–$346	$10–$130	$256–$879	$37–$419
Michigan	$109–$346	$10–$125	$276–$882	$39–$415
Washington	$82–$284	$8–$98	$213–$712	$30–$326
Total for All U.S. States	$6,100–$9,100	$2,500–$3,800	$13,600–$20,400	$7,800–$12,400

EXHIBIT 13.5   Sales Tax Losses—Top 10 States

- Internet Tax Freedom Act (1998)
- Uniform Electronic Transactions Act, *UETA* (1999)
- 2000/31/EC, EC Directive on Electronic Commerce (2000)
- Electronic Signatures in Global and National Commerce Act, *e-Sign* (2000)
- Uniform Computer Information Transactions Act, *UCITA* (2000)
- EU Internet VAT Directive (2002)

EXHIBIT 13.6   Taxation and Commerce—Notable Regulatory Events

business as well as business-to-consumer transactions), (2) the collection and use of customer data and statistics, and (3) the protection of a consumer's right to privacy.

Privacy

In *Database Nation: The Death of Privacy in the 21st Century*,[26] Simson Garfinkel points out that 30 years ago, the Nixon administration created a commission to study the effect of computers on privacy. They drafted the **Code of Fair Information Practices**, a set of rules that stated: (1) there should be no secret data banks of personal information; (2) if your name or personal information is in a data bank, you should have the right to see it; (3) if your records contain errors, you should have the right to correct them; (4) information collected for one purpose should not be used for other purposes without the consent of the person who is the subject of the information; and (5) organizations should protect information in their possession. Due to the Watergate scandal and changing presidents, no law was ever enacted that supported these guidelines. Perhaps if it had been, many of the battles being fought today over privacy on the Internet would be moot, since many of those battles are based on the very principles in the Code of Fair Information Practices.

Admittedly, the Internet has allowed websites to collect increasing amounts of data on their visitors at a scale unknown in marketing history. The process of **profiling**, in particular, which uses software "cookies" to identify and track user behavior, has received considerable and increased attention from regulatory bodies. If visitors engage in **trusting behavior** (purchasing or selling goods, banking, obtaining health information, using e-mail or instant messaging, joining and participating in communities that include the exchange of personal information), websites collect even more data. With the advent of preference matching technology (employed at sites such as CDNow), sites can "learn" from previous visits and tailor what they offer to a returning customer.

Figuring out how U.S. Internet users feel about privacy issues is difficult. Public research firms have found that 50 percent of Americans feel that they themselves, as Internet users, would be the most appropriate group to set the rules on privacy; 24 percent feel that the government should be responsible for setting those rules; and only 18 percent are confident that Internet companies should set them.[27] At the same time, some of the most recent data suggest that Americans are very concerned about privacy issues: 87 percent of Americans worry about incurring financial loss because of disclosure of credit card information; 89 percent fear that health-related websites might give out data about them; and 72 percent are "very concerned" that their insurance companies might limit or deny coverage to them because of sites they have visited.[28] According to data collected by the Pew Internet & American Life Project, 60 percent of all Americans are very concerned about privacy issues, with 54 percent of Internet users expressing a similar concern.[29]

Interestingly enough, what people *believe* about privacy online differs from how they *behave* online. According to the same Pew survey, more than two-thirds of those worried about privacy issues continue to engage in trusting behavior online. The survey noted as one of its key conclusions that "the actual incidence of unpleasant events is modest and the incidence of criminal events online is miniscule." In addition, the survey concludes that "a great many Internet users do not know the basics of how their online activities are observed and they do not use available tools to protect themselves."[30] Exhibit 13.7 shows how the range of personal activities that users engage in on the Internet has increased, despite threats to their privacy.

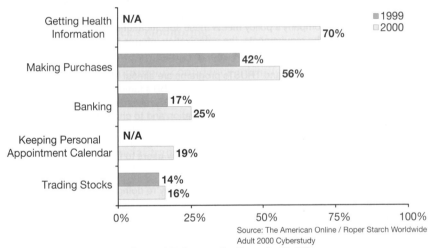

EXHIBIT 13.7   Americans' Private Online Activities

Understandably, industry and government have not been able to respond in a way that satisfies all online users and privacy advocates and addresses all online privacy concerns. The government originally expected the industry to regulate itself, with privacy policies and **privacy seals** from companies such as TRUSTe, which began as an organized group of sponsoring companies in 1997 and has grown to nearly 2,000 licensees. Indeed, evidence in a survey conducted by the Progress and Freedom Foundation in 2001 suggests that websites are collecting less information, perhaps in response to privacy concerns. Among the 100 most popular domains, the proportion collecting "personally identifying information" other than e-mail fell from 96 to 84 percent; a random sample of sites with at least 39,000 projected weekly visitors showed a decline from 87 to 74 percent.[31]

However, the same survey found that less than 50 percent of the most popular sites display privacy seals from TRUSTe (the largest provider) or BBBOn-Line.[32] Recently, sites have begun to implement **Platform for Privacy**

way for the integration of digital activity into business transactions. In Europe, a directive on a community framework for electronic signatures (Directive 1999/93 EC) and attendant legislation have played a similar role.

The government has shadowed the development of communications security at every turn. The Clinton administration's attempt to have computer manufacturers install a "backdoor" to all U.S.-made machines via the so-called Clipper Chip is one example of the engagement of government with this issue. When the attempt to ban alternative forms of encryption failed, the government attempted to subsidize the development of the chip. The government has simultaneously turned to other means—including regulating that regardless of whatever software is used there be a "backdoor" for government agencies, accessible with a court order.[36]

The courts have had to balance the concerns of these governmental agencies—including those created in response to the terrorist threats and actions of September 2001—with the constitutional rights to privacy and due process.

Current Status

When it comes to privacy and security, industry and government have engaged in a sometimes contradictory pattern of behavior. On the industry side, the implementation of P3P technology continues apace as a means of certifying a level of privacy. At the same time, sites seem to be taking an increasingly legalistic approach to privacy. In Europe, where there are stricter laws protecting privacy in general, most governments require marketing programs to be **opt-in**, which allows customers to choose to have their information shared with others in exchange for more personalized sites, marketing, and special offers. In the United States, however, many websites' marketing programs are **opt-out**, meaning that the burden of protecting private information lies with the customer.

In the last few years, the government's regulatory response to privacy issues has accelerated. The United States has seen significant regulation or legislation in a number of key areas: the protection of the privacy of children (Children's Online Privacy Protection Act, 1998, and the Children's Internet Protection Act, 2001); the coordination of commercial privacy policies with Europe (Implementation of the U.S. Department of Commerce's Safe Harbor Principles, 2002); the protection of data collected by financial institutions (Gramm-Leach-Bliely Act, 2000); and the ability of the government itself to balance the interests of privacy against threats by criminal or terrorist organizations (The U.S.A. Patriot Act, 2001).

Regulatory bodies have not been far behind. In August 2000, the Federal Trade Commission (FTC) submitted to Congress its report on online profiling by e-commerce firms. The report accepted the proposal of the Network Advertising Initiative (NAI), which stated that its members would not use "personally identifiable information about sensitive medical or financial data, information of a sexual nature, or Social Security numbers for marketing purposes." The proposal also stated that privacy policies must be "clear and conspicuous" and advertisers had to give "robust" notice before they combined a user's click-stream data with any of their personal information. Furthermore, if the user protested, the advertiser had to give the user the option to opt-out.[37]

At the same time, the FTC is itself not uniformly behind any one set of measures. FTC commissioners stand divided on the question of whether legislation is required in order to protect consumer privacy. However, in the spring of 2002, there were at least 34 Internet privacy bills working their way through Congress. Most generally follow the FTC's guidelines, proposing that websites be required to have clear privacy policies. These bills advocate that websites let customers know what data the company is collecting, inform them about what the company intends to do with those data, and give customers a chance to opt-out of having the company share those data with third parties.

One particular bill, sponsored by Sen. Ernest F. Hollings and dubbed the Online Personal Privacy Act, has won the support of many consumer advocates. The bill would require sites to obtain permission from visitors (opt-in) before collecting any personal data that could be used to identify them in the future. It would also allow anonymous information to be used for marketing purposes only if the user consents. Another bill, sponsored by Sens. Conrad Burns and Ron Wyden, would give consumers the chance to view and modify their data and provides stiffer penalties for violators.

State governments have also begun to take action against what they view as privacy violations. For instance, financial services legislation gives states the latitude to enact tough financial privacy laws and to limit how financial companies use their customers' data. While this legislation was intended for offline companies, it will also have an effect on how online financial companies use customer data. In June 2000, the Michigan attorney general formally notified several U.S. websites that the state may file lawsuits against them unless the sites' privacy policies explained how they share visitors' information with advertising services such as DoubleClick and Netscape Communications.[38] Also in September 2000, Missouri filed suit against More.com (now Puritan.com) claiming the health and nutrition retailer shared customer information with third parties in direct conflict with its stated privacy policy.

As noted earlier, the European Union and some of its members have taken a harder line on the privacy issue, and they did so earlier than the United States. Beginning with Directive 95/46/EC of the European Parliament and of the Council of October 24, 1995, "on the protection of individuals with regard to the processing of personal data and on the free movement of such data," the European Union has aggressively pursued the protection of individual privacy, starting with its use of the opt-in policy.[39] In addition, some countries have taken additional steps to secure privacy rights: In the spring of 2002, the United Kingdom announced the Data Protection Act, which banned the monitoring of Internet use and e-mails (as well as the use of hidden cameras) in the workplace.

One thing is certain: U.S. privacy advocates are unsatisfied with the government's attitude toward regulation. When the FTC recommended its guidelines to Congress in 2000, many privacy advocates believed they did not go far enough. The Electronic Privacy Information Center's response: "We do not see why Internet advertisers, who could create far more detailed profiles of the personal lives of Americans than any of the sectors currently subject to legislation, should be able to escape the fundamental obligations that would otherwise be established by law." Orson Swindle, an FTC commissioner, called the decision "embarrassingly flawed."[40]

With regard to encryption, regulation will continue to manage the tradeoff between the security of personal and business transactions and the need to uncover and prevent illegal activities. Some critics are concerned that the efforts of industry leaders to set security standards open the way to compromises of that security (or to monopolistic exploitation of those standards). On the other side of the issue stand law enforcement agencies that call for the increased ability to intercept communications in order to prevent criminal or terrorist activity. The 2001 U.S.A. Patriot Act and the 2001 Council of Europe Cybercrime Convention, for example, provide increased means for the surveillance and interception of secure transmissions by law enforcement agencies.

One of the landmark constitutional privacy cases, *Katz v. United States* (1967), highlights the ways in which the ambiguities in the U.S. Constitution ensure that the issues of security and privacy remain contentious for some time to come. The case concerned the constitutionality of a wiretap on the phone lines outside a suspect's home. Justice Potter Stewart's decision, which could also apply in the context of Internet security, made the unusual claim that the Fourth Amendment protected "people, not places" and overturned the use of wiretaps that did not intrude into private space but nevertheless invaded individual privacy. Subsequent decisions surrounding privacy have struggled with applying the intentions of 18th century thought to the implications of 21st century "virtual" spaces and "virtual" identities.[41] Exhibit 13.8 summarizes recent notable regulatory events in privacy and security.

- European Parliament Directive 95/46/EC on personal data (1995)
- Child Online Privacy Protection Act, *COPPA* (1998)
- Gramm-Leach-Bliley Act (2000)
- Implementation of U.S. Safe Harbor Provisions (2000)
- U.S.A. Patriot Act (2001)
- Children's Internet Protection Act, *CIPA* (2001)
- U.K. Data Protection Act (2002)

EXHIBIT 13.8   Privacy and Security—Notable Regulatory Events

Business Impact

Businesses have responded in very different ways to the mixed messages of government regulation and growing public concern over privacy and security. Some have tightened their privacy policies to assuage consumers' concerns, while others have loosened their privacy policies to afford them more room to leverage customer data. While businesses have increased the amount of commercial activity on the Internet, many have engaged in security audits of their network systems in the wake of the September 11, 2001, terrorist attacks.

In September 2000, Internet travel site Expedia.com expanded its privacy policy to give consumers more control over their personal information. Under the revised policy, the company will not sell or rent customer information, and customers have the ability to add, change, or remove any personal identifiers from the site. Expedia also hired accounting firm PricewaterhouseCoopers to verify whether it was following its written privacy policy; the company passed the audit.

At the other end of the spectrum is Yahoo, which announced changes to its policy long after it began to collect data on users. Yahoo explained that it would provide information to "trusted partners who work on behalf of or with Yahoo under confidentiality agreements" and that these companies "may use your personal information to help Yahoo communicate with you about offers from Yahoo and our marketing partners."[42] TRUSTe, which was involved in discussions with Yahoo about the change, eventually approved it, admitting that there was a need to balance privacy concerns with ongoing—and natural—shifts in business strategies. Industry advocates note that the selling of customer information has been a long-established practice in the offline world of catalogs and magazines.[43] Interestingly enough, although the change of policy set off a violent reaction among privacy advocates, research suggests that users remained unfazed by it: According to one study, of the nearly 1.1 million users who viewed Yahoo's new privacy policy opt-out page in the four weeks between March 25 and April 1, 2002, only 73,000 users (roughly 7 percent) chose the option.[44]

Even the federal government came under fire when it was found that its own websites did not conform to the privacy policy standards endorsed by the FTC—and that its websites aimed at kids did not follow recently legislated guideline restrictions and were compiling information on children under 13. The government countered that it was not required to adhere to the FTC's standards. Nevertheless, government sites have started to modify their data-gathering policies.

While many Internet companies are afraid of government regulation, which they believe could curb their revenue by limiting the amount of information they can collect or by preventing them from selling their customer databases, they might actually suffer more if the government does not get involved. Unfortunately, the contradictory views of Internet users provide no guide for business. While users continue to be concerned about the security of their transactions and the maintenance of their privacy on the Internet, the degree to which users are informed about the issues surrounding privacy and security remains unclear. No matter what the government does in the next few years, some will like it, others will not, and it will have an effect on how Internet companies are run and how revenue on the Internet is generated.

Content: Copyright

Perhaps the most significant effect of the Internet's ability to distribute content has been on intellectual property protection. While **trademarks** and **patents** have also been affected, shaping existing copyright law to meet the challenge of new technology has proved to be one of the biggest and most immediate challenges for Internet businesses and consumers today. As with other efforts at regulating the Internet, policy has been shaped by legislative, judicial, and governmental action. The speed of innovation fostered by the Internet has tended to keep regulation one step behind practice.

A **copyright** is not intended to give the creator of a work perpetual blanket ownership and control of that work. Rather, it is meant to strike a balance, for a limited time, between protecting a creator's work and letting the public

---

Drill-Down

Trademarks

As the Internet grew more popular in the late 1990s, a new type of "entrepreneur" emerged—the cybersquatter. Cybersquatters registered domain names of famous corporations and people with the hope that the party would pay large amounts of money for the privilege of using the URL. And, during the initial Internet frenzy, companies were willing to pay: Bank of America bought Loans.com for $3 million and eCompanies bought Business.com for $7.5 million.

In December 1999, President Clinton signed a law that banned cybersquatters from intentionally registering names that are already trademarked. But trademark suits continue, mostly now among small and medium-size companies that cannot easily claim license to the domain name. To win a suit, the offended person or company must prove either that consumers will be confused by the site or—when the trademark is famous enough—that the site will dilute the distinctive quality of the trademark. In October 2000, singer Madonna sued for the right to use Madonna.com, a site that had been an adult-entertainment portal site. The Internet Corporation for Assigned Names and Numbers (ICANN)—one of the regulating bodies for domain names—sided with Madonna.[45]

With new top-level domain names being added, trademark suits are sure to rage on, and ICANN will have to decide if Madonna also has the right to Madonna.biz, Madonna.us, and Madonna.info.

---

use it so that both can prosper. According to the Patent and Copyright Clause in the U.S. Constitution (Article I, Section 8), "Congress shall have Power . . . To promote the Progress of Science and useful Arts, by securing for limited Times to Authors and Inventors the exclusive Right to their respective Writings and Discoveries." In a more recent landmark 1991 decision, Justice Sandra Day O'Connor noted:

> The primary objective of copyright is not to reward the labor of authors, but "[t]o promote the Progress of Science and useful Arts." To this end, copyright assures authors the right to their original expressions, but encourages others to build freely upon the ideas and information conveyed by a work. This result is neither unfair nor unfortunate. It is the means by which copyright advances the progress of science and art.[46]

Copyright law, then, must walk a fine line between ensuring that incentives to creation and innovation exist (in the form of ownership protection and the revenue that results from it) and protecting the public interest by allowing others to build freely upon the thought and expression of the past. The debate over copyright protection on the Internet has seen forceful argument by partisans on both sides of this issue; interestingly enough, the party lines have extended around the globe. And while the arguments have raged on, the advance of Internet technology to create, store, display, and distribute content has easily sprinted ahead, carrying the general public along with it.

At the opening of the 21st century, three keystone pieces of legislation govern the distribution of content in ways that have important implications for the Internet: the Copyright Act of 1976, the Fair Use Doctrine (part of the

Copyright Act of 1976), and the Digital Millennium Copyright Act of 1998 (see Exhibit 13.9). The Copyright Act of 1976 protects literary, musical, dramatic, motion picture, and architectural works, as well as sound recordings. It gives the owner of the copyright the ability to, among other things, reproduce the work, create derivative works based on that work, distribute copies of the work, and perform the work publicly.[47]

- World Intellectual Property Organization Treaty presented to the United Nations (1996) (35 countries, including the United States, had ratified the treaty as of March 2002)
- Digital Millennium Copyright Act, *DMCA* (1998)
- *Universal City Studios Inc., et al. v. Corley* (2001)
- Court-ordered shutdown of Napster (2002)

EXHIBIT 13.9   Copyright—Notable Regulatory Events

The Copyright Act, though, also gives the public the right to **fair use** of the work. Under fair use, people can use the work for educational, critical, commentary, reporting, or parody purposes. A person can also use the work if he or she creates a new work of value, only uses a small amount so that it does not constitute most of the work, or if the new work does not have a negative effect on the market for the original.

The **Digital Millennium Copyright Act** was signed into law in 1998 by President Clinton. While the law is complicated and has many provisions, there are two main parts of interest for most businesses. The first is the implementation of provisions in the World Intellectual Property Organization (WIPO) treaties that prohibit the circumvention of copyright protection systems. This part makes it a crime for someone to go around a "technological protection measure" that was created by the copyright owner to keep people from stealing the work. The second part states that a copyright owner cannot hold an online service provider liable if one of its subscribers infringes on the owner's copyright. To be protected, though, the online service provider must agree to remove the infringing material and/or terminate the subscriber as soon as it becomes aware of the infringement.[48]

As discussed in Chapter 12, MP3 files are digital sound files that are smaller than conventional sound files and therefore easier to download. These files have caused problems for the record industry. With the advent of file-sharing applications, it has become easier for users not only to download music and other content from other media (tapes, CDs) but also to find similar files from strangers and download them. While before it would have taken time for someone to make a copy of a CD on a cassette tape (where there would also be a loss of sound quality), digital music, MP3 files, and file-swapping applications all converged to make it easy for millions of Internet users to swap pirated music with one another. With MP3 and various file-sharing programs, one copy had the potential to become millions of copies at digital or near-digital quality.

This threat caused the entertainment industry, including the Recording Institute Association of America (RIAA) and a number of film studios and entertainment companies, to go on the offensive, filing suits against companies that provide these services, most notably My.MP3.com, Napster, and Morpheus. The offline music industry has yet to find an optimal way to access the millions of music lovers on the Internet; it has also come to blows with the consumer electronics and technology industries, as the manufacturers of computers, MP3 players, and CD players attempt to keep pace with an insatiable demand for music on these technologies by consumers. Another outcome of this battle has been the emergence of new digital-rights management technology, which is expected to be able to stamp each file with an identifying number and watermark, ensure that the file goes through approved channels, and track where the file goes. Record companies hope this technology will enable them to offer their products online, without having to risk unauthorized copying.

Websites that either store or facilitate the transfer of copyrighted materials defend their right to make content available to users on a number of grounds. They decry the increased commodification of content in response to its increased availability on the Internet, citing long-term practices in music, art, and literature for incorporating and building previous work into new work. They question the extent to which they are liable for all of the uses (including but not exclusively those involving copies of copyrighted material) to which individuals put their services. They cite previous nonrestraining responses to copy technology by both the courts and the entertainment industry, and question the necessity of extending the term of copyright from its original 14 years to the life of the author plus 70 years. They also point out that the security technology embedded in some CDs causes computers to crash if users attempt to play the CDs on in-computer music systems.

Whether or not pirating a copy of the latest pop single is infringing on the "useful arts," there is no doubt that, without copyright laws, many businesses and industries would not be able to survive. So far, it is mostly the music industry that has grappled with the copyright issues raised by new technology. Their efforts to protect their investments have been increasingly vigorous. But other companies with established copyrights are now seeking to extend those rights—to date, Congress has extended the length of copyright protection 11 times. However, all companies that create intellectual property—whether in the form of film, books, artwork, or sewing patterns—will sooner or later confront the copyright issue.

Current Status

In the battle over ownership of content on the Internet, those who regulate that content have not delivered a consistent message. While the courts have tended to lean toward the copyright holders, much of the proposed legislation protects Internet users. Laws that would allow users to make digital recordings of CDs they have purchased and store them on the Internet have been suggested, and bills allowing companies to do the same thing have been drafted. Sen. Orrin Hatch, a songwriter himself, has been a vocal proponent of both users and copyright holders, supporting centralized services such as Napster because he feared that users would go to decentralized—

and less controllable—systems such as Gnutella and Freenet. The biggest question is whether the courts will continue to find in favor of the companies suing for copyright infringement, or if they will start leaning the other way, trying to maintain the balance between copyright holder and consumer.

Two of the biggest copyright issues—the term of copyright protection and the boundaries of content ownership—have been hotly debated in the courts. One such case, which is currently pending before the Supreme Court, is *Eldred v. Ashcroft*. The plaintiff, Eric Eldred, created an online library that contained HTML versions of works that had gone out of copyright. Confronted with the extension of the terms of the copyright law, Eldred challenged the constitutionality of that extension on two grounds. First, he argued that the extension exceeded the powers granted to Congress in the Constitution. Second, he claimed that the extension upset the delicate balance between encouraging and restricting creative expression, thereby threatening the First Amendment's free-speech protections.

Neither the District Court nor the Federal Appeals Court agreed with Eldred. According to both rulings, Congress could grant extensions to the term of copyright for specified times. What they could not do was grant *unlimited* extensions. In addition, the courts upheld the immunity of copyrights from examination under the First Amendment. Critics saw this as the latest salvo in the war to completely "propertize" culture.[49] Ultimately, the Supreme Court upheld the lower courts in January 2003.

Another highly contested copyright case is *Universal City Studios Inc. et al. v. Corley*. The case calls into question one of the more controversial parts of the Digital Millennium Copyright Act, which outlawed the distribution of technology that could circumvent copyright protection in the form of passwords or security codes or programs. Corley's website posted a copy of the decryption computer program "DeCSS," which is designed to circumvent "CSS"—the security software that movie studios used on DVDs to prevent illegal copying. Corley's claims were similar to Eldred's, although he added two additional points: (1) that the software he invented and posted was actually a form of "expression," and therefore that actions to restrain him from publishing it on the Internet threatened his First Amendment right to free speech, and (2) that the Digital Millennium Copyright Act's prohibition violated protections of fair use of copyrighted materials.[50]

Business Impact

How copyright law will affect Internet content in the future has yet to be determined. However, recent activity seems to suggest that content businesses should review their policies on copyright protection. Thus far, the RIAA has been the most aggressive force in the attempt to police the use of copyright on the Internet, although movie studios and entertainment conglomerates have also begun to crack down on perceived copyright violations. Through 2002, RIAA has carried its battles with file-sharing services such as Napster and Kazaa into the courtroom, and its most recent activity against Audiogalaxy, in the spring of 2002, indicates that it will continue to use the courts to strictly enforce existing copyright legislation. The movie and television studios have begun a vigorous campaign to restrict the use of their proprietary content, focusing largely on fan websites.

Drill-Down

The Great Copyright Debate: Finding "Commons" Ground

The Internet—with its ability to distribute perfect digital copies of songs, books, movies, photographs, articles, and other content with the click of a mouse—has spawned a new dilemma and debate about copyright and intellectual property rights. But as the entertainment industry fights to maintain control over its products (and equally zealous file-swappers scramble to keep the digital pipes flowing), at least one organization is proposing a modest but promising alternative.

The group, called Creative Commons, is the joint project of several prominent law and technology scholars who are concerned that increasingly restrictive copyright laws are blocking access to creative works that are the building blocks of future progress and innovation. Their goal: Carve out a small portion of cyberspace in which ideas, images, words, and sounds are not property to be guarded but resources to be shared—resources that can help to fuel new generations of art, insight, and innovation. They plan to accomplish this by deploying online tools that allow content creators—artists, writers, musicians, filmmakers, and others—to voluntarily share some or all of their work with others and make it simple for those seeking royalty-free material to find the materials they need to create their own works.

"If, for example, an artist wants to make her music available for noncommercial use, or with just attribution, our tools will help her express those intentions," explained Stanford University professor and Creative Commons chairman Lawrence Lessig. "Computers will then be able to identify and understand the terms of an author's license, making it easier for people to search for and share creative works."

Creative Commons ultimately hopes to create what it calls an intellectual property conservancy, which, much like a land trust or nature preserve, will amass and donate to the public domain its own repository of creative works. Whether Creative Commons will succeed in its ambition to expand the free flow of digital content within the context of existing copyright and intellectual property law is far from certain. But many who fear that creativity and innovation may be the ultimate victims of the escalating intellectual property wars are hoping that it does.

Free Speech

The right to free speech is protected in the United States, in the European Union, and in other countries. At the same time, in interpreting this right, the needs of society must be balanced against the potential for the abuse of this right. No society recognizes the absolute right of free speech—words that incite violence, for example, are clearly not protected in the constitutions of most nations. On the Internet, people enjoy their right to free speech as never before—they enter chat rooms, put up postings on bulletin boards, and offer their opinions on everything from books to sex. The Internet has created an unprecedented forum for ideas and expression, and, interestingly, it has offered individuals an equally unprecedented opportunity for anonymous participation in this forum. In so doing, the Internet poses still another set of regulatory challenges. What constitutes harmful expression on the Internet? Who should determine what constitutes harmful expression? How far should regulation of expression extend in this new realm?

In the United States, the Supreme Court has come down hard against censorship. In the European Union and elsewhere, however, some topics of discussion have been declared harmful and illegal—those surrounding the social and political activities of neo-Nazi groups, for example—and governments have tried to control their expression vigorously, even outside the European Union's borders. Some countries have gone even further. Amendments to Australia's Broadcasting Services Act ban access to websites lacking content ratings or that are X-rated. Swedish laws have banned "illegal descriptions of violence" and "racial agitation" and require the owners of electronic bulletin boards to remove such content or render it inaccessible. Swedish courts have levied fines against newspapers for anonymous statements to their online discussion boards.[51] In considering the Internet and free speech, courts, legislatures, and governments have tended to cluster their regulatory efforts on two issues: (1) obscenity and pornography and (2) the potential harm of "hate speech," words that incite others to violence against particular groups or ideas.

Current Status

Most countries have laws that protect individuals against libel and slander—expression of falsehoods that threaten or directly attack personal character. The broad reach of the Internet has compounded the sensitivity to the spread of false information. If people feel they have been slandered, they often must sue the Internet service provider for the identity of the offender before they can actually sue the offender himself. ISPs often refuse to release the identities of their customers. For example, the courts ruled that America Online and Yahoo had to reveal information about the identities of eight people who anonymously posted defamatory comments in a Yahoo financial chat room that suggested Eric Hvide, CEO of Hvide Marine, was guilty of securities violations. Hvide resigned from the company, saying that the allegations ruined his career.[52]

While U.S. companies will make small concessions for their websites' international audiences—for example, Amazon agreed to stop selling copies of *Mein Kampf* to German readers, and the search engine Google blocked links to websites hosted by an extreme German leftist group that provide instructions on how to sabotage railway equipment—they are not willing to abandon the right to free speech on behalf of citizens of other countries.

In 2000, two antiracist French groups brought suit in France against Yahoo for allowing the sale of Nazi memorabilia on its auction sites. While Yahoo France did filter the Nazi objects for French citizens, Yahoo refused to block those citizens from accessing the auctions through its other sites. Even though Yahoo says that it forbids "hateful or racially, ethically, or otherwise objectionable materials," it still hosts many online chat clubs devoted to neo-Nazism and other such causes.[53] The French court ordered Yahoo to block French citizens' access to these sites or face stiff fines. However, Yahoo then turned to the U.S. courts, which ruled that Yahoo did not have to comply with the order.[54]

The issue of Internet pornography presents an equally complex and emotional set of regulatory challenges. The regulation of what communities consider "obscene" has been the source of many pitched legal battles throughout the 20th century, in the United States and elsewhere. When approached as a general issue, few inside or outside a courtroom can agree on what constitutes "obscene" material and the potential harm of such material. Most tellingly, recent efforts at regulation have attempted to narrow the issue substantially, targeting areas of unified public concern—child pornography, in particular. In a recent poll, 92 percent of Americans said that they were concerned about child pornography, and 50 percent of Americans cite child pornography as "the single most heinous crime that takes place online."[55]

The bulk of the legislation on this issue was drafted in the late 1990s in response to increased public awareness of and anger about the issue. Some of the more notable legislative acts include the Child Pornography Prevention Act of 1996 (CPPA), the Communications Decency Act of 1996 (CDA), the Child Online Protection Act of 1998 (COPA), and the Children's Internet Protection Act of 2001 (CIPA). All were challenged almost immediately after being signed into law, mostly because of their broad definitions of what constitutes obscene and harmful material, as well as the threat they posed to websites' free-speech rights. In 1997, the Supreme Court ruled the CDA unconstitutional; in 2002, it ruled the CPPA unconstitutional as well. COPA, while upheld in part in a May 2002 ruling, has been returned to the lower courts for further adjudication.

Lesser means of regulating content have fared no better. Web filters installed on school computers to keep students from visiting inappropriate sites, for example, have come under fire from free-speech advocates and library associations. In May 2002, a federal three-judge panel in Philadelphia ruled such filters unconstitutional. Exhibit 13.10 lists some notable recent free-speech regulations.

- *Reno v. ACLU, CDA Case* (1997)

- *Yahoo Inc. v. La Ligue Contre le Racisme et al.* (2001)

- *Ashcroft v. Free Speech Coalition* (2002)

- *Ashcroft v. ACLU* (2002)

EXHIBIT 13.10   Free Speech—Notable Regulatory Events

Business Impact

The effect of free speech on Internet businesses remains to be seen. The intentions of those who seek to prevent or to punish harmful expression—either "hate speech" or pornography—may be laudable, but critics note that, once put into place, regulations that touch upon these issues have a tendency to expand to cover more ambiguous issues. For example, the U.S. federal prohibition against child pornography was expanded to cover "virtual pornography"—images that appear to depict minors but are in fact computer generated. In overturning the CPPA, Justice Anthony Kennedy noted in his opinion that the extension of regulation from the real to the virtual directly threatened the imaginative and creative processes that have driven art and literature through time.[56] Internet users' senses of where to draw the line varies widely. Indeed, the National Research Council has declared that no single technical method will protect children from pornographic content.[57]

While the commercial service nature of the Internet is important, the original purpose of the Internet was to build community and to share content, and these founding elements remain a core part of many Internet businesses. The regulation of content, then, will have wide business implications. For instance, Amazon.com's ability to incorporate user reviews of books, and the largely unfettered discussion boards active on many websites, attest to the positive impact of community on commerce. Governmental regulations could have a profound impact on both e-commerce business and the user experience.

Drill-Down

Keeping Up with the Regulations

The hectic pace of regulatory change regarding the Internet requires regular monitoring of the websites of various agencies, courts, and watchdog organizations. Here are a few that can be helpful:

North America

(*www.fcc.gov*)
The Federal Communications Commission website. The FCC is responsible for regulating interstate and international communications by radio, television, wire, satellite, and cable. The site provides regulatory news, press releases, and information organized by what it terms "major initiatives," which include consumer information, emerging technologies, global communications, industry regulation, and universal access.

(*www.copyright.gov*)
United States Copyright Office, Library of Congress information site. An essential starting place for research on U.S. and international copyright issues, laws, and regulatory actions.

(*www.uspto.gov*)
U.S. Patent and Trademark Office. Helpful information on U.S. patent and trademark laws and regulatory decisions.

(*www.ftc.gov/privacy/index.html*)
Federal Trade Commission privacy initiatives. The Federal Trade Commission is charged with administering and enforcing regulations related to competition and consumer protection.

(*www.gseis.ucla.edu/iclp/hp.html*)
The UCLA Online Institute for Cyberspace Law and Policy. A good starting point for legal research on e-commerce issues.

(*www.unbsj.ca/library/subject/cyberlaw.htm*)
The University of New Brunswick's St. John Ward Chipman Library for Legal, Privacy, and Security Issues in Electronic Commerce. An excellent portal for international research across a number of relevant issues.

(*cyber.law.harvard.edu*)
Berkman Center for Internet & Society. Portal page for Harvard Law School's program on e-commerce law.

European Union

(*europa.eu.int/information_society/index_en.htm*)
European Union Information Society website. The EU portal to a variety of issues, initiatives, and regulations relating to the information society. This is a helpful starting point for research on EU regulatory issues. Particularly helpful are its law and e-commerce pages.

Summary

1. How is the Internet currently regulated?

There is no systematic regulation of the Internet—no international body that has absolute authority, and, in most cases, no one national body to oversee it. The Internet is regulated through a combination of local, regional, and national government organizations. In most countries, a combination of laws created by legislative bodies, administrative decisions by other governmental organizations (the Federal Communications Commission in the United States, for example), and precedents set by court decisions govern the way that the Internet works in that country and with other countries.

2. What are the challenges the Internet has brought to regulation?

The two major challenges the Internet has brought to regulation are the speed with which new technology is introduced and the lack of physical borders. The rapid pace at which new technology is introduced has an effect on issues such as privacy and intellectual property; the Internet's lack of physical borders has an effect on issues such as taxation and gambling. Both have implications for free speech.

3. What are the main regulation issues affecting the Internet today?

The five main issues are access, taxation, privacy and security, intellectual property, and free speech. To benefit from the Internet, people must be able to access it, and there are regulatory issues on both sides of the supply issue—those who provide services and those who may use them. Most countries control the companies that provide Internet access and decide how they reach customers, which customers they may reach, with whom they must share supply services, and what fees that they may charge for those services. On the customer side, there remains a concern that some users are being left behind, either because it is too expensive to bring Internet services to where they live or because they cannot afford those services even if they are available. Taxation is a big issue because e-commerce companies do not have to collect sales tax on their customers' purchases. While this is an advantage to customers, it costs the states billions of dollars a year. Security is an issue because the assurance that transactions are confidential, complete, and authentic allows for true electronic commerce. Privacy is an issue because Internet companies have new technology that can track a user's every movement. Intellectual property has become an issue because new technology makes it easy to copy high-quality music files and trade them over the Internet. Free speech has become an issue because the Internet now allows millions of people to speak their minds anonymously.

Exercises

1. Visit the Creative Commons website (*www.creativecommons.org*). What information does a business that wants to register its content need? For content creators, what are the advantages of following the Creative Commons path? What are the disadvantages? What are the advantages for those who want to use content? What are the disadvantages?

2. Select either the Federal Communications Commission website (*www.fcc.org*) or the European Commission's e-commerce website (*europa.eu.int/information_society/topics/ebusiness/ecommerce/3information/law&ecommerce/index_en.htm*). Both sites highlight a number of ongoing initiatives. Select one and discuss its regulatory implications.

3. Select one U.S. online business and one European online business. Go to their privacy pages and compare and contrast them. Can you make any general statements about the two? Draft a list of necessary changes that would have to be made in order for one company to do business with the other. Compare your list to the terms and conditions of the Safe Harbor principles on the U.S. Department of Commerce's Safe Harbor site (*www.export.gov/safeharbor/index.html*).

Key Terms

Endnotes

digital divide	privacy seals	patent
open access	Platform for Privacy Preferences (P3P)	copyright
privacy issues	opt-in	fair use
Code of Fair Information Practices	opt-out	Digital Millennium Copyright Act
profiling	trademark	
trusting behavior		

[1]Justice Sidney A. Thomas, Majority Opinion, *AT&T Corp. v. City of Portland*, 216 F.3d 871 (Ninth Circuit, 2000), (URL: http://www.fcc.gov/ogc/documents/opinions/2000/99-35609.html).

[2]"Directive 2000/31/EC of the European Parliament and of the Council of 8 June 2000 on certain legal aspects of information society services, in particular electronic commerce in the Internal Market (Directive on electronic commerce)."

[3]*In the Matter of Use of the Carterfone Device in Message Toll Telephone Service*, 13 FCC 2d 420 (1968).

[4]*First Computer Inquiry*, Final Decision and Order, 28 FCC 2d 267 (1971).

[5]John B. Morris, *Broadband Backgrounder: Public Policy Issues Raised by Broadband Technology* (Washington: Broadband Access Project of the Center for Democracy and Technology, 2000) (URL: http://www.cdt.org/digi_infra/broadband/backgrounder.shtml#IE). Also Adobe Acrobat file available at the Center's website, 6.

[6]"U.N. Launches Information, Communication Technologies Task Force," Xinhua News Agency, 20 November 2001.

[7]"Message from the U.N. Secretary General," ITU News, April 2002.

[8]Michael K. Powell, "Remarks of Michael K. Powell, Chairman Federal Communications Commission, at the Broadband Technology Summit, US Chamber of Commerce, Washington, D.C. April 30, 2002" (URL: http://www.fcc.gov/Speeches/Powell/2002/spmkp205.html).

[9]See *Regulation of Broadcasting Distribution Undertakings that Provide Non-Programming Services*, No. 96-1, Canadian Radiotelecommunications and Telephone Commission, January 30, 1999 (URL: http://www.crtc.gc.ca/archive/eng/Decisions/1996/DT96-1.htm).

[10]*AT&T Corp. v. City of Portland*, 216 F.3d 871 (standaardize/footnote #1) (Ninth Circuit, 2000), (URL: http://www.fcc.gov/ogc/documents/opinions/2000/99-35609.html).

[11]For example, *GTE Service Corp. v. Federal Communications Comm.*, 205 F. 3d 416 (D.C. Ciruit, 2000) (URL: http://www.fcc.gov/ogc/documents/opinions/2000/99-1176.html). This ruling upheld the FCC requirement that ILECs provide access to offices and exchanges.

[12]The FCC has set up a Merger Compliance Oversight Team to monitor recent common carrier mergers' compliance with FCC conditions (these include the SBC/Ameritech merger, Bell/Atlantic GTE merger, Bell Atlantic/NYNEX merger, and the Qwest/US West merger). For background information about this FCC oversight see the MCOT pages at http://www.fcc.gov/wcb/mcot/. For one response to GTE/Bell Atlantic, see "Public Hearings Set for GTE Network Modernization Plan and GTE/Bell Atlantic Merger," News Release, Pennsylvania Public Utilities Commission, 4 March 1999 (URL: http://puc.paonline.com/press_releases/Press_Releases.asp?UtilityCode=TP&UtilityName=Telecommunications&PR_ID=51&View=PressRelease).

[13]For a summary of DSL issues, see Morris, *Broadband Backgrounder*, 30.

[14]Ibid., 35–36. For a darker view of the possibilities latent in increased control of the Internet by cable broadband providers see Lawrence Lessig, *The Future of Ideas* (New York: Random House, 2002).

[15]Lessig, *The Future of Ideas*, 218–233.

[16]Audrey Selin, *3G Mobile Licensing Policy: From GSM to IMT-2000—A Comparative Analysis* (Geneva: International Telecommunication Union, 2002), (URL: http://www.itu.int/osg/spu/ni/3G/casestudies/GSM-FINAL.pdf), 11-16, 33–37.

[17]Federal Communications Commission, "News Release, February 14, 2002: FCC Launches Proceeding to Promote Widespread Deployment of High-Speed Broadband Internet Access Services" (URL: http://www.fcc.gov/Bureaus/Common_Carrier/News_Releases/2002/nrcc0202.html).

[18]See Federal Communications Commission, "News Release, March 14, 2002: FCC Classifies Cable Modem Service as 'Information Service' " (URL: http://www.fcc.gov/Bureaus/Cable/News_Releases/2002/nrcb0201.html). On efforts in concert with the Department of Commerce to determine a 3G spectrum see Federa! Communications Commission, "Third Generation ('3G') Wireless" (URL: http://www.fcc.gov/3G/).

[19]*Fox Television Stations Inc. v. FCC*, 280 F. 3d 1027 (D.C. Circuit, 2002) (URL: http://www.fcc.gov/ogc/2002opin.html).

[20]Yochi J. Dreazen, "Appeals Court Orders FCC to Overhaul Network Rule," *The Wall Street Journal*, 27 May 2002. The case at issue is *US Telecom Association v. FCC,* and it is available from the D.C. Circuit website at http://pacer.cadc.uscourts.gov/common/opinions/200205/00-1012a.txt.

[21]Federal Communications Commission, "Declaratory Ruling and Notice of Proposed Rulemaking," FCC 02-77, 14 March 2002 (URL: http://www.fcc.gov/Daily_Releases/Daily_Business/2002/db0315/FCC-02-77A1.doc).

[22]Mark Wigfield, "Appeals Court Orders FCC to Explain Plan to End ISP-Connection Payments," *The Wall Street Journal*, 6 May 2002.

[23]William F. Yancey, Gregory W. Mitchell and Dana E. Lipp, "Electronic Commerce Snares Sellers in Multistate Tax Web," *Ryan & Company*, 7 December 1999.

[24]Paul Hofheinz, "EU Approves New Rules on Taxation of e-Commerce," *The Wall Street Journal Online*, 7 May 2002.

[25]Stefanie Olsen, "California Governor Vetoes Internet Tax Bill," *CNET News.com*, 25 September 2000 (URL: http://news.cnet.com/news/0-1007-200-2861946.html).

[26]Simson Garfinkel, *Database Nation: The Death of Privacy in the 21st Century* (Sebastopol: O'Reilley & Associates, Inc., 2000).

[27]Introduction by Representative Cliff Stearns, Subcommittee Chair, Committee on Energy and Commerce, House of Representatives, 107 Congress, Subcommittee on Commerce, Trade and Consumer Protection, "Opinion Surveys: What Consumers Have to Say About Information Privacy," 3.

[28]Ibid., Testimony of Lee Rainie, Director, Pew Internet & American Life Project, 10.

[29]Susannah Fox, *Trust and Privacy Online: Why Americans Want to Rewrite the Rules* (Washington D.C.: Pew Internet & American Life Project, 2000) (URL: http://www.pewinternet.org/reports/toc.asp?Report=19).

[30]Ibid., 2.

[31]William F. Adkinson, Jr., Jeffrey Eisenach, and Thomas M. Lenard, *Privacy Online: A Report on the Information Practices and Policies of Commercial Websites. The Progress and Freedom Foundation, Special Report* (Washington, D.C.: Progress and Freedom Foundation, March 2002) (URL: http://www.pff.org/publications/privacyonlinefinalael.pdf.).

[32]Ibid., 25, 28.

[33]For more on P3P see the W3C website at http://www.w3.org/P3P/; on adoption, see Adkinson, Esienach, and Lenard, *Privacy Online*, 26.

[34]Diane Anderson and Keith Parine, "Marketing the Double Click Way," *The Industry Standard*, 6 March 2000 (URL: http://www.thestandard.com/article/display/0,1151,12400,00.html).

[35]Steve Lohr, "Microsoft, I.B.M. and VeriSign to Cooperate on Web Security," *New York Times*, 11 April 2002.

[36]Lawrence Lessig, *Code and Other Laws of Cyberspace* (New York: Basic Books, 1999), 47–49.

[37]Paul Coe Clark III, "FTC in Middle of Privacy Fray," *Communications Today via COMTEX*, 1 August 2000.

[38]Brian Livingston, "Do Privacy Policies Really Protect You?" *CNET News.com*, 30 June, 2000.

[39]Directive 95/46/EC of the European Parliament and of the Council of 24 October 1995 on the protection of individuals with regard to the processing of personal data and on the free movement of such data (URL: http://europa.eu.int/comm/internal_market/en/dataprot/law/).

[40]Chris Oaks, "FTC Commish: Regulate Thyself," *Wired News*, 11 October 2000 (URL: http://www.wired.com/news/politics/0,1283,39344,00.html).

[41]*Katz v. United States*, 389 U.S. 347 (1967) (URL: http://caselaw.lp.findlaw.com/scripts/getcase.pl?court=us&vol=389&invol=347).

[42]Yahoo Privacy Center Page (URL: http://privacy.yahoo.com/privacy/us/).

[43]Saul Hansell, "Seeking Profits, Internet Companies Alter Privacy Policy," *New York Times*, 11 April 2002.

[44]Saul Hansell, "The Yahoo Privacy Storm That Wasn't," *New York Times*, 13 May 2002.

[45]Eric J. Sinrod, "Upside Counsel: Madonna.com: No Longer a Legal Virgin," *Upside Today*, 24 October 2000.

[46]Justice Sandra Day O'Connor, Opinion, *Feist Publications Inc. v. Rural Telephone Service Co.*, 499 US 340, 349 (1991) (URL: http://www.arl.org/info/frn/copy/fairuse.html).

[47]U.S. Copyright Office, "The Basics of U.S. Copyright Law" (URL: http://www.gigalaw.com/articles/2000-all/loc-2000-03-all.html).

[48]For a more detailed explanation of the DMCA, see the paper written by Jonathan Band, "The Digital Millennium Copyright Act" (URL: http://www.arl.org/info/frn/copy/band.html).

[49]Lessig, *The Future of Ideas*, 122–23, 196–199. Lessig is a critic of such an extension and has served as an advisor to Eldred.

[50]*Universal City Studios Inc. et al. v. Corley*, No. 00-9185 (Second Circuit, 2001) (URL: https://www.tourolaw.edu/2ndCircuit/November01/00-9185.html).

[51]American Civil Liberties Union, "Brief of Amici Curiae Center for Democracy and Technology, *American Civil Liberties Union et al., in support of Appellee Yahoo! Inc.*, in the matter of *Yahoo! Inc. v. La Ligue Contre le Racisme et L'Antisemitisme et al.*," Appeal No. 01-17424 U.S. Ninth Circuit Court of Appeals (URL: http://www.aclu.org/court/yahoo_9th_cir.pdf).

[52]"Companies Increasingly Suing Their Online Critics," *The Denver Post via COMTEX*, 15 January 2001.

[53]Keith Perine, "The Trouble with Regulating Hate," *The Industry Standard*, 24 July, 2000 (URL: http://www.thestandard.com/article/display/0,1151,16967,00.html).

[54]Nick Wingfield, "U.S. Judge Rules Yahoo Can Ignore French Order Blocking Nazi Content," *The Wall Street Journal*, 9 November 2001.

[55]Testimony of Lee Rainie, p. 10.

[56]Justice Anthony M. Kennedy, Opinion, *Ashcroft v. Free Speech Coalition*, (00-795) 198 F.3d 1083, Affirmed (URL: http://a257.g.akamaitech.net/7/257/2422/16apr20021045/www.supremecourtus.gov/opinions/01pdf/00-795.pdf).

[57]"There's No Easy Way to Protect Kids from Web Porn, Study Finds," *The Wall Street Journal*, 2 May 2002.

Contributing Authors
(in alphabetical order)

Jennifer Barron joined Monitor Group in 1985 as a strategy consultant. Ms. Barron has a broad range of experience in helping clients solve business problems, with a particular focus on competitive positioning and marketing strategies.

Ms. Barron is a principal and founder of Monitor's marketing strategy group, Market2Customer. She has been instrumental in driving the growth of the group and overseeing product development and new business development initiatives. Ms. Barron is currently actively involved in helping clients with brand design and delivery issues.

Ms. Barron graduated from Dartmouth College with an honors degree in economics. She received her master's in business administration from Harvard Business School.

Yannis Dosios is a former Monitor Group consultant. While at Monitor, Mr. Dosios worked in a number of industries, including e-business, telecommunications, entertainment, high-tech, consumer products, and the non-profit sector. His work has primarily focused on market analysis; corporate strategy; streamlining of activities, processes, and systems; and identification and development of new business concepts. He received a bachelor's in mathematics from Harvard University. Outside of work, Mr. Dosois enjoys traveling, playing tennis, and watching international movies.

Ian Findlay joined Marketspace in August 2000 as a director of its technology practice, Q. Mr. Findlay establishes standards and oversees the implementation of Marketspace's infrastructure, internal systems (including, e-mail, LAN/WAN connectivity, desktop, server, hosting), and software development. In addition, Mr. Findlay advises clients on the use of technology within their organizations, especially the development of software that leverages Internet-based technologies. He also manages Marketspace's network of relationships with technology implementation companies.

Prior to joining Marketspace, Mr. Findlay spent more than 12 years with a variety of network and technology consulting firms in the United States. After founding Internet consultancy Marketing Engineers in Boston, he sold that organization to the London-based consultancy Conduit Communications. There, he oversaw many of the firm's largest technology engagements, especially those involving complex database transactions, workflow process management, and XML-based content. Mr. Findlay holds a bachelor's

487

degree in history with a focus on computer science from Trinity College in Connecticut. He is a member of MIMC (Massachusetts Interactive Media Council) and a nationally ranked triathlete.

Peter Giorgio is the director of software development at Marketspace. As a member of Q, Marketspace's technology center, he oversees the architecture, design, and quality implementation of all of Marketspace's development projects. In addition, Mr. Giorgio advises Marketspace's clients on how to appropriately embed technology in their business strategy.

Mr. Giorgio joined Marketspace from Conduit Communications and Razorfish (which acquired Conduit in 1999), where he oversaw the architecture and development of many of the firm's largest e-commerce projects. Prior to Conduit, Mr. Giorgio attained the rank of captain in the United States Air Force. While in the Air Force, he taught computer programming (Java and object-oriented programming and design), developed logistics support systems, and managed government contractors.

Mr. Giorgio earned a bachelor's degree in computer science from Amherst College. When not hunched over his keyboard in a dark corner or schooling his colleagues in the finer points of the jump hook, he can often be found sprawled on the floor of the living room as a human jungle gym for his two children.

Colin Gounden is the head of Marketspace client services and leads the firm's largest client engagements and strategic client relationships. He is a veteran of more than 10 years of technology strategy and business strategy consulting in North America and Europe.

Before joining Marketspace in 2000, Mr. Gounden was director of strategy at Razorfish, where he spearheaded many large digital strategy engagements. Prior to Razorfish, he was CEO of the U.S. operations of London-based Conduit Communications, a consulting firm that he sold to Razorfish in 1999. As the founder of Conduit's technology services arm, Mr. Gounden specialized in the use of Internet technology to support organizational change.

Before joining Conduit, Mr. Gounden was with IBM, where he designed and developed business software for large organizations. Among his other early accomplishments: surviving the fixed-income trading-floor jungle at various merchant banks in London and winning an undergraduate research scholarship at Harvard for his study of the auditory systems of bats.

Leo Griffin is a leader of Marketspace's Los Angeles office. He has worked in the United States, the United Kingdom, Spain, Italy, Canada, and Russia. Prior to joining Monitor Group, Mr. Griffin worked for an Internet startup. He received a bachelor's degree in industrial economics at the London School of Economics and received a master's degree in business administration with distinction from Kellogg School of Management. When not at work, he enjoys biking in the Santa Monica mountains.

Joseph Hartzell is a former consultant at Monitor Group. While with Monitor, Mr. Hartzell worked in biotechnology, health insurance, and manufacturing.

Prior to working in management consulting, Mr. Hartzell cofounded an Internet startup and spent several years in marketing management at network equipment manufacturers. He received a bachelor's degree in business administration from the University of California at Berkeley. Outside of work, Mr. Hartzell enjoys surfing, sailing, and scuba diving off the California coast.

Ellie Kyung is a consultant with Marketspace's New York office. Since joining Monitor in 1998, she has focused primarily on the development of marketing and branding strategy, working closely with Monitor's Market2Customer group. Ms. Kyung's client work has been focused in the healthcare and e-commerce industries. Her research work has focused on branding, new business development, and the digitalization of information. She graduated cum laude from Yale University with a dual bachelor's degree in economics and international studies.

Dickson Louie is principal of Louie & Associates, a San Francisco consultancy that provides business development, marketing research, and competitive analysis to media companies. Prior to establishing Louie & Associates, Mr. Louie spent 13 years in the newspaper industry. From 1984 to 1995, he was a member of the management team of the *Los Angeles Times* and its parent company, Times Mirror. More recently, Mr. Louie served as business development and planning manager for *The San Jose Mercury News*. In 1996, Mr. Louie was appointed as a research associate at Harvard Business School, where he authored more than 20 case studies for Marketspace, including those on Amazon.com, CBS Evening News, New York Times Electronic Media Company, QVC, and Monster.com.

Mr. Louie is a graduate of California State University, Hayward, where he received his bachelor's degree in business administration with a minor in journalism in 1980, and of the University of Chicago, where he received a master's degree in business administration in 1984.

Dorsey McGlone is a consultant for Marketspace. Prior to joining Marketspace, Ms. McGlone worked at a high-tech startup that built and sold speech-activated, wearable computers. Since joining Marketspace in September 2000, Ms. McGlone has worked on a variety of projects with both startups and established companies, as well as internal projects profiling venture capital investments and the venture-capital community. She received a bachelor's degree in English language and literature from the University of Virginia in 1991 and a master's degree in business administration from Harvard Business School in 2000.

Nancy Michels has been a consultant with Monitor Group since 1992. Over the course of her career at Monitor, she has worked in healthcare, technology, financial services, and industrial manufacturing. Her work has focused primarily on marketing strategy, including customer segmentation, market assessment, competitive analysis, and brand positioning. She also has experience in distribution analysis, new-product development, process design, and organizational change management. In her work with Marketspace, Ms. Michels concentrated on online branding. She is currently working with the marketing department of a large biotechnology company on a new product launch.

Ms. Michels has also been a faculty member in Monitor's marketing training program for new consultants and is a professional development adviser for other consultants. She graduated magna cum laude from Brigham Young University with a bachelor's degree in economics and received a master's degree in business administration from Harvard Business School. Ms. Michels resides in San Francisco with her husband, David, and daughter, Elise.

Rafi Mohammed has been a consultant with Monitor Group since 1998. His work has focused on the networked economy, broadband, and online service marketing and development strategy. He is also the coauthor of the textbook *Internet Marketing*. Prior to joining Monitor, Dr. Mohammed had his own media strategy consulting practice in Los Angeles and worked on deregulatory issues at the Federal Communications Commission in Washington, D.C.

Dr. Mohammed holds a Ph.D. in economics from Cornell University and economics degrees from the London School of Economics and Boston University. His academic research has focused on media and business strategy topics.

Mark W. Pocharski is an officer and global account manager in Monitor Group's marketing strategy group. Mr. Pocharski works with B2B and B2C clients in a variety of industries, including consumer packaged goods, consumer financial services, pharmaceuticals, beverages, business telecommunications, health insurance, and natural gas. He has managed client relationships in North America, Europe, and Asia.

Mr. Pocharski's recent projects include developing an integrated online/bricks-and-mortar new-business offering for a major U.S. consumer products company; turning around the growth trend for a leading consumer financial-services company with online and bricks-and-mortar marketing initiatives; devising a growth of strategy for a major beverage brand; refreshing the brand personality for a leader in skin-care products; creating a set of innovative product offerings for and introducing a new product-development process to a major U.S. telecommunications player; designing and implementing a segment-based marketing strategy for a major U.S. health insurance company; creating an account-management program for a national energy company; and redesigning the roles and service offerings of market research groups for global leaders in consumer packaged goods and pharmaceuticals.

In addition to client project work, Mr. Pocharski designed and teaches a strategic marketing course for clients.

Mr. Pocharski received a master's degree in business administration from Harvard Business School. He graduated cum laude from Dartmouth College with a degree in economics and government.

David Ruben is senior editor at Marketspace, where he has helped to produce both an online magazine and a weekly television show about business and the Internet. Prior to joining Marketspace, Mr. Ruben was a freelance print and television journalist, writing for a wide variety of national magazines and working on *NOVA* and several other national series for PBS. He has also been an editor at several newspapers and magazines and worked as a community organizer.

Mr. Ruben graduated from Hamilton College with a degree in history and philosophy. He lives in the Boston area with his wife, two children, and (gulp) new puppy.

Marco Smit is a former consultant with Monitor Group. He spent more than five years consulting in Europe, Asia, and the United States for a variety of industries, including biotechnology, high-tech, consumer products, financial services, the nonprofit sector, and e-business.

Mr. Smit holds a master's degree in economics from Erasmus University in Rotterdam, where he studied economic integration with a specialization in financial derivatives. He also studied strategy at the ESSEC Business School in Paris. He is a fluent French, German, Dutch, and Bahasa-Indonesia speaker.

Steve Szaraz's work wih Marketspace Center focuses on the capture, development, and distribution of Marketspace Center's knowledge assets. He came to Marketspace Center from Monitor Group, where he was a part of the firm's knowledge management team and managed Monitor Group's Global Research capabilities. He worked with clients in the beverage, pharmaceuticals, financial services, and specialty chemicals industries.

Prior to joining Monitor Group, Dr. Szaraz taught at Harvard University. He also served as an assistant dean of Harvard College. He received his bachelor's degree in history and literature, his master's degree in history, and his Ph.D. in the history of American civilization from Harvard University.

Tobias H. A. Thomas is an officer and global account manager of Monitor Group's marketing strategy group. He is cofounder and leader of Market2Customer's Web-based marketing services group. In addition, Mr. Thomas is the head of M2C's GrowthPath® Application Group, which enables Monitor's clients to systematically identify and capture new growth opportunities.

Mr. Thomas is one of the primary developers of the GrowthPath®, Customer Portrait®, and Action Segmentation™ frameworks, as well as many of the other core technologies used in M2C's Web-based marketing services group and Monitor client engagements today. In addition, Mr. Thomas has developed effective marketing, business-unit, and corporate strategies for clients in a variety of industries, including consumer packaged goods, financial services, telecommunications, chemicals, metals, travel, and beverages, often doubling their historical rate of growth. Mr. Thomas's most recent client work includes developing detailed local and national consumer, brand, and channel strategies and frameworks for a global beverage company; creating targeted-offer channel strategies for a telecommunications client; and building the internal marketing capabilities of a leading investment bank.

Mr. Thomas received a master's degree in business administration from Harvard Business School, where he was an honors student, and a bachelor's degree with honors in chemical engineering from Queen's University in Canada.

Michael Yip joined Marketspace in 2000 as a member of its research and development team and served as project manager and writer for the textbook *e-Commerce* and its companion book, *Cases in e-Commerce.*

From 1992 to 1999, Mr. Yip worked in international treasury and finance at Sony Pictures Entertainment, where he developed foreign exchange hedge strategies and managed all companywide foreign exchange transactions, cross-border funds transfers, and international lines of credit and letters of credit.

Mr. Yip has also worked in film and television production. He has been a studio engineer, a production manager of national television commercials, and a producer for Jim Henson, where he developed interactive video- and game-controller devices. He was also a faculty head and taught graduate and undergraduate courses in television production and new technologies at New York University's Tisch School of the Arts.

Mr. Yip is a graduate of the University of California at Berkeley, where he received his bachelor's degree in psychology, and New York University, Tisch School of the Arts, Institute of Film and Television, where he received a bachelor's degree in fine arts.

Eugene Wang is a former Monitor Group consultant. Prior to joining Monitor, Mr. Wang worked with several Web-based companies in a variety of areas, including finance and business development. He has also spent significant time working as an administrator of an elementary after-school program. Mr. Wang graduated with a bachelor's degree in business administration from the University of California at Berkeley.

Glossary

A

acquiring bank   A financial institution that a merchant works with to process credit cards. The acquiring bank typically processes credit card transactions through the credit card networks and then deposits the funds into the merchant's bank account.

actionable segmentation   Segmentation that is easy to recognize, readily reached, and can be described in terms of its growth, size, profile, and attractiveness, but does not provide much insight into customer motivations.

adaptability   The ability of a system to adapt to changes in its function.

aesthetics   How a site looks, created by visual choices such as colors, graphics, photographs, and fonts.

affiliate program   Directs users to affiliated websites through links or links embedded in site banners or other advertising materials.

analog   Processes and transmits electronic information using a continuous varied amplitude, frequency, or phase of an electronic signal and/or carrier. Analog technology is also used for transmitting voice data over telephone wires and broadcasting AM and FM radio and TV.

analyst reports   Data sources that are a blend of primary market data on a particular topic and an analyst's view of the market.

angel   Wealthy individual who invests personal capital in startups in exchange for equity.

B

backbone network   The major wide area network to which other networks attach to form the Internet.

Balanced Scorecard   Introduced by Harvard Business School professors Robert Kaplan and David Norton in response to their perception that managers overwhelmingly focus on short-term financial performance. They argued that firms must "balance" their financial perspective when analyzing other domains of the business such as internal business processes and customer responses.

bandwidth   The amount of data that can be transferred by or through a device in a given amount of time (often measured in kilobytes per second or megabytes per second).

banner advertisements   Electronic billboards that come in a variety of types and sizes. A single website often displays multiple banners.

bootstrapping   The process of using personal resources to finance the early stages of a startup.

brand equity   Combination of assets that can be viewed from both the firm's and the customer's perspective.

branding   Concerns the consumer's perception of the offering—how it performs, how it looks, how it makes one feel, and what messages it sends to others.

broadband   A type of data transmission with connectivity speeds exceeding 128 kilobits per second.

broadcast communication   A one-way information exchange from organization to user, with no mechanism for user response.

business-logic layer   Layer of website responsible for implementing the basic rules of the system according to the operating rules of the business.

business-model metrics   Measurements that capture the subcomponents of the business model: the value proposition, egg diagram, resource system, and financial metrics.

business model   An online business model requires four choices on the part of senior management: (1) the specification of a value proposition or "value cluster" for targeted customers; (2) an online offering, which could be a product, a service, and/or information; (3) a unique, defendable resource system; and (4) a revenue model.

business plan   A document that provides a framework for testing the business from conception through early development to capitalize on strengths, compensate for weaknesses, and serve as a resume for potential investors.

business-to-business (B2B)   The full spectrum of e-commerce that can occur between two organizations, including purchasing and procurement, supplier management, inventory management, channel management, sales activities, payment management, and service and support.

business-to-consumer (B2C)   E-commerce businesses that sell goods to consumers (for example, Amazon.com, Yahoo.com, and Schwab.com).

C

cable modem   High-speed (approximately 2 to 3 megabits per second), broadband Internet connection delivered over cable lines.

capital infrastructure   The financial and management communities that enable the creation of new business.

change-management process A framework for identifying problems within a project, prioritizing the problems, assigning the task of resolving the problems to an individual or team, and tracking the progress of these efforts until all problems are resolved.

circuit-switched networks Networks in which only one data transfer can occur at a given time.

click stream Series of links that a user clicks on when using the Web.

click-through rate The number of times a link is "clicked."

client A computer that is connected to the host computer or server on a network.

client/server architecture A system in which a central server is used to store information that is accessed and acted upon by any number of client machines connected to the server through a network.

clustering Building a system based on smaller, less expensive machines rather than a few large, complicated, and expensive machines. In this system, the machines are configured to share the load for a website, often with each machine handling a few requests at a time.

Code of Fair Information Practices Created by the Nixon administration to study the effect of computers on privacy. The code is comprised of five rules set forth by the commission that are designed to protect personal information by restricting what companies can do.

commerce The sale of goods, products, or services.

commercial bank loan An installment loan in which a business borrows a certain amount of money, for a specified length of time, with a fixed or variable interest rate.

communication The dialogue that unfolds between a website and its users.

community The interaction that occurs among site users.

comparables method Placing a value on a company by comparing

it to other companies that are similar.

connection The extent of formal linkages between the site and other sites.

consumer-to-business (C2B) Business transactions that occur when consumers band together to form and present themselves as a buyer group to businesses. These groups may be economically motivated, as with the demand aggregator Mercata.com, or socially oriented, as with the cause-related advocacy groups at SpeakOut.com.

content All digital subject matter on a website.

content matrix Shows what screens will be required in order to satisfy the user case, and defines what content will be required on each screen.

context The aesthetic and functional look-and-feel of a website (for example, graphics, colors, and design features).

co-opetition Companies that are both competitors and collaborators at the same time.

copyright The legal right of writers, publishers, and other creators to the exclusive ownership of their works.

corporate ventures Large corporations that set up venture funds as a subsidiary to make investments on behalf of the parent company.

customer decision process The process a customer goes through in deciding how to purchase and dispose of goods.

customer metrics Measurements intended to assess the management of customer relationships by the firm. Includes both customer interface metrics and customer outcome metrics.

customer relationship management (CRM) Technology system that helps the company serve, satisfy, and retain customers. CRM systems help companies store data about their customers as well as help employees better communicate and serve customers.

customer support/handling processes Process that handles customer questions, either when the customer is on the website or once the customer has completed a transaction.

customization The personalization of communications between users and a website.

D

data layer System layer whose main function is to provide fast, reliable access to the data needed to run the system.

debt financing The type of financing in which a business borrows a certain amount of money for a specified time period and repays the principal with interest in regular payments.

destination site Provides almost exclusively site-generated content with very few links to other websites.

digital A binary language of computers that allows for easy generation, processing, and transmission of signals with the assistance of microprocessors. The binary language is a series of discrete bits represented by 0 or 1.

digital certificate A piece of software provided by a trusted third-party certification authority that contains a person's or company's public encryption key and verification of that person's or company's identity.

digital divide The gap between people who have computers (and/or computer skills) and people who do not.

digital lifestyle The idea that, as media-based household appliances become digitally based and interconnected, they will become the basic commodity of human interactions.

Digital Millennium Copyright Act (DMCA) Signed into law in 1998 to implement the provisions of the WIPO treaties, which prohibit the circumvention of copyright protection systems, and to state that a copyright owner cannot hold an online service provider liable if one of its subscribers infringes on the owner's copyright.

digital subscriber line (DSL) A set of digital telecommunications protocols designed to allow high-speed data communication over the existing copper telephone lines between users and telephone companies.

direct communications One of the categories of market communications. This type can take many forms, including the use of the classic business-to-business sales representative calling on accounts, retail sales clerks, and telephone customer sales representatives, as well as the use of direct marketing and telemarketing.

direct competitors Companies offering similar or competing products.

direct marketing Marketing that involves directly contacting customers (typically by phone or mail) with the intent of making an immediate sale.

distributed architecture System of server, loosely coupled across dispersed networks that work together to deliver a website.

domain name The name-based address of a website or other server that is mapped to the server's IP address (e.g., *www.yahoo.com*).

Domain Name System (DNS) Gives each computer on the Internet an address comprised of easily recognizable letters and words that could be used instead of a numeric IP address.

due diligence A careful process on the part of a potential investor to check on the validity of a business plan and the expertise of any individuals involved. During this process, references are checked, management team individuals interviewed, and business ideas tested. Potential customers may be interviewed about the likelihood of purchasing or using the company's product or service.

E

e-commerce Technology-mediated exchanges between parties (individuals or organizations), as well as the electronically based intra- or interorganizational activities that facilitate such exchanges.

egg diagram Maps the products and services of a particular company (or website) onto the customer decision process.

e-mail Messages sent and received electronically via telecommunication links, as between microcomputers or terminals.

encryption Technology that uses complex mathematical formulas to encode and decode information.

enterprise resource planning (ERP) Allows a business to establish an internal digital nervous system whereby data is shared electronically—using a company intranet—among corporate managers.

equity financing The type of financing in which a business exchanges a portion of ownership for cash, and the investor expects financial return in the future as the value of the business goes up.

evaluation and compensation systems The systems within an organization that are set up to evaluate and reward performance. Compensation can include monetary and nonmonetary rewards.

Extensible Markup Language (XML) A language written in SGML, XML is a flexible way to create common data or information formats and to share both the format and the data with other applications or trading partners. XML provides an organization and its trading partners with a consistent method for sharing information. XML differs from traditional data format mechanisms in that it provides not only the data but also a tag or description of each piece of data.

F

fair use Allows any property that has a copyright to be used for educational, critical, commentary, reporting, or parody purposes.

FAQs Frequently asked questions typically listed on a website to help users find the answers to common questions about the site.

financial capital The funding that an entrepreneur needs to attract to run the business.

financial information Information about the financial status of a company; financial information can include data such as income statement, balance sheet, statement of cash flow, industry research, annual and quarterly reports, SEC filings, stock market reports, market and industry comparison data, and analyst reports.

financial metrics Measurements that capture the revenues, costs, profits, and balance sheet metrics of the firm.

financial performance method The valuation of a company based on earnings or potential earnings that applies a discount rate to determine the present value of the cash flow.

fit The extent to which each of the 7Cs individually supports the business model.

flat-file databases Single-computer files that store all of the information for a system.

flexibility The ability of a system to adapt to changes in its function.

four key environments The four elements—customer, technology, company, and competition—that must be considered when assessing a market opportunity.

function The usability of a site, or how much information is displayed on the site, as opposed to how aesthetic the site is.

functional matrix Representation of the sections of a website in which functionality and content are shared, which allows it to take into account any unique requirements that a particular section might have.

functional specification   Provides a highly detailed guide to what every page on a website does.

functionality   The functions that a system must implement.

G

general online communications   A category of communications that includes banner ads, e-mail, viral marketing, sponsorship agreements, affiliate programs, partnerships, customer information, and online transaction.

Graphics Interchange Format (GIF)   A graphic file format containing binary data that will display an image when viewed with the proper software and hardware.

H

holding company   Large corporations that exchange cash for equity in a startup company and often are the majority stakeholder for an extended period of time.

host   A computer containing data or programs that another computer can access through a network.

HTML (HyperText Markup Language)   The most common text-based tagging language for creating documents and setting up hypertext links between documents on the Web.

hub site   A website that provides a combination of site-generated content and links to sites of related interest.

human assets   The employee resources that a firm has. These include employees at all job levels, from upper management to administrative to technical to creative.

human capital   The business team, made up of the entrepreneur, management team, strategic advisors and partners, and logistical advisors and partners.

human resource management process   Process by which a company upgrades its human resource capabilities in a manner that is in line with the value proposition.

I

implementation metrics   These metrics measure the effectiveness of a company's human resources program as well as its processes, organizational structure, systems (including information, incentives, and rewards), coordination mechanisms, culture and management style, and technology systems.

incubator   A company that offers services to new companies in exchange for an equity stake. Some common services include coaching, information technology, public relations, recruiting, office space, and legal and accounting services.

indirect competitors   Companies that offer products that attract the same customers or develop technologies, platforms, or offerings that indirectly compete.

information technology (IT)   Technology systems that help organize and give access to information in a business.

initial public offering (IPO)   The sale of shares to public investors of a company that has never been traded on a public stock exchange.

innovation   New ideas, plus action or implementation that results in an improvement, gain, or profit.

interactive communication   A two-way communication between an organization and a consumer.

interactive television   A service that allows users to e-mail, chat, and surf the Internet with a set-top box and dial-up modem while watching TV.

interactivity   The ability to conduct two-way communication between a user and a website.

Intermediaries   Well-connected individuals in the investment community who match a startup with the right investors and, in some instances, acquisition targets.

internal business process metrics   Measurements that focus on operations inside the company. In particular, this set of metrics focuses on the critical value-adding activities that lead to customer satisfaction and enhanced shareholder value.

Internet Protocol (IP)   A set of rules for packet routing over the Internet and many private networks.

IP address   A string of numbers indicating where a website is located, consisting of four groups of numbers separated by decimal points.

J

Joint Photographic Experts Group (JPEG)   A graphic file format that contains binary data that will display an image when viewed with proper software and hardware.

K

keys   Pieces of software that let users of encryption software ensure that only intended recipients of information are able to view it.

L

learning and growth metrics   Learning and growth metrics broadly capture the employee, information systems, and motivation.

life cycle of a company   This cycle includes four stages of development: startup, acquisition of customers, monetization, and maturity.

local area network (LAN)   A group of connected computers that spans a few square kilometers or less.

logical architecture   Defines the system in terms of its software components and the desired functionality of those components.

logistical advisors and partners   Paid, outsourced parties that can provide missing skill sets for a company on an as-needed basis.

M

mainframe architecture Type of architecture in which the system built around a single, monolithic computer that is shared by all users on the system.

management team Group that orchestrates the strategic direction and operations of a startup.

manufacturing and distribution processes Also known as supply chains; how a company manufacturers and distributes its goods.

market communications All the points of contact that the firm has with its customers. This includes the obvious offline communications such as television advertising, promotions, and sales calls, as well as emergent advertising approaches on the Internet.

market opportunity analysis framework An organizing framework designed to look systematically for unmet or underserved needs. The framework has seven stages: identify the unmet and/or underserved customer need, identify the specific customers a company will pursue, assess advantage relative to competition, assess the company's resources to deliver the offering, assess the market readiness of the technology, specify the opportunity in concrete terms, and assess opportunity attractiveness.

market research Online market research firms collect primary customer data through online surveys or customer submissions. These firms tend to put a strong emphasis on site usability, customer satisfaction, and traffic level. Offline market research includes surveys, experiments, and focus groups.

market opportunity metrics These measurements assess the degree to which a firm can accurately gauge its market opportunity. Generic indicators include the ability of the firm to target the most attractive segments, the ability of the firm to understand and map competitors' strategy evolution, and the ability of the firm to track the evolution of target segment needs.

marketing and branding metrics These measurements focus on communication and branding effectiveness; they include metrics to evaluate marketing communication effectiveness and metrics related to brand strength.

marketspace The digital equivalent of a physical-world marketplace.

meaningful segmentation Segmentation that generates real insight on customers but is difficult to address.

media infrastructure The various communications companies and their channels of communication, such as radio, television, newspapers, and magazines, used in mass communication with the general public.

media proliferation The emergence of new sources of mass media since the 1960s.

media-usage fragmentation A trend in which, as media sources have dramatically risen, the audience for each of those sources has declined.

Metcalfe's Law The value of a network to each of its members is proportional to the number of other users [which can be expressed as $(n^2 - n)/2$].

metrics Measurements by which companies can assess the progress and health of their online businesses. Metrics include benchmarks such as sales, margins, profit, and market share, as well as metrics that reflect the entire strategy of the company.

mobile wireless technology Allows users to access the Web and receive e-mail via handheld devices that use relatively low bandwidth.

MP3 The acronym for the standards specifications to the MPEG-1 Audio Layer-3.

MPEG-1 A computer file format and compression specification for motion video with audio.

N

n-tier architecture A website architecture system that is built around smaller, more manageable parts (more than two discrete modules).

Net marketplaces Exchanges that facilitate the interaction and exchange of e-commerce transactions among buyers, sellers, and other trading partners.

networked economy A business evnironment in which companies create value largely or exclusively through the gathering, synthesizing, and distribution of information; formulate strategy in ways that make management of the enterprise and management of technology convergent; compete in real time rather than in cycle time and operate in constantly responsive dialogue with their customers and markets; operate in a world characterized by low barriers to entry, near-zero variable costs of operations, and intense, constantly shifting competition; organize resources around the demand side; and manage relationships with customers through screen-to-face channels and interfaces.

new-to-the-world value New offerings that create value for customers. Examples include radically extending reach and access, building community, enabling collaboration among multiple people across locations and time, and introducing innovative functionality or experience.

O

object-oriented database Database that encapsulates all data into different types of objects.

offering The specific product or service a company offers to its customers.

open access The argument that broadband providers should be regulated to avoid the emergence of a monopoly.

opportunity nucleus   A set of unmet or underserved need(s).

opportunity story   First rough outline of a business plan; should include information about the target segment, value proposition, customer benefits, needed resources and available resources, revenue source, and revenue size.

opt-in   Marketing programs in which customers choose to have their information shared with others, in trade for more personalized sites, marketing, and special offers.

opt-out   The option for users to exit a company's marketing program.

organizational convergence   The increasing ability of a business to deploy multiple digital platforms (consisting of both human and technological assets) against tactical or strategic goals.

organizational culture   The pattern of shared values, beliefs, and assumptions that influence opinions and actions in a company.

P

packet   A short block of data (often a piece of a larger file) transmitted in a packet-switching network.

packet switching   A method of data transmission in which small blocks of data are transmitted rapidly over a channel dedicated to the connection only for the duration of the packet's transmission. Not all packets, even for the same file or message, necessarily follow the same route.

page schematics   Simple drawings or diagrams that serve as a conceptual layout for what each page on the site will look like.

patent   A grant that gives the owner the sole right to make, use, and sell his invention.

payment and billing processes   Processes that allow a company to correctly and efficiently collect money from its customers and pay its vendors.

payment gateway   Provides merchants with real-time authorizations for credit cards.

peer-to-peer (P2P)   Exchanges that involve transactions between and among peers or consumers. These exchanges may or may not include third-party involvement, as in the case of the auction-exchange eBay.

Performance Dashboard   Standards that reflect the health of a business, comprising of five categories of metrics: opportunity, business model, customer interface and outcomes, branding and implementation, and financial.

permission marketing   Customers agree to share personal information in exchange for receiving targeted market communications; presumes successful marketing campaigns can be created by establishing a mutually beneficial and trusting relationship between the firm and its customers.

personalized online communications   A category of market communications that includes personalized permission e-mail, personalized recommendations, personalized advertisements, personalized webpages, and personalized e-commerce stores.

personalization   A form of customization initiated by the user that enables the user to modify site content and context based on consciously articulated and acted-upon preferences. The user can make layout selections and content source selections.

physical architecture   Defines the hardware of third-party software needed to host and maintain a site.

Platform for Privacy Preferences (P3P)   An XML-based language that facilitates the matching of a site's privacy policy to the preferences of users on their browsers.

plug-in   A software program that extends the capabilities of a Web browser or other application, also known as an add-in.

portal site   A website that consists almost exclusively of absolute links to a large number of other sites.

postmoney valuation   The value of the company immediately after an investment.

premoney valuation   The value that the investor puts on the company before making an investment.

presentation layer   Layer of a website responsible for all communications with a user's computer.

privacy issues   There are three main privacy issues: (1) security and privacy or sensitive consumer information related to online sales and services transactions, (2) the collection and use of consumer data and statistics, and (3) the protection of a consumer's right to privacy.

privacy seals   A seal issued by a company such as TrustE that sets guidelines for how companies can collect and use their customers' information.

processes   The patterns of interaction, coordination, communication, and decision-making that employees use to standardize how work is done.

processing power   The amount of data that can be processed at a given time.

profiling   Identifying users and tracking their behavior through the use of cookies.

project plan   Lays out the checkpoints, milestones, and resources that are expected to be required to move the project forward to completion.

proxy server   A computer that forwards packets from a company's internal network of PCs to the Internet. Many proxy servers also cache information to improve performance on the network.

public policy infrastructure   The laws and regulations that influence strategies, technology, capital, and media in business.

R

red herring A preliminary prospectus that is sent to the SEC for review.

redundancy Having two or more of an essential component configured so that if one fails, the other can take over.

reinforcement Complementarity—or synergy—among each of the 7Cs.

relational database Database in which data are store in a series of tables.

reliability The amount of time a system can be expected to be available to its users.

resource allocation processes Formalization of the tradeoffs and prioritizations that a company makes when choosing which opportunities to pursue.

resource system A unique combination of resources within and outside of a firm that delivers promised benefits.

revenue model How a company plans to generate revenue.

router A computer or appliance in a network that handles data transfer between computers.

S

satellite system A system that enables wireless technology through satellites that orbit the earth. Three proposed systems for satellite Internet access include geostationary, medium earth orbit (MEO) and low earth orbit (LEO).

scalability The ability of a system to be extended to handle a greater load.

Secure Electronic Transaction (SET) A protocol that facilitates the secure authentication of credit card transactions on the Web as well as other payment processing issues, such as debit card transactions and credits back to credit cards.

Secure Sockets Layer (SSL) An encrypted "tunnel" automatically set up between a user's browser and a Web server that ensures secure communication between them.

security (when referring to capital) An IOU from a company to an investor that offers investors a share of ownership.

security (when referring to technology) The ability of a system to prevent illegal or inappropriate use of its data and to deter cybercriminals and hackers.

segmentation The process of dividing the diverse population of target customers into homogenous segments, any of which may be selected as the one to be reached with a distinct marketing mix.

sense and respond An approach to strategic development that focuses on quick responses to market developments.

servers Computers that store and transmit information to the browsers to be displayed.

7Cs Framework Framework for customer interface. The seven Cs are context, content, community, customization, communication, connection, and commerce.

simple rules strategy A point of view that strategy is about simple decision rules (for example, only acquire firms with less than 75 employees).

site map A hierarchical view of the proposed website that encompasses all of the primary pages.

spam Unsolicited marketing messages sent by e-mail or posted on newsgroups.

standards Rules that companies agree to adhere to so that their products can interact.

startup Beginning stage in the life cycle of a company. The goal is to develop a platform for rapid growth by building a strong team and creating a flexible site.

strategic advisors and partners A group comprising the advisory board, board of directors, and strategic alliance companies that provide strategic direction and advice and help attract potential investors.

streaming audio Sound files that allow a computer user to listen to a file while it is still downloading, rather than waiting until the file is completely downloaded to listen to it.

streaming video Video files that allow a computer user to watch a file while it is still downloading, rather than waiting until the file is completely downloaded to watch it.

strength of association The intensity with which the target consumer links a particular word, phrase, or meaning to a particular brand.

supply chain The suppliers, contract manufacturers, and distributors that a company utilizes as sources of materials and services to manufacture a product. The supply chain is focused on the activities (plan, execute, control) related to meeting needs based on a combination of an organization's capacity and its suppliers' capacity.

switching cost The cost—both financial and personal—of switching from one business or product to another. In the offline world, these costs could include having to find a new business, drive there, and taking time to become familiar with the store. In the online world, these costs could include searching for a new online business, taking time to become familiar with the website, and taking time to register on the site. Offline switching costs tend to be greater than online switching costs.

systems Routines or established procedures for any aspect of the organization.

T

tailoring A form of customization initiated by a website that enables the site to reconfigure itself based on past behavior by the user or by other users with similar profiles.

These sites can make recommendations based on past purchases, filter marketing messages based on user interests, and adjust prices and products based on user profiles.

technical convergence The evolution and migration of various media content (news, information, and entertainment) from traditional analog media platforms (print, audio, and video) to a digital platform or cross-platform where all content will be accessible through various digital devices.

technology infrastructure The foundations of an Internet system that enable the running of e-commerce enterprises. One-half of the technology equation is the hardware backbone such as the routers, servers, fiber optics, cables, and modems. The other half includes software and communication standards that run on top of the hardware.

Telecommunications Act of 1996 The first major overhaul of federal laws regulating the communications industry since 1934. With the passing of this Act, emphasis was changed from a regulation-based industry to a market-based industry to allow for increased competition.

telemarketing Marketing by a salesforce over the telephone.

template pages A page that is repeated more than once, usually on a section of the site that has multiple pages of similar content.

10-step branding process Branding framework that includes 10 steps: identify the brand audience; understand the customer; identify key leverage points in customer experience; continually monitor competitors; design compelling and complete brand intent; execute with integrity; be consistent over time; establish feedback systems; be opportunistic; and invest and be patient.

term sheet A nonbinding description of the proposed deal between the financier and the entrepreneur.

trade credit Credit extended to a business by its suppliers.

trademark A name or symbol that identifies a project and is officially registered, limiting the use of that name or symbol to the owner of the trademark.

traditional mass media communications One of the categories of market communications. Consists of television (network, cable, and local), print media (including high circulation newspapers and magazines), and national and local radio.

Transmission Control Protocol (TCP) Software that ensures the safe and reliable transfer of data.

trapped value Untapped market potential that can be unlocked by creating more efficient markets or more efficient value systems, enabling easier access, or disrupting current pricing power.

trusting behavior Activities that consumers pursue when they trust a website, such as purchasing or selling goods, banking, obtaining health information, using e-mail or instant messaging, and joining and participating in communities that include the exchange of personal information.

U

unit testing Testing in which the module, by itself, is made to do exactly what is expected of it.

unique pages Pages that have a design that is different from any other page on the site.

uniqueness The degree to which a brand is distinct, relative to other brands.

URL (Uniform Resource Locator) An address used for websites that makes them easier to remember than the underlying numerical IP address to which they are mapped.

usage occasion What task users want to accomplish when they visit a site.

use case How a user and a system interact in order to accomplish a specific goal.

user experience How a user perceives and interprets stimuli from a website.

user intentions Each task the user is trying to accomplish when he or she visits a site, and what process the user expects to go through to be successful.

user persona Fictitious, archetypal example of a real user that allows the development team to focus on the collective core needs of the users within a group.

user type The discrete types of users that will use the site.

V

valence The degree to which the association with a product is positive or negative.

valuation Determination of a company's worth.

value chain According to Michael Porter, a value chain represents the collection of activities that are performed to design, produce, market, deliver, and support a product. A firm's value chain and the way it performs individual activities are a reflection of its history, strategy, approach to implementing its strategy, and the underlying economics of the activities themselves.

value cluster A form of value proposition that includes multiple forms of each part: (1) the choice of target customer segments, (2) a particular focal combination of customer-driven benefits that are offered, and (3) the rationale for why the firm and its partners can deliver the value cluster significantly better than competitors.

value proposition Construction of a value proposition requires management to specify three items: (1) choice of target segment, (2) choice of focal customer benefits, and (3) rationale for why the firm can deliver the benefit package significantly better than its competitors in the same space.

value system An interconnection of processes and activities within and among firms that creates benefits for intermediaries and end consumers.

venture capital   A form of funding in which firms invest money in companies in exchange for stock. Venture-capital firms seek opportunities that will return 5 to 20 times their initial investment within five years; venture-capital financing is generally done in rounds where there is an expected path to liquidity.

venture-capital firms   Private partnerships or closely held corporations that raise money from a group of private investors and invest in companies in exchange for an equity stake.

venture-capital method   Values a company by determining a terminal value for a potential investment by using either a "multiple" or terminal value technique, but with a much larger discount rate.

video-game console   Video-game system with the potential to access a wide range of broadband services on the Internet.

viral marketing   A marketing method in which messages are spread via person-to-person contact and users are encouraged to pass the marketing message along to others. Also called word-of-mouth marketing.

W

Web browser   A program that translates the hypertext markup language of the World Wide Web into content that users can understand (usually in the form of webpages).

Web host   A company that rents the use of its high-bandwidth Internet access and Web servers to other companies.

Web server   A computer that processes requests from browsers for documents over the Web.

webpage   A document on the World Wide Web usually consisting of an HTML file and files linked to it, such as images or scripts.

website   A series of linked webpages that are maintained or owned by the same organization. A website typically consists of a homepage that allows navigation to the remainder of the webpages on the website.

wide area network (WAN)   Technology that allowed engineers to build networks to connect computers and LANs separated by large geographical distances.

WYSIWYG editors   (WYSIWYG stands for "what you see is what you get.") Programs that conceal the markup language from the user, allowing him to create the page in the exact look that he wants without dealing with tags and codes.